Africa Yearbook

Africa Yearbook

Politics, Economy and Society South of the Sahara in 2015

VOLUME 12

Edited by

Jon Abbink
Sebastian Elischer
Andreas Mehler
Henning Melber

BRILL

LEIDEN | BOSTON

Want or need Open Access? Brill Open offers you the choice to make your research freely accessible online in exchange for a publication charge. Review your various options on brill.com/brill-open.

Typeface for the Latin, Greek, and Cyrillic scripts: "Brill". See and download: brill.com/brill-typeface.

ISSN 1871-2525
ISBN 978-90-04-31478-8 (paperback)
ISBN 978-90-04-33323-9 (e-book)

This book is printed on acid-free paper and produced in a sustainable manner.

Contents

Preface

In May 2003, the Africa-Europe Group for Interdisciplinary Studies (AEGIS) encouraged some of its member institutions to publish an *Africa Yearbook* with a wider international appeal. The African Studies Centre in Leiden (ASC), the Institute of African Affairs in Hamburg (IAA) and the Nordic Africa Institute in Uppsala (NAI) – all very active AEGIS centres with similar profiles – accepted this challenge and their joint efforts first bore fruit in the initial volume of the series in 2004. In 2007, the Dag Hammarskjöld Foundation in Uppsala (DHF) joined this international project, while the NAI ended its involvement with the fifth volume, published in 2009. As from 2014, the DHF ended its collaboration, and from the 11th volume the NAI re-joined the collaborating institutions, ensuring the *Yearbook*'s continued publication. In a subsequent further step towards strengthening the collaboration, the University of Florida also decided with this volume to join the network of institutions. We take this opportunity to thank Rolf Hofmeier for his solid support as one of the previous editors for many years; he remains a member of the team as a contributor.

As in previous volumes, the country-specific articles cover domestic politics, foreign affairs and socioeconomic developments in the states of sub-Saharan Africa during the calendar year under review. While we recognise the impossibility of finding fully objective indicators for the relative importance of each of the states covered by the *Yearbook*, the length of the country-specific articles aims to reflect the approximate weight of each country. The four sub-regions are also introduced by means of an overview article. Further overviews summarise general continental developments and European-African relations.

The *Yearbook* is based on scholarly work, but is oriented towards a wider target readership, including students, politicians, diplomats, administrators, journalists, teachers, practitioners in the sphere of development cooperation and business people. Without forcing the individual contributions too much into a straitjacket, the volume is primarily concerned with providing factual (though not necessarily neutral) information. Each issue, in focusing almost exclusively on developments during a particular calendar year, provides a completely fresh annual overview of events and thereby adds to the cumulative record of on-going developments.

In November 2012, the *Yearbook* received the prestigious biennial Conover-Porter Award for outstanding Africa-related reference works from the African Studies Association and the Africana Librarians Council in the USA. This was an encouraging sign that the *Yearbook* has become a permanent and appreciated feature in Africanist publishing. The same year, thanks to a generous arrangement by Brill, the Africa Institute of South Africa joined as an African co-publisher, thereby greatly enhancing local distribution on the continent.

This is the twelfth consecutive volume of the *Yearbook*, and we are proud to have already covered more than a decade of African affairs in what we believe is a solid scholarly contribution towards a better understanding of and more knowledge about SSA countries. Brill has now taken the initiative to compile country-focused chronologies, with separate books published in the meantime on Mozambique, Ghana and Namibia based on the *Yearbook* chapters. More may follow, hopefully showing the value of information steadily accumulated over time and enhancing accessibility to readers with a main interest in one specific country.

Once again we wish to express our gratitude to all the contributors for their collaboration in this endeavour; to the partner institutions in AEGIS for encouraging us to embark on this ambitious project; to Carol Rowe for her meticulous language editing; to Bas van der *Mije* for his unfailing coordinating assistance; and to Brill Publishers for their continued commitment. And last but not least, we would once again like to thank our participating institutions for their on-going support.

The Editors
(Gainesville, Freiburg, Leiden and Uppsala, June 2016)

List of Abbreviations

ABN	Autorité du Bassin du Niger (Niamey)
ACP	African, Caribbean, and Pacific Group of Countries (Lomé/Cotonou Agreement)
ADF	African Development Fund (Tunis)
AfDB	African Development Bank (Tunis)
AFD	Agence Française de Développement (Paris)
AGOA	African Growth and Opportunity Act
AI	Amnesty International
APR	African Peer Review
APRM	African Peer Review Mechanism
AU	African Union (Addis Ababa)
BCEAO	Banque Centrale des Etats de l'Afrique de l'Ouest (Dakar)
BEAC	Banque des Etats de l'Afrique Centrale (Yaoundé)
CAR	Central African Republic
CBLT	Commission du Bassin du Lac Tchad (N'Djaména)
CEEAC	Communauté Economique des Etats de l'Afrique Centrale (Libreville) = ECCAS
CEMAC	Communauté Economique et Monétaire de l'Afrique Centrale
CEN-SAD	Community of Sahel-Saharan States (Tripoli)
CEPGL	Communauté Economique des Pays des Grands Lacs (Gisenyi/Rwanda)
CFAfr	Franc de la Communauté Financière Africaine (BCEAO; BEAC)
COMESA	Common Market for Eastern and Southern Africa (Lusaka)
CPLP	Comunidade dos Países de Língua Portuguesa
DAC	Development Assistance Committee (Paris)
DDR	Disarmament, Demobilisation and Reintegration
DFID	Department for International Development (London)
DRC	Democratic Republic of the Congo
EAC	East African Community
ECA	Economic Commission for Africa (United Nations; Addis Ababa)
ECCAS	Economic Community of Central African States (Libreville)
ECF	Extended Credit Facility (IMF)
ECOMOG	ECOWAS Ceasefire Monitoring Group
ECOWAS	Economic Community of West African States (Abuja)
EDF	European Development Fund (Brussels)
EIB	European Investment Bank (Luxemburg)
EITI	Extractive Industries Transparency Initiative
EPA	Economic Partnership Agreement
ESAF	Enhanced Structural Adjustment Facility (IMF)

EU	European Union (Brussels)
FAO	Food and Agricultural Organisation (Rome)
FDI	Foreign Direct Investment
FTA	Free Trade Area
GDP	Gross Domestic Product
HDI	Human Development Index (UNDP)
HIPC	Heavily Indebted Poor Countries
HRW	Human Rights Watch
ICC	International Criminal Court
ICG	International Crisis Group
ICGLR	International Conference on the Great Lakes Region
IDA	International Development Association (Washington)
IDP	Internally Displaced Person
IFAD	International Fund for Agricultural Development (Rome)
IFC	International Finance Corporation (Washington)
IGAD	Intergovernmental Authority on Development (Djibouti)
ILO	International Labour Organisation (Geneva)
IMF	International Monetary Fund (Washington)
IOC	Indian Ocean Commission (Quatre Bornes)
IORA	Indian Ocean Rim Association (Ebène/Mauritius)
MDGS	Millennium Development Goals
MDRI	Multilateral Debt Relief Initiative
MRU	Mano River Union (Freetown)
NEPAD	New Partnership for Africa's Development
NGO	Non-Governmental Organisation
OAU	Organization of African Unity
ODA	Official Development Assistance
OECD	Organisation for Economic Cooperation and Development (Paris)
OIC	Organisation of the Islamic Conference (Jeddah)
OIF	L'Organisation Internationale de la Francophonie
OPEC	Organisation of Petroleum Exporting Countries (Vienna)
PALOP	Países Africanos de Lingua Oficial Portugesa
PPP	Purchasing Power Parity
PRGF	Poverty Reduction and Growth Facility
PRSC	Poverty Reduction Support Credit
PRSP	Poverty Reduction Strategy Paper
PTA	Preferential Trade for Eastern and Southern African States (now COMESA)
SACU	Southern African Customs Union (Pretoria)
SADC	Southern African Development Community (Gaborone)
SAF	Structural Adjustment Facility (IMF)
SDR	Special Drawing Right (IMF)

SSA	Sub-Saharan Africa
TI	Transparency International
UAE	United Arab Emirates
UEMOA	Union Économique et Monétaire Ouest-Africaine (Ouagadougou)
UMA	Union du Maghreb Arabe
UN	United Nations (New York)
UNCTAD	United Nations Conference on Trade and Development (Geneva)
UNDP	United Nations Development Programme (New York)
UNEP	United Nations Environment Programme (Nairobi)
UNECA	United Nations Economic Commission for Africa
UNESCO	United Nations Educational, Scientific and Cultural Organisation (Paris)
UNHCR	United Nations High Commissioner for Refugees (Geneva)
UNICEF	United Nations Children's Fund (New York)
UNSC	United Nations Security Council
USAID	United States Agency for International Development (Washington)
WFP	World Food Programme (Rome)
WHO	World Health Organisation (Geneva)
WTO	World Trade Organisation (Geneva)

Factual Overview (as of 31 December 2015)

West Africa

Country	Area (in sq km)	Population (in m)[1]	Currency	HDI (2015)	Head of State	Prime Minister
Benin	112,622	10.6	CFA Franc	0.480	Boni Yayi	
Burkina Faso	274,122	18.5	CFA Franc	0.402	Roch Marc Christian Kaboré	
Cape Verde	4,033	0.5	Cape Verdean Escudo	0.646	Jorge Carlos Fonseca	José Maria Pereira Neves
Côte d'Ivoire	322,462	23.3	CFA Franc	0.462	Alassane Ouattara	Daniel Kablan Duncan
Gambia	11,295	2.0	Dalasi	0.441	Yahya Jammeh	
Ghana	238,500	27.7	Cedi	0.579	John Dramani Mahama	
Guinea	245,857	11.0	Guinean Franc	0.411	Alpha Condé	Mamady Youla
Guinea-Bissau	36,125	1.8	CFA Franc	0.420	José Mário Vaz	Carlos Correia
Liberia	111,370	4.5	Liberian Dollar	0.430	Ellen Johnson- Sirleaf	
Mali	1,240,000	16.7	CFA Franc	0.419	Ibrahim Boubacar Keïta	Modibo Keïta
Mauritania	1,030,700	3.6	Ouguiya	0.506	Mohamed Ould Abdel Aziz	Yahya Ould Hademine
Niger	1,267,000	18.9	CFA Franc	0.348	Mahamadou Issoufou	Brigi Rafini
Nigeria	923,768	181.8	Naira	0.514	Muhammadu Buhari	
Senegal	197,162	14.7	CFA Franc	0.466	Macky Sall	Mahammed Boun Abdallah Dionne
Sierra Leone	71,740	6.5	Leone	0.413	Ernest Bai Koroma	
Togo	56,785	7.2	CFA Franc	0.484	Faure Essozimna Gnassingbé	Komi Sélom Klassou

Central Africa

Country	Area (in sq km)	Population (in m)	Currency	HDI	Head of State	Prime Minister
Cameroon	475,442	23.7	CFA Franc BEAC	0.512	Paul Biya	Philémon Yang
Central African Republic	622,984	5.6	CFA Franc BEAC	0.350	Catherine Samba-Panza (interim)	Mahamat Kamoun (interim)
Chad	1,284,000	13.7	CFA Franc BEAC	0.392	Idriss Déby Itno	Kalzeube Pahimi Deubet
Congo	342,000	4.8	CFA Franc BEAC	0.591	Denis Sassou-Nguesso	
DR Congo	2,344,855	73.3	Congolese Franc	0.433	Joseph Kabila	Augustin Matata Ponyo Mapon
Equatorial Guinea	28,051	0.8	CFA Franc BEAC	0.587	Teodoro Obiang Nguema Mbasogo	Vicente Ehate Tomi
Gabon	267,667	1.8	CFA Franc BEAC	0.684	Ali Bongo Ondimba	Daniel Ona Ondo
São Tomé and Príncipe	1,001	0.2	Dobra	0.555	Manuel Pinto da Costa	Patrice Trovoada

Eastern Africa

Country	Area (in sq km)	Population (in m)	Currency	HDI	Head of State	Prime Minister
Burundi	26,338	10.7	Burundi Franc	0.400	Pierre Nkurunziza	
Comoros	1,862	0.8	Comoran Franc	0.503	Ikililou Dhoinine	
Djibouti	23,200	0.9	Djiboutian Franc	0.470	Ismail Omar Guelleh	Abdoulkader Kamil Mohamed
Eritrea	124,320	5.2	Nakfa	0.391	Isaias Afewerki	
Ethiopia	1,121,900	98.1	Birr	0.442	Mulatu Teshome	Hailemariam Dessalegn
Kenya	569,259	44.3	Kenya Shilling	0.548	Uhuru Kenyatta	
Rwanda	26,338	11.3	Rwanda Franc	0.483	Paul Kagame	Anastase Murekezi
Seychelles	455	0.09	Seychelles Rupee	0.772	James Michel	
Somalia	637,600	11.1	Somali Shilling	n.a.	Hassan Sheikh Mohamud	Omar Abdirashid Ali Sharmarke
(Somaliland)	137,600	3.5	Somaliland Shilling	n.a.	Ahmed Mohamed Mahamoud 'Silanyo'	
Sudan	2,505,805	40.9	Sudanese Pound	0.497	Omar Hassan Ahmad al-Bashir	
South Sudan	619,745	12.2	South Sudanese Pound	0.467	Salva Kiir Mayardit	
Tanzania	945,087	52.3	Tanzania Shilling	0.521	John Magufuli	Majaliwa Kassim Majaliwa
Uganda	197,000	40.1	Uganda Shilling	0.483	Yoweri Kaguta Museveni	Ruhakana Rugunda

Southern Africa

Country	Area (in sq km)	Population (in m)	Currency	HDI	Head of State	Prime Minister
Angola	1,246,700	25.0	Kwanza	0.532	José Eduardo dos Santos	
Botswana	581,730	2.1	Pula	0.698	Seretse Khama Ian Khama	
Lesotho	30,344	1.9	Lesotho Loti	0.497	King Letsie III	Bethuel Pakalitha Mosisili
Madagascar	592,000	23.0	Malagasy Ariary	0.510	Hery Rajaonarimampianina	Jean Ravelonarivo
Malawi	118,484	17.2	Malawian Kwacha	0.445	Peter Mutharika	
Mauritius	2,040	1.3	Mauritian Rupee	0.777	Ameenah Gurib-Fakim	Sir Anerood Jugnauth
Mozambique	799,380	25.7	Mozambiquen Métical	0.416	Filipe Nyusi	Carlos Agostinho do Rosário
Namibia	824,269	2.5	Namibian Dollar	0.628	Hage Gottfried Geingob	Saara Kuugongelwa-Amadhila
South Africa	1,219,090	55.0	Rand	0.666	Jacob Zuma	
Swaziland	17,364	1.3	Swazi Lilangeni	0.531	King Mswati III	Sibusiso Dlamini
Zambia	752,614	15.5	Zambian Kwacha	0.586	Edgar Lungu	
Zimbabwe	390,580	17.4	Zimbabwean Dollar	0.509	Robert Gabriel Mugabe	

(Population figures are for mid-2015 according to Stiftung Weltbevölkerung, www.weltbevölkerung.de)

List of Authors

Jon Abbink
Senior researcher at the African Studies Centre, Leiden University, and research professor at the Department of Anthropology at VU University, Amsterdam, abbink@ascleiden.nl

Kwesi Aning
Director, Faculty of Academic Affairs and Research (FAAR), Kofi Annan International Peacekeeping Training Centre, Accra, Ghana, Kwesi.Aning@kaiptc.org

Nancy Annan
Researcher, Faculty of Academic Affairs and Research (FAAR), Kofi Annan International Peacekeeping Training Centre, Ghana, Nancy.Annan@kaiptc.org

Alfred Babo
Scholar in Residence at the Lewis Global Studies Center, Professor of African Studies and Anthropology, Smith College, Northampton, USA, ababo@smith.edu

Alice Bellagamba
Professor of Cultural and Social Anthropology, Department of Human Sciences for Education "Riccardo Massa", University of Milan-Bicocca, alice.bellagamba@unimib.it

Heinrich Bergstresser
Media Consultant, Freelance Research Associate of the Institute of African Affairs in Hamburg and Freelance Tutor of Deutsche Gesellschaft für Internationale Zusammenarbeit GIZ, Germany, heinrich.bergstresser@web.de

Keratilwe Bodilenyane
Lecturer, Department of Political & Administrative Studies, University of Botswana, Keratilwe.Bodilenyane@mopipi.ub.bw

Emmanuelle Bouilly
PhD student, CESSP, Department of Political Science, Université Paris 1 Panthéon Sorbonne, Paris, France, emmanuelle.bouilly@yahoo.fr

Marie Brossier
Assistant Professor of Political Science, Departement of Political science, Université Laval, Québec, Canada, marie.brossier@pol.ulaval.ca

Brett Logan Carter
Assistant Professor, School of International Relations, University of Southern California, blcarter@usc.edu

Lewis Dzimbiri
Professor of Public Administration, Chancellor College, University of Malawi, proflewisdzimbiri@gmail.com

George Dzimbiri
Lecturer at the Department of Business Administration, the Polytechnic, University of Malawi, gdzimbiri@poly.ac.mw

Daniel Eizenga
Doctoral Candidate, Department of Political Science, University of Florida, USA, deizenga@ufl.edu

Sebastian Elischer
Ph.D. (2010) in Comparative Politics, Jacobs University Bremen, is assistant professor of comparative politics at the University of Florida, selischer@ufl.edu

Lansana Gberie
Academic and Writer, Ottawa, Canada, lagberie@yahoo.com

Christine Hackenesch
Researcher, German Development Institute / Deutsches Institut für Entwicklungspolitik (DIE), Bonn, Germany, christine.hackenesch@die-gdi.de

Joseph Hanlon
Visiting Senior Fellow, Department of International Development, London School of Economics, UK and Visiting Senior Research Fellow at the Development Policy and Practice Centre of the Open University, UK, j.hanlon@open.ac.uk

Ketil Fred Hansen
Associate Professor in Modern African History, University of Stavanger, Norway. ketil.f.hansen@uis.no

Kurt Hirschler
Freelance Political Scientist, Hamburg, Germany, kurt_hirschler@web.de

Nicole Hirt
Freelance Research Associate, Institute of African Affairs, GIGA German Institute of Global and Area Studies, Hamburg, Germany, e-mail: nicole.hirt@giga-hamburg.de

Rolf Hofmeier
Former Director, Institute of African Affairs, GIGA German Institute of Global and Area Studies, Hamburg, Germany, hofmeier@giga-hamburg.de

Laura James
Affiliated lecturer, Department of Politics and International Studies (POLIS), University of Cambridge, UK, lmj35@cam.ac.uk

Amin Kamete
Senior Lecturer, Urban Studies, School of Social and Political Sciences, University of Glasgow, Scotland, UK, amini.kamete@glasgow.ac.uk

Niels Keijzer
Researcher, German Development Institute / Deutsches Institut für Entwicklungspolitik (DIE), Bonn, Germany, niels.keijzer@die-gdi.de

Christoph Kohl
Researcher, Peace Research Institute Frankfurt, Frankfurt am Main, Germany, kohl@hsfk.de

Dirk Kohnert
Retired Deputy Director, Institute of African Affairs, GIGA German Institute of Global and Area Studies, Hamburg, Germany, Kohnert@giga-hamburg.de

Daniel Large
Assistant Professor at the School of Public Policy, Central European University, Budapest danlarge@gmail.com

Gabrielle Lynch
Associate Professor of Comparative Politics, Department of Politics and International Studies, University of Warwick, UK, g.lynch@warwick.ac.uk

Joseph N. Mangarella
Lecturer at the Université de Panthéon-Assas (Paris 2), Adjunct Professor at INSEEC, PhD candidate at the Africa Studies Center, Leiden, and at the Free University of Amsterdam, joseph.mangarella@gmail.com

Richard R. Marcus
Professor and Director, The Global Studies Institute and the International Studies Program, California State University, Long Beach, USA, richard.marcus@csulb.edu

Andreas Mehler
Director of the Arnold Bergstraesser Institute and professor of Political Science at the University of Freiburg, andreas.mehler@abi.uni-freiburg.de

Henning Melber
Director emeritus, Dag Hammarskjöld Foundation, Uppsala, Sweden, henning.melber@dhf.uu.se

Sanusha Naidu
Research Associate, Department of Political Science, University of Pretoria, and Senior Research Fellow with the Institute for Global Dialogue, South Africa, sanushanaidu72@gmail.com

Senzwesihle Ngubane
General Manager Operations at the African Centre for the Constructive Resolution of Disputes (ACCORD), Durban, South Africa, senzo@accord.org.za

Helena Olsson
Political Scientist and Staff Member at the Department of Sociology, Uppsala University, Sweden, helena.olsson@soc.uu.se

Claes Olsson
Political Scientist and Editor at Global Publications Foundation, Uppsala, Sweden, claesolsson@globalpublications.org

Krijn Peters
Associate Professor in Armed Conflict & Post-war Reconstruction, Department of Political & Cultural Studies, Swansea University, UK, k.peters@swansea.ac.uk

Fanny Pigeaud
Journalist, France, Fanny.pigeaud@gmail.com

Marisha Ramdeen
Senior Programme Officer at the African Centre for the Constructive Resolution of Disputes (ACCORD) in Durban, South Africa. Marisha@accord.org.za

Edalina Rodrigues Sanches
Postdoctoral Research Fellow at the Institute of Social Sciences-University of Lisbon, the Portuguese Institute of International Relations-New University of Lisbon and the Centre for Social Science Research-University of Cape Town, ersanches@ics.ul.pt

Anita Schroven
Researcher at Pasteur Institute, Paris and Max Planck Institute for Social Anthropology, Halle/Saale, schroven@eth.mpg.de

Jon Schubert
Senior Research Fellow, SPP1448 'Changing Stateness in Africa', Centre for Area Studies, University of Leipzig, jon.schubert@uni-leipzig.de

David Sebudubudu
Professor of Political Science and Dean of the Faculty of Social Sciences, University of Botswana, Sebudubu@mopipi.ub.bw

Gerhard Seibert
Associate professor at the Universidade da Integração Internacional da Lusofonia Afro-Brasileira (UNILAB), São Francisco do Conde, Bahia, Brazil, mailseibert@yahoo.com

Tor Sellström
Ph.D.hc (Uppsala 2011), researcher and writer. His latest book is Africa in the Indian Ocean: Islands in Ebb and Flow (Brill; 2015). tg.sellstrom@gmail.com

Claudia Simons
Researcher at German Institute for International and Security Affairs, Berlin, Germany, Claudia.Simons@swp-berlin.org

Roger Southall
Professor Emeritus, Department of Sociology, University of the Witwatersrand, and Research Associate in Political Studies, University of Cape Town, South Africa, Roger.Southall@wits.ac.za

Alexander Stroh
Assistant Professor of African Politics and Development Policy, University of Bayreuth, Germany, alexander.stroh@uni-bayreuth.de

Susan Thomson
Assistant Professor of Peace and Conflict Studies, Colgate University, Hamilton, USA, sthomson@colgate.edu

Stef Vandeginste
Lecturer, Institute of Development Policy and Management, University of Antwerp, Belgium, stef.vandeginste@uantwerpen.be

Klaas van Walraven
Researcher, African Studies Centre, Leiden, The Netherlands, walraven@ascleiden.nl

Volker Weyel
Consultant, Former Editor-in-chief 'Vereinte Nationen' (1977–2004), Bonn, Germany, volker.weyel@outlook.com

Bruce Whitehouse
Director, Global Studies Program, Associate Professor of Anthropology, Lehigh University, USA, bruce.whitehouse@lehigh.edu

Douglas Yates
Professor of Political Science at the American Graduate School in Paris, France, douglas.yates@ags.edu

PART 1

Sub-Saharan Africa

Jon Abbink, Sebastian Elischer, Andreas Mehler and Henning Melber

The worldwide fall in demand for primary commodities and the rapid drop in oil prices impacted on the resource-based economies in SSA. Some of the bigger economies (Nigeria, Angola, South Africa) and some of the most oil-dependent states (Chad, Equatorial Guinea) were most affected, though economic growth continued on a modest scale for many countries, not least thanks to more diversified economic relations with the new global players. In terms of continental governance, Agenda 2063 set a new programmatic agenda for the AU, while the controversies around the ICC remained a topical issue. The APRM stagnated further and restrictions limiting the activities of civil society remained common practice by governments. There were elections in 14 states, with some modest overall democratic gains and a reduction in military conflicts. Presidential term limits remained a contested issue. The negative effects of climate change were evident in the deterioration of the natural environment and remained a matter of concern, as did the issue of migration. The effects of the strongest-ever recorded El Niño resulted in an increase in food insecurity, especially in Southern Africa.

Africa in the Global Economy

Across the board, African national economies, of both resource-rich and resource-poor countries, continued to show growth, but doubts persisted as to the durability and independence of this expansion. Developments showed a *mixed picture*, with growth on the quantitative side and above the world average, but on the other hand global dependency remained, especially in mounting long-term debts, along with growing inequality and social and political-economic problems for large numbers of unrepresented, marginalised peoples and social groups. Substantial illicit financial outflows (estimated at between $ 53 bn and $ 56 bn a year) and corruption remained major problems. While elections seem to be now a permanent feature of the political landscape, a lack of developed consultative democratic structures backed up by solid rule of law and working justice systems prevented most citizens from challenging government policies and programmes. In October, the *IMF* lowered its estimate of the continent's overall economic growth to 3.75%, citing as causes the drop in commodity prices (e.g., oil), decline in world trade growth, national deficits, trade imbalances and weakening competitiveness. Exceptions showing higher growth were Mozambique, Ethiopia, Togo and Tanzania. The December figure for SSA gave growth at 3.5%, South Africa having one of the lowest rates, with only 1.3%. East Africa was the African region with the highest growth figure.

 | DOI 10.1163/9789004333239_002

Africa received a *net financial inflow* of an estimated $ 208 bn (mostly investment), 1.8% lower than in 2014, although ODA funding increased by 4% to $ 56 bn. Another major source of income was remittances, which reached some $ 64 bn. Inflation remained moderate, averaging 7.4%, though some countries experienced an exceptionally high rate: South Sudan (41.1%), Malawi (21.2%) and Sudan (16.9%). Only a few countries (e.g., Ethiopia, Kenya, Mauritius, Namibia, Rwanda) took serious initiatives towards *diversification and industrialisation* (manufacturing), generally seen as a better road to sustained economic development than the intensification of resource extraction (as in Angola, Eritrea, Equatorial Guinea, Uganda, Botswana and Sudan). A problem was that industrial sector investments were sometimes very supply-based (following top-down state investment plans) and not sufficiently geared up to export demand. In many fast-growing countries, the construction sector was a major driver. A 'High-level Expert Group Meeting on the Role of the Extractive Industries in Africa towards Sustainable Development and Inclusive Growth', held in February in New York under the auspices of the UN Office of the Special Advisor on Africa, drew attention to "the importance of harnessing the full potential" of Africa's natural resource endowments and "to employ the competitive advantage offered as an engine for inclusive economic growth", next to underlining the "crucial role of industrialization". However, the policy linkages and the strategies for attaining equity and respect for the rights of all 'stakeholders', including local peoples, were unclear.

The *agricultural sector* registered growth, but only where weather conditions were favourable and investment conditions had improved. The sector was mostly not a chief priority for major government investment. In some countries in the Horn and Southern Africa, droughts or local flooding kept the agrarian sector vulnerable, along with a disadvantagious property regime in states where all land was state property. The continent's *trade balance* remained negative: total exports grew to a value of over $ 570 bn, the lion's share being goods sent to the new partners, India and China (although there was a slowdown with the latter). The *total value of African imports* was about $ 540 bn, but with huge differences between countries. Various reports noted that the share of intra-African trade remained at only 11% (compared with 30% in Asia), too low to fuel local economic growth.

According to the World Bank's *Doing Business* report, 23 of the 51 African countries surveyed improved their ranking, with the biggest rises in Uganda, the Seychelles, Kenya and Mauritania, although scores declined for Rwanda, Zambia and Gabon. In many countries, armed conflict and regional inequalities of various kinds impeded economic stabilisation and overall development, notably in areas of Islamist violence (Northern Nigeria and the Lake Chad area, Niger, Kenya, Somalia, Egypt, Libya, Mali), while other countries struggled with post-conflict issues and domestic repression and dissent (Equatorial Guinea, the DRC, Rwanda, Ethiopia, Eritrea, Angola). Tourism, a business sector sensitive to security incidents, declined somewhat, with 3% fewer arrivals (down to 53 m) and down by 8% in North Africa.

As the Ebola crisis receded, the three countries most affected by it humanly and financially – Guinea, Sierra Leone and Liberia – started on their way to recovery.

Throughout the year, dozens of high-level policy and talking head *meetings on the African economy* were held by international and donor organisations, together with African government delegations and institutions. During 25–31 March, the 8th 'Joint AU-ECA Annual Meetings of the AU Conference of Ministers of Economy and Finance and the ECA Conference of African Ministers of Finance, Planning and Economic Development' took place at ECA Headquarters in Addis Ababa (Ethiopia) to discuss the theme 'Implementing Agenda 2063 – Planning, Mobilizing and Financing for Development'. Cape Town (South Africa) was the scene on 3–5 June of the 25th annual meeting of the World Economic Forum on Africa, a global forum with participants from business, government and civil society, which discussed ways to accelerate inclusive growth and bring about sustainable development in Africa, including optimising information and communications technology and the digital revolution, which was also central at the 'Transform Africa Summit' in Kigali (Rwanda), in October. During the year various ECA meetings were also held on sustainable development challenges, e.g. by the Committee on Sustainable Development and the Africa Regional Forum on Sustainable Development (on 16–15 June). On 2–4 November, the African Economic Conference took place in Kinshasa (DRC), organised by the AfDB, OECD and UNDP, on 'Addressing Poverty and Inequality in the Post-2015 Development Agenda', to assess the impact of 'inclusive growth strategies' in Africa. The closing document of the conference noted that the "prevalence of poverty, the high cost of doing business in the continent, governance failures caused by overdependence on primary commodities, weak health infrastructure, lack of gender equality, low quality of education and lack of credible data" were the chief issues hampering inclusive economic growth in Africa. A plea was made to have "inclusive developmental states" take a greater role in economic transformation. From 30 November to 3 December, the ILO held its 13th African Regional Meeting at ECA headquarters in Addis Ababa to address workers' rights and productive employment issues in Africa in the context of the emerging global agenda for sustainable development, the Sustainable Development Goals, and the AU's Agenda 2063. It yielded the 'Addis Ababa Declaration: Transforming Africa through Decent Work for Sustainable Development', issued on 3 December.

A major event, with significant economic ramifications for the future was the *December COP-21 Paris Climate Change conference*, which set out new plans and financial schemes to tackle the world-wide climate problem, including support for poorer, developing countries to gear up renewable energy sources. In a potentially important move, the AU announced during the COP-21 Paris climate change conference that its members would mobilise $ 20 bn to develop at least 10 GW of renewable energy on the continent by 2026 – to be funded partly from the $ 100 bn pledged by developed countries in 2009. In various countries, initiatives to invest in durable and renewable energy sources were started, with South Africa's investments in 'green energy' increasing by 329% to $ 4.5 bn, Morocco spending some $ 2 bn., and Uganda about $ 1 bn.

The annual *African Economic Outlook 2016* report by the AfDB, OECD and UNDP noted that future economic development was strongly dependent on "unlocking the potential of African cities". The number of people living in cities in 2015 rose to some 475 m, i.e., double the figure for 1995. Rapid urbanisation created burdens but also possibilities for further economic dynamics, provided the environment and service infrastructure could keep up, which was the case in few African cities. Comprehensive urban policy, with citizen participation, was yet to be developed.

Under the the IMF and the World Bank's HIPC *debt relief scheme*, most indebted African countries (34 in total) had reached completion point in earlier years, being relieved of much debt. In 2015, only Chad was accepted, in April, as a candidate for debt relief to the tune of $ 1.1 bn. The status of three 'pre-decision point' countries (Eritrea, Sudan and Somalia) remained unclear and was put on hold because of their arrears, lack of performance and faulty policy environment. The IMF made an Article IV Consultation visit to Somalia, the first in 25 years.

Africa's *international economic relations* showed growing and deepening contacts with global players such as China, India, the EU and the USA. The last organised the 14th AGOA Forum on 24–27 August in Libreville (Gabon). In October, the 3rd India-Africa Forum Summit was held in New Delhi, with Indian Prime Minister Narendra Modi noting that the India-Africa relationship was emotionally and historically strong, and "... beyond strategic considerations". And not to be outdone, on 4–5 December at the 6th Forum on China-Africa Cooperation in Johannesburg (South Africa), China offered the continent development investments of $ 60 bn (including $ 5 bn in grants and interest-free loans and $ 35 bn in loans and export credits), along with promises to help industrialisation.

Migration, particularly to Europe, revealed that the African growth story was partly a myth and excluded millions from employment, education and life chances. In North Africa, especially Libya and Morocco, hundreds of thousands of people congregated to take the first chance they could to cross the Mediterranean illegally. This was a flow separate from the conflict- and war-induced waves from Syria and adjacent countries, and consisted mainly of economic migrants. For instance, thousands left Senegal, not known as a country in distress. However, many migrants also originated from countries where repression and violent conflict were a daily experience: Among the Mediterranean-route migrants from Africa were some 46,000 Eritreans and about 34,000 Nigerians (Eurostat figures). Also *within* Africa, illegal migration was a serious problem, with South Africa, for example, hosting some 300,000 asylum seekers and many more foreign immigrants. As a rule, African governments ignored the migrant crisis and did not develop policies to tackle it.

The AU and the APRM

The AU's activities were dominated by policy plans for long-term development ('Agenda 2063') and for the security infrastructure, as well as by responding to ongoing crisis challenges. AU forces continued to be deployed in Somalia (AMISOM) and in Darfur. Numerous meetings were held that saw the *adoption of several ambitious new plans*. On 30–31 January, the 24th Summit of the AU (the first of the biannual gatherings) took place at its Addis Ababa headquarters, where the 2015 roadmap for the AU's vision, known as 'Agenda 2063', was officially adopted, as prepared by the AU Commission, and with seven lofty long-term goals, such as a single air transport market, better higher education and an 'E-university', a commodities strategy, a free trade area, an 'African passport', common financial institutions, and an end to armed conflicts. The 24th summit took place under the theme of 'Women's Empowerment Year and Development for the Concretisation of Africa's Agenda 2063'.

A somewhat bad turn for the AU was the increasing tendency towards anti-Western rhetoric among its members and the choice on 30 January of Zimbabwean President Robert Mugabe (aged 90) as the AU's chairperson for the year. Younger politicians and African youth criticised this and called for reform and rejuvenation of the Union. In September, a survey of *Ignite The Youth* (an international society of youth activists in Africa) on the relationship between youth and the AU showed that the organisation was perceived by 67% of respondents "to have failed the African youth", and it received an overall public rating of 3.2 out of 10 (832 respondents from 24 African states). This 24th AU summit session's theme of *women's empowerment* was followed up in the 25th session, held from 7 to 15 June in Johannesburg, where the first ten-year implementation plan was adopted. Future moves toward the Continental Free Trade Area-Negotiating Forum (CFTA-NF) were also discussed, as well as the end of the Ebola virus epidemic. At this meeting, actress and UN goodwill ambassador for refugees Angelina Jolie gave an impassioned speech, pleading for an end to global violence against women. In a July meeting of the AU in Addis Ababa, again under stifling Ethiopian security arrangements that also had a domestic purpose, the most prominent guest was US President *Barack Obama*, who was visiting Ethiopia (and Kenya) for the first time. On 28 July, he gave a candid and good-humoured address, calling for Africa to create more (economic) opportunity for the next generation, reduce corruption, "expand freedoms" and "broaden democracy" on the continent.

In ongoing efforts to develop the *governance structure of the AU* and its member countries, the Secretariat of the African Governance Architecture (AGA) Platform and the AU Department of Political Affairs held a consultation with the AU Permanent Representative Committee on 2–4 September in Arusha (Tanzania), where the AGA operationalisation process was reviewed. Following up on this, the

Fourth High Level Dialogue on Democracy, Governance and Human Rights, convened by the AU Commission, took place on 7–8 December in Kigali and focused on 'Women's Equal Participation and Leadership in Political Parties'. This flowed into the inaugural meeting of the Political Heads of the AGA Platform members in on 9–10 December, also in Kigali. All such events (there were many more) revealed the AU's skills in developing a culture and capacity for extended political negotiation as well as meeting stamina (resembling EU proceedings), but produced few concrete results in better governance on the ground. And the words of AU Commissioner for Political Affairs Dr Aisha Laraba Abdullahi during the Kigali meeting, applauding "... the leadership of Rwanda as a shining example for women participation in Africa and indeed the world", clearly showed the highly propagandistic value of such gatherings.

In AU's relations with the EU, next to challenges of security and sustainable growth, the issue of *migration* again took a prominent place, against the background of ongoing streams of political refugees and socio-economic migrants to Europe, with the largest contingent from Eritrea but many also coming from other countries that were not marred by deep repression or violent conflict. On 11–12 November, the AU-EU Valletta Summit on Migration took place and adopted another action plan. On 22 April, the AU and EU held their annual College-to-College meeting in Brussels, on the basis of the 'Joint Africa EU-Strategy Roadmap 2014–17'. The EU supplied about 80% of the AU's programme budget, including € 1.6 bn for the African Peace Facility. On 20 October, EU Foreign Affairs Representative Federica Mogherini visited the AU in Addis Ababa for talks with the AU foreign affairs commissioner, and a joint statement was duly released re-affirming their commitment to strengthen partnership.

The concretisation of the AU's complex *peace and security architecture* – consisting of: a) the 15-member Peace and Security Council, the standing organ of the AU for prevention, management and resolution of conflicts, b) the (projected) African Standby Force (ASF) of a potential 20,000 troops, and c) the African Capacity for Immediate Response to Crisis, and some subsidiary bodies – made limited further progress. It was originally scheduled to be fully ready in December but did not meet this deadline. However, in October-November, an ASF continental field training exercise, coded AMANI AFRICA II, was conducted, hosted by SADC in Lohatla (South Africa), with over 5,500 military, police and civilians participating.

While most of the nine *peace-keeping missions* in Africa were under the UN flag, the AU continued its mission Somalia (AMISOM) and its part of the joint mission in Darfur, the African Union-United Nations Hybrid Operation in Darfur (UNAMID). ECOWAS kept an AU-approved small mission in Guinea-Bissau. Violence and tensions in Libya, the DRC and the CAR, as well as Egypt's political situation, remained points of AU concern, as did Islamist terror (in Libya, Somalia, Kenya, the Sinai, and elsewhere). The AU 'Regional cooperation initiative for the elimination of the Lord's Resistance Army' (RCI-LRA or RTF, see more below) did not fulfil its end goal.

During the year, AMISOM lost dozens of African soldiers to terror attacks by the Islamist al-Shabaab movement, bringing the total number of victims since 2007 to at least 2,000 (although AMISOM did not release casualty figures). Military action against the violence of the Boko Haram terror movement in northern Nigeria was not taken by the AU as a body, but by the member-states adjacent to its areas of operation: Cameroon, Chad, Niger and Nigeria. Lack of political consensus among member states and overwhelming dependence on foreign funding (72% of the $ 522 m operational budget came from donors, led by the US and the EU) continued to limit the AU's rapid response, efficacy and commitment. On 31 January, during the 24th summit, AU leaders repeated an initiative to impose new taxes, so as to end this over-dependency on foreign funds, which was seen as unsustainable and politically undesirable. In addition, about half of the member states were in arrears with their contributions.

During the year, the crisis in Burundi, triggered by President Pierre Nkurunziza's controversial (third) term extension, took much of the AU's attention. Its *Peace and Security Council* adopted resolutions on Burundi on 9 July, 6 August and most strongly on 17 October at its 551st meeting, but it did not intervene or mediate as a collective body, although AU Commissioner for Peace and Security Smail Chergui lauded Uganda's President Museveni, appointed by the heads of state of the EAC, for his mediation efforts in June. In December, the AU threatened to send in a 5,000-strong force, called the African Prevention and Protection Mission in Burundi (MAPROBU), but the Burundian parliament rejected its formation on 23 December and no decision had been taken by year's end. On 18 December, the AU Commission authorised a 30-person four-day AU Short-Term Observation Mission to monitor the general elections in the CAR, held on 27 December.

The AU's outstanding issues with the *ICC* – which it accused of 'bias' – were not solved, although the African head of the ICC, Chief Prosecutor Ms Fatou Bensouda (from The Gambia), reiterated that the AU's criticism "did not match the reality". She also said that "... all cases with the exception of Kenya, Sudan and Libya, were at the request of African states asking for the ICC's intervention". The ICC had dropped the case against Kenyan President Uhuru Kenyatta, though not for lack of evidence, but the latter still saw fit to rail against the Court again during the 24th AU Summit. In another affront to the ICC, South Africa refused to arrest the war crimes-indicted Sudanese President Omar al-Bashir during his visit to Pretoria on 13–15 July.

The *APRM*, Africa's self-assessment mechanism for good governance (since 2003), was on the agenda at various AU meetings. By December, 35 of the 54 African countries had acceded to the APRM. During the year, 'base review missions' were carried out in Djibouti, Senegal, Sudan and Chad. Second reviews of Kenya, Rwanda, South Africa and Nigeria were prepared. The review comprised not primarily political structures, but more emphatically economic features regarding development goals and achievements, anti-corruption measures, financial administration, etc. With the introduction of the AU's Agenda 2063 and the AGA, the APRM faced increasing risk of playing third fiddle, though both Agenda 2063 and AGA attributed an important role to the APRM to turn vision into action. However, commitments to the APRM remained disappointing. Most member states had not regularly paid their annual minimum contribution of $ 100,000 and three had never made any financial contributions – including Liberia, whose President Ellen Johnson Sirleaf chaired the APRM Forum of Heads of State and Government, its highest decision-making body, between May 2013 and June 2015. It also faced massive problems in filling the vacancy at the helm of the secretariat, which had had no permanent chief executive officer since 2008. The last interim CEO held office from June 2014 until the beginning of 2016. The regular intervals originally anticipated for countries to come under review had also not yet been implemented; no country had so far conducted a full 'second generation' review, and not a single review had taken place since January 2013.

The *Extraordinary APRM Forum of Heads of State and Government* scheduled for 10–11 September in Nairobi (Kenya) to address critical challenges facing the APRM system was cancelled only four days before the set date with no official reasons being offered. An effort to reanimate the APRM was the establishment of the Pan African Parliament's (PAP) APRM Network. At the PAP plenary session on 7 October, four earlier country review reports on Algeria (2007), Burkina Faso (2008), Uganda (2009) and Lesotho (2010) were presented. Given more recent developments in several of these countries, this further underlined the APRM's current weaknesses more than any strengths or relevance. Observers agreed that the APRM faced a crucial future in which it must either regain credibility or vanish completely.

Democracy and Elections

For a tenth consecutive year, the North American NGO Freedom House reported a worldwide *decline in democracy*. In SSA there were only minor changes after 2014 had seen a notable downturn. The number of countries classified as 'free' fell slightly from ten in 2014 to nine; the number of countries classified as 'partly free' increased from 20 in 2014 to 21; the number of countries classified as 'not free' fell from 21 in 2014 to 20. Countries with a noticeable drop in political and civil liberties included Angola and Burundi. In Angola, this was due to an increase in government repression of the media, political activists and religious groups. Burkina Faso and Nigeria recorded visible improvements. Burkina Faso held its most successful presidential and legislative elections ever and subsequently saw the installation of a civilian government. Contrary to what many sceptics had predicted, Nigeria experienced comparatively peaceful and fair executive and legislative elections, which resulted in the first ever opposition victory at the national level. The CAR, Equatorial Guinea,

Eritrea, Somalia and Sudan featured on Freedom House's list of countries as among the worst in the world for democratic freedoms.

In terms of *elections*, it was a very busy year for SSA as voters cast their ballots in 14 states. Zambia, Lesotho, Burkina Faso, Burundi, the CAR, Chad, Côte d'Ivoire, Ethiopia, Guinea, Niger, Nigeria, Sudan, Tanzania and Togo went to the polls in presidential and/or legislative elections. South Sudan's first election since Independence in 2011, originally scheduled for June, was pushed back to 2017 as a result of violence. In some countries, elections offered an opportunity to consolidate democratic governance. In others, elections were seen as a new beginning after years of violence. The elections in Nigeria, Sudan, Burundi, Burkina Faso and the CAR deserve particular attention given the international headlines they created.

In Côte d'Ivoire, Nigeria and Burkina Faso, elections suffered from shortcomings and domestic criticism. However, in the last two, elections consolidated or at least stabilised previous *democratic gains*. This was especially the case in *Burkina Faso*, which underwent its first-ever competitive elections. The elections had originally been set for October. However, in September the presidential guard overthrew the transitional civilian-led government after it had passed an electoral code that effectively banned supporters of former long-term ruler Blaise Compaoré from contesting the election. The military coup proved unsuccessful and elections finally took place in late November. The presidential election was won by Roch Kaboré of the People's Movement for Progress, who received 53% of the vote in the first round. The elections were viewed as credible and legitimate by the international community. For the first time in many years, *Nigeria* received positive headlines. For the first time since the country's return to democracy in 1999, the ruling People's Democratic Party's hold on the presidency was under threat. Former military leader Muhammadu Buhari won a close but decisive victory over the incumbent, Goodluck Jonathan, in one of the most contested elections on the continent. In *Côte d'Ivoire*, President Alassane Ouattara won more than 83% of the votes cast in the first round of the presidential elections, a victory made possible by a fragmented opposition and an economic boom. Despite major political controversies between government and opposition, observers declared the elections peaceful and transparent.

The elections in *Sudan* and *Burundi* did more harm than good. In Sudan, the second multiparty elections after 2010 resulted in more of the same as incumbent President Omar al-Bashir won the presidential election by a landslide. The majority of opposition parties boycotted the elections. In Burundi, President Nkurunziza's decision in April to seek a third term plunged the country into its most serious crisis since the end of the civil war in 2005. Dozens were killed before the 21 July election, which saw weeks of demonstrations, a failed coup in May and clashes between rebel soldiers and loyalists, as the government took harsh measures against opposition protesters. The weeks of protests and violence forced more than 175,000 people to take refuge in neighbouring countries. The UN Electoral Observation Mission in Burundi observed media freedom restrictions and violations of human rights and other fundamental freedoms in the run-up to the elections. Similar concerns were expressed by the AU, the EAC and the ICGLR.

The outcome of the long-awaited elections in the *CAR* was not known by the end of the year. The elections, originally scheduled for 18 October, were delayed several times, and voters finally went to the polls on 30 December. The elections were supposed to end the violent conflict that had begun in late 2012 with the Séléka rebel group's march on the capital, Bangui. Numerous challenges overshadowed the run-up to the elections including on-going violence, lack of funds, voter registration issues and a lack of personnel to supervise the elections. No presidential candidate received more than 50% of the vote. Following the annulment of the results of the National Assembly elections by the Transitional Constitutional Court, the second round of presidential and new parliamentary elections could not take place till 2016.

Across the continent, several countries saw government attempts to restrict the *freedom of civil society*. In Kenya, government officials attacked civil society groups who supported the prosecution of President Kenyatta and Vice President Ruto by the ICC. Kenya also targeted civil groups who documented abuses by security forces in the context of anti-terrorism efforts. Sudan expelled humanitarian organisations from Darfur in response to the March 2009 ICC arrest warrant for President Omar al-Bashir, and shut down groups that publicly promoted justice and human rights. Uganda's parliament adopted an act that, if signed into law, would permit prison sentences of up to three years for leaders of independent groups that shirked broad and undefined "special obligations", including engaging in any act "prejudicial to the interests of Uganda". Unsurprisingly, most governments violating human rights did so whenever term limits threatened their continuation in power. This was the case in Burundi and in the DRC, where human rights defenders and pro-democracy youth activists were jailed, beaten and threatened after organising peaceful protests and speaking out against the possible extension of President Joseph Kabila's term beyond the Constitution's two-term limit.

The Reporters Without Borders' World Press Freedom Index noted a worldwide *decline in press freedoms*. Congo was particularly affected after a difficult year for independent news outlets. The government stepped up its witch-hunt of critical journalists, at times resorting to extreme violence. In South Sudan, constant harassment of news organisations made press freedom virtually nonexistent. In Côte d'Ivoire and Madagascar, press freedom improved as political uncertainty decreased. According to Freedom House, there was not a single SSA country where the press was rated as free. Several countries experienced significant declines in press freedom including Gambia, Burundi, Zimbabwe, Sudan, Swaziland, Sierra Leone and Ghana. As in previous years, Eritrea and Equatorial Guinea were among the worst countries in the world for journalists.

Unconstitutional Rule, Coups and Armed Conflict

Burkina Faso was the scene of a dramatic coup attempt that failed utterly. On 16 September, the Regiment of Presidential Security (RSP), loyal to ex-president Blaise Compaoré and headed by Gilbert Diendéré, detained transitional President Michel Kafando, Prime Minister Yacouba Isaac Zida and members of his cabinet. The transitional government had originated in the crisis of October 2014 when demonstrations took place in response to attempts by Compaoré to extent his 27 years in power by changing the Constitution. The RSP briefly seized control of the capital Ouagadougou, denounced the transitional government's electoral law (which prohibited Compaoré followers to stand for elections) and proclaimed the establishment of a new junta to oversee the elections envisaged for 11 October. However, the coup leaders failed to establish themselves fully and were condemned by African leaders, ECOWAS, the AU and the UN. More importantly, the coup met with resistance from large parts of the army. On 23 September, loyalists to the transitional government regained control of Ouagadougou and were able to restore Kafando as interim president. This was greeted with joy in the capital and also came as a relief to most international actors. However, the suspected implication of Guillaume Soro, former rebel leader and parliamentary speaker in neighbouring Côte d'Ivoire (where Compaoré lived in exile) created major diplomatic tensions between the two countries.

As in previous years, *presidential term limits* were debated in many African countries. The turmoil in Burkina Faso in 2014, which had led to a "pro-democracy coup" and the failure of an "anti-democracy coup attempt" plus regime change in 2015 did not go unnoticed in other countries, but Congo's President Sassou Nguesso nevertheless found his situation safe enough to go ahead with changing the Constitution in order to allow him to stand for further terms. This was greeted with protests by demonstrators (and by diaspora groups in Paris). His counterpart in the DRC, Joseph Kabila, was quite obviously tempted to follow suit. The case of Burundi's Pierre Nkurunziza was rather more specific. His intention to run for a further mandate split the political scene, which was already operating under severe strain. On 5 May, the Constitutional Court ruled that Nkurunziza's candidature would be legal, based on an interpretation that his first mandate, during a transitional phase, would not count. This interpretation resulted in a failed bloody coup attempt (13–15 May), when parts of the army set out to overthrow the regime. The coup attempt in turn triggered acts of repression on a scale unprecedented since the end of the civil war, including the murder of opposition politicians, as well as revenge assassinations of top state representatives. In the course of the year, over 350 people died and more than 215,000 fled the country. The presidential elections in July confirmed Nkurunziza in office but were declared undemocratic by most of the international community, and were unable to calm the situation. Fears of a return to ethnic pogroms and genocide were voiced both domestically and externally.

The CAR was on the way to return to *constitutional rule* with the holding of a referendum and the first round of presidential elections, but the interim government and legislative body were still operating by the end of the year. In Lesotho, the crisis of 2014 was partly resolved with the holding of early (and peaceful elections). It was debatable whether the declaration by Gambia's President Yahya Jammeh on 10 December that his country would from now on be an 'Islamic republic' was in conformity with the Constitution. Jammeh explained that Islam was the religion of most citizens and that the nation should break away from its colonial past, thus continuing on his course over recent years to turn his back to the Commonwealth and on the West in general. ECOWAS, having strict rules on unconstitutional rule, did not respond to this declaration. Coincidentally, the Federation of African Journalists and three individual Gambian journalists filed a legal claim before the ECOWAS Court on 7 December to challenge the pervasive culture of persecution, violence and injustice towards journalists in Gambia.

In most African war zones, the *intensity of conflict abated* in comparison with 2014. This was obvious in the CAR and the DRC, and also in Mali. The MINUSCA mission in the CAR was able to control most, though not all, hotbeds of violence and there were sporadic local confrontations, mostly in the centre of the county and in the capital Bangui. The DRC saw a number of military operations to unseat local militias in the east, but none were of comparable size to those in the past. A *peace agreement in Mali* signed in June by the government and a Tuareg-led rebel coalition initially brought hope of an end to years of turmoil but expectations quickly faded when it was difficult to implement. The UN and Algeria were the main drivers of the peace process. The peace accord called for the creation of elected regional assemblies but did not establish autonomy for northern Mali. Though direct confrontations were on the decline, Mali did not disappear from international headlines as it was the base for several terrorist groups. On 20 November, a breakaway al-Qaeda faction, the so called al-Mourabitoun, took 170 hostages and killed 20 people in an attack on the five-star Radisson Blu hotel in the heart of Mali's capital, Bamako. Nine hours after the beginning of the attack, security forces from Mali, France and the USA stormed the hotel together, freed the hostages and killed two of the hostage-takers. Even in South Sudan, where the political crisis was far from over, the number of fatalities recorded by the Uppsala Conflict Data Programme fell, but still numbered 1,125 dead. In comparison, the *Boko Haram* insurgency was much more serious and continued to claim lives, mostly in north-east Nigeria, but also in neighbouring Niger, Chad and Cameroon. In Nigeria, Boko Haram attacks and state-led repression accounted for most of the nearly 9,000 deaths in violent conflicts recorded, and the numbers of deaths related to Boko Haram also increased in all neighbouring countries (particularly Cameroon, where a singular suicide bombing in the regional capital Maroua claimed 33 lives and sent shock-waves round the whole country). The other steady source of concern was in Somalia, where around 1,200 deaths were recorded. A major terrorist incident was a suicide attack on a hotel in Mogadishu on 26 July, which caused 13 deaths. The *al-Shabaab* militia again claimed several terrorist attacks in Kenya. Most attention was received by the attacks on Garissa University College, where nearly 150 people were killed, but there was also an attack on Mandera, and on a bus on the Nairobi–Mandera highway created shock. Largely ignored by international media were on-going confrontations in Sudan, both in Darfur and in the Blue Nile region, were largely ignored by the international media. According to the *Uppsala Conflict Data Program*, the number of fatalities in Sudan over the year rose to 2,518.

International engagement in Africa's violent conflicts remained high, mostly via peacekeeping operations, though in some cases a peace agreement including all major conflict parties was not in place. According to the German-based Center for International Peace Operations (ZIF), the following major UN-sponsored peacekeeping missions were in place by September: MONUSCO (DRC; with 18,694 combat troops); UNAMID (Sudan (Darfur), 14.585; a hybrid mission in conjunction with the AU); UNMIS (South Sudan, 11,529); MINUSCA (CAR, 9,254); and MINUSMA (Mali, 9,159). The missions already established for a considerable time in Côte d'Ivoire, Liberia and Abyei (Sudan) were still of a substantial size, totalling around 5,000 combat troops. These large UN missions were in some cases accompanied by smaller specialised EU operations, such as EU Training Missions in Mali and Somalia. More importantly, the AU in its own right conducted the largest military mission on the continent, i.e. AMISOM in Somalia, with 21,645 soldiers. In some of these missions, the police component was substantial (Darfur, Liberia, Côte d'Ivoire, the CAR, the DRC and Mali, with over 1,000 police personnel each) but even so it was doubtful that this component was strong enough for the tasks assigned to it, which did not include combat. France had the single most important military mission, the Sangaris mission, in CAR. Finally, two major regional alliances fought against insurgencies: the Multinational Joint Task Force (MJTF) to fight Boko Haram included forces from Nigeria, Niger, Chad, Cameroon and Benin, and was supported by intelligence officers from France and, from October onwards, about 300 US soldiers. The MJTF had an estimated 10,000 soldiers and suffered a heavy blow in January, when its headquarters in Baga (Nigeria), were overrun by Boko Haram elements, who subsequently destroyed the town. The Task Force of the Regional Cooperation Initiative for the Elimination of the LRA (consisting of forces from Uganda, the DRC, South Sudan and the CAR, supported by US special forces) had an estimated 2,285 troops. Both task forces struggled to become more efficient. Despite the LRA's generally small numbers (though they were very fluid and depended on the rate of abductions), the latter mission did not seem to be particularly successful. However, both the inaccessible terrain and local alliances with rebel groups, plus suspected support from the government of Sudan, made the elimination of the LRA and more particularly the capture of dreaded warlord Joseph Kony a difficult enterprise. 2015 was not the easiest year for peacekeepers as more and more reports about (mostly sexual) abuse came to light. UN headquarters belatedly deemed it necessary to concentrate strongly on such cases and to sanction individuals and entire contingents.

Piracy in the Indian Ocean and in the Gulf of Aden and the coastal region of the Horn of Africa continued to decline, according to the Annual Report on 'Piracy and Armed Robbery against Ships' published by the International Maritime Bureau. The total number of attacks fell from 55 in 2014 to 35 and there were none off Somalia, which had been hardly imaginable only few years earlier. The High Risk Area of Somalia was sensibly reduced by 55% on 1 December, though experts warned that piracy threats remained and that the presence of the EU naval mission would still be needed. In contrast, attacks by pirates continued to be recorded in the Gulf of Guinea and concentrated in the coastal region of Nigeria (14), Congo (5), the DRC (3) and Guinea (3), i.e. those areas remained risky and aggressors were mostly well armed and extremely violent. Taking hostages and mistreating the crew over periods of a few days was not unusual. Early in the year, pirates armed with AK47s hijacked a product tanker in Nigerian waters and took hostage all nine crew members. The robbers transferred oil to an unidentified vessel. As the tanker moved into Ghanaian waters, the local navy intervened and arrested the pirates. Following this event, five assaults in Nigerian waters resulted in the kidnapping of a total of 19 crew members. After negotiations, 14 abducted crew memers were released. Thus, the overall number of crew taken hostage in the African region increased, but such incidents took place exclusively off Nigeria. The Nigerian authorities reacted by expanding their capability. As part of a security operation named 'Pulo Shield', over 1,600 suspected pirates and militants in the Niger Delta Region were detained by the Nigerian military. With 50 vessels, 200 barges and specialised weaponry, the security forces appeared well equipped.

Epidemics and Disasters

Sub-Saharan Africa remained the global region most affected by *HIV/AIDS*, with an estimated 19 m or 70% of all people living with HIV, including 88% of the world's HIV-positive children. SSA registered an estimated 1 m new HIV infections during the year, a decline in new infections by an estimated 14% compared with 2010. AIDS treatment had reached over 10 m people. Some 60% of HIV positive patients were receiving antiretroviral therapy, and new infections among children had declined by two-thirds compared with 2010. Despite continued high figures, SSA was the only region that had registered a consistent drop in new infections after 2010, but AIDS remained the number one cause of death among adolescents, followed by diarrhoeal diseases and malaria. The *Ebola* virus disease epidemic, which had by early 2015 led to a total of almost 25,000 confirmed deaths since its outbreak in Sierra Leone, Liberia and Guinea, was brought under control with only a few new cases reported during the year. Various *cholera* outbreaks were reported from provinces in the DRC and in Tanzania, while Niger suffered from a wave of meningococcal meningitis, although cases of meningitis in general had dropped significantly over recent years. Communicable diseases and other conditions still predominated in SSA, but *non-communicable diseases*, such as cardiovascular diseases, cancers, diabetes and chronic respiratory diseases were projected to become the leading cause of death by 2030.

Natural disasters remained an on-going feature. The scale of weather-related events raised questions as to the extent to which they were a result of climate change, which may have exacerbated *floods* and droughts. In January, torrential rains flooded parts of Malawi and the devastation made close to a quarter of a million people homeless. In March, floods in Angola killed several people. In June, a flood in Accra (Ghana) killed more than 150 people sheltering from rain, while many victims died as the result of setting a petrol filling station at fire. An estimated 20,000 residents in and around Ouagadougou suffered from heavy rains in August.

The massive *drought* that developed towards year's end in Ethiopia and Southern Africa, with life threatening consequences for millions of people, was linked to and considered the direct result of a monster El Niño. Sea surface temperatures from December were much warmer than at any time since records began. A measured increase of 2.2°C was much higher than those during recent massive El Niños in 1997/98 and 1982/83 (which both saw an increase of 1.6°C). From mid-year, South Africa was already experiencing one of the worst droughts ever recorded, with devastating consequences for farming communities. Lack of sufficient rainfall also meant that the water shortage in Namibia brought massive problems. *Food security* in the sub-region declined drastically and millions of people in several countries were reliant on initiatives by their governments to survive. Droughts in Angola, Botswana, Malawi, Namibia, South Africa and Zimbabwe had major impacts on staple foods and cash crops. This resulted in decreased means of sustenance and income, and contributed to increased migration into urban areas or across borders. Botswana allocated emergency funds to livestock farmers to ease the worst drought conditions in 30 years. Southern Africa's total production forecast was down by about 7% from 2014, according to FAO's 2015 Crop Prospects and Food Situation report.

The level of *man-made violence* in countries such as Mali, the CAR and South Sudan added to the pressure on humanitarian aid. While a report on the State of the Humanitarian System recorded fewer emergencies in recent years, the numbers of refugees and IDPs had grown as a result of conflict-related violence, often with little to no meaningful humanitarian assistance for the victims. According to a humanitarian action advocate, the humanitarian system was "failing to protect people in conflict situations" and unable to give these people appropriate assistance. He said: "I would much rather be waiting for aid in a typhoon hit country than I would in Central African Republic."

PART 2

African-European Relations

Christine Hackenesch and Niels Keijzer

Although the main route to Europe lay further east in the Mediterranean, Africa-EU relations continued to be dominated by what has since been dubbed the 'refugee crisis'. Unfortunately, on this key issue European and African interests could not be further apart: while most African governments would welcome increased opportunities for legal migration to Europe, the EU was politically not willing and therefore not able to move in this direction. (Unless indicated otherwise, in this chapter the abbreviation EU refers to the European Union and its Member States.) Instead, and contrary to its nature as a trade liberalisation project, the EU's discourse accentuated the desire to 'manage' migratory flows and tackle 'root causes' of migration.

The year's key political moment for EU-Africa relations was the *Valletta Summit on Migration* on 11–12 November, a high-level meeting convened by the EU to discuss the subject with Africa. The most important outcome of the meeting was the launch of a dedicated *EU Trust Fund for Africa*, whose aim was to foster stability and contribute to better migration management. In her first ever public address to the AU, European Commission Vice President and High-Representative for Foreign Affairs and Security Policy Federica Mogherini had argued on 20 October: "It is not about giving money in exchange for keeping migrants in the region, or having them returning. It is not an exchange. It is finding the resources to address a common interest: managing together the migration flows in all their aspects." For the Trust Fund, the EU moved funds that would otherwise have been jointly programmed with Africa into a setup that gave the EU a greater say. This was an indication that, in contrast to the EU's political discourse, the EU and Africa remained far from pursuing a common approach on migration and development.

Beyond these 'inter-continental' trends, European media and political interest focused once again on African crises at the national level, including slow progress in South Sudan, a deteriorating situation in Burundi, and substantial lingering conflicts in almost all African regions. Terrorist threats posed by Boko Haram and al-Shabaab and debates around 'third terms' for African heads of state particularly raised EU concerns. These crises, as well as the political uncertainty affecting the European project as a whole, showed that bilateral relations remained at the core of EU-Africa relations.

Migration

A key moment was the launch of the 'Emergency Trust Fund for Stability and Addressing Root Causes of Irregular Migration and Displaced Persons in Africa'

 | DOI 10.1163/9789004333239_003

during the Valletta Summit. In press releases, the EU typically referred to the *Trust Fund* as the antithesis of the stereotypical EU development cooperation intervention, namely as a mechanism allowing for 'fast delivery' and quick as well as visible results. The majority of its € 1.8 bn budget was raised from EDF reserves. The Trust Fund was in principle resourced by the European Commission and the member states. However, the original idea that member states would match the Commission's contribution was not implemented and, by November, EU member states had managed to collectively provide only a little over € 78 m (including contributions by Norway and Switzerland). The economic and political drivers of forced migration in Africa were nonetheless long-term development issues. Shifting such resources to address an issue that had been framed in security terms was clearly problematic and cast a shadow on the EU's development policy. First indications of programmes agreed in 2015 raised considerable doubts about the extent to which the Trust Fund would finance different kinds of intervention from those undertaken via the normal programming channels. Additional contributions by the non-EU member states Norway and Switzerland, who were represented in the Trust Fund management structure, while African and European parliaments were excluded, added to concerns over whether it could convincingly present itself as a development instrument rather than an EU measure to respond to its own security concerns.

Observers believed that the programmes financed by the Trust Fund, although designed and delivered in new ways, might face the same old challenges of (non-) effectiveness as EU development cooperation writ large, including prominently the fact that sustainable results hinged on the partner's interest, commitment and contribution. In this light, the low additional financial contributions made to the Trust Fund by EU member states, along with the EU's decision, taken in the same period, to provide a much larger amount of funding to one country – Turkey – than to the entire continent of Africa, triggered disappointment on the part of many African governments. In this context, towards the end of the year the EU adopted plans to review the European Neighbourhood Policy (ENP), which also affected Africa. The ENP had been adopted in 2004, an optimistic period during which the EU's 'big bang' enlargement was finalised, but events in recent years in both eastern and southern Europe were challenging the EU's long-term development objectives in the regions, while also exposing its inconsistent and undisciplined application of conditionality. The ENP was thus to be adjusted to accommodate both the changing EU regional dynamics and the changes that had occurred within the EU itself in the more than ten years since the ENP's adoption.

'Maiden Speech' of the EU High Representative to the AU

On 20 October, Federica Mogherini became the first EU High Representative to address AU member states at the organisation's headquarters in Addis Ababa (Ethiopia). She began by quoting Nelson Mandela, who had described Africa as a region of vast yet untapped potential, using his words to emphasise Africa's economic and human potential. She considered realisation of the latter more challenging and, referring to the need for Africa to create 18 m new jobs per year, called for a shift in relations with the EU from aid to investment. Only towards the end of her speech did she become more explicit about the refugee crisis but, to counteract the EU's symptom-fighting tendencies, she also maintained that "geography and history make us natural and almost indispensable partners". While relatively down-to-earth and not containing any breaking news, Mogherini's speech represented a symbolic and important next step in deepening EU-Africa dialogue beyond the bilateral level, and an important stepping stone towards the next EU-Africa Summit, scheduled for 2017.

While *'third terms'* had become a prominent issue in African election debates, the EU had not developed a broader consensus or strategy on how to respond to various attempts by African presidents to change the constitution of their countries in order to stay in power for more than two terms. In *Burundi*, the EU sought to put pressure on the president to step down and was active in contributing to the de-escalation of the mounting violence, although with limited success. In *Burkina Faso*, the EU had been taken by surprise by the popular uprisings in 2014 against President Compaoré's attempts to stay in power. While the EU had done little in response to the short-term crisis then, it strongly supported the longer-term political process that led to the elections in November. In *Rwanda*, the EU criticised President Kagame's steps to change the constitution in order to run for election again in 2017, while remaining relatively silent overall. The EU did not comment on the referendum on 25 October in the Republic of *Congo*, which opened the way for constitutional change to allow President Denis Sassou Nguesso to run for a third term. Constitutional changes to allow for a third term were also expected in the *DRC*. In light of the experience gained from Burundi and the EU's positioning in other cases, it seemed unlikely that the EU would take a strong critical stance there. Despite its own high ambitions, these crises pointed to the obvious limitations of the EU as an external actor: in the case of Burundi, EAC member states did not strongly engage, although a meeting in Dar es Salaam (Tanzania) in May did provide the opportunity for a failed coup attempt in Bujumbura (Burundi). Their decision to appoint Ugandan President Yoweri Museveni as mediator gave the wrong signal, given that the plank of his 38-year rule clearly left him ill-equipped to remove the splinter from President Nkurunziza's eye.

Eastern Africa / Horn of Africa

The European Council adopted the Horn of Africa Regional Action Plan (2015–20) on 26 October. The Action Plan outlined the EU's comprehensive approach towards the region and sought to implement the EU Horn of Africa Strategic Framework, adopted in November 2011. The Action Plan aimed at better combining the EU's various instruments (development and humanitarian aid, Common Security and Defence Policy missions, etc.) to support peace, stability and sustainable and inclusive growth in the Horn of Africa. Since 2011, three main issues affecting the EU's interests in the region had gained prominence: violent extremism, migration and forced displacement, and the influences of the wider region on the Horn. The EU therefore identified five priorities for its cooperation with the region for the coming five years: supporting regional security and stability; fighting against migration and forced displacement; countering radicalisation and violent extremism; supporting youth and employment; and human rights, rule of law and democratic governance.

The EU continued to support negotiations between the two parties in the *South Sudan* conflict under the aegis of IGAD, but the lack of progress in these talks prompted the EU to release a statement in February calling for closer involvement by the international community in resolving the conflict. Not least in response to the long series of brokered and subsequently violated ceasefire agreements, the EU decided in March to provide € 5 m to IGAD through the Africa Peace Facility in support of a so-called monitoring and verification mechanism. This mechanism sought to monitor violations of the ceasefire agreement, including monitoring the public communication between the parties in order to inform measures to be put in place by regional authorities to increase leverage with the parties to the conflict. In view of the lack of progress made and in response to violations of ceasefire agreements, the EU imposed Common Foreign and Security Policy (CFSP) sanctions on two South-Sudanese military leaders in July, thus beginning to add tougher measures to the existing package of mediation facilitation. On 26 August, South Sudan's President Salva Kiir finally signed the peace agreement already endorsed by other South-Sudanese parties in Addis Ababa earlier that month. The EU welcomed the agreement but reiterated the need for a lasting ceasefire and unhindered access for humanitarian operations.

The worsening of the political and security situation and escalation of violence in *Burundi* was equally high on the EU's agenda throughout the year and of great concern not only with regard to Burundi itself but also for peace and stability within the wider Great Lakes region. In the run-up to presidential elections, President Pierre Nkurunziza made it clear that he would not step down. On 25 April, he formally announced that he would seek a third mandate, arguably against the provisions in the Constitution, which set a limit of two terms. His decision caused unrest and demonstrations by the opposition, which the government violently repressed. The elections finally took place on 21 July, after the Constitutional Court's interpretation of the Constitution affirmed that Nkurunziza had only served one regular term and was eligible to stand for one more, and against requests from regional leaders (EAC and AU) to further postpone the elections.

To prevent an escalation of the situation, the EU early on engaged the Burundian government in intensified political dialogue under Article 8 of the Cotonou

Agreement, with meetings on 17 October and 9 December 2014, 23 January and 5 March. The EU had planned to deploy an election observation mission (EOM), led by Chief Observer David Martin, a Member of the European Parliament. However, in light of severe restrictions on independent media, excessive use of force against demonstrators and a climate of intimidation for opposition parties and civil society, European Commission Vice President and High Representative Mogherini felt that not even the minimal conditions for an EOM were in place and decided on 28 May to suspend the mission. In response to the escalating violence and growing number of refugees leaving Burundi for neighbouring countries, the EU increased its humanitarian aid to € 9 m between April and July. By July, around 175,000 people had fled the country, mostly to Tanzania, Rwanda, the DRC and Uganda. Total EU humanitarian aid for the Great Lakes region over the year amounted to € 56.5 m. On 1 October, the European Council adopted CFSP sanctions against Burundi. Four persons whose activities were viewed by the EU as particularly obstructive to achieving a political solution to the current crisis were banned from travelling to the EU, but President Nkurunziza himself was not sanctioned in order to keep dialogue channels open. In addition, on 8 December, the EU formally opened consultations under Article 96 of the Cotonou Agreement – a process that could lead to the suspension or reduction of aid funds and the limiting of new EU support to humanitarian measures. The opening of Article 96 consultations had already been debated ahead of the elections, but it was decided to first await and support regional action. Moreover, as Article 96 consultations were seen as a "measure of last resort" (once referred to as the "nuclear option" by the EU's former development commissioner Andris Piebalgs), the EU wanted to explore all other options first.

On 13 December, Mogherini and European Commissioner for International Cooperation and Development Neven Mimica issued a joint statement arguing that the "dramatic deterioration in the situation requires a determined response". Mogherini and Mimica urged that a political process and inter-Burundian dialogue be started immediately, mediated by Uganda and the AU. The EU announced that it would make financial support available to support this political dialogue. Throughout the year, the EU sought to closely engage with the UN Secretary-General's Special Envoy Said Djinnit, who was supposed to facilitate the mediation, and with the AU and the EAC to reach a consensus between international actors and Burundian officials on how to proceed. In June, the EU supported the EAC summit call to postpone the elections to allow time for the necessary conditions of peace, security and stability to be put in place.

Relations with *Rwanda* had started to deteriorate in 2012, when the UN Expert Group published a report accusing the Rwandan government of supporting rebel groups in the eastern DRC. In 2015, relations became tense when the government initiated a modification of the Constitution to allow President Kagame to run for a third term in the 2017 presidential elections. The EU and some EU member states such as the UK (as well as the USA) openly criticised the Rwandan government for changing the Constitution. Kagame condemned the criticism via Twitter in a series of emotional tweets. Rwanda's relations with the UK were at a particularly low level in the summer, when the head of Rwanda's intelligence services, Karensi Kareke, was arrested in London on the basis of a Spanish warrant on charges of participating in war crimes in the immediate aftermath of the genocide. He did not stay long in British custody, however, and was released on grounds of procedural errors; Cherie Blair, wife of former prime minister Tony Blair, was his defence counsel in court.

The run-up to the elections in *Ethiopia* in May was characterised by tense relations with the EU and other international partners. The EU considered internally whether to deploy an EOM but finally decided against it (and was also not invited to do so by the Ethiopian authorities). The EU had been cautious from the start about deploying another EOM, after the difficult experiences in May 2005, when the government had brutally repressed opposition demonstrations after the elections, and the difficult experiences in May 2010, when the EU EOM was not allowed to present its final report in Addis Ababa (setting a precedent in the history of EU EOMs). The spokesperson of the European External Action Service (EEAS) stated that the pre-election process was peacefully concluded and that the elections were largely peaceful and orderly. However, he criticised the arrest of many journalists and opposition politicians, the closure of some media outlets and the restriction of opportunities for the opposition to engage in the election campaign, reminding all parties that they should adhere to the provisions of the African Charter on Democracy, Elections and Governance.

The EU did not comment on or criticise the outcome of the elections (the ruling Ethiopian Peoples' Revolutionary Democratic Front took all the seats in parliament), but instead, relatively soon after the elections, sought to 'upgrade' its relations with Ethiopia. A bilateral meeting on 20 October between Mogherini and Ethiopia's Minister of Foreign Affairs Tedros Adhanom resulted in a joint statement whose main message was that the relationship between Ethiopia and the EU would be 'elevated' to a *Strategic Partnership*. The statement identified private sector development, migration and peace and security as the key focus for regular political dialogue in the future. It avoided the issue of the mass protests that had taken place in the Oromia region over the expansion of the municipal boundary of the capital, Addis Ababa, which had threatened the eviction of farmers from their land. With this statement – an interesting example of what the EU refers to as 'economic diplomacy' – the EU refrained from reacting when the protests escalated, until 23 December, when it issued a timid statement calling on both parties to enter into dialogue and refrain from violence and inflammatory statements. The European Parliament, on the other hand, was more outspoken and "strongly condemned the recent use of excessive force by the security forces in

Oromia and in all Ethiopian regions, the increased cases of human rights violations and abuses".

Central Africa

In March, the EU deployed a new Military Advisory Mission (EUMAM) in the *CAR*. The EU Force (EUFOR), which had been set up in 2014, ended its mandate and was closed on 15 March. Its objective had been to provide support towards achieving a secure environment in the Bangui area, before an African peacekeeping mission could take over. Concerns were raised, however, that EUMAM was considerably smaller than its predecessor and that its size was thus not commensurate with its ambitious objective. On 26 May, the EU convened an international conference on the CAR in Brussels, focusing on the country's humanitarian needs, recovery and resilience-building. This event followed almost a year after the EU, France, Germany and the Netherlands jointly launched the EU Bêkou Trust Fund for the CAR, when the European Commission announced that it would increase its assistance to the CAR to a total of € 72 m, consisting of humanitarian aid (€ 10 m), budget support (€ 40 m) and a new contribution to the EU Trust Fund for the CAR (€ 22 m). It thus increased its profile as one of the biggest donors to the country as it was gearing up for elections scheduled for late December (and a second round in January 2016). The EU welcomed the constitutional referendum held on 13–14 December to prepare for the parliamentary and presidential elections and took it as a positive sign that the CAR was determined to move on from the era of transition.

The EU also closely followed political developments in the *DRC*. The EU delegation together with local representatives of EU member states published a statement criticising persistent human rights violations in the *DRC*, particularly in the eastern parts of the country. The EU welcomed the new electoral law on 25 January but, on various occasions, urged the Congolese government to allow for an electoral process within a climate of freedom of expression and association and raised particular concern when the head of the electoral commission resigned on 10 October. On 19 November, the EU welcomed President Kabila's decision to launch a national dialogue, which was intended to smooth the way for the organisation of presidential and legislative elections in November 2016.

West Africa and the Sahel Region

Throughout the year *Boko Haram* continued to absorb considerable European foreign policy energy directed towards the African continent. In February, EU foreign ministers adopting a detailed political statement that emphasised upfront the wider regional threats caused by the insurgency, with particular reference to Cameroon, Chad and Niger. The statement also underlined the limited direct role available to the EU, as it felt that the countries directly affected were responsible for protecting their civilians, but it also pledged its support for and approval of regional and continental security operations. In June, the EU pledged € 21 m in humanitarian aid to support populations in Nigeria and affected neighbouring countries. Following terror attacks in Cameroon in July, the EU reaffirmed the worsening of the security situation in the countries around Lake Chad.

As with the Horn of Africa, the European Council adopted a *Regional Action Plan for the Sahel* (2015–20) on 20 April, as a framework for implementing the EU Strategy for Security and Development in the Sahel (adopted on 21 March 2011 and revised on 17 March 2014). The Action Plan sought to reaffirm the EU's continued engagement and its support for sustainable and inclusive political and socioeconomic development in the Sahel region. It focused on four main areas: the prevention and countering of radicalisation; the creation of appropriate conditions for youth; migration and mobility; and border management, the fight against illicit trafficking and transnational organised crime. On 7 June, Mogherini and EU Commissioner for Humanitarian Affairs Christos Stylianides met in Brussels with the foreign ministers of the five Sahel countries (Burkina Faso, Mali, Mauritania, Niger and Chad) to discuss the Action Plan. The five Sahel countries set up the 'Sahel G5' as an institutional framework for regional cooperation in the area of security and development. The EU and the G5 agreed to complement the Action Plan with a regular and structured political dialogue, in parallel with dialogues at the bilateral and regional level. On 20 November, Mogherini joined the 3rd Sahel G5 summit in Chad, where she announced the new support programme for Chad from the 11th EDF (€ 101 m).

The EU welcomed the signing of the peace agreement in *Mali* on 20 June. The EU had supported the mediation process, led by Algeria and involving a broad range of regional actors (ECOWAS, AU, neighbouring countries and the UN). The EU supported the peace process with considerable development aid funds. Under the 11th EDF, the EU allocated € 615 m for the period 2014–20 of which € 300 m was to be disbursed by the end of the year. The EU provided direct support to the state budget, the education sector and the creation of jobs for youth. The EU Capacity Building Mission (EUCAP Sahel Mali) was formally launched on 15 January for a period of two years with the objective of supporting the Malian government to ensure stability and maintain the state's monopoly on power throughout the country. The mission also provided advice and training for the police forces (Gendarmerie and Garde Nationale), while closely coordinating and working with other international partners. In addition to EUCAP, the EU continued to maintain its military training mission in Mali, which trained and advised the Malian Armed Forces with a view to restoring their military capacity to enable them to engage in combat operations aimed at restoring the country's territorial integrity.

Southern Africa

Even though the EU's trade sanctions on *Zimbabwe* had been lifted in August 2014, a travel ban and asset freeze on President Mugabe and the first lady and an arms embargo had been retained. Following a review in February, the EU decided to give Zimbabwe € 234 m in aid under the 11th EDF. The EU agreed to allow Mugabe to travel to the EU on an exceptional basis during his year-long chairmanship of the AU, if travelling on AU business. The EU's Official Journal reported, however, that EU governments were not yet convinced that Mugabe had changed enough to merit a definite lifting of restrictions. Diplomatic circumspection paid off in that there were no Mugabe-EU incidents during his period as AU chairman.

The EU voiced concern in June when *South Africa*, a signatory of the Rome Statute establishing the *ICC*, did not arrest the Sudanese President Omar al-Bashir during his visit to Pretoria. Al-Bashir faced an international arrest warrant for alleged crimes in Darfur. The South African government consequently publicly considered withdrawing its signature from the Rome Statute.

While the European Commission and External Action Service were silent on the shrinking of political spaces and increasing human rights violations in *Angola*, the European Parliament adopted a critical resolution on 9 September. The Parliament raised concern that the military and intelligence services had become drivers behind human rights violations and urged the European Commission to take relevant steps in accordance with Articles 8, 9 and 96 of the Cotonou Agreement, if the situation did not improve.

Election Observation

2015 was again a busy year on the electoral front, with 14 African states organising national elections. Each year, the High Representative identifies a number of countries where *EU EOMs* could be deployed, in consultation with the Council of Ministers and the European Parliament. Feasibility missions are subsequently carried out to determine whether an observation mission would be advisable, feasible and useful, and to determine conditions for the host government to ensure the EU mission could operate fully and credibly.

This year, elections in Nigeria, Tanzania, Guinea and Burkina Faso were covered by EU EOMs. All elections were complicated in their own way, and showed that the EU did not pick easy battles. *Tanzania's elections* were organised in a context of a weakening ruling party, with the complicating element of separate parliaments for mainland Tanzania and the island of Zanzibar. This EOM, with 141 observers, was the largest undertaken during the year. In its final statement, the EU announced that the elections were vigorously contested and largely well managed but was also critical that the decision-making processes of the electoral management bodies were not fully transparent. Moreover, in a joint statement with observers from the AU, SADC and the Commonwealth on 29 October, the EU expressed strong concern at the situation in Zanzibar and called for transparency in the electoral process.

In *Nigeria*'s history books, 2015 will probably claim a prominent place, with the opposition winning elections for the first time since the transition from military rule in 1999. President Goodluck Jonathan's early and unambiguous acceptance of defeat paved the way for a peaceful handover to Muhammadu Buhari after elections that the authorities had earlier postponed because of the Boko Haram insurgency in the North. The EU deployed a mission comprised of observers from 26 EU member states as well as Norway and Switzerland, making a total of just 90 observers – rather low given the large population and land size of this federal state. The observation report attested to highly competitive elections that were marred by incidents of violence, abuse of incumbency at state and federal levels, and direct attempts at manipulation. Recommendations were put forward but no characterisation of the election as a whole, with the report acknowledging that the observation sample was not representative. These experiences should lead to some reflection as to whether EOMs in their current form are fit for purpose when applied in large nations.

In *Guinea*, the EU deployed a 72-member observation mission. The EU delegation cited "massive deficiencies" ahead of polling but its post-election report concluded that the process overall was "valid".

The last EOM of the year was deployed for elections in *Burkina Faso* on 29 November, following the 2014 uprising and forced departure of President Compaoré, who had ruled the country for 27 years. His party was banned from running a presidential candidate but was still able to participate in the parliamentary election. The presidential election was won by Roch Marc Christina Kaboré with 53% of the vote in the first round. While wealthier candidates clearly gained advantages during campaigns in this largely rural country, the elections were widely heralded as the most open and transparent that the country had experienced. More than 17,000 national and international observers scrutinised the legality of the elections, including 80 officials from the EU's mission.

EU Member States' Relations with African Countries

France's President Hollande hit the headlines on 17 December when he denounced his country's brutal colonial rule over Algeria. He was also the only European head of state at the AU's 50th anniversary celebrations. The Franco-African 'Elysée Summit for Peace and Security in Africa' on 6–7 December in Paris was attended by 53 delegations from African countries, representatives from France and a range of international and regional organisations (the UN, AU, EU, AfDB, IMF and World Bank). The choice of peace and security, economic partnership, development and climate change as overarching topics for the summit stressed the search for areas of mutual interest, but also reflected the real and increasing competition for French influence and interests in the continent.

2015 saw some high-level visits from *German* politicians to African countries. President Gauck visited Tanzania in February, using the occasion to give a speech to the EAC. Foreign Minister Steinmeier travelled to Mozambique, Zambia, Tanzania and Uganda in November, together with a delegation of German parliamentarians and representatives from the private sector. While development topics and foreign policy considerations took the limelight, German commercial interests continued to be on the rise, too. In this context, it is noteworthy that in September over 300 entrepreneurs from Africa and Germany gathered in Berlin for the first German-African Business Summit. Steinmeier's discourse at the event highlighted that relations with the continent were ever more convincingly moving from a traditional emphasis on aid towards trade, though he also commented on various political issues such as the ignoring of constitutional term limits by some African heads of state.

In December, the *United Kingdom*'s Foreign and Commonwealth Office and DFID jointly launched a public consultation on the UK government's relations with Africa. A month earlier, the UK adopted its new bilateral aid strategy, which, among other reforms, increased the role of other government departments in managing the country's Official Development Assistance budget. Moreover, the strategy put a strong focus on fragile and conflict-affected states, including Syria and other countries in the MENA region. Support for Africa was only mentioned as part of the UK's engagement with countries where the UK had strong historical, cultural and diaspora links.

In November, the *Netherlands*' Prime Minister Mark Rutte led a delegation to South Africa with the aim of further deepening trade relations between the two countries. The delegation turned out to be the largest Dutch trade mission to Africa so far. In response to the Paris terrorist attacks, Rutte returned to the Netherlands after the first political-level meetings. Despite this engagement, the Dutch government did not seem to have many concrete plans with regard to EU-Africa relations during its upcoming presidency of the EU in the first half of 2016.

The 2030 Agenda on Sustainable Development and the Paris Agreement on Climate Change

In October 2014, the president of the UN General Assembly had appointed the permanent representatives of Ireland and Kenya as co-facilitators to lead the negotiations on the *post-2015 development agenda*, which formally started following the publication of the UN Secretary-General's Synthesis Report in December 2014. During the 7th AU-EU 'college to college' meeting, the respective Commissions committed themselves to intensive cooperation in the post-2015 negotiations and the negotiations for a legally binding agreement on climate change in December.

The successful adoption in September of the ambitious 2030 Agenda for Sustainable Development shed a positive light on the European and African co-facilitators and provided a much-needed measure of success to the multilateral system. There were high expectations that the EU would be as assertive in implementing the agenda as it had been in negotiating it, but the remainder of the year saw the political energy of the EU's leadership being largely absorbed by managing the so-called 'refugee crisis'.

One exception was the EU's strong role in the successful conclusion of the 21st Conference of Parties on climate change in Paris in December, in which both the hosting country France and the European Commission advancing the EU's position played important roles in achieving a successful outcome. One key effort to this end was to set up a Coalition of High Ambition, with which all African states associated themselves with the exception of South Africa as a member of the BASIC group (Brazil, India, South Africa and China), a group of countries more reluctant to a act in a way that might impinge on their own national development priorities and those of developing countries as a whole. The conference testified to the potential for more opportunity-driven cooperation between the EU and Africa outside of their formal (and in the case of the Cotonou Agreement legal) cooperation frameworks.

Future of EU-ACP Relations

June marked the 40th anniversary of the *ACP*, created by the 1975 Georgetown Agreement. In 1975, the Group had founded itself following the conclusion of a cooperation agreement earlier that year between the then 46 ACP states and the European Economic Community. Building on the series of Lomé Conventions, the Cotonou Partnership Agreement was agreed in 2000 to govern cooperation between the EU and the then 78 ACP states in the areas of trade, development cooperation and political dialogue. Africa played an instrumental role in the negotiations leading to the first cooperation Convention in 1975, and in fact constituted the roots of the ACP through its earlier Yaoundé Conventions with Europe during the 1960s. However, African states have different views on the continuing relevance of the agreement and the topic has not been a frequent issue of debate at the AU headquarters in Addis Ababa. The EU launched preparations for its mandate for negotiations on what might govern its relations with the ACP after the expiry of the Cotonou Agreement, which were due to start no later than September 2018. It did so by convening expert roundtables in different EU member states, which fed into a Joint Consultation Paper by the European Commission and EEAS launching a public consultation between October and December. The result of the public consultation was meant to become a key element of the Commission's impact assessment to inform its proposed EU negotiation mandate.

Significantly, the ACP had started its preparations several years before the EU, with the 2012 ACP Summit of Heads of State mandating an Eminent Persons Group (EPG) under the chairmanship of Nigeria's former president Olusegun Obasanjo, as well as a working group of Brussels-based ambassadors. Both groups had been given similar terms of reference and had been expected to finalise their working documents in 2014. This was achieved in November 2014 in the case of the Ambassadorial Working Group but the completion of the EPG's report was delayed after the 2014 Summit in Suriname was cancelled. The ACP was now likely to adopt the basis for its negotiating position at its next summit in Papua New Guinea, scheduled for June 2016.

PART 3

West Africa

Sebastian Elischer

Contradictory developments shaped West Africa's trajectory in 2015. Nigeria and Côte d'Ivoire experienced peaceful elections, which proved wrong many sceptics who had predicted the opposite. Economic growth rates and investment in national infrastructure were encouraging and confirmed the positive trends of previous years. At the same time, a number of brutal autocratic governments managed to consolidate their power base either through rigged elections or through the deployment of their security apparatus. Islamic terrorism remained a major security challenge, with serious implications for civil liberties and human rights. Almost all West African nations remained stuck at the bottom of the HDI as positive growth rates failed to translate into visible improvements for most citizens. Despite national and international efforts to end the Ebola epidemic, Liberia, Guinea and Sierra Leone only slowly managed to become Ebola-free.

Regime Dynamics and Human Rights

The quality of West Africa's political regimes and the willingness of incumbents to respect basic human rights differed significantly across the sub-region. In a number of countries, democratic processes were well-entrenched, even though the democratic process left much to be desired. Others had recently undergonc democratic transitions or were in the process of putting their political systems back together, often after years of conflict. The Mano River countries struggled to return to normality as the health crisis continued to overshadow all other domestic issues. A final group of countries remained under autocratic rule with little hope for improvement.

In Cabo Verde, Benin, Ghana, Senegal and Niger *democratic processes* and compliance with basic human rights standards remained the norm, with these five countries generally regarded as the *democratic showcases* of the region. While Cabo Verde and Benin experienced relative political tranquillity, Senegal, Ghana and Niger saw intense political debates. In Ghana, there appeared to be a real danger that the fallout over the ongoing electricity crisis and the run-up to the 2016 elections might turn violent and undermine the political gains of the last two decades. In Niger, divisions between government and opposition parties deepened further.

The decision by *Cabo Verde*'s ruling parties to approve a 64% salary increase for the president, government members and parliamentarians led to popular protest. Many called on President Jorge Carlos Fonseca to veto the decision and it was ultimately taken off the parliamentary agenda. This indicated that, the despite all its

 | DOI 10.1163/9789004333239_004

shortcomings, the political elite remained somewhat responsive to its citizenry. *Benin* experienced its *7th parliamentary elections* since the return of multi-party democracy in the early 1990s. The results took away the parliamentary majority of the president's coalition and President Yayi was unable to push through any constitutional amendments. Up to the legislative elections, allegations that he wanted to change the law so that he could run for a third term had dominated political debate. Yayi's lack of a parliamentary majority thus ended speculation about a future constitutional crisis.

In *Senegal* controversial *institutional debates* shaped the start of the second part of President Sall's term in office. In June, parliament passed a bill that limited the presidential term to five years and prohibited MPs from switching parliamentary parties during the parliamentary term. After months of internal debate within the governing coalition, Sall announced that a national referendum (scheduled for 2016) would decide whether these reforms would be enacted into law. The trial of Karim Wade, the son of former president Abdoulaye Wade and a former minister of energy, divided the political landscape. Accusations of nepotism in the presidential entourage remained a consistent feature in domestic politics. In *Ghana* large sections of the population protested against the seemingly endless power shortages, which turned into a *severe electricity crisis* on an unprecedented scale. A high number of civil society organisations and the business community became involved in these protests. In July, President Mahama escaped an *assassination attempt*. The relationship between the opposition and the government was poisonous and left little room for cooperation. Violence escalated within Ghana's main opposition party, the National People's Party, and led to the killing of several party functionaries. The inability of the ruling party to solve the electricity crisis and the unwillingness of all major political actors to work against violence cast serious doubts on Ghana's longstanding reputation as a showcase of democracy in West Africa. *Niger* was rocked by religious riots. Initially peaceful protest against the 'Charlie Hebdo' cartoons in Zinder in January quickly escalated into violence, which resulted in *the pillaging of churches* and the destruction of the French cultural centre; 45 people were wounded and five were killed. In Niamey, rioters destroyed dozens of churches, hotels and other establishments associated with Western influence. In July, religiously-motivated violence occurred in Maradi. One year before the next presidential and parliamentary elections, tensions between the government of President Issoufou and the opposition worsened. Debates about electoral procedures, *arbitrary arrests* of journalists, allegations about the involvement of opposition figure Hama Amadou in a baby smuggling ring and the banning of opposition rallies overshadowed the run-up to the elections scheduled for 2016.

After the overthrow of President Blaise Compaoré by a popular insurrection in 2014, *Burkina Faso* underwent a democratic transition. It experienced *significant blowbacks but also progress* on its journey towards democracy. Following the promulgation of a law that effectively outlawed the political activity of many well-established politicians, the presidential guard staged a *military coup* against the transitional government, but this received little or no public support and was short-lived. Together, international actors and the national military reinstated the transitional authorities, affording them the necessary support to organise *elections* and inaugurate a *new government* by the end of the year. The democratic transition process in *Guinea Bissau* also underwent several upheavals, which reflected the country's previous unstable trajectory. Throughout the year, the relationship between President Vaz and Prime Minister Pereira deteriorated, ultimately resulting in the *dismissal of the popular prime minister*. The formation of a new government proved contentious and tedious. *Corruption* and *crime* remained major concerns.

Nigeria, Côte d'Ivoire and *Mali* continued as *electoral democracies*, coming to terms with a history of large-scale intra-state violence. Nigeria and Côte d'Ivoire made noticeable progress, but *the future of the Malian state* remained more questionable than ever before. The overall human rights record of all three countries was disappointing.

Against predictions to the contrary, the *Nigerian presidential, parliamentary and gubernatorial elections* took place as scheduled. The presidential elections resulted in a *peaceful transfer of power* from Goodluck Jonathan to Muhammadu Buhari, and the parliamentary elections provided the former opposition with a clear mandate to govern. In the months following the election, the Buhari administration reshuffled the hierarchy of the security forces, but *suicide bombings* still went on unabated and kidnapping for ransom remained rampant. The precarious security situation in most parts of the country had serious implications for Nigeria's human rights record. In *Côte d'Ivoire* the first *presidential election* after the contentious 2010 election took place. Deep divisions within the two main parties and heated debates about the impartiality of the electoral supervisory body shaped the run-up to the elections. Although the political scene remained deeply divided between supporters and opponents of former president Gbagbo, the *peaceful re-election* of President Alassane Ouattara stabilised the country. The internal security situation remained precarious: the number of child kidnappings increased dramatically and a number of prisons saw the escape of inmates. Due to violence by *Islamist groups*, insecurity was rampant in northern *Mali*. Despite a peace agreement between the central government and the northern Tuareg rebels, attacks by Islamists on UN personnel and civilian targets spread across the country. To make matters worse, the government of President Ibrahim Boubacar Keita continued to lose legitimacy because of its *poor governance record*.

Political and social life in Guinea, Liberia and Sierra Leone was overshadowed by the long-term consequences of the *Ebola* outbreak. In *Guinea*, the postponed presidential elections provoked ethnic clashes, which eventually gave way to *free and fair elections* and the re-election of President Condé. Human rights violations nevertheless remained a permanent feature in Guinean politics. In *Liberia*, politics continued to be fractious, even at the height of the Ebola crisis, as *corruption allegations* haunted the administration of President Ellen Johnson Sirleaf. Instances of mob violence and *vigilantism* severely tested the capability of the police. In *Sierra Leone*, President Koroma *sacked Vice President Samuel Sam-Sumana*, who was accused of fuelling violence and attempting to form a breakaway party. This provoked protests by civil society organisations and the opposition. In all three countries, human rights considerations were overshadowed by government attempts to control the Ebola epidemic.

Togo, Mauritania and Gambia *lacked democratic procedures*. The human rights situation in all three countries remained dismal. In *Togo*, President Faure Gnassingbé secured his *third five-year term*, thus strengthening the autocratic grip of the Gnassingbé clan, which had been in power since 1967. The government postponed democratic reforms indefinitely. In *Mauritania*, government and opposition failed to engage in any meaningful dialogue. As the opposition had boycotted the previous election, the government of President Mohamed Ould Abdel Aziz enjoyed free reign. Under pressure from the UN and international donors, the government adopted a *new anti-slavery law*. Anti-slavery and human rights organisations expressed concerns that the law threatened the freedom of NGOs to operate independently. After the failed coup attempt against him in 2014, *Gambia*'s President Yahya Jammeh brutally *cracked down* on members of the army, journalists, civil servants and the relatives and friends of the alleged plotters. Jammeh's unilateral declaration of Gambia as an 'Islamic Republic' led to condemnation by religious clerics and the diaspora.

Socioeconomic Developments

According to the AfDB, West Africa's projected growth rate was 5%, a slightly less encouraging figure than in previous years. With the exception of East Africa, West Africa remained the most dynamic sub-region of the continent. This positive development was reflected in the projected growth rates of individual countries. However, macroeconomic figures said little about the dire living conditions of most citizens. All West African countries remained stuck at the bottom of the HDI. Ghana and Cabo Verde were the usual outliers.

Ghana's electricity crisis continued to hamper economic growth and seriously threatened to affect the positive economic trajectory the country had taken since the early 1990s. Unsurprisingly, Ghana's projected growth rate (3.9%) contracted in comparison with previous years. In *Cabo Verde economic recovery remained slow* because of unfavourable global and national economic conditions.

The *three economic powerhouses* in the region, Nigeria, Côte d'Ivoire and Senegal, continued to grow at roughly the same rates as in 2014. In *Nigeria*, robust growth (estimated at around 7%) was threatened by macroeconomic challenges, particularly *exchange-rate volatility* and *falling global oil prices*. Both had a negative impact on public-sector spending. Plummeting oil and gas prices fell below the $ 40 per barrel mark by the end of the year. The decline highlighted Nigeria's overdependence on its main export commodities and developments on the international energy market. The ongoing military confrontation between the Nigerian army and Boko Haram eradicated trade and commerce in much of Northern Nigeria. The *national currency* came under pressure at the end of the year. *Côte d'Ivoire* recorded the *highest projected growth rate* (7.9%) in the region. The government invested in social programmes, including a *social housing scheme* and *national health insurance*, and continued to invest heavily in infrastructural projects. In *Senegal*, projected annual GDP growth reached 5.4% (up from 4.3% in 2014). On the one hand, this was due to good harvests and the growth of the livestock sector. On the other, Senegal benefited from a *generally favourable economic environment*. Price competitiveness improved thanks to the 2.6% depreciation of the CFA franc and a significant inflation differential with other countries.

Growth rates were also very encouraging in Niger, Mali, Benin, Mauritania, Burkina Faso and Togo (all between 4.0% and 5.5%, depending on the source and country). Being located in or near the *Sahel*, all were affected by *climate change* and generally adverse structural conditions. The *solid growth rates* confirmed the upward trend of the previous decade, but national growth rates were heavily *dependent on agricultural output* and rain. Disappointing harvests caused the decline of economic growth rates in a number of countries. In *Niger*, French *uranium conglomerate Areva* announced that it had suffered a total loss of € 4.8 bn in 2014. In addition, oil production was hindered by labour disputes, mechanical failures and arguments with the state petroleum company over price controls. *Mali's economic output* was also disappointing compared with 2014. This slowdown was partly attributed to setbacks in the agricultural sector, with late rains and poor fertiliser quality causing the country's cotton harvest to fall short of its forecasted level. In both Niger and Mali, the *fight against Islamic terrorism* deterred economic investment and led to the destruction of local infrastructure. In contrast to Mali, *Benin's cotton production improved* and rose by almost one-third. In *Mauritania*, unpredictable weather conditions meant that agricultural production was impossible to predict. The country also experienced *large-scale strikes* throughout the first quarter of the year. *Burkina Faso*'s democratic transition did not have any positive effect on its economic predicament. All principal economic sectors faced challenges. Late rains led forecasters to anticipate that cotton production would not meet projections for the 2015/2016 growing season. Compaoré's departure from the presidency also coincided with a variety of *disputes at several mining locations*. In *Togo*, economic growth remained strong because of *public investment* in national road networks, mining and port infrastructure, as well as productivity gains in agriculture and the recovery of global commodity prices. Cotton production increased by 45%, thanks to good weather and the government project to improve the agricultural sector. Across the Sahel, governments *invested heavily in infrastructure*.

The socioeconomic impact of *Ebola* in *Liberia, Sierra Leone and Guinea* included *job losses, smaller harvests and food insecurity*. According to the World Bank, Ebola *killed more than 11,000 people* in the three countries combined, including more than *500 health workers*. At the end of the year, all three countries were declared Ebola-free and public services improved slowly. At the macroeconomic level, there were some *signs of recovery*. Liberia's projected growth rate stood at 3.8%, an increase of 2% compared with 2014. Guinea's growth rate showed a very moderate recovery from 0.6% to 0.9%. The Sierra Leonean economy failed to recover. The estimated growth rate stood at -2.5%, a fall of over 8% compared with previous years. All three countries remained dependent on *donor funding* and goodwill. By the end of the year, the World Bank Group had mobilised $ 1.62 bn in financing for Ebola response and recovery efforts to support the countries hardest hit by the epidemic. This included $ 260 m for Guinea, $ 385 m for Liberia and $ 318 m for Sierra Leone.

The economies of Guinea-Bissau and Gambia also suffered from the Ebola outbreak and *political uncertainty*. *Guinea-Bissau* reversed its economic fortunes to the better and showed *visible improvements*: GDP was projected to rise by 4.7%, double the growth rate in 2014. In addition, tax revenues and electricity and water supplies exceeded expectations. 2015 was also a good year for agriculture as the production of rice was expected to rise by one-third. The harvest of cashew kernels, the country's main cash crop, reached a record high. In *Gambia*, the economy was predicted to grow by 4.7%, a significant improvement over 2014, the positive estimate being all the more surprising given the *low agricultural output* due to climate change and erratic rainfall patterns. The dramatic lack of civil and political liberties, high youth unemployment and low agricultural harvests continued to force many Gambians youths to attempt *illegal migration* to Europe.

Regional Cooperation and Foreign Affairs

The four major regional organisations, ECOWAS, the community of Sahel-Saharan states (CEN-SAD), the MRU and the Liptako-Gourma Authority, differed significantly in terms of their activity and output.

ECOWAS remained the most significant regional actor. In May and December, ECOWAS hosted ordinary sessions of the ECOWAS Authority of Heads of State and Government. The summit in May took place in Accra (Ghana) and elected Senegalese President Macky Sall as *new ECOWAS chairman*. Sall took over from Ghana's President John Dramani Mahama. At the summit, the heads of state agreed to temporarily drop the proposal to restrict presidents in the sub-region to two terms in office. The summit in December took place in Abuja (Nigeria). Peace and security matters, particularly the *new cross-border threats* in the ECOWAS region, dominated the meeting. The heads of state and government issued a final communiqué in which they stated that religious dress codes that made identification of individuals difficult considerably hindered actions geared towards protecting people and property. This was widely seen as an initiative to discourage Muslims from wearing hijab. In May, ECOWAS celebrated its *40th anniversary*. Its achievements were highlighted at the ordinary summit in December. In September, Nigeria's President Buhari hosted an *extraordinary summit in Abuja*. The meeting examined the unfolding political crisis in Burkina Faso. The ECOWAS heads of state and government called on the military junta in Burkina Faso to hand over power to the interim administration immediately.

As in previous years, ECOWAS was involved in *election observation missions* and military interventions. In March, it sent an observer mission to elections in Nigeria and declared the elections free and fair. Also in March, ECOWAS called on the Togolese government to postpone that country's elections. Despite widespread concerns about electoral manipulation, ECOWAS congratulated Faure Essozimna Gnassingbé on his swearing-in as president of the Republic of Togo. ECOWAS also deployed a short-term electoral observation mission with 133 observers to Burkina Faso. In September, ECOWAS extended a security force in Guinea-Bissau into 2016 to help protect state institutions amid a political crisis that left the country without a government. Also in September, ECOWAS chiefs of defence staff met in Dakar (Senegal) to discuss sustaining the multi-national approach to end security-related challenges within the region.

In February, the *ECOWAS parliament* discussed the *Supplementary Act*, which foresaw the enhancement of the powers of the ECOWAS Parliament. The ratification of the act would allow ECOWAS parliamentarians to be elected through an electoral college by their national parliaments. It would also usher in a new parliament, whose role would be one of co-decision making and subsequently law making in areas to be defined by the heads of state and government. During the year, the ECOWAS parliament called on the South African government to punish the perpetrators of recent xenophobic attacks in South Africa and have them prosecuted at the ICC.

The presidents of the *MRU* – Liberia, Guinea and Sierra Leone – organised a summit in Conakry (Guinea). They committed the organisation and its members to achieving "zero Ebola infection", but the MRU displayed no other signs of activity. UEMOA hosted an ordinary summit on 19 January. The Liptako-Gourma Authority and CEN-SAD remained dormant.

At the bilateral level, Nigeria, Ghana, Senegal and Benin were the region's most active countries on the diplomatic stage. On 19–22 July, Nigeria's President Buhari paid a state visit to the USA and held bilateral discussions with President Barack Obama on 20 July, when the US administration offered its assistance in tracking down millions of dollars' worth of stolen assets. Washington committed $ 5 m in support for the fight against *Islamist insurgencies*. In addition to support from the

USA, Nigeria secured financial support from the United Kingdom for the fight against terrorism. Abuja also fostered military cooperation with countries in the Lake Chad region in order to coordinate efforts to defeat Boko Haram on the battlefield. Ghana continued to demonstrate its commitment to ECOWAS and the AU. Senegal became a non-permanent member of the UNSC in October, and was elected onto the executive board of UNESCO for a four-year term in November. Senegal's President Sall negotiated the release of three leaders of the 'Y en a marre' movement, who had been arrested for undermining the DRC's internal security. After 72 hours in police custody, the Senegalese activists were released and returned home. Together with his counterpart from Benin, Sall also led a special ECOWAS mediation team to negotiate a peaceful conclusion to the crisis in Burkina Faso. Sall was the first African head of state to be hosted by King Salman, the new king of Saudi Arabia. Sall pledged his support for the Saudi military intervention against Shiite rebels in Yemen.

Niger, Mauritania and Mali were heavily involved in various *anti-terrorism measures*. All three derived much of their international legitimacy from their unflinching support for American and French military intervention in the region and the formation of African-led multinational military contingents. The UN and the EU continue to play a key role in the stabilisation of Mali, which remained the most serious security challenge in West Africa. The Multidimensional Integrated Stabilization Mission in Mali (MINUSMA) by now included over 10,200 uniformed personnel (military and police peacekeepers), 578 international civilian personnel, and 682 local civilian staff. By year's end, MINUSMA had suffered more casualties than any other peacekeeping mission on earth, with 61 peacekeepers killed in action since the beginning of the mission in 2013, 16 of them during 2015.

A number of bilateral relations remained tense or took a turn for the worse. *Relations between Gambia and Senegal* worsened after Senegal's refusal to extradite Gambian citizens accused of plotting a coup against President Jammeh in December 2014. The relationships between Benin and Burkina Faso and between Benin and Nigeria suffered from minor *border disputes*. Ghana's relations with Côte d'Ivoire suffered as the two countries battled over the disputed marine borders. In Liberia's border region with *Côte d'Ivoire*, there were instances of cross-border attacks and reports of illegal farming.

Benin

Alexander Stroh

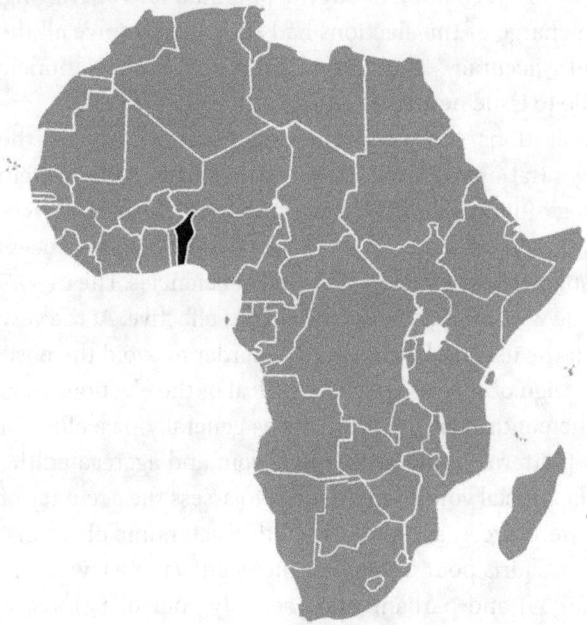

After years of heated debate about President Yayi's intention to modify the Constitution in order to allow him to run for a third term, April's parliamentary election results took away the government's majority. Therefore, unilateral constitutional amendments became impossible, the political debate cooled down and focused on the candidates who were preparing their election campaigns. The election procedure confirmed Benin's reliance on democratic processes. Meanwhile, the country continued to experience moderate economic progress and major corruption scandals. Though the domestic security situation remained stable, Benin assumed more regional responsibility in the fight against jihadist terrorism, given the imminent threat of jihadi attacks at home and growing international pressure to join international efforts to combat terrorism.

Domestic Politics

The upcoming parliamentary and presidential elections had dominated the political debate for a long time before the official start of the electoral campaign. On 26 April, the one-chamber National Assembly was elected for its seventh four-year

 | DOI 10.1163/9789004333239_005

term since the country's return to multiparty competition in 1990. Election day was marked by serenity and routine, although almost the opposite qualities had characterised the pre-election period. Heated debate about the computerised electoral roll ('Liste Electorale Permanente Informatisée': LEPI) had long shaped the domestic debate and given rise to speculation about the potential for vote rigging. The administration bodies in charge of the elections had struggled to solve all the controversies about the LEPI's accuracy. The 'Commission Électorale Nationale Autonome' (CENA) was unable to issue new voter cards in time.

Various civil society organisations had very efficiently joined forces in the 'Plateforme Électorale des Organisations de la Société Civile du Bénin'. With the help of the Dakar-based Open Society Initiative for West Africa (OSIWA), it set up a website, used social media tools, closely observed every stage of the electoral process and immediately pushed for solutions whenever it detected deficiencies. The CENA's solution on the voter cards issue was not much appreciated but effective. At the very last minute, the CENA allowed the use of old voter cards in order to avoid the postponement of the elections. Foreign observers were less critical of the elections than domestic ones and praised the conduct of the elections as generally peaceful. On election day, the civil society platform set up a situation room and aggregated the results simultaneously with the official vote count in order to assess the accuracy of the results. The official results were largely accepted by political actors and observers.

Boni Yayi's party, the 'Forces Cauris pour un Bénin Emergeant' (FCBE), won the largest share of the votes (30.3%) and parliamentary seats (33 out of 83). As in the past, no party managed to win a parliamentary majority. The two largest opposition groups together took the same number of seats as the FCBE. The electoral alliance 'Union fait la Nation' (UN) won 13 seats with 14.3% of the votes and the 'Parti du Renouveau Démocratique' (PRD) gained ten seats with 10.4%. The alliance led by the party 'Renaissance du Bénin' (RB) finished fourth, taking seven seats with 7.1% of the votes. The PRD and the RB had successively left the UN alliance after the last presidential election, when the alliance had failed to beat the incumbent President Yayi. The PRD stayed in opposition, whereas the RB had approached the presidential camp. The new parliament remained fragmented, with another seven electoral alliances and individual parties winning seats. On 20 May, the freshly constituted National Assembly elected opposition candidate and PRD party president Adrien Houngbédji as its president. Houngbédji – a leading figure in Benin's politics for over 25 years and the UN's candidate for the helm of state in 2013 – had already twice served as the head of the National Assembly (1991–95 and 1999–2003). His election was an important victory for the opposition, although Houngbédji was not allowed to run for the state presidency because the Constitutional specified an age limit of 70 years for presidential candidates.

The National Assembly continued to use the governor's palace in Porto-Novo, despite it being too small to conduct parliamentary business satisfactorily. The contractor and the minister in charge had repeatedly promised that the construction of the new buildings alongside the Ouémé River would be finished by 30 November. Several ministers had been dismissed in connection with corruption and mismanagement of the prestigious construction project since the launch of the project in 2009. Yayi was keen to conclude the project before leaving office and visited the site at least three times during the year (22 May, 17 October and 13 December) to put pressure on project managers. At his last visit, the completion was well behind schedule. Minister of Urban Affairs Noël Fonton's attempts to explain the situation included references to insecurity caused by Boko Haram and the workers' lack of motivation, but unions rejected the reproaches and pointed to ongoing mismanagement. The state had at least spent CFAfr 14 bn (more than € 21 m) on the project.

The election result meant that Yayi was unable to push through any constitutional amendments. Up to the legislative elections, allegations that he wanted to change the law so that he could run for a third term had dominated political debate. The president had been unable to create a minimum level of trust among his opponents, although he constantly affirmed his intention to leave office after ten years in Marina Palace. Having lost his majority in parliament, the third-term debate faded away and discussion turned towards the presidential candidates, who began to prepare their campaigns.

Presidential elections were due in February 2016 and so debate about the future political leadership remained centre stage and political positioning and repositioning continued after the parliamentary elections. For a long time it remained unclear whether Yayi would support any presidential candidate. Early rumours had produced the name of retired army general Robert Gbian. However, since his electoral alliance – 'Alliance Soleil' – underperformed in the parliamentary polls (gaining 6.7% of the vote and four MPs), he no longer appeared to be a promising candidate. Yayi's brother-in-law and long-serving minister Marcel de Souza was also considered a potential frontrunner but Yayi eventually threw his support behind Lionel Zinsou, a Franco-Beninese economist and a complete newcomer to the domestic political scene. He had been living in Paris and his appointment as prime minister by Yayi on 18 June took many by surprise. He was nominated as the FCBE's presidential candidate only five months later.

Zinsou was a 'Southerner' in the terms of country's political geography and decended from a well-respected family, being the nephew of former president Emile Derlin-Zinsou. Yayi's rhetoric revealed his strategy to combine his own political weight as the outgoing president from the northern part of the country with Zinsou's southern background. On 26 December, the prime minister's helicopter crashed immediately after take-off in Parakou. The accident gave rise to speculation about a political attack but it transpired that a combination of environmental conditions and human error had caused the crash. Zinsou escaped unharmed.

By the year's end, businessman Patrice Talon had also started his presidential campaign. A fierce political enemy of Yayi, he had returned to Benin in December after more than three years in exile in France. Talon – a financial heavyweight and influential networker with excellent relations to private media outlets – had been a key supporter behind Yayi's election 2006 election campaign, but had later come into conflict with Yayi. In October 2012, Talon was accused of attempting to murder the president and, in February 2013, of plotting a military coup. An international arrest warrant was issued and was only lifted in May 2014 when Yayi pardoned Talon for crimes in which the latter had always sharply denied any involvement. Rumours about his candidacy emerged by midyear and, on 1 October, the weekly 'Jeune Afrique' published an interview in which Talon confirmed his intention to run for president. Apart from Talon and Zinsou, three other promising candidates were expected to run: former prime minister Pascal Irénée Koupaki, the well-established northern politician Abdoulaye Bio-Tchané, and Sébastian Ajavon, another millionaire and businessman – all of them opponents of Yayi.

In May, police searched the home of MP Candide Azanaï, which led to public protests, and tensions rose after the police violently broke up the demonstrations. There were no reports that anyone was seriously injured, but the incident underlined again the low level of tolerance of any government restrictions of civil liberties.

On 14 October, Mathieu Kérékou, a former military dictator (1972–91) who had later served two more terms as a democratically elected president (1996–2006), died at the age of 82. He was a political icon and had always been primarily seen as a disciplined soldier, so the first commemoration ceremony in his honour took place at Camp Guézo, the main army barracks in central Cotonou. Later, he was buried in the northern town of Natitingou in his native region. Yayi declared a week of national mourning.

In early November, the president of the national media commission, Adam Boni Tessi, stopped the publication of the daily newspaper 'Le Matinal', which had featured a story claiming that a court had asked the state to compensate businessman Patrice Talon for an incorrect public award process. According to the newspaper, Yayi had rejected the court order, indicating his scorn for justice. 'Le Matinal', which had frequently been sued for libel in the past, was run by Charles Toko, a close business associate of Patrice Talon.

The political importance of football became obvious when the Council of Ministers decided to withdraw the licence of the 'Fédération Béninoise du Football' (FBF) on 27 March. Two days later, gendarmes – robustly armed, according to FBF officials – occupied the FBF headquarters in Porto-Novo. The minister for sport argued that the bad management of the federation justified this draconian measure and the Confederation of African Football (CAF) had indeed suspended Benin from all under-17 activities for a period of two years on 4 September 2014. The FBF under-17 team had allegedly included players past the age limit on several occasions. The FBF president, Augustin Ahoevouenbla, claimed that the government was pursuing an agenda against him because of his political background: he was a senior member of parliament in Adrien Houngbédji's opposition PRD. FIFA secretary general Jérôme Valcke officially protested on 9 April, reminding the government of the FIFA statutes that guarantee the full independence of national associations. Various FIFA and CAF officials visited the country four times during the year (4 April, 3–5 May, 22–23 July, 1–2 November) arranging for the appointment of a so-called 'normalisation committee' to organise FBF elections by early 2016. The seven committee members were appointed on 9 November but FIFA dismissed two of them as soon as 18 December for irreconcilable internal conflict. Ahoevouenbla, who had meanwhile become head of the PRD's parliamentary party, had not been a committee member. Football consumed about one fifth of the national budget for sport.

Foreign Affairs

Benin deepened its involvement in regional politics beyond formal activities such as hosting the ordinary summit of the West African Economic and Monetary Union (WAEMU) on 19 January. On a bilateral level, the governments of Benin and neighbouring Niger held their first joint council of ministers on 6 January. Niger's geographic position makes it largely dependent on the transport corridor to Benin's port of Cotonou, and Benin started to support the government in Niamey in the fight against Boko Haram in a conjoint mission with Togolese troops. It was also agreed that Benin would contribute 800 troops to a multinational combat force of 8,700 men based in N'Djamena (Chad) to fight the jihadist terror network more effectively. When French President François Hollande visited Cotonou on 1 July, his main message was to encourage Benin to contribute more in the battle against jihadism in the region. Beyond its regional military engagement, Benin was contributing a total of 1,500 security personnel to UN missions by the year's end, almost all in the three ongoing UN missions in Côte d'Ivoire, the DRC and Mali.

ECOWAS entrusted President Yayi and Senegal's President Macky Sall with mediating in neighbouring Burkina Faso when a military coup threatened to end the democratic transition in September. However, Sall and Yayi were unable to negotiate a proposal that would satisfy all actors: pro-democratic forces in Burkina Faso firmly refused to endorse the agreement the two presidents had drafted, claiming that it made too many concessions to the putschists. Sall and Yayi's mission thus failed, while the coup in Burkina Faso ended without heavy bloodshed as the putschists surrendered.

Though relations with neighbouring states were generally peaceful, Foreign Minister Nassirou Bako-Arifari had to deal with two long-standing border demarcation issues. On 16 January, he travelled to Ouagadougou (Burkina Faso) to prepare for the WAEMU summit. In his meeting with Transitional President Michel Kafando, the border dispute in the Kourou/Koalou zone, a small area between the Pendjari River and the border triangle with Togo, became an issue because of recent allegations that Benin was not respecting the territory's neutrality (agreed by the two countries in 2009). The status of the zone had been disputed since 1980, with the case pending before the International Court of Justice. Some 3 km of the main road between Benin and Burkina Faso cross the zone, which has meant that the issue has attracted recurring attention. The second latent border dispute re-emerged in November, when Benin's gendarmerie entered 16 villages in the Okuta district, which Nigeria considered to belong to its own territory. Various Nigerian media outlets reported that local traditional authorities were accusing Benin of an invasion. 'The Vanguard Newspaper' (Lagos) cited the Emir of Okuta confirming that Beninese flags had been hoisted but later dismantled by his followers. 'The Guardian' (Lagos) explained to its readers that the artificial border drawn between the British and French had not taken into account the common cultural and economic activities of the Bariba, who lived on both sides of the imperialist divide. National authorities played down the conflict.

Socioeconomic Developments

On 11 December, the IMF's Executive Board applauded Benin for concluding a third consecutive year of solid economic growth, which stood at around 5%. The Fund identified Nigeria's economic slowdown as the main risk to Benin's development but also urged further customs and tax reforms, accelerated structural reforms (generally by privatisation), greater diversification and judicial reliability. The USA shared this generally positive assessment. On 12 September, Washington approved a second grant of $ 375 m from the Millennium Challenge Account.

International aid – mainly from the EU – brought into service the second phase of the Greater Cotonou drinking water supply system on 24 January. According to the national water supply company SONEB and government sources, the project served more than 2.3 m people in the country's largest metropolitan area, giving four out of five residents direct access to clean water. Thanks to the project, it became possible for water charges that users had to pay to SONEB could be reduced by more than 50% to CFAfr 50,000 p.a. Shortly afterward, the Netherlands withheld development aid in response to large-scale corruption in a water supply project. According to the Dutch, CFAfr 3 bn (almost € 4.6 m) had been embezzled. Minister Barthélémy Kassa, a longstanding ally of President Yayi, was dismissed over the scandal. However, a motion to lift Kassa's immunity as a member of parliament was defeated by the votes of the FCBE and four opposition MPs, protecting him from prosecution. Surprisingly, the affair did not affect Benin's bilateral relationship with other donors.

Energy production remained one of the focal points of the government's economic policy. On 1 May, Yayi visited the Maria Glèta power plant to push for the completion of the 80 MW production site. On 6 May, the president received the representative of an international plant construction company that was to build another 200 MW power station. The government aimed at a total production of 1 GW to reach energy self-sufficiency in 2016. According to the office of the president, the Islamic Development Bank, the state of Iran and private foreign investors were proposing the construction of three more plants with a combined capacity of 650 MW. Renewable energy sources were designated to bring a minimum level of electricity supply to all 105 county towns. In October, recently appointed Prime Minister Lionel Zinsou announced an initiative to bring electricity to the three-quarters of the population who then had no access. He promised to provide solar power kits to every family in the country in addition to the installation of some 100 micro power plants. It was also planned that the energy parastatal SBEE ('Société Béninoise d'Énergie Électrique') would introduce an electronic payment system: the prime minister estimated that time wasted at SBEE counters caused considerable economic damage.

Cotton production in the 2014/2015 harvesting season rose by almost one-third compared with 2013/2014. The target of 359,000 tonnes was exceeded by 34,000 tonnes. The cotton sector remained Benin's primary industry and largest employer. The production target for the 2015/2016 season was set at half a million tonnes. Besides cotton, re-export trade through the port of Cotonou was the most important business. Logistics and transport infrastructure were therefore a key to economic growth. A new traffic management system began to operate at the port of Cotonou which aimed at massively facilitating the process by which forwarding companies collected freight. Car drivers in Cotonou expected a welcome side effect. Extended waiting times for lorries transporting heavy freight had long obstructed road traffic in the city. The new handling scheme improved the situation. Regarding long-distance transport routes, two priority projects were central: the upgrading of the motorway from Cotonou to the Nigerian border in the east and the construction of the railway line toward the Nigérien border in the north. The presidents of Benin and Niger had jointly celebrated the inauguration of the first section between Niamey and Dosso on Nigérien soil in 2014, and they finally launched the infrastructure project connecting Cotonou with Parakou in the north and Porto-Novo in the east on 19 March. President Yayi and Prime Minister Rafini of Niger had already opened the renovated main station in downtown Cotonou on 14 January. Vincent Bolloré, the French CEO of Bolloré logistics and construction company, who had won the contract, had joined the two politicians for this event. Benino-Gabonese businessman Samuel Dossou contested the award process in court, however, and, on 19 December, the Court of Appeal in Cotonou ruled in favour of Dossou's company, Petrolin, and the judges ordered Bolloré to immediately stop construction work. On 5 November, another French company (Geftarail) also contested the award process before the International Court of Arbitration, and the ECOWAS Court of Justice and Arbitration had earlier ordered Benin to pay CFAfr 131 bn (approximately € 200 m) to one of Patrice Talon's companies in another award process case. The government had appealed and the final decision was pending at year's end.

Despite previous government declarations that it would fight fuel trafficking from Nigeria into Benin, the informal trade in fuel, 'Kpayo', remained omnipresent at the roadsides. On 2 November, a truck full of Kpayo exploded in Dantokpa market, destroying more than 700 shops according to press reports. Casualties were fortunately limited because the incident occurred at 1 am.

Two cultural events attracted particular attention. On 8 February, Angélique Kidjo received her second Grammy Award for the best world music album. President Yayi had welcomed the world-famous Beninese artist at his presidential palace on 9 January. In June, the Zinsou Foundation celebrated its tenth anniversary. The charity promoted the fine arts in Cotonou and made notable efforts to bring creative education and the world of art museums to school children. The Zinsou Foundation was managed by a member of the respected Zinsou family, of which Prime Minister Lionel Zinsou and former president Émile Derlin-Zinsou were members.

Burkina Faso

Daniel Eizenga

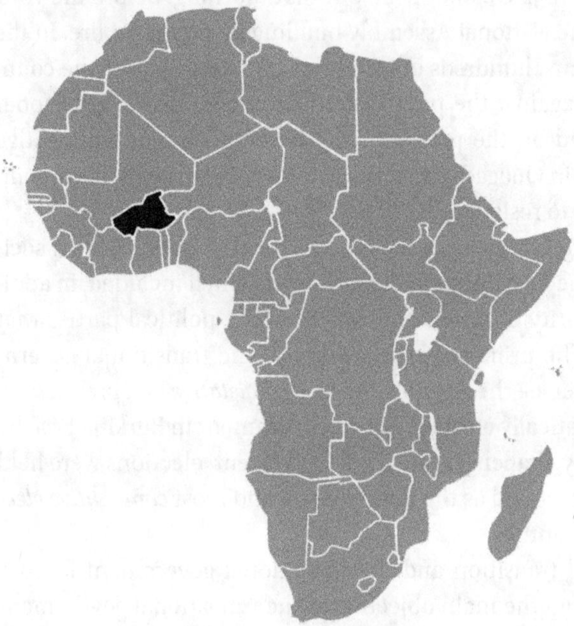

Following the removal of Blaise Compaoré by a popular insurrection in 2014, the transitional government that oversaw the return of an elected civilian government in 2015 overcame several challenges. The former presidential guard mounted a coup, temporarily derailing the political transition and forcing the government to postpone elections. Together, international actors and the national military reinstated the transitional authorities, affording them the necessary support to organise elections and inaugurate a new government by the end of 2015. Foreign relations with Côte d'Ivoire were tense because it provided refuge and support to former president Compaoré. In addition, the security situation in Mali and the larger Sahel region further deteriorated, spilling into Burkina Faso for the first time. Economically, the country faced declining growth in 2015 but, despite economic challenges, the transitional government was able to reform the mining sector and address several concerns of the country's labour unions and civil society organisations.

Domestic Politics

Burkina Faso's domestic politics during 2015 took place in the wake of the 2014 popular insurrection and consequent ousting of former president Blaise Compaoré.

 | DOI 10.1163/9789004333239_006

He and his political party, the 'Congrès pour Démocratie et le Progrès' (CDP), had been in power since launching a military coup in 1987. In October 2014, CDP leaders had attempted to modify *Article 37 of the Constitution* so that Compaoré would be allowed to run for re-election in 2015. The National Assembly had been scheduled to vote on the amendment on 30 October 2014, but that morning, before the vote, crowds had streamed into the National Assembly building and set it on fire. In the days leading up to these events, hundreds of thousands of people across the country had gathered in protest against the proposed amendment. On 30–31 October 2014, protesters had marched on the presidential palace and the administrative headquarters of the military in Ouagadougou, the capital city. This massive mobilisation had forced Compaoré to resign from office.

Following *Compaoré's resignation*, leaders of the political opposition, civil society and the military established a *transitional government*, which included, in addition to these leaders, a minority of representatives from the political parties that had supported Compaoré. The primary responsibility of the transitional government was to organise and oversee the administration of *legislative and presidential elections* to restore a democratically elected civilian government in Burkina Faso by the end of 2015. Despite many challenges and a postponement, elections were held on 29 November and were described as the freest, fairest and most *competitive elections* ever to be held in the country.

Nevertheless, the political transition and the transitional government faced a variety of challenges. Although the main objective of the transitional government was to organise and hold elections, the transitional authorities decided to enact *several reforms* in an effort to improve the overall state of civil liberties. President of the transition's legislative body, the 'Conseil National de la Transition' (CNT), Cherrif Sy, pursued many legal initiatives during his tenure. He also established several subcommittees charged with producing recommendations on how to reform several state bureaucracies including the military, which had not originally been outlined in the transitional government's charter. Some of these reforms were approved with widespread support, including the adoption of much stricter *anti-corruption legislation* on 5 March and a set of laws aimed at *combating violence against women and children* on 8 September. Other reforms, however, were hotly debated in public, causing social divisions. For example, reforms to the laws concerning the media included a *decriminalisation of libel* and defamation, making them civil offences and removing the possibility of jail sentences, although the fines associated with these offences were now increased. Some journalists argued that the fines had risen so much that they would effectively put them out of business.

The most heated political reforms dealt with modifications to the *electoral code*. Not all of these changes caused controversy but there was widespread disagreement over the CNT's proposal to exclude politicians who had supported Compaoré's attempt to modify Article 37 in 2014. Members of the CNT justified their position on the basis of the massive popular opposition there had been to modifying limits to presidential terms.

On 7 April, 75 of the 88 members of the CNT supported the exclusion proposal and Transitional President Michel Kafando ratified the modification to the electoral code on 9 April. Members of the CDP and its allies in the CNT opposed the reform and immediately began a campaign to fight it both by trying to stir up public outcry and by bringing a case to the courts of ECOWAS. It appeared that their efforts would prove successful when the ECOWAS Court of Justice invalidated the electoral reform on 13 July, declaring its anti-democratic spirit to be contrary to the ECOWAS charter. However, the Burkina Faso Constitutional Court upheld the reform on 25 August and *barred more than 50 politicians from running* in either the legislative or presidential elections. Among those excluded were Eddie Komboïgo (the president of the CDP), Djibrill Bassolé (Compaoré's foreign affairs minister), and Gilbert Noël Ouédraogo (president of the 'Alliance pour la Démocratie et la Fédération-Rassemblement Démocratique Africain', one of Burkina Faso's oldest political parties and a former ally of the CDP).

The exclusion of so many well-known politicians sparked *significant public debate* in the media. In response, the CDP held a number of political rallies in major urban centres such as Bobo Dioulasso and Ouagadougou. The rallies received limited popular support, making it clear that the CDP had lost at least some of its ability to mobilise the masses. There was also limited support from *civil society*; many civil society organisations, such as the 'Association des Amis de Blaise Compaoré', that had mobilised supporters for Compaoré and the CDP during the debates over the reform of Article 37 in 2014 had disbanded after the subsequent popular insurrection. Eventually, Compaoré's *presidential guard*, the 'Régiment de Sécurité Présidentielle' (RSP), *staged a coup*, taking President Kafando, Prime Minister Isaac Zida, Minster of Public Works Augustin Loada, and Minister of Housing and Urban Development Réné Bagora hostage at the presidential palace on 15 September. The coup was led by the head of the RSP, General Gilbert Diendéré, and was the culmination of a tense debate between the RSP and the transitional government regarding the RSP's future.

Under Compaoré, the RSP had been an elite unit within the military under Compaoré's rule and had received significant financial support as well as arms and training superior to those provided to the rest of the military. Compaoré frequently used the RSP for 'special operations', which were widely believed to involve illicit and highly profitable activities. After Compaoré's resignation, Diendéré and a unit of the RSP had provided as escort when he fled to Côte d'Ivoire. With Compaoré's departure, members of the RSP were concerned for the future of their unit.

Initially their hopes rested with Lieutenant Colonel Yacouba Isaac Zida, second-in-command of the RSP, who had been appointed to the office of the prime minister of the transition by Kafando in November 2014. However, in an attempt to gain public support, Zida did not protect the elite unit and instead supported *legislation to disband the RSP*, creating substantial tensions between the transitional government and the unit's leaders. Three times prior to the September coup – on 30 December 2014, 4 February and 30 June – RSP soldiers sought to take hostage, or arrest the prime minister. On 14 September the *National Reconciliation and Reform*

Commission, which had been established by Zida, submitted a 500-page document to the prime minister, recommending that the RSP be disbanded. While the RSP justified its coup in light of the exclusion of certain pro-Compaoré, and thus pro-RSP, political elites from the upcoming elections, there is little doubt that the Commission's recommendation also played an important role.

The coup received little or no public support. *Demonstrators against the coup* took to the streets hours after the RSP took the leaders of the transition hostage. In response, the RSP methodically sent patrols into the streets, dispersing demonstrators by shooting into the crowds. On 17 September, RSP patrols continued as RSP spokesman Lieutenant Colonel Mamadou Bamba announced the establishment of the 'Conseil National pour la Démocratie', a country-wide curfew to be observed from 7.00 pm, and the *disbanding of the transitional government*. In response, Cheriff Sy declared himself acting president of the transition in place of Kafando and Zida and went into hiding. Sy managed to regularly dispatch communiqués protesting the coup, demanding the release of the RSP's hostages, and supporting the national military, which up to this point had remained inactive.

ECOWAS was heavily involved in *negotiations following the RSP-led coup*. Unlike the AU and the French and American embassies, which all called for the release of Kafando and the reinstatement of the transitional government in a categorical rejection of the coup and Diendéré's 'Conseil National pour la Démocratie', ECOWAS sent a delegation of ECOWAS leaders including then President Macky Sall of Senegal and President Thomas Boni Yayi of Benin, who arrived in Ouagadougou, to mediate between political and civil society leaders and the RSP. During meetings on 18–20 September, Sall and Yayi developed a provisional agreement and they then flew to Abuja (Nigeria) for a *special session of ECOWAS* on 22 September, where all sitting presidents of ECOWAS countries were to discuss and vote on the provisional deal.

However, the *provisional agreement attracted widespread criticism* amongst the leaders of Burkinabè civil society, including Cherif Sy, then the self-declared transitional president. It later emerged that Sall and Yayi had met with Kafando, who had been released by the RSP and given safe haven at the French ambassador's residence, but without discussing the proposed plan with him. The 13-point deal outlined by Sall and Yayi therefore seemed only to take into consideration the demands of the RSP and Diendéré, such as provisions restricting the transitional government from passing any legislation except that required to schedule and hold elections. The deal would also have overturned the reform to the electoral code that barred certain politicians from running in the elections and postponed any and all proposed reforms to the military until an elected government could take power.

Following the ECOWAS mediation attempts and *country-wide demonstrations* against the coup, the regular army, led by Chief of Staff General Pingrenoma Zagré, mobilised in support of the transitional government on 21 September. Three detachments were sent from military bases around the capital, Ouagadougou, to surround it and demand the surrender and disarmament of the RSP. At this point, on 23 September, the ECOWAS leaders meeting in Abuja called for the RSP to disarm and surrender as well as for the immediate reinstatement of Kafando and the transitional government.

Without the backing of the national military, the RSP had lost its bargaining position. On the morning of 23 September, Zagré and Diendéré signed an agreement detailing the *surrender and disarmament of the RSP* and the *reinstatement of the transitional government* and by that evening Kafando had resumed his position as transitional president. On the same day, ECOWAS sent a delegation including the presidents of Benin, Niger and Ghana to ensure the reinstatement of the transitional government. Kafando's first action was to call an extraordinary meeting of the Council of Ministers on 25 September, during which members formally decided to completely disband the RSP. This decision caused tensions to flare up among some RSP hardliners, who on 27 September refused to disarm or to give up their barracks. On 29 September, the military launched an operation that included the shelling of the RSP's barracks to force their surrender. The *RSP eventually laid down their arms*, and the regular army took control of the barracks on 30 September.

Prior to the military's assault, General Diendéré fled the barracks, sought refuge at the Embassy of the Holy See in Ouagadougou and implored his soldiers to surrender to avoid more bloodshed. He was taken into custody from the Vatican Embassy by the National Gendarmerie on 1 October. In addition to Diendéré, Djibrill Bassolé, Mamadou Bamba and 11 others were arrested in connection with the coup. Fourteen individuals and four political parties suspected of being involved in plotting the coup had their *assets frozen* by the Justice Department. Many of them had already left the country, including the wife of Diendéré, Diallo Fatou Diendéré who had been a CDP parliamentary minister under Compaoré, CDP president Eddie Komboïgo and CDP vice president Léonce Koné.

On 14 October, as a result of the coup, the elections originally scheduled for 11 October were rescheduled for 29 November. Despite the political turmoil brought on by the coup, the *election date* held and a close race between two candidates developed during the official campaign period, which began on 8 November. The *two frontrunners* were Roch Marc Christian Kaboré, leader of the 'Mouvement du Peuple pour le Progrès' (MPP), and Zéphirin Diabré president of the 'Union pour le Progrès et la Changement' (UPC).

Several *international partners gave support for the organisation of the elections*. Taiwan, a long-time ally of Burkina Faso and which remained the only African country to recognise Taipei's claim to sovereignty, donated several computers and other technological equipment to aid Burkinabè election officials, including solar-powered printers and computers used for the biometric election registration drive. On 2 September, Nigeria donated 20 vehicles with the approval of newly elected President Muhammadu Buhari in fulfilment of the Nigerian government's March pledge to help with the logistics of the elections. On 5 May, France contributed roughly € 3 m to support the functions of the 'Commission Electorale Nationale Indépendante' (CENI) and Constitutional Court in training police, polling staff, election observers and the presidents of regional electoral commissions in legislative procedures concerning the electoral process. Several other EU countries also donated funds to support the administration of these elections.

During the electoral campaign, Kaboré was heavily criticised by his rivals for his close relationship with the CDP prior to 2014. In fact, many MPP members were former CDP members who had broken away in early 2014, led by Kaboré, who, with Salif Diallo and Simon Compaoré (no relation to the former president) led a mass resignation of CDP party members in protest against the plan to modify the constitution. These three politicians had been prominent members of the CDP, serving in several ministerial posts under Compaoré. The former CDP members then created the MPP with Kaboré as its president, Diallo as vice president, and Simon Compaoré as second vice president. The MPP quickly joined ranks with Diabré's UPC, helping to organise widespread social mobilisations against another term for Compaoré in 2014.

Diabré had also worked with the CDP and served as a minister under former president Compaoré, but in 2010 he had created the UPC. In the 2012 legislative elections, the UPC had won the second-largest number of seats in the National Assembly, and so Diabré had become the formal leader of the political opposition. Despite the fact that Diabré had led the opposition during the popular insurrection of 2014, Bénéwendé Sankara (no relation to Thomas Sankara), former leader of the opposition, criticised Diabré and Kaboré for being former collaborators with Blaise Compaoré. These criticisms did little to hurt the two candidates, however, and it was widely speculated that the MPP profited from their past ties to the CDP through its well-established patronage and political networks.

The Constitutional Court announced the official and *final election results* on 15 December. Kaboré won the presidential election with slightly more than 53% of the votes cast, and Diabré came in second with just under 30%. Twelve other candidates participated in the contest, but none received more than 5% of the vote. While the CDP did not have a candidate running in the presidential election, the party did contest several of the seats in the National Assembly. The *legislative election results* suggested that the CDP continued to enjoy significant support throughout the country as it came in third with 18 of the 127 total seats, behind the MPP's 55 and the UPC's 33. The other 21 seats were split between 11 different parties. These results meant that the *MPP failed to establish a majority* in the legislature and would need to form a coalition with parties that could guarantee the support of nine more members. By the end of the year, it was widely believed that the MPP would not have trouble obtaining the necessary support from the smaller parties but, ironically, the CDP was to align with the UPC in opposition to the MPP. None of the candidates or parties contested the results and local and international election observers congratulated the CENI for their part in the *free and fair administration of the elections.*

Kaboré was inaugurated into office on 29 December, and on the same day Salif Diallo was elected as the new president of the National Assembly. At the end of the year, the office of prime minister, and consequently many ministerial positions, remained empty, but with Kaboré and Diallo inaugurated and elections successfully complete, domestic politics in Burkina Faso appeared to have come to the end of a period of political instability.

Foreign Affairs

Because the transitional government was in power during 2015, Burkina Faso's foreign policy was rather limited. The security situation in *Mali* remained a primary focus because it shares sections of the Burkinabè northern and western borders. The *Sahel G5*, formed in 2014 with Mali, Niger, Mauritania and Chad to combat the growing threat from terrorist groups in the Sahara-Sahel region, especially northern Mali, met for a second time on 12 May in Niamey (Niger). After the meeting, all member states signed a commitment to further *inter-state cooperation* to bolster the region's security, but tangible results of the meeting remained elusive and the security situation continued to deteriorate.

On 4 April, prior to the Sahel G5 meeting, *armed men ambushed a security patrol* guarding a mine located in northern Burkina Faso and kidnapped a Romanian national. This was the first such kidnapping in Burkina Faso, despite its proximity to Mali and Niger, where such attacks had become common in recent years. Then, on 9 October, roughly 50 *gunmen killed three Burkinabè gendarmes* in Samorogouan, near Burkina Faso's western border with Mali around 300 km south-west of Ouagadougou. The government later claimed that the attack was linked to jihadist groups based in Mali who may have intended to aid the RSP coup in September. On 26 November, 13 individuals identified as Burkinabé and Malian Tuareg were arrested in connection with the attack. On 16 December the *French Embassy warned its citizens against travel* to a national park in eastern Burkina Faso, stating that Malian jihadist groups were believed to have set up camps in the park in hopes of kidnapping European tourists visiting the park during the December-May hunting season. Each of these events highlighted the increasingly complicated and *deteriorating security situation.*

Relations with *Côte d'Ivoire* also became more complicated as former president Blaise Compaoré had sought and received refuge there in 2014. In addition, on 17 November 2014, Ivorian President Alassane Ouattarra had signed a document authorising Compaoré's naturalisation as an Ivorian citizen. On 16 July, the CNT voted to charge Compaoré with high treason along with other crimes related to his attempt to modify the Constitution in 2014. Later, on 21 December, Burkina Faso's military court issued an *international arrest warrant for Compaoré* hoping for his extradition, but it did not take place because Côte d'Ivoire does not extradite its citizens.

Further complicating relations between the two countries were a series of *tapped phone conversations* that allegedly took place between Djibrill Bassolé – under arrest for helping to plot the RSP coup – and Guiallume Soro, former Ivorian prime minister and current president of the Ivorian National Assembly. In these conversations, Soro and Bassolé allegedly discussed the possibilities of supporting the then on-going coup led by Diendéré. It was claimed that Soro offered to help finance the coup and the assassination of Cherif Sy and Salif Diallo. Soro completely denied any connection with the coup or any involvement in the recorded conversations but relations with Côte d'Ivoire, where some 500,000 Burkinabè migrant workers reside, were understandably tense by the end of the year.

Socioeconomic Developments

The political transition did not dramatically improve the country's economic situation. Burkina Faso remained *one of the poorest countries on the planet*. In the UNDP's annual 'Human Development Report', it fell from 181st to 183rd out of 187 countries and territories. In the World Bank's annual 'Ease of Doing Business Report', Burkina Faso ranked 143rd out of 189 countries, just below the 25th percentile, albeit above several other African economies. *Real GDP growth* also slowed, with the Economist Intelligence Unit estimating growth to be 3.5% compared with the 4.0% recorded in 2014. Nevertheless, officials managed the economy relatively well considering the number of challenges faced by the transitional government.

Domestic social factors did not bolster the economy during the transition either. At the start of the transitional government, several *civil society organisations*, emboldened by their recent success in bringing down the Compaoré regime, continued to pressure the transitional government through the use of 'ruecratie' tactics or a type of 'politics of the street'. Organisations such as the 'Coalition National contre la Vie Chère' (CCVC), composed of unions, consumers' associations and human rights groups, continued to mobilise supporters, holding *public protests* on a wide range issues. On 4 February, the CCVC ran a countrywide sit-in demanding a reduction in the price of petrol. This was later picked up by the trade union conglomerate, 'Unité d'Action Syndicale' (UAS), which held a 48-hour general strike on 17–18 February. UAS also called for judicial action against former Compaoré regime authorities believed to be involved in corruption and rights abuses. During the strike, UAS threatened to organise national protest marches if their demands were not promptly addressed by the transitional authorities. Although the transitional government did not respond immediately, it did begin to address the demands of these civil society organisations.

Corruption had been rampant under Compaoré. While Burkina Faso's ranking in TI's 'Annual Corruption Perceptions Index' had fluctuated over the previous five years, this reflected score changes in other countries on the index because Burkina Faso's score had remained the same during that period. However, on 18 August, the CNT authorised the judiciary to pursue *two high profile corruption cases* concerning the former infrastructure and development minister, Jean Bertin Ouédraogo, and the former security minister, Jerome Bougouma, who were being held in Ouagadougou's main prison. Despite these arrests and the aforementioned legislation aimed at taking a tougher stance on corruption, by the end of the year it seemed unlikely that the new administration would actively pursue a strong anti-corruption agenda. The newly elected President Kaboré and other leaders of the MPP had all actively participated in the past practices of the Compaoré regime and might be heavily implicated in corruption charges brought against former Compaoré officials.

The transitional authorities reopened two significant *political murder cases* in a further attempt to address grievances raised by 'ruecratie' actors. First, the assassination of former president and revolutionary leader *Thomas Sankara* had long been ignored by the Compaoré regime because of Compaoré's alleged involvement in the murder. Sankara had been killed along with 12 others in 1987, when members of his presidential guard opened fire on them, allegedly following Compaoré's orders. On 4 March, after reopening the Sankara case, the transitional government, in a symbolically significant decision, authorised the exhumation of Sankara's body. The UN Human Rights Council and the African Court on Human and Peoples' Rights (ACHPR), based in Arusha (Tanzania), had previously called for this and for an autopsy on Sankara's remains, but the Compaoré regime had ignored these international appeals.

Under transitional President Kafando, the Sankara case was transferred to the judicial wing of the military. On 25 March, Minister of Justice Joséphine Ouédraogo announced that a military tribunal would conduct an investigation into Sankara's assassination, a process which began with the exhumation of his body on 25 May. An autopsy was carried out on Sankara's remains and a report was released on 13 October. DNA results were not immediately available, but the presumed corpse of Sankara was described as being "riddled with bullets", supporting the narrative surrounding Sankara's death. Doctor Diébré Alidou had signed Sankara's death certificate, stating that he had died of natural causes and so he was charged with complicity in covering up the assassination. On 7 December, General Gilbert Diendéré, already imprisoned and facing charges related to the September coup, was charged with complicity in Sankara's murder, along with Diendéré and ten other less senior members of the RSP.

The second case re-opened by the transitional government concerned *Norbert Zongo*, an investigative journalist who had been found dead with three others in 1998. Zongo had been investigating the involvement of President Compaoré's brother, François, in the murder of his driver, David Ouédraogo. On 5 June, the ACHPR reviewed the Compaoré regime's investigation of Zongo's murder and ordered the Burkinabè authorities to resume the investigation in an effort to find, charge and try the perpetrators of the murders of Zongo and his compatriots. The ACHPR also ordered the government of Burkina Faso to pay compensation in the amount of roughly $ 16,000 to the families of Norbert Zongo and the three others killed in the attack. While the government accepted the ruling of the court, by the end of the year relatively little progress on the reopened investigation had been made public.

The principal economic sectors also faced challenges. Late rains led forecasters to anticipate that *cotton* production would not meet projections for the 2015/2016 growing season. Additionally, world cotton prices dropped to a six-year low. While the low prices were unlikely to dramatically affect overall production in Burkina Faso owing to a lack of alternative crops, the reduced prices combined with poor weather conditions did reduce the expected profits for farmers.

Compaoré's departure from the presidency coincided with a variety of disputes at several *mining* locations. Some speculated that the increased altercations were a result of the popular view that those close to Compaoré profited disproportionately in the booming mining sector. In many cases, incidents occurred between local populations and mining company employees. For instance, in January it was reported that equipment belonging to the Canadian firm True Gold had been damaged by local people at the Karma gold project, halting the development of a new mine.

In addition to the turbulent atmosphere following Compaoré's fall from power, the transitional government announced that it would review the government's *mining code* and conduct a complete audit of the sector. In March, the CNT received a revised version of the code from the Ministry of Mines and Energy, which included several new stipulations increasing the overall regulation of the sector. The reformed code included measures to increase support for local communities by using local goods, services and labour, as well as requiring mining companies to contribute to a fund for environmental protection and local economic development. The code also clarified contract terms and eliminated the possibility of income tax exemptions, imposing a 27% income tax rate across the board. The new code was adopted by the CNT on 26 June.

Finally, the 24th biannual 'Festival Panafricain du Cinéma et de la Télévision de Ouagadougou' (FESPACO) took place from 28 February to 7 March. FESPACO is an *internationally recognised film festival* and arguably the largest in Africa. Despite the popular uprising and subsequent political instability, Burkinabè authorities successfully organised and held the festival, which was attended by thousands of movie-goers. French-Moroccan filmmaker, Hicham Ayouch won the Golden Stallion of Yennenga, the prize for the best feature film with his film entitled 'Fièvres'. Abderrahmane Sissako's film 'Timbuktu' was also screened despite some initial controversy. The film depicts the Malian city of Timbuktu in 2012, during its occupation by al-Qaida-affiliated jihadist groups, who implemented harsh forms of Sharia law. Festival organisers initially stated that they would not screen the film because of security concerns in the Sahel region. However, when faced with public disappointment, the government reversed their decision, assuring attendees that security arrangements would be put in place to ensure their safety. FESPACO took place without incident, helping to ensure the continued development of tourism in Burkina Faso.

Cabo Verde

Gerhard Seibert

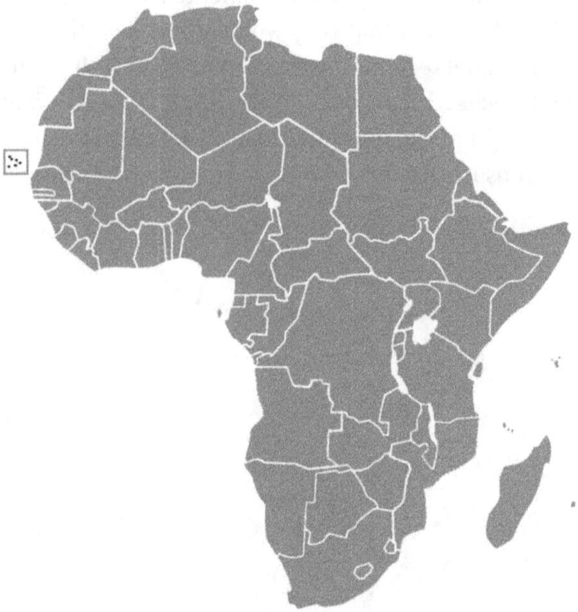

Despite the downward economic trend that affected all sectors of the economy, the number of tourist arrivals increased. In addition, tourism received the largest foreign investment project ever made in the sector. An attempt to considerably increase the incomes of political office holders was blocked by a presidential veto in response to spontaneous popular protests. Despite considerable diplomatic lobbying by the presidency and the government, Finance Minister Cristina Duarte failed to be elected as head of the AfDB.

Domestic Politics

On 23 January, the ruling 'Partido Africano da Independência de Cabo Verde' (PAICV) held its 14th congress. The delegates confirmed the election of Janira Hopffer Almada as new party leader. Almada had already received the support of ordinary party members on 14 December 2014. She appointed Manuel Inocêncio Sousa, Eva Ortet and José Maria Gomes Veiga as first, second and third vice presidents, respectively. Besides a list presented by Almada, two other lists were presented by Felisberto Vieira and Cristina Fontes Lima, both of whom Almada had defeated

 | DOI 10.1163/9789004333239_007

in the December 2014 party leadership vote. The three lists competed in the *elections of the members of the National Council* (CN) and the National Jurisdiction and Supervision Commission (CNJF). Almada succeeded with the election of 32 member of the CN, while Vieira secured 14 and Lima four members. In the CNJF elections, Alamada's list took five members, Vieira's two and Lima's none. The three leaders praised the results as having strengthened intraparty democracy.

On 25 March, the PAICV, 'Movimento para a Democracia' (MpD) and 'União Cabo-verdiana Independente e Democrática' (UCID) approved a 64% salary increase for the president, government members and parliamentarians as part of a *reform of the Statutes of Political Position Holders*. This provoked widespread popular protests on 30 March, with calls urging President Jorge Carlos Fonseca to veto the decision, which many decried as a 'national shame'. Under the new statutes, the adjusted monthly salaries of all office holders were indexed to the highest one – the president's – which was increased from CVE (escudo) 170,000 (€ 1,540) to CVE 280,000 (€ 2,540). The president eventually vetoed the new statutes on 9 April and asked parliamentarians to revise the bill, arguing that he could not ignore public protests in times of economic crisis. Subsequently, due to a lack of consensus on the revised statutes, the PAICV and MpD decided to remove the issue from the parliamentary agenda.

On 1 August, the law on the general scheme ('regime geral') of the *privatisation of public enterprises* was approved by the 37 deputies of the ruling PAICV against 27 votes of the opposition MpD and UCID. The MpD deputy and former prime minister, Carlos Veiga, justified his party's position on the grounds that the law appeared only half a year before the end of the legislature and lacked the transparency, rigidity and exemptions that were imperative for privatisations. In turn, Finance Minister Cristina Duarte (PAICV) declared that the revision of the privatisation law was motivated by the desire to prepare the ground for the next privatisation round. Accordingly, the government's main intention was to limit the extent to which the state intervened in the private economy and to reduce public debt. On 7 December, Fonseca vetoed the law, arguing that it allowed the privatisation of public enterprises by direct sale, which was difficult to reconcile with the public interest.

On 24 November, Prime Minister José Maria Neves announced the *dismissal* of Minister of Infrastructure and Maritime Economy Sara Lopes in what he said he considered an ordinary cabinet reshuffle and announced that he would take over her portfolios until the end of the legislature, while Maria de Jesus Miranda, hitherto secretary of state for foreign affairs, was appointed deputy minister of infrastructure and maritime economy. During a parliamentarian debate, Lopes had been accused by the opposition of being responsible for the sinking of a ferryboat off Fogo Island on 8 January, which had killed 15 people, but she firmly responded that the government had done everything that should have been done in that case. Neves denied that there was any connection between the incident and Lopes' dismissal. On 23 December, PAICV leader Janira Hopffer Almada left her position on the executive as minister for youth, employment and human resources development to fully dedicate herself to preparations for the legislative elections on 20 March 2016.

Foreign Affairs

On 14 February in the Vatican, Pope Francis consecrated Santiago's Bishop Arlindo Gomes Furtado as one of 20 new cardinals. *Bishop Furtado became the first cardinal of Cabo Verde*, Africa's first diocese, founded in 1533, and one of the 15 new cardinals eligible to vote in a papal conclave. A government delegation headed by Neves attended the ceremony.

Diplomatic activities prioritised relationships with Portuguese-speaking countries and also with China. On 28 January, Prime Minister Domingos Simões Pereira of *Guinea Bissau* arrived in Praia for a three-day visit. Neves and Pereira signed four bilateral agreements covering the mutual promotion and protection of investments, premises to house diplomatic missions, the establishment of a mechanism for bilateral political consultations and a general friendship and cooperation treaty. Both heads of government stressed their commitment to strengthening bilateral cooperation in all sectors.

During a four-day visit to Guinea-Bissau that began on 16 July, Neves declared that Cabo Verde owed an enormous debt to the Guinean people, since the liberation struggle of both countries was fought in Guinea-Bissau. He promised to promote cooperation in the maritime, security and public administration sectors. During his visit, Neves met with Prime Minister Domingos Simões Pereira, President José Mário Vaz, and President of the People's National Assembly Cipriano Cassamá, as well as with leaders of political parties represented in parliament and the local Cabo Verdean community. Neves and Pereira agreed to establish of a *strategic partnership between the two countries*, including a biennial summit of their heads of government.

On 30 January, President Fonseca participated in the 24th Ordinary Session of the Assembly of AU Heads of State and Government held in Addis Ababa (Ethiopia) on the theme 'Year of Women's Empowerment and Development'. In meetings with acting ECOWAS chairman President John Dramani Mahama of Ghana and other leaders, Fonseca took the opportunity to lobby for the *candidacy of Finance Minister Cristina Duarte as new head of the AfDB*. However, in the elections on 28 May, Duarte came only third with 10.3% of the votes cast, while the Nigerian candidate, Akinwumi Adesina, was elected new AfDB president with 58.1%.

On 14 February, China's outgoing ambassador, Su Jian, promised that his country would increase annual development assistance to Cabo Verde from $ 25 m in 2014 to $ 30 m. Jian stressed that Cabo Verde was the African country that received most

Chinese aid in per capita terms. For 2015, the ambassador announced the construction of an agricultural products processing centre, an experimental solar energy project, and a new modern campus for the public 'Universidade de Cabo Verde'. Further, he announced the donation of two Chinese patrol boats for the local coast guard by March. Su Jian was replaced as ambassador by Du Xiaocong, hitherto deputy director of the Africa Department at Beijing's Foreign Ministry.

Fonseca left for Johannesburg (South Africa) on 11 June to participate in the *25th AU Heads of State and Government Summit.* The next day, during a stopover in Luanda (Angola), Fonseca met with the local Cabo Verdean community. He declared that he was aware of the great challenges that Cabo Verde was still confronting after 40 years of independence and declared his commitment to solving the many problems his compatriots encountered at home and abroad. On his return from Johannesburg on 16 June, Fonseca had dinner with Angolan businessmen in Luanda and was received by Angolan President Eduardo dos Santos. He told the Angolan business community that the establishment of partnerships between entrepreneurs of the five Portuguese-speaking African Countries (Palop) was beneficial for all.

On 26 June, *Portugal*'s Defence Minister José Pedro Aguiar-Branco was in Praia to sign a *bilateral agreement on technical-military cooperation* to strengthen military cooperation with Cabo Verde. Portugal's military aid included the training of marines, military police and coast guard. Technical-military cooperation between the two countries also included the permanent presence of Portuguese military in the Centre for Military Instruction in Mindelo, São Vicente, and the joint participation of Cabo Verdean and Portuguese military in peace maintenance operations.

As part of a tour of four African countries, on 1 September *Brazil*'s Foreign Minister Mauro Vieira visited Cabo Verde, one of Brazil's principal cooperation partners in Africa, a major recipient of Brazilian university scholarships, and, since 2013, host to a Brazilian Naval Mission Centre ('Núcleo de Missão Naval'). Vieira held talks with his local counterpart, Jorge Tolentino, as part of the third meeting of the Mechanism of Political Consultations and of Cooperation between the two countries, created in 2009. In addition, he was received by Fonseca, Neves and President of the National Assembly Basílio Mosso Ramos.

On 4 November, Neves left for a four-day tour of *Angola*, his last foreign visit as prime minister. He participated in the commemorations for the 40th anniversary of Angola's Independence and met with local authorities and businesspeople. Neves stressed the importance of Angolan private investments for the development of Cabo Verde. During a visit to Cabinda, he said he considered Angola a strategic actor in the transformation not only of Southern Africa, but of the whole continent. He also met with the Cabo Verdean communities in Luanda, Benguela and Cabinda to say farewell as prime minister.

On 2 December, Fonseca and Foreign Minister Tolentino travelled to Johannesburg to participate in the *2nd Forum on China-Africa Cooperation* (FOCAC) held on the theme 'Africa-China Progressing Together: Win-Win Cooperation for Common Development'. The event was considered to be of great importance for Cabo Verde, given the $16 bn in Chinese investments expected for the period 2016–18. On 5 December, Fonseca participated in a group meeting of 17 African presidents with Chinese President Xi Jinping.

Socioeconomic Developments

On 29 January, Portugal suspended a credit line of € 200 m used to finance the *social housing programme 'Casa para Todos'* created by the Cabo Verdean government in 2009. When the credit line ended, Cabo Verde had only used € 115 m of the total amount. However, Cabo Verde had failed to contribute the 10% of the overall sum as stipulated in the credit agreement. Subsequently, the construction works slowed down or were suspended altogether. In May and June, 'Imobiliária Fundiária e Habitat' (IFH), the agency in charge of the programme, settled debts of CVE 500 m (€ 4.5 m) owed to the companies. On 14 October, the government approved the issue of obligations worth CVE 850 m (€ 7.7 m) on behalf of IFH to facilitate access to low-cost housing for disadvantaged sections of the population. By that time, the construction of 2,188 houses had been completed, equivalent to 34.6% of the 6,010 houses scheduled for the first phase of the programme. After the government had fulfilled its contractual obligations, on 8 December, the Portuguese government endorsed the state-owned 'Caixa Geral de Depósitos' to extend the credit line for the housing programme by € 85 m.

On 20 February, the government sold its 10% stake in the 'Banco Comercial do Atlântico' for CVE 464 m (€ 4.2 m) as part of its privatisation policies. On 7 August, the government provided the local branch of 'Novo Banco' (formerly 'Banco Internacional' established in 2010 and owned by the Portuguese Banco Espírito Santo Group that went bankrupt in August 2014) with seven government-owned buildings located in Praia, estimated to have a value of CVE 149 m (€ 1.4 m), which 'Novo Banco' was to sell to increase the state's share by augmenting the institution's capital stock. If 'Novo Banco' failed to sell the buildings, they would revert to being state property. The transaction was aimed at strengthening the bank's financial standing in order to attract new private investors.

Despite ongoing financial troubles, on 2, 3 and 5 June the *national airline* TACV ('Transportes Aéreos de Cabo Verde') inaugurated new international weekly flights from Praia to Providence RI (USA), Bissau, and Recife (Brazil). The connection to Providence replaced the former connection between Praia and Logan airport in Boston MA. The change provoked protests by the Cabo Verdean community in Boston because of the longer distance to T.F. Green airport in Providence and a ticket price increase from $ 1,300 to $ 1,700. On 17 December, TACV initiated another direct weekly connection from Sal to Rotterdam (The Netherlands). The government had already provided TACV with a loan of CVE 155 m (€ 1 m) on 15 February to settle operational debts and on 28 July the 'Instituto Nacional de Providência Social' (INPS) acquired corporate bonds issued by TACV worth CVE 475 m (€ 4.3 m). On 9 September, the state-owned 'Caixa Económica de Cabo Verde' agreed to lend TACV a further CVE 350 m (€ 3.2 m) with a five-year term to finance the maintenance of the company's aircraft. In addition, on 13 August, the government approved the disbursement of $ 3.9 m for the annual lease of three ATR72 planes for inter-island connections. Despite these consecutive financial injections, on 18 December, the International Air Transport Association Clearing House temporarily suspended TACV for non-payment of debts.

On 15 June, the *fish cannery Frescomar* opened a new production line for tuna processing in São Vicente that was expected to create about 400 new jobs. Manuel Monteiro, vice-president of Frescomar's board of directors, announced that his company was expanding further since it was concluding the refurbishment of the fishing complex in Cova de Inglesa and would soon start renovating the old Salmar factory on Sal Island, which would generate another 100 and 120 new jobs, respectively. On 22 July, Frescomar won the public tender for a ten-year concession for the operation of the freezer complex in Porto Grande, Mindelo. In 2014, the company's exports had totalled € 25 m, equivalent to 50% of Cabo Verde's exports.

Tourism attracted several foreign investments. On 10 June, 'Cabo Verde Investimentos' and Matiota Investments signed an agreement on the renewable 50-year concession on a 5,000 m^2 plot in Laginha, Mindelo, for the construction of the four-star 240-bed Tulip Laginha Hotel. The hotel represented an investment of € 32 m, of which more than half was expected to be financed externally, and included a conference hall, casino, shopping mall and parking for 70 vehicles.

On 23 July in Macau, Tourism and Investments Minister Leonesa Fortes and the Chinese businessman David Chow, Cabo Verde's consul in Macau and CEO of Macau Legend Development Ltd, the owner of entertainment and casino gambling facilities in the Chinese city, signed a 75-year concession agreement, renewable for 30-year periods, on the construction of Cape Verde Integrated Resort and Casino. The *luxury tourism project* budgeted at $ 250 m, included buildings, infrastructure, a marina, parking area, sports complex and a casino, to be constructed on a total area of 17 ha on the islet of Santa Maria and parts of the Gamboa beach in Praia, which faces it. The huge investment was expected to create 2,100 jobs and receive 12,000 people a day for shopping, leisure, sports and cultural activities.

On 12 November, Neves and the mayor of Praia, Ulisses Correia e Silva, attended the laying of the foundation stone of the Praia Hilton Hotel, the group's second hotel in the archipelago. The five-star hotel project included 201 rooms on 14 storeys and a leisure area with a swimming pool and spa.

Over the entire year, the number of visiting *tourists increased* by 4.4% from 539,621 in 2014 to 569,387, while the number of overnights increased by 6.8%. Great Britain was the principal origin of visitors with 22.2% of the total, followed by Germany (13.4%), Portugal (10.9%) and Belgium and the Netherlands (10.6%). Sal was the most visited island with a 43.2% share of tourist entries.

Côte d'Ivoire

Alfred Babo

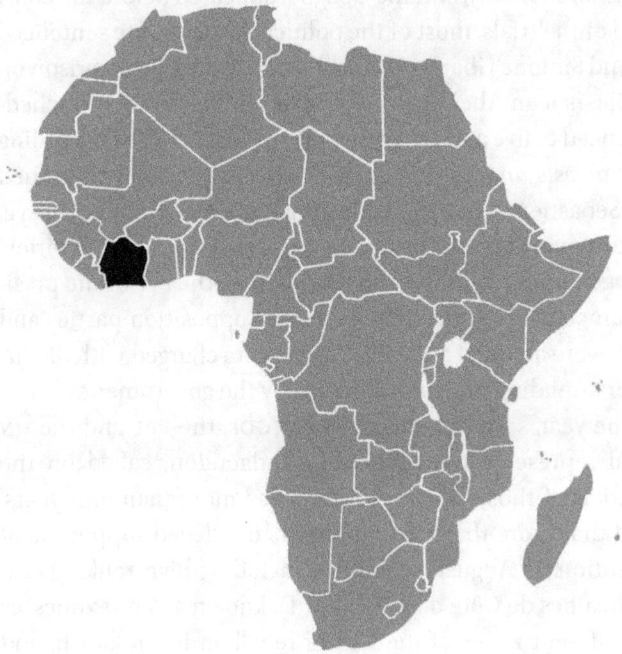

The first presidential election after the contentious 2010 polls attracted widespread national and international attention. On the one hand, the country witnessed the consolidation of the governing coalition. On the other, it saw the disintegration of the opposition. After being rescheduled several times, the trial of supporters of former president Gbagbo, indicted for their alleged role in the post-election violence of 2010–11, took place in Abidjan. As in the past, the judicial system was biased in favour of the incumbent. After the ousted president of Burkina Faso, Blaise Compaoré, found refuge in Côte d'Ivoire, relations with Burkina Faso turned sour. However, the challenging political environment did not stand in the way of positive macroeconomic and social developments.

Domestic Affairs

The year started with the trial of 83 supporters of the ousted former president Laurent Gbagbo, including several high-ranking political and military leaders. The members of the former regime were charged with offences against national security

 | DOI 10.1163/9789004333239_008

before the Criminal Court of Abidjan. The *trial of former ministers* Jean-Jacques Béchio and Georges Armand Ouégnin began on 5 February and of former prime minister Gilbert Aké N'Gbo, and the former ministers Alcide Djédjé, Christine Adjobi, Ettien Amoikon, Raphaël Dogbo and Joseph Kata Kété on 10 February. All pleaded not guilty. The former first-lady, Simone Gbagbo, appeared before the court on 23 February. At the end of the trials, most of the political leaders were sentenced to several *years in prison* and Simone Gbagbo was sentenced to 20 years in prison on 10 March. The military officers Jean Abéhi and Séka Séka, whose trial was rescheduled to August, were sentenced to five and 20 years in prison, respectively. According to an AI report, *arbitrary arrests and detentions* of Gbagbo supporters continued during the year. In May, Sebastien Dano Djédjé, Justin Koua and Hubert Oulaye, high-ranking leaders of the main opposition party, the 'Front Populaire Ivoirien' (FPI), were arrested. Between mid-September and October, on the eve of the presidential election, more than 50 people, mostly members of opposition parties and civil society organisations, were arrested and jailed. They were charged with disturbance of public order after attending protests repressed by the government.

During the course of the year, several human rights NGOs, the FPI and the UN secretary-general's special representative, Aïchatou Mindaoudou, called on the government to start the trials of those who had been jailed more than four years. The AI report highlighted that more than 200 supporters or alleged supporters of Gbagbo remained in detention. In August, 20 officers, including high-ranking officers of the 'Forces Républicaines de Côte d'Ivoire' (FRCI), known as 'com-zones' as they were commanding different zones of the former rebellion in the north, and some traditional hunters, 'dozos', from the north, who had participated in the 2011 war, were charged by the investigating judge, but the charges did not lead to any arrests. In parallel with the judiciary process, as part of the *reparations* for the 2010 post-election war victims, 200 people received cheques worth a total of CFAfr 1 m. According to the 'Programme National de Cohesion Sociale', by the end of the year more than 1,000 had received compensation.

The *presidential election* dominated the political discourse. Early in the year, observers and opposition parties were already raising concerns about the credibility of the electoral institutions. February saw the *sudden resignation of Francis Wodié*, the chair of the Constitutional Council (the country's highest court), which was mandated to validate the candidacies and the results. Some opposition parties alleged that he had been subjected to pressure from the government and the ruling party, the 'Rassemblement des Républicains'. Apprehension grew when he was replaced the following day by *Mamadou Koné*, a close friend of President Alassane Ouattara. Despite opposition protests, Ouattara kept Youssouf Bakayoko as president of the 'Commission Electorale Indépendante' (CEI). He was not trusted by opposition parties because of his controversial role in the 2010 post-electoral crisis.

The run-up to the elections led to deep divisions within the country's two major political parties, the 'Parti Démocratique de Cote d'Ivoire – Rassemblement Démocratique Africain' (PDCI-RDA) and the FPI. Division appeared in the PDCI-RDA when three of its leaders – former prime minister Konan Banny, Minister Essy Amara and Representative Konan Kouadio Bertin – refused to endorse Konan Bédié's support for the incumbent, Alassane Ouattara. The three dissidents failed to get the party's support and the party decided to endorse Ouattara at its convention on 28 February. Ouattara fought the election under the banner of the 'Rassemblement des Houphouétistes pour la Démocratie et la Paix', a coalition that included the PDCI-RDA.

The FPI experienced profound *divisions* between one group led by former prime minister Affi NGuessan and another led by Aboudramane Sangaré. While the former argued that the party should participate in the October election, the latter demanded the release of former president Gbagbo from jail in The Hague before the party would participate in any presidential election. The crisis escalated as the two factions organised separate party congresses to elect a presidential candidate. During the extraordinary congress on 5 March, NGuessan was ousted from the party presidency and replaced by Sangaré. NGuessan responded by suspending all those who had attended the extraordinary congress, and he then filed a lawsuit to contest Sangaré's presidency. On 3 April, Affi was declared the legal president of the FPI by the Court of First Instance of Abidjan. On 31 April, the faction led by Sangaré organised a convention in Gbagbo's village, Mama, where participants proclaimed Gbagbo the new president of the FPI and called for a boycott of the national presidential election. This group, known as 'FPI-Sangaré', subsequently formed a new alliance with other parties on 15 May, and this alliance gathered candidates from the PDCI-RDA, a number of smaller parties and members of civil society. Together they formed the '*Coalition Nationale pour le Changement*' (CNC). The 'FPI-Affi' organised another convention a few weeks later on 22 May in Abidjan and nominated N'Guessan as its presidential candidate.

In order to counter widespread suspicion regarding the electoral system, the CEI tried to improve the transparency and reliability of the process, including the introduction of a new system for reporting local poll results to the CEI's headquarter in Abidjan. In addition, it set up a biometric authentication system and 'anti-fraud' tablet computers in all polling stations. The tablets held voters' biometric data including name, fingerprints, photograph, and a secret code that could be used only once for the vote. The registration process started on 1 June and was initially scheduled to end on 30 June, but registration was low during this period. Although the deadline was extended to 12 July, only 6,300,142 people enrolled out of a total of 9 m eligible voters (according to the 2014 registration census). Thus, about 2.3 m–3.3 m potential new voters did not register to vote. Other factors that lowered participation were *calls for abstention and boycott* from prominent opposition parties including the FPI and the 'Liberté et Démocratie pour la République', the low rate of electoral ID collection by voters, and the *withdrawal of prominent candidates* such as former prime minister Konan Banny and former minister Essy Amara, just before the polls, leaving a total of ten candidates. The electoral campaign for the first round opened on 9 October and ended on 23 October. Ivorians voted peacefully on 25 October and Alassane *Ouattara was re-elected* with 83.6% of the vote, defeating Affi, who ran under the banner of the FPI and came second with 9.2% of the vote, in spite the controversies surrounding the turnout. The CEI initially announced a *turnout* of 60% on 26 October, but this proved to be controversial due in part to the problems with registration. A prominent civil society organisation monitoring the election, 'Plateforme pour l'Observation des Elections en Côte d'Ivoire', gave a figure of 53%. Finally, the CEI lowered its estimate and announced the turnout to be 52.8%.

Throughout the year, security was the government's dominant concern, largely due to a new form of criminality – the growing number of *child abductions*. In January, 21 children were kidnapped and only one was found alive. On 28 January, the government announced a strategic plan to fight child kidnapping and deployed 1,500 security personnel and increased police patrols in risky areas of the economic capital, Abidjan. The *escape of inmates* from several prisons in Abidjan and in the countryside in Bouaké, Korhogo and Agboville was an additional security concern and the authorities increased the number of prison guards to 2,000. According to public authorities, the DDR programme, which ended in June, reintegrated 55,000 former combatants out of 64,000, that is over 80% of all former combatants. Many sceptical voices questioned the validity of these statistics, claiming that the government had deliberately exaggerated the figures in the run-up to the presidential election. It was widely assumed that many fighters were still unaccounted for and, even though the security situation had improved, the persistence of land disputes in the west remained a serious problem.

In addition to the internal security issue, the country also faced attacks on its borders and *terrorist threats* from outside. In August, seven alleged jihadists were arrested and deported to Mali. FRCI positions were repeatedly attacked. An attack at Olodjo, on the Liberia border, caused the death of seven soldiers, and another attack occurred in Nougoua at the Ghanaian frontier on 26 December.

Foreign Affairs

Côte d'Ivoire remained a constructive member of the AU and continued to help solve regional problems. In April, in the aftermath of the controversy about the first round of the Togolese elections, President Ouattara intervened on behalf of the AU in order to ease the political climate. In addition, the country continued to strengthen its relationship with *Morocco*. Early in January, an economic forum gathered Moroccan and Ivorian investors in Marrakesh and King Mohammed VI visited Côte d'Ivoire in June. Together with Ouattara, he launched in Abidjan the 'Bay of Cocody' project, to include the construction of a viaduct, an urban park, a marina and leisure areas, as well as commercial facilities. In addition, 46 partnership agreements between the two countries were signed between 2 and 5 June and the Moroccan king donated two tonnes of medicine for the fight against AIDS. Moroccan businesses accounted for 22% of companies in Côte d'Ivoire. Ouattara also reactivated relations with *Egypt* in March, when Egypt's Prime Minister Ibrahim Mahlab visited Abidjan to explore economic cooperation.

Relations with Burkina Faso and Ghana declined. A *diplomatic crisis with Burkina Faso* broke out when recordings of phone conversations between Guillaume Soro, the president of the Ivorian National Assembly, and Djibril Bassolé, the former minister of foreign affairs of Burkina Faso, were leaked on social media. The conversations revealed the involvement of Ivorian authorities in the failed military coup in Burkina Faso in September. In addition, the Burkinabe Ministry of Justice issued an international arrest warrant on 21 December for its former president, Blaise Compaoré, who had gone into exile in Côte d'Ivoire, for the murder of Thomas Sankara. These two issues poisoned diplomatic relations between the two countries. Côte d'Ivoire denied the involvement of its National Assembly president and refused to execute the arrest warrant.

The relationship with *Ghana* suffered when, in late December, unidentified armed assailants attacked the Ivorian military post in Noé on the frontier. In addition, the two countries had long disagreed over the demarcation of their *maritime border*. They had decided not to exploit the offshore oil resources located within the disputed zone but Ghana, nevertheless, bypassed the agreement and granted exploration permits in the area. On 29–30 March, Côte d'Ivoire lodged a complaint before the International Tribunal for the Law of the Sea, in Hamburg, Germany, where adjudication of the dispute remained pending at year's end.

Côte d'Ivoire maintained its privileged relations with France and explored new ones with Israel. In the first half of the year, trade between Côte d'Ivoire and *France* grew by 9%, mainly due to an increase in French imports (+ 16.7%). Apart from economic cooperation, the two countries agreed in July to lift the *visa requirement* for diplomatic passport holders. A diplomatic crisis almost occurred on 7 December, when the judge in a Parisian court issued a warrant against the president of the National Assembly, Guillaume Soro. The judge was processing the investigation related to a complaint filed by Michel Gbagbo – Laurent Gbagbo's son – for mistreatment when he was held in prison without trial in 2011 by Soro's former rebel forces. This warrant against the second most influential politician in Côte d'Ivoire was considered inappropriate by the Ivorian government. In Abidjan, the Ivorian minister of foreign affairs summoned the French ambassador on 8 December and delivered his protest. According to the Ivorian side, Soro was in Paris on state business to participate in the COP21 conference and so enjoyed *diplomatic immunity*. This 'crisis' ended with Soro's rapid departure for Côte d'Ivoire shortly thereafter.

Côte d'Ivoire revived its relationship with *Israel*. On 28 July, the president of the Ivorian National Assembly led a delegation of representatives to Israel where they were welcomed by his counterpart, Yuli Eldestein. The two countries signed a parliamentary cooperation agreement. Relations with the USA improved further. Côte d'Ivoire was granted $ 500 m on 16 December by the Millennium Challenge Corporation program. In addition, after a wait of 15 years, Abidjan was authorised by the US Transportation Security Administration to operate *direct flights* to USA.

The Ivorian government tried to get financial support from the World Bank, the EU, the IMF and the Islamic Development Bank (IDB). The World Bank celebrated the 50th anniversary of its activities in Abidjan on 25 June and used this opportunity to disburse an interest-free loan of $ 100 m designed to improve transportation infrastructure between Côte d'Ivoire and Burkina Faso. The EU pledged € 200 m to reduce fossil fuels. In September, an IMF delegation recommended the disbursement of € 65 m under the ECF. Côte d'Ivoire also received support from the IDB through a loan agreement of CFAfr 77 bn, which financed the extension of the northern highway between the political capital Yamoussoukro and the town of Tiébissou.

Socioeconomic Developments

Côte d'Ivoire pursued several important socio-economic *infrastructure projects*. On 21 March, the head of state inaugurated the 'Philippe Gregory Yacé' bridge built in Jacqueville (South) at a cost of CFAfr 22.5 bn. The China Harbour Engineering Company began the construction of the new industrial zone, called PK 24, and was expected to invest at least CFAfr 60 bn in this project. In order to implement its national development plan, the Ivorian government raised CFAfr 150 bn in Islamic bonds. An agreement with the Islamic Corporation for Private Sector Development was concluded on 17 September. In addition, *electricity generation* improved when the extension of the Azito power plant in Abidjan became operational on 30 June. A new 139 MW turbine, with capacity for clean power generation of 430 MW, brought the national capacity up to 1,772 MW, representing a 10% increase in the country's power production. From 5 May onwards, the public *banking sector* underwent restructuring. The programme foresaw the privatisation of four banks, the 'Banque de Financement de l'Agriculture' (BFA), Versus Bank, Nsia-Banque and the 'Société Ivoirienne de Banque'. The privatisation process was eventually expected to provide the country with around CFAfr 32.4 bn. As part of the process, the BFA was liquidated because of its permanent deficit.

The government attempted to reduce social inequality. An extensive programme of *social housing* was assigned to 39 real estate companies, with more than 80% of sites located in Abidjan, where demand was high. Statistics showed a deficit of 200,000 affordable homes and a total deficit of 400,000 houses across the country. A healthcare system called '*Couverture Maladie Universelle*' was finally implemented and more than 200,000 people were enrolled in the new system by August. On 29 April, the government signed a decree prohibiting the manufacture, marketing and use of risky skin lightening products.

The government also increased *public sector wages*. In May, a total of 1,116,098 employees received an increase in their salaries ranging from CFAfr 13,787 to CFAfr 142,940. The literacy rate rose to 56.9%. In July, a presidential decree established *compulsory education* for 6–16-year-olds. The compulsory education project was expected to cost CFAfr 700 bn, most of it to cover the wages of 5,000 new secondary school teachers.

Agricultural production improved due to the expansion of a new *cocoa* plant: the 'Centre National de Recherche Agronomique' yielding an average of 1.5 tonne/ha boosted the national production of cocoa beans and, in June, Côte d'Ivoire was still ranked as the world's largest producer of cocoa beans (40% of the global harvest). The recent 2014–15 campaign resulted in a record harvest of about 1.8 m tonnes. Prices rose by about 20% from CFAfr 850 per kilo in 2014 to CFAfr 1,000. *Processing* capacity also improved. With the inauguration of the cocoa factory Olam Cocoa Processing on 7 March in San Pedro (South), the country now had 12 shredders. According to the International Organization of Coffee and Cocoa, Côte d'Ivoire was the number one nation for cocoa bean processing. The country also began to produce chocolate, a more lucrative business. On 18 May, a chocolate factory with a production capacity of 10,000 tonnes per year (using one-third of the country's total bean production) was opened in Abidjan by the French corporation Cemoi. The *smuggling* of cocoa beans into neighbouring countries became an issue. Even though cocoa beans were seized at the border with Liberia, several illegal operators continued to be active. At the end of the 2014–15 season, *cotton* production reached a record 450,000 tonnes, up 11% from the previous season, making Côte d'Ivoire the third largest regional producer behind Burkina Faso and Mali. However, a declining world market for cotton meant that the increased production did not translate into higher export earnings. Prices declined from $ 0.87 (CFAfr 390) per pound during the 2014–15 season to $ 0.69 (CFAfr 310) in 2015. National production of *cashew nuts* reached 700,000 tonnes, with Côte d'Ivoire now the world's leading producer of cashew together with India. In this sector, turnover rose from CFAfr 200 bn in 2013 to CFAfr 337 bn in 2015 and cashew nut producers saw their incomes rise by 68%, according to Minister of Agriculture Mamadou Coulibaly Sangafowa.

Overall, the agricultural and infrastructural results contributed to a generally favourable macroeconomic performance. An IMF delegation visited Côte d'Ivoire in September. Its report highlighted the strength of the country's economic performance and particularly emphasised the *low inflation rate* and the robust GDP growth. However, the IMF was slightly more pessimistic about the annual growth rate and estimated it at 7.9%, compared with the 9.4% announced by the government. In September, another IMF mission headed by the deputy director of the

IMF's Africa Department revised the growth forecast to 8.4%. With a score of 74%, according to the Africa Performance Index (API), Côte d'Ivoire ranked first in the economies of the CFAfr zone, making the Ivorian Ministry of Economy the best performing institution in terms of tax governance, institutional framework and internal factors such as GDP growth, management of inflation and public debt. According to the 2015 Doing Business report, Côte d'Ivoire was among the ten African economies that had made the most progress since the 2014 edition.

Despite these positive economic performances, challenges remained. The cost of living remained high: on 21 May, the government announced an increase in charges for household electricity from 1 June. Even though the government did not initially apply this measure, many citizens complained in December that they had noticed an increase of their electricity bills. Extreme poverty still affected about 46% of the population, according to the National Institute of Statistics.

Gambia

Alice Bellagamba

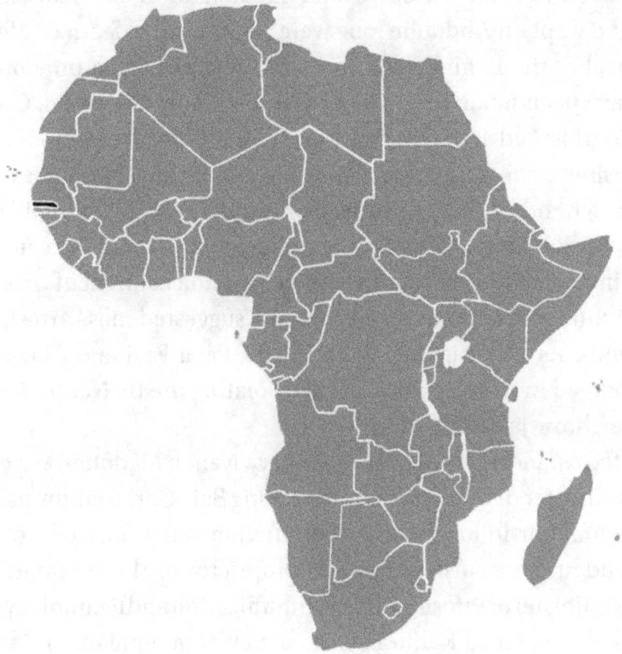

After the foiled coup of 30 December 2014, Yahya Jammeh's government strengthened security measures. State repression affected members of the army, journalists, civil servants and the relatives and friends of the alleged plotters who had sought refuge abroad. A number of surprising political moves took place during the year, including sweeping electoral reforms, presidential pardons for over 250 detainees, the banning of female genital mutilation and Jammeh's declaration of the Gambia as an Islamic republic. The country's economic performance deteriorated and the level of public debt rose dramatically.

Domestic Politics

President Yahya Jammeh and his government reacted harshly to the *foiled coup of 30 December 2014*. Its leader, Lamin Sanneh (an ex-army colonel and commander of the Presidential Guard, who had left the Gambia with his family in 2012 to seek asylum in the USA), was killed with three other assailants during the operation. Another attacker died the following day, while the rest of the plotters sought refuge

© KONINKLIJKE BRILL NV, LEIDEN, 2016 | DOI 10.1163/9789004333239_009 in Senegal and Guinea Bissau. Jammeh confirmed the position of the Gambian army by declaring that the coup was a terrorist attack by Gambian dissidents based in Germany, the UK and the USA. However, contrary to this, on 30 March, a court martial convicted six members of the Gambian army. Private Modou Njie, Lieutenant Colonel Sarjo Jarju, Lieutenant Amadou Sowe and Lieutenant Buba Sanneh, Captain Buba K. Bojang and Captain Abdoulie Jobe were sentenced to death or life imprisonment. Their appeal at the Banjul High Court was rejected on 10 June on the basis that it should have been made through the Gambia Court of Appeal. On 8 April, the Banjul High Court issued arrest warrants for Cherno Njie, the Gambian-American Texas-based businessman accused of financing and masterminding the foiled coup, together with eight other alleged plotters: Mustapha Faal, Alhajie Saidy Barrow, Papa Faal, Baboucarr Bai Lowe, Musa Sarr, Landing Sonko, Lamin Njie and Aisha Jallow. The charges included multiple counts of treason, concealment of treason and other offences. Online media reports and rumours suggested mass arrests of their relatives and friends. As US residents, Cherno Njie, Papa Faal and Alagie Saidy Barrow were also charged in the USA for allegedly violating the US Neutrality Act in their attempt to overthrow Jammeh.

The failed coup prompted *cabinet reshuffles*. On 5 January, Neneh Mcdouall Gaye returned to the cabinet as minister of foreign affairs, replacing Bala Garba Jahumpa, who was reassigned his former portfolio of works, construction and infrastructure. Sheriff Bojang, an independent journalist, editor and proprietor of the 'Standard Newspaper', was appointed minister of information, communication and technology. On 8 January, Lamin Nyabally replaced Kalilu Bayo as secretary general and minister of presidential affairs. In the same announcement, the president relieved Basiru Mahoney of his duties as minister of justice. Until the reappointment of Mama Fatima Singhateh as attorney-general and minister of justice, the Ministry of Justice fell under the purview of the Ministry of Higher Education, Research, Science and Technology headed by Babucarr Senghore. On 14 January, Lamin K. Mboge, a private legal practitioner, was appointed solicitor general at the Ministry of Justice, and his appointment was revoked the same day without reason or explanation. At the Ministry of Finance and Economic Affairs, Kebba Touray was relieved of his duties as cabinet minister on 16 March. Abdou Colley, the former minister of finance and economic affairs was reinstated. Aki Bayo was relieved of his cabinet duties as minister of lands and regional government on 15 November but was reinstated in the same post 11 days later. On 23 November, Deputy Secretary General Sulayman Samba was promoted to secretary general and head of the civil service, and minister responsible for presidential affairs in place of Lamin Nyabally, who had been relieved of his duties and appointed as the new minister of fisheries on November 18. In a twist of events, a 29 December press release from State House announced the dismissal of Sulayman Samba and of Minister of Agriculture Ismaila Sanyang.

The *repressive grip of Jammeh's regime* did not spare media houses, members of the judiciary and religious leaders. Immediately after the foiled coup, on 1–4 January, the Gambian authorities ordered 'Teranga FM', an independent radio station, to stop broadcasting. Its managing director, Abdoulie Ceesay, was detained overnight on 1 January before being given conditional bail. He had to report daily to the police station. On 2 July, he was picked up and detained by the National Intelligence Agency (NIA). He was released on 13 July but, on 17 July, he was forced into a vehicle by agents suspected to be from the NIA. On 25 August, Ceesay was charged with six counts of sedition and publication of false news with intent to cause public alarm. On 26 November, the arrest and removal of Ebrima Jaiteh, the magistrate of Brikama Magistrates Court, provided a stark example of Jammeh's efforts to control the judiciary. Jaiteh had presided over two landmark cases: the trials of two senior managers of the Gambia Ports Authority and of Imam Moheideen Hydara, who had been arrested in 2014 for allegedly disobeying a presidential order to observe the Muslim Eid prayer on a prescribed date. In both cases, Jaiteh discharged the accused, to the displeasure of the government. Three imams were also arrested and detained: Sheikh Omar Colley, an imam of a mosque in Jabang Borehole, was arrested on 15 October, Alhaji Ousman Sawaneh, the imam of Kanifing South Mosque, on 19 October, and Imam Gassama of Dasilami village in Lower Fulladou West District, Central River Region, on 2 November. The reasons for these arrests remained unknown.

In light of the strained relations with many development partners and the lack of donor funding to complete major development projects, Jammeh had developed a tactic of scapegoating members of his cabinet and other government officials for his failing policies or stalled projects. For instance, Ebrima Jawara, the son of former president Jawara, along with the former permanent secretary Ada Gaye and four other staff members on were charged 7 September with 13 counts of economic crime, five counts of abuse of office and six counts of neglect of official duty.

Presidential elections were scheduled for 1 December 2016. The opposition parties presented an electoral and constitutional reform proposal to the Independent Electoral Commission (IEC), which included a term limit for the presidency, fresh demarcation of electoral constituencies and the involvement of civil society institutions in the selection of IEC commissioners. The opposition also called for the neutrality and non-involvement of civil servants in the electoral process and the extension of the electoral franchise to Gambians in the diaspora. The IEC vehemently rejected these proposals and introduced a new electoral law, which required presidential candidates to pay a fee of $ 12,630 for registration, a steep increase from the previous $ 252. The fee for National Assembly candidates was raised to $ 1,263. The reform was ratified into law by the president on 20 July. On 29 December, National Assembly members also passed a bill that sought to increase the number of National Assembly members from 48 to at least 53. As a component of the memorandum of understanding between the IEC and the National Council for Civic Education, a community sensitisation exercise on supplementary voter registration was started in December. Lack of adequate resources rendered many opposition parties unable to appoint enough agents to oversee the voter registration process. This inadequate transparency of the process led many to fear duplication of voters and the registration of minors and ineligible people from across the border.

On 3 July, in contrast to the frequency and intensity of illegal detentions and sackings, the president, acting in accordance with his constitutional powers, pardoned over 250 prisoners serving time at the Mile Two central prison. The list of names included Modou Gaye, a former deputy inspector general of police, who was serving a life sentence for his involvement in an attempted coup. Other surprising moves followed. On 25 November, Jammeh banned the age-old traditional practice of *female genital mutilation* (FGM). Although a few pundits criticised the announcement as a political move to score dividends with young female electors in the 2016 elections, the ban was received well by prominent gender activists and FGM victims. On 10 December, Jammeh surprised the nation and the international community with a declaration that "as from today, Gambia is an *Islamic Republic*". Although the official reason given was to preserve the country's religious identity as a Muslim nation, critics in the Gambian diaspora alleged that Jammeh was trying to win foreign aid from the Gulf States, and also rebranding his image in time for the December 2016 elections. Opposition political leaders and some religious clergy condemned this statement as not only unconstitutional, but also divisive and threatening to peaceful co-existence between the Christian minority and their Muslim fellow citizens. The Peoples' Democratic Organisation and Independent Socialism party in an editorial urged Parliament to commence impeachment proceedings against Jammeh.

Foreign Affairs

Relations with Senegal remained volatile throughout the year. The presence of the 30 December coup plotters in Senegal and the refusal of Senegal to extradite them to the Gambia brought simmering tensions to the boil. Senegal refused to comment, and Jammeh bitterly condemned the Senegalese authorities for their silence. The absence of Senegal's President Macky Sall at the landmark Golden Jubilee Independence celebration on 22 February was a clear indication of the rift between the two heads of state. On 15 November, in the border town of Farafenni, Jammeh described Sall as a "puppet in Western hands" and urged Senegalese citizens to outvote their president for the benefit of their nation. The following day, Senegal closed the border without explanation. Contrary to ECOWAS agreements on the free circulation of people and goods, border restrictions became the default strategy the two governments use to settle diplomatic grievances.

Relations between the Gambia and *the West* deteriorated further. On 5 June, Agnes Guillaud, the chargée d'affaires of the EU Delegation to the Gambia was declared persona non grata. No official reason was given for her expulsion from the country. In December, the EU announced the suspension of € 13 m in funding. After a lengthy diplomatic hiatus between Banjul and Washington, Ambassador-Designate C. Patricia 'Pat' Alsup arrived in the Gambia on 6 November. In December 2014, the USA had excluded the Gambia from AGOA trade preference over allegations of illegal detentions and torture of citizens as well as Jammeh's strong position against homosexuality.

Socioeconomic Developments

According to estimates, about 48% of Gambians were living below the poverty line. The rural-urban economic and development gap remained high. *Low agricultural output* due to climate change and erratic rainfall patterns significantly reduced the government's export earnings and also widened the poverty gap, having particular effect in rural areas. The 2014 groundnut trade season did not start until 8 January. Farmers sold the greater part of their harvest at bargain prices to intermediaries across the border in Senegal. In addition to lack of civil and political liberties, high youth unemployment and low agricultural harvests continued to force many Gambian youths to attempt illegal migration to Europe. In his budgetary speech to the National Assembly, Finance and Economic Affairs Minister Abdou Kolley predicted that the 2016 fiscal year would be difficult, as the country would continue to grapple with *growing levels of public debt.* Domestic debt now accounted for almost half of the country's debt stock. The economic impact of the regional Ebola outbreak on tourism and the delayed summer rains in 2014, together with unrestrained government expenditure, resulted in increased domestic borrowing and widened the country's balance of payment and fiscal deficit, which increased from GMD (dalasi) 11.3 bn in 2013 to GMD 20.7 bn. Consumer price *inflation* fell to 6.7% in December, from 6.9% in December 2014. This was ascribed to the decline in food inflation to 4.8% in December from 8.4% in December 2014. The governor of the Central Bank announced that non-food inflation had increased to 5.2% in December from 4.8% in December 2014. Frequent border closures with Senegal and the disruption of trade between the two countries had a strong impact on the Gambian economy, which remained highly vulnerable to external shocks.

In order to spur economic growth and to curb the rapid depreciation of the dalasi against other the US dollar and the pound sterling, the government instituted a number of *monetary reforms* and fiscal consolidation measures. One was the requirement that approval be obtained from the office of the president for foreign currency exports exceeding $ 10,000. This directive, announced in a press release on 4 May, warned that violators would risk forfeiture of their money to the state and resulted in almost a week of interruption of Western Union transfer services to customers. On 25 February, the Central Bank of the Gambia introduced new dalasi currency notes, and new denominations of GMD 20 and GMD 200 notes. The image of Jammeh on the new notes raised eyebrows among many Gambians who remembered his condemnation of former president Jawara's image on the old dalasi notes. The undue *interference of government in the free market economy* further lowered the trust of foreign investors in spite of official efforts to promote free trade. Bern Georg Diedrich, a German national, was deported by executive directive to Germany on 16 January. He had arrived in the Gambia in 1989 and bought land at Tranquil Wullingkama for investment purposes. After a land dispute with Alieu Barry, the High Court had delivered judgment in his favour in 2013. Nonetheless, officials from the Physical Planning Department, backed by about a dozen police personnel, had evicted him from his property on 18 December 2014. On 27 May, Hussain Tajudeen, the proprietor of TAJCO, was ordered to leave the country within 72 hours for allegedly engaging in unacceptable business practices. This decision was rescinded barely a month later. Tajudeen had already had a similar experience, having been expelled from the Gambia in June 2013, only to later be granted a 'presidential pardon' that allowed his return and the resumption of his business operations. According to the World Bank's 2015 Doing Business report, the Gambia ranked 138th out of 189 countries.

Lack of public investment and donor support severely compromised the *health sector*. Gambians had to travel to the capital city for treatment and had to pay for examinations and medicines even in public institutions. Families who could not count on the financial support of relatives abroad faced severe difficulties in the management of their health problems, especially in rural areas, where health facilities continued to be few and poorly equipped.

Ghana

Kwesi Aning and Nancy Annan

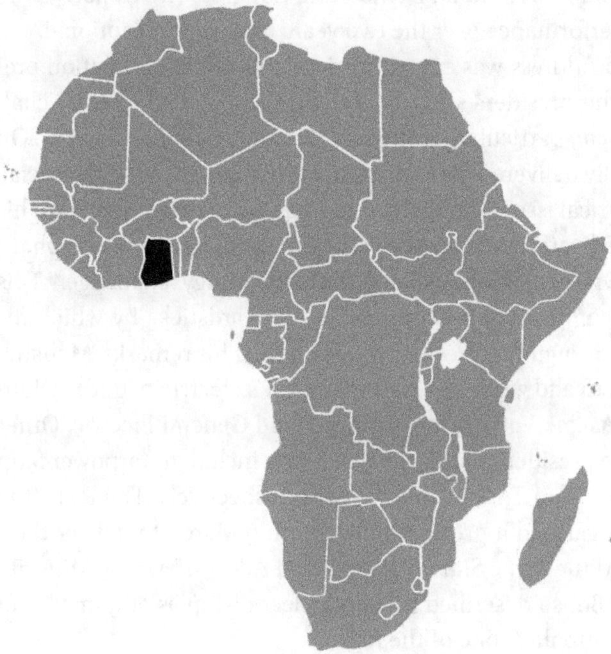

President Mahama and his National Democratic Congress experienced a challenging time. Incessant power irregularities, fire outbreaks and corruption allegations overshadowed an otherwise relatively peaceful year. Violent intra-party clashes within the New Patriotic Party dominated the political debate across the country. The release of a video recording of corrupt judges, and controversy over political advertising on buses and the Africa Middle East Resources Investments scandal shaped socio-economic issues.

Politics

At the beginning of the year, President John Dramani Mahama encouraged Ghanaians not to "lose hope" in his government and to expect a new year with new opportunities. On 7 January, he assured Ghanaians of his continuous dedication to serving the country. The celebration for the second anniversary of Mahama's taking office was met with *criticism of the president* from the public and the opposition New Patriotic Party (NPP). On 10 January, for example, the NPP Women's Organiser

 | DOI 10.1163/9789004333239_010

Otiko Afisa Djaba on a media platform accused Mahama of failing to deliver his 'Better Ghana Agenda'. She labelled Mahama a "de-facto president" who had been thrown into leadership due to the ill-health of his predecessor the late president John Evans Atta-Mills. Her criticisms were met with a sharp rebuttal from Abigail Mensah, a member of Mahama's National Democratic Congress (NDC) party, who said that the president's performance over the two years had been exceptional.

The State of the Nation Address was eagerly anticipated as the population prepared anxiously to hear the president's responses and plans for addressing challenges from the previous year, particularly with regard to the *power fluctuations*. On 26 February, Mahama finally delivered his address in Parliament. Among the social, health, economic and political issues highlighted, energy was central. To assure his fellow Ghanaians of his dedication to addressing the energy dilemma, he emphatically declared, "I, John Dramani Mahama, will fix this energy challenge." This pronouncement, though comforting, became one of the yardsticks by which his government was assessed throughout the year. In concluding his remarks, Mahama outlined his five-year plan to add 3,665 MW to the country's electricity grid, including supplies from Sunon Asogli, Volta River Authority and General Electric. Other companies included in the president's *emergency solution* included Karpower Ship and Alstom Power Rentals, from Turkey and the UAE, respectively. The NPP (the minority in Parliament) organised a press conference on 9 March to deliver their version of what they called the "True State of the Nation Address", where Minority Leader Osei Kyei Mensah-Bonsu described Mahama's leadership as "abysmal" and as having resulted in a "shambolic" state of the nation.

Several *civil protests* took place in response to the erratic power outages and other socio-economic challenges. On 18 February, the NPP organised its "Won Gbo" (meaning "we are dying") demonstration against the endless power challenges and to pressure the government into keeping to its promises. This was followed by a *dumsor* (power fluctuation) vigil organised by a well-known Ghanaian actress, Yvonne Nelson, on 15 April to compel the government to end the energy crises in the country. Although most civil protests were incident free, the demonstration organised by the Let My Vote Count Alliance (LMVCA) on 16 September turned violent, with reports of injuries, police brutality against protestors and 20 arrests, including that of a prominent NPP member, Gabby Asare Otchere-Darko. The LMVCA was joined by other groups such as the Movement for Change and the Alliance for Accountable Governance, calling on the Electoral Commission (EC) to collate and produce a *new electoral roll*, after allegations that the existing register was inaccurate. *Labour strikes* also took place. On 4 March, the business community shut down all their operations in order to undertake strike action against the enforcement of the Ghana Conformity Assessment Programme (G-CAP) and the Advanced Shipment Information regulations, which they believed demanded more tariffs and would "aggravate their already harsh conditions". The G-CAP, which had been launched in August 2014, sought to charge, among other fees, 5% fees for pre-shipment, verification fees of $ 200–$ 300, registration fees of $ 375, and $ 300 per inspection for used vehicles, as a way of curbing the import of sub-standard products. The strike resulted in the suspension of the G-CAP by the Ministry of Trade and Industry on 6 March. The Polytechnic Teachers Association of Ghana (POTAG) followed up with an indefinite strike on 15 May, accusing the government for failing to pay their book and research grants. Their strike shut down polytechnics across the country for over two months, forcing the Parliamentary Select Committee on Education to give them a hearing on 21 July. Just after the POTAG strike, the National Association Graduate of Teachers also began a strike on 16 May calling on the government to resolve inconsistencies in the payment system.

On 24 July, the nation was brought to a standstill over the news of the *attempted assassination* of President Mahama. The perpetrator, Charles Antwi, was arrested for carrying a double barrelled gun to the Ringway Gospel Centre where the president was worshipping with his family. The offender claimed that the president's leadership was poor so he wanted to eliminate him and take over the presidency. He was sentenced to ten years in jail on 26 July.

Intra-party conflict was rife, with notable violence leading to the demise and injury of some members. Although these incidents occurred within various parties, the most highlighted was the *chaos and conflict within the NPP*. On 31 January, a voice tape was released accusing the NPP National Chairman Paul Afoko and NPP General Secretary Kwabena Adjei Agyapong of conspiring to prevent Nana Akuffo-Addo, the flagbearer, from winning the 2016 elections. Northern Regional Chairman Daniel Bugri Naabu was suspected to be behind the tape but he vehemently denied the accusation. As the year unfolded, the chaos within the party turned violent. On 6 May, the vetting of NPP parliamentary candidates in Asante Akyem North Constituency, Ashanti region, was marred by *violence* with members brawling, insulting and attacking each other, leading to one member being injured. Moreover, on 20 May, Upper East Regional Chairman Adam Mahama was attacked with acid by unknown assailants alleged to be party members, which led to his death on 21 May. In an attempt to bring calm within the party, Akuffo-Addo promised to address the internal mayhem and called for unity during one of his campaign tours on 28 September.

Despite Akuffo-Addo's assurances and pleas, *violence continued* to escalate. On 27 October, NPP General Secretary Agyapong was attacked at the party headquarters by some members, who broke the back windscreen of his car. On 6 November, another death was recorded when Abubakar Saddiq, a staunch party member, was stabbed in the Asawase constituency, Ashanti region, during clashes between Akuffo-Addo and Afoko loyalists. The internal conflict became so intense that, on 23 October, National Chairman Afoko was given an *indefinite suspension* by the National Executive Committee, who accused him of undermining Akuffo-Addo's presidential ambitions for 2016. This decision further stoked tensions within the party, as was demonstrated by the violent clashes between the party's private security group the 'Invincible Forces' and Afoko loyalists, who stormed the NPP headquarters on the same day, resulting in several injuries. On 8 December, there were gunshots in Chorkor, a suburb of Accra, where NPP member Joshua Attoh Quashie was intending to host an anti-Akuffo-Addo press conference. Shortly afterwards, on 10 December, General Secretary Agyapong and Second Vice Chairman Sammy Crabbe, who were alleged to be close allies of Afoko, were also suspended for their demonstration of contempt at the party's decision to suspend the national chairman.

While the NPP had elected its *flagbearer* and *running mate* in 2014, several other political parties began their selection in 2015. On 26 September, the Great Consolidated Popular Party elected Dr Henry Lartey, son of its late founder Dan Lartey, as flagbearer and national chairman for the 2016 elections. On 21 November, Mahama recorded a massive 95.1% endorsement, with 1,199,118 of the 1,260,954 valid votes, to become the NDC flagbearer. On 13 December, the People's National Convention (PNC) party elected Dr Edward Nasigre Mahama as its presidential candidate for the 2016 elections. He received 492 votes while his opponent, Hassan Ayariga, had 426. The 2016 elections would be the fifth attempt for the veteran, who had run in the 1996, 2000, 2004 and 2008 elections.

The selection of the *running mate for President Mahama* created headlines within the year. Prior to the selection, there were speculation and mixed views about Mahama's choice. Some called for the removal of Vice President Paa Kwesi Amissah-Arthur as his running mate while others wanted him to stay. On 19 January, former Ashanti regional deputy minister Samuel Yaw Adusei wrote an article indicating the importance of Mahama keeping Amissah-Arthur as his running mate in order to secure victory. In contrast, on 28 November, the Ga-Adangme Youth wing of the NDC called for the removal of Amissah-Arthur as the president's running mate, questioning the vice president's loyalty and competence: "We feel this is a strong indictment on the capability of the Vice-President to inspire any confidence in our electioneering campaigns, let alone lead the party in 2020." Notwithstanding much speculation, Mahama went ahead on 7 December to announce the choice of Amissah-Arthur as his running mate.

The EC was also at the centre of attention. On 25 June came the landmark appointment of Charlotte Kesson Smith Osei as its new chair, the EC's *first female chair* since independence. She replaced Dr Kwadwo Afari Gyan, who was heading for retirement after 20 years of service to the EC. Her appointment came in the wake of accusations directed by the NPP and other concerned citizens against the EC and Mahama's government over discrepancies in the 2016 voter's register. Pressure mounted when the NPP organised their 'New Voters Register Now' press conference on 18 August, where they alleged that the country's electoral roll was bloated with over 76,286 foreigners (predominantly Togolese) and requested the compilation of a new register. The party followed up with another submission on 22 September, claiming to have identified an additional 2,096 cases of multiple and double registration. NDC General Secretary Johnson Aseidu Nketia interjected on 28 September, labelling the NPP's claims "illogical" and "absurd". To assess the claims, the EC on 24 October set up a five-member panel to investigate and receive proposals from other political parties. To this end, the EC hosted a two-day forum on 29–30 October to hear from concerned parties. However, after thorough investigation, the EC issued a statement on 30 December, discrediting the NPP allegations.

Foreign Affairs

President Mahama's diplomatic calendar commenced with a visit to *Brazil* on 1 January for the inauguration for a second term of President-elect Dilma Rousseff, who had become Brazil's first female president after winning the elections in 2010. On 14 January, *Spain*'s ambassador to Ghana, Maria J. Allonso, paid a courtesy call on Vice President Amissah-Arthur at Flagstaff House to express her country's gratitude to Ghana for supporting Spain's bid for a seat on the UNSC. The two nations also discussed future bilateral cooperation.

Mahama began his bilateral engagements for the year with a state visit to *Germany* on 18 January. The president held private talks with Chancellor Angela Merkel and President Joachim Gauck on ways to strengthen bilateral relations and economic cooperation between the two countries. With their diplomatic relationship dating back to the 1960s, Ghana had been a beneficiary of Germany's contributions since 1961 to the tune of € 1.3 bn. On 19 January, the two leaders also discussed issues relating to terrorism, pandemics, regional insecurity, energy, vocational training and economic partnership at a press conference held in Mahama's honour. Acting in his capacity as ECOWAS chairman, Mahama also put forward a proposal for a *regional taskforce* to fight Boko Haram. Merkel welcomed this initiative and assured ECOWAS of Germany's support while debunking the perception that Europe was unconcerned about insecurities in Africa. Following his meeting with Merkel, Mahama addressed the Business Forum for the African Association in Germany on 20 January. This meeting, organised by the Delegation of German Industry and Commerce in Ghana (AHK Ghana) highlighted potential bilateral business ventures and projects in agriculture, energy, oil and gas and mining. While the meeting was taking place, there were *protests* by Ghanaians on the streets of Berlin against the incompetence of the Mahama government. They held placards and shouted: "Dumsor dumsor, we need light, dumsor dumsor we don't have light", "Mahama is a thief", "NDC cocaine party".

On 9–11 March, Mahama took up an invitation from President Seretse Khama Ian Khama of the Republic of *Botswana* to visit to his country. Botswana and Ghana had enjoyed close relations, with the latter contributing teachers, engineers and artisans to support Botswana's development. Key highlights of the visit included the signing of a memorandum of understanding (MoU) to deepen partnership on consolidating *good governance and commerce* between the two countries. Mahama's meeting with the Ghanaian community on 10 March was perhaps the most controversial part of his visit. During the meeting, the president said: "I have seen more demonstrations and strikes in my first two years. I don't think it can get worse ... It is said that when you kill a goat and you frighten it with a knife, it doesn't fear the knife because it is dead already ... I have a dead goat syndrome." These remarks earned Mahama criticism from many Ghanaians. On 12 June, policy analyst for the PNC Atik Mohammed said that Mahama's "dead goat syndrome" statement demonstrated his lack of concern for the plight of the people of Ghana.

Ignoring the naysayers, Mahama consolidated Ghana's ties with *Italy* by embarking on a state visit on 15–18 July. On 16 July, he had bilateral discussions with President Sergio Mattarella and Prime Minister Matteo Renzi on economic partnership and other outstanding projects. The president also performed a flag raising ceremony for the Milan Expo 2015 and held meetings with Ghanaian and Italian business owners on 17 July.

Despite diplomatic ties with several countries being consolidated, Ghana-*Turkey* relations was nearly marred on 21 January when it was reported by Deputy Minister of Communications Ato Sarpong that 11 websites of the state's internet portal had been hacked by a well-known Turkish hacking group, Alsancak Tim, forcing a 48-hour shut-down of the websites. To remedy the situation, the Turkish ambassador, Nesrin Bayazit, paid a courtesy call on Vice President Amissah-Arthur on 23 January to affirm her country's commitment to supporting Ghana to apprehend the offenders. Ghana's relations with *Côte d'Ivoire* continued to suffer as the two countries continued to battle over their *disputed marine borders*, which had started in 2010 over Ghana's oil field in Cape Three Point, when Côte d'Ivoire reportedly started claiming part of the fields run by Tullow Oil. Ghana had submitted the case to the Special Chamber of the International Tribunal for the Laws of the Sea in 2014 after ten failed attempts at bilateral negotiation. On 25 February, a few months before the hearing, Côte d'Ivoire submitted a petition requesting the Tribunal to place an injunction on all Ghanaian oil activities within the disputed area, but the Tribunal ruled on 24 April that Ghana be allowed to continue with ongoing projects, while banning new exploratory drilling until the final verdict in 2017. Many Ghanaians were aggrieved over Côte d'Ivoire's claims. On 29 April, Kwaku Baako, editor of the Ghanaian private newspaper 'Crusading Guide', vented his frustrations with the Ivorians, calling them "insincere, inconsistent and dubious".

In the midst of the diplomatic scuffle between Ghana and Côte d'Ivoire, President Mahama continued to show his unconditional support for West Africa's largest economy, *Nigeria*, by attending the investiture of President-elect General Muhammadu Buhari on 29 May. Buhari was declared the winner of Nigeria's much anticipated elections on 31 March after securing approximately 15.4 m votes, beating the incumbent Goodluck Jonathan, who won 12.9 m.

On the *regional and continental fronts*, Ghana continued to demonstrate its commitment to ECOWAS and the AU. On 16–17 January, Ghana hosted the High Level Coordination Meeting of *ECOWAS* Heads of State and Partners to discuss initiatives towards addressing Ebola and other pandemics in the sub-region. The meeting was concluded with a press conference to discuss the growing terrorist activities in the sub-region. Immediately after the ECOWAS meeting, Mahama attended the 24th Ordinary Session of the Assembly of Heads of State and Government of the *AU* in Addis Ababa (Ethiopia) on 29–31 January. Prior to the official summit, Mahama met with the ECOWAS heads of state on 29 January and addressed the AU Peace and Security Council, highlighting the sub-region's proposal for a region-wide force to fight Boko Haram. During the official summit on 30 January, AU Commission Chair Nkosazana Dlamini-Zuma welcomed Mahama's proposal, calling for countries to contribute to the force. At the end of the meeting, 7,500 troops were pledged. On 19 May, Mahama hosted the 47th Ordinary Session of ECOWAS Heads of State and Government in Accra. Among other things, the meeting discussed the 2015 provisional report of the ECOWAS Commission, the report of the 74th Ordinary Session of ECOWAS Council of Ministers, and the report of the 34th Meeting of the Mediation and Security Council. At the end of the summit, Mahama handed over the chair of ECOWAS to President Macky Sall of Senegal. On 22 September, Mahama attended an emergency extraordinary session of the ECOWAS Authority of Heads of State and Government to deliberate on the political conundrum in Burkina Faso after the 17 September coup d'état.

At the international level, Mahama began his engagements by travelling to Rome to open the 38th meeting of the IFAD Governing Council in Rome (Italy) on 16 February. In his opening speech, Mahama promised that his government "would not hesitate to reject any agricultural programme that took away the direct benefits from farmers and gave them to technocrats". Ghana was currently benefiting from IFAD loans and grants worth over $ 271.5 m. On 29 September, Mahama attended the annual *UN General Assembly* meeting in New York. Addressing the General Assembly, he assured global leaders of Ghana's commitment to the achievement of the sustainable development goals and also entreated his European counterparts to "relocate more industries and products to Africa" in order to prevent *large migrant flows* to Europe. On 29 November, Mahama travelled to Malta for the 2015 Commonwealth Heads of Government Meeting, which highlighted issues such as peace and security, governance, sustainable development and migration.

Energy, agriculture, youth employment and economic development were the pivotal focus of Mahama's diplomatic engagements. As a result, on 24–27 August, Mahama embarked on a four-day visit to *Mauritius* to conclude the signing of three MoUs on mutual visa exemptions, bilateral trade and tertiary exchange programmes. On 29 September, Ghana and *Togo* began consultation over the construction of dam over the River Oti, which lies along their borders, to supply energy to both countries. This was followed by the signing of two partnership agreements between Ghana and *Columbia* on 16 October to support sports and youth entrepreneurship in both countries. This marked the first political between the two countries since the opening of the Colombian mission in Ghana in 2013. On 19 November, Ghana and Germany signed a € 34 m three-year financial cooperation agreement (2015–17) in Accra. The funding was expected to support renewable energy, agriculture, waste management and governance. Finally, on 10 December, Ghana signed two framework of agreements with the Republic of *Korea*, the Framework Agreement on Grant Aid and the Framework Arrangement on the Concessional Loans from Economic Development Cooperation Fund, which aimed at providing concessionary loans and technical support to Ghana. Under the agreement, Ghana was expected to access about $ 200 m between 2015 and 2017.

Socioeconomic Developments

The *African Cup of Nations* (AFCON) began on 17 January. The three-week long competition. held in Equatorial Guinea, sparked enthusiasm among many Ghanaians as well as raising debate about the competence of new Black Stars coach Avram Grant to bring home the trophy. The former Chelsea boss had been appointed on 7 November 2014, making the AFCON his first major tournament. Unfortunately for Ghana, their excitement ended when the national team lost 9–8 to the Ivorians, after penalties in the final on 8 February.

On 12 March, the minister of finance was forced to present a revised *budget* to Parliament after the initial version had been approved in December 2014. The reason for the recall was linked to "funding gaps, overestimations and incorrect projections" that had been identified in the budget. In addition, the minister also presented a supplementary budget to Parliament on 21 July after a comprehensive review. The 2016 budget, which was submitted to Parliament on 13 November, revealed *appreciable progress* made during the year, including the completion of the Atuabo Gas Infrastructure Project, expected to produce 180,000 metric tonnes of liquefied petroleum gas, the installation of the 250 MW Africa Middle East Resources Investments (AMERI) and 225 MW Karpower projects to address the power fluctuations, the completion of the Kpong water supply expansion and rehabilitation, which produced 20 m gallons a day for Greater Accra, and the construction of roads in rural and urban areas.

Despite these highlighted achievements, there were also some major *socioeconomic downturns*. For example, according to the 2016 budget, the country's 2015 public debt rose to a total of $ 24,285.1 m from $ 21,733.5 m in 2014, and the continuous erratic power outages affected the income and production of many companies; 17.5% inflation was recorded in September; and the cedi depreciated by 4.8%, 12.6% and 7.8% against the US dollar, the pound sterling and the euro, respectively.

According to Price Water House Coopers, Ghana's over dependence on imports contributed to the *cedi depreciation.* To make matters worse, the government on 14 December, increased electricity and water tariffs by 60% and 67%, respectively, which generated civil uproar. Mahama's government blamed the drop in crude oil prices (from $ 90 to $ 45 per barrel) on the global market as the cause of Ghana's economic woes.

As already indicated, the incessant power fluctuations that had characterised the whole of 2014 continued. The protracted *dumsor* caused major losses for many domestic and foreign companies and organisations as well as the state. On 27 February, it was reported that the Ghana Port and Harbour Authority, a state agency, had lost over $ 100,000 as a result of a 24-hour power outage at Tema Harbour. Subsequently, on 20 May, research conducted by the Institute of Statistical, Social and Economic Research of the University of Ghana, Legon, led to the publication of a rather disturbing revelation that businesses were losing $ 2.2 m every day and $ 686.4 m annually because of the energy crisis. By 2 June, the work force was worried when the Ghana Employers Association indicated that about 12,000 jobs had been lost during the first half of the year and predicted 50,000 more losses if the situation was not resolved. Businesses such as Multi-Media, Citi FM and the Ghana Broadcasting Corporation complained of deteriorating conditions caused by the crisis.

Linked to the energy enigma were frequent *fire outbreaks.* On 5 January, there were reported fire eruptions at the Achimota Market and the Melcom Warehouse (a private enterprise), which damaged many goods. According to the Ghana National Fire Service, there were about 160 fire outbreaks across the nation between 1 and 7 January. This worrying trend continued throughout the year. On 13 January, an inferno occurred at the Central Medical Stores of the Ghana Health Service, destroying much needed medical supplies and costing the state a whopping GHS (cedi) 237.7 m ($ 61,838,200). This resulted in public agitation over the potential negative impact on medical distribution that might be caused by the damage. However, on 15 January, Minister of Health Dr Kwaku Agyemang-Mensah assured Ghanaians that the incident would not affect drug distribution. Perhaps the most disturbing fire outbreak occurred on 3 June, when the country witnessed the shocking deaths of over 150 people in a firestorm that erupted at a gas filling station at the Kwame Nkrumah Circle in Accra. The president declared three days of mourning for the victims. By 11 August, 2,707 fire outbreaks had been recorded, leading to the loss of property worth GHS 10, 244,493 ($ 2,665,130).

Corruption and fraud allegations were widespread. Government officials and civil servants were accused of engaging in corrupt activities. On 27 January, the medical superintendent of the Essikado District Hospital, Western Region, Dr N.K. Ametewee, was apprehended for conning the National Health Insurance Authority (NHIA) out of GHS 415,439 ($ 108,077). Upon his arrest, it was revealed that Ametewee had also suborned the NHIA auditing team with a cheque for GHS 5,000

($ 1,300.76) to conceal the transaction. On 29 January, the Majority Leader in Parliament Alban Bagbin expressed his disappointment at the country's tolerance of corruption, which, he said, made it difficult to resolve.

On 22 September, Ghana's democratic governance was tested when a highly acclaimed *investigative journalist*, Anas Armeyaw Anas, released a video recording showing 34 judges and magistrates, seven policemen, five state attorneys, bail contractors and over 100 court clerks taking bribes. His two-year investigation exposed state officials extorting bribes of between GHS 100 and GHS 1,000 ($ 26–$ 260), while others took livestock and farm produce in exchange for justice. This raised questions about the transparency of state institutions, especially the judiciary, which was the focus of the video. To address the issue and calm tensions, Chief Justice Georgina Wood established a committee of inquiry on 23 September. After thorough investigation, 21 judges including eight Circuit Court judges and 13 district magistrates were dismissed by the Judicial Council on 7 December. On 14 December, Minister of Power Dr Kwabena Donkor was accused of overlooking the inflation of the actual cost of the *AMERI contract*, which was expected to purchase teno gas turbines to supply the nation with 250 MW of electricity. According to the Norwegian newspaper 'Verdens Gang', which first released the news, a Pakistani Norwegian, Umar Farooq Zahoor, had inflated the figures, charging the state over $ 510 m for the turbines, priced at $ 220 m on the market, costing the nation an extra $ 290 m. Donkor released a statement that day calling the allegations "false, misleading and a gross misrepresentation of the facts" and indicated that the government's contract was with AMERI Group and not the said fraudster. Amidst the AMERI scandal, Minister of Transport Dzifa Attivor also came under fire on 16 December for spending over GHS 3.6 m ($ 936,549) to emblazon the 116 state-owned *Metro Mass buses* with the photographs of the current and former presidents. The situation worsened when Kwaku Mensah Abeiku, manager of Crystal Concept, the agency delegated to oversee this operation by the contracted Smartys Management, indicated on 17 December that his agency had charged GHS 11,600 ($ 3,018) and not the amount announced to parliament by the minister. Chief of Staff Julius Debrah ordered an investigation into the case on 17 December. In the midst of the civil agitation, the shamed minister handed in her resignation on 23 December.

Guinea

Anita Schroven

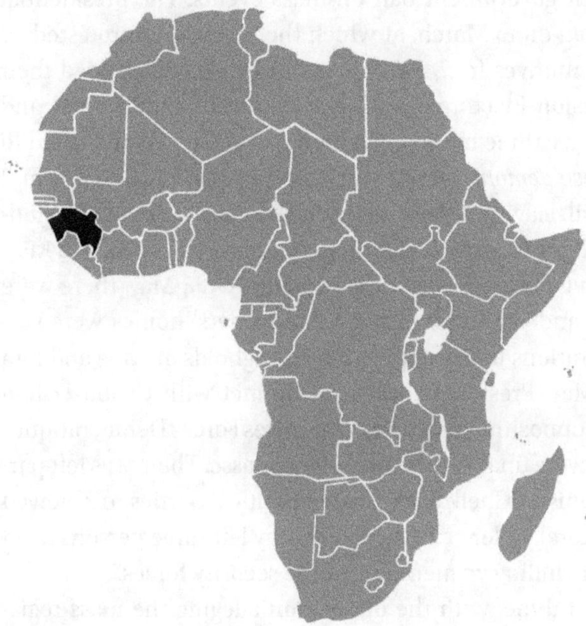

The year saw Guinea firmly in the grip of the Ebola outbreak, slowing economic progress and influencing domestic and international political relations. In addition to the Ebola-related challenges, economic slow-down heavily affected the national economy, leading to rising market prices and weakening of the domestic economy. The comparatively peaceful re-election of President Condé continued the formal democratic process while at the same time revealing the deep estrangement between the wider population and the government – a lack of trust revealed in epidemiological as well as political and security measures taken by the government. While there was progress in the expansion of civilian control over the security forces, little advancement was made with regard to their accountability.

Domestic Politics

The year began with preparations for *presidential elections*, which were postponed over the course of the year due to the Ebola outbreak. Since the choice of electoral operators, including SAGEM and Waymark, had caused tensions between political parties in previous years, a new contract was signed with the French company

GEMALTO to prepare and carry out the 2015 presidential elections. Throughout the year, opposition parties remained dissatisfied with the timetable for local elections, due since 2010 and called for them to take place before the presidential elections, and opposition rallies took place on 7 and 22 January – despite the ongoing Ebola outbreak and the consequent government ban on mass events. The presidential election schedule was released on 10 March, at which the opposition protested by withdrawing their 51 representatives from Parliament. They also suspended their cooperation in the 'Commission Electorale Nationale Indépendante' (CENI) and called for more demonstrations; three main opposition parties signed an accord to that effect on 24 March. These *demonstrations* started on 13 April in Conakry and spread nationwide on 23 April, leaving at least two dead, dozens wounded (including innocent bystanders) and more arrested. Demonstrations continued into May, with opposition parties calling for a new election schedule. On 4 May, there were demonstrations in Conakry, and prominent opposition leaders' homes were surrounded by police. Demonstrations in the opposition strongholds of Labé and Pita remained peaceful. On 20 May, President Alpha Condé met with Cellou Dalein Diallo, the leader of the main opposition party, the 'Union des Forces Démocratiques de Guinée' (UFDG), but they were unable to resolve the impasse. Their MPs left parliament in protest. Justice Minister Cheik Sacko called political parties to renewed negotiations on 25 May. Electoral violence in April and May left three persons dead and more than 200 injured, including 77 members of the security forces.

Voter enrolment ended on 6 June, with the opposition alleging the mass registration of minors in government strongholds, such as Kankan, where the highest numbers of new voters were registered. Sixty-five thousand voters were registered abroad. Led by the justice minister, election negotiations with international participation started on 18 June, which caused the postponement of local elections into 2016. On 20 August, opposition and government parties signed an accord calling for a revision of the electoral register and the composition of the CENI, and controversially suggesting that Hadja Ramatoulaye Bah, a former minister and wife of the leader of the 'Parti Guinéen pour la Renaissance et le Progrès' (PGRP), should head the CENI. However, the long-term CENI president, Bakary Fofana, remained in post. With UN, AU, ECOWAS and Francophonie-mediation, government and opposition parties signed a power-sharing deal on 14 September, which laid down the procedures for the coming local elections in such a way that they could be prepared without the ruling party 'Rassemblement du Peuple Guinéen' (RPG) dominating the process. At the same time, this accord ensured that major opposition parties did not withdraw from the presidential elections, for which the campaigning period was about to start.

Ex-junta leader Moussa Dadis Camara had announced his future presidential candidacy in May with support of the newly founded party, 'Forces Patriotiques pour la Démocratie et le Développement' (FPDD), which predominantly represented the interest of the Forest Region, Camara's home region. Hee enjoyed popular support there, as manifested by demonstrations in N'Zérékoré on 7 May, when several of his supporters were arrested and detained in local and Conakry prisons. In June, Camara met with main opposition leader Diallo with a view to joining forces for the presidential elections but, on 9 July, he was indicted for complicity in the attacks of September 2009, known as 'Bloody Monday'. On 21 September, he withdrew his candidacy and refused to endorse another candidate. His political plans remained uncertain as protection in his temporary home in Burkina Faso was fading after the ousting of Blaise Compaoré.

Electoral campaigns led to the first violent clashes in Koundara on 19 September, with 35 opposition members arrested, 25 of whom were still in prison at the end of the year. Sporadic violence during election week left 13 dead and many more injured or arrested, continuing the ethnic tensions between majority Malinké supporters of Condé and predominantly Fulbe supporters of Diallo. Condé's illustrious re-election team included Minister of State Ibrahima Kassory Fofana, who had been minister of economy under Lansana Conté (president from 1984 to 2008), the director of the National Social Security Fund, Malick Sankhon, and the Director of the Conakry Port, Mamadouba Sankhon. The *elections* were held on 11 October with a turnout of 68% and were deemed 'largely free and fair' by international observers from ECOWAS and the EU, even though observers noted problems with the identification of voters, ballots without envelopes and other administrative shortcomings. The Constitutional Court confirmed the results and dismissed the complaints of four presidential candidates on 31 October. Condé was declared the winner of the presidential elections in the first round, with 58% of the votes cast, over runner-up Diallo with 31%. International human rights bodies called for political parties to show restraint and respect the rule of law after the election to avoid heightened ethnic violence. Diallo immediately rejected the results but refused to call on the Constitutional Court, citing his lack of confidence in their independence, but he demanded the release from prison of all UFDG supporters. On 3 November, nine prisoners were released while 27 remained in jail. Diallo continued to refuse to join the future government, increasing internal party tensions with his vice president, Amadou Bah Oury, who had returned to Guinea after four years in exile, having been pardoned by the president for his alleged implication in the 2011 coup attempt.

Condé was sworn in and inaugurated for his second term on 14 and 21 December, respectively, and brought the opposition's second runner-up, Sidya Touré and his secretary-general Baidy Aribot of the 'Union des Forces Républicaines' (UFR) into the government fold, thus strengthening the division within the opposition and enlarging his ruling Rainbow Coalition. Condé was expected to not recall most of the ministers in his first government as most of them had been heavily criticised for their performance. He announced that his economic councillor, Abdoulaye Magassouba, would lead the key Ministry for Mining. Condé also changed the portfolio of Minister Kalifa Gassama Diaby from human rights to national unity, marking his willingness to respond to international concerns over the *ethnicisation of politics*. The lack of judicial response to the security forces' violence and killing nevertheless remained a mark on Condé's government, even though it was lauded for implementing codes of conduct within the police and strengthening civilian control over security forces and police deployment through June's Public Order Bill. This bill had been widely discussed in relation to the police's right to disburse demonstrations as soon as one person was suspected of carrying a firearm. Another controversial point was the illegality of spontaneous assemblies. Overall, the bill received positive reactions as it further limited the scope for the deployment of the military in cases of domestic unrest. The continuing *security sector reform* favoured the training of the army and gendarmerie, while neglecting the training and equipment of the police. The police in their turn stood accused of using lethal force and committing mass rapes at opposition rallies that took place throughout the year.

In January, opposition and *human rights* organisations alleged that Condé had changed the laws governing the 'Institution Nationale Indépendante des Droits Humains'. The importance of human rights was highlighted on 9 November, when a riot in the overcrowded Conakry civil prison left a dozen inmates and guards injured.

On 2–4 February, demonstrations took place in Labé over alleged changes in civil service regulations, leaving about 24 members of the security forces and 25 civilians injured. Protests erupted in this opposition stronghold after news spread that long-established civil servants were to be moved to other parts of the country.

A UN employee and former minister, Thierno Alioune Diaouné, was killed on 6 February. Suspects were charged in a local court in May but no trial date had been set by the end of the year. On 19 September, Colonel Jean Dougou Guilavogui, president of the Union of Retired Military Personnel was arrested for treason, with the charges later changed to contempt of the Head of State and the army. Fellow unionists were arrested during a demonstration demanding his release on 29 September and many of them were still being held in prison without trial at the end of the year.

On 5 October, journalist Thierno Amadou Camara was beaten by supporters of Condé in Siguiri, after he published on rivalries within the ruling RPG. Reporters Without Borders stated that the government controlled the High Authority for Communication in a way that interfered with the *freedom of the press*. After the journalist Chérif Diallo disappeared without trace on 13 July, his colleague at the privately-owned TV station 'Espace TV', Moussa Moise Sylla, and some of his family members were shot at on 31 December. All of them survived the incident.

Inter-communal violence broke out in Touba, a popular place of Sunni pilgrimage, over the construction of a new mosque, leaving two dead, many more injured and several vehicles and buildings destroyed. On 20 November, Interior Minister Mahmoud Cissé, Secretary of State for Religious Affairs El Hajd Abdoulaye Diassy and his deputy were dismissed by the president for incompetence in managing the dispute and the ensuing violence.

Foreign Affairs

In January, Condé participated at the World Economic Forum in Davos, discussing the Forum's Africa Strategic Infrastructure Initiative, together with South Africa's President Jacob Zuma.

On 22 April, Condé met French President François Hollande in Paris. The visit took place after a one-week trip to the USA, where Condé met with political allies, business partners and party chapters of the RPG.

On 24 June, the *UN Universal Periodic Review* lauded Guinea's improvement in civilian oversight of all security forces and especially the army, and the decrease in incidences of torture. At the same time, however, the report highlighted the need to reform the judicial and prison systems in line with international standards. The report also criticised the fact that the judicial system had not made any progress towards the indictment of senior members of the security forces accused of crimes committed in September 2009 in the events known as Bloody Monday, when more than 150 persons were killed and unknown numbers of women were raped by the military. In July, the prosecutor of the *ICC*, Fatou Bensauda, visited Guinea to follow up the Guinean judiciary's progress in this matter. She emphasised that the ICC served as a last resort if the Guinean judiciary proved unable or unwilling to prosecute those most responsible for the so-called Bloody Monday massacre. Former leader of the transitional government, General Sekouba Konate, met with Bensauda twice to hand over a list of 50 persons who, according to him, were most responsible for the massacre. However, no action had been taken against any of the named persons by the end of the year, apart from one lower-ranking soldier, whose trial had begun. Throughout the year, multiple reports by human rights bodies remarked on the general level of impunity for all Guinean security forces. Also in July, Army Chief of Staff General Namory Troaré visited Angola to sign a variety of *military cooperation* treaties with Angola's Minister of Defence João Lourenço. Guinea continued to support the UN mission in Mali (MINUSMA), with Guinean troops stationed in Kidal.

The president and other members of the government met with their regional counterparts on several occasions. The government sought close cooperation with the Sierra Leonean and Liberian governments in order to coordinate efforts against the continuing outbreak of *Ebola Virus Disease* (EVD). This was assisted by the UN Mission for Ebola Emergency Response and the Organisation for International Migration. The MRU and ECOWAS were also involved in such efforts. In this regard, the Prefecture Forécariah and the Sierra Leonean District of Kambia signed a *cooperation accord* in the border town of Pamelap on 5 May for the sharing of contact tracing information and diagnostic facilities between the two countries in this region of highly mobile populations.

Socioeconomic Developments

The ongoing *Ebola outbreak* caused unrest and political tension throughout the year. On 14 January, two men were killed in a village in coastal Guinea over accusations that they had brought EVD there. On 6 February, members of the public clashed with police over the arrest of an imam who had led a funeral for an Ebola victim. Since 2014, funerals had become strictly regulated, but the population often failed to comply with these new regulations. In another incident in Forécariah in February, about 58 people were charged with attacking a team of EVD workers who were accused of spreading the virus. In March, Condé declared a *national health emergency*, which remained in place until June. In the capital and other regions, large sections of the population continued to resist measures designed to contain the spread of the virus and, as a result, security forces had to accompany national and international health professionals. At times, the government had to close down hospitals treating EVD cases; the government also limited the mobility of populations living in areas where there were renewed outbreaks of EVD. Visits to health facilities dropped by 50% over the course of the outbreak, revealing both the lack of trust in public health infrastructure and the need to increase capacity in terms of both staff and equipment.

On 29 December, the government declared the EVD outbreak to be over. The country remained on heightened alert for a further 90 days, as required by WHO. Overall, Guinea suffered from EVD for nearly two years, longer than the neighbouring countries and with a higher mortality rate (2,536 of 3,804 suspected and confirmed Ebola cases resulted in death). In addition, 110 health workers died during the EVD outbreak, resulting in a further weakening of the country's fragile healthcare system.

Because of the EVD outbreak, Guinea experienced unprecedented international attention, including the deployment of foreign military personnel, humanitarian aid and closer ties with its former colonial power. The IMF created the Catastrophe Containment and Relief Trust in February and Guinea became a major beneficiary. On 28 April, the IMF reported that Ebola had limited Guinea's growth rates by negatively affecting agriculture and service industries and by halting mining and infrastructure projects. Condé reported his country's post-Ebola recovery plans to the IMF's spring meeting, which resulted in budget and debt-service assistance of $ 390 m to the three most-affected countries. Guinea received $ 63.6 m from the IMF through the ECF, $ 39.8 m from its Rapid Credit Facility Programme and $ 29.4 m in debt relief.

It was only thanks to these loans that Guinea was able to manage its financial obligations. The revision and execution of the 2015 national budget of about $ 7,282.9 m was strongly influenced by EVD, which led to revenue shortfall, lowered tax income and increased expenditure, especially in the healthcare sector, causing a fiscal deficiency of about 7.1% of GDP. Real *GDP* growth was estimated at -0.2, with GNI $ 480 per capita, mainly secured by bauxite production, which was less affected by EVD than iron ore exports in the same period. Here, the world market price dropped by 39% in the course of the year, a development disastrous for Guinea's *revenues*. And bauxite export revenues, too, were remarkably lower than the pre-EVD-estimated 4.3% GDP. The agricultural sector contracted by about 2% and services and manufacturing also continued contracting over the year. The government aimed to recover some of the tax losses by introducing a mobile phone call tax of GNF (franc) 1per minute. The economic slump in 2014 and 2015 resulted in systematic reviews of the PRSP, as poverty was expected to have risen significantly and with a long-term effect.

Inflation rates averaged 9.4% over the year, with food inflation reaching up to 10.3% in June and July, which was a significant improvement on 2014.

Guinea ranked 139th with a score of 25 on the Corruption Perception Index, and 10th on the Fragile State Index. With regard to economic potential, it ranked 139th on the Economic Freedom Index, and 171st on the World Bank's Doing Business Index.

The *World Bank* provided funding for direct food aid and agricultural assistance for the planting season in April. On 7 May, the IMF reported a 0% growth forecast for 2015 as a consequence of the "heavy social and economic toll" of the Ebola outbreak, the political uncertainties due to the presidential elections and the lowering of global commodity prices. On 20 May, the World Bank approved a $ 15.1 m programme to extend maternal and under-five health and nutrition programmes in Faranah and Labé, where about 52% of the population were female and 20% of the population under five years old. The programme included training for front-line health workers. On 21 October, the AfDB approved a Post Ebola Recovery Social Investment Fund of $ 33.3 m to benefit Guinea, Liberia and Sierra Leone. Hosted by the MRU Secretariat, the programme would target water and sanitation programmes. In Guinea, about 29 % of households had no access to toilet facilities.

With only 6% of small and medium-sized firms able to access the credit they needed, Guinea needed $ 900 m to develop this vital part of its economy. The World Bank approved $ 22 m for the West Africa Regional Fisheries Programme's Guinea Programme for the governance of fishery and improvement of artisanal fishing capacities. On 27 May, Guinea and Canada signed a foreign investments agreement. In June, the Africa Finance Corporation provided a € 30 m loan to upgrade the road between Kissidougou and Kankan, the motorway connecting Conakry with Ouagadougou (Burkina Faso) and Dakar (Senegal), thus improving trade infrastructures.

After three years of construction, the *Kaléta Hydropower station* went into operation in September. A Chinese-Guinean cooperation project with a contract value of $ 446.2 m, it would export about 30% of its 965 GWh per year to Guinea-Bissau, Senegal and Gambia under the ECOWAS inter-connection programme, whose infrastructure is in turn supported by World Bank funding. In June, the Guinean government signed a € 11.3 m contract with the French company Veolia to provide energy management services to the state-owned Electricité de Guinée.

Despite the halting of many direct investments due to the global economic slow-down and EVD, *mining* continued to be a central issue. Arcelor Mittal and Sable Mining were in dispute over railroad access to Guinea's iron ore deposits in the Nimba Mountains on the Liberian border. While ArcelorMittal was using the Liberian state-owned railway to Buchanan port, it had to allow others to use the railway's surplus capacity. Sable Mining required more capacity for its development-stage explorations in Guinea, where Condé was keen to show much awaited progress in the mining sector before presidential elections in October. Condé supported Sable Mining, which had strong relations to his family and to Aboubacar Sampil, a long-time friend of the Condé family.

Mining exploitation in the forest region has so far only been possible via the Liberian railway connection, a route less favoured by the Guinean government than direct investment in a trans-Guinean railway that would allow iron ore exportation through Guinea directly. However, these mining and infrastructure processes remained slow throughout the year, with mining conglomerates ArcelorMittal, BHP Billiton, Rio Tinto, Benny Steinmetz and other international players involved in negotiating, suing and coalescing between themselves, pushing potential domestic revenue from the world's largest iron ore deposit Simandou further into the future. Only at the end of November did the Guinean government agree with Rio Tinto, Chinalco and the IFC on details for future exploitation of the southern half of the Simandou deposits.

With the *FBI investigating* the Simandou dealings of the Benny Steinmetz Group Resources, which implicated a wife, son and brother-in-law of late president Lansana Conté, Swiss investigators also started interviewing witnesses in Conakry in July to explore potential corruption charges linked to Swiss nationals. Amongst the interviewees were the governor of the Central Bank, Louceny Nabé, a former mining minister.

President Condé personally negotiated with Chinese investors for new bauxite exploitation on the northern coast, where UK-based Alufer Resource Ltd had already begun exploring for the so-called Bel Air Project. In July, British government officials intervened on behalf of Alufer's interests directly with Condé, who in turn facilitated Boké Mining's explorations in his home region of Boké, without directly involving the Ministry of Mining.

Guinea-Bissau

Christoph Kohl

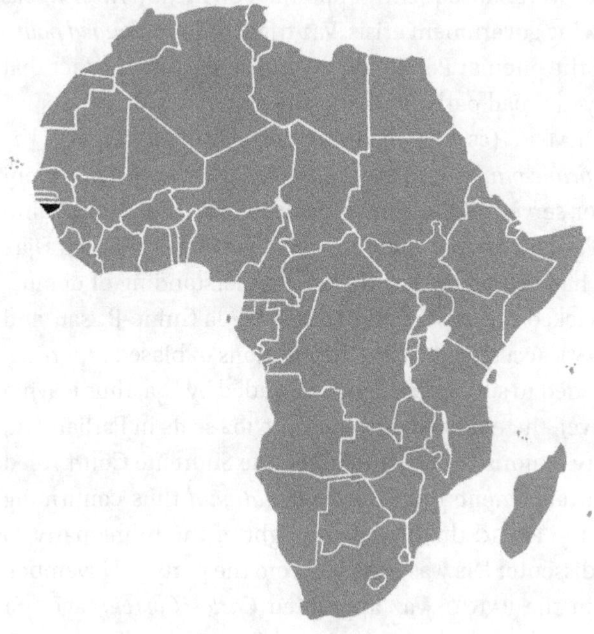

Positive developments marked the beginning of the year: an international donor conference in March resulted in higher donations and credit commitments than expected. Political stability, enhanced governance, and significant infrastructural improvements resulted in economic recovery and widespread popular confidence. However, by the second half of the year deep political divisions emerged between Prime Minister Domingos Simões Pereira, who was also the president of the 'Partido Africano da Independência da Guiné e Cabo Verde' (PAIGC), and President José Mário Vaz (PAIGC). Eventually, Vaz dismissed the all-party government, which resulted in constitutional controversies. The new government, headed by PAIGC veteran Carlos Correia, remained unstable due to divisions both within the ruling PAIGC and with the second largest party, the 'Partido para a Renovação Social' (PRS), which remained absent from the new government.

Domestic Politics

In early 2016, the relationship between President Vaz and Prime Minister Pereira deteriorated. The head of state demanded a greater say in government politics and

 | DOI 10.1163/9789004333239_012

his own parallel budget, which the Constitution did not provide for. Differences between Vaz and Pereira were evident in the appointment of a new interior minister: after months of negotiations Octávio Inocênvio Alves succeeded Botche Candé on 6 March. Candé had been dismissed in 2014. New heads of the Public Order Police and the National Guard were subsequently appointed on 14 May. After weeks of rumours and talk of a brewing government crisis, Vaz triggered a *prolonged political crisis* when he dismissed the popular Pereira on 12 August, despite the fact that the prime minister still enjoyed broad parliamentary backing.

Without consulting the PAIGC (as the majority party in Parliament), *Vaz appointed Baciro Djá as new prime minister* on 22 August. Djá, PAIGC vice president and a former defence minister, served as minister of the prime minister's office until 23 June, when he resigned. Parliament and the PAIGC had strongly criticised Djá's unilateral appointment and had vetoed it. Djá's dubious understanding of democracy became clear when he sacked the heads of the 'Televisão da Guine-Bissau' and 'Radio Difusão Nacional' (RDN), accusing the state-run stations of biased reporting. On 4 September, the PRS decided to support a coalition headed by Djá, thus leaving the anti-Djá coalition. However, the PRS held only 41 of the 102 seats in Parliament, so Djá lacked a parliamentary majority. On 9 September, the Supreme Court ruled Djá's nomination (and his arrangements) to be *unconstitutional* thus confirming the view of Parliament and the PAIGC that it was the right of the ruling party to propose a candidate. PAIGC dissenter Djá was expelled from the party in November.

Following a proposal from the PAIGC, Vaz appointed *Carlos Correia*, aged 81 and three times head of government, as the new prime minister on 17 September. However, the *formation of a new government* proved difficult as Vaz rejected Correia's list of candidates, criticising the high percentage of members of the previous government. Tedious negotiations combined with international pressure and an ECOWAS mediation team headed by Olusegun Obasanjo eventually paved the way for a new government, which formally took office on 12 October. While the PRS remained absent from participation, two smaller parties, the 'Partido da Convergência Democrática' and 'União para a Mudança' continued in the new executive, which consisted to a significant extent of members of the Pereira government. Two portfolios (interior and natural resources) were not assigned because of disagreement between Vaz and Correia. Geraldo Martins (PAIGC) was reappointed finance minister. Vaz repeatedly questioned the integrity of unnamed government members, contributing to political instability. In a vote of no confidence on 23 December, 15 PAIGC parliamentarians, among them businessman and Pereira adversary Braima Camará, joined with the opposition PRS in not supporting the government. As a result, Parliament adjourned until January 2016. Vaz's alignment with PAIGC dissenters and the PRS was reconfirmed when he dismissed Attorney-General Hermenegildo Pereira on 25 November, who was recognised for his impartial fight against corruption. Vaz replaced him with António Sedja Man (PRS). The same day, Dionísio Cabi, also from the PRS, became the new head of the Audit

Court. The new attorney-general's perception of his office became apparent when he announced on 4 December the suspension of a regular political discussion programme on RDN – a decision that he withdrew after criticism some days later.

Public administration continued to encounter numerous problems. The public procurement agency was often bypassed. The number of state employees had grown considerably after the 2012 coup, leading to 30% increase in staff costs. For the first time since its establishment in 1992, the Audit Court presented a report for the years 2009–2010 on 25 September. Its president, Vasco Biague, objected that no one in the government was actually controlling public spending. On 4 August, the government announced a new civil service pay framework and higher salaries for 2016.

In January, it became known that the government was striving for the adoption of a *local administration bill* and local elections by 2017 and Parliament approved a draft bill on 13 July. (There currently are no independent local administration bodies.) According to reports in November, which, however, did not go into detail, parliamentary discussions of *constitutional reform* – put on hold in 2001 – to eliminate legal uncertainties and inconsistencies made crucial progress.

Corruption remained an issue but serious attempts were made to investigate cases: in February, the Public Ministry filed investigations against Foreign Minister Mário Lopes da Rosa (PAIGC), a former fisheries minister, and the prosecutors confiscated his passport in July, accusing him of embezzlement. State Secretary of Youth, Culture and Sports Tomás Gomes Barbosa, who had served in the Fisheries Ministry in 2009–2012 under Prime Minister Carlos Gomes Júnior (PAIGC), was also summoned by the Public Ministry in July, accused of being involved in unloading spoiled fish. State Secretary Idelfrides Fernandes was temporarily arrested in June illicitly selling diplomatic and official passports. To ensure more transparency, the government had decided in January to withdraw diplomatic and official passports after the end of the respective official's journey. Investigations against government members provoked the PAIGC in July to blame the public ministry for 'attacks' – allegations that the attorney-general rejected, accusing the government of manipulating the judiciary. In July, Parliament waived the immunity of a PAIGC member accused of embezzling money from the public pension fund.

Crime was also a concern. Armed robberies of kiosks committed by young men became a problem in some of Bissau's neighbourhoods. As a result, military commandos patrolled some suburbs from October onwards. Even security personnel were involved in crime: in February, a soldier was sentenced for selling arms to rustlers in Buba. Five policemen were suspended in April for stealing power cables in Bissau. In July, the 'Liga Guineense dos Direitos Humanos' (LGDH) made public the case of a man who was beaten to death by policemen in a police station in Bissorã. In the same month, a Sierra Leonean citizen charged with robbery accused the police of demanding money to release him. It was reported in July that 200 individuals had been registered in Bissau as a result of a campaign in May to track illegal weapons. On 22 November, the judicial police detained a policeman for assisting drug-traffickers. On the positive side, the Inter-Governmental Group against Money Laundering in West Africa removed Guinea-Bissau from its list of non-cooperating countries.

Former general chief of staff José Zamora Induta, who had been illegally dismissed and detained in 2010, returned from his Portuguese exile on 21 July. Induta's residence was guarded by security officials, putting him de factor under (undeclared) house arrest in August. On 22 September, he was officially imprisoned on remand in the Mansôa barracks: the military jurisdiction accused him of being involved in political assassinations (including the killing of then state president João Bernardo 'Nino' Vieira in 2009) and an alleged military coup attempt on 21 October 2014. The High Court ordered his release on 11 November, but the Military High Court reopened the case in December.

Foreign Affairs

International donors rewarded Guinea-Bissau's good performance with commitments. The results of an international roundtable conference in Geneva on 25 March, in which 70 countries and institutions participated, exceeded all expectations: pledges, two-thirds of them grants, worth € 1.3 bn to support the government's 'Terra Ranka' (The Country Rises) strategic plan for 2015–2020 were made. Brazil cancelled 95% of Guinea-Bissau's debts, and the EU and the World Bank resumed activities and lifted sanctions. Guinea-Bissau continued to rely heavily on development cooperation: various projects in the governance, infrastructure, employment, education, agriculture, health and ecology sectors were concluded or implemented. Among the donors were China, Japan, Morocco and Portugal, as well as the AfDB, CPLP, EU, IMF, and the UN.

Bilateral and diplomatic relations with Cabo Verde, suspended since 2012, were normalised in January, after both countries signed various cooperation agreements. Relations with Mauritania improved in June with the signing of three agreements. Reports in January said that Guinea-Bissau had accumulated debts to the UN amounting to more than $ 600,000, threatening the country's voting rights in the General Assembly. King Mohammed VI of Morocco visited Bissau on 28–30 May; Guinea-Bissau supported Morocco's accession to the CPLP in return for development support.

Security sector reform remained relevant, involving Angola, the AU, Brazil, Cabo Verde, the CPLP, China, ECOWAS, the EU, Portugal, Timor and the US, which were active or expressed the intention of strengthening their support. On 18 February, the UNSC extended the mandate of UNIOGBIS (United Nations Integrated Peacebuilding Office in Guinea-Bissau) for one year until 29 February 2016. For the first time, UNIOGBIS's objectives, such as national reconciliation, consulting with relevant institutions, and the coordination and mobilisation of international assistance, were specified in the resolution. Portugal relaunched its military cooperation in March. On 19 May, ECOWAS extended the mandate of its peace mission in Guinea-Bissau (ECOMIB) to 31 December. The EU continued its support for the country's detention facilities; the LGDH reported in June that conditions in police detention continued to be unacceptable. The UN Peacebuilding Support Office and the UN Peacebuilding Fund signed a Peacebuilding Priority Plan for 2015–2017 with the government on 30 July. In November, it was reported that the World Bank had reviewed defence and security spending. After years of discussion, a military pension fund was put in place and the first of 2,000 military officials were expected to retire by the end of the year.

Drug-trafficking continued to be a problem. In February, four Bissau-Guinean drug mules continued to be detained in Togo. In July, a Bissau-Guinean was arrested at Casablanca airport, and another in Praia, both arriving from Brazil. In November, a drug mule, arriving from Morocco, and in March and February two more, one a Nigerian, were arrested at Bissau airport. The EU decided in February to integrate Guinea-Bissau into its anti-drug programme Seaport Cooperation (SEACOP).

The Interior Ministry announced on 1 July that from 2016 the EU would support the country in monitoring its *terrestrial and maritime borders*. The authorities arrested 300 foreigners who had no residence permit in Bissau on 12 February, and another 500 in October.

Socioeconomic Developments

The IMF estimated on 28 October that *GDP* was expected to rise by 4.7%–5% in 2015. The country attracted several new companies (working in, e.g. cultivation, cement and fenestration). *Tax revenues* exceeded expectations with an increase of 60% in 2014, the IMF said in February; only 20–25 of the taxes came from the hinterland. To improve tax compliance, the government began to control the documentation of imported goods and, in July, reformed tariffs on car imports. Portugal and the US supported reforms in the fiscal sector, while Guinea-Bissau recruited fiscal consultants with the help of the AfDB. On the negative side, it was reported in April that many enterprises were not paying social insurance contributions.

The *electricity and water supplies* improved considerably. The capital experienced regular power supply and even some towns in the interior benefited from these improvements. The AfDB approved a € 9 m loan and a € 7.7 m grant in June to improve the worn and inadequate power distribution grid in Bissau. It was also expected that a new power station with an initial capacity of 15 MW would be built in Bissau from 2016 at a cost of CFAfr 15 bn. In July, the government announced plans for the construction of a thermal power station in Buba. By 2017, the government would start receiving electricity from a hydroelectric dam being built on the River Gambia by the 'Organisation pour la Mise en Valeur du Fleuve Gambie' (OMVG), run by Gambia, Guinea, Guinea-Bissau and Senegal. The OMVG said in April that it also planned to construct a dam near Bafatá at a cost of € 80 m. The government signed agreements with the AfDB for about CFAfr 11 bn in November for the construction of an OMVG interconnection network. On 25 June, the World Bank signed an agreement to provide $ 78 m to construct a line between the Kaleta dam in neighbouring Guinea and Bissau. On 30 September, the AfDB approved a € 121.5 m OMVG package, part of a € 937.5 m international project with multiple donors, including the World Bank. With international support, a water supply system was inaugurated in Catió and Bafatá and it was announced on 27 July that the Portuguese public company 'Águas de Portugal' would help to upgrade Bissau's water supply network.

2015 was a good year for *agriculture*: the production of rice was expected to rise by one third to 170,000 tonnes. The harvest of cashew kernels, the country's main cash crop, reached the record high of 180,000 tonnes, bringing an income of about $ 164 m and making Guinea-Bissau the sixth-largest producer. 20% of GDP and 85% of jobs depended on cashew. The price for cashew paid to farmers also rose to CFAfr 250–350 per kg. The smuggling of cashew (about 90,000 tonnes in 2014) to avoid taxation remained a problem; officials were involved.

A new three-year *fisheries* agreement was concluded with the EU in January, requiring the EU to pay € 9.2 m a year and an additional contribution of € 3 m for fishery projects. On 21 June, China announced the construction of a fish plant in Bissau, creating 400 jobs. To fight illegal fishing, the Guinea-Bissau authorities introduced in May a satellite-based control system for all fishing vessels. The EU helped Guinea-Bissau to acquire three vessels to combat illegal fishing while South Korea donated two boats worth € 118,000. This was necessary as in April and May alone the 'Serviço Nacional de Fiscalização e Controle de Actividades de Pesca' (FISCAP) confiscated three Chinese vessels that were fishing illegally. FISCAP cleared and destroyed several illegal camps used by fishermen from neighbouring countries.

Timber exports rose significantly to 37,000 tonnes in early 2015, signifying a state income of about € 15 m before the government prohibited the export of timber from 1 April to fight illegal logging. A significant number of containers loaded with illegally logged timber were seized during the year. In December, the government imposed a five-year moratorium on timber exports.

Transport infrastructure improved. Streets and roads in and around Bissau were constructed or upgraded. In January, the government announced plans to acquire three ships to link the islands with the mainland. In February, EuroAtlantic increased its flights to Lisbon and in June 'Transportes Aereos de Cabo Verde' (TACV) resumed its flights to Bissau, which had been suspended after the 2012 coup. Plans were announced in the same month to found 'Air Guiné-Bissau', with the government holding 40% and the Romanian Tender Group 60%, and, in July, to privatise the port of Bissau, and a public tender for the construction of a dry port in Bissau was launched in August. Also in August the government announced plans to construct two bridges in Bissau and Farim and a connection to Catió.

Mining operations continued, with some hiccups: Bauxite Angola, which was accused of bribing politicians, stopped its infrastructure activities in mid-2015. The exploitation of heavy sands by the Russian company Poto near Varela faced resistance from local residents citing ecological concerns. In March, a court had ordered the suspension of Poto's mining activities. In November, the Canadian GB Minerals announced plans to exploit phosphate near Farim from 2018, and the Nigerian Petroplus received a contract for petroleum exploration.

In February, Guinea-Bissau joined the Afreximbank, which promotes and finances trade in Africa. There were media reports in November that the Ivorian 'Banque Atlantique' would open a branch in Bissau.

Communications public companies Guiné Telecom (fixed network) and Guinétel (mobile) were out of operation, having been *de facto* bankrupt since 2014. The Angolan Unitel showed interest in Guinétel in March and the government announced on 27 July that it planned to transform Guiné Telecom into an infrastructure provider. Terrestrial and satellite lines remained unreliable; according to media reports in May, the World Bank approved a loan of $ 35 m to connect Guinea-Bissau with undersea telecommunication cables by 2017. Also in May, the government announced the liberalisation of the Internet. From January, 'Correios de Portugal' took over international mail exchange.

Cyclone Fred hit the country in late August, causing floods in coastal areas, including parts of Bissau, and killing seven fishermen.

Liberia

Lansana Gberie

The year was in large part dominated by the Ebola Virus Disease (EVD) outbreak, though WHO tentatively declared the outbreak over on 9 May. The economy suffered throughout the year, largely as a result of falling commodity prices. Corruption scandals, including some related to misappropriation of funds meant to combat the EVD epidemic, dominated the political scene, revealing the depth of public distrust of national institutions and the inefficiency of state bureaucracy. The debate between and within political parties was highly divisive. Although the UN Mission in Liberia suggested that it might soon be leaving the country, its military and administrative capacity remained untouched. Liberia's foreign policy was dominated by the government's attempts to attract development funds to combat the consequences of the EVD epidemic.

Domestic Politics

EVD transmission had begun to subside by the beginning of the year, though Liberia was still virtually held hostage to many of the effects and ramifications of

 | DOI 10.1163/9789004333239_013

the outbreak. By 11 January, 8,331 Liberians had been infected and 3,538 had lost their lives to the virus, according to figures released by WHO. In the same week, the country recorded only seven new infections. This contrasted sharply with what was happening at the height of the outbreak in August and September 2014, when Liberia was recording more than 300 new cases of the virus every week. In fact, by 20 February, the EVD situation had so improved that the government lifted the curfews it had imposed on several parts of the country, including the capital, Monrovia, and announced that it was reopening its borders with neighbouring countries on 22 February, although those countries continued to maintain closed borders. At that point, the government announced that there were only five confirmed cases of EVD in the entire country.

Politics remained fractious even at the height of the EVD crisis. After the certification, on 3 January, of 12 of the 15 newly-elected senators by the *National Elections Commission* (NEC), six of the losing candidates filed a complaint to the NEC challenging the results of their polls. The most prominent case was that filed by *Henrique Topka*, former president of Cuttington University and a candidate for the ruling Unity Party, who had lost to *Jewel Howard-Taylor* of the National Patriotic Party (NPP), the ex-wife of former president Charles Taylor and a prospective presidential candidate for the 2017 election. Topka had lost by a sizeable margin to Howard-Taylor, but he alleged that her vote tally had been inflated in three precincts of Bong County. Most observers believed that there was no rigging and a simple recount would confirm Howard-Taylor's victory. A magistrate concluded that the disputed figures had been the result of a simple error, and that Howard-Taylor had won fairly. Topka, however, appealed the decision in the Supreme Court and the matter dragged on until August, when the Supreme Court upheld Topka's petition and ordered a new vote. At that point, Topka, hailing the court's decision as "a victory for not just my supporters but the new democratic dispensation in Liberia", announced that he had no intention of running again and requested that the money for the re-run be instead diverted towards the completion a technical college in the county. The certified senators had already taken the oath of office and presented their credentials to the 53rd Legislature on 12 January. On 12 February, the senators elected *Armah Jallah*, of Gbarpolu County, as president pro tempore of the *Senate*. A senator for the NPP – which had been founded by Charles Taylor – he had first been elected to the senate in 1998, won re-election in 2011, and again won a by-election in December 2014.

Corruption allegations against the Speaker of the House of Representatives Alex Jenekai Tyler led in January to minority opposition members demanding his resignation and calling on the dilatory *Liberia Anti-Corruption Commission* (LACC) to investigate him. Tyler stood accused of circumventing public procurement laws in relation to a $ 25,000 consulting fee, but he declined to appear before the LACC. A highly influential member of the Unity Party with close ties to President Ellen Johnson-Sirleaf, Tyler, who served as the Representative for the 1st District of Bomi

County (to which he had been elected in 2005), resigned in October in order to be able to run for president in 2017. Tyler had built for himself an extravagantly appointed house on the highway from Roberts International Airport to Monrovia, triggering speculation about the sources of his wealth. It was generally believed that Sirleaf and major foreign companies in Liberia routinely bribed members of the legislature to have important mineral laws passed or appointments confirmed, and Tyler was persistently alleged to be at the centre of the graft. The LACC made known to Tyler in January that it was investigating improper consulting fees paid to him as well as the expenditure of $ 1.2 m allegedly provided for 'public consultations' – code for executive bribery of the legislature – in connection with draft petroleum legislation in 2013. Tyler struck back, inviting the LACC, itself reputedly not above board, to account for its expenditure for the fiscal years 2012 to 2015.

Allegations of corruption or misuse of state funds surfaced again on 23 February, when charges were brought against a former member of the House of Representatives and eight former board members and employees of the *National Oil Company of Liberia* (NOCAL), including a newly-elected senator. Ten NOCAL employees were arrested. The alleged corruption dated back to 2006 and related to the practice of bribing members of the legislature to facilitate the easy, uncritical ratification of contracts involving the NOCAL in 2006 and 2007. Amidst the scandal, Sirleaf proposed an ameliorating measure: during her annual address to the legislature on 26 January, she made clear her intention to propose the establishment of a specialised criminal court with jurisdiction over corruption crimes. She also proposed granting the LACC direct powers to prosecute. By year's end, the LACC was empowered to prosecute any case it referred to the Ministry of Justice if the ministry declined to prosecute within 90 days.

Public outrage at the initially slow and fitful response to the Ebola (EVD) outbreak was rekindled in April after the General Auditing Commission (GAC) reported to the Senate on the use of funds by the *Ebola Task Force*. The audited funds amounted to $ 13 m, disbursed at the height of the outbreak from 1 August to 31 October 2014. The auditors concluded that $ 850,000 had been improperly spent, including tens of thousands of dollars paid to a public relations firm, and tens of thousands of dollars more paid to state security agencies and the Ministry of State for Presidential Affairs. The report, issued on 7 April and published on the GAC's website, noted that the "conduct of the affairs of the National Ebola Trust Fund were marred by financial irregularities and material control deficiencies". In response, the Ebola Task Force issued a statement on 13 May, acknowledging its lack of compliance with the required public financial management and procurement laws on grounds that it was operating in an emergency situation that made it "unrealistic and unreasonable" to expect its activities to be fully compliant with established rules. Predictably, though the auditor general encouraged the Senate to urgently consider the report and its recommendations, by year's end there was no indication that this had been done. Sirleaf, who had never been personally implicated in corrupt dealings, demonstrated on 24 August that she could act decisively when she dismissed *Thomas Kaydor*, the deputy minister for foreign affairs responsible for international cooperation and economic integration, for inappropriate conduct as part of an investigation into the alleged misuse of funds from the government of Japan. Also in April, she suspended the managing director and comptroller of the National Port Authority, who was under investigation by the LACC. In November, five senior officers of the *Drug Enforcement Agency*, including the chief of intelligence and the deputy chief investigator, were dismissed following allegations of extortion and bribery. By year's end, the LACC had received 29 allegations, 25 of them involving serving state officials, of which it investigated six cases and recommended one for prosecution. Liberia scored 37 points out of 100 on TI's corruption perceptions index – more or less the average for the past ten years.

A potentially destabilising development relating to amending the *Constitution* involved a recommendation by a national constitutional conference on 2 April to designate Liberia as a *Christian nation*. The conference, which attracted 500 delegates, was organised by the Constitutional Review Committee (CRC), which had been set up by Sirleaf in 2013 to recommend changes to the country's Constitution to bring about greater national cohesion and stability. The Christian state proposal was one of nine – whittled down from 25 – that the CRC had agreed to be discussed at the conference, before being submitted to Sirleaf. It would then require a two-thirds vote in favour in the legislature and majority endorsement at a referendum before becoming law. Besides needlessly inflaming religious passions, the amendment, if passed, had potential practical consequences. The state currently subsidised private schools, most of them run by Christian or Muslim groups, with neither taking precedence. This would change if Liberia became a Christian state. Muslim groups promptly staged a protest in Gbarnga when the CRC adopted the proposal, and many observers feared that, if ratified, it might lead to widespread sectarian violence, for which there were precedents, albeit infrequent. In October 2004, riots between Christians and Muslims in Monrovia had led to the deaths of half a dozen people and the burning down of churches and an Islamic school. UN troops, displaying overwhelming force, had put down the violence. Clashes between the two groups in Lofa County in 2010 had led to at least four deaths and the destruction of property. Nevertheless, proponents argued that Liberia had been founded as a Christian state, that the overwhelming majority of its population was Christian, and that Liberia's recent woes had been caused by its lapse into 'immorality' since the introduction of the current 1986 secular Constitution. They cited the disputed 2008 National Population and Housing Census, with figures giving Liberia's population as 85.6% Christian, 12.2% Muslim, 0.6% adherents of indigenous religious beliefs, 1.5% persons who claim no religion, and less than 1% members of other religious groups. Sirleaf rejected the proposal, as did several political parties in a joint statement on 6 April. However, two key senators, Jewel Howard Taylor and Prince Yormie Johnson, campaigned in favour, as did the powerful Council of Churches.

By year's end, the Senate had not commenced consultations on the proposal, as was required before it could be submitted to a referendum.

A more unifying development was the declaration by WHO on 9 May that Liberia was *free of Ebola*. The front-page headline of a local paper captured the national mood of triumph over adversity: "Ebola Crushed!" A subsequent flare up of EVD cases, beginning on 29 June, with a new death that was quickly followed by five cases of infection linked to that index case, was declared over in September. However, a new outbreak was detected in Montserrado County on 19 November. The outbreaks were limited and quickly contained but, by year's end, Liberia had still not been completely freed of the virus.

As in previous years, instances of mob violence and vigilantism severely tested the capability of the police, which at year's end had 5,170 personnel, 18.6% of whom were women. *Violent protests* by 200 local youth on 26 May at Golden Veroleum Liberia's oil palm plantation in Sinoe County resulted in the looting of warehouses and damage to company vehicles. They were protesting at the company's alleged failure to conduct sufficient consultation with local communities before signing concession agreements. Previously, on 7 May, 40 company employees who were seeking salary increases had detained senior company officials in a violent protest. In both instances, the Liberia National Police, spread thin in the area, were incapable of effective intervention, and the UN's military and police units had to be deployed to support them in restoring stability. On 12 October, armed robbers killed two security guards at the China Union iron ore mine in Bong County and, on 26 October, 50 former employees of a private security company broke into the premises of Arcelor Mittal Liberia in Grand Bassa County in protest against the failure to pay benefits allegedly owed to them.

On 30 September, *riots* broke out in Ganta after residents found the body of a 20-year old motorcyclist and, assuming that it was the result of ritual killing – an occasional occurrence in the county – proceeded to damage and loot private property and then attacked the local police station. More than 60 persons were arrested in connection with this incident and were awaiting trial at year's end.

On 15 September, Sirleaf submitted a report and a letter to the speaker of the House stating that her government had implemented or was well advanced in implementing "the majority" of the recommendations of the 2009 report of the *Truth and Reconciliation Commission*, and she left open "for future consideration" by the legislature the establishment of a *special war crimes court* as recommended by the Commission. This was in response to the UN Human Rights Council's Universal Periodic Review for Liberia, published in May. The government accepted 147 of the 187 recommendations made by the Council, including on issues related to sexual and gender-based violence, access to justice and economic, social and cultural rights. Sirleaf also, for the first time, accepted in principle the criminalisation of female genital mutilation. Some recommendations, including those related to the rights of lesbian, gay, bisexual and transgender persons and the abolition of the death penalty, were simply noted.

The next presidential elections were scheduled for November 2017, but positioning for the polls began in earnest as the Ebola outbreak waned. The respected Minister for Foreign Affairs *Augustine Kpehe Ngafuan*, a prospective presidential candidate for the Unity Party, tendered his resignation, which Sirleaf accepted on 9 October. On the same day, she dismissed Minister of Internal Affairs *Morris Dukuly*. Liberia's most famous businessman, *Benoni Urey*, registered the All Liberian Party in early August and launched it amidst fanfare in November, declaring himself a presidential candidate. His party added to 14 registered political parties in Liberia, 11 of which were represented in parliament. Also campaigning to be president were 70-year-old Vice President *Joseph Nyumah Boakai* and *George Oppong Weah*, who had been elected to represent Montserrado County in the Senate in December 2014. Weah had first contested for president in 2005, and had lost to Sirleaf.

Foreign Affairs

On 27 February, US President Barack Obama hosted President Sirleaf at the White House, where he praised her for her "extraordinary" leadership in the Ebola crisis. The *USA* had led the Ebola containment efforts in Liberia, deploying over 3,000 troops in 2014 to build holding and treatment centres and dozens of medical personnel through the Center for Disease to help combat the epidemic. On Sirleaf's initiative, on 15 February the leaders of the MRU had endorsed a comprehensive regional health strategy to prevent the cross-border transmission of infectious diseases and promote post-Ebola socioeconomic recovery.

In a mark of the esteem in which she was held abroad, *Sirleaf* was selected by her colleagues to be spokeswoman for the leaders of the three West African countries worst affected by Ebola – Liberia, Sierra Leone and Guinea – at donor meetings in Washington and Brussels in March to discuss post-Ebola reconstruction issues. She was also seriously discussed as a candidate to replace Ban Ki-moon as UN Secretary-General when Ban's final term expired in 2016. A 'New York Times' editorial on 22 August listed her name, along with Christine Lagarde, among "accomplished world leaders" who should be actively considered for the post.

Liberia's frontier region with *Côte d'Ivoire*, a perennial area of security and diplomatic concern, remained largely calm during the EVD outbreak, in part because the borders were sealed. However, incidents of sporadic violence and reports of illegal farming in the areas bordering Côte d'Ivoire continued to be reported. A particularly deadly attack on 2 December, when armed militia struck at Ivorian security forces 20 km from the border with Liberia, caused significant concern in both countries, though no evidence of Liberian involvement was established. The attack resulted in 11 deaths and the flight of 38 persons into Liberia. Sirleaf had announced the reopening of the border between the two countries on 20 February, but the Ivorians had not reciprocated.

At an international Ebola recovery conference hosted by the UN Secretary-General on 10 July, pledges of more than $ 5 bn for the three most affected countries were made, of which Liberia received pledges of $ 812 m towards the implementation of the *Economic Stabilization and Recovery Plan* for recovery and resilience projects from 2015 to 2017.

Socioeconomic Developments

The socio-economic outlook remained bleak, largely because of a sharp decline in exports caused by Ebola and plummeting commodity prices. The shortfall was only partially offset by Ebola-related donor assistance and lower oil prices. The drop in *iron ore* prices caused Liberia's three largest producers – Acelor Mittal Liberia, Putu Iron Ore Mining Inc., and Western Cluster Limited – to scale back their operations, leading to significant job losses and cuts in tax receipts by the government. Acelor Mittal reduced its workforce by 20%, which meant that 270 employees were laid off. All three companies axed employees, suspended construction work on railroads and ports, and requested tax waivers from the government. The Liberian Central Bank reported a fall of 34% in iron ore output, and that export earnings had fallen from $ 61.4 m during the last quarter of 2014 to $ 32.2 m during the first quarter of 2015. Iron ore had displaced rubber as Liberia's chief export earner a few years earlier.

Rubber, which in 2010 accounted for 59.2% of Liberia's export earnings and 36.5% of GDP, accounted for only 25% of export earnings in the first quarter of 2015. Prices of rubber had by the first quarter of 2015 plunged by 75% in five years, from $ 2.53 per lb. in 2011 to about $ 0.60. Investments by Firestone Inc., which maintained the world's largest rubber plantation (or farm, its preferred term) in Liberia, was seriously affected. The company had invested about $ 160 m since the end of the civil war to rebuild Liberia's crumbling or looted infrastructure, replant trees and build schools and hospitals. It currently employed 8,000 Liberians, and about 80,000 Liberians were living on its concessions area of 118,990 acres. Firestone claimed to be losing $ 40 m annually as a result of the plummeting of rubber prices, and its Liberia manager speculated in August that the company's senior management could face increased pressure to divest if the situation did not improve – which could be catastrophic for the Liberian economy.

Moreover, *offshore oil* prospects appeared to be disappointing. There were no commercially viable finds, though a two-year bidding process run by NOCAL, British-based Ernst and Young and Norway's TGS-Nopec Geophysical Company, which had started in 2014, had by year's end attracted bids from, among others, New York-based Kosmos Energy, Liberty Petroleum Corporation and Nigeria's Pillar Oil and Platform Petroleum Limited. Chevron suggested it would be pulling out of Liberia. Anadarko withdrew from the country in July, relinquishing its oil block. However, in October ExxonMobil announced plans to spud its oil blocks in late 2016 or early 2017. NOCAL faced criticism for incompetence and corruption. In December, the EITI annual report for Liberia criticised NOCAL's organisational inadequacies, including failure to make available background information on the oil and gas sector, particularly on the companies operating, their ownership shares in the licences, historical transfers of ownership between the companies and related matters.

Sirleaf submitted the draft *national budget* for 2015/16 to the legislature on 2 June. It totalled $ 604 m, a fall of 4.9% from the previous budget. Of this, $ 252.1 m (41.7%) was allocated to civil service salaries, $ 79.4 m to education, $ 73.0 m to the health sector and $ 23.2 m to the Social Development Fund. The budget projected that $ 465.6 m would be raised through domestic revenue, with the remaining funds to be provided by grants and donor budget support programmes ($ 66.2 m), loans ($ 58.6 m) and the surplus from the 2014/15 fiscal year ($ 13.6 m). On 22 July, the House of Representatives approved a budget of $ 622.7 m, which was followed by Senate concurrence on 6 August.

By year's end, some 40% of household heads who had been working before the EVD epidemic and had lost their jobs during the crisis were still unemployed. About 80% of Liberians did not have formal sector *employment*.

Mali

Bruce Whitehouse

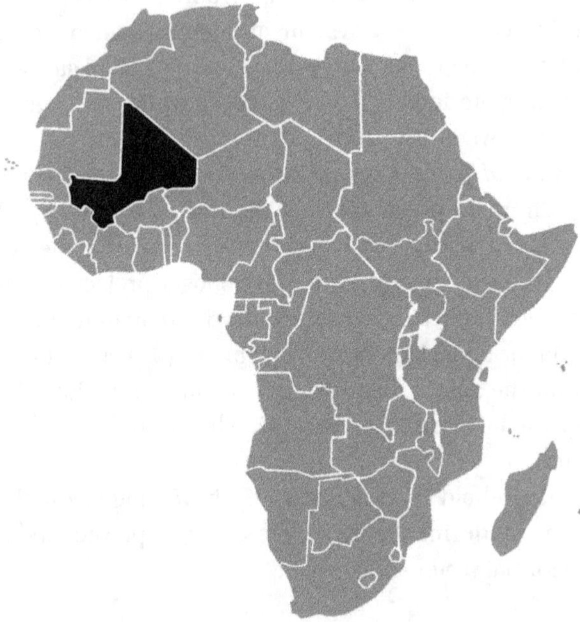

2015 brought renewed hope for a lasting settlement to the conflict between Mali's government and northern rebels that had divided the country for three years. Although a peace agreement was successfully negotiated, insecurity continued to be rampant in northern Mali, largely due to violence by Islamist groups. For the first time, this violence spread to other parts of the country and included brazen terrorist attacks on civilian targets in cities. Militants routinely targeted UN peacekeepers and employees. The Malian government maintained close ties with France and other donor governments while also strengthening its relations with new international partners. Mali's economy grew more slowly than in 2014 but showed prospects for a better performance in 2016.

Domestic Politics

The Malian authorities and their partners in north-west Africa and beyond sought to shore up the country's *peace process with Tuareg separatist rebels* that had begun in 2014. Prime Minister Modibo Keita, named by President Ibrahim Boubacar Keita

 | DOI 10.1163/9789004333239_014

to lead the government after Moussa Mara's resignation in January, worked with Algerian mediators and rebel leaders to draft an agreement that would transfer many powers from the central government to regional and local officials. Fighting continued to flare up between various armed groups, however, sometimes drawing forces of the UN Multidimensional Integrated Stabilisation Mission in Mali (MINUSMA) into the conflict. Following skirmishes between pro-government militia fighters and rebels of the separatist 'Mouvement National pour la Liberation de l'Azawad' (National Movement for the Liberation of Azawad, or MNLA) near the northern village of Tabankort in January, a MINUSMA helicopter fired on MNLA forces, killing five; a MINUSMA spokesperson said this was to protect peacekeepers who had come under fire. UN officials later proposed creating a buffer zone around Tabankort to prevent further fighting, but scrapped the plan after violent protests erupted outside MINUSMA headquarters in the city of Gao. Protestors accused MINUSMA of siding with the MNLA, and some reportedly threw rocks and petrol bombs. Three protestors were shot dead by MINUSMA guards. A UN investigation later found that the guards' lethal response was unauthorised and excessive.

Peace negotiations between Prime Minister Keita and rebel leaders resumed in Algiers in February. The *Accord for Peace and Reconciliation in Mali* (or 'Algiers accord') that these negotiations produced satisfied the Malian government's main conditions – recognition of Mali's territorial integrity and its secular, unitary state – while also meeting rebel demands for recognition of Mali's cultural diversity and for a more 'balanced' distribution of development resources. The Algiers accord aimed to address multiple issues underlying the cycle of violence that had prevailed in northern Mali since the 1960s, notably by devolving power from the national to the regional and local levels. It provided a framework for several new institutions, including a national senate, elected regional governors and regional legislatures, and local police forces; it also called for shifting 30% of state revenue from the central government to local authorities. The accord generated fierce criticism among rebels and government loyalists alike, however. Many rebels resisted the treaty, holding out hope for the creation of an independent homeland in the north; in contrast, many government supporters felt the deal endangered national unity by granting too many concessions to the rebels. Protests against the accord were held both in Bamako and in the northern rebel stronghold of Kidal, and several authorities within the rebel coalition refused to endorse the document. Although government and rebel representatives initialled the accord at a March ceremony in Algiers, many rebel leaders and their supporters continued to reject the document. Tensions peaked in April and May after pro-government militia forces took the northern town of Ménaka from MNLA fighters, sparking combat between pro- and anti-government forces in multiple locations throughout the north. The UN reported that 60,000 residents were displaced by renewed fighting. After the violence subsided, the Algiers accord was finally signed in Bamako by senior government and rebel leaders on 20 June. MINUSMA officials moved to curb a new round of skirmishes in

August by creating a security zone around the town of Anefis. While implementation of the reforms called for by the Algiers accord was slow, no further fighting had broken out between government forces and the MNLA or other former separatist rebels by year's end. The MNLA remained in complete control of Kidal, where there had been no official Malian government presence since May 2014.

Despite undeniable progress in the peace process between the government and Tuareg rebels, Mali's security situation remained dire as *asymmetric attacks by Islamist militants on Malian and UN personnel* persisted. These attacks reportedly took the lives of 82 members of the Malian security forces and another 12 members of MINUSMA during the year, with dozens more injured. Armed with suicide bombs, improvised explosive devices, rockets, mortars, and firearms, groups including al-Qaida in the Islamic Maghreb (AQIM), Al Mourabitoune (an offshoot of AQIM), Ansar Eddine and the Macina Liberation Front carried out assaults on Malian army or MINSUMA bases in six of the country's nine administrative regions. Attacks on Malian and UN convoys, patrols and positions remained especially prevalent in the northern regions of Gao, Kidal and Timbuktu, which had witnessed endemic unrest since 2012. In May, the UN estimated that 78 attacks had targeted MINUSMA personnel since the beginning of the year. At least 60 civilians were also killed by armed groups, mainly in northern Mali. Militants of MUJAO (the 'Mouvement pour l'Unicité et le Jihad en Afrique de l'Ouest', or Movement for Oneness and Jihad in West Africa) executed at least three civilian truck drivers working for the UN and Red Cross in the north. A Dutchman kidnapped from Timbuktu by AQIM fighters in 2011 was rescued by French troops in April, but two other foreign hostages (from South Africa and Sweden) remained in AQIM custody and were shown on a video the group released in June.

In a new and destabilising trend, *Islamist attacks on government and UN targets spread southward* into areas previously untouched by Islamist violence. In Bamako during the month of May, a MINUSMA peacekeeper was shot dead, another wounded and a Malian security guard wounded in two separate attacks later claimed by Ansar Eddine. In June, Ansar Eddine claimed responsibility for two more attacks on Malian government posts in the Sikasso region near the border with Côte d'Ivoire. In September, militants reportedly affiliated with the Macina Liberation Movement attacked an isolated police post in the Mopti region, 5 km from the Burkina Faso border; two policemen and two civilians were killed. The following month, the Malian armed forces launched coordinated anti-terrorist operations in the Mopti and Sikasso regions.

Al Mourabitoune also orchestrated a series of high-profile *terror strikes on civilian targets*. They began with an assault on a Bamako nightclub in March that killed five civilians, including two foreign UN employees. Malian security forces later killed one suspected perpetrator of the nightclub attack and arrested three alleged accomplices. In August, gunmen struck a hotel frequented by UN civilian contractors in the central town of Sévaré; four militants died along with nine civilians and four Malian soldiers. On 20 November, an attack on Bamako's Radisson Hotel killed 20 people – six Malians, six Russians, three Chinese, two Belgians, one American, one Israeli and one Senegalese. Both perpetrators were killed by Malian and French security forces following a siege lasting several hours, and two suspected accomplices were later arrested. These attacks signalled a change of tactics by Islamist militants operating in Mali: prior to 2015, Bamako, Sévaré and other towns in central and southern Mali had been free of terrorist violence. In response to rising insecurity, the Malian government postponed local elections, and on 21 December declared a ten-day state of emergency that was later extended into March 2016.

Political violence notwithstanding, the regime of President Ibrahim Boubacar Keita remained generally stable throughout the year, despite scandals over poor governance. Criticism of Keita's regime ramped up in the Malian press, with opposition politicians (most notably Tiébilé Dramé of PARENA, the 'Parti pour la Renaissance Nationale' or Party for National Rebirth) increasingly calling out the government for alleged corruption in affairs including the importation of adulterated fertiliser and the allocation of subsidised tractors by the presidency. In September, Prime Minister Modibo Keita formed a new government consisting of 31 ministers, and conspicuously kept Bocary Tréta, who, as minister for rural development, had been embroiled in the fertiliser scandal.

Foreign Affairs

Maintaining existing relations with international partners and forging new ones was a top priority of the government of President Keita, who made 32 trips abroad and visited 18 different countries over the course of the year.

In light of multiple threats to its security and stability, Mali continued to preoccupy the international community. The *UN*, through its Multidimensional Integrated Stabilization Mission in Mali (MINUSMA) mission, maintained the largest military presence in the country, including (as of June) over 10,200 uniformed personnel (military and police peacekeepers), 578 international civilian personnel, and 682 local civilian staff. By year's end, MINUSMA had suffered more casualties than any other peacekeeping mission on earth, with 61 peacekeepers killed in hostile actions since the beginning of the mission in 2013; 16 of those deaths occurred during 2015. Tensions between the UN and Malians were evident. Polls showed that most Malians did not believe MINUSMA was fulfilling its mandate to protect civilians. Speaking in May, President Keita called MINUSMA's impartiality and effectiveness into question. In December, MINUSMA head Mongi Hamdi stepped down after one year in office amid complaints about his weak leadership. He was replaced by Mahamat Saleh Annadif, former Chadian foreign minister.

The *EU* also played a role in boosting Malian security through the EU Training Mission (EUTM) based in the town of Koulikoro, 100 km north of Bamako. This mission, established in 2013, provided instructors from European armies to train units of the Malian armed forces. It graduated its sixth training battalion in February and its seventh in December; units previously trained by the EUTM also returned for additional exercises. The EUTM also expanded its activities to include training in defence procurement and instructing units of Mali's National Guard and paramilitary police (gendarmerie). Germany took command of the mission in July, succeeding Spain in that role.

President Keita maintained close ties with former colonial power *France*. Following the January attack on the Paris offices of the satirical magazine 'Charlie Hebdo' that killed 12 people, Keita attended a solidarity march in Paris with French President François Hollande. In April, France forgave € 65 m of Mali's bilateral debt. In October, President Keita again visited Hollande in Paris, this time receiving a pledge of € 360 m in aid for the period 2015–2017. The French military also kept a significant presence in Mali in the form of Operation Barkhane, which was active in targeting the leaders of Islamist militant groups on Malian territory; 1,000 French troops were stationed in Mali as part this operation, with 2,000 more in neighbouring countries.

Other donor nations also contributed to peacekeeping and security sector reform. *Denmark* announced in October that it would send 45 troops and a transport aircraft to join MINUSMA; a month later, *Germany* decided to commit 650 troops to MINUSMA. *Japan* partnered with the UNDP to upgrade Mali's National Police Academy. The *USA*, for the first time since suspending bilateral military cooperation with Mali after the 2012 coup d'état, sent trainers to work with the Malian armed forces; in October, a detachment of US Marines participated with Malian paratroops and National Guard troops in a disaster response and humanitarian aid exercise. After the terrorist attack on Bamako's Radisson hotel in November, however, the US government scaled back its presence in Mali by cutting its embassy staff and evacuating its Peace Corps aid programme in the country; it also advised its citizens against travel to Mali.

Mali strengthened bilateral ties with *Turkey*, which President Keita visited three times in 2015. During an official visit to Ankara in February, Keita promised to close down private schools linked to Turkish dissident Fethullah Gülen at the request of the Turkish government, which was campaigning to curb the Gülen movement's influence in several African countries. In return, Turkey's President Recep Tayyip Erdoğan pledged to open new schools and to increase bilateral trade with Mali. The following month, Mali's minister of housing and urban development signed an agreement with a Turkish firm to create a public-private partnership with the goal of financing the construction of 20,000 units of subsidised housing. These initiatives came on the heels of an elaborate mosque construction project in Bamako funded by the Turkish Ministry of Religious Affairs.

Malian citizens encountered a number of dangers abroad. In June, the government of *Gabon* deported hundreds of African migrants whose presence on Gabonese territory was deemed to be unlawful; press reports indicated that at least 89, and as many as 300, of these migrants came from Mali. In September, hundreds of Malians were among the more than 3,000 people killed during a stampede at the annual hajj pilgrimage in Mecca (*Saudi Arabia*). Mali's Ministry of Religious Affairs later estimated that 312 Malians had lost their lives in the incident, and another 34 remained unaccounted for.

2015 also saw the first appearance by a defendant charged with war crimes committed during Mali's conflict at the ICC in The Hague. In September, Ahmad al-Faqi al-Mahdi stood accused of ordering the destruction of ten historic mausoleums and monuments in Timbuktu during that city's 2012 occupation by Islamist militants. Faqi was alleged to be a member of the group Ansar Eddine.

Socioeconomic Developments

Mali's economy lost momentum in 2015, with the annual economic growth rate dropping below 5%, down from over 7% in 2014. This slowdown was partly attributed to setbacks in the *agricultural sector*, with late rains and poor fertiliser quality causing the country's cotton harvest to fall short of its forecasted level of 650,000 tonnes. The rice harvest, by contrast, came in at 2.45 m tonnes, up 13% from the previous year; other cereal harvests were similarly high. *Manufacturing* also declined, but industrial food production was set to expand, with the announcement of Chinese financing worth over € 150 m for four new factories.

In the *mining sector*, which generates one-quarter of Malian state revenue, gold production for the year was 50 tonnes, on a par with the 2014 total. Four tonnes were produced by artisanal miners and the remainder by industrial mining operations. Industrial production was forecast to increase in 2016 due to the planned expansion of existing mines and the opening of new mines in southern and western areas of the country. The Ministry of Mines estimated that remaining reserves amounted to 600 tonnes, or roughly 12 years at the current production rate.

Several major *infrastructure projects* were announced. In the transportation sector, these included a € 1.3 bn contract awarded to the China Railway Construction Corporation to refurbish railway service between Bamako and Dakar (Senegal), and a € 168 m AfDB loan to fund a new highway linking Bamako with the port of San Pedro (Côte d'Ivoire). Initiatives to help meet Mali's growing demand for electricity included a € 30 m deal with the Eranove group to build a 42-MW hydroelectric dam at Kenié, 30 km outside Bamako, and a € 52 m agreement with Scatec Solar to construct a 33-MW solar power plant near the city of Ségou.

Lagging *human development indicators*, however, showed the impact of ongoing insecurity in Mali and throughout the region. School enrolment declined by

11.4% nationally from 2011, mainly due to unrest in the north. 136,000 Malian refugees remained in neighbouring countries, and in March the UN estimated that 3 m Malians were suffering from hunger. In September, a child who had recently come to Bamako from Guinea was found to have polio, stoking fears of a resurgence of the virus, which had previously been eliminated from the Malian population. This occurred only a year after an outbreak of the Ebola virus caused six deaths in Bamako.

Mauritania

Helena Olsson and Claes Olsson

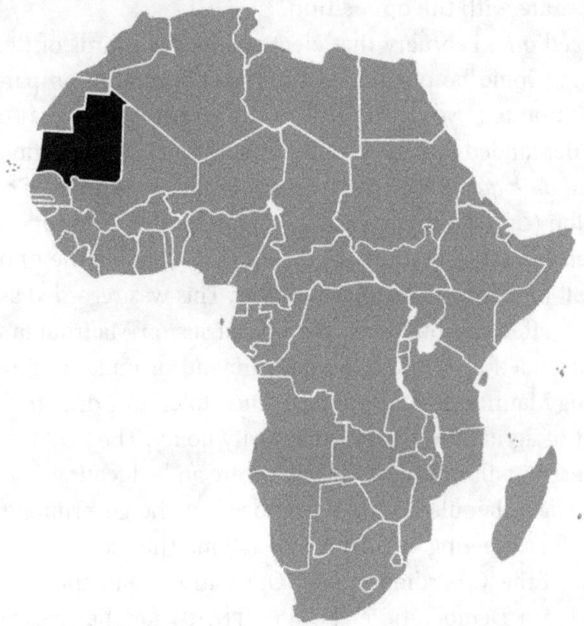

The failure to establish a dialogue between the government and the opposition dominated the political climate. Elections for one-third of Senate seats were postponed and the major opposition group, the 'Rassemblement des Forces Démocratiques' (RFD), ignored the government's initiative for a national dialogue. Instead, the RDF organised street campaigns trying to exploit public frustration over the government's inability to reduce poverty and unemployment. Regional security remained problematic. Potential security threats arising from terrorist groups in neighbouring countries dominated the foreign policy agenda. Mauritania reasserted its role as a regional mediator as President Aziz remained chairperson of the 'G5 du Sahel'. Although the government's main economic policy focus was on macroeconomic stability and attempts to boost the role of the private sector, it failed to agree a new three-year programme with the IMF. A four-year fisheries accord with the EU was signed and was expected to boost the fishing sector considerably.

 | DOI 10.1163/9789004333239_015

Domestic Politics

Opposition fragmentation meant that the ruling 'Union pour la République' (UPR) was able to consolidate its grip on power. President Mohamed Ould Abdel Aziz had little need to cooperate with the opposition.

The government announced on 4 February that elections for two-thirds of the Senate, planned for March 15, would be postponed. Most of the opposition parties had expressed their intention to boycott the vote. At the end of February, RFD leader Ahmed Ould Daddah demanded that the president should, as a precondition for the long-awaited *national dialogue* between government and opposition, dissolve the electoral commission (CENI) and promise to adhere to the Constitution and to agree on a government of national unity. As this did not happen, the RFD rejected the government's call for dialogue on 25 September. This was regarded as a setback for President Aziz's efforts to build a wider consensus on Mauritania's political future. The RFD continued to criticise the government for undermining the country's unity, destroying Mauritanian traditional values, tolerating drug trafficking and mismanagement of agriculture and food security policy. The RDF further highlighted the government's failure to provide healthcare and education.

A new national dialogue was scheduled for 7 November, but the government opted out hours before the first meeting with the opposition. The government refused to meet the demands of the 'Co-ordination de l'Opposition Démocratique' and the 'Forum National pour la Démocratie et l'Unité' (FNDU) for the release of political prisoners and the dissolution of the security apparatus, although the FNDU announced its readiness to resume the dialogue. The election of Ahmed Salem Ould Bouhoubeiny – former dean of the 'Batônnier de l'Ordre National des Avocats' (Mauritanian Bar Association) – as FNDU chairman on 16 October probably contributed to this new approach. Nevertheless, the opposition did not accept the president's invitation to join the government.

Although Mauritania did not experience any terrorist attacks, the *regional terror threat* dominated the security discourse. Many state resources went into the military instead of being invested in infrastructure or social welfare. On 21 April, international media reported that Younis al-Mauritani, a senior al-Qaida leader, had been jailed for 20 years in Mauritania for "terrorist activities". On 17 June, international media reported that a court in Mauritania had convicted three men of "belonging to a terrorist organisation and possession of terrorist propaganda"; they were sentenced to between five and ten years in prison. The names and ages of the men were not specified. On 27 June, a jihadist group, 'Ansar Dine', claimed responsibility for an attack in the Malian city of Nouara close to the Mauritanian border.

On 15 January, Biram Dah Abeid, president of the 'Initiative pour la Résurgence du Mouvement Abolitionniste' (IRA) and a prominent candidate in the 2014 presidential elections, IRA vice president Brahim Bilal Ramdhane and Djiby Sow, president of 'Association Kawtal Djélitaré', were sentenced to two years in prison by a court in Rosso for their involvement in a peaceful 'La Caravane de la Liberté' protest on 11 November 2014. The purpose of the protest had been to draw attention to landowners' exploitation of marginalised citizens, and to educate marginalised groups about *land ownership rights*. The judgement was regarded as a signal of the authorities' determination to constrain the activities of the country's anti-slavery movement. The UN expressed its deep concern and urged an independent investigation, and AI called for the prisoners' immediate release. However, the case did not cause any major foreign protests.

A new *anti-slavery law* was adopted on 21 August, replacing the previous law of 2013. The law made slavery a crime against humanity and doubled the prison term for slave owners to 20 years. The law was welcomed by the UN Human Rights Council but anti-slavery and human rights organisations expressed concerns that new draft legislation threatened the freedom of NGOs to operate independently and might undermine the new anti-slavery law and the ability of NGOs to work with victims. The level of slavery in Mauritania remained the highest in the world, with some 150,000 people living as slaves, according to the Global Slavery Index. On 10 December, Justice Minister Brahim Daddah announced that the government had ordered the creation of three special courts to try slavery cases. However, the main challenge remained the reluctance of state officials to use these legal tools.

Despite a government-sponsored national commission to fight *corruption* (launched in September 2014), the government was subject to minimal scrutiny as a consequence of the extremely fragmented state of the opposition. While the government continued its efforts to convince international partners and investors that it was committed to fighting corruption, there were no clear signs that it was being reduced.

Foreign Policy

Mauritania's engagement with international partners on issues other than security remained limited, while efforts to enforce *security cooperation* with Western and Arab countries continued. On 9 April, President Aziz made an official visit to Saudi Arabia. The Nouakchott Process on the enhancement of security cooperation and the operationalisation of the African Peace and Security Architecture continued. A 34-state (including Mauritania) Islamic Military Alliance to Fight Terrorism was announced by Saudi Arabia on 15 December.

On 29 January, the Mauritanian centre for crisis monitoring, alerts and management ('Centre de Veille, d'Alerte et de Conduite des Crises') was inaugurated. The project is funded equally by NATO and the Canadian Department of Foreign Affairs as part of a national system for crisis management and disaster monitoring, and it covered in its first stage the areas of Nouakchott, Nouadhibou, Rosso and Nema.

With regard to cooperation with the *Maghreb region*, Mauritania maintained a precarious balance between the two major regional powers, Morocco and Algeria. A minor diplomatic dispute with Algeria occurred on 15 April, when news articles in the Mauritanian online news portal 'Al-Bayan' accused Morocco of flooding Mauritania with drugs. Belkacem Cherouati, first counsellor at the Algerian embassy in Nouakchott, was expelled and accused of interference in Mauritania's internal affairs and of jeopardising a possible rapprochement between Morocco and Mauritania. In addition, the website's editor, Moulaye Brahim Ould Moulaye M'Hamed, was questioned by police and accused of damaging Mauritania's relationship with Morocco by spreading lies and false allegations. The official explanation given by the Mauritanian authorities was that the article published by 'Al-Bayan' misrepresented a report on Western Sahara presented by UN SecretaryGeneral Ban Ki-moon to the UNSC on 10 April. During a regional tour by Ban's envoy Christopher Ross in February and March, President Aziz had drawn attention to some negative impacts of the conflict, particularly the arrival of a considerable amount of cannabis. Aziz stressed that cannabis posed a serious threat to the security of all countries of the Sahel-Saharan region because it financed criminal groups, extremists and terrorists.

Mauritania's decision on 3 August to release Sanda Ould Bouamama, a prominent spokesman for 'Ansar Dine' and also closely associated with al-Qaida in the Islamic Maghreb, caused resentment in neighbouring Mali. Bouamama had dual Mauritanian and Malian citizenship and had been delivered to the Mauritanian authorities in 2013. It was speculated that the release was actually part of an effort to consolidate Berabiche support for the recent northern Malian peace agreement. On 28 August, officials from Mauritania and Mali agreed on an increase in joint patrols, the sharing of intelligence and the pursuit of radicals across their shared border.

On 16 June, the International Organisation for Migration launched a two-year project on enhancing the collective capacity for managing borders and for protecting border communities between Mauritania and Mali. The project would be financed by the government of Japan through a grant of $ 3 m for conflict prevention and peace building.

On 26–28 July, Sudan's President Omar al-Bashir took part in the two-day regular summit in Nouakchott on the *Great Green Wall* initiative, aimed at planting a wall of trees in Africa to combat desertification. The visit took place despite the ICC's arrest warrant issued against him in 2009 on charges of genocide, crimes against humanity and war crimes. Mauritania is not a signatory to the Rome Statute.

On 9–16 September, President Aziz visited *China* and discussed enhanced *capacity cooperation* through building steel and cement plants and increased cooperation in animal product processing and exploitation of marine fisheries. On 7 December, the Senate adopted a bill authorising the ratification of a cooperation agreement in the field of security, signed on 26 May between Mauritania and *Spain*, which focused on information and communication technologies, specialised vocational training and exchange of information. The agreement was expected to be an important tool for reducing illegal migration.

Socioeconomic Developments

On 1 January, the National Assembly approved a $ 5.1 bn *budget* for 2015. The budget deficit stood at 2.6% of GDP. The budget foresaw a reduction in government spending on subsidies and goods and services. An IMF report stated that employment in the formal sector represented only 13% of total employment. For the vast majority of the population who were not employed in the formal economy, safety nets were mostly provided by local underfunded state agencies, NGO programmes and extended family networks. Migrants also provided important support through remittances. However, the UNDP estimated that 42.8% of the population were living in "severe poverty".

On 4 June, the IMF concluded that Mauritania was facing a severe terms-of-trade shock as a result of the drop in iron ore prices on the world market. Accordingly, there was no progress in reducing the national debt burden. *Economic growth* slowed and the IMF estimated GDP growth to be around 2%, down from 6.6% in 2014. Consumer price inflation was expected to rise to an annual average of 4.4%.

The PRSP ended in 2015. The government was determined to design a new programme and was particularly committed to achieving *fiscal stability*. The 'Banque Centrale de Mauritanie' continued to manage a flexible exchange-rate regime in order to enhance the competiveness of the export sector. The main infrastructure projects were focused on overland electricity lines, a water supply system and a new airport, as well as highway construction.

Organisations representing formal sectors of the economy had the capacity to mobilise members and engage with the state. This was demonstrated by *strikes*, including large-scale strikes at the plants of the 'Société Nationale Industrielle et Minière' in Zouerate and Nouadhibou during the period January–March, including general strikes on 30 January and 3 March. The employees demanded a wage increase that had been promised in 2014. An agreement was reached on 2 April.

On 1 June, the US-based Kosmos Energy chief executive, Andrew Inglis, announced a major *gas* discovery in the deep offshore area, close to Senegalese waters. This was good news, especially since Ireland's Tullow revealed in January that it would scale back its exploration activity in the Banda gas field, and the only producing *oilfield*, Chinguetti, had seen production drop. On 24 November, President Aziz opened the country's first wind energy plant in Nouakchott. The overall cost of the project was estimated at $ 51 m and it was co-funded by the Arab Fund for Economic and Social Development.

On 10 July, a new, four-year protocol to the *Fisheries Partnership Agreement* with the EU was initialled and provisionally applied on 16 November. Annual compensation from the EU was limited to € 100 m ($ 114.5 m) per year, and the ceiling on fishing was set at 225,000 tonnes/year. This programme was designed both to protect local fish and to maximise fishing revenue. It was also expected to increase the European fishing companies' interest in investing in local processing arrangements and in training or recruiting more local staff. The agreement required 60% of fishing crews on EU boats to be Mauritanian. A longer-term agreement was also expected to create more stability and avoid the previous almost continuous negotiation of two-year agreements. Fishing cooperation with China continued to play an important role. Three Chinese high-seas fishing companies were engaged in fishing product processing: China National Fisheries Corporation, Shanghai Fisheries General Corp. (Group) and Fuzhou Hongdong Pelagic Fishery Corporation.

With almost half of the population living in conditions of extreme poverty, environment changes presented a major threat to the livelihoods of many people. The unpredictable weather conditions continued to mean that agricultural production was impossible to predict. The Integrated Food Security Phase Classification estimated that 1.3 m people were facing *food insecurity*. Of these, nearly half a million were expected to fall into severe food insecurity and be unable to meet their food needs without external assistance. Around 21,000 were estimated to be suffering extreme food insecurity, or the near complete loss of their livelihoods. The shortage of funding led to 50,000 Malian refugees receiving reduced food rations, which at times met only about half their nutritional needs, after WFP cut rice rations by more than half in June, from 12 kg to 5.4 kg.

In November, international media reported that a growing number of Syrian *refugees* were trying to escape to Europe via Mauritania. The new escape route included a flight from Syria to Mauritania (3,000 miles) and a subsequent overland trip on the ancient salt roads from Mali through the Sahara. Around 300–500 Syrian refugees and asylum seekers were estimated to be living in Mauritania, and around one in ten of them had tried to cross into Mali and head for Europe, according to the Mauritania representative for the UNHCR, Sebastien Laroze. Mauritania was one of the few countries where Syrians could arrive without visas after Algeria imposed visa restrictions early in the year.

Efforts to strengthen the *business environment* led to some success following liberalisation policies. In the World Bank's 2016 Doing Business report, Mauritania moved up eight places, to 168th (out of 189 countries). The *tourism* sector continued to suffer heavily from the fragile security situation. Most Western countries advised visitors against all travel to several provinces and against all but essential travel to the rest of the country, including the Nouakchott-Nouadhibou corridor, and to avoid all demonstrations.

Niger

Klaas van Walraven

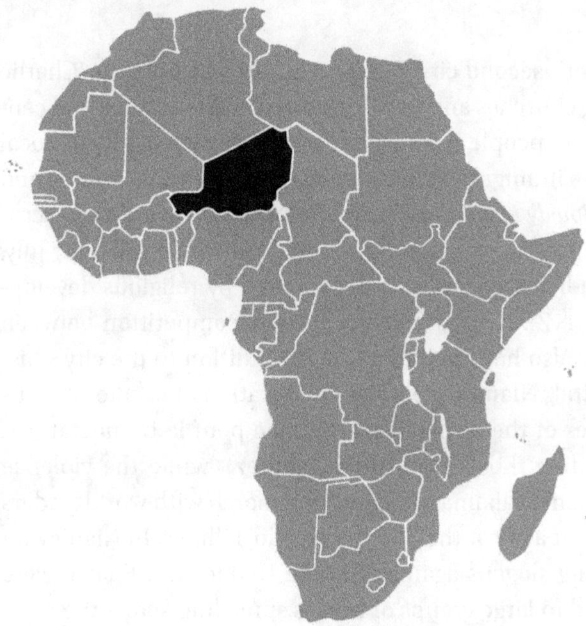

The capital Niamey was struck by religiously inspired violence. Riots started in the central-eastern cities of Zinder and Maradi in protest against a cartoon of the Prophet Muhammad in the French magazine 'Charlie Hebdo' after Islamist gunmen killed cartoonists in Paris. Christian churches, bars and other establishments owned by non-Muslims were the targets of attack. Not necessarily related to this, the war against Boko Haram in the south-east began in earnest, marked by a spate of attacks, killings and counter-guerrilla operations. The flow of refugees and IDPs grew to record levels, leading to a serious humanitarian crisis in the south-east. Tension between the government and opposition mounted ahead of the 2016 presidential and legislative polls. The main opposition candidate for the presidency, Hama Amadou, who had fled to France in 2014 after being charged with involvement in a baby-trafficking scandal, returned to Niger in November to prepare for his campaign. He was immediately detained. With political temperatures rising and the country facing mounting security threats, media freedom came under pressure. The rough evacuation of civilians from Boko Haram operation zones worsened the picture. Towards year's end high-ranking army officers were arrested, accused of plotting to overthrow the government. Food security was precarious owing to

 | DOI 10.1163/9789004333239_016

the previous year's poor harvests and compounded in the south-east by the Boko Haram crisis. GDP growth declined because of depressed uranium and oil prices.

Domestic Politics

On 16 January, rioters in Niger's second city, Zinder, protested against the 'Charlie Hebdo' cartoons by pillaging churches and burning down the French cultural centre. In the ensuing violence, 45 people were wounded and five were killed. Local Christians (often West African immigrants) found shelter in a military barracks and Protestant church. The *religiously inspired violence* showed that government scrutiny of imams had not prevented the emergence of jihadi Salafi beliefs: on 17 July, the violence spread to Maradi, a city traditionally affected by religious developments in Northern Nigeria. In Zinder, however, economic competition between Christians and Muslims may also have played a role, in addition to the city's historical rivalry with the capital, Niamey. Political connotations became obvious through attacks on the offices of the ruling 'Parti Nigérien pour la Démocratie et le Socialisme' (PNDS) (including those in northern Agadez), while the violence erupted in the wake of President Mahamadou Issoufou's march with world leaders in Paris on 11 January to protest against the 'Charlie Hebdo' killings. In Niamey on 17 January, protesters shouting slogans against 'Charlie Hebdo' and France were dispersed by tear gas. This led to large groups of rioters spreading across the capital, destroying dozens of churches, hotels, drinking establishments, an orphanage and a Christian school, and companies owned by French people or West African immigrants. Security forces managed to protect Niamey's Catholic cathedral, but five people were killed and more than 120 were injured. The government declared three days of national mourning.

Although President Issoufou emphasised that he had participated in the Paris march to protest against terrorism while in no way approving of 'Charlie Hebdo', the damage had been done. The *riots' political significance* became clearer on 18 January. The coalition of opposition parties, the 'Alliance pour la Réconciliation, la Démocratie et la République' (ARDR), refused to cancel a meeting already scheduled to protest against the government's record but now the authorities (Ministry of the Interior) banned the meeting. Ninety people were arrested, among them several opposition representatives. The leader of the 'Convention Démocratique et Sociale', Mahamane Ousmane, accused the president of using the opposition as scapegoat to divert attention from his own mistakes. Thus, Issoufou's aspiration to play a more visible role in the international fight against terrorism may have led him to underestimate the fallout of participating in the Paris march. However, frustrations over the effectiveness of Issoufou's divide-and-rule tactics also encouraged opposition forces to take more to the streets and use anti-system rhetoric.

With the 2016 elections looming, *political tension worsened*. The main opposition, the 'Mouvement National pour la Société de Développement' (MNSD) of Seini Oumarou, and the third party in the country, the 'Mouvement Démocratique Nigérien' (Moden-Lumana) led by Hama Amadou, risked implosion. In January, Interior Minister Hassoumi Massaoudou validated one of two rival MNSD congresses, which had been held the previous November. His decision played into the hands of MNSD Secretary-General Albadé Abouba, who also held the post of presidential adviser. After the January riots, the opposition ended its dialogue with the government, while the administration accused the opposition of prior knowledge of the violence. On 6 June, thousands of youths took to the streets of Niamey and called for the fall of the government. Political debate was extremely bitter, although this in itself indicated the vibrancy of Niger's political culture. However, on 19 August, NGO platform 'Alternative Espace Citoyen' called on all major political actors to engage in dialogue. In September, the UN expressed concern about the political climate. On 17 August, 30 parties, unions and civil society groups established a joint opposition alliance, the 'Front Patriotique Républicain'. It accused the Constitutional Court of presidential bias, calling for its dissolution. In its legally required review of presidential candidates, the Court had published negative statements about several opposition contenders.

Electoral procedures became an arena for altercations between the opposition and the government. On 4 June, a three-week registration process for the electoral register began. On 1 November, after rumours of lost registration records circulated in the media, thousands of people joined a march in Niamey to call for the exercise to be repeated. The electoral calendar fixed by the independent Electoral Commission (whose composition was contested) was also criticised. On 30 July, the first round of the presidential polls was scheduled to take place on 21 February 2016, simultaneously with the legislative elections. The presidential run-off (if necessary) was scheduled for 20 March 2016. Municipal elections were set to take place on 9 May 2016 – a change from previous practice when municipal elections were held before the national elections. While government and opposition agreed on 12 December on an audit of the electoral register, the latter withdrew from the exercise three days later. The threat of an opposition boycott hung in the air and the government accused the opposition of bad faith.

President Issoufou praised his *government record* extensively. He boasted of his efforts in the field of education and claimed that he had succeeded with his agricultural improvement programme. Infrastructural prestige projects such as the start of construction of the Niamey-Parakou railway were seen as electoral vote winners. On 25 February, Issoufou appointed Foreign Minister Mohamed Bazoum as minister of state at the Presidency to oversee his re-election campaign. Bazoum was succeeded at the Foreign Ministry by Aïchatou Kané Boulama, governor of the Niamey region.

On 7 November, the PNDS announced Issoufou's candidature. Hama Amadou was nominated for Moden-Lumana on 13 September at a conference in Zinder, but when he returned from France on 14 November he was detained over a 2014 baby-trafficking scandal. This did not stop Amadou, the political tycoon and king-maker (of Mahamadou Issoufou, among others) from continuing to exercise influence. Amadou won one legal battle when on 30 January a court in Niamey threw out the charges against those involved in the baby-trafficking case on the grounds that the parentage of the children concerned was unclear. Amadou maintained that the case was politically motivated. In July, an appeals court reversed the previous judgment, deciding that the case could go to trial. Towards the end of the year, Amadou was denied bail on procedural grounds. The administration's efforts to hinder Issoufou's *presidential rivals* by any means, including incongruous efforts that betrayed the authoritarian reflexes of Nigérien politics, provoked the opposition's anger. On 7 November, the supporters of CDS leader Mahamane Ousmane fought police in Zinder to protest against the banning of a CDS congress that was planning to nominate Ousmane as its presidential candidate. Like the MNSD, the CDS split into pro- and anti-government wings. Ousmane was confronted with a rival for the CDS candidacy, Abdou Labo, who was close to the government but ironically also tainted by the baby-trafficking scandal. While much of this infighting took place by way of court action (a testimony to the judiciary's relative independence), Ousmane launched his own party towards the end of the year to safeguard his presidential bid. Former minister Amadou Boubacar Cissé withdrew his party from the presidential coalition and announced his own candidacy at the end of October. The government retaliated by questioning him when he submitted the paperwork required for his candidacy. MNSD chair Seini Oumarou only had his candidacy secured when the appeals court of Niamey confirmed the legitimacy of his leadership and had the faction of Secretary-General Albadé Abouba expelled – Abouba set up his own movement.

All these developments left the opposition heavily fragmented, which made an Issoufou victory likely. On 13–14 December, the PNDS headquarters were struck by gunfire. The PNDS blamed the attack on the opposition ARDR. However, in the wake of this attack the administration arrested several high-ranking military officers, accusing them of a *coup attempt*. Most details on this had not become known by year's end.

The government's authoritarian reflexes were especially felt by representatives of civil society and the media. On 18 May, the director of 'Alternative Espace Citoyen', Moussa Tchangari, was arrested on charges of having links with Boko Haram. Tchangari had criticised the evacuation of residents of the Lake Chad region in the wake of an attack by insurgents, leaving thousands of people without support or shelter. On 27 May, Tchangari was released but the charges of endangering national security were maintained. Around this time, another activist, Nouhou Arzika, was also detained on similar charges (having revealed that soldiers were complaining of a lack of equipment in the struggle against Boko Haram). The state *human rights* commission denounced what it presented as a wave of arbitrary detentions in the context of the war against Boko Haram, claiming that some individuals had been tortured. The government played down the issue but circles around the president admitted that Interior Minister Hassoumi Massaoudou had played things rough. Overall, Niger still scored fairly well in terms of civil liberties, reflecting the vibrancy of its civil society.

The *Boko Haram war* began in earnest. On 3 January, insurgents staged a bloody attack on the Nigerian town of Baga on Lake Chad (the last stronghold of the Nigerian army in the state of Borno). Chadian and Nigérien army troops, which had helped defend the town, withdrew, dissatisfied with Nigeria's military commitment. However, in a video message Boko Haram also threatened Niger and in a renewed offensive its forces began to encroach on the country's borders. Numerous young Nigériens had recently been recruited to the movement's ranks, attracted by the promise of financial gain. The authorities mobilised thousands of soldiers, gendarmes and intelligence operatives to reinforce security. On 6 February, Boko Haram attacked the town of Bosso on Lake Chad, leading to fierce fighting with Niger's military, who reported more than 100 insurgents killed. A few days later a *suicide attack* took place in the market of the provincial capital Diffa, causing at least six deaths and numerous injuries; that same day, Boko Haram fighters attacked the convoy of Niger's defence minister. On 9 February, insurgents attacked Diffa prison. Government forces repelled the assault. That same day the National Assembly approved the dispatch of troops back into Nigeria and the next day, a two-week state of emergency was imposed.

As Chadian forces came to the rescue, thousands of civilians began to leave the Diffa region for Zinder. On 17 February, unidentified fighter planes appeared over the village of Abadam, which straddles the border with Nigeria. One dropped bombs on the Nigérien side of the village, hitting a funeral procession and *killing 37 mourners*. Nigeria denied responsibility and Chad declined to comment; both countries had jet fighters active in the region (locals claimed to have seen Nigerian colours on the planes). On 18 February, the Nigérien army clashed with Boko Haram on an island in Lake Chad; 23 people were reported dead. At least 19 civilians were killed in an attack on three islands on 1 March, with many victims burnt alive. By then the authorities had reported 24 casualties among police and the military besides more than 500 on the side of Boko Haram, with another 200 of its fighters detained. This was partly the result of the Nigerian army's renewed efforts to win back territory. On 8 March, Niger and Chad launched major air and ground strikes inside Nigeria. Their troops recaptured the village of Damasak and nearby Malam Fatori, seizing large quantities of weapons and detaining dozens of insurgents. Between 200 and 300 Boko Haram fighters were reported killed, in addition to 19 Chadian soldiers and five Nigériens. Independent verification was impossible. With Chadian forces redirecting operations towards Cameroon, Boko Haram attempted to infiltrate back into Niger near Bosso on 30 March. Their forces were pushed back by Nigérien and Chadian troops. Locals spoke of intense aerial operations.

On 25 April, Niger's army suffered its *worst losses* when insurgents attacked a poorly equipped military post on Karamga, an isolated island in Lake Chad: 74 people were killed including 46 military personnel, and more than 30 soldiers went missing, while 156 insurgents, who came to Karamga in motorised canoes, were reported killed. The government ordered the population on the islands (more than 25,000 people) to leave for the mainland, abandoning them to their fate in makeshift camps. On 13 May, village chiefs who remained behind were arrested and accused of lack of cooperation with the authorities. Towards the end of May, the state of emergency in the Diffa region was extended for a further three months. This included a ban on the use of motorbikes (a favourite means of transport for Boko Haram), while women were prohibited from wearing burqas, which were used by suicide bombers.

Later in June, Chad's air force carried out attacks on Nigérien territory in retaliation for Boko Haram bombings in its capital N'Djaména. On 24 June, the Nigérien government reported that it had killed 15 insurgents and captured 20 while destroying motorbikes and an armoured vehicle. The operation came in the wake of a Boko Haram attack near Gueskérou, which led to the death of 38 civilians, including several women and children. On 11 July, *insurgents packed with explosives* again attacked Diffa prison and, on the 15th, in the wake of a Chadian-Nigérien troop withdrawal from the Nigerian town of Damasak, insurgents killed 15 villagers near Bosso, after which the Nigérien military pursued and killed some 30 attackers and destroyed numerous motorbikes. In an attack on the village of Dagaya, militants slit the throats of five civilians. August saw a relative lull in the fighting.

By September, the authorities were reporting that more than 1,000 suspected militants had been detained, but 6,000 villagers fled after an attack on Ngourtoua at the end of the month. On 1 October, insurgents killed two government soldiers near the border village of Baroua; in the ensuing fighting, which lasted five hours, an army vehicle was destroyed. On 4 October, two suicide attacks on a military camp and mosque in Diffa left five civilians, one policeman and the four insurgents dead. On 20 October, two soldiers were killed in a suicide attack on Boulongori, near Diffa. Four insurgents were killed and a number detained after an entire night of fighting. Despite the imposition of a new two-week state of emergency on 14 October, another attack took place on 27 October on the village of Ala, where militants killed 13 people and wounded three. Vehicles, houses and shops were burnt. In a major *counter-insurgency operation* in early November, army troops arrested 20 militants after a soldier had been killed by a remotely-controlled bomb near Lake Chad. On 11 November, some 25 civilians were killed in an attack on a village in the Bosso district; 20 militants were reported killed by the military.

The hostilities, unprecedented in the region, led to a *severe humanitarian crisis*. With some 100,000 Nigerians present in the Diffa region, pressure on food supplies increased. The government issued an appeal for international relief, while UNHCR set up camps to cope with the influx. In the course of the February hostilities, 50,000 IDPs made their way to Zinder. In June, the EU announced that it would provide € 21 m in aid to more than 1.7 m people in the Diffa region. By November, 200,000 people, a third of the region's population, had become displaced. WFP hoped to be able to distribute food to over 120,000 people in the course of the year.

Foreign Affairs

Niger's foreign policy agenda was dominated by the fight against Islamist terrorism – in both the Saharan region and the Lake Chad area. As a consequence, the traditional ties with *France* remained good. President Hollande visited Niamey on 18 July in the course of a West African tour. While he called on African leaders to respect constitutional term limits, France remained reluctant to criticise the authoritarian reflexes of Niger's government. When President Issoufou met his French colleague at a breakfast meeting in Paris on 2 June, they focused on the situation in Libya and Mali and the war against Boko Haram. Relations with the *United States* were driven by similar dynamics. Deputy Secretary of State Antony Blinken visited Niamey on 9 July. In October the Americans donated two military aircraft and some 30 military vehicles to improve border surveillance.

Relations with *Chad* were marked by close cooperation in the struggle against Boko Haram, while ties with *Nigeria* improved following the arrival of Muhammadu Buhari in power on 29 May. As a northerner, Buhari appeared to be committed to ending the insurgency. Following his inauguration, Buhari visited the capitals of neighbouring countries for talks and came to Niamey on 3–4 June.

On 20 January, Niger received delegates from some 20 countries to discuss the establishment of a multinational military force. On 9 February, the AU facilitated a meeting in the Cameroonian capital Yaoundé to encourage the formation of a regional force projected to number 8,700 troops. The CBLT-inspired taskforce was now set to start at the end of March. Two weeks earlier, the chiefs of defence staff of Niger, Nigeria and Chad had met for talks in Abuja (Nigeria) and decided to establish a Joint Operations Headquarters. Follow-up talks in Abuja on 9–11 June, which were also attended by Cameroon and Benin, ended in formal agreement to establish what was called the Multi-National Joint Task Force (MNJTF). The MNJTF would replace the current ad hoc arrangement and would be led by a Nigerian, with a Cameroonian as second-in-command; headquarters were projected to be in N'Djaména.

Socioeconomic Developments

Growth was expected to fall to 4.3% as a result of the poor 2014 harvest and declining oil and uranium prices. The *budget* came under pressure from rising expenditure on defence and increased spending related to the 2016 elections. On 25 May, the National Assembly increased expenditure to CFAfr 732.4 bn. Some 60% of spending was earmarked for public investment projects (which carried electoral significance for President Issoufou).

The *rains* started late but led to floods that affected at least 20,000 people; more than 2,000 homes were destroyed. *Cereal harvests* were mixed, with an overall deficiency expected to lead to food insecurity for at least 2.8 m people (15.7% of the population), particularly in the war-torn south-east.

French *uranium* conglomerate Areva announced that it had suffered a total of € 4.8 bn in losses in 2014. Difficulties with projects in other parts of the world and depressed uranium prices were to blame. As a result, it was decided to discontinue development of the huge mine of Imouraren. Only 40 of the 225 people employed at the site would be retained. In another development, workers at Areva's Somaïr mine in Arlit staged a strike on 7–9 April in protest against the non-payment of bonuses earned in 2014. The other northern city, Agadez, benefited increasingly from *illegal migration*. Many West Africans en route to North Africa stayed temporarily in the town, whose income from tourism had plummeted in recent years as a result of growing insecurity. On 11 May, the National Assembly criminalised human trafficking, to which police and customs officials habitually turn a blind eye in exchange for bribes.

Oil production at the refinery in Zinder was hindered by labour disputes, mechanical failures and arguments with the state petroleum company SONIDEP over price controls. Cheap black market oil imports from Nigeria also undermined Niger's production for the domestic market. The production of *butane gas* increased, stimulated by government consumer subsidies in efforts to fight deforestation. Production now reached 44,000 tonnes a year. Wooded areas in the south of the country had been reduced by a third in the previous 25 years. Funding for the opencast *coal* mine and power plant in the Tahoua region was completed; it would help reduce dependence on power imports from Nigeria.

China signed two accords with Niger on 26 August involving grants and loans worth CFAfr 13.5 bn and CFAfr 9 bn, respectively. This should, amongst other things, allow Chinese construction of a third bridge in Niamey across the River Niger. China was now Niger's principal trading partner, ahead of France. Chinese investments totalled some $ 4.7 bn and Niger boasted some 30 Chinese companies, providing employment to some 6,000 people.

In mid-August, the conventions for the construction of the Niamey-Parakou railway were signed with French conglomerate Bolloré, which would finance the costs in return for 40% of the shares in the operating company, BENI Rail (the states of

Niger and Benin would take 10% each, the rest going to private investors from both countries). The railway would link the capital with the port of Cotonou in Benin and would be used primarily for freight. In the course of the year, construction on the long-awaited project began.

A meningitis *epidemic* struck in seven of the eight regions. The west, including the capital, was particularly affected. The vaccination campaign was hindered by shortages (over half of the 1.2 m doses required were available) and by the fact that the outbreak, not uncommon in Niger, involved a rare strain of the disease. By May, the government had recorded more than 6,600 cases, with a death toll of 443.

Nigeria

Heinrich Bergstresser

The March and April elections at the federal and state level dominated the political scene. For the first time in Nigeria's history, a sitting president was voted out of office. Muhammadu Buhari won decisively and was given a strong political mandate. An improved election commission conducted the most credible elections yet in Nigeria's history, although it had initially appeared that the postponement of the elections would derail the whole election process with unforeseeable repercussions. However, at the end of the day, the political class and the vast majority of the elites demonstrated their willingness and ability to stabilise the Fourth Republic. The new government intensified the fight against the Islamist insurgency in the North-East, which improved the security situation as a whole. However, Buhari faced economic challenges amplified by plummeting oil and gas prices.

Domestic Politics

The most prominent issues were the *general elections*, scheduled for 14 February (presidential and National Assembly), 28 February (gubernatorial and state assemblies), and the ongoing threat of Boko Haram. At the beginning of the year, all eyes

 | DOI 10.1163/9789004333239_017

were on the elections, in which the incumbent President Goodluck Jonathan, a Christian from the Niger Delta, and the former military dictator and three-time presidential candidate Muhammadu Buhari battled for the presidency, a repeat of the previous election in 2011. While Jonathan, of the ruling People's Democratic Party (PDP), kept his vice president, Namadi Sambo, a Muslim from the North as running mate, Buhari, of the All Progressives Congress (APC), named former Lagos state attorney general, Yemi Osinbajo, a Christian from the South-West. The other 12 aspirants and their respective running mates played little to no role in the outcome

At the start of the year, logistical and technical problems within the *Independent National Electoral Commission* (INEC), along with the ongoing Islamic insurgency in the North, meant that only two-thirds of the 67.4 m registered voters had collected their 'Permanent Voters' Cards' (PVCS). Accordingly, the INEC extended the collection deadline until 8 February. At this point, doubts were raised as to whether the elections would take place at all, given the undercurrent of political change in favour of Buhari. However, the ability of the APC to seal a strong alliance between the North-West and South-West, which Nigeria had last seen on the eve of the civil war, presented Jonathan with an insuperable challenge, despite the fact that the presidency and the PDP had a level of resources no other candidate could hope to match. In fact, the credibility of Jonathan and the PDP had already reached a nadir from which they never really recovered. Moreover, the APC was able to demonstrate unity and stayed away from any provocative language during the election campaign.

On 22 January, at Chatham House in London, Sambo Dasuki, the national security adviser, insinuated that elections would not take place as scheduled. This was the prelude to similar indications by the security agencies, who were about to commence a six-week special campaign against the Islamist insurgents in the North-East and would not be available to support the planned elections. Thus, on 7 February, the well respected INEC chairman, Attahiru Jega, announced that *the polls* would be shifted to 28 March (presidential and National Assembly), and 11 April (gubernatorial and state assemblies). Although the elections were delayed, they still met the constitutional deadline.

Soon afterwards, the two main presidential contenders accepted the postponement and the incumbent pledged that the new president would be sworn in on 29 May, the day that marks the beginning of a new presidential term. In addition, the INEC extended the deadline for collecting the PVCS to 8 March and almost 80% of the registered voters eventually collected their cards. The uneven distribution pattern, however, indicated a comfortable lead of the North over the South, which was to a large extent related to the fact that many former pro-Jonathan voters, particularly from the Igbo heartland in the South-East, abstained from the election process. In the final analysis, this paved the way for Buhari to win by a clear margin. These issues notwithstanding, there was much uncertainty in the days and weeks that followed, as to whether the INEC could withstand the mounting pressure from influential inner government and security circles. The card reader issue in particular became a serious bone of contention since the *biometric machines* had been put in place in order to prevent and reducing electoral malpractice. Furthermore, the INEC had selected top personnel from tertiary institutions as returning officers. Against this background and the general political climate for change, it emerged that forces close to the government had advocated either a postponement or an indefinite delay of the elections.

Finally, the *INEC's determination* prevailed, with the support of the business community and well known tycoons such as Aliko Dangote, the international community and a broad alliance of civil society groups such as the Nigerian Civil Society Situation Room. The latter mobilised people to cast their vote and closely monitored events.

The presidential and National Assembly elections on 28 March, in which 31.7 m accredited voters eventually took part, was well covered by the media and it soon became clear that the expected change was in the offing. On 31 March, hours before the official announcement of the results, *Jonathan conceded defeat*, thereby confirming that the electorate, for the first time in Nigeria's history, had voted out a sitting head of state. Buhari polled closed to 54% (28.6 m votes) and won by a large margin of almost 2.6 m. Consequently, on 1 April, the INEC declared Buhari the winner. Buhari immediately accepted the mandate.

The results for the bicameral National Assembly resembled the results from the presidential elections. The APC won a landslide victory, securing an absolute majority in both the 109-member Senate and the 360-member House of Representatives.

A fortnight later, on 11 April, the PDP suffered another humiliating defeat in the gubernatorial and state assembly elections. While state assembly elections were held in all 36 states, only 29 gubernatorial mandates were contested because the tenure of seven sitting governors had not yet expired. Nineteen APC front runners triumphed, while the PDP won nine states, all but two (Gombe and Taraba) in the South. In some rare cases such as in Imo, Taraba and Abia states, results were inconclusive and supplementary elections were to be held two weeks later. The outcome of the elections was a *sharpened North-South divide*, which shaped the political landscape.

Most observers saw the poll as the most credible in Nigerian history, despite some shortcomings and lapses with regard to card readers and logistics. There were also some *violence*, in the form of election-related killings and isolated bomb blasts, various forms of aggression, arson and hijacking of election materials in a number of states. Such incidents occurred mainly during state elections. Moreover, the PDP did not challenge Buhari's victory in court, which, together with Jonathan's attitude towards the defeat, might indicate a constructive change in the political culture, at least in the medium term.

Nevertheless, 680 results, most of them for parliamentary seats, were challenged at *election tribunals* and in the courts, although these cases were for the most part dismissed. In Rivers state, the tribunal annulled the outcome of the gubernatorial election that saw Nyesom Wike of the PDP victorious, a ruling that was upheld by the Court of Appeal on 16 December. In Taraba, however, the election tribunal's verdict of 7–8 November in favour of the defeated APC candidate, Ms Aisha Alhassan, led to a violent clash between supporters of the two parties, leaving at least 12 people dead. On 31 December, the November verdict was repealed in favour of the PDP candidate Darius Ishaku. Ms Alhassan vowed to appeal. On 3 November, the Abia state tribunal had dismissed the petition by the All Progressives Grand Alliance (APGA) candidate, Alex Otti, challenging the INEC's decision to declare the PDP candidate Okezie Ikpeazu the winner. On 31 December, however, the Court of Appeal rejected the supposed winner and directed the INEC to make arrangements for Otti's swearing in. Shortly before, on 18 December, a court nullified the election of PDP Governor Udom Emmanuel of Akwa Ibom state and ordered a re-run within 90 days. At the end of the year, the controversial verdicts on these four gubernatorial election results, together with other less disputed cases, were still pending at the Supreme Court.

The gubernatorial election in Kogi state, not due until 21 November, became a focal point of *legal wrangling* after the ballot was declared inconclusive and the APC candidate, Abubakar Audu, who was on the verge of winning against the sitting PDP governor, Idris Wada, died before the final result could be announced. In a disputed process, Yahaya Bello, the runner-up in the APC primaries, eventually replaced the deceased and, following supplementary elections on 5 December, was declared governor elect.

In Bayelsa state, the ballot on 5 December was marred by *malpractices and violence* and was eventually cancelled in southern Ijaw. Accordingly, the INEC fixed supplementary elections in the affected areas to take place on 9 January 2016. The incumbent, Seriake Dickson, had a clear lead and was widely expected to win.

With only hours to go before the end of his tenure, the outgoing president signed six bills into law, among them the Tobacco Control Bill, and issued 72 radio licences to dubious clients. However, he refused to sign the adopted constitutional amendments titled 'Fourth Alteration Act 2015'. A *silent power struggle* between the outgoing executive and the legislature over sensitive clauses relating to a reduction in the power of the executive had been going on since 2010, and was eventually brought before the Supreme Court. Legal experts, backed by a Federal High Court, had originally insisted that amendments passed by the National Assembly and backed by the necessary majority of at least two-thirds of all the 36 state assemblies must be signed by the president. The then president abided by the contentious verdict and in early 2011 put the first constitutional amendments into force. The National Assembly rejected this argument and the issue was left pending for years.

Against the backdrop of an imminent change of government, the court suggested defusing some clauses, particularly that concerning the presidential power to put constitutional amendments into force. However, given the fact that the

Constitution offers no clear guidance, the court was reluctant to take a final decision on such a fundamental issue. Eventually, on 26 May, both sides agreed on minor constitutional amendments such as a pension for life for the National Assembly's leadership, the admission of independent candidates, reformed citizenship, the president's annual state of the nation address and a simplified process to deregister political parties, which Jonathan vowed to sign into law. He ignored the agreement, however, and the whole alteration process collapsed.

Buhari was sworn in on 29 May. After the inauguration of the 8th legislative period on 9 June, the overwhelming APC majority in the House of Representatives elected the APC members Yakubu Dogara from Bauchi State and Yusuf Lasun from Osun state as speaker, and deputy speaker, respectively. One month later, and after a lot of political wrangling, on 9 July, APC-senator Olubukola Saraki from Niger state emerged as senate president, while PDP-senator Ike Ekweremadu from Enugu state was somewhat surprisingly returned as his deputy. Interestingly, the *distribution of power* among the top three positions in the Nigerian political system was not balanced between the six geo-political zones, since it excluded the South-South from where Jonathan originates.

In successive steps between his inauguration and the forming of a cabinet in November, Buhari dissolved almost all federal parastatals and agencies and appointed new personnel. In addition, he immediately made appointments to *key positions within the presidency*, including the then president of the Nigerian guild of editors, Femi Adesina, as chief spokesman (30 May), Alhaji Ahmed Idris as the new accountant general of the federation (25 June) and Ms Amina Bala Zakari as acting chair of the INEC following the departure of Attahiru Jega, whose five-year term expired on 30 June. Later in the year, however, on 21 October, Ms Zakari was replaced by Mahmood Yakubu and appointed as INEC commissioner, representing the North-West. Lawal Musa Daura was named as the new director general of the Department of State Security (DSS; also known as the State Security Service: SSS) on 2 July, retired Major General Babagana Monguno was appointed national security adviser and retired Brigadier P.T. Boroh became the coordinator of the amnesty programme for former militants in the Niger Delta. In August, further important appointments were made, such as that of Emmanuel Ibe Kachikwu as head of the Nigerian National Petroleum Corporation (NNPC), Babachir David Lawal as secretary to the government of the federation and Alhaji Abba Kyari as the president's chief of staff.

More than five months after his inauguration, on 11 November, the president presented his *cabinet*. The number of ministries had been reduced from 29 to 24 and, in a deft move, security and law related portfolios were given to the crisis-shaken North, while key positions concerning finance and the economy were handed over to appointees from the economically better off South, in particular from the South-West. Two retired high-ranking military officers, Mansur Maman Dan Ali and Abdulrahman Bello Dambazau, emerged as defence minister and minister of the interior, respectively, the latter including authority over the police force, while Abubakar Malami took over at the Ministry of Justice. Ms Kemi Adeosun was appointed minister of finance, former Lagos governor Babatunde Raji Fashola was given the Ministry of Power and Infrastructure, another former governor, Rotimi Amaechi from Rivers state, was named minister of transportation, and Udoma Udo Udoma minister for budget and national planning. As expected, the president kept the decisive Petroleum Ministry – a repeat of Olusegun Obasanjo's approach during his incumbency – but called on the head of the NNPC, Kachikwu, to oversee the ministry's day-to-day business. In addition, Buhari approved the appointment of 18 new permanent secretaries in the federal civil service, some of whom were recruited from private sector fields such as banking and engineering.

Against the backdrop of the still *precarious security situation*, Buhari enforced wide-ranging changes within the military. Immediately after his inauguration, he directed the army to move its 'central command and control centre' to the Borno state capital Maiduguri, a move in which he hoped to consolidate 'Operation Zaman Lafiya' previously known as 'Operation Lafiya Dole'. This operation – the fight against Boko Haram - was placed under a unified command structure coordinating GOC 3 and 7 Divisions.

In a sweeping shake-up on 13 July, all service chiefs were retired and replaced. Major General Abayomi Gabriel Olonishakin became chief of defence staff, Lieutenant General Tukur Yusuf Buratai emerged as army chief of staff, Rear Admiral Ibok-Ete Ekwe Ibas was promoted to navy chief of staff, and Air Vice-Marshal Sadique Abubakar became air force chief of staff. Air Vice-Marshal Monday Riku Morgan took over the position of defence intelligence chief. On 4 August, the senate confirmed these appointments. Prior to that, on 31 July, the new army chief of staff had handed over command of the Multinational Joint Task Force (MNJTF) to Major General Iliyasu Isah Abbah.

At the end of July, more than 300 army officers of the upper echelons, including some *General Officers Commanding* (GOC), were redeployed. Major General Adeniyi Oyebade became commander of the GOC 1 Division. Major General L.C. Ilo took over the GOC 2 Mechanized Division, and Major General Hassan Umaru emerged as commander of the GOC 3 Armoured Division. Less than six months later, on 18 December, Umaru replaced Major General Yusha'u Mahmood Abubakar, appointed in August, as commander of 'Operation Zaman Lafiya'; Brigadier M.S.A. Aliyu took over GOC 3. However, Major General I.H. Edet was appointed commander of the GOC 81 Amphibious Division, while Major General Ibrahim Attahiru became the new head of the GOC 82 Airborne Division. Only Major General Lamidi Adeosun, appointed in January by the previous government, was kept on as commander of the GOC 7 Infantry Division, garrisoned in Maiduguri. A few weeks later, in early September, the air force and the navy also undertook a major shake-up, redeploying most of their senior officers.

In addition to the shake-up and redeployment, president Buhari and his government inherited a number of *serious military problems*. For instance, on 16 January, more than 200 soldiers of the GOC 3 Armoured Division had protested against their dismissal a few days earlier. Shortly thereafter, on 22 January, 22 officers were court-martialled in Lagos, among them Brigadier J.O. Komolafe and 14 colonels, for alleged cowardice and desertion. In Abuja, on 11 March, another batch of 30 officers, including another brigadier, Enitan Ransome-Kuti, a member of the famous Kuti-family in Yorubaland, suffered the same fate, being held responsible for failing to repel terrorists who had attacked the headquarters of the MNJTF in Baga at Lake Chad in January. Later in the year, on 15 October, it emerged that the first count of 'cowardly behaviour' against Ransome-Kuti was struck out and he was given a six-month prison term and dishonourably discharged from the army for neglecting his military duties.

On 20 May, the Nigerian army disclosed that about 579 officers and soldiers were facing *general court martial* in Lagos and Abuja for various offences such as insubordination, cowardice, refusal to carry out orders and indiscipline. In addition, it was reported that hundreds of rank and file soldiers had been dismissed. On 22 May, the soldiers, sentenced to death in December 2014 for alleged mutiny, filed a suit before a civil court in Abuja to prevent the army from executing them. In July, another group of sacked soldiers hauled the army before the National Industrial Court to seek redress. On 2 August, the new chief of army staff ordered a legal review of all court martial verdicts and, on 3 September, the army confirmed the pardon and reinstatement of more than 3,000 of some 5,000 convicted soldiers. In addition, on 19 December, all death sentences were commuted to ten year' imprisonment, a decision that could still be challenged in a civil court. Earlier, on 21 September, 5,000 soldiers fighting Boko Haram were promoted in a measure aimed at boosting their morale. Previously, around mid-year, it was reported that the challenges of the Islamist insurgency and conflict within the army had led to the re-engagement of retired officers to serve as consultants and instructors at the artillery school in Kachia, Kaduna state. At year's end, it transpired that within 12 months the army was intending to raise another division in the North-East.

The *police forces* also underwent major changes. Much to the surprise of the public, the then president Jonathan, on 21 April, sacked the inspector general of police, Suleiman Abba, whom he had appointed only in August 2014. Hailing from the North, Abba had allegedly acted in bad faith in the run-up to the state elections in Rivers state by ignoring an order from the presidency to recall the deployed assistant inspector general, Tunde Ogunshakin. It was surmised that the presidency considered Ogunshakin sympathetic to the outgoing Governor Amaechi and his party (APC), and that he would not allow the PDP to win.

Solomon Arase, a deputy inspector general of police from the South, emerged as inspector general and retained his appointment under the new president. At the end of August, Ms Olabisi Kolawole was named as the police force's spokesperson, the first woman to hold this position. A redeployment of all commissioners of police in the 36 states and the capital Abuja and of most of the assistant inspector generals followed suit. At the same time, the new leadership enforced a presidential order calling for immediate *withdrawal of police security for VIPs* who were not entitled to the service. Until then it had been common practice for the political class and self-proclaimed eminent business people to make improper use of policemen for their personal security. Last but not least, 260 senior police officers were promoted and, at the end of September, the police service commission reinstated more than a dozen officers and recalled and/or retired several others, thereby reversing their unfair dismissal. In addition, between late August and early September a purge hit the top echelon of the State Security Service (SSS), including Gordon Obua, Abdulrahman Mani and Ms Marilyn Ogar and dozens of other senior staff. On 27 November, Buhari appointed 30 new judges to the Federal High Court in line with the recommendations of the National Judicial Council.

Over the course of the year, the once precarious security situation in the crisis-ridden North-East improved, thanks to *a new and massive military campaign* that began in mid-February. The improvement allowed for elections to take place in most parts of the affected area. As in previous years, however, Adamawa, Borno and Yobe states were the main targets of the *Islamist insurgency*. The deadly attack on the MNJTF base in Baga only a few days after New Year's Eve, which cost hundreds of lives, as well as suicide bomb attacks in Damaturu (Yobe state) and Maiduguri (Borno state) on 9 and 10 January, heralded yet another year of the insurgency. Eventually, some 2,000 persons were killed during the attacks and counter-attacks, bringing the total number of victims, at a rough estimate, to 20,000. However, the number of injured persons is not known, and is certainly several times higher. In addition, the number of IDPS rose close to 2 m.

Early in the year, the army and the air force began a large-scale operation that included the use of drones. On 21 February, Baga was recaptured and, in late April, military forces, backed by air strikes, started to invade Sambisa Forest, the insurgents' last known stronghold. It was reported that Boko Haram fighters stoned to death some of the women they had abducted as security forces approached. Towards the end of the year, all areas but Sambisa Forest were retaken and some 2,000 abductees, mostly women and children, were rescued. Two months earlier, on 28 October, the army had published photographs of 100 top suspected Boko Haram terrorists. By year's end, the effects were at best mixed, since only very few suspects had been arrested. In one case, on 18 December, the army had to set free one Abubakar Sadiq who had been wrongly detained a month earlier.

This notwithstanding, *suicide bombings* went on unabated, mostly undertaken by young girls, most of whom were probably unaware of their deadly mission. Yola, the capital of Adamawa state, more or less considered out of reach of terrorist attacks, was eventually hit on 17 November, just days after Buhari's visit. The bomb blast killed more than 30 people. Shortly after Christmas, on 28 December, two bombers struck a market in Madagali, the headquarters of the local government of the same name, claiming more than 25 lives. At the same time, only days after Buhari had claimed that the war against Boko Haram had been 'technically won', Maiduguri was hit for the umpteenth time, causing more than 30 casualties.

Kano state and the capital of the same name along with the Federal Capital Territory Abuja, as well as Gombe, Kaduna and Plateau states, suffered similar attacks, though not on the same scale as before. For example, on 24 February, a suicide bomb attack killed more than two dozen persons in a bus at a motor park in the Kano state capital along Zaria Road. Another blast occurred on 6 July outside the Umar Ibn al-Khattab mosque, located along the same road, when a teenage girl detonated explosives after she had been prevented from entering. Fortunately no one else was killed. On 18 November, a market in Turani local government in Kano State was hit by a twin blast, claiming at least 15 lives. On 27 November, some 20 members of the Muslim Brethren, also known as the Islamic Movement of Nigeria, who consider themselves 'Shiites', were killed by a bomb blast near Kura Town, on their way from Kano to the sect's main base in Zaria in neighbouring Kaduna state, where they were to participate in the Ashura festivities.

A day after Buhari's *address to the nation* on the occasion of the 55th Independence Day on 1 October, a twin blast occurred in the urban districts of Kuje and Nyanya within greater Abuja, claiming the lives of 15 and three persons, respectively; dozens were seriously wounded. Much earlier, on 2 April, a young woman had dropped a bag at a shop within a motor park in Gombe town. The improvised explosive device went off, killing more than a dozen people, including six soldiers. In Plateau and Kaduna states, almost 50 people lost their lives in two bomb attacks in the state capital Jos (5 July) and at least two dozen were killed by a bomb in Sabon Gari, a local government within greater Zaria.

In North-Central Nigeria, including the Middle Belt states, cattle rustling, disputes over grazing rights and rights over fertile land led to deadly skirmishes in which hundreds of peasants, herdsmen, soldiers, policemen and uninvolved citizens lost their lives. In early July, for example, even as far as Zamfara state in the far north, gunmen raided some villages in Birnin-Magaji local government, killing dozens of people and taking their livestock. Despite the alarming number of deadly clashes in Benue and Taraba states, Barkin Ladi and Riyom local governments in Plateau state remained the focal point of *sectarian and ethnic clashes*, in which mainly ethnic Birom and Fulani were involved. One of the cruellest incidents occurred in Foron Town on 2 May, when a church building of the Church of Christ in Nations was set on fire, allegedly by Fulani herdsmen; 27 worshippers were killed, including the pastor Luka Gwom. In the days and weeks that followed, the situation spiralled out of control in both local government areas. Eventually, on 13 August, the new Plateau state governor, Simon Lalong, imposed a dusk-to-dawn curfew.

Over the course of the year, the crisis in the North and the general elections kept public attention away from the unabated spread of bank robbery and organised crime throughout the country, particularly in the South, and from a number of disturbing incidents in the *Niger Delta and the Bight of Biafra*. According to the International Maritime Bureau, 14 incidents were reported during the period under review, with nine vessels boarded, though many attacks were believed to have gone unrecorded. For example, on 3 February, a tanker sailing under a Maltese flag was attacked while waiting to load at Qua Iboe in Akwa Ibom state. One crew member was killed and three others were taken hostage. A French oil industry supply vessel came under attack on 8 April, when pirates kidnapped three Nigerians. In another incident in the eastern Cross River state, pirates on speed boats attacked the marine police armoury in the state capital Calabar, making away with two gun boats and caches of weapons. The authorities denied claims that officers were killed.

On Good Friday, 3 April, ethnic Urhobo militants blew up a gas pipeline in Delta state, allegedly drawing attention to their exclusion from lucrative protection contracts with the NNPC. Barely a month later, on 29 April, militants from the same ethnic minority in the state claimed responsibility for two explosions that rocked two major trunk lines in Ughelli north and south local governments. Following the navy's destruction of 50 illegal camps in Burutu local government area in Delta state on 11 October, the Federal High Court in Lagos, on 30 October, convicted seven men to jail terms of 12 years each for *unlawful dealings in petrol*, ordering the forfeiture of their vessel and the assets of the convicts' company.

Kidnapping for ransom, mostly targeting Nigerians, remained quite rampant, particularly in the southern and south-western parts of the country. On 1 April, five local members of staff of a subsidiary of ExxonMobil were kidnapped in Akwa Ibom state by unknown gunmen. In neighbouring Rivers state, the vice chancellor of the Ignatius Ajuru State University, Ms Rosemond Green-Osagholu, was taken hostage on 20 June as she was leaving the campus. At least temporarily, Ekiti state somehow became a hub for this profitable business. For example, on 7 May, a former chief medical director, Patrick Adegun, was taken hostage, along with his wife Kikelomo. The following day, a university lecturer, Femi Omisore, suffered the same fate, with his driver killed during the incident. On 15 May, three women along with their husbands and children were abducted on their way from Oyo to Ekiti state. Eventually, the captors dropped the men and the children while the women were driven away. Emmanuel Akingbade, a Catholic priest of the diocese in the state, who was taken hostage on 9 June, was held captive for several days.

In neighbouring Kogi state, a US citizen and missionary of the Free Methodist Church, Ms Phyllis Sortor, spent more than three months in captivity after being kidnapped on 23 February. Prior to her release, on 25 May, a state high court judge, Samuel Obayomi, was attacked and abducted and his orderly shot dead on the spot. He eventually had to spend more than a month in his captor's custody. The well-known former politician, septuagenarian Olu Falae, was kidnapped on his farm in Ondo state on 21 September. He survived his kidnapping unscathed, as did the vast majority of abductees. However, the killing of Samuel Okpara, a medical doctor who was taken hostage on 20 February in Port Harcourt, and the discovery of the decomposing body of a university lecturer, Paul Erie, in Edo state on 1 October, underlined the fact that the *citizens' everyday life was still vulnerable*. Erie had allegedly died at the hands of his captors soon after being kidnapped on 16 June. The former vice chancellor of the Federal University of Technology in Akure, Ekiti state, 79-year old Albert Ilemobade, was killed on 22 June by two of his servants, who were intending to steal his car. Soon afterwards, both were apprehended. One Catholic priest and lecturer, Dennis Osuagwu, was murdered by a kidnap gang in Imo state on 15 August; and an Israeli citizen lost his life, when he resisted a kidnap attempt in Abuja on 9 September.

Against this backdrop, the newly elected Rivers state governor, Nyesom Wike, assented on 7 August to an amended *kidnap prohibition law*, stipulating that persons convicted of this crime would forfeit their assets to the state.

Despite a *great deal of crime*, the police forces, in conjunction with the DSS broke up several notorious gangs, particularly during the second half of the year. One of the cruellest crimes however, occurred on 16 September in Ogun state, where ten DSS operatives were killed in Arepo area by pipeline vandals who were siphoning off fuel. Earlier, towards the end of July, the DSS in Imo state had arrested a notorious gang leader, simply named Chibueze but popularly known as 'Vampire', alleged to have kidnapped and killed individuals in their dozens. Prior to that, on 6 July, Lagos state police command had smashed a gang that had carried out various robberies on waterways and highways in the state, including a bank in Lekki peninsula, where, on 12 March, three policemen and two civilians had been killed. In early October, while half a dozen ethnic Fulani herdsmen, suspected to be the kidnappers of Olu Falae, were detained in Ondo and Niger states, Lagos state police command claimed to have arrested some 100 suspects in September alone for offences ranging from armed robbery to kidnapping, murder and sophisticated fraud. On 28 October, the police in Imo state smashed the gang of one Musa Isah, alias Yahaya Ibrahim, that had killed Reverend Father Osuagwu.

The precarious security situation in most parts of the country had serious effects on *human rights*. On 4 June, AI maintained that the Nigerian military was responsible for the deaths of more than 8,000 prisoners detained during the campaign against Boko Haram; more than 7,000 had starved to death or died of disease, while some 1,200 were executed without trial. The military vehemently denied these allegations. Despite this accusation, AI was permitted to open an office in Abuja on 13 October. Earlier, on 10 June, the Federal High Court in Enugu acceded to the prosecutor's application to proceed in secret with the trial of members of the 'Biafra Zionist Federation'. The leader, Benjamin Onwuka, and some of his followers were charged with treason for crimes allegedly committed in 2014. No verdict had been reported by year's end. On 12 December, a motorcade of the Army Chief of Staff Buratai made headlines when it was attacked on its way to a ceremony in Zaria, allegedly by members of the so-called Shiites; the soldiers opened fire without warning, causing dozens of fatalities. In a climate of reciprocal accusations, the official investigation into the grisly incident commenced rather reluctantly. The above is nowhere near a complete list of the terror-attacks, counter-attacks, kidnappings and murders that took place during the year .

On 27 November in Abuja, the Federal High Court turned down an application by the DSS aimed at quashing the decision of the National Human Rights Commission (NHRC) to pay compensation in the so-called 'Apo killings case'. The NHRC had held the government responsible for the *extra-judicial killings* of eight squatters in September 2013 and awarded monetary compensation to the victims' relatives. In 2010, an amended act had made the Commission's decisions and recommendations legally binding and enforceable by the courts.

On 25 June, after a secret trial in an upper *sharia court* in Rijiyar Lemo in Kano state, nine people, including a cleric, were sentenced to death for blasphemous statements. Four others, arrested with those convicted, were found not guilty and were discharged. The sentences had not been carried out by year's end. The charge of murder brought against a 15-year-old girl was eventually dropped by a Kano state High Court on 20 May. At the age of 14, she had allegedly poisoned her 35-year old husband and four others. However, the constitutional legality of the death sentence was upheld on 24 April by the Supreme Court, when it rejected the appeal of a convicted armed robber.

As the unprecedented scale of corruption under the previous government gradually became clear, Buhari vowed to take drastic measures in his *anti-corruption campaign*. Despite the appointment of Ibrahim Mustafa Magu as the new chairman of the Economic and Financial Crimes Commission on 9 November, it had not gained any significant momentum by the end of the year. The serious charges against the former national security adviser, Sambo Dasuki, were considered as the litmus test for the government's ability to convict high ranking officials of the previous government on charges of looting public funds. In addition, controversial multimillion dollar contracts between the ousted government and former Niger Delta militia leaders such as Mujahid Dokubo-Asari and Government Ekpemupolo, alias Tompolo, came under severe scrutiny.

Foreign Affairs

Over the course of the year, the new leadership reshaped Nigeria's foreign policy. The fact that US Secretary of State John Kerry was present at Muhammadu Buhari's inauguration on 29 May was a strong indication of the *gradual improvement of relations with the USA*. The visit was a clear sign of the Obama administration's willingness to strengthen diplomatic relations, which had become severely strained under former president Goodluck Jonathan. The attendance at the ceremony of the head of the US Africa Command, General David Rodriguez, confirmed America's renewed commitment to cooperation with Nigeria.

From 19–22 July, Buhari paid a state visit to the USA and held bilateral discussions with President Barak Obama on 20 July, in which the US administration offered its assistance in *tracking down millions of dollars of stolen assets*. In addition, it committed $ 5 m in support for the MNJTF's fight against Islamist insurgencies. However, the trip produced a disappointing result with regard to military assistance as Buhari failed to secure an arms deal. On the positive side, USAID agreed on 11 June to expand its humanitarian assistance to north-eastern Nigeria to the tune of some $ 44 m.

On 2 November, Musa Jack Ngonadi, believed to be the son of former military leader Yakubu Gowon, was released from prison and deported. He had served more than half of a 40-year sentence for his involvement in a drugs cartel.

As in previous years, *legal issues shaped the relationship with Britain*. Days before his inauguration, president-elect Buhari undertook a six-day trip to the UK (22–27 May) where, on 23 May, he held discussions with Prime Minister David Cameron. As expected, the meeting focused on the Islamist insurgency and the UK's continuing commitment to provide military training and intelligence support. The timing of this visit had the effect of avoiding publicity in the run-up to the inauguration, which was attended by British Foreign Secretary Philip Hammond.

At the end of March, 36 year-old Ms Franca Asemota was arrested in Edo state by the National Agency for the Prohibition of Trafficking in Persons and extradited to the UK, where she was wanted for *trafficking young women and underage girls* to Europe using Heathrow Airport as a transit hub. On 1 April, Woolwich Crown Court sentenced Jeffrey Okafor to a minimum 17-year jail term. The verdict ended a murder case and manhunt after Okafor had stabbed another Nigerian, Carl Beatson-Asiedu, to death in 2009. The victim was a well-known DJ on the club scene. Using his brother's passport, the culprit had fled to Nigeria where he was eventually apprehended and extradited to the UK in 2014. His brother, Junior Okafor, had already been given a four-year jail term in 2010 for assisting an offender. In a similar case, 39-year old Abdul Adewale Kekere-Ekun was sentenced on 7 September to life imprisonment for a murder committed in 2001. He had fled to Nigeria in a bid to escape prosecution but was arrested in February 2015 for identity theft offences, which revealed that he was on a UK wanted list.

On 2 October, former minister for petroleum resources, Ms Diezani Alison-Madueke, was temporarily arrested in London by the UK National Crime Agency over allegations of corruption perpetrated during her tenure as minister. Shortly thereafter, the UK government formally asked Nigeria to assist in investigating her activities as minister. In another corruption case, former bank manager Erastus Akingbola had been tried for serious fraud at the Federal High Court in Lagos, but on 20 February, the Court of Appeal ordered his retrial, basing its decision on the verdict of a UK court in 2014. In 2012 the Federal High Court had cleared Akingbola of all charges for lack of diligent prosecution. Once again, these incidents highlighted the fact that *numerous wealthy Nigerians owned expensive, luxury real estate in the UK*. The NGO African-British Returnees International claimed in February that Nigerians spent at least £ 300 m a year on British education.

Probably the most spectacular international corruption case involved a former minister for petroleum, Dan Etete. On 15 December, Southwark Crown Court in London prevented the release of $ 85 m to Etete's allegedly fraudulent Malabu Oil & Gas Company in Lagos. The money was seized at the request of Italian prosecutors who were investigating a disputed oil deal worth more than $ 1 bn, involving Etete's company, the multinationals Shell and ENI, and the Nigerian government under then president Jonathan.

Due to the Islamist insurgency in the Lake Chad region, Nigeria's relationships with African countries focused on the West African region. Towards the end of February, military chiefs from Nigeria and the four neighbouring countries began finalising their ambitious strategy for the creation of an 8,750-strong force aimed at taking on Boko Haram. N'Djamena, the Chadian capital, would serve as the overall command centre. By May, however, during a state visit by Chad's President Idriss Déby, it emerged that the strategy was too ambitious, although the military chiefs met again in N'Djamena on 20–21 August. Nigeria's *structural web of arrogance, corruption, incompetence and shame* and the deep-seated and long-existing mutual mistrust between Nigeria and the neighbouring francophone states undermined and delayed potentially promising cooperation. Moreover, the weakness of Cameroon's and Niger's security forces offered Boko Haram an opportunity to regroup after they had been largely driven out of Nigerian territory.

On 11 June, an extraordinary meeting of heads of state and government of the Lake Chad Basin Commission and Benin met in Abuja and approved *Nigeria's retaining the leadership of the MNJTF*. Cameroon's President Paul Biya did not attend the meeting, being represented by senior staff member from the Ministry of Defence, but he did receive Buhari in Yaoundé on 30 July. Apart from endorsing the commitment made at the extraordinary meeting, Biya and his guest agreed to complete the demarcation of the common land border before the end of the year. Earlier, on 13 June, the Buhari had attended the 25th AU summit in Johannesburg (South Africa). On 7 September, he paid a one-day state visit to Ghana, where he held talks with President John Mahama; he welcomed Togolese President Faure Gnassingbé on 10 September and, on 22 September, hosted an extraordinary meeting of ECOWAS, which aimed at resolving the impasse in Burkina Faso.

Buhari's busy travel schedule provoked sceptical reactions both within elite circles and amongst the public. He attended the G-8 summit in Germany (7–8 June), and travelled twice to Paris, for a three-day state visit on 14–16 September, and later, to address the summit on climate change, which began on 30 November, flying in the meantime to New Delhi to participate in the India-Africa Forum (26–29 October). On 23 November, he attended the summit of the Gas Exporting Countries Forum in Tehran (Iran) and was in Malta on 27 November to participate in a meeting of the Commonwealth Heads of Government.

Nigeria's relations with the UN remained friendly. On 9 January, the UN Secretary-General Ban Ki-moon announced the appointment of Major General Salihu Uba as the new commander of the UN Mission in Liberia (UNMIL). On 8 July, Nigeria abstained from voting on a UNSC resolution that would have dubbed the 1995 massacre at Srebrenica a 'crime of genocide'. Despite Nigeria's abstention, the resolution still had the necessary majority, but Russia eventually vetoed it. On 23 August, Ban Ki-moon arrived in Nigeria on a two-day official visit, and Buhari addressed the UN General Assembly on 28 September.

On 24 September, *a stampede in Mecca* (Saudi Arabia), caused by a collapsed crane, killed several hundred pilgrims on the Hajj. The number of injured was much higher. The first northern female newspaper editor, Bilikisu Yusuf, and the Chief Imam of the Sultan Abubakar III Jumaa'a Mosque in Sokoto were among the more than 200 Nigerian victims.

On 28 May, Akinwumi Adesina, was elected as the 8th president of the *AfDB Group* and took over on 1 September. He was the first Nigerian to occupy this position after Nigeria's previous bids had failed three times. On 24 July, Ms Arunma Oteh was appointed vice president and treasurer of the World Bank with effect from 28 September.

Socioeconomic Developments

Plummeting oil and gas prices fell below the $ 40 per barrel mark by the end of the year. The decline had a serious impact on the economy and highlighted Nigeria's overdependence on its main export commodities and developments on the international energy market. The national currency immediately came under pressure. By New Year's Eve, the exchange rate of the naira had fallen to NGN 300 to the dollar in the parallel market as against the official rate of NGN 197, stubbornly maintained by the Central Bank of Nigeria (CBN) and the government.

Earlier in the year, on 20 May, the spokesman of the then president confirmed that Jonathan, without the usual fanfare, had signed into law the *federal budget 2015*, totalling NGN 4.5 trn ($ 22.6 bn). The budget was based on a benchmark of $ 53 per barrel of crude oil and a production level of some 2.2 m b/d. It was slightly smaller than the previous budget and took the price fluctuations for oil into consideration. On 18 November, the new government sent a supplementary budget of NGN 465 bn to the National Assembly in order to cover fuel subsidies and gasoline imports. On 1 December, both chambers eventually approved an even higher budget of NGN 574 bn, but this increase was to fund a special military operation in the crisis-ridden North-East.

Despite the *volatile global oil and gas market*, shrinking foreign reserves of some $ 32 bn and a depleted excess crude account of just $ 1.7 bn at mid-year, President Buhari approved a rescue plan of NGN 1.2 trn on 6 July in order to help ailing states' budgets and and local governments. In addition, the CBN disbursed a special intervention fund to the states in the form of soft loans, repayable over a 20-year period at an interest rate of 9%. The fund was set up with the sole purpose of paying outstanding salaries. In September, in line with the government's anti-corruption campaign, the bank set up a nationwide monitoring mechanism to ensure that the fund was not diverted for other purposes.

On 22 December, the president presented his *2016 budget proposal* before a joint session of the National Assembly. The budget, totalling NGN 6.08 trn was based on a crude oil price of $ 38 per barrel and a production estimate of 2.2 m b/d and was aimed at reviving the economy by massively increasing capital expenditure. The government accepted a deficit of some NGN 2.22 trn, equivalent to 2.1% of Nigeria's GDP, which, unsurprisingly, gave rise to concern both inside and outside of Nigeria about the government's ability to handle financial and economic affairs.

Much earlier, at the end of January, the CBN had already commenced the Federal Government's Independent Revenue e-Collection Scheme, a platform to support the collection and remittance of all government revenue to a consolidated account domiciled with the CBN. This marked the beginning of the full implementation of a *Treasury Single Account (TSA) system* in Nigeria aimed at ensuring the accountability of government revenue, enhancing transparency and avoiding the misapplication of public funds. This controversial move forced the commercial banks to act as collection agents and, on 17 September, led to the governor of the CBN, Godwin Emefiele, trying to refute their claim that the policy had provoked a liquidity crisis. As early as 24 June, Emefiele had to defend the bank's decision to tighten foreign exchange control by excluding 41 items from the interbank forex market, an action some economic analysts criticised. Interestingly, the National Assembly rejected the TSA initiative, maintaining its role as an independent body of the constitutional order and triggering a silent power struggle with the presidency. By year's end, the issue had not been resolved.

Despite increasing economic hardship, the 2015 Global Wealth Report indicated a *rising number of Nigerian millionaires*, some 15,400, three times the number recorded in the previous study, published in 2000. Against this background, unsurprisingly, four Nigerian banks, including FirstBank of Nigeria and Zenith Bank, were among the top 500 banks worldwide.

As in previous years, Nigeria kept its position as Africa's largest and most lucrative telecommunications market with more than 140 m subscribers spending about

NGN 200 bn on calls every month. In addition, there were almost 90 m users of the Internet, although the vast majority were still dependent on the outdated mobile technology GSM. In October, however, this booming sector suffered from an act of negligence on the part of the South African MTN Group, Africa's leading provider, which controls more than 40% of the Nigerian mobile phone market. MTN was fined $ 5.2 bn by the Nigerian Communications Commission (NCC) for refusing to deactivate almost 40 m improperly registered SIM cards. All competing companies had abided by the order, which was designed to undercut Boko Haram's communication capacity. For its part, MTN tried to have the heavy fine reduced. The NCC offered a 25% deduction of the original fine, payable by 31 December. The MTN in turn rejected that offer and challenged the fine in the Lagos Federal Court.

Last but not least, on 8 November in Chile, the Golden Eaglets retained the U-17 World Cup after defeating Mali 2-0.

Senegal

Emmanuelle Bouilly and Marie Brossier

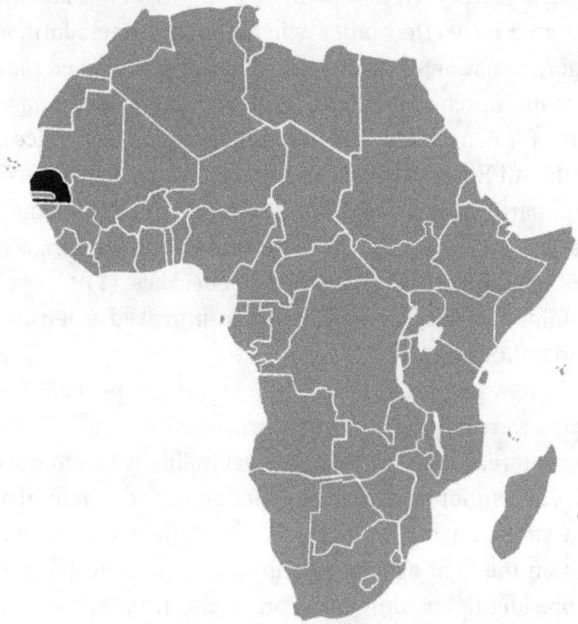

Corruption scandals and violations of human rights dominated the political discourse. Debates on constitutional reform, particularly the reduction of the presidential term, and the forthcoming presidential elections resulted in infighting between and within political parties. In foreign affairs, Sall continued Senegal's role as a major regional actor in a number of fields such as terrorism and migration.

Domestic Politics

Criticism of *nepotism in the presidential entourage* was a consistent feature in domestic politics. The press, civil society and the opposition criticised the 'Faye-Sall' dynasty for providing access to positions of power for members of the families of President Macky Sall and his wife, Marieme Faye Sall. In January, the 'Alliance Sauvons le Sénégal' and its leader, Babacar Mbaye Ngaraf, lodged a complaint at the 'Office de Lutte contre la Fraude et la Corruption' (OFNAC) against Aliou Sall, President Sall's brother and manager of Petro-Tim Limited Company, which was suspected of having been granted two oil exploration licences because of its proximity

 | DOI 10.1163/9789004333239_018

to the president. In the past, Aliou Sall had been accused of benefiting from illicit sales of shares to Timis Corporation. As well as being the mayor of Guédiawaye (a suburb of Dakar), he also became head of the 'Association des Maires du Sénégal' and the 'Union des Elus Locaux' on 22 January and 12 May, respectively. The 'Association Nationale des Elus Départementaux' claimed that political favouritism was at play. A major political scandal erupted on 18 December, when Lamine Diack, former president of the International Association of Athletics Federations, confessed that he had organised a major corruption scheme to oust former president Abdoulaye Wade from office. In exchange for concealing Russian athletes' doping practices, he had received € 1.5 m from the All-Russia Athletic Federation, which he had used to fund a variety of opposition parties, including the 'Alliance Pour la République' (APR) in the 2009 and 2012 election campaigns. On 19 December, Oumar Sarr, MP and deputy general secretary of the 'Parti Démocratique Sénégalais' (PDS), was arrested on charges of disseminating false news. The arrest provoked extensive criticism from civil society and politicians.

President Sall implemented a new set of reforms to improve *judicial and political transparency*. On 12 January, MPS were informed of the reform of the Criminal Code and the Code of Criminal Procedure, which brought Senegal in line with international conventions. On 29 May, Sall announced the presentation in Parliament of a bill that would guarantee a lawyer for anyone facing a trial. On 26 June, Parliament ratified the ECOWAS protocol on the fight against corruption, which Senegal had signed in 2001. Sall granted a presidential pardon to 432 prisoners on 25 September. On 2 October, OFNAC and the EU signed an 18-month contract for € 264 m to promote integrity in the management of public and private affairs.

Controversial institutional debates affected the start of the second part of Sall's term in office. On 25 June, a group of 23 MPS from the parliamentary majority party 'Benno Bokk Yaakar' (BBY), along with two opposition MPS from the 'Parti Socialiste' (PS) (Awa Gueye Diop and Cheikh Seck), proposed a bill to amend 22 articles regarding the procedures of the National Assembly. It limited the presidential term limit to five years and was meant to stabilise parliamentary factions. The bill attracted strong criticism as it prohibited MPS from switching parliamentary parties during the parliamentary term, but it was nevertheless passed on 29 June. Regarding the debate on the reduction of the presidential term from seven to five years, President Sall announced on 18 March that he would hold a referendum in May 2016. If the 'yes' camp won, the next presidential election would be held in February 2017. However, this proposal failed to meet with the approval of the presidential coalition as well as among opposition parties. On 2 April, President Sall's advisers strongly recommended that he call off the referendum. On 3 April, Pape Diop, the leader of the opposition 'Coalition Convergence Bokk Gis Gis' and a former head of the Senate, proposed bringing forward the date of the presidential elections. On 13 April, Sall formally asked his party officials to end the debate on the referendum and to focus on issues related to the implementation of the 'Plan

Sénégal Emergent' (PSE) instead. Despite Sall's an intervention by Sall on 11 May, the PS called for the referendum to be brought forward from May 2016 to the autumn of 2015. Sall indicated that he would refer the question about the referendum to the Constitutional Council in early 2016, to which he appointed new members known for their morality and impartiality: on 26 June, Pape Oumar Sakho, former first president of the Supreme Court, became the new president of the Constitutional Council, with Malick Diop appointed as its vice president and Ndiaw Diouf and Ndiaye Mandiogou as regular members. On 14 September, Sall confirmed that the referendum would be held in 2016.

The trial of Karim Wade, the son of the former president Abdoulaye Wade and a former minister of energy, continued to feature on the judicial and political agenda. Karim Wade had been prosecuted by the 'Cour pour la Répression de l'Enrichissement Illicite' (CREI) since April 2013 on charges of embezzlement of state funds during his father's presidency. On 20 January, he refused to present himself before the CREI. On 3 February, his defence lawyers accused the state of bribing witnesses. On 6 February, Minister of Justice Sidiki Kaba refused Abdoulaye Wade's request for his son's case to be heard by the High Court. In reply to the banning of a demonstration in Guediawaye and at Place de l'Obélisque in Dakar on 23 and 29 January, the pro-Wade camp organised an unauthorised march in front of the presidency on 31 January. This led to violent clashes with the police, during which Abdoulaye Wade broke through a police checkpoint and announced that he was "ready to give his life" for his son. The prefect eventually authorised the protest march on 4 February. Opposition parties and civil society organisations such as the 'Mouvement du 23 Juin' expressed their concern over the possibility that the protests could lead to an escalating cycle of violence. On 26 February, AI reported serious *violations of human rights* including torture, the violation of freedom of assembly and the controversial existence of the CREI, which they claimed violated human rights in the justice process. Wade's lawyers contested the CREI's constitutionality, arguing that the CREI did not have jurisdiction to prosecute a former minister as this was the prerogative of the High Court. On the same day, former prime minister Souleymane Ndiaye Ndéné claimed that Abdoulaye Wade bore some responsibility for this escalation. The tension between the pro-Wade camp led by the PDS and the government increased on 17 March with the arrest of three PDS officials, including Amadou Sall (a former minister of justice and Karim Wade's defence lawyer), for insulting the president and undermining state security. Meanwhile, the anti-Wade camp maintained its support for the CREI. On 23 March, Moustapha Diakhate, chairman of the ruling BBY, called for calm and respect for the decisions of the court and, on 24 March, the CREI handed down its ruling: Karim Wade and some of his co-defendants were convicted of illicit enrichment involving an amount of CFAfr 69 bn. He was sentenced to six years in prison and a fine of CFAfr 138 bn. The same day, his defence lawyers announced that they would petition the Supreme Court to quash the CREI's ruling. A demonstration against the verdict planned by Abdoulaye Wade was cancelled *sine die* at the request of the general caliph of the Mourides on 26 March. On 1 April, the NGO 'Rencontre Africaine des Droits de l'Homme en Afrique' called on the government to investigate the trial. On 7 May, the UN Working Group on Arbitrary Detention accused the Senegalese authorities of arbitrarily detaining Karim Wade and called on the government to compensate him. His lawyers welcomed the recommendation but Minister of Justice Sidiki Kaba argued that the UN lacked authority on domestic rulings and the government denounced the recommendation as biased on 26 June. On 20 August, the Supreme Court rejected Karim Wade's appeals and confirmed the CREI ruling. The Karim Wade camp announced that it would continue to contest the ruling of the courts.

Political forces began to prepare for the *2016 presidential elections*. President Sall and his party rallied support throughout the year. On 27 January, former prime minister Aminata Touré was named as Sall's campaign director and his candidacy was endorsed on 23 March by Landing Savané, the leader of the 'And-Jëf/Parti Africain pour la Démocratie et le Socialisme' (AJ/PADS) and on 12 May by Serign Modou Kara, the leader of the 'Parti de la Vérité pour le Développement'. On 22 October, eight political parties of the Macky2012 coalition launched a movement called 'Les Républicans Domou Rewmi' to support the president's re-election. Important political elites such as former president Abdou Diouf came out in favour of Sall's candidacy on 28 December. Among the opposition, a number of new political parties emerged, including, on 26 February, the 'Parti Justice et Développement', which aimed to turn Senegal into a new Dubai. The 'Taxawu Jotna' party was created on 30 April to support the candidacy of Khalifa Sall, the mayor of Dakar. The 'Union Nationale pour le Peuple' endorsed former prime minister Souleymane Ndéné Ndiaye on 29 May. On 8 July, several opposition parties (PDS, Rewmi, AJ/PADS, 'Bokk Gis Gis', 'Front pour le Socialisme et la Démocratie/Benno Jubël' (FSD/BJ), 'Union Centriste du Sénégal' (UCS) and the 'Union pour le Renouveau Démocratique') accused the APR and the Ministry of the Interior of committing fraud by creating fake national identity cards, thus endangering the on-going revisions of the electoral lists. The PS experienced internal debates which saw the confrontation of two presidential candidates from different generations: Ousmane Tanor Dieng, the party's historical leader, against Khalifa Sall, a younger party executive and mayor of Dakar since 2009.

The PDS was weakened by *internal conflicts over leadership*, which remained entirely in the hands of Abdoulaye Wade's family and his proxies. On 23 March, in order to contest Karim's detention, PDS officials nominated him as their official candidate for the next presidential elections. On 15 April, PDS party officials disagreed over whether Abdoulaye Wade should remain the party's general secretary until 2017. This eventually led to the creation of a splinter group headed by Modou Diagne Fada, a PDS official, former minister and chairman of the 'Groupe Parlementaire des Libéraux et Démocrates' within the National Assembly. The open conflict led Wade to remove Fada from its role as the PDS spokesperson on 16 June. Violence between the two groups broke out (punching and face-to-face threats) on 30 June. With the opposition trying to mobilise against Sall's candidacy from 22 May, Fada invited the opposition parties on 9 June to support a joint candidate to drive Macky Sall from power. Although Fada managed to gather a broad parliamentary alliance including the PDS, Rewmi, UCS, 'Bokk Gis Gis', FSD/BJ and AJ/PADS on 13 October, he was excluded from the PDS on 16 October after 20 years of membership. The PDS announced on 19 October that Karim Wade was to remain its nominee for the 2017 elections, despite his conviction in August. Abdoulaye Wade announced his intention to take over the leadership of the 'Groupe Parlementaire des Libéraux et Démocrates' on 27 October.

Debates about Islam were dominated by regional and international terrorism. On 3 February, the prefect closed a mosque in one of Dakar's western districts to avoid the risk of clashes and disturbances between Sunni and Shi'a Muslims. On 5 June, the 'Réseau Ouest-Africain pour l'Édification de la Paix' highlighted the potential for an increase in religious extremism in Senegal. Following the attacks in Bamako (Mali) in late November, President Sall expressed his concerns about Islamist radicalisation and announced a ban on the full-face veil for women on 20 November, which provoked a heated debate.

Promising measures were taken regarding the continuing *separatist conflict in the south-western Casamance region*. On 20 March, female members of the 'Comité Régional de Solidarité des Femmes pour la Paix en Casamance' called for the government to get involved in the peace negotiations. However, on 13 April, hostilities restarted between national and rebel forces. Twelve forest farmers who had been taken hostage by rebel groups were released unharmed on 14 July after a week in captivity. On 11 November, the national media lamented that only a few citizens appeared to be aware of the negotiations between the government and the 'Mouvement des Forces Démocratiques de Casamance'.

Foreign Affairs

Senegal became a *non-permanent member of the UNSC* on 16 October, and was elected onto the executive board of UNESCO for a four-year term on 11 November. President Sall attended several international meetings: the 70th UN General Assembly in New York on 29 September, the OIF Economic Forum in Paris on 26 October, the G20 Summit in Antalya (Turkey) on 16 November, and the UN conference on climate change in Paris on 30 November. On 20 July, the long-expected trial of former Chadian president Hissène Habré, in exile in Senegal since 1990, opened before the 'Cour d'Assises des Chambres Africaines Extraordinaires' hosted in Dakar.

Terrorism particularly affected diplomacy. On 11 January, President Sall joined the rally in Paris to condemn the terrorist attacks on 'Charlie Hebdo'. Some Senegalese politicians and religious leaders criticised his participation, considering it a sign of support for the cartoonists, and thus for blasphemy. Public opinion also deplored the fact that no such march had been organised in solidarity with Nigeria or northern Mali. Sall stated that he had expressed his solidarity with victims' families and the French people, as Senegal believed in freedom of speech. However, on 15 January, he banned two French newspapers that put a cartoon of the Prophet Mohammad on their front pages. A march against these cartoons was organised in Dakar on 24 January. French and Senegalese officials met in Dakar on 11 February to revise the CFAfr 460 m 'Plan d'Action Contre le Terrorisme' launched two years earlier. They decided to reinforce training for the Senegalese police, army, magistrates and intelligence agency. Dakar hosted the second International Forum on Peace and Security in Africa on 9–11 November. Sall advocated a moderate and tolerant Islam, and called for regional cooperation against jihadists. After new terrorist attacks in Paris in November, Sall condemned them as "barbaric acts". They led to the death of a Senegalese woman. On 20 November, two days after the deadly hotel siege in Bamako had killed a Senegalese worker, Sall visited Mali's President Keïta to offer his condolences, and announced three days of national mourning.

International and illegal migration was another important issue. In February, the government repatriated 400 Senegalese from Libya while a Mediterranean shipwreck killed at least 250 others in April. From January to April, 1,187 Senegalese migrants succeeded in reaching Italy by boat. At the Euro-African Summit on Migration held in Malta on 11–12 November, Sall urged the EU to remove the "politique de barricades", and to ensure that migrants' rights were respected. He had already made the same appeal at the UN General Assembly in September. The government had to cope with the deportation of 52 illegal Senegalese workers from Gabon in August and 75 more in December. On 1 October, Minister of Foreign Affairs Mankeur Ndiaye flew to Mecca, where 34 Senegalese were victims of a stampede during the annual pilgrimage.

Senegal maintained its active *diplomacy on the African continent*. Sall negotiated the release of three leaders of the 'Y en a marre' movement who had been arrested for undermining the *DRC*'s internal security after a meeting in Kinshasa on 15 March. After 72 hours in police custody, the Senegalese activists were released and returned home. Sall also led a special ECOWAS mediation team to negotiate a peaceful conclusion to the crisis in *Burkina Faso*. Sall proposed the return of the ousted transitional government led by Michel Kafando in exchange of an amnesty for the putschists. Kafando had warned he had "serious reservations" about this proposal, adding that he had not been invited to the talks, which Sall vehemently denied. Sall did not attend the ceremonial reinstatement of Kafando on 23 September. Relations with *Guinea-Bissau* were also erratic. On 25 March, at the request of the Guinea-Bissau authorities, Sall took part in the International Donors' Conference for Guinea-Bissau held in Brussels, where he strongly supported the economic development strategic plan presented by his counterpart José Mário Vaz. On 9 August, Sall invited Vaz to Dakar for discussions about the political crisis in Guinea-Bissau, but failed to deter him from dissolving his government and removing his prime minister. On 18 December, the two countries opened discussions about the renegotiation of their cooperation agreement signed in 1993, including the Guinea-Bissau/Senegal joint management area. Relations with *Gambia* worsened. Although Dakar had condemned the failed coup against President Jammeh on 31 December 2014, Gambia decided to close its frontiers on 20 January. Tensions rose again when a Senegalese chief prosecutor ordered the autopsy of the exiled former Assets Management and Recovery Corporation director, Abdoulie Tamba, who had died in suspicious circumstances in Dakar on 2 February. On 14 April, Jammeh publicly declared Sall to be his 'enemy' and accused him of sheltering regime opponents.

By contrast, relations with *Guinea* improved after Senegal reopened its land border on 26 January following the end of the Ebola crisis. On 6–8 August, Guinea's President Condé visited Dakar. A military cooperation agreement, including joint border patrols, was discussed, and a memorandum of understanding in the field of hydro energy was signed. On 22–24 October, Senegal and *Mauritania* signed nine cooperation agreements in the fields of health, higher education, energy and transport, and agreed to build a bridge at Rosso over the Senegal River. Senegal maintained its close connections with *Morocco*: in May, King Mohammed VI spent a week in Dakar during which 13 cooperation agreements were signed regarding education, tourism, health, customs, sanitation, fisheries, handicrafts, agriculture and banking. On 25 May, the Moroccan-Senegalese economic impetus group was officially set up to foster partnership between the two countries' private sectors, and monitor the implementation of private-private and public-private agreements.

President Sall visited Saudi Arabia and Turkey in April, South Korea in June and Portugal in September. He also attended the Africa-India Summit in New Delhi on 29 October, and the Africa-China Summit in Johannesburg (South Africa) on 4 December. Sall was the first African head of state to be hosted by King Salman, the new king of *Saudi Arabia* from 30 March to 2 April. Sall pledged his support for the Saudi military intervention against Shiite rebels in Yemen. One month later, he announced that 2,100 Senegalese soldiers would be sent to Yemen, which was strongly criticised by opposition parties and human rights organisations. In return, Saudi Arabia made a commitment to grant CFAf 73 bn for budget aid, rural electrification, hospitals and higher vocational education.

The year ended well on 16 December, when the Board of Directors of the Millennium Challenge Corporation selected Senegal as eligible to develop a second compact.

Socioeconomic Developments

Senegal benefited from a *favourable economic environment.* Price-competitiveness improved thanks to the 2.6% depreciation of the CFA franc and a significant inflation differential with other countries (*inflation* was close to zero in Senegal). While the structural *trade deficit* remained high (CFAfr 1716.1 bn), it fell as the value of exports grew faster (+8.9%) than that of imports (+3.4%), particularly as a result of the drop in oil prices on the world market. This fall allowed the state to reduce its subsidies to the 'Société Nationale d'Electricité du Sénégal' from CFAfr 66 bn to CFAfr 27 bn. The gain was reallocated to priority sectors identified by the PSE, such as social welfare, infrastructure and agriculture. For example, the 'Programme d'Urgence de Développement Communautaire' promoting access for rural populations to basic social services received CFAfr 19.4 bn and the budget for fellowships and study grants received CFAfr 36 bn, an increase of CFAfr 8 bn. CFAfr 5.4 bn was allocated to the 'Programme des Domaines Agricoles Communautaires' for the creation of agribusiness clusters for young people.

In January, President Sall launched the construction of *several major infrastructure projects*, including the Thiès-Touba highway, a thermal power plant at Cap de Biches and a second university in Dakar. He also inaugurated a new fishing wharf, built at a cost of CFAfr 1.5 bn in Soumbedioune on 26 May. In February, Sall announced a CFAfr 200 bn programme for the development of the landlocked Sedhiou region and launched a programme to open up the Casamance region, including a 50% rebate on the Dakar-Ziguinchor boat shuttle, a ten-year tax holiday for tourism operators, and the modernisation of the port of Ziguinchor funded with CFAfr 10 bn from The Netherlands.

The CFAfr 2,824.4 bn *state budget* showed a 4.2% increase in resources thanks to the effective collection of fiscal and non-fiscal revenues. As expenditure rose modestly by 4.1% due to the rationalisation of both administrative expenditure and interest charges on the public debt, the *state deficit* remained stable at CFAfr 389 bn. Senegal relied on the successful issue of treasury bonds and on loans. The state launched a ten-year Eurobond in the amount of $ 500 m on 23 June, and a ten-year bond loan on the domestic market for CFAfr 50 bn on 30 October. The economy's dependence on *donor aid* did not lessen. On 22 July, the World Bank approved a $ 70 m loan for water supply and sanitation facilities in urban areas. On 30 October, the 'Banque Ouest-Africaine de Développement' approved a CFAfr 45 bn loan for three projects: CFAfr 10 bn for sanitation in ten towns, the same amount for the electrification of 177 villages, and CFAfr 25 bn for the building of a power supply loop. On 7 April, the 'Agence Française de Développement' and Senegal signed a convention agreement for € 30 m for the agriculture and health sectors. On 7 May, the IMF mission chief in Dakar launched a new three-year 'Instrument de Soutien à la Politique Economique' to sustain the PSE, whose implementation rate was judged satisfactory despite some delays in disbursements from the Islamic

Development Bank and the World Bank. The IMF managing director, visiting Dakar on 30 January, had already expressed satisfaction with overall Senegalese macro-economic performance.

The annual GDP growth reached 5.4% compared with 4.3% in 2014. The *primary sector improved* thanks to good harvests and the growth of the livestock sector. The fishing sector lagged behind and fell by 1%, still dealing with adverse weather conditions and over-fishing. Production of all cereals rose significantly (+82%), as did groundnuts (+68%) and cotton (+17%). This performance was achieved thanks to good rainfall and better access to land and farm equipment, which received government subsidies of up to 70%. Areas under cereal production increased by 45% compared with 2014. Encouraged by the progress made in rice production, which reached almost 1 m tonnes (+64%), President Sall stated that Senegal would achieve rice self-sufficiency in 2017. The strong growth rates in the *secondary sector revived* (+6.2%) was driven by the chemicals, power, construction and building materials sectors, with reported growth up by 32.4%, 5.8%, 7%, and 13.6%, respectively. On the other hand, extractive industries declined by 8.8%. After its recapitalisation in 2014, 'Industries Chimiques du Sénégal' started to show promising signs of recovery and produced over 1 m tonnes of phosphates. The government sought a buyer for the two ailing Suneor and Transrail companies. The state temporarily nationalised Suneor, the main processor of peanuts, after Advens Group, the main shareholder, withdrew its assets on 26 October. On 7 December, the Senegalese and Malian governments chose to unilaterally terminate the concession contract of Transail, an Advens Group affiliated company in charge of the Dakar-Bamako railway, which had been in debt for years. The *tertiary sector* maintained its good track record (+4.1%). The *abolition of the visa system* from 1 May (it had been introduced in July 2013) did not reverse the plummeting of the tourism sector.

Several *law reforms* were passed that impacted on the economy. In January, a draft Mining Code was presented to the National Assembly. Its overall objective was to increase state royalties and revenues from the mining sector for local communities, while still maintaining an attractive environment for investors. A bill prohibiting plastic bags, and a new Fisheries Code to reinforce the conservation of marine stocks and the penalties for illegal fishing, were passed in April and June, respectively.

Wage employment in the modern sector grew by 2.6% due to a strong 9.6% growth of the workforce in the tertiary sector, in contrast to employment in the secondary sector, which was down by 3%. The *unemployment rate* reached 13%. A number of *social conflicts* occurred during the year. Doctors and health sector employees went on strike in April and August, commuter train employees in April, and the garbage collectors of Dakar in May, calling for better working conditions or wage increases. The public *education sector* remained a burning issue. On 3 February, in front of the Education Office in Dakar, the 'Syndicat Autonome de l'Enseignement Supérieur' (SAES) burnt the law governing university governance, which had been adopted in

December 2014. The unions were defending academic freedom from attempts to make places on universities' boards available to private companies. On 17 March, the SAES and the government reached an agreement amending 12 of the law's 22 articles, which were eventually passed on 18 December. Members of secondary school education unions went on strike six times during the year, calling for the implementation of the February 2014 memorandum of understanding. The unions and the government agreed on an implementation plan for the memorandum on 17 April. On 3 August, when President Sall came to inaugurate new university buildings on the Dakar campus, his motorcade was stoned by students shouting 'Justice!' for their comrade, Bassirou Faye, who had been killed in 2014. On 12 October, Sall met union leaders in order to avoid tensions in the new school year, and announced a special grant of CFAfr 5 bn for the education sector.

Sierra Leone

Krijn Peters

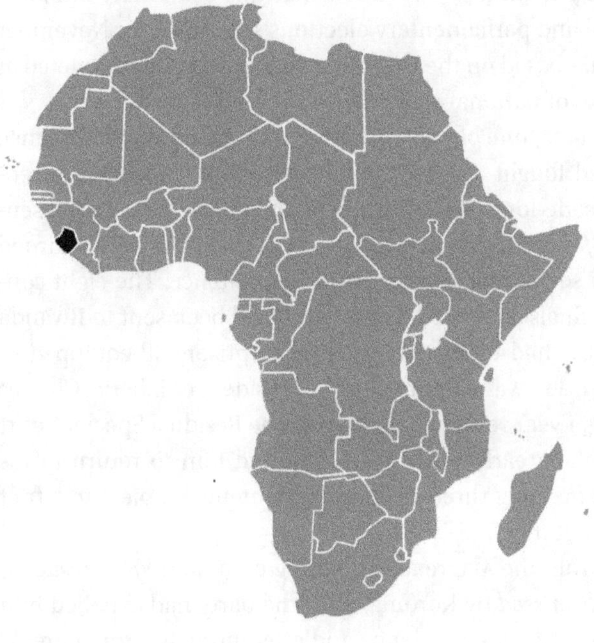

For the second year in a row, life in Sierra Leone was dominated by the Ebola epidemic. Although the disease peaked in the last months of 2014, the beginning of 2015 still saw hundreds of new cases reported each month. Gradually, these numbers declined and the last case was reported in September, allowing President Koroma to declare Sierra Leone 'Ebola free' in November, although vigilance continued to be required. Economically, the country was hit by the epidemic and the collapse in world market prices for iron ore. GDP contracted by more than 20%, although expectations were that the country would bounce back sooner rather than later. On the political front, little happened. The main event was Koroma's dismissal of Vice President Sam-Sumana. There were no indications that the president would not complete his second term, with elections scheduled for late 2017.

Domestic Politics

In February, President Ernest Bai Koroma was forced to postpone the National Housing and Population Census (NHPC), following criticism that his political party,

 | DOI 10.1163/9789004333239_019

the All Peoples Congress (APC), would be over-represented on the NHPC's management committee and that restructuring of electoral district boundaries might have an impact on the *electoral register* in favour of the Northern Province – the ruling party's stronghold. The new date for the commencement of the census was announced to be December 2016, but it was feared that this could have a knock-on effect on the presidential and parliamentary elections scheduled for November 2017, as electoral registration –based on the NHPC – would have to be completed at least one year before the date of national elections.

On 12 March, Moinina Fofana, one of the top commanders of the Civil Defence Forces – the militia that had fought against the Revolutionary United Front rebels during Sierra Leone's decade-long civil war (1991–2002) and who had been sentenced by the *Special Court for Sierra Leone* (SCSL) to 15 years in prison – returned from Rwanda where he had served nearly 12 years of his sentence. The eight convicted Sierra Leone war criminals convicted by the SCSL had been sent to Rwanda to serve their time, as the UN had found Sierra Leonean prisons ill-equipped to house the convicts. The exception was warlord-turned-president of Liberia, Charles Taylor, who was serving his 50-year sentence in the UK. The Residual Special Court for Sierra Leone granted Fofana early release, and allowed him to return to his native town of Bo for the remaining three years of his sentence, subject to "strict conditions and stringent monitoring".

On 18 March, tensions within the APC reached boiling point and *Vice President, Samuel Sam-Sumana, was dismissed* by Koroma, after the party had expelled him on 6 March. He was accused of fuelling violence and attempting to form a breakaway party. On 14 March, while he was still under self-imposed quarantine following the death of one of his bodyguards from Ebola, Sam-Sumana went into hiding when armed troops started to surround his house. He subsequently tried to claim asylum at the US embassy, stating that his life was in danger. A few days after Sam-Sumana's dismissal, Victor Bockarie Foh, Sierra Leone's ambassador to China and formerly APC secretary-general for over a decade, was appointed as the new vice president. Most opposition parties and civil society organisations, such as the Sierra Leone Labour Congress and the Sierra Leone Bar Association, rallied behind Sam-Sumana, and stated that they would not recognise Foh as vice president. Sam-Sumana then launched a legal challenge against the president's ruling, claiming that he had not been appointed by the president but elected under the Constitution of Sierra Leone. Having adjourned on 9 April, the Supreme Court unanimously rejected the injunction on 5 May and, on 9 September, ruled against Sam-Sumana, arguing that he was responsible for his own downfall because of his expulsion from the APC.

Foreign Affairs

On 15 February, at a local summit in neighbouring Guinea, the presidents of Sierra Leone, Guinea and Liberia, pledged to eradicate Ebola in their respective countries by mid-April. This was a highly ambitious goal, illustrated by the fact that just two days before the summit, 700 homes in Freetown were placed under quarantine, following new cases in the area.

On 2 March, SN Brussels Airlines hosted Koroma at its Belgium headquarters, where it confirmed its ongoing commitment to serving Lungi International Airport.

During an Ebola summit at the World Bank/IMF spring meetings in April in Washington DC, Koroma, together with President Sirleaf of Liberia and President Condé of Guinea, presented his *Ebola recovery plans*. The summit was attended by global development leaders, including World Bank President Jim Yong Kim.

On 29 June, the Africa50 initiative, supported by the AfDB and intended to serve as a new infrastructure investment platform, held its Constitutive General Assembly in Casablanca (Morocco). Member countries, including Sierra Leone, had so far contributed $ 830 m. The aim of Africa50 was to mobilise African savings and private sector finance, and act as a public-private investment bank for infrastructure development in Africa.

Socioeconomic Developments

On 20 January, the World Bank Group released a report, 'The *Economic Impact of Ebola on* Sub Saharan Africa: Updated Estimates for 2015', which stated that the pre-Ebola growth rate for Sierra Leone of 8.9% had been brought down to a 2% contraction of the economy. The only positive finding in the report was that it recognised that one particular worst case scenario – that the epidemic might affect the wider region beyond the MRU countries – was unlikely to materialise. Three days later, on 23 January, the ban on the movement of people in six of the country's 14 districts was lifted. The ban had negatively affected rural areas and consequently resulted in a shortage of local food production.

On 5 February, the IMF announced a debt relief package for Sierra Leone, Liberia and Guinea worth $ 100 m and indicated that it was willing to release an additional $ 160 m in concessional loans. According to estimates by the World Bank, almost 180,000 people had lost their jobs since the start of the epidemic. The first week of February still saw 76 new Ebola cases reported in the country, although this was less than half of the 184 new cases reported in the first week of the previous month and a long way down from the 500 new cases per week at the peak of the crisis in November 2014.

In February, the Audit Service Sierra Leone, mandated by the Constitution, submitted its report to Parliament on the *(mis)management of Ebola funds*, covering the period May to October 2014. Corruption within the Ministry of Health and Sanitation was confirmed regarding tens of millions of US dollars meant for Ebola treatment centres, ambulances and pay for Ebola health workers.

On 3 March, representatives of UN organisations pledged their support at an international conference in Brussels, organised by the EU, under the heading 'Ebola: from emergency relief to assistance to recovery'. Participants were the UN Secretary-General's Special Envoy on Ebola, Dr David Nabarro, WHO Director-General Dr Margaret Chan, and Head of UNDP Helen Clarke. The number of Ebola cases had fallen throughout March, giving hope that the end of the epidemic was in sight. Nevertheless, the country remained extremely vigilant and on 27 March the government imposed another three-day lockdown to give health workers the opportunity to check for unreported cases of Ebola virus disease (EVD).

In early April, WHO reported that in the week up to 5 April only nine new cases of EVD had been reported and, on 14 April, schools across the country started to reopen after being closed for more than eight months. The closure had affected nearly 2 m children. On 17 April, the World Bank pledged another $ 650 m to help the Ebola recovery process, making its total pledge $ 1.6 bn for the three affected countries, Sierra Leone, Liberia and Guinea. The announcement followed new estimates of how much the epidemic was costing Sierra Leone, with GDP losses put at $ 1.4 bn. It was estimated that the 2014/15 crisis did $ 2.2 bn of economic damage, only partly offset by international *Ebola recovery funds*. With such an enormous loss in GDP, it was particularly pleasing that on 21 April, Sierra Rutile, active in the country for nearly half a century, announced the construction of a $ 44 m dry mine at Gangama. This was a much welcomed investment in a country hit by the collapse of the iron ore industry. Sierra Rutile currently employed nearly 2,250 people and this new investment would create jobs both in the construction of the mine and during its operation. The first phase of the two-phase project was expected to bring down the company's total operating cash costs to $ 595 per tonne, making it one of the foremost low-cost/high quality producers on the global market.

On 4 May, a *Social Safety Net* programme was initiated. Financed by a $ 7 m grant from the IDA, in addition to $ 1 m from the Sierra Leone government and $ 300,000 from UNICEF, it allowed for repeated cash transfers to more than 20,000 extremely poor households affected by Ebola. In August, the board of executive directors of the World Bank approved an additional $ 10 m for the Social Safety Net programme to provide direct cash support. Francis Ato Brown, the World Bank's country manager for Sierra Leone, applauded the Social Safety Net system for being able to reach the poorest families, who were particularly hard-hit by the negative impact of EVD. More than 7,000 people were estimated to benefit from these additional funds. On 5 June, President Koroma and President Condé of Guinea released a joint statement in which they announced that they would extend the reinforced emergency measures in their countries until 30 June because of the persistence of the epidemic.

On 8 July, Palo Conteh, head of the government's National Ebola Response Centre, stated that the 6:00 pm to 6:00 am curfew – put in place in June as part of Operation Northern Push – had been indefinitely extended in the worst-affected communities in north-west Sierra Leone. Two days later, on 10 July, a UN summit pledged $ 3.4 bn to support Sierra Leone, Liberia and Guinea's struggle against Ebola. This was just over the amount estimated by the UN be needed to cover the three countries' national recovery plans. The total amount pledged so far was more than $ 5 bn, with pledges from both multi-lateral organisations such as the AfDB ($ 745 m), the Islamic Development Bank ($ 360 m) and the EU ($ 500 m), and bilateral donors such as the UK ($ 381 m), the USA ($ 266 m) and Germany ($ 220 m).

As an indication of the progress made in combating the Ebola epidemic, in August officials lifted the ban on sporting events and nightclubs, although, on 7 August, Koroma urged that "all Ebola prevention protocols, including temperature screening of employees and customers and the prevention of overcrowding" needed to be observed. The following month, the deadly disease struck again, and hundreds of people were quarantined on 14 September following the death of a 16-year-old girl from Ebola. The case was probably the result of sexual transmission. It became increasingly evident that the virus could be transmitted by Ebola survivors long after they had been declared free of EVD, as it survived in bodily fluids. However, *on 27 September the last Ebola patient was discharged* from a special medical centre and the north of the country saw its quarantine restrictions lifted, which triggered the start of the 42-day period in which, if no new cases were reported the country would be declared Ebola free. Previous experiences showed that this was by no way a secure process.

Flash-floods are a recurring problem in Freetown during the rainy season, exacerbated by bad planning and dwellings erected illegally in flood-prone areas. In early September, thousands of people had to leave their homes when they were destroyed by floodwater, and were forced to remain in temporary camps. A five-hour storm flooded over 20 neighbourhoods and Connaught Hospital. The dead toll was put at ten.

In September, the IMF estimated that *GDP would contract by around 15%*, revising downwards earlier forecasts, as a result of the Ebola crisis triggering increased health-related spending and lower agricultural production, on top of the collapse of the iron ore mining industry. Following the closure of the African Minerals and London Mining iron ore mines, about 7,500 people lost their jobs. In the first half of the year, gold exports dropped from 11,751 grams in January to under 4,000 grams in July. Diamond exports fell by 50%. Even taking into account seasonal variations in export figures, it was clear that the Ebola outbreak had affected the mainly rural workforce in both industries. Following a two-week visit during the first half of September by an IMF team to study structural reform measures, the IMF head of mission, Jon Wakeman-Linn, stated that to maintain macroeconomic stability a strong policy commitment was pivotal, which he said would result in long-term growth. Special reference was made to the socio-economic impact of the Ebola crisis and the collapse of the mining industry, more specifically to the cessation of iron ore mining due to plummeting world market prices.

On 21 October, a grant of just over $ 33 m was approved by the AfDB to create a Post Ebola Recovery Social Investment Fund to help the Ebola-affected MRU countries in their implementation of their National Post Ebola Recovery strategies. AfDB's Director for Human Development Sunita Pitabmer said: "Building on lessons learned from the response, recovery efforts should ensure that people and their communities are at the centre of the recovery process. The regional nature of this epidemic calls for regional solutions to leverage economies of scale, systems strengthening, improved governance, communication, coordination and community involvement." The fund, managed by the MRU Secretariat, aimed to reach 2,000 vulnerable children and 5,000 Ebola survivors.

On 7 November, during a ceremony in the presence of President Koroma and WHO representative Anders Nordstrom, Sierra Leone was *declared Ebola free.* People took to the streets to celebrate the news. This followed 42 days – double the maximum incubation period – with no new EVD cases. Nordstrom said: "The world had never faced an Ebola outbreak of this scale and magnitude and the world has never seen a nation mobilising its people and resources as Sierra Leone did." The Ebola outbreak had dominated the life of the country's citizens for much of 2014 and 2015 and took the lives of nearly 4,000 Sierra Leoneans. The official end of the epidemic triggered a three-month surveillance period to stem any new outbreaks as soon as possible. More than 220 health workers died during the epidemic, severely undermining the country's already fragile and weak health infrastructure. Before the Ebola crisis, the country already had the fifth-worst ratio of doctors to population in the world. Cases of malaria and measles had already risen and a World Bank report entitled 'Healthcare Worker Mortality and the Legacy of the Ebola Epidemic' indicated that maternal deaths could increase by 74%. As a short-term measure, around 1,300 expatriate health workers were active in the three most affected countries. However, in the longer term, an additional 43,000 health workers (midwives, nurses and doctors) needed to be hired across the MRU countries.

On 16 November, the IMF Executive Board finished its third and fourth reviews of Sierra Leone's achievements under the three-year ECF. This triggered the disbursement of just over $ 46 m. The deputy managing director and acting chair, Min Zhu, spoke of the economic challenges that the country would face now that it was declared Ebola free. Specifically, he referred to the drop in iron ore prices, which had resulted in the closure of the main iron ore mines, and its knock-on effect on the wider economy and the government's fiscal budget.

On 17 December, the AfDB signed off on a $ 20 m loan for the construction and operation of a *new power plant.* It was hoped that the frequently recurring blackouts that plagued the capital city, Freetown, would become a thing of the past, and that the new plant would significantly raise the percentage of the population with access to electricity from its current low of 10%. The heavy fuel oil plant would have a 50 MW capacity and would be located in the Kissy area of eastern Freetown. Once operational, it would increase the generating capacity of the existing grid by more than 50%.

At the end of the year, Finance and Economic Planning Minister Kaifala Marah stated that the economy had contracted by 21%, inflation would reach 10% and revenue shortfalls would rise to nearly 5% of GDP. On the other hand, the Ebola crisis also resulted in more foreign currency inflows, having a positive effect on the current account balance and foreign reserves accumulation. However, the minister expected that, with the EVD crisis over, the economy would be recovering, producing growth figures close to 20% by 2017.

Endemic corruption remained a key problem. The Afrobarometer research group, together with TI in its 'People and Corruption: African Survey 2015', found that, while neighbouring Liberia had the highest rate of bribery, with nearly 70% of those interviewed stating that bribes had to paid to access public services, Sierra Leone came second (jointly with Cameroon and Nigeria), with between 40% and 50% of interviewees indicating the need to pay bribes to public servants. Reporting corrupt officials remained at a low of around 10%, despite government efforts to provide anonymous reporting mechanisms.

Togo

Dirk Kohnert

The presidential elections of 25 April resulted in a victory for the incumbent, Faure Gnassingbé. Thus, he secured his third five-year term, strengthening the autocratic grip of the Gnassingbé-clan, which had been in power since 1967. The institutional and constitutional reforms that would have been required for free and fair elections and which the opposition parties, civil society and international donors demanded, were postponed indefinitely. Nevertheless, the international community declared the elections free and fair, given their security interests in the region. Economic growth remained stable at about 5% p.a., although economic growth rates were not inclusive and benefitted the few. The business climate improved considerably.

Domestic Politics

Presidential elections had initially been envisaged for March and opposition and civil society groups pressed all the more urgently for constitutional and institutional reforms of the electoral system, which were assessed as a necessary precondition for free and fair elections. According to an Afrobarometer survey in October 2014, 85% of the population were in favour of procedural reforms, calling for the reestablishment of a limit on presidential terms, which the late head of state Gnassingbé

 | DOI 10.1163/9789004333239_020

Eyadéma had abolished in 2002 by an illegitimate amendment of the 1992 constitution. However, government and opposition could not agree on either the scope or the timetable of the reforms.

After two weeks of futile consultations, the draft electoral reform law was rejected at the end of January. Although the Constitutional Court had ruled that the polls should be held between 17 February and 5 March, Minister of Territorial Administration Gilbert Bawara announced that the elections would be delayed till mid-April, citing mainly logistical issues.

Opposition groups did not object because they felt that they would benefit from additional campaigning time, but were divided on the question of whether to boycott the elections, given these unfair conditions. In February, the 'Comité d'Action pour la Renouveau' warned the opposition and the international community not to participate in an "ongoing electoral charade". The opposition increasingly moved away from putting forward a joint opposition candidate, which was the only way to challenge the incumbent effectively. Given the biased electoral system, discord within the opposition, and the strength that the ruling party 'Union pour la République' (UNIR) had acquired, a victory for any opposition candidate seemed unlikely. In February, international and national human rights organisations, including the Truth and Reconciliation Commission (CVJR), the 'Collectif des Associations Contre l'Impunité au Togo' and the 'Plateforme Citoyenne Justice et Vérité' (PCJV), had advocated political reforms, warning that failure to implement them could lead to electoral violence. Nevertheless, a majority within the newly formed opposition coalition 'Combat pour l'Alternance Politique en 2015' (CAP 2015) was in favour of contesting the elections and supported Jean-Pierre Fabre, the leader of the main opposition party, the 'Alliance Nationale pour le Changement'.

The *presidential elections* took place on 25 April, with about 3.5 m people entitled to vote. The disputed electoral system stipulated that the president would be elected for a five-year term, the winner being the candidate with the most votes after a single round of voting. That is, the winner did not need to have an absolute majority in the first round, as stipulated by the controversial 2002 amendment to the constitution, which favoured the incumbent. Apart from the incumbent, Faure Gnassingbé, and the leading opposition candidate, Jean-Pierre Fabre, there were three other contestants from smaller opposition parties: Aimé T. Gogué of the 'Alliance des Démocrates pour le Développement Intégral', Gerry K. Taama, the leader of 'Nouvel Engagement pour le Togo', and Mohamed Tchassona Traoré of the 'Mouvement Citoyen pour la Démocratie et le Développement'.

After three days of quarrelling and tension within the Electoral Commission ('Commission Électorale Nationale Indépendante'; CENI), its president announced the results on 28 April – prematurely, as 28 of the 42 reports of the local electoral commissions had not yet been examined in plenary – and declared that *Faure Gnassingbé* had won an absolute majority with 58.8% of valid votes, against 35.2% for Jean-Pierre Fabre (CAP 2015) and 3% for Aimé T. Gogué. AU, ECOWAS and UN observer missions declared the polls free and fair, despite opposition complaints on

30 April that irregularities had taken place. A confidential report of an EU electoral mission, prepared between 12 March and 7 May, which was leaked to the press on 26 October, confirmed these claims. The report recognised the generally peaceful conduct of the polls but criticised irregular high rates of voter registration (99.9% nationwide), based only on simple testimony, notably in the northern districts, where support for the incumbent had historically been high: Centrale and Kara-Binah (137%), Bassar (121%), Dankpen (177%), Doufelgou (117%), Kozah (114%), Kéran (109%) and Assoli (106%). Registration rates were significantly lower in regions considered to be the stronghold of the opposition (especially the Maritime region). In addition, the reported voter turnout was higher in the north. According to the CENI, turnout was initially estimated at about 53% nationwide, i.e. at least 10% lower than at the previous presidential elections in 2010 (64%), but this was later adjusted to 61% without explanation. The fall in turnout compared with the previous polls was interpreted as a sign of growing voter fatigue, which may have been aggravated by the boycott called for by smaller opposition parties and a potentially high number of voters who could not cast their vote because of technical problems, especially in the Maritime region. On 3 May, the Constitutional Court ratified the result, which was not challenged by the CAP 2015 because it did not believe in the impartiality of the Court, given its composition and similar decisions in the past.

Thus, Faure Gnassingbé easily secured a *third five-year term in office* and thereby the extension of the autocratic rule of the Gnassingbé family, which had already been in power for 48 years, a world record, topped only by North Korea, as pointed out by the international NGO 'Tournons La Page'. The opposition had little opportunity to challenge the regime through democratic elections, given the extensive influence and material resources that were at the government's disposal. Apart from the biased electoral system and the state-controlled media, the opposition was subjected to additional forms of judicial and financial repression, including a policy of divide and rule, combined with a carrot and stick strategy, and systematic weakening of the opposition's local power base. The last had been effected by, among other things, the replacement of local mayors and communal councillors by special delegates nominated by the administration in 2001, and, most importantly, by the endless postponement of local elections since 1987.

After the resignation of Prime Minister Ahoomey-Zunu on 22 May, the president appointed *Selom Komi Klassou* as the new premier on 5 June. The 55-year-old Klassou, an Ewe originating from Notsè, and regarded as a hardliner and long-time ally of the Gnassingbé regime, had been a member of the politbureau of the former unity party, the 'Rassemblement du Peuple Togolais' (the antecedent of the ruling UNIR), and had served as cabinet minister under both the late dictator Eyadéma and his son Faure. He had also been the campaign manager in the disputed 2005 presidential election, which had assured Faure's succession to his late father Eyadéma on the latter's death. On 28 June, Klassou announced his *new cabinet*, reduced from 26 to 23 members. It included four women (a cutback from 26% in 2013 to 17%), including the third most important member of the government, Victoire Dogbé, director of the presidential cabinet, who kept her portfolio as minister of grassroots development, youth and youth employment. Twelve former cabinet members were reappointed, including Minister of Foreign Affairs and Cooperation Robert Dussey, and Minister of Security Colonel Yark Damehane. Adji Otèth Ayassor became the only minister of state, overseeing the Ministry of Economy and Finance, which now merged with the Planning Ministry and thus became a 'super-ministry'. Gilbert Bawara, former minister of territorial administration, became minister of labour and social dialogue, responsible for, among other things, relations with civil society organisations, including labour unions. Abli Bidamon, former chief of Togolese customs, was awarded the strategic Ministry of Mines and Energy in recognition of his loyal service in the CENI. The junior coalition partners, the 'Union des Forces de Changement' (UFC) and 'Convergence Patriotique Panafricaine', kept the Ministries of Environment (André Johnson) and Higher Education (Octave Broohm), respectively, while the former foreign minister Elliot Ohin (UFC) was demoted to minister without portfolio to the prime minister. The Defence Ministry remained (as it had since 2008) in the hands of the president, apparently as precaution against possible coup attempts.

All in all, Togo was still rated as an 'authoritarian regime' in the democracy index of the Economic Intelligence Unit (London). In the global ranking of the independent Democracy Ranking Association (Vienna) published on 29 December, Togo was ranked 110th of 113 countries. The population was becoming increasingly frustrated by the regime's inability to initiate meaningful reforms. According to the World Database on Happiness (an index of subjective wellbeing), the Togolese came among the lowest of the 149 countries surveyed, and the UN World Happiness Report of 2015 ranked Togo as the lowest country worldwide, a drop since the previous report of 2005–7.

The regime delayed the implementation of most of the *recommendations for reform* made by the CVJR in 2012. In March, the government established an 'Haut Commissariat pour la Réconciliation et le Renforcement de l'Unité Nationale', supplemented by a civil-society platform, the PCJV, in order to accelerate implementation. The National Human Rights Commission ('Commission Nationale des Droits de l'Homme'; CNDH) complained of a lack of resources and of the government's unwillingness to cooperate. A bill to improve the composition and organisation of the CNDH, particularly with respect to the prevention of torture, was adopted in Parliament in mid-October. On 31 December, the CNDH handed to the government its report on the violence that had ensued following a government attempt to implement a nature conservation project in Mango (Northern Togo) without due popular consultation. In November, the intervention of the army to quell the local population's protests had resulted in eight deaths. AI and CAP 2015 activists called for an independent inquiry, the release of 11 persons detained in the Dapaong prison, and reparations for the families of the victims.

In late December, the government adopted a bill for the creation of a response force composed of retired military personnel to improve national security. On 28 December, another bill, providing guidelines for regional planning, was passed in parliament in order to enhance the national policy of comprehensive regional planning as enacted in the council of ministers in 2009.

Foreign Affairs

At the *ECOWAS* summit in Accra (Ghana) on 19 May, the heads of state dropped a proposal to restrict West African presidents to serving two terms in office. Togo and Gambia, the only ECOWAS members who had not yet introduced the limit, were reportedly the driving forces behind the rejection of the proposal.

Unlike in 2010, the *EU* did not send a delegation to observe the presidential elections because its recommendations concerning the previous 2010 and 2007 elections had not been implemented. However, the EU did assist the electoral process by, for example, co-funding 1,200 national election observers, a project launched by the 'Concertation Nationale de la Société Civile au Togo', a network of 53 civil society organisations founded in 2002. Jérome Leyraud, an expert commissioned by the EU to monitor the elections, was expelled from the country shortly after his arrival in late March because of his critical remarks in a 2013 EU report on the parliamentary elections. Togolese Commissioner of Economy and Finance Adji Otèth Ayassor had already in February asked the resident representative of the IMF, Werner Keller, to leave the country ahead of schedule because of his outspoken criticism of the hesitant implementation of the IMFS recommendations. The IMF responded by announcing the temporary closure of his office in Lomé one month later.

In February, *Germany* provided € 245,000 for the formation and training of administrators and local leaders (prefects, village heads, etc.) within the framework of a UNDP programme in order to guarantee their political neutrality in the electoral process.

At the Togolese government's request, the OIF assigned a committee of experts to assist the CENI from 14 March to 8 April in drawing up the electoral register. At the end of its mission, the OIF stated that the electoral register was incomplete but could nevertheless be accepted because it was not contested by the opposition.

During an official visit to Lomé in March, UN Deputy Secretary General Jeffrey Feltman expressed his concern about standards of democracy and the transparency and credibility of elections. UNDP, among others, had supported the formation of an 8,000-strong security force to oversee the presidential elections ('Force Sécurité Elections Présidentielles; FOSEP 2015). In June, the UN High Commission for Human Rights closed its office in Lomé, which had been founded in 2006 to tackle human rights issues arising from political violence during the 2005 presidential elections. On 11 February, a UN working group on Togo had sought in vain the release of Kpatcha Gnassingbé, the president's half-brother, imprisoned in 2009 on charges of involvement in an alleged coup attempt, and of other prisoners facing the same charges, citing lack of evidence.

Following the terrorist attack on the newspaper 'Charlie Hebdo', on 11 January, Faure Gnassingbé attended a gathering in Paris of 50 world leaders, who met to show their solidarity with France. He underlined that his presence was also to make his European colleagues understand that *terrorism* had to be countered worldwide and to make them aware that he considered it to be the same evil, even if it took different forms in Africa. On 15 December, Saudi Arabia announced the formation of an Islamic military alliance to fight terrorism. The initiative was explicitly not restricted to countering the so-called Islamic State, but was intended to combat all forms of terrorism worldwide, and included 34 member countries. Besides ten Islamic countries, including nations with large and established armies such as Pakistan, Turkey and Egypt, 20 African countries joined the alliance, including Togo, Nigeria and Ivory Coast.

At the end of September, Faure Gnassingbé addressed the 70th session of the UN General Assembly in New York on the progress made by his country in achieving the MDGs. Some days after the adoption of the new 17 sustainable development goals (SDGs), the UN selected Togo to host the first workshop of the working group of Francophone African countries to prepare for the implementation of the SDGs. According to the UN coordinator, Khardiata Lo N'Diaye, this was in recognition of Togo's constructive role in preparing the new SDGs agenda up to 2030.

After the abortive coup in Burkina Faso on 16 September, led by Gen. Gilbert Diendéré, the former chief of President Blaise Compaoré's security guard, Cote d'Ivoire and Togo were accused of having supported the coup attempt, according to international press reports based on the preliminary findings of an investigative commission in Ouagadougou.

The Forum on *China*-Africa Cooperation held its first summit on African soil in Johannesburg (South Africa) on 5 December. The summit was attended by most African leaders, including Faure Gnassingbé, who met Chinese President Xi Jinping one day before the opening. The latter praised the political and economic cooperation with Togo since the establishment of diplomatic ties in 1972 and pledged to strengthen cooperation in infrastructure projects (roads and development of the Lomé port area as a transregional industrial hub), agriculture and the health sector.

Socioeconomic Developments

Real *GDP growth* remained strong because of public investment in national road networks, mining and port infrastructure, as well as productivity gains in agriculture and the recovery of global commodity prices. It had averaged 5.6% in 2013–14 and was projected to remain at this level up to 2018, with inflation staying well below the UEMOA convergence rate of 3%. Industry was the fastest growing sector, last but not least because of recent developments in the key clinker and cement production, including the huge Heidelberg Cement plant in Tabligbo, 80 km north-east of Lomé, which opened in March, with capacity for annual production of 1.5 m tonnes.

Nevertheless, real GDP per capita remained below the UEMOA average and, importantly, growth was not inclusive. According to the latest available figures, income distribution had worsened (Gini coefficient increased from 0.36 to 0.39, 2006–11), and poverty remained high (although declining from 62% in 2006 to 59% in 2011) and, according to the IMF country report released in November, geographically concentrated in rural areas and the north. Moreover, the high level of public investment resulted in a visible increase in *public debt*, rising from 46% of GDP in 2012 to 58% in 2014, which the IMF viewed as unsustainable, although the current account deficit of recent years was projected to improve marginally to 12.5% in 2015 as result of lower oil prices.

Secondary income, especially private *remittances and donor grants* continued to be vital for the balance of payments. About 2 m Togolese were living abroad – 1.5 m within Africa and about 500,000 overseas. Remittances from the Togolese diaspora played a significant role in development. According to OECD statistics for 2014, Togo ranked high on a global scale not only for ODA per capita ($ 91 in 2011, ranked 17th) but also for remittances ($ 52 per capita, ranked 7th). Remittances had steadily increased by 7% over the previous decade and represented 8% of GDP or CFAfr 182 bn ($ 333 m) in 2014.

Tax revenues were expected to rise to 16.8% of GDP in 2015 because of improved revenue collection, but the fiscal deficit was expected to widen from 4.5% of GDP (2014) to 5.1%. The increase was due to public expenditure apparently related to the elections. Against this background, the general *budget* for 2016, approved by Parliament on 30 December, was based on optimistic predictions. With CFAfr 1,002.2 bn (€ 1.524.5 m) in expenditure to be set against CFAfr 962,8 bn in revenue (of which CFAfr 575 bn was projected internal revenue, compared with CFAfr 480 bn in 2014), the budget deficit of CFAfr 39.4 bn was to be financed mainly from extraordinary revenue.

Several *road projects* to improve national and trans-national trade flows were agreed upon in May. They included the upgrading of the vital transit axis Lomé–Ouagadougou that connected the deep-water port of Lomé not only with projected mining areas in northern Togo but also with the landlocked neighbouring countries of Niger and Burkina Faso, thus improving Togo's role as a major commercial and transportation hub within West Africa.

Apart from public works, private *commercial investments* were also implemented. A fertiliser plant managed by the 'Compagnie des Intrants Agricoles du Togo', a branch of the French Mambo Group, began production in the port area of

Lomé in June with an installed capacity of 400,000 tonnes per year. It was to profit from the nearby phosphate mines, like an even bigger $ 1.4 bn *phosphate mining and fertilisers* project with a nominal annual production of 3 m tonnes of phosphate rock concentrates, 500,000 tonnes of phosphoric acid, and 1.3 m tonnes of fertiliser, using energy supplied by the new West African Gas Pipeline. This huge project was the biggest of its kind in West Africa and was contracted in September between the government and a consortium of the Israel-based Elenilto and the Chinese state-owned Wengfu. Based in Kpémé near Lomé, it would significantly contribute upon completion in 2018 to Togo's main export (phosphates represented 11% of total exports in 2014) and to the resurgence in exploration and development of the sixth-largest phosphate mine in Africa. However, notwithstanding the recovery of the ailing phosphate production, which had increased by 9% to 1.2 m tonnes in 2014, equipment constraints slowed down production, and operational accidents and strikes affected the production of clinker and cement.

Cotton production, a major export earner, increased by 45% from 77,850 tonnes of cotton grain in the previous season (2013–14) to 113,000 tonnes in 2014–15, thanks to good weather and the government project to improve the agricultural sector ('Projet d'Appui au Secteur Agricole'; PASA) with an investment of $ 75.5 m over six years. The PASA particularly emphasised cash crops, such as cotton, cacao and palm oil and the government tried to reduce dependency on some 18,000 tonnes of imported palm oil by assisting the Mauritanian company Kaylan Agrovet Investments to plant some 52,000 palm trees on 250 ha at Agou (south-west Togo), to be extended to 1,000 ha by 2016. The group invested $ 65 m, including for the construction of an oil-mill with an annual capacity of 24,000 tonnes of oil by 2022. The *coffee* harvest was expected to yield 11,000 tonnes by the end of the cropping season, compared with 5,000 tonnes before the start of the PASA.

The *business climate* improved considerably. According to the 2015 Doing Business Report, Togo's country ranking improved by 15 places from 164th in 2014 to 149th, the third-best improvement worldwide, although starting from bottom place. Its rating in the Heritage Foundation's index of economic freedom also improved, by 3.1 points from 2014, resulting in Togo being ranked 138th of 166 countries worldwide and 30th of 46 countries in SSA.

On occasion of the annual Ramadan festivities on 17 July, El Hadj Inoussa Bouraïma, president of the most important Togolese Muslim organisation, the 'Union Musulmane du Togo', warned of the ambitions of terrorist groups to propagate Islam by violent means and declared that jihadis had no place in Togolese society. Although there had been no history of Islamist terrorism in Togo, the faithful who had gathered for the festival in Kégué stadium in Lomé were, for the first time, searched by security forces.

PART 4

Central Africa

Andreas Mehler

The transition from crisis to a somewhat more stable situation in the CAR was counter-balanced by serious confrontations between both the Chadian and Cameroonian security forces and the originally Nigeria-based Boko Haram insurgency and continued armed confrontations in the eastern DRC, though arguably of less intensity than in the past. Heads of state in the sub-region proved particularly stubborn in trying to maintain their grip on power, although elections were held in only one country in the sub-region. Historically low prices for crude oil on the world market hit the oil exporting countries severely. Among the sub-regional organisations, CEMAC relocated its headquarter back to Bangui (CAR) and gave up plans for a sub-regional airline, while CEEAC confirmed its status as the most important international forum in Central Africa.

Democracy and Elections

As in previous years, the sub-region demonstrated lower levels of democratic achievement than West, Eastern and Southern Africa. With the notable exception of São Tomé and Príncipe, all the other countries in the sub-region were rated 'not free' by Freedom House, and similar agencies came to the same conclusion. For example, the Bertelsmann Transformation Index, rating only the five most populated countries, put all of them in the category of 'hard-line autocracies', though – at least partially in contradiction – two of them (the DRC and the CAR) were also marked as 'failing states'. In fact, at least with regard to the CAR, it was difficult to assume that a transitional government under international tutelage could exert any form of autocratic rule.

After numerous postponements, the first leg of presidential elections took place in the *CAR* shortly before year's end, surely representing a major step towards terminating the transitional period that had started in early 2014. The elections were preceded by a constitutional referendum that was interpreted not only as a necessary condition, but also as a test-run for holding elections in a highly volatile security situation. No elections were held in any other country of the sub-region. Quite to the contrary, members of the *Chadian* National Assembly extended their own mandate – legally due to expire in the summer – until 2017. The official line was that the census, which made it possible to issue biometric identity and voting cards, could not be completed in time and this served as the justification for postponing elections till after presidential polls scheduled for early 2016. Controversies over the electoral law, the electoral register and the entire electoral process impeded the

 | DOI 10.1163/9789004333239_021

holding of provincial elections in the DRC and posed serious challenges for holding national elections, also planned for 2016.

In contrast, preparations were underway to allow the mostly autocratic regimes of the region to extend the mandates of mostly unpopular presidents. This was most visible in the case of *Congo*, where President Denis Sassou Nguesso engaged into political and technical preparations for a constitutional referendum. Unlike other autocrats eager to get a third term in office not provided for in an existing constitution, Sassou Nguesso had to overcome three high legal hurdles specified in the Congo Constitution. Those included the specific stipulation of only one possible re-election (after 2002 and 2009), a further regulation that set an age limit for presidents at 70 (Nguesso being already 71) and a particularly strict regulation that the number of a president's terms in office could not be changed by a simple amendment to the Constitution. It was therefore obvious that only a completely new constitution would solve matters and that a referendum on the new constitution would be needed if the president's wish was to be fulfilled. This referendum was finally held on 25 October. According to official figures (fiercely contested by the opposition) some 92% of voters endorsed the new Constitution – though the high turn-out of 73% looked barely credible. The referendum opened the way for Sassou Nguesso to obtain a further mandate in elections scheduled for 2016. Even the sub-region's oldest president, Paul Biya of Cameroon (born 1933) gave indications that he could be interested in a further re-election in 2018, when he would have served 36 years in office.

The 'third-term controversy' situation in the sub-region was as follows: In Chad, provisions to limit presidential mandates had been scrapped in 2006, and in Cameroon in 2008; Congo now joined this group of countries, while the DRC's President Kabila was heading towards the same goal. President Obiang Nguema in Equatorial Guinea had no such constitutional obstacles and was safely jockeying for his sixth re-election in 2016. There were no term limits either in the case of Gabon, where President Ali Bongo Ondimba was preparing to start a second mandate in 2016. Both the new constitution in the CAR just adopted by referendum and that in São Tomé and Príncipe stick to a two-term limit.

Instability, War and Peace

Confrontations in the CAR occurred strictly on a local level, mostly along a notional borderline separating zones of influence of at least three different Séléka factions and territories under the vague control of so-called Anti-balaka groups. Locally, communities supported different armed groups, but the meta-narrative of a mostly interreligious conflict (Christians against Muslims) was increasingly unable to claim credibility. This may have been linked to the fact that a good part of the Muslim population had already fled either to safe havens or to neighbouring countries.

In addition, AI reported from some places that Anti-balaka militia had forced Muslims to convert to Christianity. The capital Bangui was again the scene of a major act of violence when a neighbourhood bordering the PK5 area, including a Protestant church, was razed to the ground. Pope Francis visited Bangui in November and contributed to the calming down of religious tensions.

The Lord's Resistance Army (*LRA*), operating mostly in the DRC and the CAR, but occasionally also in South Sudan, was not fully defeated though there were more signs of decline. The arrest of LRA commander Dominic Ongwen in January was a highly publicised event. Ongwen testified to the weakness of the dreaded militia and was transferred to The Hague to face trial before the ICC. However, LRA leader Joseph Kony remained at large. He managed to ally with other locally armed groups, obviously including some Séléka units (who also claimed that they had originally detained Ongwen before handing him over to US forces, but had not received the promised reward).

The DRC's eastern provinces were the scene of further military actions, mostly against armed movements combating regimes in neighbouring countries, but operating on Congolese soil. Unilaterally, government forces launched a large-scale military operation against the pro-Hutu 'Forces Démocratiques de Libération du Rwanda' (*FDLR*) in January without the participation of the UN Force Intervention Brigade, which came as a surprise after the intense joint preparations for the operation. The 'Front National de Libération' (FNL), a rebel movement that aimed to overthrow Burundi's President Pierre Nkurunziza, was also targeted by government forces in South Kivu province, but this time with support from the international peacekeeping mission MONUSCO, although Kinshasa was also concerned about groups of pro-Nkurunziza 'Ibonerakure' militia crossing the frontier in pursuit of FNL fighters. Finally, the Ugandan Allied Defence Forces operating in North Kivu continued to clash with government forces. Further to the north, in Ituri, the 'Force de Résistance Patriotique en Ituri' (*FRPI*) was constantly in and out of negotiations with the government, and the security forces managed to win a few battles against them over the course of the year.

The *Boko Haram* insurgency, originating in north-east Nigeria, posed serious security challenges to Chad and Cameroon. Both countries tried to coordinate their military efforts (including with Niger and Nigeria) within the CBLT framework. Attacks in Cameroon's Far North region and in Chad's Lake Chad area became increasingly violent and claimed many lives (potentially over 1,000 in total). Suicide bombings, including in Cameroon's provincial capital Maroua, where 33 were killed in July, caused panic beyond the localities where they occurred. The Chadian government ordered the inhabitants of some islands in Lake Chad to relocate to IDP camps. Both countries stepped up their military actions and constantly claimed success in their anti-terrorism efforts. However, repression resulted in many arbitrary arrests, including of children, and it was significant that the governments made no tangible efforts to complement purely military strategies with political, social or cultural programmes to reduce the attraction of a movement that was clearly not recruiting in Nigeria alone. Boko Haram issued direct threats to both governments.

The most recent upsurge in refugees from Syria may have obfuscated the fact that the sub-region remained a major source of refugees, as well as having to cope with significant refugee inflows from elsewhere. The DRC had, according to UNHCR, a "total number of concern" in nearly 3 m people, of whom 1,555,112 were IDPs, 736,837 returned IDPs and 541,291 refugees from neighbouring countries. UNHCR statistics indicated that there were 471,100 refugees from the CAR at the end of the year, making it the seventh-largest country of origin worldwide. Cameroon (267,500), the DRC (107,900), Chad (63,400), and Congo (23,700) were the most important host countries for them. The number of CAR refugees in Congo and the DRC declined fractionally over the year as 21,632 returned to their country of origin. The number of IDPs in the CAR also declined from over 400,000 to 216,392 at year's end. Cameroon and Chad also had important numbers of IDPs protected or assisted by UNHCR (92,657 and 51,999 respectively).

Human Rights

The severe human rights violations perpetrated by the *Boko Haram rebellion* and the *responses by governments* in Cameroon, Chad (and Nigeria) were a major source of concern. AI issued a report in September ('Human rights under fire: Attacks and violations in Cameroon's struggle with Boko Haram') and estimated the number of civilians killed by Boko Haram from January 2014 to September 2015 to be at least 380. The Cameroonian security forces were at best only marginally less brutal and arrested over 1,000 suspected Boko Haram sympathisers. Controls on mosques and Qur'an schools became daily practice.

The humanitarian, social and political consequences of the serious confrontations in the CAR became more tangible during the year. AI issued a report titled 'Erased identity: Muslims in ethnically-cleansed areas', highlighting forced conversion from Islam to Christianity in some localities. An open letter to Pope Francis by 18 human rights organisations published on the occasion of his CAR trip appealed to him to focus on Muslims who had to hide their faith under threat from Anti-balaka militias. A separate substantial AI report motivated by human rights abuses in the diamond sector focussed on supply chains and smuggling. It pinpointed weaknesses in the Kimberley Process from which the CAR was suspended as a result of its civil war. In July, the CAR was in principle allowed to resume diamond exports from some areas under government control and subject to certain conditions (but official diamond exporting did not resume during the year). However, it was obvious that diamond smuggling, at least from rebel-held territories, continued and enriched the treasury of Séléka rebel factions. In the same context, the US-based Enough project issued a report on 'Warlord business' on 17 June, which focussed on profit-driven illegal operations by the CAR's violent armed groups. HRW, in a shorter report on 15 December, documented acts of sexual violence against women and girls by armed militia men in Bangui.

In a report issued on 25 May, AI documented arbitrary detentions, deportations, torture, rape and other crimes of sexual violence, persecution and other inhumane acts in the context of the so-called operation *Mbata ya Bakolo*, a repressive action by security forces from the Republic of *Congo* against mostly DRC citizens; about 180.000 DRC nationals were deported in 2014.

The manifest threats against lesbian, gay, bisexual, transgender and intersexual (*LGBTI*) persons in *Cameroon* remained a source of concern. A fact-finding mission initiated by the 'Fédération Internationale des Droits de l'Homme' had toured Cameroon in 2014 and published its report on 25 February in conjunction with the Human Rights Defenders Network in Central Africa, the 'Maison des Droits de l'Homme au Cameroun' and the association African Men for Sexual Health and Rights. The report referred to "alarming proportions" of threats and physical assaults against LGBTI human rights defenders in Cameroon. The hostility was not limited to this sector, however; NGO activists in the forestry sector were equally under pressure.

The overall human rights situation was certainly no better in *Chad*, where Djeralar Miankeol, director of Association Ngaoubourandi, an NGO working on land use and settler-herder conflicts, was arrested after criticising the corrupt practices of judicial officers in a radio programme. He was convicted on 7 July of "insulting the judiciary" and given a two-year prison sentence plus a fine; AI named him as a 'prisoner of conscience'. Repression in Chad was a daily practice.

A joint report by Global Witness and AI on problematic due diligence examinations by US-based firms using minerals from the *DRC* analysed 100 reports filed by companies under a section of the so-called Dodd-Frank Act – a law that required companies listed on US stock exchanges to check whether their mineral purchases were funding warring parties in Congo and to report on the findings. After the identification of the law's minimum requirements, the report evaluated whether companies had met them and found that 79 companies were failing and 21 complying. A report by the Enough project focussed particularly on gold mining. It claimed that trade in illegally mined "conflict gold" was fuelling high-level military corruption in the eastern DRC. Gold was smuggled out of the country mainly by road to Uganda and Burundi. Numerous shorter reports highlighted human rights violations in the context of armed conflict, such as an HRW report on the killing and displacement of civilians, particularly Pygmies, by ethnic militias in northern Katanga (DRC).

A substantial part of *ICC* activity focused again on the Central African subregion. In the case against former DRC vice president Jean-Pierre Bemba for crimes against humanity perpetrated by his militia in the CAR (mostly in 2002), closing statements had already been made in 2014. However, in a separate process, the relevant Chamber found there was substantial evidence that Bemba and his supporters had committed offences against the administration of justice in connection with witness statements (between the end of 2011 and 14 November 2013). These charges included corruptly bribing witnesses to give false testimony and presenting false evidence. In the case against Bosco Ntaganda, who was accused of war crimes and specifically recruitment of child soldiers, little progress was made after the unanimous confirmation of charges in 2014.

Separate from the ICC, a spectacular court case at Special African Chambers began in Dakar (Senegal) against former Chadian dictator *Hissène Habré*. An estimated 40,000 people may have been killed by Chadian security forces under Habré's supreme command between 1982 and 1990. Extra-judicial executions, disappearances and rape were among the accusations. The Court was established within the Senegalese court system and was able to work on copious documentation of the crimes against humanity perpetrated by Habré when he was in office. International NGOs had carried out intensive enquiries over many years and some 70 survivors ready to testify against Habré showed their satisfaction that the trial could finally begin. Habré's strategy was to portray himself as the victim of an illegal court action.

In implicit acknowledgement of the limited capabilities of the ICC, the transitional legislative body of the CAR voted into law a new hybrid Special Court, but it was unclear when it would be established, not least because of unclear funding.

Socioeconomic Developments

With the MDG period reaching its end, the global conclusions of the UN system were unsurprisingly positive but differed between world regions, with SSA showing relatively less progress or outright stagnation. In the absence of reliable comparable data, one could only assume that this was also the general assessment for the Central Africa sub-region. Data from the World Development Indicators (not available for Equatorial Guinea or the Republic of Congo) showed a positive long-term trend in many aspects, though probably below expectations for some. While life expectancy at birth stood at 55.9 years in Cameroon (up from 51.9 in 2000), it was 64.9 years (up from 59.3.) in neighbouring Gabon, attesting to the latter's greater success. Under-5-mortality rates in six countries differed markedly. Though steadily declining, the rate stood at 138.1 per 1,000 in Chad, three-times worse than São Tomé and Príncipe (47.3) and well above Gabon (50.8), Cameroon (87.9) and even the DRC (98.3), but only slightly above the war-torn CAR (130.1). Despite this bad result, the Chadian government showed little inclination to deal with structural problems and was the country in the sub-region that allocated by far the highest proportion of its GDP to military expenditure (2.8%).

The IMF's World Economic Outlook (published in April 2016) painted a differentiated picture of the sub-region, which fared less well overall than in 2014, undoubtedly linked to the slump in crude oil prices on the world market – at least four out of eight countries being heavily dependent on oil exports. After record growth in 2014, the DRC was credited once again with a high *GDP growth* rate of 7.7%. Cameroon had the second highest with 5.9%, followed by moderate growth rates in the CAR (4.3%), Gabon and São Tomé and Príncipe (both 4%), though low and sharply reduced growth rates were given for Congo (2.5%) and Chad (1.8%), and Equatorial Guinea's economy shrunk again by a staggering 12.2%. The AfDB's African Economic Outlook briefly explained the decline in Congo by the government's response to falling oil revenues, namely cutting infrastructure investment. Cameroon's relative economic success was explained by "solid and broad-based growth driven by agriculture and forestry, construction, industry and oil production". Gabon's government received praise for its continuing investment programme, despite lower oil revenues. The AfDB explained the DRC's performance with the expansion in agriculture, services and industry plus increases in mineral production. Towards the end of the year, the BEAC, the central bank of the CEMAC zone, had put the *budgetary deficit* of its member states at an average of 4.2% of GDP (up from 2.8% in 2014), despite emergency budget cuts in four countries – in Equatorial Guinea investment spending was even reduced by 57%.

The sub-region's low ranking in the Index of Economic Freedom (Heritage Foundation) was once again confirmed. Three countries continued to be in the 'mostly unfree' category (Gabon, São Tomé and Príncipe, and Cameroon) and five in the worst category of 'repressed' economies: Chad, the CAR, the DRC, Congo and Equatorial-Guinea ranked between 165th and 173rd out of 178, with Equatorial Guinea losing 4 index points. The World Bank's 'Doing Business' report contained similar messages, with the first three countries placed in the same order, and the CAR again ranking worst.

Sub-regional Organisations

CEMAC held its ordinary summit in Libreville (Gabon) on 12 May with only four heads of state attending (Chad, Congo, Equatorial Guinea, Gabon), and two governments represented by either the prime minister (CAR) or another high-placed official (Cameroon). Boko Haram and the CAR crisis took centre stage, and the summit confirmed the intention to re-establish the organisation's headquarters in Bangui (CAR) from where it had been removed to Libreville in the midst of the violence in March 2014, and the CEMAC Commission did in fact return to Bangui in July. The age-old project to establish a sub-regional airline (Air CEMAC) was abandoned by the summit without comment. In accordance with routine, Equatorial Guinea's President Obiang Nguema took over as chairman of CEMAC from Gabon's President Ali Bongo Ondimba at the end of the summit. At the level of the associated Union Economique de l'Afrique Centrale, an ordinary council of ministers meeting was held in Malabo (Equatorial Guinea) on 23 October, when the process for liquidating the phantom airline was discussed in more detail.

As in previous years, *CEEAC* outpaced CEMAC in overall importance, as was visible even in the number of high-level meetings held. CEEAC held an extraordinary summit on security issues under the aegis of its peace mechanism COPAX in Ndjaména (Chad). President Idriss Déby Itno was able to welcome the heads of state of Cameroon, the CAR, Congo, Gabon and Equatorial Guinea. The DRC was not represented, even at ministerial level. On 25 May, an ordinary summit was held again in the Chadian capital, with five heads of state attending and the DRC again absent. Finally, on 25 November, an extraordinary summit was held in Libreville; here, Congo's Sassou Nguesso and the host, Ali Bongo Ondimba, were the only presidents attending, with other member states sending ministerial representatives. The summit focused almost entirely on the upcoming elections in the CAR in the prevailing difficult political and security situation. These top-level events were complemented with many more technical meetings on the expert level. One of these focused on (positively) reviewing the joint military exercise Loango 2014 (19–20 May 2014). CEEAC was also active at an inter-organisational level, holding joint meetings with ECOWAS (on fighting the Boko Haram insurgency) and ICGLR (to discuss the sociopolitical situation in the CAR).

While the *CBLT* did not hold a formal meeting on its main mission (i.e. halting the desertification of the Lake Chad Basin), the organisation served as a framework to discuss military cooperation in the region to combat the Boko Haram threat. Experts from all four members states met in Yaoundé (Cameroon) on 5–7 February and finalised the operational documents of the Multinational Joint Task Force in the presence of representatives of the AU Commission and other relevant organisations (CEEAC, ECOWAS, the UN, the EU and OIC). The Central African Forests Commission held just one ordinary council of ministers conference in January in Bujumbura (Burundi).

Members of the ICGLR, under Angolan chairmanship, met twice on a presidential level in March and May in Luanda (Angola). An extraordinary meeting of the Committee of Ministers of Defence took place in October with the participation of Angola, Burundi, the CAR, Congo, the DRC, Kenya, South Sudan, Uganda and Zambia. The agenda was dominated by security and humanitarian issues in the DRC, Burundi, the CAR and South Sudan.

Cameroon

Fanny Pigeaud

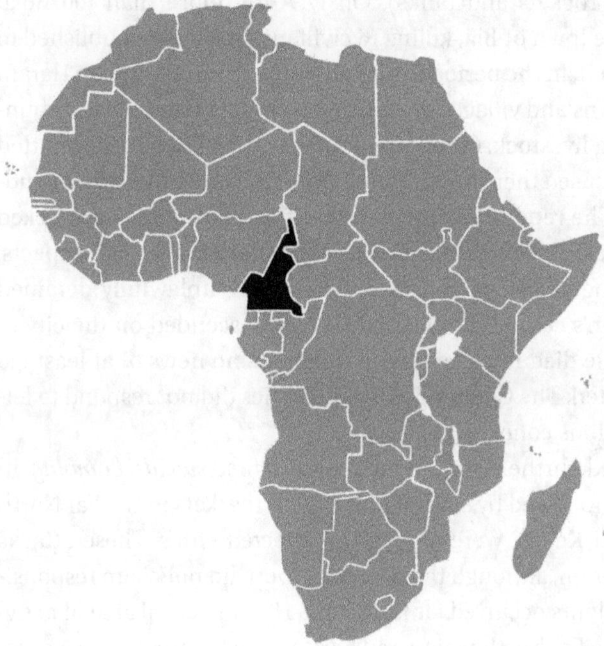

On the political front, a minor cabinet reshuffle took place at the end of the year. Security remained a major problem in the Far North region with armed attacks and suicide bombings attributed to the Nigerian-based Boko Haram movement, which had killed hundreds of people. The East region was also affected by insecurity, with regular incursions by armed gangs, probably coming from the CAR. Cameroonian security forces were accused of human rights violations in the Far North. On the economic front, the country was able to adjust well to the fall in crude oil prices, but corruption scandals continued. Analysts were becoming increasingly concerned about the rapid increase in the country's debt.

Domestic Politics

Boko Haram's insurgency in the Far North region dominated the news throughout the year. For the first time, the leader of the group, Abubakar Shekau, threatened

 | DOI 10.1163/9789004333239_022

President Paul Biya directly in a 17-minute video posted on 5 January: "Paul Biya, if you do not put an end to your evil plan you'll be entitled to the same fate as Nigeria (...). Your soldiers can do nothing against us," Shekau said. As in 2014, Boko Haram engaged in guerilla style warfare, deploying small raiding forces, but they also operated as an army capable of deploying hundreds of fighters armed with heavy artillery (including rockets and tanks). On 17 April, more than 100 Boko Haram fighters stormed the town of Bia, killing 16 civilians. In a report published in September, AI estimated that, in the period from mid-2014 to mid-2015, Boko Haram had attacked dozens of towns and villages, killing nearly 400 civilians, burning hundreds of homes and looting livestock. Cameroonian security forces also committed violence in response. AI accused them of numerous *human rights violations*, including summary executions. The report documented that the security forces attacked villages, destroying homes, killing civilians and arresting more than 1,000 suspects, including children as young as five. About 84 children were unlawfully detained for six months at a children's centre after security forces descended on the city of Guirvidig. At least 25 people died in custody, and there was no news of at least 130 others who had been arrested. The Cameroonian authorities did not respond to letters from AI expressing serious concern.

In July, terrorism gained further prominence with a first *suicide bombing* in Fotokol. The bombing was followed by several more, all in markets in the Far North region: Mora, Kolofata and Kaliari were among the affected cities. These attacks were attributed to Boko Haram, although the terrorist group did not claim responsibility and some of the incidents occurred far from Boko Haram's usual area of activity. In Maroua, capital of the Far North region and located 400 km from the Nigerian border, 33 people were killed in several suicide bombings in late July. In December, two suicide attacks killed at least four people at Waza, a town bordering Nigeria and Chad. These attacks appear to have been committed by children, teenagers or socially vulnerable women, who were unwittingly carrying the explosives, some of which were triggered by remote control. After the first suicide bombings, committed in Fotokol by two women wearing burqas, the governor of the Far North region decided to ban the garment.

Terrorism in the north had an impact on major cities in the south. After the suicide attacks in Maroua, inhabitants of Yaoundé and Douala also became afraid. Controls on roads and at bus stations nationwide were tightened by police, primarily in Yaoundé and Douala. In Yaoundé, in the popular neighbourhood of Briquetterie, known for its large Muslim community, the police raided houses and mosques in July. According to local newspapers, dozens of people were arrested. Minister of Communication Issa Tchiroma Bakary said that these sweep operations had led to the arrest of many suspects in several regions of the country. *'Vigilance committees'* made up of residents were set up in some localities to fight the terrorist group by providing security forces with information. Local authorities equipped the committees with binoculars, torches, mobile phones, etc. Some members were armed with clubs and machetes. Their role was hailed by President Biya in his end-of-year address: he spoke of the "legitimate exercise of civil defence" and portrayed such committees as "models" for the nation. Worried voices asked what these committees would become after the end of the 'war'.

Actions by Boko Haram and indiscriminate retaliation by the army both had severe humanitarian consequences: the number of IDPs grew dramatically. The UN Office for the Coordination of Humanitarian Affairs estimated that they numbered 117,000 in March. Many had abandoned their farms, which directly aggravated malnutrition in an area that was still recovering from a decade of periodic drought. In addition, according to UNICEF, by the end of the year, only one of the 135 schools that had closed in 2014 because of the conflict with Boko Haram had re-opened.

On 28 February, thousands of Cameroonians demonstrated in Yaoundé to denounce the terrorist group's atrocities and to support the Cameroonian army. However, the march, officially organised by a few journalists and a private newspaper editor, did not receive unanimous approval. Critical observers denounced political exploitation, if not outright manipulation, by a few regime members. Some ministers had in fact joined the march, including Minister of Defence Edgard Alain Mebe Ngo'o, Minister of Labour Grégoire Owona, and Tchiroma. It should be noted that the authorities in Cameroon rarely allow *demonstrations*, much less participate in them. Some local analysts claimed that the event, presented by its organisers as a civil movement, was in fact secretly financed by the minister of defence.

There was general questioning of the real identity of the Boko Haram fighters. The idea that the terrorist group concealed Western interests became increasingly widespread among the population. Professor Jean Emmanuel Pondi of the International Relations Institute of Cameroon, who was not known to be close to the Biya regime, publicly stated the view that the attacks on Cameroon were related to its wealth, which "some countries want to seize" and he also spoke of a plot to destabilise the country.

Apart from the Far North region, other areas of the country also faced significant security issues throughout the year. In Adamawa, armed gangs, allegedly coming from the CAR, conducted dozens of *kidnappings* for ransom throughout the year. Between July and December, the authorities counted 76 hostage takings in the region. The departments of Vina and Mbéré were the most frequently targeted and several raids by armed gangs were also reported in the East, on the border with the CAR. Seventeen people, including a mayor and four traditional chiefs, were abducted in March in the village of Babio, close to Garoua Boulaï. According to the Ministry of Communication, the hostages were taken to the CAR.

On 2 October, Biya finally carried out a minor *government reshuffle*, which had in fact been expected since the legislative and municipal elections of September 2013. The president kept Philemon Yang as prime minister but Minister of Defence Mebe Ngo'o was replaced by Joseph Beti Assomo, formerly governor of the Littoral region. Mebe Ngo'o, who was said to have grown up in Biya's house, was known for his extravagant life-style – his official motorcade was similar in size to the president's, for example – and he was also suspected of using the army's human and material resources for personal purposes, while the soldiers fighting against Boko Haram were experiencing difficult conditions on the ground. On 9 September, about 200 soldiers wearing UN blue helmets marched over 4 km from their base in Ekounou, a popular area of Yaoundé, through the town centre towards the army headquarters, demanding their unpaid bonuses. They were part of the 1,260 *Cameroonian contingent with the UN mission in the CAR* (MINUSCA). This was the first time that soldiers had marched in the streets of the capital. The government deployed heavily armed troops to block streets and impede their passage, but the minister of communication stated that the contingent would quickly be paid. Mebe Ngo'o's removal was therefore popular, but also matched other calculations: Known for lavishly funding numerous private media outlets, Mebe Ngo'o seemed in fact to have been demoted by Biya because of his supposed presidential ambitions (a fate shared by others from Biya's inner circle). A few weeks later, Mebe Ngo'o, who was shifted to the significantly less important Ministry of Transport, was summoned by the military court to answer several cases of corruption filed against him. Meanwhile, his successor symbolically spent 31 December in the Far North with the troops in Kidimatari. Mebe Ngo'o had never visited the front line.

Biya, aged 82, still showed no desire to leave the presidency. On the contrary, many signs indicated that he was planning to stand for *re-election in 2018*. For example, numerous 'motions of support' came from members or elites of the ruling party, calling for his re-election. In the past, Biya had always used these expressions of support published by the state media to justify his decision to stand again for election as president. The population, for their part, sarcastically noted that, during Biya's traditional speech on 31 December, Cameroon experienced a huge power outage as he was speaking about the need for adequate and permanent sources of energy. The minister of energy announced that the power cut was due to crows nesting on connections and electrical installations.

Foreign Affairs

On 21 February, French Foreign Minister Laurent Fabius came for a short official visit to Cameroon. Biya received him in the context of tense relations between the two countries, as was the case in 2014. Officially, Fabius came to Yaoundé – staying less than 24 hours – to express the support of *France* for Cameroon in the fight against Boko Haram. Some Cameroonian commentators, however, felt that this visit was primarily intended to rebut allegations that France had connections with and was supporting Boko Haram, and wanted to use the terrorist movement to destabilise Cameroon. During his visit, Fabius had to repeat many times that France was a friend of Cameroon

On 3 July, French President François Hollande made a state visit to Cameroon to meet with Biya, the first visit by a French president since 1999. However, the visit lasted only a few hours, showing that the relationship between Hollande and Biya was still complicated. The visit was part of the French presidency's campaign for the UN conference on climate change (COP21), which was hosted by France a few weeks later, in December. Hollande needed the votes of African countries for the adoption of the forthcoming Paris agreement. During his visit, Hollande also met with leaders of political parties represented in the National Assembly, without distinguishing between opposition parties and the presidential party. At a joint press conference with Biya, he made an important statement that went almost unnoticed in France but was much commented on in Cameroon: the French president implicitly recognised *the repression by the French army* in Cameroon in the 1950s of the 'Union des Populations du Cameroun' (UPC), a political party calling for independence. In the late 1950s, tens of thousands of UPC members had been massacred by the French army, including the UPC leader, Ruben Um Nyobe, who was killed in 1958. The repression continued after independence in 1960 and was led by the Cameroonian army, under the supervision of French officers. Hollande spoke of "tragic episodes" and of "repression", and gave assurances that he wanted the archives to be opened to historians. Thus, Hollande became the first French president to speak of this period in the history of the two countries. Until then, French officials had always denied the extent of French repression and, in 2009, the then French Prime Minister François Fillon had publicly refused to admit that the French had killed people in Cameroon. Hollande's statement broke a taboo, observers noted. According to some Cameroonian analysts (and also noted in the French press), the French authorities' new attitude was due to the rise of anti-French sentiment in Cameroon, the increasing influence of China, which had won numerous large public contracts in Cameroon, and France's desire to reclaim its diminishing influence/control. The Cameroonian historian Achille Mbembe said that Hollande was seeking to eliminate grievances against France without having to pay anything.

A television channel based in Yaoundé, Africa Media, was sealed off after airing accusations that France and the USA were supporting Boko Haram. The 'Conseil National de la Communication' (CNC) justified its decision by claiming that some guests of the channel from politics, academia and civil society had openly and repeatedly accused Paris and Washington of supporting Boko Haram. The presenters of some of the incriminated programmes were also suspended for six months by the CNC.

In November, Cameroon agreed that the *USA* would establish a drone base in Garoua (North), and accepted the deployment of 300 US soldiers. The contingent was officially sent to conduct airborne reconnaissance operations in the region, to help fight terrorism and to provide intelligence to the multi-national task force being set up to fight Boko Haram. The USA gave assurances that their troops deployed in Cameroon were armed only for their own protection and security, and that they did not have a combat mission. Off the record, some Cameroonian officials expressed concern, admitting that Cameroon would not have the means to control their activities. Some residents of Garoua were convinced that the USA was in fact interested in exploiting oil reserves believed to be situated along Cameroon's border with Chad.

To everyone's surprise, the *Chadian army* entered Cameroon on 17 January to fight Boko Haram. Many Cameroonians were sceptical about this operation, as the role of Chad in the region had been at least ambiguous: Chadian President Idriss Déby Itno had at one point been suspected of himself having links with Boko Haram. It was also widely known that Déby and Biya did not have a good relationship. In early November, Chad suddenly withdrew its troops from Cameroon without any official announcement.

In July, the new *Nigerian President Muhammad Buhari* made a two-day visit to Cameroon. Biya greeted him on his arrival at Yaoundé airport. The two heads of state held talks about ways to defeat Boko Haram. This meeting took place two months after a state visit by the Nigerian president to Chad and Niger. Analysts said that the visit would help erase the climate of mistrust between Cameroon and Nigeria, after years of relations strained because of the border dispute over Bakassi. Cameroon had for some time been accused by Nigeria of dragging its feet over tackling Boko Haram and Cameroon complained of Nigeria's refusal to grant Cameroonian forces the right to pursue them onto Nigerian soil. It should be noted that Biya did not attend Buhari's inauguration in May.

Socioeconomic Developments

Cameroon suffered from the *drop in world oil prices*, but the economy showed remarkable resilience. Indeed, the fall in oil revenues was partially offset by an increase in production. The start of production at the Bojongo field and the reactivation/optimising of mature fields in the Rio del Rey basin (Inter-Inoua Barombi, Barombi Northeast and Padouk) were part of this strategy. According to the 'Société Nationale des Hydrocarbures' (SNH), production reached 102,586 b/d on 21 April, a level last achieved in 2002, and 35 m barrels were produced over the year. On 31 December, oil and gas production was up about 26% year-on-year. Gas production reached 12.5 bn ft^3. The SNH paid the treasury CFAfr 378,536 bn – substantially more than the budgeted annual target of CFAfr 264,25 bn.

The *state budget* increased slightly over the budget for 2014: revenues and budgetary expenditure were set at CFAfr 3,746 bn, compared with CFAfr 3,312 bn in 2014, an increase of 13.1%. Investment represented CFAfr 1,150 bn, up from CFAfr 1,000 bn in 2014, operating costs were estimated at CFAfr 2,159 bn, (an increase of CFAfr 150.7 bn compared with 2014) and the public debt service was CFAfr 302.8 bn. The government expected a GDP growth rate of 6.3% and an inflation rate of around 3%. While

GDP had been expected to rise to 6.1% in 2014, it reached only 5.1%, according to the IMF. The Ministry of Finance deemed growth insufficient to signal a real takeoff of the economy and to reduce poverty, estimating that Cameroon had the potential to reach annual rates above 10%.

One of the main barriers to growth lay in the recurrent shortcomings of the *port of Douala*, entry and exit point for 95% of imported and exported goods. Ship-owners constantly assessed Douala as one of the world's most disastrous port sites, citing the silting up of the access channel and the absence of modern infrastructures to cope with the intensity of traffic. The passage of goods took 22 days, i.e. five times longer than at the port of Durban (South Africa), according to a World Bank study.

To reverse the trend, there were high expectations concerning the *deep water port* that was being built in Kribi, in the south of the country. Some platforms were already operational. On 26 August, Prime Minister Philemon Yang announced that a consortium of the French companies Bolloré and CMA CGM and the China Harbour Engineering Company had been awarded the operation of the container terminal of the port of Kribi. Another consortium made up of French group Necotrans and the Cameroonian Kribi Multi Port Operators won the management of the multi-purpose terminal. Operations were planned to start at the port in the second quarter of 2016. These projects were expected to create 10,000 direct jobs. Cameroon was projected to earn 1.5% of growth each year, once the complex was fully operational, according to official – and optimistic – projections that saw the new port as a 'hub' capable of capturing maritime traffic through the Gulf of Guinea.

Insecurity in the Far North and in the East also impacted on the economy and government finance: the maintenance of 6,000 men in 14 bases was, of course, expensive. Yaoundé also had to provide the fuel for the 2,500 Chadian soldiers fighting alongside Cameroonians. *Corruption* was another major constraint on economic development: Cameroon remained one of the most corrupt states in the world. TI placed it at the head of the most corrupt African countries, with only Liberia rated worse. The public 'Commission Nationale Anti-Corruption' (CONAC) in a report on 2013 released in 2015 pointed to the issuing of false pay slips, the inflation of officials' salaries and pensions, the processing of false driving license, fraudulent billing for services, etc. The Commission noted numerous problems in delivering false patents, and the issuing of false tax stamps by illicit stamp machines, even within Directory General of Taxes. The CONAC also highlighted the opacity of the 'Bureau de Gestion du Fret Terrestre', which, according to the CONAC president, had "become a state within the State". The government did not take any major measures to fight corruption: there was no notable progress on 'Operation Epervier', launched by Biya in 2006 to fight corruption at the official level, apart from court rulings against two 'big men'. A special criminal court sentenced former finance minister Polycarpe Abah Abah to 25 years in prison for embezzling CFAfr 6 bn to buy houses and cars. Abah Abah, formerly a powerful minister, in jail since 2008, appealed his sentence. The former general manager of the state-owned bank 'Credit Foncier du

Cameroun', Joseph Edou, and his deputy were sentenced to 15 years in prison for embezzlement.

The *business climate remained poor*, and Cameroon plummeted ten places in the World Bank's 'Doing Business 2015'. Several reports also stated that Cameroon, with 40% of its territory still forested, had failed to make progress in tackling illegal logging since the conclusion, in 2010, of a Voluntary Partnership Agreement between Cameroon and the EU. According to the EU, this agreement was intended to provide a legislative framework within which to detect and ensure the traceability of timber; put in place government and independent verification procedures to certify that all timber exports from Cameroon to European markets had been procured, felled, transported and exported legally, in order to provide a basis for the legal management and exploitation of the Cameroonian forests; and reinforce the application of forestry regulations and governance. But a report by an independent auditor financed by the EU showed that none of the logging companies working in Cameroon, including European companies, were compliant with Cameroonian laws.

To improve the situation, the government launched its first *Eurobond* at the end of the year: € 750 m (CFAfr 462 bn), issued at a yield of 9.5% for a weighted average life of ten years. This loan was part of a plan to mobilise CFAfr 1,000 bn to finance a three-year emergency plan to accelerate the country's economic growth. However, part of this programme was used to refinance a debt of $ 164 m owed by the 'Société Nationale de Raffinage'. In December, the AfDB approved a loan of € 24 m (CFAfr 15.7 bn) to the Kribi Power Development Corporation, to extend the gas power plant of Kribi. This project, 'Kribi II' was planned to add 125 MW, to bring the total capacity of the plant to 341 MW. It was supposed to address the energy deficit, estimated at 100 MW, while demand was believed to be growing grow annually by 8%. € 35 m or 25% of the cost would be paid by the shareholders (government and Globeleq). The rest would come from international donors (IFC, AfDB, EIB, the Netherlands Development Finance Company, Proparco and the 'Banque de Développement des Etats de l'Afrique Centrale') and national donors (Standard Chartered Bank Cameroon, Afriland First Bank, 'Société Commerciale de Banque Cameroon', 'Banque Internationale du Cameroun pour l'Epargne et le Crédit', and 'Société Générale Cameroun') that had supported 'Kribi I'.

All of these loans were seen as worrying by many analysts, who considered that Cameroon's medium-term economic health was threatened by a *high level of indebtedness*. Indeed, in a report on the economic prospects of Africa, the IMF calculated that Cameroon's debt had almost doubled in four years from 15% of GDP to just over 30%. The rating agency Fitch Ratings stated in December that, although the debt was still below the average in Africa, it had accelerated sharply in the last five years and that, although Cameroon's dependence on the oil sector was low (its hydrocarbon exports accounted for only 2% of its GDP), the amount of state investment projects appeared to be too high in proportion to its financing capacity. They also said that Cameroon remained dependent on Chinese loans and was trading less with its neighbours, and estimated that Cameroon was at the end of a political cycle, with many uncertainties about Biya's succession, reinforced by security issues.

Negotiations took place between the government and the two main *mobile phone operators*, the French group Orange and the South African MTN (which had 10 m subscribers and about 60% of the market), for the renewal of their licence, but the talks were difficult as the two operators wanted to reduce the price asked by the government (CFAfr 75 bn or € 114 m). They finally agreed on a renewal of their licences for 15 years, until February 2030. In addition, the government allowed the two firms to start offering third and fourth generation (3G and 4G) services. The third-largest mobile operator Nexttel, owned by Vietnam's Viettel Group, had received approval to offer 3G services when it was launched in 2014. According to statistical data, only 6% of Cameroon's population had Internet access, among the lowest rates in Africa, despite there being more than 16 m mobile phone subscribers.

Central African Republic (CAR)

Andreas Mehler

This was a year of progress towards the end of a prolonged transition from civil unrest to democratic rule and limited stability, despite the general precariousness of all achievements. A peace forum and the referendum on a new constitution prepared the ground for holding the first round of presidential and legislative elections shortly before the end of the year. However, renewed hostilities in the centre of the country around Bambari and Kaga-Bandoro and above all a number of serious confrontations in the capital Bangui reminded both the population and the international community that the overall situation remained volatile.

Domestic Politics

On 7 January, interim President Catherine Samba Panza nominated the 22 members of the Preparatory Commission for the Bangui Forum, an elite gathering designed to create reconciliation and set the stage for the *final period of the transition to constitutional rule*. Local consultations in preparation for the Forum were launched

 | DOI 10.1163/9789004333239_023

by this commission at the end of January; they met with organisational difficulties (reportedly just 4,000 people took part in some selected cities outside the capital) and with outright scepticism, especially in areas controlled by the Muslim-based Séléka alliance. About 400 Muslim demonstrators took to the streets of Bangui on 23 January to protest against their perceived under-representation in that process. Facilitators of the consultations on 11 March held their final workshop and produced a synopsis of the fears and desires of the population. On 27 February, four former prime ministers, the vice president of the transitional parliament ('Conseil National de Transition', CNT) and the president of the Bangui Forum preparatory committee, plus some political heavyweights, signed an appeal for national reconciliation at the Rome headquarters of the Community of Sant'Egidio, a well-known peace-making organisation supported by the Catholic Church. The *Bangui Forum* was eventually able to take place on 4–11 May, with 600 participants representing the transitional government, rebel groups, civil society, religious groups and the prefectures, as well as refugees and neighbouring countries. It produced a list of recommendations, *inter alia* to postpone elections from July to later in the year (and therefore to push back the end of the entire transition) as well as the introduction of a truth, justice and reconciliation commission (building on the work of local peace committees). At the margins of the Forum, an accord was signed on 5 May between the government and representatives of ten armed movements to stop the recruitment of children, the so-called 'Pacte Républicain' was agreed, which – amongst more vague principles – called for the installation of a Special Criminal Court, and a DDR and repatriation agreement was signed on 10 May. The Séléka wing under Ali Darassa released about 400 child-soldiers from its ranks on 14 May as one tangible consequence of the Forum's appeal. The creation of the Special Court, already discussed within the CNT before the Forum, was imminent after the promulgation of the relevant legislation on 3 June, but it was unclear who would provide the funding for this form of transitional justice.

The *transitional bodies* enjoyed little popular support and complaints about corruption were frequently voiced. Interim President Samba-Panza made adjustments to her *government* three times over the year. On 16 January, she changed the positions of four ministers: four new faces entered and four left the government. Most significant was the promotion of Marie Noëlle Koyara from minister of rural development to the position of defence minister, the first time since independence that a woman held this position. The next reshuffle, on 21 July, saw the arrival of Sébastien Wénézoui, one of the prominent anti-Balaka leaders, and of a new foreign minister. On 29 October, Samba-Panza again slightly restructured the transitional government and made only a few new appointments, the most notable being the removal of the two ministers responsible for security issues – after the serious wave of violence that hit Bangui – including Koyara, who was replaced by the well-known judge Joseph Bindoumi. Mahamat Kamoun remained prime minister throughout. The former Séléka alliance continued to provide three minor ministers (who were, however, officially banned from their organisations), while anti-Balaka groupings felt underrepresented with only Sébastien Wénézoui as environment minister.

The political-military movements appeared to be weakened by ever-growing *fragmentation*. In the anti-Balaka camp, Wénézoui started a reconciliation campaign with Muslims and created his own party, as did his most visible rival, Patrice Edouard Ngaïssona. Within the former Séléka alliance, Nourredine Adam, leader of the potentially biggest faction, the 'Front Populaire pour la Renaissance de Centrafrique' (FPRC), took the most uncompromising stance, *inter alia* by appealing for a boycott of the 13 December referendum, and one day later declaring an autonomous 'Republic of Logone' in the north-eastern part of the country (with Kaga-Bandoro as its provisional capital). In contrast, Ali Darassa, heading the second most important party, the 'Union pour la Paix en Centrafrique' (UPC), invited his followers to vote in the referendum. In the end, 93% of those who voted (with a 38% turnout) voted in favour of a text that had not circulated widely, and consequently was never publicly discussed. In a country plagued by violent political overthrows the most important innovation of the *new Constitution* was potentially the exclusion of all coup, mutiny or rebel leaders from political office (Art. 28) plus the creation of a senate as a chamber to represent the 'territorial collectivities' (i.e. above all the prefectures; Art. 73).

The *security situation* remained a source of serious concern, with various local constellations producing different forms of confrontation. After the arrest of Chadian warlord Baba Laddé on CAR territory in late 2014, UN peacekeepers of the 'Mission Multidimensionnelle Intégrée des Nations Unies pour la Stabilisation en République Centrafricaine' (MINUSCA) quickly deported this embarrassing prisoner on 2 January to Chad, where he was immediately jailed. The overall stability did not improve, however. The MINUSCA mission even had to learn that it could itself trigger escalation, when it arrested the anti-Balaka leader Rodrigue Nagibona (aka Andilo) on 17 January. Andilo followers kidnapped a French humanitarian worker two days later (she was released on 23 January) and Minister of Youth and Sport Armel Sayo, himself the leader of an armed movement ('Révolution et Justice') on 25 January (he was released on 10 February). This made it clear that MINUSCA was not even able to protect government officials. Even more embarrassing for MINUSCA was that, on 28 September, 677 detainees (about one-third of whom were anti-Balaka elements) managed to escape from the Ngaragba prison in Bangui. Sexual misconduct on the part of some MINUSCA personnel also undermined the acceptance of the mission.

The *Christian-Muslim divide* continued to be salient, at times translating into direct confrontations between ex-Séléka forces claiming to protect Muslim minorities and anti-Balaka groups claiming to represent local or Christian majorities and/or involving peacekeepers, but such conflicts were only superficially religious in content. In Mambere Kadei prefecture, a series of confrontations between Fulani herders from Cameroon and anti-Balaka groups led to the killing of 40 civilians on 2 May. Clashes between Mbororo herders and the local population in mid-May caused the death of nine civilians and the displacement of more than 1,460 people from surrounding villages to Kaga Bandoro. The main religious leaders, Archbishop Dieudonné Nzapalainga (Catholic Church), Imam Kobine Layama (Muslim community) and the Reverend Nicolas Guerekoyame-Gbangou (Evangelical churches) constantly called for moderation and were most clearly the opinion-leaders with a peace agenda. They were highly praised outside the country, but could not prevent all ethno-religious confrontations on the ground. After a fatal attack on a Muslim taxi-driver in Bangui at the end of September, severe communal clashes erupted in in the city, which led to 77 people being killed and 400 injured; in addition, about 30,000 were forced to flee their homes and entire neighbourhoods were burnt to ashes. Guerekoyame-Gbangou narrowly escaped when angry Muslim youths searched for him in a retaliatory move on 26 September; two Catholic churches were destroyed. This did not prevent *Pope Francis* travelling to the CAR on 29 November with his anticipated message of peace and tolerance; his schedule included a visit to a mosque under siege by Christian militias in Bangui. The Pope's visit was greeted from all sides as sending an important signal for a possible return to coexistence.

In the previous month, on 26 August, clashes had erupted between militias in Bambari, causing thousands to flee their homes. Ethnic or religious motives were certainly at work, but all the armed factions were more visibly in pursuit of *material aims*, e.g. of controlling mining sites and trade roads. In fact, extensive areas of the country, particularly the border zones to the east and the north, were not under government control. Infighting within the former Séléka alliance sometimes ended in bloodshed. Smaller groups also continued to be a threat more locally. According to a detailed account by Dominic Ongwen, a commander of the Lord's Resistance Army, who was captured by a Séléka group and handed over to US forces in January, the size of this movement had dramatically shrunk to only 38 fighters in the CAR. In the western and northern border zones with Chad and Cameroon, anti-Balaka groups and the armed movements 'Front Démocratique du Peuple Centrafricain' (FDPC) and 'Révolution et Justice' challenged state authority, although the latter was represented by its leader within government. MINUSCA tried to secure main road corridors, but also robustly combated the FDPC, although FDPC leader Abdoulaye Miskine, who had boycotted the Bangui Forum, stated that his movement was not creating instability as the UN claimed, and pointed instead to Boko Haram elements infiltrating from Cameroon. At year's end, some 450,000 *refugees* plus 450,000 *IDPs* (together roughly 20% of the population of 4.8 m) were waiting for conditions to improve to allow their return.

Arranging for refugees and IDPs to vote was one of the organisational challenges in the preparation for the elections, but the plans seem to have worked at least for refugees in Cameroon and Congo. Building on the experience of the referendum the transitional authorities, particularly the 'Autorité Nationale des Elections' (ANE), felt confident enough to hold the *first round of both legislative and presidential elections* on 30 December, three days later than planned according to the repeatedly adjusted timetable. As in every previous smooth election in the CAR (1993, 1998, 1999), the logistics relied heavily on military transport provided by external troops. On 8 December, the Constitutional Court excluded ten declared candidates from the contest, most importantly the anti-Balaka leader Patrice-Edouard Ngaissona (for his numerous infractions to the law) and former president François Bozizé (because he was not resident in the CAR). It was clear that strong international pressure was exerted to exclude Bozizé (who was under UN sanctions), but this was not mentioned in the court ruling. The decision, immediately condemned by Bozizé, triggered violence in Bangui; five people were killed in the PK5 district and confrontations also occurred on the same day in Batangafo. Thirty candidates were allowed to stand, including sons of former presidents (Patassé, Kolingba), former prime ministers (Dologuélé, Touadéra, Ziguélé) and former ministers. Their chances were largely unclear, given that free elections had not been held since 1999 – Bozizé had strongly manipulated elections under his rule. The ANE did not announce the election results until early January 2016.

Foreign Affairs

The CAR remained a constant item on the agenda of the *UNSC*. MINUSCA, established in April 2014, became fully operational in spring. On 28 April, the UNSC passed a resolution to renew the MINUSCA mandate and authorised a slightly increased limit of 10,750 military personnel, including 480 military observers and staff officers and 2,080 police personnel. The deployment figures remained below that maximum until the end of the year. Within MINUSCA, the 1,552 international police personnel were particularly important for security. At year's end, some 9,110 blue-helmets provided substantial security coverage but without being able to fully control the vast territory. On 17 November, in preparation for the election phase, the UN Secretary-General asked for and received from the UNSC a temporary deployment of 300 personnel from the quick reaction force in Côte d'Ivoire under an inter-mission cooperation arrangement. On 17 December, the UNSC decided to add Haroun Gaye (FPRC leader in Bangui) and Eugène Ngaïkosset (aka 'the butcher of Paoua') to its sanctions list for incitement to violence in the preparatory phase of the elections. African governments (particularly Chad and Kenya) had not applied the travel ban against Bozizé and Adam, raising doubts as to the effectiveness of the sanctions regime.

The *EU*-sponsored mission of 700 soldiers focusing on Bangui ceased in March in line with its mandate; a small military advisory mission remained on the ground, however, in order to promote security sector reform. Additionally, after a reduction in the size of the force in April, France still had some 1,500 to 1,700 of its *Sangaris* mission troops on the ground – and it was also contributing soldiers to the MINUSCA and EUFOR RCA (EU Force in the CAR) missions. It was clearly the most important security actor in the country.

The MINUSCA mission faced several crises in which it had to deploy force – and took a few *casualties*. On 10 April, a reported 300–400 partially armed demonstrators attacked the MINUSCA camp in Kaga Bandoro, wounding 10 peacekeepers. Around Mbres, MINUSCA and French forces engaged in robust actions to stop conflicts between Fulani and ex-Séléka on the one hand and anti-Balaka troops on the other. MINUSCA also investigated attacks like one in Kouango at the end of April, confirming that 36 abandoned villages were found, including 27 that had been totally or partially burned down. The UNSC condemned in the strongest terms an attack on a MINUSCA convoy travelling from Damara to Ngerengou, during which one peacekeeper from Burundi was killed and another injured. Similarly, it expressed shock at an attack on a MINUSCA checkpoint in the divided town of Batangafo, which followed an outbreak of violence in the local IDP camp. One peacekeeper from Cameroon was killed in the incident.

CEEAC also devoted much energy to the CAR crisis. Meeting in N'Djamena (Chad) on 25 May, the Conference of Heads of State and Government authorised a 'technical' extension of the transition to 31 December in order to permit the transitional authorities to organise the elections appropriately. An extraordinary summit in Libreville (Gabon) on 25 November focused on the upcoming elections in the CAR. Mediator Sassou Nguesso (Congo) was not the best-loved man in Bangui as he had in late 2014 initiated *parallel peace talks* in Nairobi (Kenya) with former presidents Djotodia and Bozizé, both under UN sanctions, in clear contradiction of the Bangui Forum idea and drawing on the support of the Kenyan government. The transitional government rejected the separate peace process on 25 January, not least because it was itself not represented in Nairobi. On 14 April, Bozizé and Djotodia signed a 'Nairobi declaration' in the presence of Kenyan President Uhuru Kenyatta and Vice President William Ruto, who were both under indictment at the ICC. Observers quickly termed the deal meaningless. The Cessation of Hostilities Agreement, signed on 23 July 2014 in Brazzaville, had provided for an implementation mechanism, including a Follow-up Commission and a Technical Committee. The UN Secretary-General noted that these did not adequately monitor or prevent the frequent violations of the agreement, thereby indirectly also criticising Sassou Nguesso. Djotodia (for Séléka) and one anti-Balaka leader had signed the Cessation of Hostilities Agreement on 8 April, prior to the Nairobi declaration.

The *AU* also paid close attention to events in the CAR and hosted several meetings of the International Contact Group for the CAR under the co-chairmanship of Peace and Security Commissioner Smail Chergui and Congolese Defence Minister Richard Mondjo. The AU Commission convened a DDR Sensitisation at the AU headquarters on 25–26 November

On 21 December, the *UN Panel of Experts* issued a substantial report on the war economy that had taken root and on infractions of the sanctions regime, pointing at sub-regional involvements and repercussions. *Cameroon*, temporary home to close to 250,000 refugees from the CAR, remained particularly exposed to the crisis. On 8 January, Cameroonian authorities arrested an arms dealer in Kenzou. A sizable proportion of smuggled CAR diamonds reportedly went through Cameroon, contributing to the a growing criminalisation of the economy. Truck drivers in Garoua-Boulai on the Cameroonian side of the border took strike action (in June, August and October) in protest against the inability or unwillingness of both MINUSCA and the official armed forces to protect them from attacks by the FDPC and unidentified gangs.

The *Sudanese* authorities were believed to at least tolerate illegal trade in coffee and sugar from Séléka-occupied territory in the CAR. Séléka fighters and commanders could travel to both Chad and Sudan without any hindrance, and Nourredine Adam in particular maintained his networks in the neighbouring country. However, there was *fierce competition between the three main Séléka factions* over the lucrative control of trade routes to Sudan. Sudanese arms traders dominated the market in the eastern part of the CAR. According to the UN Panel of Experts, *Chadian* security and military personnel were constantly committing human rights violations against CAR nationals, including killings, looting and destruction, forced displacement, extortion, illegal detention and violation of the right of return of CAR refugees in Chad), an allegation rejected by N'Djamena. Although officially closed, the common border could be passed unilaterally by Chadian traders pursuing business in the CAR, but not by ordinary CAR nationals. Chadian security forces mobile checkpoints were present as far as 25 km inside the CAR. Chad and the *DRC* each hosted more than 90,000 CAR refugees.

Socioeconomic Development

After a dramatic fall of 36% in its *GDP* in 2013 and a mere 1% growth in 2014, the Economist Intelligence Unit estimated the CAR's economic growth at 3.3% for 2015. Some sectors were slowly recovering, most notably agriculture and trade, but the formal CAR economy remained in limbo. Humanitarian aid had replaced market relations in large parts of the country, while armed movements controlled most of the illegal trade in diamonds, gold, cattle and other products. In the south-west, some anti-Balaka leaders even managed to obtain official mining licences.

With high demands on every side, e.g. for the restructuring of the security sector, the government, with its limited means, was barely able to make an impact. An increase in expenditure meant that the *public finances* fell back into a deficit, which the Economist Intelligence Unit estimated at 5.1% of GDP. The IMF disbursed $ 7.9 m in March and $ 11.8 m in October within its Rapid Credit Facility. After the conclusion of the Bangui Forum, the EU committed itself to additional funding from a development trust ('Fonds Bêkou'; with contributions from France, Germany and the Netherlands) including € 40 m of critically needed budgetary support.

The UN Panel of Experts provided detailed information on the *illegal trade routes* of conflict minerals out of the CAR in which armed movements or individuals were involved. The picture painted was one of widespread plunder. The government saw as one of its crucial aims the reestablishment of orderly practice in the diamond trade. In fact, the country remained suspended from the Kimberley Process Certification Scheme, which translated into a ban on official diamond exports. By an administrative decision, this ban was partially lifted in August for production zones under government control (i.e. in the west), if transparency prevailed and on condition that safeguard conditions would be met. It was also hoped that this decision would facilitate the export of stocks (60,000 carats with an estimated value of $ 7 m) accumulated since early 2014. It also meant that all diamond production in the east and the centre would still fall under the sanctions; there were few signs that this could change in the immediate future.

According to the UN Office for the Coordination of Humanitarian Affairs (OCHA), 2.7 m Central Africans were still in need of *aid* and 1.4 m. people were affected by food insecurity at the end of the year. Shortly before year's end, the UN OCHA humanitarian response plan had received $ 319.9 m, representing only 52% of total funding requirements (with the USA and the EU being the major donors). Humanitarian organisations complained of frequent targeting by armed groups.

Chad

Ketil Fred Hansen

Many deadly attacks committed by Boko Haram on Chadian soil made the Déby Itno regime take a number of counter-terror measures, including declaring a state of emergency in some parts of the country. Additionally, the massive fall in the oil price on the world market seriously affected the public purse. Payment of salaries in the public sector and scholarships for students were delayed or cut, causing many demonstrations and strikes. In July, the trial of former president Hissène Habré for crimes against humanity, war crimes and torture started in Dakar (Senegal).

Domestic Politics

Idriss Déby Itno maintained his firm control over the country and its populace in his 25th consecutive year as president. Persistently issuing presidential decrees, a total of 2,441 during the year, he governed Chad more or less as he saw fit. Two major *government reshuffles* occurred. On 23 August, eight ministers were dismissed from the government. Of the 11 newly-appointed ministers, six had previously

 | DOI 10.1163/9789004333239_024

served as ministers under Déby. According to rumours in N'Djamena, the president had initially intended to appoint one of his sons, Zakaria Déby, as minister of the environment. However, also according to rumours, the president's private secretary and wife, Hinda Déby, made him change his mind. Newspapers and blogs reported that she increased her influence considerably over the year. However, Minister of Foreign Affairs Mossa Faki Mahamat was also reported to be gaining influence over Déby, managing to get many of his friends and relatives appointed. One of Faki Mahamat's cousins, Mahamat Al Mastour Asseid, was appointed minister of livestock, only to be replaced on 26 December. The same happened to the husband of one of Faki Mahamat's nieces, Mahamat Ali Hassane, who was appointed minister of territorial administration on 23 August but quickly replaced on 26 December.

While one of Déby Itno's older brothers, Daoussa Déby Itno, continued to serve as minister of post and telecommunications throughout the year, one of his younger brothers, Saleh Déby Itno, who served as director of customs, was removed from his post and imprisoned on 24 October. He was accused of corruption when police found bank notes worth some $ 220 m in his residences. However, he served less than a month in prison before he was released, giving more flesh to already flourishing accusations of *nepotism* around President Déby Itno and his clique's inner circle. Only a few months earlier, on 18 August, Déby signed a decree allowing each of his two sons, Zakaria and Mahamat, to buy a 1000–1200 m^2 plot in the new, luxurious commercial centre under construction in N'Djamena at very favourable prices.

On 20 July, the Extraordinary African Chambers started the trial against Chad's former president *Hissène Habré* in Dakar (Senegal). Accused of war crimes, crimes against humanity and torture during his presidency (1982–90), Habré (aged 73) protested loudly and violently in court against the trial. As Habré's appointed lawyers did not appear in court when the case started, the presiding judge stopped the proceedings on 21 July, suspending the trial until 7 September for the court-appointed defence to be able to prepare. When the trial resumed, guards followed Habré into the courtroom early every day so that he was already seated when the judges, the witnesses and the audience arrived. Habré usually appeared wearing a turban and sunglasses and remained completely silent when the prosecutor tried to question him, having said earlier that he did not recognise the legitimacy of the court. For more than three months, close to 100 witnesses gave testimony against him, most of them Chadian nationals selected from among 2,500 victims interviewed by pre-trial investigating judges. Significant time and attention were granted to the victims. Especially rare and important was the focus given to women testifying about sexual abuse committed both by Habré himself and by his armed forces and police. National and foreign human rights researchers and forensic experts also testified, as did a French doctor who had treated 581 torture victims. Parts of the trial were broadcast on television in Chad. This was the first time in history that a court of one country had prosecuted a former president of another country for alleged human rights crimes. A 'New York Times' editorial called it "a transformative moment for justice in Africa". The verdict was expected by the end of May 2016.

Fighting *Boko Haram*, in both Nigeria and Cameroon as well as in Chad, was one of the foremost priorities of the Chadian regime. On 17 January, 1,500–2,000 Chadian troops supported by 400 military vehicles and a few combat helicopters arrived in northern Cameroon. A few days later, on 29 January, Boko Haram killed three Chadian soldiers and wounded many more in a clash near the northern Cameroon village of Fotokol. On 24 February, Chadian troops reported having killed 207 Boko Haram militants in the Nigerian town of Garambu for the loss of only one of their own soldiers. After that, revenge was taken several times for the Chadian army's participation in fighting Boko Haram. Prior to Déby's decision to send troops into neighbouring Nigeria and Cameroon, no attacks related to Boko Haram had taken place on Chadian territory, but after February, numerous *attacks* with significant fatalities took place in Chad. An attack during market day in Tchokou Telia village on 3 April killed seven people at random. Much more severe were two simultaneous attacks on 15 June in N'Djamena, when assaults on a police station and a police school killed 38 and wounded around 100.

On 17 June, President Déby issued a *decree prohibiting women from wearing the burqa* throughout the territory as one response to terror, but with little immediate effect. In the early morning of 29 June, Chadian police officers headed for a Boko Haram den in Diguel quarter in the outskirts of N'Djamena. Boko Haram suicide bombers surprised them, killing five police officers, while six Boko Haram militants were killed. Two weeks later, on 11 July, a female suicide bomber blew herself up while she was being searched at the entrance to N'Djamena's central market, killing 15 people, including police officers and market guards. Investigation teams managed to capture ten Boko Haram members responsible for these attacks in June and July. On 28 August, they were all sentenced to death and executed the following day at a military training camp near Massaguet, some 60 km north of N'Djamena. The main organiser of weapons and ammunition smuggling from Chad to Boko Haram in Nigeria and Cameroon, Bana Fanaye (alias Mahamat Moustapha), was among those executed. Numerous weapons used by Boko Haram originated from Chad. In September, the Boko Haram insurgency on several islands in Lake Chad caused numerous deaths. The Chadian authorities requested the population on 23 islands to evacuate to IDP camps on one of the lake's larger islands. Close to 50,000 Chadians fled their homes as a result of Boko Haram activities in the Lake Chad area between July and September. On 10 October, a Boko Haram suicide attack in Baga Sola, on the border of Lake Chad, killed 41 and wounded 48. Another bomber killed two in Ngouboua village and wounded a dozen on 8 November. Then, on 9 November, Déby imposed a ten-day state of emergency on the region, which was a few days later extended to last until 22 March 2016. The state of emergency gave the regime the authority to ban the movement of people and vehicles, search homes, recover arms and detain people for longer periods without trial. Nevertheless, on 5 December another 27 persons were killed and some 80 wounded in the region when three suicide bombers attacked people at the market on Loulou Fou, a small island on Lake Chad.

By the end of the year, Chadian troops stationed in Cameroon and Nigeria to fight Boko Haram had returned home, but the fight against Boko Haram was not over. In June, the army had started recruiting another 10,000 troops to increase their regular forces and by the end of the year the 70,000 troops equipped with T-55 combat vehicles, M-24 and M-25 attack helicopters and Russian-made Mig-29 jet fighters made the *Chadian army* the largest and best-equipped army in Central Africa and among the strongest on the entire continent. Mahamat Deby Itno, one of the president's sons, commanded the tough and resolute presidential guard throughout the year.

Domestic insurgent groups based in the north-eastern parts of Chad were not very active during the year. Their military strength and popular support had decreased significantly and so it seemed unlikely that they would attain their ultimate goal of taking state power by force. However, *ethnic violence and random banditry* posed serious security problems both in the north-eastern parts of the country and in the Tibesti region.

On 27 February, the members of the *National Assembly* voted to prolong their own mandate until 2017. Under the Constitution, the mandate should have ended on 20 July but the elections originally scheduled for 20 September were now postponed. The reasons invoked were that the biometric census was not complete and that the presidential election should take place before legislative elections.

Towards the end of the year, *preparations for the presidential elections* (planned for 10 April 2016) were in full swing. On 26 October, the long-planned biometric census started and was expected to be completed for the entire country in 45 days. The stated goal of the operation was to reduce the chances of double voting and to make it impossible for foreigners to vote. However, the biometric census process was strongly criticised by numerous opposition parties and human rights groups, who claimed that many foreigners who supported the regime were counted, while Chadians supporting the opposition were not included in the census. By the end of the year, some 6 m potential voters had been registered. Taking into account the demographic layout of Chad's official 12 m inhabitants, the number of recognised voters looked exceedingly high. Protesters claimed that a figure of 6 m voters indicated a total population of 20 m. The company that originally gained the contract to carry out the biometric census, the 'Société de Commerce Général de Construction et de Transport' (SOGECT), was owned and run by Abderahaman Hassan Mahamat Itno, a nephew of the president. However, after serious complaints, the government took control of the census itself – while SOGECT claimed CFAfr 34 bn (€ 52 m) for breach of contract.

Although Déby had not officially declared himself a candidate for the 2016 presidential election by the end of the year, no one doubted that he would do so. However, speculation about the *health of the head of state* was rife. In April, Déby was apparently very sick and did not appear in public for more than a week. Rumours had it that one of his sons, Mahamat Déby Itno, was preparing to take over power. After some ten days, Déby re-appeared in public in relatively good shape, but he travelled regularly to Paris for medical treatment at the American Hospital in Neuilly, including prior to the COP21 conference in Paris in November.

Other candidates also waited for a date closer to the election to officially announce their candidature, but it was clear by the end of the year that major *opposition leaders* would not boycott the upcoming presidential election this time. It was also close to certain that both Saleh Kebzabo of the 'Union Nationale pour le Développement et le Renouveau' and Ngarlejy Yorongar of the 'Fédération Action pour la République' would be candidates in the presidential election.

The *media* were not able to report freely. A programme on national television containing an interview with Aberaman Kollamalah, who had taken part in the attempted coup d'état in February 2008 and had just published a book about the incident, was taken off air on 2 April, which led the well-known journalist Jean Bosco Manga to resign. On June 23, Chadian police expelled Laurent Correau, a French journalist working for 'Radio France Internationale', while he was preparing to broadcast on the Habré law case. A huge number of human rights organisations and media worldwide protested against the expulsion. Political opponents mostly opted to be active on various weblogs with IP addresses outside Chad as state and private media were mostly tightly controlled.

Foreign Affairs

Chad enjoyed firm military support from Western powers, especially the USA and France, to fight terrorism throughout the year. Western powers perceived the regime as a relatively stable area in the midst of a troubled region. With serious social upheavals and political conflicts in neighbouring Sudan, Libya and CAR, together with Boko Haram insurgency in neighbouring Cameroon and Nigeria, Western powers were eager to maintain the political status quo despite the regime's dubious human rights record. On 17 January, the AU authorised the transfer of the head-quarters of the 8,700-strong anti-Boko Haram Multinational Joint Task Force (MNJTF) from Northern Nigeria to N'Djamena and on 6 March, approved an increase of up to 10,000 troops for the MNJTF.

As part of the Trans Sahara Counter Terrorism Partnership (TSCTP) supported by the US Africa Command (AFRICOM), the annual military training *'Exercise Flintlock'* was conducted in Chad in February and March. With participants from

28 countries, some 1,300 troops trained in combat patrols and practised real-world counter-terrorism missions, supposedly against Boko Haram, for three weeks. The 2015 Flintlock exercise was the largest ever. With an annual budget of $ 90–160 m since its inception in 2005, the TSCTP was among the most important military anti-terror programmes in Africa.

France's military force 'Opération Barkhane' established to fight terrorism and secure French interests in the Sahel and Central Africa, inaugurated on 1 August 2014 in N'Djamena, continued throughout the year. France engaged some 3,000 troops in the operation covering Sahelian countries from Mali in the west to Chad in the east. 'Opération Barkhane' replaced the smaller French 'Opération Epervier' (1986–2014), which had deployed only about 1,000 troops, also based in N'Djamena. Political relations between Chad and France were cordial and intense. Déby was invited by President François Hollande for an hour-long one-to-one meeting in the Elysée Palace in Paris on 14 May. Hollande praised Déby for Chad's active participation in the fight against Boko Haram and also emphasised the role Chadian troops had played in fighting Islamist rebels in northern Mali. Déby tried to lobby for his Minister of Finance Bedoumra Kordjé to be put forward as a candidate for the position of director of the AfDB. (Kordjé lost to his Nigerian rival on 26 May.) On 5 October, Déby was once more at the Elysée Palace at Hollande's invitation, but the visit was not reciprocated. French diplomats warned that, for security reasons, French citizens should not travel to Chad unless absolutely necessary, and more specifically not to the Lake Chad and the Tibesti regions.

Chad and *Sudan* continued their friendly relations. On 28 January, Déby travelled to Khartoum for a two-day official visit, discussing regional crises (in Libya and the CAR), Sudan's military offensive in Darfur and the situation for Sudanese refugees in Chad with the his Sudanese counterpart Omar al-Bashir. On 9 October, Déby arrived again in Khartoum to participate in the inauguration of Sudan's National Dialogue conference and was welcomed by al-Bashir at the airport. Déby had in fact managed to persuade three main leaders of Darfur's rebel armed factions to sign the Doha Document for Peace in Darfur and to participate in the National Dialogue conference. By the end of November, more than 40,000 Sudanese refugees in eastern Chad had voluntarily returned to their homes in Ambaro, Korney and Al-Tina in northern Darfur.

On 17 June, all the foreign ministers of the *G5 Sahel* met together for the first time with *EU* representatives in Brussels (Belgium) to discuss security issues related to Boko Haram, the political situation in Libya and Islamist unrest in Mali. They had as one of their goals the establishment of regular meetings between the G5 Sahel and the EU. On 20 November, G5 Sahel heads of state, presided over by Déby, met in N'Djamena to discuss how to strengthen their joint efforts against Boko Haram and other Islamist militant groups in the region.

On 23 December, UN Secretary-General Ban Ki-moon nominated the Chadian former minister of foreign affairs and head of UN peacekeeping forces in Somalia,

Mahamat Saleh Annadif, as his special representative for *Mali* and head of the UN peacekeeping force MINUSMA.

Socioeconomic Developments

In April, Chad took the necessary steps to finally reach completion point within the *HIPC* initiative launched in 1996 by the World Bank and the IMF for conditional debt relief. Chad was the 36th and last African country to achieve this status. As a result, both institutions cancelled debts of $ 1.1 bn. On 24 June, creditors within the Paris Club also cancelled debts owed by Chad to the tune of $ 62.6 m. In December, the World Bank awarded a grant of $ 18 m for work on reforming the country's public budgets and making them more transparent.

Students and teachers staged numerous strikes and demonstrations. On 26 January, high school students in Doba protested against a decision by the minister of education to bar all pupils who had failed their 2014 baccalaureate exams with marks below 5/20 from re-sitting before 2016. The demonstrations were violently suppressed by the Chadian police, resulting in two deaths (one student and one passer-by). Students also demonstrated in Ndjamena on 8 and 9 March. The police used brutal force against the protesters and at least one student was killed. A new law forcing motorcyclists to wear helmets sparked off demonstrations among youngsters, students and motorcycle taxi drivers in many cities on 23 March. Demonstrations turned violent in N'Djamena, where three people were killed by the police. As an act of solidarity, the University and many high schools in the capital locked down for days. On 7 April, teachers in N'Djamena went on strike for a little over a week in protest over the non-payment of their salaries. On 25 July, the special intervention police force stopped a protest march organised by students at N'Djamena University and the National Teachers College. The Ministry of Education had not paid student scholarships for the past six months. Similar strikes and police repression occurred on 11 November in N'Djamena and in December in N'Djamena, Abeche and Pala.

The humanitarian situation was a source of concern. Despite a 10% increase in production of the main staple crops (millet, sorghum, rice and maize), Chad was one of eight countries in the world classified by the Global Hunger Index as experiencing "alarming hunger", based on high child mortality and general malnutrition. Chad continued to host *refugees* from many neighbouring countries, although the total number fell slightly. Approximately 300,000 refugees from Sudan continued to live in eastern Chad, together with 65,000 from the CAR. An estimated 15,000 from Nigeria fled to Chad fearing Boko Haram, most of them just after the attacks in Baga village in January. In addition, some 40,000 Chadians in the Lake Chad area were sporadically internally displaced during July and August as a result of acts of terror by to Boko Haram.

Congo

Brett Logan Carter

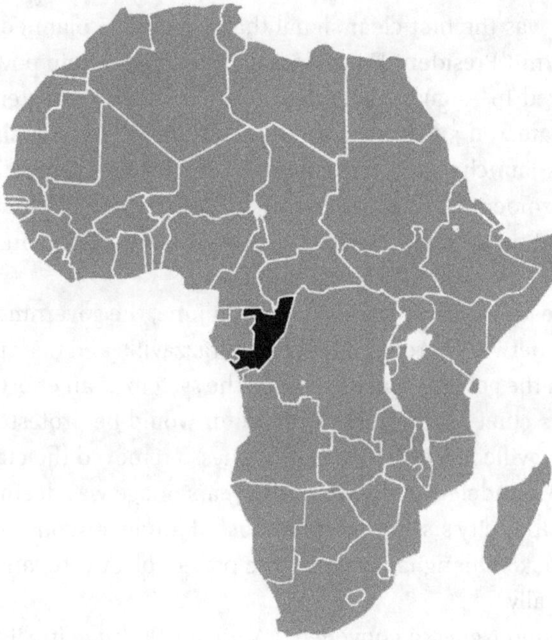

On 22 October, President Sassou Nguesso staged a constitutional referendum, which left him poised to extend his rule for at least another decade. Decried by the political opposition as a "constitutional coup d'état", the referendum elicited massive protests across the country. Sassou Nguesso expected citizens to mobilise in protest and, in the months prior to the referendum, he prepared himself politically. In March, in order to further increase his control over the country's oil sector, Sassou Nguesso promulgated a new Hydrocarbons Law. In August, he announced a new government, which excluded two long-standing ministers who had criticised the impending constitutional revision. Abroad, Sassou Nguesso continued to fashion himself as the region's elder statesman, especially as Western governments condemned both the constitutional referendum and his record of economic mismanagement. China emerged as Congo's chief export destination, accounting for 52% of the country's total exports. As oil production declined and global prices fell, the government's fiscal position deteriorated and public debt increased.

 | DOI 10.1163/9789004333239_025

Domestic Politics

On 31 December 2014, the 'Parti Congolais du Travail' Central Committee had convened to determine whether to support the constitutional referendum and, to no one's surprise, the Committee announced its support on 1 January. Although the vote itself was a formality, it was the first clear signal that the regime planned to revise the Constitution to permit President Denis Sassou Nguesso to retain power when his second term expired in August. Congolese citizens quickly registered their disapproval. A month later, on 5 February, a range of civil society organisations and opposition parties launched the Republican Front for the Respect of Constitutional Order and Democratic Alternance (FROCAD), led by Paul Marie Mpouélé. FROCAD denounced the impending constitutional revision as a "constitutional coup d'état".

The regime moved to shore up its *repressive apparatus*. In June, the government installed a video surveillance network throughout central Brazzaville and near the Maya-Maya airport. Although the government advertised the system as an effort to improve traffic circulation, its chief purpose was to monitor would-be protesters. On 6 July, as tensions in Brazzaville intensified, Sassou Nguesso removed the city's long-serving prefect, Benoît Moundélé-Ngollo, who at 72 years of age was deemed unable to effectively oversee the city's security apparatus. Moundélé-Ngollo was replaced by Pierre Cébert Ibocko-Onangha, formerly the prefect of Cuvette and a longstanding Sassou Nguesso ally.

Between 13 and 17 July, Sassou Nguesso convened a *National Dialogue* in Sibiti, Lékoumou, to discuss the "evolution of the country's political institutions", a euphemism for the constitutional revision. The Dialogue, presided over by André Obami Itou and Firmin Ayessa – among Sassou Nguesso's most trusted allies – was denounced as a charade by the political opposition, who ultimately boycotted it. The Dialogue served to propose the government's terms for a constitutional revision. Delegates conceded more legislative oversight to the executive, the appointment of a prime minister, and a reduction in the length of presidential terms from five years to seven. On the crucial question of the limit to the number of terms a president could serve, however, the Dialogue announced that participants were divided. Later in the year, the Dialogue's failure to achieve consensus allowed Sassou Nguesso to justify a constitutional referendum as a principled deference to popular sovereignty.

Sassou Nguesso announced a *new government* on 11 August, dismissing the two ministers who had publicly opposed the constitutional revision: Claudine Munari, a former Lissouba ally from Bouenza region, and Guy Brice Parfait Kolélas, leader of the 'Mouvement Congolais pour la Démocratie et le Développement Intégral'. As replacements, Sassou Nguesso selected a pair of young politicians whose family pedigrees would prove politically useful for the referendum ahead: Jean-Marc Thystère Tchicaya and Euloge Landry Kolélas, Guy Brice Parfait's brother.

Although Thystère Tchicaya was less popular in Pointe-Noire than his late father, the appointment removed the spiritual centre of the city's opposition. By persuading Euloge Landry Kolélas to accept his brother's place, Sassou Nguesso further undercut potential *opposition* from the Pool region. Sassou Nguesso also renewed his alliance with Laurentine Milongo, widow of the late André Milongo, founder of the 'Union pour la Démocratie et la République' (UDR-Mwinda), who had remained among the Pool region's most popular opposition leaders until his death in 2007. Just before their dismissal, Kolélas and Munari founded the Initiative for Democracy in Congo (IDC), along with three other former Sassou Nguesso allies who staunchly opposed the constitutional revision: Charles Zacharie Bowao, René Serge Blanchard Oba, and André Okombi Salissa. The IDC quickly agreed to an alliance with FROCAD.

On 22 September, Sassou Nguesso finally announced the *constitutional referendum.* As expected, the Constitution would be advertised as "more democratic" than its predecessor. It reduced the length of presidential terms from seven years to five, called for the appointment of a prime minister, and gave the National Assembly greater oversight authority. Perhaps more importantly, from Sassou Nguesso's perspective, the new Constitution forbade the extradition of Congolese citizens and granted presidents lifetime immunity from prosecution. The Constitution even specified that the transgression of these provisions would be counted as treason. By ushering in a new republic, the new Constitution enabled Sassou Nguesso to circumvent the term limits imposed by its predecessor. The timing of the announcement was strategic. It occurred just three days after the 11th African Games, held in Brazzaville, and after it became clear that both President Pierre Nkurunziza of Burundi and President Paul Kagame of Rwanda would also brave international condemnation to secure third presidential terms. Having committed himself to the referendum, Sassou Nguesso moved quickly. It was scheduled for just five weeks later, on 25 October. Congolese citizens responded angrily. On 27 September, only five days after the referendum was announced, opposition leaders organised a protest attended by some 30,000 people, easily the largest since Sassou Nguesso's return to power in 1997 and possibly larger than those that had forced him to convene the 1991 National Conference. Rather than suppressing protesters, Sassou Nguesso organised a 'mega concert', which was ultimately boycotted even by the headliner, Roga Roga. Congo's pro-democracy activists coordinated their efforts via social media, and days later the hashtag "#SassouFit" emerged as the rallying cry, a clever phonetic play on 'ça suffit' ('that's enough').

Protests intensified as the referendum approached. Sensing the possibility of a Burkina Faso style revolution, the regime responded brutally: one Pointe-Noire protest led to more than 30 deaths. The regime shut down SMS text messaging, limited Internet access, and placed several opposition leaders under house arrest. Hoping that Western governments would force Sassou Nguesso to abandon the "constitutional coup d'état", as they called it, the political opposition organised a series of protests in Paris and Washington. Finally, in the days before the referendum, the opposition called for a boycott.

The referendum was held on 25 October. Days later, the regime claimed that some 73% of eligible voters went to the polls, with 92% of votes cast endorsing the *new Constitution*. In reality, most Brazzaville polling stations were deserted until late afternoon, when the regime began bussing in its few supporters – many of whom had been paid to vote – to create the illusion of participation. The new Constitution was promulgated on 6 November and the presidential election was scheduled for 20 March 2016.

The year concluded just as Congo's political parties were selecting their candidates for the March 2016 presidential elections. As they did so, Sassou Nguesso sought to placate the political opposition by appointing a *prime minister* from the country's southern regions. Martin Mberi, among former president Pascal Lissouba's chief aides and a senior minister in several Lissouba governments, emerged as the principal candidate. After having publicly opposed the constitutional revision in 2014, Mberi toured the southern regions of Niari, Lékoumou, and Bouenza between 12 and 23 December, attempting to generate public enthusiasm.

Foreign Affairs

Sassou Nguesso's efforts to secure a constitutional revision dominated his foreign policy. Early in the year, Western governments voiced their opposition. On 3 June, the US State Department affirmed the Obama administration's opposition and, on 7 July, French President François Hollande issued his objection directly to Sassou Nguesso. Indeed, the Élysée Palace broke protocol by not laying the red carpet at the palace entrance when Sassou Nguesso arrived.

Sassou Nguesso's bilateral relationship with *France* was further strained by the ongoing 'biens mal acquis' corruption investigation. French authorities seized three major properties owned by the Sassou Nguesso family: in June, the French justice department seized Villa Suzette, a mansion located in Yvelines, just west of Paris and, in August, the French government seized two apartments, in Neuilly-sur-Seine and Courbevoie. In February, police officers searched a fourth property, also in Neuilly-sur-Seine, during which they seized more than $ 300,000 in cash alone. Sassou Nguesso continued in his efforts to persuade Hollande to block the investigation, but still to no avail. In September, Sassou Nguesso chose Alain Akouala-Atipault, who until August had served as the minister of special economic zones, to succeed Henri Lopès as ambassador to Paris; Akouala-Atipault, one of Sassou Nguesso's most loyal aides, had been a frequent critic in Brazzaville of the 'biens mal acquis' investigation. Paris declined his credentials.

However, as violence in Burundi spiralled out of control, Western governments softened their opposition to the constitutional revision. After Congolese protesters called on Hollande to block the revision on 20 October, Hollande stated that was Sassou Nguesso's right as president to consult his people in a constitutional referendum and that the people would have to respond. "Then, once the people have been consulted [...] we must always be careful to unite, to respect, and to make peace." Members of the Congolese opposition declared Hollande's statement a "knife to the back". Even the French daily 'Le Monde', normally friendly to Hollande's Socialist government, led with the headline, "The African press denounces the complicit support of François Hollande to President Sassou Nguesso."

As bilateral relationships with Western governments deteriorated, Sassou Nguesso redoubled his efforts to court regional allies. In April, he financed Faure Gnassingbé's re-election campaign in *Togo*; Gnassingbé repaid his generosity by visiting him in Oyo, his native village, on 15 May. In September, Sassou Nguesso coordinated a $ 40 m transaction between Lucien Ebata and President Alassane Ouattara of Côte d'Ivoire, which provided the Ivorian government with liquidity at a crucial moment. Sassou Nguesso continued to serve as the official mediator for the crisis in the CAR. Although his relationship with Transitional President Catherine Samba-Panza was strained by year's end, Sassou Nguesso actively courted the two leading candidates to succeed her in the February 2016 presidential elections.

As in years past, Sassou Nguesso pursued ever closer bilateral relationships with *China, Russia, Turkey, Brazil* and *India*. In July, to much fanfare, the Sassou Nguesso government welcomed a delegation from the Agricultural Bank of China (ABC), among the largest financial institutions in Beijing. The ABC and the Congolese government jointly established the 'Banque Sino-Congolaise pour l'Afrique', with the Bank's founding capital contributed in roughly equal measure by the two countries; local journalists reported that the Sassou Nguesso family owned roughly 12%. The Brazzaville office represented only the eighth international branch of the ABC, and the first in Africa. In September, the Sassou Nguesso government signed an agreement with Turkish firm BTP Summa to build a 'Cité Gouvernementale in central Brazzaville, which would ultimately house the country's central administration.

Socioeconomic Developments

As oil prices declined, the regime sought new revenue streams to purchase political support. On 25 March, Sassou Nguesso approved a new *Hydrocarbons Law*, which was designed to enhance his ability to distribute patronage. The law featured three critical provisions. First, the state oil company, 'Société Nationale des Petrôles du Congo' (SNPC), was given exclusive authority to grant oil and gas concessions. In practice, this move gave Denis Christel Sassou Nguesso, the president's son and the SNPC's deputy director, even more authority to organise the oil sector to the regime's benefit. Second, the law stipulated that the government's share of oil revenue would be at least 35%. Finally, and perhaps most importantly, nationally held private companies would receive at least a 15% share in all production sharing agreements. Only two such companies enjoyed the technical capacity to participate meaningfully in production sharing agreements: Africa Oil and Gas Corporation and Orion Oil. Although owned by Denis Gokana and Lucien Ebata, respectively, both firms were effectively controlled by Sassou Nguesso.

Congo's nominal GDP reached $ 14.2 bn, at a growth rate of about 1%. This represented a significant decline; in 2010, Congo's growth rate had reached nearly 9%. The slowing growth rate was driven almost entirely by declining oil reserves and global market prices. The oil sector continued to account for some 75% of government revenue and 80% of foreign exchange earnings. Congo produced only 241,000 b/d, down from over 300,000 in 2013. Reflecting this, Congo's total exports declined as well, from $ 10.5 bn in 2013 to $ 5.85 bn in 2015. China emerged as Congo's chief export partner by a substantial margin, accounting for 52% of total exports. Australia, Congo's second leading export partner, accounted for just 8.3%.

As commodity prices declined, the government's fiscal position rapidly deteriorated. Although reserves at the central bank constituted 20% of GDP – the highest percentage in the region – external public debt increased to 47% of GDP, up from 20% in 2010. The government's current account deficit reached 8% of GDP. Declining oil prices forced the government to take corrective fiscal measures. Based on an oil price assumption of $ 70 per barrel, in May the Council of Ministers adopted a supplementary budget based on an oil price of $ 55. As a result, Standard & Poor's downgraded Congo's bond rating from B+ to B, while Fitch downgraded Congo's Issuer Default Rating from Stable to Negative. The inflation rate was 2.1%.

Democratic Republic of the Congo

Claudia Simons

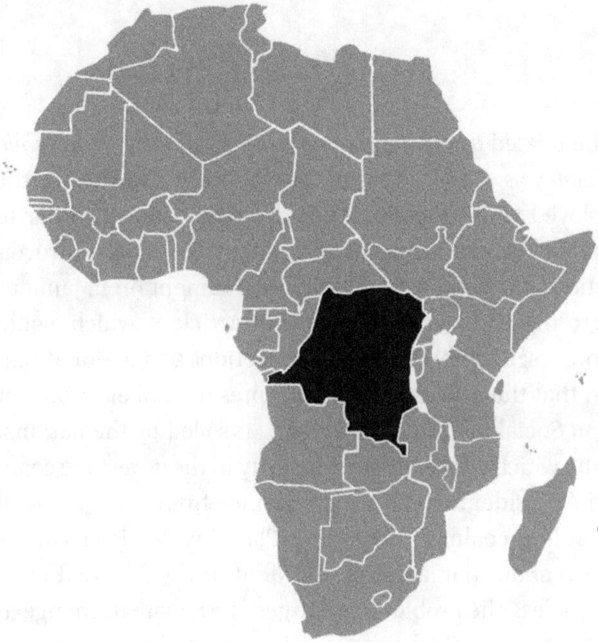

The year was marked by debates and protests around the elections that were to begin with provincial elections in 2015 and culminate in presidential polls in 2016. The government engaged in various strategies to prolong its hold on power, despite the constitutional term limit that banned President Kabila from serving a third mandate. The issue of a third term for Kabila was controversial within both the ruling coalition and the political opposition and led to widespread street protests, which were violently repressed by the police. Kabila called for a national dialogue to discuss the electoral process, but most opposition parties boycotted the effort. After nine years of foot-dragging on decentralisation, the existing 11 provinces were hastily carved up into 26, leading to a chaotic situation that made provincial elections impossible. The Constitutional Court was established and immediately came under criticism for allowing Kabila to appoint interim governors for the newly created provinces without elections. Cooperation between the DRC's 'Forces Armées de la République Démocratique du Congo' (FARDC) and the UN Stabilization Mission in the DRC (MONUSCO) broke down over the handling of red-listed army officers, whereupon MONUSCO was sidelined in long-awaited operations against the 'Forces Démocratiques de Libération du Rwanda' (FDLR). The security situation in the east

 | DOI 10.1163/9789004333239_026

of the country remained fragile, mainly due to fighting between the army on the one hand, and the FDLR and the Ugandan militia 'Allied Democratic Forces' on the other. The mining sector increased in importance, with copper production rising significantly.

Domestic Politics

The election process and the related question of whether President Joseph *Kabila* would stay *in office beyond 2016* was the biggest domestic political issue during the year. The government employed various strategies to delay elections in order to hold on to power, a process that became known as 'glissement'. The first controversial move was the introduction of a new electoral bill in Parliament on 12 January. The most disputed change to the *electoral law* was within Article 8, which would have tied the updating of voter registration for the 2016 elections to a national census. The opposition claimed that the census would delay presidential elections for many years. The 'Mouvement Social pour le Renouveau' (MSR) led by the national security advisor, Pierre Lumbi, which was an important party in the governing coalition 'Alliance pour la Majorité Présidentielle' (AMP), abstained from voting. Several other politicians from the ruling coalition, including Planning Minister Olivier Kamitatu, also raised concern about the law. The president of the Senate, Kengo wa Dondo, publicly called Article 8 'the problem' and urged the Senate to change it. Further pressured by mass protests in Kinshasa and other cities, the upper house amended the bill on 23 January, dropping the contested reference to a census. The proposed electoral law still remained controversial, however, as it stipulated that voter registration would be updated in line with available demographic data – without specifying how this data would be gathered. In the version of the bill that was finally enacted by Parliament on 25 January and approved by Kabila on 12 February, Article 8, and with it all references to demographic data, was taken out. Parliament also removed additions made by the Senate that made explicit reference to the constitutional time frame as binding – thereby removing a stipulation that Kabila would have to leave office in 2016.

A further controversial issue was the publication of the *electoral calendar* by the electoral commission, the 'Commission Electorale Nationale Indépendante' (CENI), on 16 February. Legislative and presidential polls were scheduled for 27 November 2016, to be preceded by provincial and municipal elections in October 2015 and several local elections in the course of 2016. The opposition immediately demanded a revision of the calendar, which they claimed was too ambitious. The fact that local and municipal elections, stipulated by the 2006 Constitution but postponed for almost ten years, were to be held before the presidential polls, was widely seen as a tactic used by the president to delay the electoral process. Related legislation that sparked controversy was the revision of constituency boundaries for local and municipal elections. This annex to the electoral law was rejected by the National Assembly and sent back to the government in March. Subsequently, a revised version was approved in an extraordinary session of the National Assembly on 25 July, only to be nullified by the Senate in its first extraordinary session on 31 July on grounds of unconstitutionality according to some and of the lack of a quorum in the Senate according to others. On 11 August, the Senate, in a second extraordinary session, adopted the text unanimously, but only because the political opposition boycotted the session. The boundary revision, which was a precondition for the holding of local and municipal elections, was a particularly sensitive issue as a voters' register on the local level was virtually non-existent and badly planned local elections would run the risk of exacerbating simmering communal conflicts.

On 4 April, the *Constitutional Court* was officially established and the nine judges were sworn in. For the first time in its history, the DRC had an institution theoretically able to judge the president and the prime minister. The Court had jurisdiction to be in charge of the upcoming presidential elections. Hitherto, this had been the remit of the Supreme Court of Justice, which had repeatedly come under criticism, particularly for its handling of the 2011 presidential and legislative elections. The nine Constitutional Court judges had been nominated the previous year and many had occupied political posts in the past. Their appointment was the prerogative of the president, Parliament and the High Council of Magistrates. The independence of the Court was immediately questioned by civil society activists, who argued that both Parliament and the Council of Magistrates were politically biased towards the president, but they nevertheless welcomed the establishment of the Court as they hoped it would speed up the many cases stalled at the Supreme Court. The first major ruling of the newly created Court brought widespread criticism. In response to a demand by the CENI, the Court ruled on 8 September that the CENI had to review the election calendar, and the entire electoral process, judging it to be financially and politically unfeasible. Notably, the provincial elections originally scheduled for 25 October were said to be dependent on the appointment of governors in provinces that had been newly created within the framework of a countrywide decentralisation.

The long-awaited *decentralisation* process had started on 11 March, when Kabila signed into law the establishment of 26 provinces to replace the current 11. While the provinces of Kinshasa, North Kivu, South Kivu, Maniema and Bas Congo remained as they had been, the provinces of Bandundu, Equateur Orientale, Kasai Oriental, Kasai Occidental and Katanga were split up into 21 smaller units. A tight time frame foresaw that the new provinces would be operational within 135 days. However, by 8 September no administrative committees had been established in the new provinces, causing the Constitutional Court not only to rule that provincial elections were unfeasible but also to call the situation 'anarchy' and demand that the government take exceptional transitional measures to restore order. Responding to this ruling, Kabila appointed 'special commissioners', mostly loyalists, for the new provinces on 29 October. A reorganisation of the country's territory had been stipulated in the 2006 Constitution but postponed ever since, so its hasty and underfunded implementation was seen by the opposition as yet another ploy to delay the electoral process. After the court ruling, the provincial and local elections originally scheduled for 25 October were simply scrapped without much comment from the government or the setting of a new date.

On 26 September, the press made public a proposed law to regulate referenda, which had been initiated a few days before by two MPs loyal to Kabila. Although the government claimed that it only wanted to define the regulations for referenda to close a legal loophole and that it did not plan to actually hold a referendum any time soon, the news sparked outrage among the opposition and civil society. Critics saw the law as yet another manoeuvre by Kabila to make it possible for him to stand for a third term, the Constitution foreseeing only three circumstances in which a referendum could be held: namely a proposed change of the capital city, of national frontiers or of the Constitution.

A further blow to the already chaotic electoral preparations came with the *resignation of the CENI president*, Abbott Apollinaire Malu-Malu, on 10 October, officially for health reasons, and its vice president, André Mpungwe, who quit on 31 October, for personal reasons. Critics feared that the demise of the two CENI chiefs was the result of political pressure by the president. Malu-Malu had headed the electoral commission during the 2006 elections, which were seen as free and fair, but not during the flawed 2011 elections, and was largely seen as an upright administrator. CENI's treasurer, Chantal Ngoy Thite, also resigned in early November. She was a member of the MSR, which broke away from AMP and formed a new opposition platform called G7 in September (see below). On 16 November, Kabila made public the appointments of Corneille Nangaa as new CENI president, Norbert Basengezi as his vice president and Pierrette Mwenze as treasurer – all members of the AMP.

Under pressure, in an address to the nation on 28 November, Kabila called for a *national dialogue* to ensure a peaceful electoral process, and announced a preparatory committee without specifying its composition or the timing of the dialogue. Kabila also said he would accept an international mediator but stated that the mediator would only step in if major problems occurred. Another statement by Kabila, namely that the DRC should start to consider a less costly electoral system, sparked criticism by the opposition, who feared that Kabila wanted to change the Constitution to put in place a system to elect the president by indirect vote, effectively allowing him to be re-elected by Parliament – potentially inspired by the example of Angola's President dos Santos. Prior to his official call for dialogue, Kabila had in May called on the opposition to engage in negotiations. Of the main opposition parties, only the 'Union pour la Démocratie et le Progrès Social' (UDPS) initially agreed to discuss how such a dialogue might be organised. This came as a surprise since the UDPS had for decades rejected most attempts by consecutive governments to talk with the opposition. On 13 September, however, the party broke off the talks and set a deadline for the government to begin the dialogue on 30 November and accept an international mediator, failing which the UDPS would withdraw their participation. On 2 December, the UN Special Envoy for the Great Lakes region, Saïd Djinnit, arrived in Kinshasa to discuss the organisation of a political dialogue.

Although the delay of elections and the possible third mandate for Kabila were the most discussed political topics throughout the year, the government remained vague on the subject. As early as 5 February, the government spokesman, Lambert Mende, announced that Kabila would respect the Constitution and repeated the statement on several occasions. However, the AMP spokesman, André Alain Atundu, declared on 31 October that it was impossible to organise credible elections under the current conditions and that they would have to be delayed by two to four years. The government quickly retracted the statement, saying that it did not represent official government policy, at the same time not denying the need for a delay. Kabila himself kept silent about the elections and his stay in power – apart from very general statements about the DRC's commitment to democracy.

The *ruling coalition was divided* over the question of a third mandate. In mid-September, seven of the AMP coalition parties founded a new opposition grouping (the G7), including the MSR and Planning Minister Olivier Kamitatu's 'Alliance pour le Renouveau au Congo' (ARC), who had voiced concern about Kabila's efforts to stay in power as early as January. The leaders of the G7 had already urged Kabila to stand down and expressed concerns about the potential delay of elections in an open letter on 5 March. On 14 September, the G7 published a second letter, accusing Kabila of a suicidal strategy to spread confusion about the elections in order to stay in power. The seven parties were thereupon dismissed from the AMP. Their members included eight ministers and the vice president of the National Assembly, and they held around 80 of the 500 seats in Parliament, amounting to a third of the ruling coalition's control of the lower house. With the consequent dismissal of G7 ministers, ten new ministers entered the government in late September and the G7 then evolved into an important opposition movement, which announced in October that it considered Moise Katumbi, the former governor of Kabila's mineral-rich home province of Katanga, to be a potential presidential candidate for the opposition coalition. The announcement came shortly after Katumbi had resigned from the ruling People's Party for Reconstruction and Democracy (PPRD) on 29 September, and he had already in December 2014 publicly urged Kabila to leave power. The politically and economically influential Katumbi had been governor of Katanga since 2007 but left his post with the division of the province into four provinces as part of the decentralisation process. Just before the end of Katumbi's mandate – and with it his immunity – Kabila's special advisor for good governance and the fight against corruption, Emmanuel-Janvier Luzolo Bambi Lessa, asked Prosecutor General Flory Kabange Numbi to investigate allegations of fraud against Katumbi and 19 other officials. Human rights activists from Kinshasa and Lubumbashi voiced concern that the initiative was political and warned of corruption show trials of political opponents. Katumbi had until recently been a very close ally of the president but in the course of the year became a potentially powerful rival to Kabila in the 2016 elections.

On 19 December, opposition parties and civil society associations established the *Citizen Front 2016*. The Front included political heavyweights such as Katumbi, the former president of the National Assembly and head of the 'Union pour la Nation Congolaise', Vital Kamerhe, the son of the historical UDPS opposition politician Etienne Tshisekedi, Félix, the secretary general of Jean-Pierre Bemba's 'Mouvement de Libération du Congo', Eve Bazaiba, and the leader of the 'Forces Acquises au Changement', Martin Fayulu. In December, discussions began about the affiliation of the G7 to the Citizen Front.

Despite this new cooperation between the political and civil *opposition*, the opposition's politics were far from coherent. The largest and most important opposition party, the UDPS, was riven by internal splits. Its ageing historical leader, Etienne Thisekedi, had been in Belgium for health reasons since 2014 and had increasingly lost influence over the party's decisions. The in-fighting mainly revolved around the question of whether the UDPS should engage in a dialogue and form part of a potential future government of national unity, as encouraged by Thisekedi's son Félix and his allies, or retain their traditional distrust of the Kabila government and stay out of any negotiations, as many officials and the traditional support base of the party wanted.

The debate about the 2016 elections and a possible third mandate for Kabila was accompanied by various *mass protests* in Kinshasa and other cities. The parliamentary vote on the electoral law on 12 January sparked a series of demonstrations in Kinshasa, Goma and Bukavu, which escalated over the following days and were met by heavy police violence. According to HRW, 41 people had died by 23 January, including 21 shot by the police. The month of March saw another peak in protests following the arrest of around 40 pro-democracy activists from the DRC, Burkina Faso and Senegal and a member of the US embassy staff, during a gathering in Kinshasa on 15 March.

On 8 December, the UN Joint Human Rights Office published a report documenting an increase of *violations of political rights and public freedoms* committed mainly by police and the national intelligence agency against political opposition, media and civil society groups. The report listed 143 human rights violations in relation to the election between 1 January and 30 September, including summary executions, excessive use of force, arbitrary detention and restrictions on the right to freedom of expression and peaceful assembly. On 15 April, MONUSCO asked the government to investigate a suspicious mass grave in Maluku district around 80 km from the capital Kinshasa. According to local authorities, 421 unclaimed foetuses, stillborn babies and homeless people had been buried there on 19 March. However, the unusual circumstances of the burial, which had taken place during the night, overseen by security forces, sparked concerns that Muluku was being used to hide the bodies of government opponents killed during protests in January. On 5 June, the families of 34 such victims filed a public request for the bodies to be exhumed.

On 17 September, the High Military Court delivered its judgement in the case of the murder in 2010 of human rights activist Floribert Chebeya and his driver, Fidèle Bazana. The convicted former police colonel Daniel Mukalayi was sentenced to 15 years in prison in a change to the death sentence handed down by the military court of Kinshasa in 2011. The court cited extenuating circumstances. Four other policemen were acquitted. On 1 July, Mukulayi's former driver, Kalala Kalao, had made surprising revelations before the court, including the existence of a third victim. The Chebeya case had attracted international attention and raised questions concerning the situation of human rights defenders, the role of security organs and impunity in the DRC.

The *security situation* in the east of the country continued to be fragile. On 2 January, a six-month ultimatum set by the ICGLR and SADC for FDLR fighters to surrender or face military action, expired. Only around 200 rank-and-file soldiers of the estimated 1,500 FDLR fighters had surrendered by then.

On 29 January, FARDC Chief of Staff Didier Etumba announced *unilateral military action* against the FDLR. The campaign was to be headed by General Bruno Mandevu and would only receive logistical and other non-combatant support from the UN. The side-lining of the UN Force Intervention Brigade (part of MONUSCO) came as a surprise as joint operations had been planned for over a year. Together with the appointment of Mandevu, this increased tensions between the FARDC and MONUSCO. Mandevu figured on an internal UN red-list of FARDC commanders excluded from cooperation as he was accused of several human rights violations, including summary executions and rape. The UN and human rights groups from the DRC called for his removal.

The *operations against the FDLR*, dubbed Sokola II, started with attacks on rebel positions in South Kivu on 24 January and in North Kivu on 26 January. External monitoring of the operations was severely restricted due to the lack of UN involvement. By July, the government claimed to have captured around 400 FDLR combatants, a number questioned by Rwanda and the UN. After a lull in July, FARDC action against the FDLR intensified in August with attacks on the rebels' strongholds in Walikale, Lubero, Masisi and Rutshuru territories in North Kivu. While Sokola II was able to dislodge the rebels from main axes, the FDLR's command, their troop strength and military capacity remained intact and FDLR leader Sylvestre Mudacumura was still at large at the end of the year. The ICC had issued an arrest warrant against him in 2012 and in 2013 the US State Department's Rewards for Justice programme had offered up to $ 5 m for information leading to his arrest.

The fate of the demobilised FDLR fighters remained uncertain throughout the year. On 22 August, the head of MONUSCO, Martin Kobler, announced the suspension of financial aid to the Kisangani transit camp, where most demobilised FDLR fighters were awaiting repatriation to Rwanda. According to Kobler, the UN did not have the means to finance fighters who were not willing to return. In an FARDC controlled camp in Kanyabayonga (North Kivu), the FARDC clashed with demobilised fighters on 25 May, after which around 50 of the camp inhabitants fled to UN sites and others disappeared.

On 5 January, the FARDC, together with the South African MONUSCO contingent launched attacks against the main bases of the Burundian rebel group 'Forces de Libération Nationale' in Uvira/South Kivu. According to MONUSCO, these surprise strikes, which also targeted some Mai-Mai groups, were the precursor to an offensive against the FDLR. With a growing political and security crisis in neighbouring Burundi, cross-border movement by the Burundian militia Imbonerakure into the DRC (and of FDLR elements into Burundi) further destabilised the province of South Kivu, mainly around Uvira.

Violence in North Kivu's Beni territory further escalated over the first half of the year. Many of the attacks were attributed by various observers to the Ugandan rebel group, the Allied Democratic Forces (*ADF*), but a lot remained unclear about the exact authorship and circumstances of many of the particularly brutal incidents. Among other things, the ADF was said to have killed two Tanzanian peacekeepers and injured 13 in Beni on 5 May and led coordinated attacks on a hospital in the town of Eringeti and a MONUSCO base in Beni on 29 November, leaving dozens of civilians, four FARDC soldiers, 12 rebels and one Malawian peacekeeper dead. MONUSCO responded with attacks on ADF positions south-east of Eringeti the following day. The FARDC had declared victory over the ADF in March 2014 but attacks continued. Since the death of the army commander of the military region covering North Kivu, Lucien Bahuma Ambamba, in August 2014, the FARDC's Sokola I operation against the ADF – since then under the lead of Brigadier General Muhindo Akili Mundos – had made very little progress and was only revived when Mundos was replaced by Brigadier General Marcel Mbangu Mashita in June. However, due to a breakdown in military cooperation between MONUSCO and the government, operations were conducted almost solely by the FARDC and were met with fierce resistance by the ADF. A restructuring of the Sokola I operation in Beni and the replacement of officers gave rise to optimism about more discipline and potential prosecution of FARDC elements for abuse of office. In fact, civil society activists had filed complaints ranging from inaction and indiscipline to complicity in the massacres. In late April (the exact date was unclear), the head of the ADF, Jamil Mukulu, was arrested in Tanzania and was extradited to Uganda on 10 July. Mukulu had been under UN sanctions since 2011 and sentenced to death in absentia by a military tribunal in Goma for the killing of FARDC Colonel Mamadou Ndala in 2014. Mukula had been the uncontested leader of the ADF for over two decades and over the years been accused by the UN Group of Experts of recruiting child soldiers, slavery and forced marriage.

Negotiations between the government and the 'Force de Résistance Patriotique en Ituri' (*FRPI*), one of the oldest local militias, which had operated in Ituri district since 2002, failed twice. In January, the FRPI withdrew from the negotiations as a consequence of the arrest of their leader Cobra Matata, who was detained on 2 January and taken to Kinshasa on 5 January accused of war crimes and crimes against humanity. A second round of negotiations failed in June, because the FRPI was unwilling to hand in arms as a sign of good will. After each round of failed negotiations, the FARDC and MONUSCO launched offensives against the FRPI. On 15 January, an attack on FRPI positions in Aveba caused the death of 21 fighters, and an offensive on 3 June killed 34 fighters and injured 46. The government had been in negotiations with the FRPI since 2014 and had already agreed on terms very favourable for the group, including an amnesty for all its members, full integration into the FARDC with retention of ranks and deployment in home areas for officers, and financial aid. In the weeks following the second offensive, MONUSCO's Martin Kobler repeatedly underlined the success in the anti-FRPI operation in order to demonstrate unity between MONUSCO and the DRC army, which had experienced increased tensions earlier in the year.

On 2 June, a group of former *Mai-Mai* fighters led by Kambale Malonga attacked Goma airport, leaving seven people dead. The assailants tried to steal ammunition from a depot at the airport. Malonga and about 20 others were arrested. Malonga was a well-known rebel who had taken part in the formation of various rebel groups, as well as demobilisation programmes, and had several times expressed disappointment with government demobilisation policies.

Foreign Affairs

The *international prosecution* of FDLR and former Rwandan participants in genocide saw some breakthroughs. On 28 September, after a four-year trial, a court in Stuttgart (Germany) sentenced the former head of the FDLR, Ignace Murwanashyaka, to 13 years in prison and his deputy, Straton Musoni, to eight years. The prosecutor had called for life imprisonment for Murwanashyaka and 12 years for Musoni. The latter was conditionally released after the verdict as he had already served almost six years in pre-trial detention and had applied for conditional release for good behaviour. Another FDLR member and presumed protagonist during the Rwandan genocide, Ladislas Ntanganzwa, was arrested in Goma on 9 December. He had been indicted by the UN International Criminal Tribunal for Rwanda in 1998 but the case had been referred to Rwandan national jurisdiction in 2012. Ntanganzwa was listed by the US State Department's Rewards for Justice programme in 2013, with a promise of $ 5m for his arrest or information leading to his arrest. Rwandan Prosecutor-General Richard Muhumuza said Rwanda was ready to try Ntanganzwa for international crimes before the Rwandan special court for genocide, and applied for immediate extradition. The government in Kinshasa, however, wanted to hear Ntanganzwa first and had him transferred to Kinshasa on 11 December, where he remained at the end of the year.

On 18 December, two former militiamen convicted before the *ICC* were transferred to Kinshasa to complete their sentences in a Congolese prison. Thomas Lubanga had been sentenced to 14 years in prison on 10 July 2012 for recruitment of child soldiers, of which he had already served more than two-thirds in the Netherlands. Germain Katanga, sentenced on 23 May 2014 to 12 years in prison for arms stocking and distribution during a massacre in Ituri in 2003, benefitted from early release and was transferred to Kinshasa for his last month in prison, in anticipation of his release scheduled for 16 January 2016.

The ICC case against the former DRC rebel leader and presidential candidate in the 2006 elections, *Jean-Pierre Bemba*, who had been tried for atrocities committed in the CAR in 2001, continued although the closing hearings had been held in December 2014 and the Court had announced a verdict without undue delay. In the meantime, Bemba's defence team applied twice for a stay of proceedings, in December 2014 and July 2015. The first application was rejected by the Court on 17 June. The ICC also rejected an appeal for interim release on 20 May and instead opened a second trial against Bemba on 29 September. In this first ever ICC trial for witness-tampering and bribery, Bemba was accused of influencing the testimonies of numerous defence witnesses, alongside his lawyer, Aimé Kilolo Musamba, another member of Bemba's defence team Jean-Jacques Mangenda Kabongo, and his political allies Fidèle Babala Wandu and Narcisse Arido. All five pleaded not guilty.

On 26 March, the UNSC extended the *mandate of MONUSCO* and its Intervention Brigade for a further year and agreed on a cut in the number of troops by 2,000. The DRC's foreign minister had wanted the force to be cut by 6,000. According to the UNSC resolution, permanent reduction and further reconfiguring of MONUSCO was subject to progress concerning its priorities, including the fight against the FDLR. A week before the mandate extension, Kobler had stated that the FDLR would be much more easily defended with the full support of MONUSCO, alluding to the breakdown of cooperation between the FARDC and MONUSCO due to controversies over red-listed officers. The most contentious issue between MONUSCO and the DRC government was MONSUCO's role in the elections. MONUSCO had been mandated to promote political dialogue and pave the way for elections, but the government's cooperation on the political process was hesitant throughout the year.

In the course of the year, MONUSCO reshuffled large parts of its political and military leadership. On 7 February, Deputy *Special Representative of the UN Secretary-General* (SRSG), the Nigerian Abdallah Wafy, who was responsible for the operations in the east of the DRC, was replaced by an American, David Gressly, who had previously served as deputy SRSG and humanitarian coordinator in Mali. The second deputy SRSG, who also served as UNDPS's main representative, the Malian Moustapha Soumaré, was replaced by the Guinean Mamadou Diallo, who had previously been regional director of the Joint UN Programme on HIV/AIDS for West and Central Africa. On 29 December, the South African Lieutenant General Derrick Mbuyiselo Mgwebi replaced the Brazilian Lieutenant General Carlos Alberto dos

Santos Cruz as force commander of MONUSCO. On 8 October, UN Secretary-General Ban Ki-moon appointed Maman S. Sidikou of Niger as the new SRSG for the DRC and head of MONUSCO. Sidikou had previously been the AU's special representative for Somalia and head of the AU Mission to Somalia. He replaced Kobler, who had served as head of MONUSCO since 2013 and been hailed for bringing an end to the M23 crisis, as well as criticised for militarising MONUSCO's policies. The departure of a leadership that was known to have significant clout and be very forceful towards both rebels active in the DRC and the FARDC added to the difficulties MONUSCO faced in playing a positive role in the DRC during rising political tensions.

Relations between the government and MONUSCO further soured after a controversial helicopter attack by MONUSCO in the central Pinga region of North Kivu Province on 5 October. According to North Kivu's governor, Julien Paluku, and confirmed by the government's spokesman, Lambert Mende, the attack killed five civilians who were returning to their homes after fleeing militia fighting. The UN denied any civilian deaths, spoke of one dead fighter and said its attack had been directed against another militia group, called Nduma Defence of Congo, and conformed with MONUSCO's mandate to protect civilians.

On 28 April, Paluku denounced the presence of the *Rwandan Patriotic Front* on DRC territory and the injuring of an FARDC soldier during a clash between the two armies. On 24 September, DRC Defence Minister Aimé Ngoy Mukena met with his Rwandan counterpart, James Kabarebe, in Kigali to discuss bilateral security matters. It was the first such meeting since the M23 rebellion in North Kivu had caused severe tensions between the two states in the second half of 2012 but was preceded by a meeting during an ICGLR summit in Luanda (Angola) on 13 May. The main points on the agenda concerned the FDLR and the surrendered M23 combatants. Apart from general statements about a reinforcement of security cooperation, the two ministers declared that they intended to set up a joint team to tackle the question of repatriation of M23 combatants cantoned in Rwanda and FDLR fighters cantoned in the DRC. After the meeting, rumours abounded in parts of North Kivu's civil society and population about secret plans between the two states to bring the Rwandan army back into DRC territory, as had been the case in 2009. Paluku denied the rumours in an official statement. Only a day after the meeting, on 25 September, Mukena was replaced and transferred to the Ministry of Oil in the course of a general cabinet reshuffle.

On 18 January, *Angola*'s President José Eduardo dos Santos visited Kinshasa. Several bilateral agreements were signed, including with regard to rail-cooperation, the exportation of Congolese copper through Angola, the resumption of Angolan state airline flights between Luanda and Kinshasa, security cooperation and potential support for the DRC's Inga Dam Project. Another agreement on the joint exploitation of offshore oilfields was signed on 27 January. The exact terms of the agreement remained unclear, sparking a controversy in Kinshasa about potential disadvantages with regard to DRC claims to offshore reserves. On 5–7 October, the

DRC and Angolan chiefs of staff met in Cabinda (Angola) to further deepen security cooperation, focusing on the training of the FARDC in Angola. This signal of closer relations came after tensions in 2014.

On 24 February, the US special envoy to the Great Lakes Region, Russ Feingold, gave his final speech at the US Institute of Peace and stepped down, and his successor, Thomas Perriello, was not appointed till 6 July. During the interim, US policy towards the DRC was managed by the Africa Bureau at the State Department and the US embassy in Kinshasa – with tangibly less assertiveness than during Feingold's 18 months in office. Feingold had been the most straightforward of special envoys in the DRC. He had invited Rwanda to end its support for M23 rebels in 2013 and before leaving office insisted that Kabila respect the Constitution, explicitly calling him to step down in 2016.

Socioeconomic Developments

As a result of the political and security crisis in neighbouring *Burundi*, thousands of Burundians and a few hundred Congolese nationals residing in Burundi fled to South Kivu's Uvira and Fizi territories from March on. In April alone, around 7,000 people arrived in the DRC and the DRC government reported a total of 15,735 Burundian refugees in South Kivu as of 28 October. Martin Kobler made a visit to Uvira to assess the situation on 5 May.

A *measles epidemic* raged in the (former) province of Katanga from March until the end of the year. As of 20 November, 39,619 cases, including 474 deaths, had been reported by the Ministry of Public Health, mostly children under the age of five. Katanga was also heavily affected by *cholera*. On 23 September, Public Health Minister Félix Kabange officially declared a cholera outbreak. As of 29 November, 19,705 cases had been reported in DRC since the beginning of the year. Apart from (ex)Katanga, with 4,565 cases, the provinces of South Kivu (4,906), Maniema (3,971), North Kivu (3,294) and ex-Oriental (2,969) were the most heavily affected. Between late October and December, heavy rains caused *floods*, leaving 20 people dead in Kinshasa and affecting thousands of people across the country. In Tshopo province (formerly Orientale province) alone, around 17,000 houses were destroyed and many more damaged.

The first quarter of the year saw a close to 14% increase of *copper production* compared with the same quarter in 2014. This was due to an increase in production at several large mines, including those operated by the Swiss mining giant Glencore. On 7 September, however, Glencore announced the suspension of its copper and cobalt production in its Katanga Mining Ltd branch for one-and-a-half years because of a drop in world market prices. Glencore said it planned to improve infrastructure at the unit in order to lower operating costs. The suspension caused a loss of income from around 290,000 tonnes of copper a year for the government, amounting to 30% of the DRC's total copper output for 2014. In recent years, copper production had been the main driver of growth and the revenues produced in the sector were urgently needed for the costly electoral process. On 6 November, copper production began at the Sino-Congolese mining project Sicomines. The Chinese state-lender ChinaEximBank provided most of the financing for the mine and announced the construction of roads, railways and other infrastructure worth $ 3 bn in return for a 68% stake in Sicomines. By June, around half of the money had been dispersed, but both funding and implementation had been more difficult than expected, according to DRC government officials. The start of production came after repeated delays due to stalled financing by ChinaEximBank, damages in the mine and electricity shortages. In order to meet the mine's electricity needs, Sicomine discussed the construction of a 240 MW, $ 660 m hydropower project in Busanga, planned as a joint venture between the Sicomines partners, the state-owned mining company Gécamines and the state-owned electricity company 'Société Nationale d'Electricité'. On 15 October, the executive secretary of the Office for the Coordination and Monitoring of Sicomines stated that all sides were aligned and that the establishment of the company tasked with the development of the project was under way. According to the company, Sicomines' annual copper output was estimated to begin at 50,000 tonnes, gradually rising to an expected 400,000 tonnes over the next two decades. The controversial joint venture between Gécamines and the two Chinese investors, China Railway Group Ltd and Sinohydro Corp., had been signed in 2007 as part of a $ 6 bn minerals-for-infrastructure deal. The deal was hailed by the DRC government as a model for sustainable mining development but criticised by the opposition and various human rights organisations for embezzlement, lack of transparency and eviction of local residents without compensation. The head of the Bureau for Coordination and Monitoring of the Sino-Congolese Program and a close ally of Kabila, Moise Ekanga, was criticised for circumventing former state actors, such as Mines Minister Martin Kabwelulu, and being answerable only to Kabila.

Splits within the ruling elite concerning *mining deals* were also evident in a dispute between the Canadian Ivanhoe Capital Corporation and Kabwelulu over the sale of 49.5% of Ivanhoe's Komoa copper project to the Chinese Zijin Mining Group, announced in May. The DRC held a 5% stake in the local operating company, Kamoa Copper SA, but had been offered an increase of 15% at market rates. Kabwelulu blocked the deal, and ordered a legal review of the sale on 16 June, arguing that he had not been consulted and that the discussions about increasing the DRC's share had not been concluded, despite Ivanhoe insisting that the company had been in regular contact with Kabila and Ekanga during the negotiations with Zijin. After Ivanhoe agreed to increase the government's stake to 20%, the deal was approved by the government on 22 September and completed on 8 December.

Despite the fall in mineral commodity prices on the world market, gold production in the two industrial mines operated by the UK's Rangold Ressources and the

Canadian Banro Corporation rose by 57% during the first half of the year compared to the same period in 2014.

Due diligence and certification systems continued to be an issue in the Congolese mining sector. A report by Global Witness and AI published on 1 May claimed that around 80% of US stock-listed companies using tin, tantalum, tungsten and gold from the DRC had failed to comply with reporting requirements as laid out in section 1502 of the Dodd-Frank Act, which required companies listed on the US stock exchange to ensure that the entire supply chain of certain minerals was 'conflict free'. The Act had previously met with criticism by the Congolese government and mining companies, as well as by the renowned Goma-based Pole Institute research centre, for being too costly, having devastating effects on the livelihoods of artisanal miners and being inappropriate for tackling the problem of militia activities. On 18 August, the US Accountability Office confirmed that most companies that had disclosed their files to the Securities and Exchange Commission in 2014, as required by the Dodd Frank Act, had been unable to determine the source of their minerals and 99% of companies had reported that they had carried out inquiries in the countries of origin – particularly the DRC – but information from suppliers had been superficial. On 20 May, the European Parliament rejected a long-awaited proposal by the European Commission and the European Parliament's Committee on International Trade for a self-certification system for importers into the EU of so called 'conflict minerals' from all conflict zones worldwide – mainly targeting the DRC – to ensure that the trade did not benefit smugglers and militias. The European Parliament instead called for a mandatory due diligence system for all importers, smelters and refiners, as well as downstream companies participating at any point in the supply chain, up to brands, retailers and final manufacturers. This implied not only the 400 European importers of conflict minerals, but around 880,000 European companies that could have simply resorted to foreign importers if the original proposal had been adopted. Although the amended bill received only a slight majority in Parliament, the latter opted for informal talks with EU member states and negotiations with the European Commission and Council in order to discuss the final version of the bill.

A long-awaited *law governing oil and gas activity* in the DRC, till then regulated by a bill of 1981, was adopted by the DRC National Assembly on 15 June and approved by Kabila in August. The law foresaw a new tax and customs regime, an increase in role of the state and private companies in the exploration and production of oil, and regulation of new permits. The Anglo-French oil and gas company Perenco – the DRC's only oil producer to date – would be exempt from the new taxes, according to the company. The French company Total and a company owned by the Israeli Dan Gertler continued to explore oil sources near Lake Albert in eastern DRC.

Equatorial Guinea

Joseph N. Mangarella

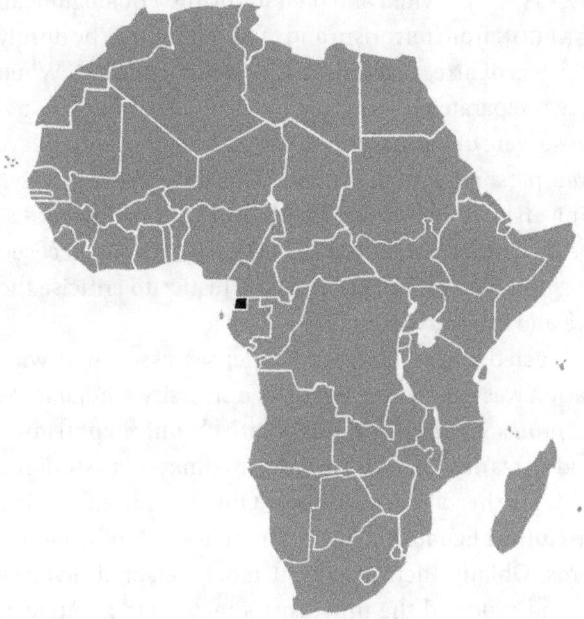

Facing chronic decline in hydrocarbons production and oil reserves, President Teodoro Obiang Nguema Mbasogo, supported by the ruling 'Partido Democrático de Guinea Ecuatorial' (PDGE), sought to maintain his decades-long grip on power. Confronted with sharp reductions in government revenue and the attendant cuts in public spending, the regime carefully redistributed patronage, suppressed dissent, and propped up Obiang's son and likely successor, second Vice President Teodoro Nguema Obiang Mangue (aka Teodorín). Summitry and the hosting of high-profile events such as the 2015 African Cup of Nations (AFCON) showcased a regime very adept at balancing the need for international recognition with obviating unwanted media attention. The regime increasingly pinned its hopes on promising liquefied natural gas (LNG) ventures.

Domestic Politics

President Obiang and the prominent Mongomo clan were clearly not willing to democratise a political system that remained among the most oppressive in the world. From 17 January to 8 February, the country hosted *AFCON 2015*, filling newly

 | DOI 10.1163/9789004333239_027

renovated venues in Bata, Equatorial Guinea's largest city, and the capital Malabo. The quick decision to rescue the football tournament after its abandonment by Morocco, while regarded by Zimbabwe's President Mugabe as 'heroic', met with protest and harsh criticism from both foreign and domestic voices. With the help of the Zimbabwean Defence Forces (ZDF), invited and paid for by the Equatoguinean regime to assist with securing AFCON from terrorism and "acts of sabotage by unruly elements and mercenaries", dozens of arrests and beatings were carried out. When crowds invaded the pitch on two separate occasions, *journalists and political opponents* speaking out against abuse were quickly silenced. Most notably, on 14 January the authorities detained three persons, one of whom, Celestino Okenve, was a retired professor from the Universidad Politécnica de Madrid who had been distributing leaflets advocating a boycott of the tournament. The authorities accused Okenve of 'destabilisation', prompting the US-based NGO EG Justice to criticise the regime's continued "repressive and arbitrary tactics".

While austerity had not affected the unbudgeted expenses associated with hosting AFCON, higher education was not spared. By April, university scholarships had fallen by a third, sparking *protests by students* fed up with chronic nepotism in the awarding of highly coveted bursaries. In mid-April, approximately 50 students were tear-gassed and arrested. Further violence caused Obiang himself to visit the 'Universidad Nacional de Guinea Ecuatorial' to obtain first-hand information on the origin of the problems. Obiang then promised more personal involvement in the bursary process and replaced the university's rector. On 25 August, repressive government tactics were deployed in tear-gassing dozens in Rebola, where a crowd was dispersed for protesting against the dismissal of a cultural centre's management team by Minister of Interior Clemente Engonga Nguema Onguene, who publicly objected to the politicised lyrics sung by one of the centre's rappers.

In late February, AI slammed the administration for abuses dating back to January 2014, claiming that *a general amnesty* for political prisoners in 2014 had not been respected as no prisoners were actually released. Furthermore, several NGOs reported that nine prisoners had been executed in 2014, two weeks prior to a moratorium on the death penalty as a condition for Equatorial Guinea's forthcoming membership in the CPLP. The regime's opponents in the 'Convergencia para la Democracia Social' chimed in and denounced the continued detention of several of their members. The regime accused AI of defamation and held that there had not been any political prisoners qualifying for release under the general amnesty. As to the charges of employing the *death penalty*, President Obiang coldly stated in a public speech before the third extraordinary congress of the PDGE that "they should have their tendons severed so that when people see them limping in the streets, they will be recognisable as thieves". The party congress took place from 8–12 November and was an occasion for the president to announce his candidacy in the presidential elections in November 2016.

The ruling clan spent the last two-thirds of the year reshuffling the country's highest administrative ranks, presumably to secure a smooth transition of power in the event of the death of Obiang, who was 73. The president began in April by *dissolving the government and reconstituting it* with little change among the upper ranks. Among the 50 top civil servants in Obiang's government, 25 served as ministers, three served as deputy prime ministers, and the rest acted in constitutional and advisory capacities. In early April, Obiang also threatened to rein in a judiciary fraught with irregularities. On 20 May, the president issued a decree allowing him to subsequently dissolve the country's entire judiciary, from lower court to Supreme Court judges – a first since the country's Independence in 1968. On 26 May, lawyer Juan Carlos Ondo Angue, a close associate of the regime, was appointed as the new president of the Supreme Court.

Further stoking suspicions that the Obiang clan continued to run the country like a family firm, the 'West Africa Newsletter' reported in October that *First Lady* Constancia Mangue Nsue de Obiang had been intimately involved in the reshuffles. The influential publication suggested she was behind the ousting of President Obiang's long-serving right-hand man, Hassan Hachem, in favour of her brother, Teodoro Biyogo Nsue Okomo, now the chief of the head of state's office. The First Lady had also been active in assuring the eventual succession of the eldest of her three sons, *Teodorín*, who on 3 August, the 36th anniversary of Obiang's power grab, was named a colonel in the army by presidential decree. The only officer to be promoted, he retained his posts as both Vice President for defence and security and vice president of the PDGE. On 25 September, Teodorín was dispatched to the UN General Assembly to deliver a formal address on behalf of the country.

Foreign Affairs

AFCON brought into sharper relief the extent of the ruling clan's regional allies. As Robert Mugabe's ZDF helped secure the tournament, he publicly congratulated Equatorial Guinea on 31 January for its commitment to hosting the tournament. After a two-day 'working visit' to Equatorial Guinea in late May, the 'Zimbabwean Independent' reported that Mugabe had returned in late June, and later claimed that the *Zimbabwean ruling family's frequent travels to Malabo* were to pursue personal business interests as prominent shareholders in companies active in Equatorial Guinea. Later in the year, Obiang re-invited contingents of the ZDF, reportedly to bolster counter-terrorism and train Equatoguinean forces, prompting opposition members in the Zimbabwean parliament to publicly question the inappropriate diversion of public resources.

By contrast, Equatorial Guinea's relations with other regional actors appeared strained. Despite having hosted a joint ECOWAS/CEMAC summit in April and the International Conference on Africa's Fight against Ebola in July, the regime maintained its *obstinacy in safeguarding its borders and territorial integrity*. During another CEMAC summit in early May, the Equatoguinean envoy unsuccessfully attempted to water down a much-heralded agreement by member states to allow free movement within the community. It thereafter became clear that Equatoguinean authorities, in conjunction with well-known, France-based attorney Jean-Charles Tchikaya, might seek legal recourse to limit the agreement's effects. The regime's tough stance on immigration was echoed again in late November, when the speaker of the Nigerian parliament called on Equatorial Guinea to act to halt the 'maltreatment' of Nigerians doing business in the country. Equatorial Guinea, which had a miniscule population of 700,000–800,000 and sizable proven hydrocarbons reserves, continued to register the highest per capita income on the continent.

Strained regional relations were also attributed to the president's personal preferences – even though economic incentives were in place to warrant collaboration – as exemplified when Obiang and other officials failed to show up for successive meetings with their counterparts in Abidjan (*Côte d'Ivoire*) in December 2014, April and June, which were scheduled to resume talks on the establishment of a joint gas company. Although the development of LNG remained a central component of the Equatoguinean regime's economic policy, sources cited by 'Africa Energy Intelligence' reported that Obiang simply did not like President Ouattara. In similar fashion, *maritime border disputes* with *Cameroon* remained unresolved, despite the promise of profitable ventures that collaboration might have brought. Although Obiang travelled to Yaoundé for the COPAX summit on regional security, swathes of Cameroon's offshore Ntem block were still claimed by Equatorial Guinea. The dispute dismayed potential investors, who cited the political risk involved, including Britain's Sterling and the US Noble Energy, both of which had urged the countries to cooperate. On 23 October, the Equatoguinean consul general in Douala (Cameroon) publicly called for a culture of peace and mutual co-existence between the two nations.

Tension again characterised Equatorial Guinea's relations with *Western actors*. Though formal relations with the *USA* appeared intact after the regime's settlement with the US Justice Department over an embezzlement case in 2014, *private legal battles and disagreements persisted.* In March, Ruben Maye Ensue Mangue, former ambassador to the USA, was sued for recovery of $ 1.2 m in payments owed to International Decision Strategies, an American lobbying firm contracted to advise Equatoguinean officials during the US-Africa summit in 2014. As the Justice Department maintained its criticism of the regime's human rights abuses, Obiang, who should have been well aware that the country's economy remained largely dependent on American oil firms, expressed frustration with their reticence to carry out new projects when he made a personal visit to Houston, Texas, in early November; the results of the business meetings were unclear.

Other legal battles plagued the regime more directly throughout the year, as Equatoguinean authorities relied on the state's attorney, Jean-Charles Tchikaya, to help them evade property seizures and paying hefty damages. In January, he helped the regime to settle a breach of contract case brought by Canadian exploration firm Brilliant Resources, Inc. which alleged that Equatorial Guinea had cancelled its permit to explore the Rio Muni region. The regime settled out of court with a payment of $ 31.5 m. In September, Tchikaya successfully obtained the release of a Boeing 777 owned by Ceiba International, Equatorial Guinea's fledgling airline. The aircraft, which had been undergoing servicing in Basel (Switzerland), had been seized by Yves Michel Fotso, the Cameroonian businessman who had pursued his claim that the government owed his bank € 76 m. Finally, in November, yet another seizure of a Ceiba 777 by Fotso was invalidated by Spanish courts.

The regime eventually appeared to make headway in resolving the ongoing *ill-gotten gains cases* brought by the French judiciary against Teodorín in previous years, though tensions with France persisted. In early February, Obiang received French Development Minister Annick Girardin, while on 5 March the newly appointed Equatoguinean ambassador to France, Miguel Oyono Ndong Mifumu, held a conference in the Hotel Pullman Montparnasse in Paris. The rhetoric aimed to clear his country's human rights record, while he publicly labelled AI a "multi-headed monster". *Courtship of the French authorities* proceeded apace in late October with the second visit of President Hollande's personal friend, socialist lawyer Pierre Mignard, to Malabo to discuss the possible resolution of Teodorín's case. This despite a scuffle with French immigration authorities in March, when eight Equatoguinean engineers bound for Germany were stopped at Charles de Gaulle Airport and held for 12 days while the authorities scrutinised their travel intentions. They were released only after the personal involvement of President Obiang and Teodorín, who responded by increasing the wait time for French nationals wishing to obtain visas to Equatorial Guinea from one to ten days.

It was no surprise, then, that Equatorial Guinea continued its *deepening partnership with China*, from which it secured a $ 2 bn infrastructure loan on 29 April during state visits there by President Obiang and Minister of Mines, Industry and Energy Gabriel Nguema Lima.

Socioeconomic Developments

The government did not take discernible measures to reduce Equatorial Guinea's *hyper-dependence on hydrocarbons*, despite its nominal commitment to diversification under its Horizon 2020 national development plan. According to most estimates, oil extraction accounted for 80% of GDP, 90% of government revenue, and 97% of all exports. *Tumbling oil prices, ageing oilfields and few prospects of new discoveries* thus meant the figures and projections for the economy and public finances remained dismal. While national oil production was estimated to have fallen from 254,000 b/d in 2014 to 230,000 b/d, the price of Brent crude tumbled from almost $ 100/b in 2014 to nearly $ 50/b. As a result, real GDP growth was estimated at between −7% and −10% over the year, a steep decline from a contraction of roughly 3% in 2014. As early as May, the Senegal-based 'Agence de Presse Africaine' reported the Equatoguinean government as having anticipated a 58% drop in its oil revenue, closely mirroring the oil price and forcing budget revisions and spending cuts in order to halt the rising public debt, estimated at a years-long high of 13–15% of GDP. Despite Equatorial Guinea having assumed the unenviable position of one of least transparent countries in the world according to the International Budget Partnership's Open Budget Survey 2015, statistical assessments by the IMF confirmed the gloomy outlook for the country in September, when it published the results of its Article IV Consultation, concluded on 20 July. Consistent with multiple other analyses, the Fund projected an unabated decline in oil revenues into the foreseeable future and highlighted the country's inadequate social and human capital spending towards diversification. Indeed, the June publication of BP's Statistical Review of World Energy 2015 forecast that all Equatorial Guinea's proven oil reserves would be exhausted by the mid-2020s.

Short-term efforts by the regime to shore up depleted savings and secure future solvency focused on procuring investment and revising the budget, while long-term efforts appeared geared towards further hydrocarbons development. Despite IMF recommendations to consolidate public spending by substituting large capital outlays for marginal increases in social spending, the government indicated the continuation of prestige projects and registered among the lowest social spending levels in the region – 25% of GDP. Though the 2015 budget projected a 5% budget deficit, the government announced on 5 September a mid-year fiscal surplus of $ 287 m. The anomaly might have gained clarity after the government's release of its 2016 budget projection, which predicted a further 13% increase in expenditure. Indeed, China Machinery Engineering Corporation was contracted, during the state visit to Beijing in late April and May, to conduct feasibility studies on a power plant in Kogo and install streetlights in Mbini, while a contract with Sinohydro was renewed in view of its noteworthy accomplishment; the government appeared well on its way to achieving full electrification under Horizon 2020.

In the longer term, the government set its sights on developing LNG as it failed to attract meaningful investment towards more oil discoveries. The results of *oilfield licensing rounds* were further delayed until 2016, as many oil majors were purportedly dissuaded not only by diminishing crude prices and depleted proven reserves but also by the requirement that domestic companies hold a minimum 35% share in all ventures. No new projects were to come on stream after Noble Energy's Alen field in 2013; only juniors such as Nigeria's RoyalGate, the USA's Vaalco and Qatari Heritage Oil appeared interested in further exploration and drilling. As for more established firms such as Hess, Marathon and ExxonMobil, only the last, in late April, signed an additional production-sharing contract with the oil and mines ministry.

While austerity appeared to rule out plans for a second *LNG* train in Punta Europa, Ophir Energy signalled its intentions to continue developing a floating LNG on block R, the touted 'Fortuna' project. In addition to interested buyers such as Total and Nigeria's Oando, Ophir signed advanced agreements with six firms in December, assuring upfront cash for it and the Equatoguinean parastatal Sonagas, which holds a 25% stake in the venture. Equatorial Guinea boasts gas reserves of up to 1.3 trn ft^3, a figure that held promise of revitalising the ruling clan's lifeblood for decades to come.

Gabon

Douglas Yates

The on-going collapse in world commodity prices hit the economy hard. Without high oil, timber and manganese prices to fund President Bongo's ambitious 'Gabon Emergent' development plans, his regime was forced to slash public spending mid-year, reshuffle the cabinet and manage an increasingly disgruntled civil society before the all-important 2016 presidential elections. Intense diplomatic activity with France and China marked the entire year.

Domestic Politics

On 12 April, opposition leader *André Mba Obame died* at the age of 57. A former prime minister under the late Omar Bongo – President Ali Bongo's father – Obame had become one of Ali Bongo's main rivals in the 2009 presidential elections. After revelations on French television that the results of those elections had been doctored, Obame attempted a failed African version of the 'Arab Spring' in 2011, and spent his final years suffering from chronic illness under the constant threat of treason charges. His premature death ended one challenge to the legitimacy of Ali Bongo's dynastic succession but opened up another as other former ministers from

 | DOI 10.1163/9789004333239_028

his father's 42-year reign tried to agree upon which of them would become the new unified opposition candidate.

Gabon's French-style dual executive system continued, with the president predominant, and members of his presidential staff easily able to out-manoeuvre cabinet ministers, including prime ministers, who are frequently dismissed or moved around by the president in cabinet reshuffles. The three most influential such presidential advisors were Chief-of-Staff Maixent Accrombessi, who controlled many of the most important portfolios in Bongo's ambitious 'Gabon Emergent' development plan, the young financial management and marketing analyst Liban Soleiman, and a former minister of mines Regis Immongault, now minister of the economy.

In mid-June, Bongo was reported to have been pressured by powerful members of his Téké ethnic group to dismiss the 'Beninois' Accrombessi and 'Somalian' Soleiman from his presidential staff. Such calls motivated major changes within the *security sector*. On 10 June, responding to Téké concerns, Bongo named a retired Téké general, Laurent Nguetsarato, to head the 'Conseil National de Sécurité' intelligence agency and supervise security services inside the country, including the 'Direction Générale de la Documentation et de l'Immigration', a police force run by Célestin Embinga Loury, who had served for a decade under Nguetsarato. Bongo also promoted another Téké general, Paul Operha, to replace Jean-Claude Ella Ekogha as the new army chief-of-staff. For his part, Operha was replaced as head of the army by another Téké general, Roch Ongaga, who hailed from Bongo's mother's home village. The influential Téké ethnic minority risked losing their privileges if the Bongo dynasty lost power. Thus, their control of the state security apparatus remained an important preparation for controlling the anticipated post-election popular unrest in 2016.

On 3 August, *Maixent Accrombessi was arrested* by French anti-corruption agents at Charles de Gaulle airport and briefly detained in Paris on money laundering charges related to revelations that a company owned by someone connected to Accrombessi had won a € 300,000 contract for military uniforms. This embarrassing arrest did not lead to his long awaited downfall, but several important changes in the presidency did take place before year's end. On 12 September, Bongo reshuffled his *cabinet*, retaining the Fang Prime Minister Daniel Ona Ondo for the third time (the Fang being the largest ethnic group in Gabon), and increasing the number of cabinet members from 34 to 41. Fang politician Paul Biyoghe Mba, who had been Ali Bongo's first prime minister, was now named as first deputy prime minister and health minister in the new 'Ondo III' government. Madeleine Berre, head of Gabon's chamber of commerce, was named minister for trade and small business. Furthermore, and most notably, a former Bongo spokesman, Yves-Fernand Manfoumbi, who had previously served as the head of the 'Direction Générale du Budget', was named on 17 December as head of the 'Bureau de Coordination du Plan Stratégique Gabon Emergent'. Manfoumbi's appointment to this key public spending post was interpreted as a political appointment aimed at purchasing consent among disgruntled Southern voters before the 2016 presidential election.

Hoping to silence his critics, who continued to say that his family had too much control, Bongo tweeted that he hoped his 12 September cabinet reshuffle would "bring together all the political forces of the nation". But he failed to create a united government ahead of the presidential election as *several of his nominees refused to accept the posts* they were offered. For example, Jean-Robert Endamane, of the mostly Fang opposition 'Rassemblement pour le Gabon', declined his nomination as minister for town planning and housing, declaring that he had never been consulted about this appointment. Jean de Dieu Moukagni Iwangou, leader of the Southern opposition 'Union du Peuple Gabonais', was offered the Ministry of Agriculture, but publicly declined to take up the post at a press conference. Iwangou had been one of the most outspoken opposition critics in the 'Front Uni de l'Opposition pour l'Alternance' (FUOPA), a *coalition of opposition parties* dedicated to ending almost five decades of one-party dominance by the 'Parti Démocratique Gabonais'. Disunity was evident, however, in FUOPA's failure to rally around a single opposition candidate. In January 2016, Jean Ping – former foreign minister and former chairman of the AU – announced that he had been selected in a closed-door meeting as the coalition's official candidate, but his selection was neither transparent nor unanimous.

Foreign Affairs

Relations with France worsened over the year, despite President Bongo's repeated efforts to make diplomatic capital out of his regular visits to France (where his family reportedly had 33 luxury properties). For example, he was the only Central African head of state present in Paris at the famous 'Republican March' of 11 January in the wake of the 'Charlie Hebdo' terrorist attack. On 5 February, Minister for Foreign Affairs Emmanuel Issoze Ngondet and Minister of the Economy Régis Immongault travelled to Paris to meet with France's Minister for Development and Francophonie Annick Girardin to discuss the *COP21* climate change conference that would be hosted in Paris. Bongo participated on 6 February in the Franco-African Forum for Shared Growth organised by the French Ministry of Economy. On 16 June, he flew again to Paris and met with French Prime Minister Manual Valls and Defence Minister Yves Le Drian while attending the Paris Air Show, an important vehicle for the French government to sell its aerospace defence technology.

Relations between the two countries were strained, however, by the arrest of Gabon's Chief-of-Ctaff Maixent Accrombessi on 3 August, at which the Gabonese government protested by recalling the newly appointed ambassador to France, Diedonné Nzengué. In order to control the damage caused to his reputation by the ongoing corruption investigation by French judges, Bongo announced on

27 August that he would renounce his share of his father's estate in France, which had been going through a long and bitter succession battle in the French courts, involving 42 legitimate heirs of the late Omar Bongo. Ali said he would give his share to fund training programmes for Gabon's youth.

On 28–29 August, France's Environmental Minister Ségolène Royal and Minister for Development and Francophonie Annick Girardin flew to Libreville to participate in the lavish 4th *New York Forum Africa*, an annual showcase for Bongo and his wife Sylvia, which involved extravagant expenditure on potential investors. The two French ministers also inaugurated the opening of a satellite programme to combat elephant poaching, built by the French space agency and funded in part by the 'Agence Française de Developpement', an initiative of President Bongo against the illegal ivory trade. While in Libreville, these ministers had personal interviews with Bongo concerning President François Hollande's initiatives on climate change.

On 10 September, Bongo travelled to Paris to meet with Hollande at the Élysée Palace to discuss the Accrombessi affair. During this official visit, Bongo told the French press that he believed his adviser was innocent of the charges, and that the manner in which he had been arrested appeared to be a "policy of sensationalism" intended to "humiliate Gabon". The French president diplomatically made no denial of the accusation. Bongo was apparently able to leverage his diplomatic support for Hollande's showcase propositions to lower carbon emissions at the COP21 climate change conference in exchange for assurances that the investigation into money laundering by his chief-of-staff would be ended.

On 10 November, Bongo travelled again to Paris to meet with Hollande at the Elysée Palace along with four other African leaders from Benin, Guinea, Ghana and Ethiopia to discuss joint resolutions for the upcoming COP21. From 20 November to 5 December, Bongo participated in the climate change conference both as president of Gabon and as the acting president of CEEAC representing its 11 member states, which include all the countries in the Congo rainforest basin, the world's second largest forest reserve after the Amazon. In his official speech, delivered before conference participants on 20 November, he called for policies to be implemented by the signatories for a cap on global warming. Bongo promised to stop the wasteful flaring of gas from Gabon's oil fields, announced the construction of new dams that would result in an energy mix of 80% hydroelectricity and 20% natural gas, and promised to protect Gabon's tropical rainforests, which cover over 80% of the country, and to preserve biodiversity.

The cooling of relations with France led Bongo to revise his resource nationalism and cultivate *stronger bilateral relations with China*. This was a policy his father had pursued at the turn of the century. On 3 December, Bongo met with Chinese President Xi Jinping in Johannesburg, ahead of the 2nd Summit on China-Africa Cooperation held that weekend in the South African capital. Praising the Bongo family – both Ali and his father – as "good friends of the Chinese people", Xi suggested that the two countries should further consolidate the political foundation of their fruitful economic relations and also intensify cultural exchange in order to improve mutual understanding between the two peoples, especially the younger generations. Xi said that his government was willing to encourage Chinese businesses to take part in Gabon's infrastructure construction and development of energy resources. Calling China an "old friend" and a "reliable partner" of Gabon, Bongo expressed his gratitude for Chinese developmental assistance and also welcomed investment in forestry and agriculture, as well as minerals. This was a dramatic change of direction of Bongo's policy, which had allowed authorities to revisit several major contracts with Chinese mining companies in recent years.

Socioeconomic Developments

Falling commodity prices hit the economy particularly hard. Economic growth stood at only 4%, compared with 5% in 2014. On 2 April, the 2015 *budget* was drastically reduced to CFAfr 2,651 bn (€ 4 bn) following revised financial guidelines to take into account the net decline in oil and manganese prices. Despite highly publicised efforts to diversify the Gabonese economy away from oil rents, around 40% of GDP was based on *petroleum*, which brought in 50% of government revenue (44% according to Moodys) and represented 85% of total exports. According to Reuters, citing a report by the Finance Ministry, crude oil production fell by around 8%, from 10.9 m tonnes to 10.0 m tons, because of ageing wells and the impact of strikes by oil workers.

The long *strike* at the country's main oil refinery, which began in 2014, resulted in a net loss for the 'Société Gabonaise de Raffinage' (SOGARA). It was originally motivated by the closing of certain medical facilities, including a radiology laboratory, at the SOGARA refinery and the layoff of five union members. More than 22,000 b/d were also lost after the total stoppage of Addax oil production following a strike called by the 'Organisation Nationale des Employés du Pétrole' on 14 April in protest against the management's refusal to apply the terms of its reconciliation agreement signed in Libreville under the guidance of two special inspectors for the oil sector. The agreement had guaranteed the retroactive payment of salaries and bonuses, improvement of working conditions and transportation, and the regularisation of illegal foreign workers. In an economy that employed around 120,000 workers, the General Directorate of the Economy indicated that the oil sector provided only a little more than 2,000 jobs at the national level, representing less than 2% of the total workforce.

The largest private employer remained the *forestry sector*, which involved hundreds of companies, 75% of which were owned by expatriates. The Gabonese Employers' Confederation, the largest association in forestry, accounted for nearly 80% of GDP and 90% of jobs in the formal sector. Preserving jobs in this sector was essential to fighting unemployment, which meant that a structural conflict existed between President Bongo's promises to protect the country's rainforests in the name of biodiversity and climate change, and his promises to promote economic growth, development and lumberjack jobs. There was rising anger among trade unionists, environmentalists and civil society groups after 38 fixed-term workers in Mbomao, Ogooué-Ivindo province were sacked on 17 February by the timber company, Rain Forest Management (RFM), a wood processing company with Malaysian investment. RFM had been locked in a lengthy dispute with the 'Entente Syndicale des Travailleurs du Gabon' union and refused to negotiate with workers who were planning to take part in trade union meetings and were threatened and intimidated. On 17 February, as the employees were returning to work, RFM called on police to evict them from their company-supplied dormitories, claiming that the workers had violated company rules. The dismissals were linked to worker protests over poor working conditions, unsanitary housing infested with rats, cockroaches and snakes, demands for legal working hours and payment of wages on time.

On 14 August, the Singapore agro-industrial group Olam Gabon, which employed some 4,400 workers in the country, opened its first factory for the processing of *palm oil* in Awala. This factory, situated 60 km southeast of Libreville, had the capacity to treat over 36 m tonnes of crude palm oil per year for export to countries in the CEMAC zone. The new factory was located on a 20,030 ha concession, of which 6,502 ha were planted with oil palms, part of a massive € 437 m agro-industrial project led by Olam Palm Gabon (60% owned by Olam and 40% by the Gabonese state), which planned to expand its plantations to 18,359 ha with two additional factories near Mouila, in the south-west of the country.

On 12 November, Moody's ratings agency affirmed Gabon's *Ba3 bond rating*, explaining in its report that it had maintained Gabon's rating in the wake of the commodities price collapse largely because of its membership in CEMAC and the CFA franc zone. Both limited the potential for external risk to translate into credit pressure as the economy adjusted to world price shocks. This was because the CFA franc remained pegged to the euro, with its convertibility guaranteed by France, and because CEMAC had relatively high foreign exchange reserves, sufficient to absorb the commodity price shock for the year. Moody's predicted that the government's balance sheet would reverse its downward trend, and that its debt-to-GDP ratio would peak at 45% in 2016, after which it would fall to 35% by 2017, a much lower level than its peers. However, Moody's rating was based on what appeared to be speculative Brent crude prices of $ 55 per barrel in 2015, $ 53 in 2016, $ 60 in 2017 and $ 68 in 2018. Dependence on oil income represented a major ongoing risk for Gabon's economy.

São Tomé and Príncipe

Gerhard Seibert

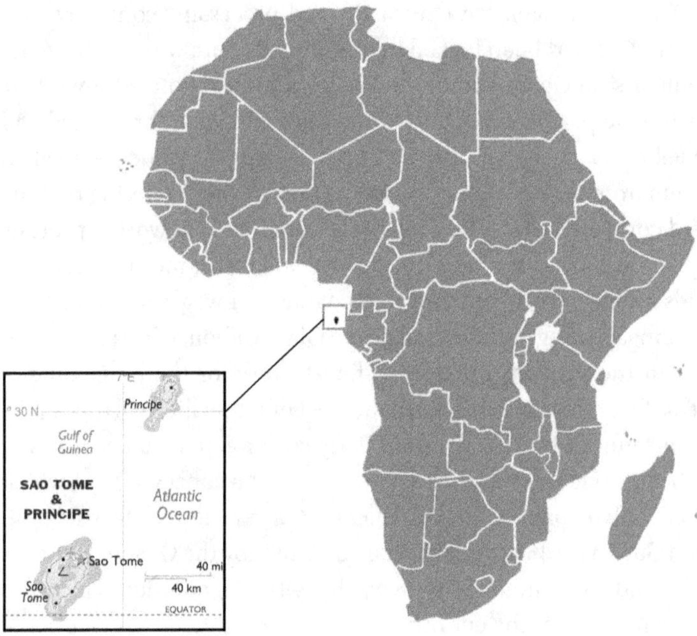

The first year of cohabitation between President Manuel Pinto da Costa and Prime Minister Patrice Trovoada ('Acção Democrática Independente'; ADI) was largely marked by mutual non-interference in each other's affairs. Both politicians were engaged in strengthening South-South cooperation, particularly with Angola, Cabo Verde and Equatorial Guinea. Government officials were eagerly selling the significance of the country's strategic location for maritime security and attracting more FDI.

Domestic Politics

Only few events aroused passionate discussion on the domestic front: On 30 January, Brigadier Justino Lima, the *chief of staff of the armed forces*, appointed only in February 2014, was forced to resign after a video published on a social media platform showed him participating in the beating up of a delinquent who had assaulted a female soldier carrying army funds. Several other high-ranking military personnel were also involved in the incident. Deputy Chief of Staff

© KONINKLIJKE BRILL NV, LEIDEN, 2016 | DOI 10.1163/9789004333239_029

Colonel Olinto Amado Paquete temporarily filled the vacancy until 3 July, when Colonel Horácio Sousa was promoted to brigadier and inaugurated as the new chief of staff.

On 16 February, *President Pinto da Costa successfully vetoed a bill* regulating conflicts of interest for parliamentary deputies, which had been approved by a majority of the ruling ADI. The president justified his veto by asserting his view that parliamentarians should not be simultaneously engaged in other paid jobs within the civil service and so receiving various incomes, which the bill would have permitted. In addition, he stated that if deputies held senior civil service positions it would jeopardise the principle of separation of powers and the political independence of the deputies, who were responsible for monitoring government actions and the civil service. In response, José Diogo (ADI), the president of the 55-member National Assembly, withdrew the bill four days later and urged his colleagues to fully respect the provisions of the current statutes, which do not allow deputies to simultaneously hold paid positions in the civil service.

On 2 March, the government decided to restore *Sãotomean citizenship* to all foreigners who were resident in the country at the time of Independence in 1975 and to their descendants. African plantation workers had been granted citizenship at Independence, but in 1996 this status had been withdrawn in a populist move to win elections. The decision to reverse this mainly benefitted former plantation workers from Angola, Cabo Verde and Mozambique. The government launched a campaign inviting applications for citizenship under these rules, which ran from 8 March to 8 August.

On 29 October, the National Assembly approved a government proposal to exempt CPLP, EU and US citizens from visa requirements for stays not exceeding 15 days. The new legislation was aimed at further increasing tourist arrivals in the islands, which had reached a record 20,500 in 2014. The *visa waiver* also applied to citizens of other nationalities who were permanent residents in the beneficiary countries.

In party elections on 15 November, the businessman Aurélio Martins was elected unopposed, with 7,792 (85%) of the votes of registered members, as the *new chairman of the opposition* 'Movimento de Libertação de São Tomé e Príncipe – Partido Social Democrata' (MLSTP/PSD). Martins had already been MLSTP/PSD leader from January 2011 until June 2012, when he had been replaced by Jorge Amado. Shortly before the vote, Elsa Pinto, a former defence minister, withdrew her candidacy and asked for the cancellation of the elections, which she considered fraudulent, citing alleged irregularities in the process. Two weeks later, during his inauguration, Aurélio Martins, a controversial figure both within and outside his party, declared that he would not be his party's candidate in the presidential elections in 2016. On the same day, Prime Minister Patrice Trovoada also publicly announced that he would not run for the presidency, since he preferred to see out his premiership, due to end in 2018.

Foreign Affairs

On several occasions, São Tomé strengthened bilateral cooperation with Angola, Cabo Verde and Equatorial Guinea, while military cooperation with Brazil, Portugal and the USA was also extended. On 13 January, Prime Minister Trovoada paid his *first official visit* after his re-election to *Angola*, São Tomé's principal bilateral creditor. He was accompanied by Minister of the Presidency Afonso Varela and Finance Minister Américo Ramos. Trovoada, who was received by Angolan President Eduardo dos Santos, declared that he was confident that, despite increasing budgetary problems caused by falling oil prices, Angola would disburse the second tranche of a $ 40 m credit line agreed in 2013 for São Tomé's budget support.

On 20 February, Trovoada, together with Foreign Minister Manuel Salvador dos Ramos and Public Works Minister Carlos Vila Nova, paid a 24-hour visit to *Equatorial Guinea*, another important bilateral creditor. Trovoada proposed to his hosts the establishment of a submarine cable connection between São Tomé and the neighbouring Equato-Guinean island of Annobón and discussed the implementation of existing cooperation agreements.

Portugal, the former colonial power, was also prominent: during an official two-day visit, Portuguese Defence Minister José Pedro Aguiar-Branco and his local counterpart Carlos Stock signed an amendment to the existing bilateral *maritime security agreement* on 18 March. In addition to Portuguese navy vessels included in the original agreement, the amendment also allowed the Portuguese Air Force to monitor São Tomé's Exclusive Economic Zone (EEZ), which is 160 times larger than the country's land surface. The agreement provided for the deployment of a military radar plane in the archipelago. During his stay, Aguiar-Branco donated two lifeboats to the local coast guard and met with Trovoada and President Pinto da Costa.

Another heavyweight in the CPLP world, *Brazil*, showed interest in a related field. During a lightning visit to São Tomé on 29 March, Brazilian Foreign Minister Mouro Vieira assured Trovoada of his country's interest in strengthening bilateral cooperation with São Tomé, particularly with regard to maritime security. Vieira stressed the importance of maritime security for merchant shipping. He also met with Pinto da Costa, to whom he handed a letter from Brazil's President Dilma Rousseff, in which she expressed her country's intention to further improve cooperation with the archipelago. In early May, Brazil deployed a nucleus of the local Naval Mission of the Brazilian Navy to assess the needs of São Tomé's coast guard, which already received training and equipment from Brazil's Navy. On 3 December, another 37 local marines concluded four month' training provided by the Brazilian Navy.

Pinto da Costa also emphasised the strategic nature of São Tomé's location for other partners. During the accreditation ceremony for the new Libreville-based US ambassador Cynthia Akuetteh on 10 April, Pinto da Costa stressed his country's need to further strengthen bilateral cooperation with the *USA* in the area of maritime security. In her response, Ambassador Akuetteh stressed that strengthening maritime security had to do primarily with support for institutional capacity building in São Tomé rather than with any US military presence in the country. However, she expressed her country's intention to extend US bilateral cooperation in the agriculture and education sectors.

On 24 April, Minister of Economy and International Cooperation Agostinho Fernandes and *Taiwan*'s new resident ambassador Jian-gueng Her signed a new bilateral cooperation agreement for budget support amounting to $ 16.2 m for the current year. One-third of this was destined for the health sector, 31% for infrastructure improvement, 20% for agriculture and the remainder for human capacity building and institutional support for the judiciary, National Assembly, the Presidency and government ministries. Fernandes stated that his government would like to see Taiwan's engagement expand in the future beyond annual budget support to private investment by Taiwanese businesspeople. The search for *foreign private investment* was clearly a top government priority. On 23 May, a government delegation headed by Trovoada left for a trip taking in France, Turkey and the United Arab Emirates. Trovoada said that his executive had already been in touch with entities associated with the private and financial sectors in the three countries, and that were interested in capitalising on the archipelago's privileged geographic location in the oil-rich Gulf of Guinea. On 13 July, Portuguese Secretary of State for Foreign Affairs and Cooperation Luís Campos Ferreira and São Tomé's Finance Minister Américo Ramos signed an agreement for a *Portuguese credit line* of € 10 m to finance private investments in agro-industry, tourism and energy. Both local and Portuguese companies were entitled to apply for credits. At the same time, the Agency for Portugal's Investment and External Trade inaugurated a local office in São Tomé, housed within the Portuguese embassy.

Various anniversaries offered opportunities for deepening diplomatic ties. On 12 July, *Cabo Verde's President Jorge Carlos Fonseca* was the only foreign head of state to attend commemorations for the 40th anniversary of São Tomé's Independence. Other foreign guests were Angolan Minister of Territorial Administration Bomito de Sousa, Algerian Minister of National Planning Amar Ghoul, and Taiwan's Deputy Foreign Minister Ko Shen-yeaw. In addition, 43 soldiers from Gabon and 34 from Equatorial Guinea participated in the military parade on Independence Day. During his talks with Pinto da Costa, Fonseca announced the extension of existing bilateral cooperation in education between the two island nations to the economic, business and renewable energy sectors.

On 3 August, President Pinto da Costa participated in the commemoration of the 36th anniversary of the coup that brought *Equatorial Guinea's President Teodoro Obiang Nguema* to power. During an official visit to São Tomé by an Equatorial Guinean government delegation comprising 48 members and headed by Obiang Nguema on 18 October, Pinto da Costa praised his colleague as a "true brother". Obiang Nguema proposed a joint enterprise with São Tomé to exploit oil in a zone of the two countries' maritime borders that supposedly had considerable oil potential.

On 11 December, the new non-resident EU ambassador, Helmut Rudolf Kulitz, and Finance Minister Agostinho Fernandes signed an agreement on *EU annual budget support* for development projects totalling € 28 m under the 11th EDF National Indicative Programme until 2020. Kulitz announced that São Tomé would in addition benefit from other EU development funds during the five-year period, provided that the funds were well managed.

Socioeconomic Developments

On 27 April, the National Assembly approved the national budget of $ 154 m for 2015 with 31 ADI votes and 17 abstentions on the part of the opposition parties MLSTP/PSD and 'Partido de Convergência Democrática'. This was almost unchanged from 2014. The largely externally supported budget was predominantly financed by non-traditional donors, such as Angola, Nigeria and Taiwan. Energy accounted for 13.1% of the total, followed by education (12.5%), health (10.6%), road maintenance (10%), agriculture (5%) and security (5%). During the debate, Prime Minister Trovoada revealed that as much as 51% of current government revenue was spent on public sector salaries.

The *banking sector* occupied some news headlines. On 27 January, the Central Bank (BCSTP) decreed a 90-day intervention in the affairs of the Angolan-owned Banco Equador, one of the seven local bank branches, because of its liquidity problems and recurrent breaking of established financial rules. Subsequently, the intervention period was extended until April 2016 because the bank failed to recapitalise. In late June, for the first time ever, the BCSTP held an *auction of treasury bills* worth STD (dobras) 75 bn ($ 3.4 m) to four African commercial banks based in the country. In turn, the banks made the treasury bills available on the secondary market. The successful auction was aimed at capturing local financial resources to finance government expenditures. On 6 August, the World Bank Group's International Finance Corporation (IFC), as part of its programme *Financing to Micro, Small and Medium Enterprises* (MSME) Globally, granted $ 3 m to the Banco Internacional de São Tomé e Príncipe (BISTP) to co-finance 50% of a new credit line for local MSMEs. The IFC's shared risk initiative, which also included Japanese government funds of $ 300,000 enabled the BISTP to provide credit at a lower cost to local enterprises. The BISTP expected the new credit line to allow small enterprises to create employment and reduce poverty through investments in modernisation, new equipment and technology, and improved business capacities.

On 7 October, the Trovoada government signed a memorandum of understanding with the state-owned China Harbour Engineering Company Ltd (CHEC) for the construction of a *deep-sea trans-shipment port* in Fernão Dias intended to serve the logistics needs of the Gulf of Guinea region. Under the agreement, CHEC was in charge of the engineering, design and construction of the entire port and promised to contribute at least $ 120 m to the total investment, estimated at $ 800 m. The port was expected to be operational in 2019. The government announced that the port would be developed under a Public Private Partnership to raise the missing $ 680 m from foreign investors.

On 14–15 October, the government held an *investor and development partner conference* called STeP IN, organised by the Portuguese communication company Companhia de Ideias. The government presented to the invited businesspeople and representatives of bilateral and multilateral donors an ambitious four-year Transformation Agenda focusing on three economic pillars: a deep-water transshipment port as a maritime hub for the Gulf of Guinea; an international airport as the regional aviation hub; and a 'do-business-easy' legal and fiscal infrastructure in dedicated areas. The oil sector was intentionally excluded because of repeated failures to discover commercially viable offshore hydrocarbons, while the agreement with CHEC on the construction of a deep-sea container port served to show the government's vision of the archipelago's future role as a regional logistics platform. Trovoada expected to considerably improve his country's capacity to execute externally financed projects and concomitantly expected the donors to significantly increase annual aid to $ 90 m until 2019 so that the ambitious development plans could be implemented.

On 26 October, more than 16 months after the closure of a restricted auction with three bidding companies for Blocks 1 and 6 of the EEZ, the National Oil Agency (ANP) signed a 28-year *production sharing contract for Block 6* with the Portuguese Galp Energia and the Dallas-based Kosmos Energy. In exchange for a signature bonus of $ 2 m, the two companies were each awarded 45% of the acreage with Galp as the operator, while the ANP retained the remaining 10% stake on behalf of the state. Under the agreement, the first eight years were allocated for seismic surveys, while the following 20 years were intended for the development and production of the block. Ten days earlier, the ANP approved the transfer to Kosmos of 100% of ERHC Energy's rights and interests in EEZ Block 11, adjacent to Block 6. Consequently, Kosmos became the operator of Block 11 with working interests of 85%, while the ANP kept the remaining 15%.

The Joint Development Authority (JDA) had already, on 9 June, signed a new production-sharing contract for *Block 1 of the São Tomé and Príncipe-Nigeria Joint Development Zone (JDZ)* with two Nigerian companies, Equator Hydrocarbons Ltd, the operator, with 56% of working interests, and Pan African Industrial Services Ltd-PAPIS Energy Solutions (35%), while Dangote Energy Equity Resources kept its original 9% interest awarded in 2004. At that time, the JDA had repeated earlier announcements that it would proceed with the deployment of non-conventional technology to speed up development activities in the block that had been abandoned by Total and Addax in 2013, following negative exploration drilling results.

PART 5

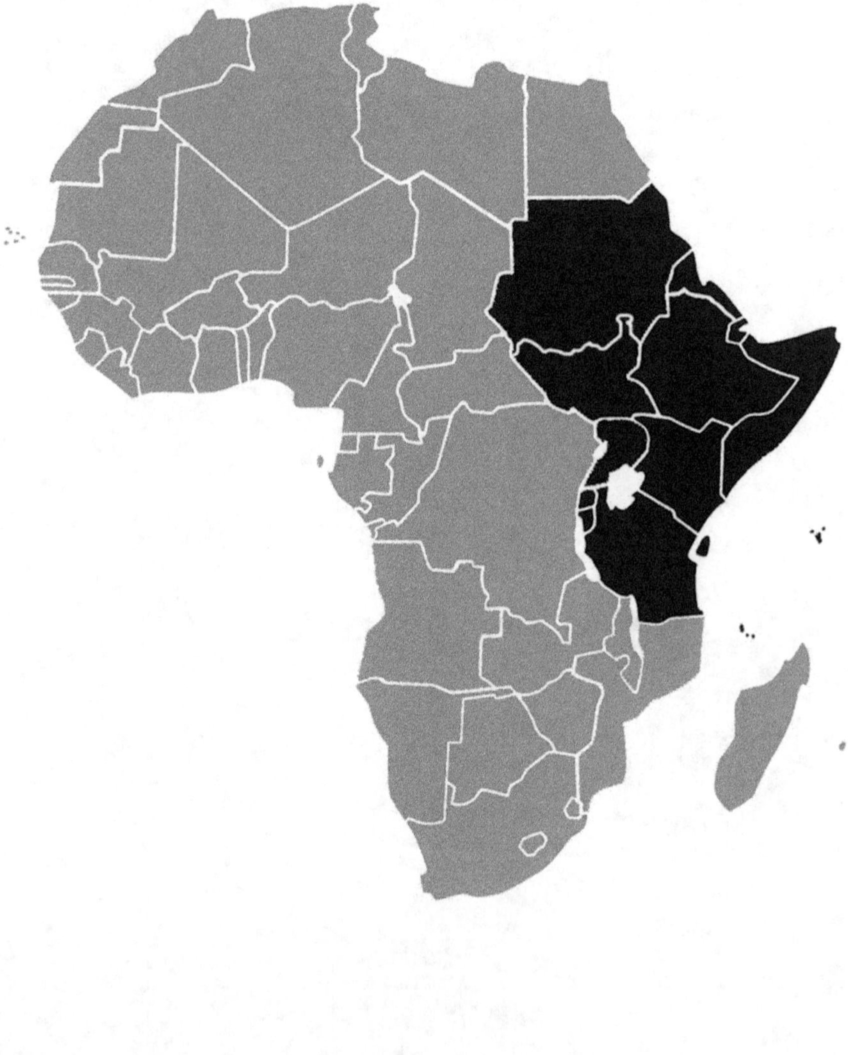

Eastern Africa

Jon Abbink

Predominant issues in Eastern Africa were: efforts to deal with the aftermath of armed conflict in South Sudan, where a truce was agreed after the devastating two-year civil conflict, and in Burundi, and elections – or rows about the delay of elections – in many countries. In no fewer than seven countries elections were held, but in no case was an opposition presidential candidate or party voted in. Political events showed a pattern of stable instability, with contestations and unresolved issues of national consensus-building. In Sudan, Djibouti and Burundi, 'elections' confirmed the incumbent presidents in power, all having extended their mandate beyond the legal limit. In Ethiopia's elections, the ruling party secured 100% of the seats in both houses of parliament. It all showed that politics in the sub-region was still a highly personalised affair and that elections were successfully coopted into vested authoritarian power structures. Only in Tanzania and Comoros were elections fairly credible. Overall, the state of political 'democracy' in the sub-region remained very precarious. Elites in power tended to suppress criticism and undermine the independence of parliaments and the judiciary. Frequent intimidation and outright repression of the independent media, including the Internet and social media, were prevalent. Accountability of the powers-that-be was limited, and their security forces usually acted with impunity.

In the wider Horn countries apart from Ethiopia, Islamist terror, mainly inflicted by the Somali insurgent al-Shabaab movement, continued unabated, with hundreds of dead in Somalia and Kenya. Sea piracy continued to decline, however, with only one fishing trawler attacked.

The Horn region was hit by another major drought, allegedly caused by the El Niño phenomenon, and led to food insecurity, death of livestock and hardship for over 19 m people, some 8.5 m of them in Ethiopia alone. Other areas saw unseasonal flooding, related to the same weather phenomenon. Projections were that this would continue into 2016. The familiar global machine of humanitarian assistance was again appealed to and set in motion, but funding commitments fell short of the amount asked for by the UN and governments.

Macro-economic development as measured in figures, such as GDP, infrastructure growth and electricity generation, saw Eastern Africa above the SSA average during the year. GDP in the sub-region increased by 6.3%, with the fastest rates of growth in Uganda, Tanzania, Ethiopia and Rwanda. Urbanisation accelerated but the extension of urban facilities and job creation did not keep up.

The continent evaluated 15 years of MDG efforts. As happened elsewhere, they were not all attained, but a UNECA report showed that the Eastern African countries had made progress in several basic areas of poverty reduction, primary education and health care.

 | DOI 10.1163/9789004333239_030

Regional organisations such as IGAD and the EAC held a spate of meetings to deal with both economic and political issues, notably conflict resolution in Burundi and South Sudan. An important result was the IGAD-sponsored agreement signed in Juba (South Sudan) in August on ending the South Sudan conflict. IGAD also tried to formulate a Regional Climate Change Strategy. The EAC, a group of six countries with 158 m people, moved slowly but steadily towards more economic integration, but the aim of political federation still remained remote, despite being the main theme of the 16th EAC summit in Nairobi (Kenya) on 20 February. The Nile issue was addressed in a new 'declaration of principles' on shared use between Egypt, Sudan and Ethiopia.

International relations highlights were the visit by US President Barack Obama to Kenya and Ethiopia and his address at the AU headquarters in Addis Ababa (Ethiopia) in July. Also, EU High Representative for Foreign Affairs Federica Mogherini made her first visit to the AU headquarters and signed agreements to intensify cooperation on development, migration issues and security, solidifying the 2014–17 Joint Africa-EU Strategy.

Eastern African countries received an average 8% share of their GDP in ODA. Impact and oversight problems of donor-funded schemes, projects and sectoral aid remained, with the World Bank in particular not studying the broader and longer-term effects of aid and its (ab)uses, and restricting itself to macro-economic issues.

Political Developments

Another round of infighting in *South Sudan* came to a close with an uneasy cease-fire agreement between President Salva Kiir (Dinka), the leader of the Sudan People's Liberation Movement (SPLM), and his perennial rival, the SPLM-in-Opposition leader Riek Machar (Nuer). These leaders, unaccountable to the wider public and not known for respecting democratic processes – came to sign a 70-page deal in the capital, Juba, in August, although not together. Kiir signed a week after Machar, on 25 August, under pressure from the UN and the leaders of Uganda, Ethiopia and Kenya, who were present, but he insisted on attaching a long list of reservations. As part of this IGAD-sponsored deal, Machar returned as vice-president – a bizarre twist which in effect sealed impunity for civil war violence. The agreement was complex and precarious in its clauses on power-sharing and joint government. Some renegade generals rejected the agreement, so to many observers it seemed a matter of time before a next round of hostilities would erupt. New in the deal was the planned installation of a Commission for Truth, Reconciliation and Healing to investigate the appalling human rights violations that had taken place during the conflict. The food security situation in South Sudan was one of the main post-conflict challenges, because the war's disruptive effects had caused scarcity, hunger and the displacement of some 2 m people from their homes and lands, as well as the destruction of fields, crops and livestock.

In neighbouring *Sudan*, the overall situation deteriorated, with continued *de facto* dictatorship, mounting economic problems and debt burdens, and a festering civil war in Darfur, out of the world's media attention, but again with major violent clashes taking the lives of thousands of civilians. The more than 2 m IDPs stayed in their camps. President al-Bashir was re-elected in a poll with little credibility. There were efforts to hold a National Dialogue to tackle the political crises (ongoing insurgencies, anti-government protests) evident since South Sudan's secession in 2011, but the ruling National Congress Party government under al-Bashir failed to create conditions for a 'dialogue' and did not give away its dominance. The opposition also remained divided and thus rather powerless. The regime strengthened its links with the Gulf States and Saudi Arabia, and relations with its neighbours, even South Sudan, remained fairly stable. There was limited economic recovery, though not dramatic, as economic diversification, investment and private sector development remained weak. The country's MDG achievements were also quite modest. The regime could not, or did not wish to, find solutions to the insecurity, armed conflict and economic misery in its more remote regions. Al-Bashir visited South Africa in July but the authorities there did not meet their obligation to arrest him and hand him over to the ICC.

Eritrea remained isolated in the region, not attending IGAD meetings, not entering into diplomatic relations with any neighbours except Sudan, and continuing to rehearse its rhetoric of self-reliance. Domestic socioeconomic and political conditions were dismal, reflected in the unprecedented numbers of younger Eritreans risking their lives to escape the country. Throughout the year, an estimated 3,000 persons per month left Eritrea illegally. Some economic growth was achieved by focusing on the expansion of the mining sector (gold, zinc, copper and potash), scheduled to become the main economic engine in the coming years. No signs of any thaw in Eritrean-Ethiopian relations were visible and the border remained highly militarised. There were few international development partners, except that UNDP maintained its programmes. In a blow to the regime, an Ethiopian rebel group that had supported President Isayas's hold on power, the Tigray People's Democratic Movement, defected and escaped with 600 men via Sudan to Ethiopia. The findings of a highly incriminating report by the UN Commission of Inquiry on Human Rights in Eritrea made waves internationally, but were immediately rejected by the regime.

In *Ethiopia*, the May national parliamentary elections passed almost as a non-event, returning the ruling Ethiopian Peoples' Revolutionary Democratic Front to power with 100% of the seats. The campaigning had been subdued and problematic, and the opposition parties scorned the result. Massive social unrest broke out with the Oromo revolt against the expansion of Addis Ababa Region and the resulting land expropriation process. This revolt led to large-scale violence, with allegations of more than 400 people killed and thousands arrested, and the government's Addis Ababa Master Plan was put on hold. September saw the inauguration of part two of the Growth and Transformation Plan for 2015–20. Notwithstanding blatant political and media repression, Ethiopia again attracted significant ODA and FDI and also issued bonds to finance its controversial Blue Nile dam. In March, a Declaration of Principles was signed between Ethiopia, Sudan and Egypt's leaders towards better cooperation on the Nile issue. GDP growth and the country's massive infrastructure building continued and, despite ongoing controversy over its negative consequences, the Gibe-III hydro-electric dam was started up. Donor countries, the IMF and the World Bank kept the donor funds flowing without bothering too much about policy implementation details, rights abuses or environmental issues.

In May, *Djibouti*'s President Guelleh was re-elected for a fourth five-year term in office, against opposition protests that were harshly repressed. In general, political conditions and media freedoms were further restricted as the year went on, with multiple arrests of opposition politicians, journalists and rights activists, and authoritarianism became more entrenched than ever. There were armed clashes between government forces and an Afar rebel movement. Guelleh solidified relations with Ethiopia with a number of new cooperation agreements, and for a hefty sum allowed China to prepare for the construction of a naval base. There was economic growth (notably through infrastructure outlays) but also an increase in inequality and poverty, aggravated by the effects of drought.

Throughout the year *Burundi* was gripped by a political crisis, purely of President Nkurunziza's making: he wanted an unconstitutional third term in office. He first delayed, then allowed the presidential-parliamentary elections, and was duly 're-elected' in July. His moves provoked popular protests all through the year and the security situation rapidly deteriorated, with the media repressed, civil society organisations threatened, and the multi-ethnic, youthful opposition chased off the streets. There were reports of disappearances and hundreds of people killed, often in summary executions. The education and healthcare systems, as well as food production, suffered badly, leading to hunger and flows of refugees, with some 250,000 moving across the borders. The president's actions became a textbook case of how to destroy a country, just as it was getting back on its feet after 2005.

In *Kenya*, the perennial wrangling continued over issues of corruption, implementation of devolution under the 2010 Constitution, and insecurity. The first two were connected, with the more than 47 new county governments formed providing great new opportunities for graft. Claims that the government was using the threat of insecurity and terrorism to outlaw criticism were much repeated and credible. The promises of the new Constitution – e.g., real devolution of power, reform of the judiciary and police, and respect for a new Bill of Rights – were not delivered. The Somali al-Shabaab radical Islamists perpetrated several massacres on Kenyan soil and also continued recruiting young local Muslims to their cause.

Uganda prepared for presidential and parliamentary elections in early 2016 and, contrary to a previous promise, President Museveni announced his renewed candidature. Opposition parties failed to unite, but Dr Kizza Kesigye of the main opposition party, Forum for Democratic Change, was nominated as his opponent. Museveni enjoyed the inevitable support of the security forces and his National Resistance Movement party. In the run-up campaigning, intimidation and various tricks were used by the state apparatus against critics. Due to the instability in the wider region, notably in South Sudan and the DRC, Uganda received new influxes of refugees. A visit by Pope Francis to Kenya and Uganda brought the two countries into the international limelight. Uganda's economy continued to grow, although more slowly than hitherto, and was on relatively firm ground. Oil production had not yet started, and expectations were somewhat lowered in view of the worldwide slump in crude oil prices.

The *Seychelles* also saw elections. Several new political parties were created in the run-up, and President Michel and his long-ruling Parti Lepep were faced with seven officially registered new contenders. Only in the second round of the presidential elections was Michel victorious by only a few hundred votes over his main challenger, Wavel Ramkalawan, of the opposition Seychelles National Party. The economy registered more growth, with further reforms to liberalise it and encourage small and medium-sized local enterprises. Tourism registered record figures. The country had by far the highest HDI ranking in the sub-region. On the international stage, the government continued efforts to present itself as a champion of the interests of small island developing states.

Comoros, a federation of three 'autonomous' islands that kept a tolerable peace, also held elections, in January–February, for the National Assembly and for communal and island councils and President Dhoinine was reconfirmed in office. There was relative political calm throughout the year, and fears of new confrontations between opposing political groups did not materialise. The economy showed no major signs of vitality, as growth figures remained low and the power and water supply infrastructure was under strain. There were protests over mounting salary arrears in the public sector and also several strikes.

In *Rwanda*, the Rwandan Patriotic Front under President Kagame consolidated its hegemonic and authoritarian rule. The government orchestrated revisions to the 2003 Constitution to allow Kagame to stand for another term in office in the 2017 elections (he had ruled since 1994), and a referendum even approved in principle that he might stay up to 2034. The regime faced little internal political opposition, as this was effectively disempowered. Tensions with donors increased, notably because of ongoing political repression and disappointment at Kagame's decision to run for a third term, but ODA disbursements held steady, with donors continuing to support the government's 'developmental agenda'. Rwanda's relations with Burundi and the DRC were also strained. Economic growth remained above the SSA average at 6.5%, despite an ambitious and costly development programme and the effects of no new foreign aid, but facilitated by the lower global energy costs and less domestic public spending. Public service delivery improved in some aspects.

Tanzania saw presidential and parliamentary elections in October. It was the only sub-region country (apart from Comoros and Seychelles) that ran an open and rather competitive contest, but the long-ruling CCM party was able to defend its majority in parliament. Its candidate John Magufuli was elected as the new president, succeeding President Kikwete who, uncharacteristically for Africa, resigned after two terms. Elections in semi-autonomous Zanzibar took place under dubious conditions, almost as usual, and were declared null-and-void. No solution to the crisis was reached before year's end. A promised referendum on a new constitution was not held. Magufuli became popular for his new leadership style, stressing discipline, cost-cutting and anti-corruption measures in state institutions. Relations with Western aid donors were slightly strained over their dissatisfaction with the lack of economic reforms and the Zanzibar election issue. Macroeconomic performance and growth continued to be significant.

In *Somalia*, there was continued insecurity and snail's pace political reform and institution-building by the federal government. It remained a divided country, dependent on the international donor community in all vital respects. Somaliland cherished its *de facto* independence and saw slow economic growth. Puntland, nominally under the Transitional Federal Government, remained an autonomous territory. Elections for the Somali Federal Government presidency previously announced for 2015 were delayed by President Mohamoud. His government's activities were burdened by clan-divisions and corruption. The country's security problems – terror by the radical jihadist movement al-Shabaab and the resulting instability – were not solved, and the disruptive attacks remained a challenge to any normalisation. Many hundreds of people were killed in various attacks. The economy grew, carried mainly by the private sector, but investments by diaspora Somalis receded somewhat, although remittances remained the largest source of income. Humanitarian problems due to food insecurity and high numbers of IDPs necessitated significant international food and medical aid again.

The *state of the sub-region* in terms of *political development, media freedoms and civic rights* remained *precarious*, with no decisive democratic culture taking root. Critics and members of opposition parties and civic movements were scrutinised, arrested or accused in court. Indexes prepared by organisations such as Freedom House, the Committee to Protect Journalists, Reporters Without Borders and HRW assigned most countries to the lower ranges. Uganda, Ethiopia, Somalia, South Sudan, Djibouti, Sudan and Eritrea were in the lowest Freedom House category, 'not free', while the rest were ranked 'partly free'. The Reporters Without Borders' *World Press Freedom list* (180 countries) ranked eight sub-region countries below 140, the rest above. Uganda, Djibouti and Burundi made a notable drop down the list. Comoros was best, placed 50th. Political rights and civil liberties declined in Eritrea (lower was not possible), Ethiopia, Burundi, Rwanda, South Sudan, Sudan and Uganda. Best were Somaliland (categorised separately) and Tanzania. The *HRW World Report* for 2015 concluded that governments in Eastern Africa had made little or no progress on human rights, with a sharp deterioration in Burundi and Ethiopia and also a decline in Uganda, notably with increased intimidation and threats against journalists and activists.

TI's *Corruption Perception Index* located some of the most corrupt countries on earth in Eastern Africa. In the EAC, Tanzania's corruption was worst, followed by Uganda, Burundi and then Kenya. Outside the EAC, Somalia was the most corrupt country, surpassing all. Following at some distance were Ethiopia and the other countries – all in all, a dismal performance illustrating the lack of political commitment of elites and the continued burdens placed on ordinary people in their dealings with the state. The World Bank's *Ease of Doing Business Index* was important and here most sub-region countries except Seychelles and Rwanda were well down in the lower half of the table, although most countries except South Sudan, Sudan, Burundi and Eritrea made improvements. Overall weak points in ease of doing business were: electricity supply, good commercial dispute resolution, trading across borders, and registering property.

There was excessive repression of Internet freedom in some countries, including Eritrea, Rwanda and Ethiopia, which maintained their obsessive surveillance, apparently for political reasons. Governments in the sub-region enacted many new laws 'regulating' Internet use and, while the principle of regulation was not disputed by the public, the growing interception and supervision by the authorities of digital media and resources and means of free expression were rejected.

The general figures on political life and freedom of expression and communication again confirmed that the picture of economic growth and dynamics was *not matched* by one of political improvement, democratic culture or societal security, and that being involved in (opposition) politics remained quite risky business.

On the 188-country *HDI*, all Eastern African countries except the Seychelles, remained in the category 'Low' (lowest of four), despite moving up several places. The HDI, although a biased and purely material index, gave at least some indication of living standards.

Transnational Relations and Conflict Configurations

The sub-region saw the end of one conflict and the start of another: South Sudan reached a ceasefire agreement and a brittle political compromise; but Burundi, which had been on the way to recovery after the end in the civil war in 2005, was plunged into violent crisis. Existing long-term conflicts in Sudan (Darfur, South Kordofan), Somalia (al-Shabaab terror; the Puntland-Somaliland border dispute), and domestic repression in Sudan, Eritrea and Ethiopia, continued.

In *South Sudan*, it was not the AU but IGAD that made a major effort to end the civil war, a two-year conflict that had seen ruthless violence against civilian populations and deeply troubling ethnicised war rhetoric. South Sudan's economy was ruined, and widespread food insecurity, poverty and displacement of people were the result. This was to be tackled by the new 'unity government', which however was a repeat of previous structures and a return of the same warlords, so no durable solution was in the offing. In the dispute between South Sudan and Sudan over the Abyei area, nothing happened, all attention being deflected by the South Sudan civil war. *Sudan*'s regime showed itself unwilling and incapably of working towards a solution for Darfur and continued its war against the Nuba Mountains population, a conflict largely forgotten by the world and not addressed by the AU. In the ongoing violence in both Sudan and South Sudan, disturbing incidents of gender-based violence and the use of rape as a 'weapon of war' were recorded.

The border conflict issues between *Eritrea* and its neighbours *Ethiopia* and *Djibouti* remained frozen, with no moves made towards a solution. Ethiopia and Sudan, however, started talks to demarcate their definitive border, addressing a problem dating from the pre-1974 imperial era. Another long-standing issue, eliminating the remnants of the originally Uganda-based Lord's Resistance Army (LRA), roaming in the DRC-CAR-South Sudan border area, was again not accomplished, a remarkable feat of incompetence on the part of the AU and EAC countries. In June, the UNSC adopted a resolution condemning "threats to security in Central Africa", directed at the LRA.

Meanwhile in *Burundi*, the conflict caused by President Nkurunziza's reckless and arrogant extension of his presidential term escalated into violence and economic upheaval, also causing trans-border refugee streams. The EAC made the major mediation efforts here, with Uganda's President Museveni taking the lead. Several rounds of negotiation were held after the June presidential elections, but without a definitive solution. In December, the AU threatened to send a 5,000-member peacekeeping force to Burundi, drawing an angry response from the country's president and parliament.

In *Somalia* (and Kenya), the al-Shabaab radical Islamist insurgent movement continued to wreak havoc, with numerous terror attacks, bringing it no political advantage but causing social disruption and death for hundreds of people – government personnel, civilians, aid workers and soldiers of the AMISOM peacekeeping forces. As before, al-Shabaab refused any political settlement, and extended its recruitment drives among young Muslims in Kenya. The Somali federal government protested against Kenyan plans to build a defensive border-wall and also accused Kenyan AMISOM soldiers of criminal activities. Tensions between the two countries thus increased. The festering border conflict between the autonomous regions of Somaliland and Puntland, based on clan-group disputes over land and identity, continued. Along the coast of Somalia there was only one *piracy attack*, against an illegal Iranian fishing trawler, whose crew were seized. A reported 46 crew members of ships captured in previous years were still held on land somewhere in Somalia.

Kenya was heavily impacted by al-Shabaab terror, as three major attacks were perpetrated on its territory: in Garissa (148 people killed), in Mandera (14 killed) and on the Nairobi–Mandera highway when a bus was ambushed (28 killed). Insecurity in north-west Kenya was serious and had significant implications for future investment and infrastructure building in connection with economic corridor development. Although not highlighted in the media, there were serious 'ethnic clashes' during the year between pastoral communities (Turkana, Samburu and Pokot) in northern Kenya, leaving at least 310 people dead and a few hundred thousand displaced. Kenyan state authority was only lightly maintained in these pastoral regions, considered marginal from a political and economic point of view.

President Museveni of *Uganda* was involved in brokering the South Sudan peace agreement signed in August, and Ugandan troops continued to participate in the AMISOM force. In October, it was announced that Uganda would withdraw its contingent of troops in South Sudan, which had been sent in late 2013 to support President Kiir against his rebel vice president. In a violent incident in Uganda, two Muslim clerics were assassinated, probably by members of an Islamist insurgent movement, the Allied Democratic Forces, active in the DRC-Uganda border area and known for gross abuses against civilians in the DRC.

Rwanda had tense relations with Burundi, Uganda and the DRC over the unresolved conflict dynamics in their border area. President Kagame suspected the presence of forces of the anti-government, Hutu-dominated, *Forces Démocratiques de Libération du Rwanda* (FLDR) in Burundi and the DRC, and tensions increased as a result of Nkurunziza's forced third term in office, which was rejected by Kagame. Rwanda also hosted some 70,000 Burundian refugees produced by the Burundi conflict. Burundi's president in turn suspected that Rwanda harboured 'coup plotters' against his regime. Tanzania took sides with Burundi, even after Nkurunziza's 're-election', because it suspected that Rwanda was supporting armed groups in the eastern DRC, as it had in previous years supported the (defeated) M-23 rebel movement against the UN Force Intervention Brigade (which included Tanzanian troops). Regional bodies such as the ICGLR and the EAC (headed by a Rwandan) were not able to come up with a solution to the tensions. The DRC came to see the some 2,000-strong FDLR forces on its territory as a threat to stability and finally started and offensive against them in the South Kivu region. The battle continued until the end of the year.

Peace-keeping activities with the participation of Eastern African forces were ongoing in Sudan: the joint AU-UN mission UNAMID in Darfur, and the UN Interim Security Force in the Abyei region (UNISFA, a 5,300-strong force, including troops from Ethiopia, Rwanda and Tanzania). In this region, a complete stalemate existed, as desired by the Sudan regime because it could reap the benefits from the Difra oilfield. The UNAMID mandate was extended in June by the AU Peace and Security Council, but talks about an exit strategy were explored, largely due to the Sudan government's ongoing sabotage of the Darfur situation and of UNAMID's work.

Uganda, Kenya, Ethiopia, Burundi and Djibouti maintained their contingents in the 22,000-strong AMISOM force in Somalia, which was hit heavily by al-Shabaab. The UN MONUSCO force and its Force Intervention Brigade in the DRC, tasked with stabilising the north-eastern border area after 2010 and succeeding the UN Organization Mission in the DRC (or MONUC), had its mandate extended, but its force reduced by 2,000 to about 18,500 troops. Its annual cost was $ 1.3 bn. It contributed to conflict prevention, demining and civilian protection but could not turn the situation round and achieve stability, given the large number of roaming armed insurgent groups in the region.

The UN Mission in South Sudan (UNMISS) was not able to intervene in the civil war (2013–15) and was restricted in its movements, but maintained its presence in the country. It tried to play a mediating and stabilising role after the signing of the Agreement on the Resolution of the Conflict in the Republic of South Sudan by Machar and Kiir in August. In October, the UNMISS mandate was adjusted by the UNSC to support the implementation of the Agreement.

Socioeconomic Developments

Economic growth in Eastern Africa, with a *6.3% GDP increase*, was above the SSA average of 3.5%, driven by increasing private consumption and donor-funded infrastructure investments. Part of this growth was due to the ongoing 'capture' of the informal economy in the formal, tax-paying structures. Internal disparities and inequalities grew, however, and many regions and social or ethnic groups remained excluded from the benefits of both growth and 'good governance', notably those in areas of large-scale land acquisitions and hydro-electric (dam) schemes, where land was expropriated with minimal compensation. Many agro-pastoral peoples were in dire straits, on top of the droughts they faced in their semi-arid regions (Somalia, Afar, Samburu, Rendille, Gabbra, Boran). High growth was experienced in Ethiopia (8.7%), Rwanda (7.6%) and Tanzania (7.1%), with sluggish growth in Sudan (3.5%), Eritrea (2.1%) and Comoros (1%), but there was near zero growth in South Sudan and Burundi due to conflict.

Growth in the sub-region outside conflict zones was hampered somewhat by the unpredictable business environments, notably for private business, by weather variability affecting agricultural output, and by relatively low energy capacity and electricity-grid connectedness. State authorities took a leading role in the economy, with investment/development plans and active state companies, but the private sector was not facilitated enough. Weather vagaries related to El Niño caused rainfall deficiency and crop failure in some areas, reducing agricultural output and livestock pastures in semi-arid areas. With regard to energy, an estimated 80% of the population in the sub-region did not have access to mains electricity. Rural areas remained most disadvantaged, and in urban areas, only about one in four people had access to electric power, although capacity in all countries increased over the year. In general, issues of energy production were high on the agenda, with countries in the region developing their oil, natural gas and hydro-electric infrastructure plans as well as power system interconnectivity, e.g., via the Eastern African Power Pool, now in operation for ten years. Ethiopia continued its programme of large hydro-electric dams construction, successfully raising funding by issuing domestic bonds, Kenya invested more in geothermal energy in the Rift Valley, Uganda built up its oil infrastructure, and Somalia's federal government and the autonomous Puntland region signed deals with foreign oil and gas prospecting companies. Sudan and South Sudan lagged behind.

Also struggling to keep up were water provision systems (only a minority of the population had access to piped water) and related health and sanitation facilities. Eastern Africa here underperformed compared with the rest of SSA, except Nigeria.

State *current account deficits* were registered in almost all countries, with higher debts in Seychelles (18% of GDP), Djibouti (16.5%), Sudan (12.8%) and Somalia (11%). Tanzania reduced its deficit by almost 40% to 7% of GDP. Almost all countries in the sub-region increased their domestic revenue generation as a proportion of GDP, but all still remained at below 20%. While the SSA overall *inflation* rate was 9.2%, the Eastern Africa average was estimated at some 6.5%–7% (discounting South Sudan). Inflation rates remained high in Sudan (14%), Eritrea (12.5%) and Ethiopia (over 10%), but low in Comoros (2%) and Somalia (1.3%), and dramatically high (due to war) in South Sudan (about 109% in December).

Urbanisation continued apace, with cities struggling to keep up with urban infrastructure and employment creation. *Unemployment* figures given in official AfDB, AU, ECA, UNDP and ILO documents were puzzling: for SSA as a whole it was estimated at 7.7% (with youth unemployment at 11.8%), and in Eastern Africa it was said to be 7.9%. These were fictitious figures, based on unclear and unreliable data. For example, World Bank statistics based on such country data gave Ethiopia a lower youth unemployment rate (7.1%) than Germany (7.6%), which is rather unlikely.

High population growth in the sub-region, continuing at around 2.7%–3%, was not matched by employment creation. With the global – and in particular China's – growth rate declining and absorptive capacity of national economies not growing sufficiently, the so-called 'demographic dividend' was not materialising. Most employment was still located in the agrarian sector, and the shift towards services and industry was slow.

As the era of the *MDGs* came to a close, it was concluded that the sub-region had made *overall progress*, especially in extending primary education, combating (but not 'eradicating') hunger and poverty, reducing child and maternal mortality, and bringing down HIV/AIDS figures. Less impressive, or not at all successful or durable, were environmental sustainability (except in a few small areas), inclusive growth and employment creation for the rapidly growing population, and social and cultural gender equality (which goes beyond assigning females in the national parliaments). The 8th MDG, "developing a global partnership for development", was much discussed and was evident in the December COP-21 Climate Change conference in Paris, as well as being quite visible in the China-Africa and India-Africa summits, although less so in AU meetings (the 24th and 25th Summits), where anti-Western rhetoric was often gratuitous and exaggerated.

Internet access and use proceeded rapidly in most sub-region countries, with average penetration rates above 20%, but the grand plans and rhetoric on information and communications technology (ICT) investment and development in Eastern Africa were not yet matched by reality. The performance of the continent in general was low: 30 of the 31 African countries in the sample were in the bottom half of the rankings on the Network Readiness Index (with 143 countries assessed). Seychelles was 74th, Rwanda 83rd and Kenya 86th (up six places), with all other East African countries below 115. Ethiopia was 130th and Burundi on 136th on this list.

FDI in the sub-region, mostly provided by China and India but also by newer investors, such as Turkey and the UAE, increased by some 11% compared with 2014. Tanzania and Ethiopia each received about $ 2 bn to $ 2.2 bn, Uganda $ 1.1 bn and Kenya almost $ 1 bn. Given the global reduction in FDI by an estimated 16%, the region was still doing well. Even so, bribery and corruption remained part of the economic and social fabric.

High *out-migration* was a predominant feature in the sub-region. It had political and socioeconomic causes, but also figured in transnational and transcontinental relations, as the large majority of people leaving for political and economic reasons tried to reach Europe, and a second preferred destination was the rich Gulf countries. A very large part of SSA migrants came from Eastern African countries, predominantly Eritrea, but also Ethiopia, Somalia and some other EAC countries.

Sub-regional Cooperation and Sub-regional Organisations

Sub-regional cooperation was severely taxed by the emerging *conflict in Burundi*, which brought divisions between countries supporting President Nkurunziza's 'election coup' and others opposing it. The *South Sudan conflict* also proved a challenge, with Uganda having intervened militarily to support incumbent President Kiir. There was a plethora of several dozen sub-regional organisations that were supposed to enhance cooperation and development, but the two dominant regional organisations were the *EAC* and *IGAD*, both of which had economic and political aims. Both organisations' budgets were substantially supported by EU countries.

The *EAC* (Burundi, Kenya, Rwanda, Tanzania and Rwanda) presented its $ 111 m annual budget, down by $ 15 m compared with 2014, and held its *16th ordinary summit in Nairobi* (Kenya) on 20 February. The EAC's general mandate was to deal with furthering regional economic integration, the single customs area, harmonising tariffs, working towards a common currency, and cross-border infrastructure, and the summit focused mainly on discussing the annual progress report on various initiatives, security issues in the region, the choice of a new chairperson, the appointment of judges to the East African Court of Justice, and lastly funding (72% of the budget was provided by donors, and several EAC member countries were in arrears). An achievement on the sidelines was a *rapprochement* between Rwandan and Tanzanian presidents Kagame and Kikwete, whose relations with each other had been tense. Plans for the *political federation* of EAC countries, the central theme of the summit and originally foreseen for completion in 2015, did not make headway. Discussions were held on Somalia's 2012 and South Sudan's 2015 applications, but neither had been accepted by year's end. The *East African Legislative Assembly* (EALA), relatively unknown as the political body within the EAC and a member-country parliament with authority, in principle, above that of national parliaments, held various sessions in Arusha (Tanzania). It discussed or adopted new legislation, such as the Cooperative Societies Bill in January, the Creative and Cultural Industries Bill in March, and an Electronic Transactions Bill, a Forest Management and Protection Bill, and the Disaster Risk Reduction and Management Bill during its October session. The Assembly also formed a Parliamentary Forum on Climate Change. On 15 November, the EALA held a four-day public hearing on the humanitarian aspects of the crisis in Burundi. Most important was perhaps the enactment of the Non-Tariff Barriers Act, which would facilitate trade. The impact of the EALA was relatively limited (but Assembly members' pay was attractive at almost $ 15,000 per month).

The *Eastern Africa Standby Force*, one of the five sub-regional multidimensional forces of the AU's African Standby Force – meant to deal with acute security threats, coups d'état, post-election violence, counter-terrorism and disaster relief response – had not reached the stage of full operationalisation in December 2014, its planned date, but it went on stand-by in 2015, headquartered in Addis Ababa, and held various exercises, e.g., in Adama (Ethiopia). Ten countries of the sub-region provided troops for this 5,200-strong force. Its eventual deployment in Burundi was vehemently rejected by that country's leaders.

IGAD's main feat was pushing through the *agreement in South Sudan* between the two warring SPLM factions led by President Kiir and former vice president Machar. It was not able to play an influential role in Somalia, although together with the AfDB it launched the Somalia Project Component of the Drought Resilience and Sustainable Livelihoods Program in November. Also important was the start in July of its implementation of a Biodiversity Management Program for Kenya and Somalia, funded by the EU. For the rest, IGAD held numerous meetings with various partners and global organisations on drought threat and disaster resilience, climate change issues, land governance, etc. Notable closer cooperation was achieved between IGAD member states Ethiopia and Djibouti, whose leaders signed a number of additional cooperation agreements in Djibouti city in March on energy, telecoms and transport, accompanied by a rhetoric of 'common destiny' and 'greater unity and integration'.

The *EU* reconfirmed its *engagement with Africa and the role of EPAs* for the continent, including the EAC (an EU-EAC EPA had been signed in October 2014), in its new Trade and Investment Policy document, published in October, which was said to redefine its relations with Africa.

COMESA, a free trade area association with nine member states from the sub-region, held its 18th summit of heads of state and government in March in Addis Ababa. The theme was "inclusive and sustainable industrialisation". Ethiopia's Prime Minister Hailemariam Dessalegn was chosen as its new chairman, succeeding the DRC's President Kabila. A partial follow-up was the COMESA-EAC-SADC heads of state and government summit on 7–10 June in Sharm al-Sheikh (Egypt), also geared to realising regional integration, with priority given to infrastructure development, industrialisation, reduction of tariffs and the free movement of business people. At this summit, the long-awaited *Tripartite FTA* was launched, though it would have to be ratified in 2016 by the 26 member states (representing almost half of the AU countries, 51% of their GDP, and a population of some 632 m).

On 17 October, the 11th Summit of the *Northern Corridor Integration Projects* (NICP) – an ambitious development initiative designed to connect landlocked countries in the sub-region and advance regional integration – took place in Nairobi. Presidents Kenyatta of Kenya, Museveni of Uganda and Kagame of Rwanda and a presidential advisor from South Sudan (the four founder countries) were present, and were joined by officials from Burundi, Ethiopia, the DRC and the AfDB. Ethiopia joined this project officially in November. The 12th NCIP Summit was held in Kigali (Rwanda) on 10 December. The NCIP's focus was on standard-gauge railway development, ICT infrastructure, oil-refinery development, power and energy transmission facilities for the wider region, and border control.

The *ICGLR* touched upon trans-border events in Eastern Africa relevant to seven members of the sub-region. It had been concerned since 2000 with security, peace and development issues, including "combating the illegal exploitation of natural resources", a topic on which three meetings were held during the year. The ICGLR was chaired by Angola and held its 10th Regional Inter-Ministerial Committee Meeting on 11 March, its 9th Extra-Ordinary Summit of heads of state and government in May, and its meeting of Ministers of Defence in October, all in Luanda (Angola). Chief topics were the security problems in the DRC, the conflict in Burundi, and the South Sudan civil war. The ICGLR pulled its headquarters out of Bujumbura (Burundi), relocating to Lusaka (Zambia). Tensions between Rwanda, Tanzania and Burundi within the ICGLR were not resolved: e.g., in October President Kagame refused an ICGLR initiative to broker his dispute with Burundi, which had lodged an official complaint with the ICGLR in September on Rwanda's alleged 'plotting' against President Nkurunziza.

Several Eastern African countries bordering the Indian Ocean were member of the IOC (Seychelles, Comoros) and the IORA (Kenya, Seychelles, Comoros, Tanzania, Somalia), but these two bodies did not undertake any significant activities. The 15th IORA Foreign Ministers' Meeting took place in Padang (Indonesia), on 23 October, and discussed collaborative activities in aquaculture, fisheries and ocean forecasting (the 'blue economy') and climate adaptation, as well as maritime safety issues.

The 16th meeting of the *Nile Basin Initiative* took place on 21 February in Khartoum (Sudan), and for the first time in five years Egypt participated. A new development in the Nile debate was the signing on 23 March in Khartoum of the *declaration of principles* on the use of the Nile waters by the leaders of Sudan, Egypt and Ethiopia. This agreement had limited value because it only dealt with the issue of the Grand Ethiopian Renaissance Dam project on the Blue Nile and did not address the larger, thorny issue of sharing all Nile waters in a comprehensive agreement by all riparian states. It was a political event, expressing the willingness of the three main countries involved to solve matters amicably and via talks, thus repairing some of Ethiopia's unilateral actions in the recent past. The agreement solved none of the issues raised by the 1999 Cooperative Framework Agreement (not signed by Egypt), nor the issue of how to determine and manage water quotas for each country in an overall riparian states' sharing agreement.

Burundi

Stef Vandeginste

The year was marked by a severe political, security and humanitarian crisis. The nomination of incumbent President Nkurunziza by his party, the 'Conseil National pour la Défense de la Démocratie – Forces de Défense de la Démocratie' (CNDD-FDD), and his re-election for a third term stood at the heart of the crisis, which split the party and destabilised state institutions. Popular demonstrations culminated in a failed coup d'etat attempt in May. These events were met with severe repression, and hundreds of civilians were executed, disappeared and/or tortured. Over 200,000 people fled to neighbouring countries. International mediation efforts were stepped up but failed to produce a meaningful result. Two new rebel movements announced an armed struggle to topple the Nkurunziza government. The crisis negatively affected Burundi's relations with most of its international partners, several of which imposed individual and/or aid sanctions. The political crisis also had a major impact on Burundi's economy and on fiscal revenue.

 | DOI 10.1163/9789004333239_031

Domestic Politics

The run-up to the 2015 general elections was characterised by mounting tensions. First and foremost, and somewhat unexpectedly, the *pre-electoral crisis* affected the dominant CNDD-FDD itself. The main cause of internal party divisions was President Pierre Nkurunziza's ambition of to renew his term in office, despite a two-term limit being laid down in the 2000 Arusha Peace and Reconciliation Agreement and – albeit somewhat ambiguously– in the Constitution. The internal opposition against a third presidential term became most visible when, in February, the national intelligence service, 'Service National des Renseignements' (SNR), addressed a memo to the president, warning against the negative consequences of a *third presidential term* for the country's stability and post-conflict recovery. In response, SNR head General Godefroid Niyombare – a Hutu and former rebel commander alongside Nkurunziza – was dismissed and replaced by General Steve Ntakarutimana. This did not end the internal party crisis but, on the contrary, symbolised Nkurunziza's decision to align himself with the more radical military wing of the party, most notably his closest aides, General Adolphe Nshimirimana and General Alain-Guillaume Bunyoni. In March, several senior CNDD-FDD dignitaries, including Nkurunziza's own spokesperson, Léonidas Hatungimana, wrote an open letter to the president asking him not to stand in the forthcoming presidential elections. They were supported by other internal opponents (also known as 'frondeurs'), whose names were not disclosed at the time but who included the speaker of the National Assembly, Pie Ntavyohanyuma, and the second vice president of the Republic, Gervais Rufyikiri. In an effort to quash the internal opposition, many dissident party officials were replaced by loyalists both within the party and in leading positions in the provincial and national administration and the diplomatic corps. After securing the loyalty of a carefully orchestrated national party congress, Nkurunziza was nominated as the party's presidential candidate on 25 April.

The nomination prompted unprecedented *mass demonstrations* in the streets of the capital, Bujumbura. Never before had Burundians, generally perceived as being quite reserved and discrete, taken to the streets in such numbers. Finding inspiration in Burkina Faso's earlier successful experience of demonstrations against a third presidential term, a widely supported and initially peaceful civil society campaign urged Nkurunziza to respect the Arusha Agreement and not to accept his nomination, but the protest had very little success outside Bujumbura. In rural areas, the CNDD-FDD had gained hegemonic control over territory, people and local administration since its coming to power in 2005. In addition, under the leadership of General Nshimirimana, the party's youth wing 'Imbonerakure' ('those who see from afar') had been trained as a parallel non-state police force, or 'militia', as the UN High Commissioner for Human Rights labelled it after his mission to Burundi in April, much to the dissatisfaction of the party leadership. The demonstration movement in Bujumbura built on the earlier, more timid protest campaign against the sharp rises in the price of consumer goods and, politically more importantly, the publicly celebrated release in February of *Bob Rugurika*, a well-known journalist and director of 'African Public Radio' (RPA), who had been arrested in January for his alleged complicity in the murder of three Catholic nuns in 2014 after suggesting that Nshimirimana had been responsible for their assassination. The large crowds celebrating his release symbolised the anger of many Bujumbura residents at the government's increasingly deplorable human rights record and poor economic governance and the lack of a tangible peace dividend ten years after the first post-conflict multi-party elections. In its response to the mass demonstrations, the government increasingly framed the protests in *ethnic terms*, that is, as being led by Tutsi minority opposition activists who were trying to pre-empt their defeat in the forthcoming elections and who, in reality, were calling for the establishment of a non-elected transitional government. While demonstrations did indeed mostly take place in predominantly Tutsi neighbourhoods of Bujumbura, the opposition to Nkurunziza's third term was political rather than ethnic and included both Hutu majority and Tutsi minority activists. Later in the crisis, a cross-border dimension was added to the ethnic framing of the anti-Nkurunziza movement. Rwanda in particular, and President Paul Kagame (Tutsi) personally, but also Belgium as the former colonial power, were the target of increasingly vehement government rhetoric against a so-called neo-imperialist campaign that allegedly had regime overthrow as its ultimate purpose.

On 27 April, a group of CNDD-FDD senators petitioned the *Constitutional Court* to interpret the Constitution on the legality of Nkurunziza' candidacy. While few observers expected the Court to be able to rule independently, there was considerable debate among the judges. The Court concluded that, despite the two-term limit and because of the ambiguity of a transitional provision in the Constitution, Nkurunziza – who had been indirectly elected by parliament in 2005 and directly elected in 2010 – could run for an additional term. The court ruling was particularly controversial because, during the court's deliberations, its vice president fled the country, citing intimidation by Nkurunziza supporters. After the ruling, the president confirmed his intention to run for a final term in office, but opponents feared that, if re-elected, he might seek to change the Constitution and remove presidential term limits altogether. Seen from that perspective, Rwanda's President Kagame, who had had his own term limits revised, thus setting an important regional precedent, was an ally of Nkurunziza. In September, the president established a National Commission for Inter-Burundian Dialogue (CNDI). During its public hearings, which were held in several provinces and which, according to the opposition, were carefully orchestrated by the regime, many interventions called for an amendment to the Constitution, including the removal of executive term limits. Like his Rwandan counterpart, Nkurunziza thus seemed to generate a public demand for the possibility that he might continue to lead the country. As an additional justification for his presidency, Nkurunziza also increasingly referred to visions in which God explained to him and his wife that he was the predestined leader of Burundi.

On 13 May, at the height of the popular demonstrations and when he was about to attend an extraordinary EAC summit on Burundi in Dar es Salaam (Tanzania), a *coup d'etat* was staged by General Niyombare and a group of dissident (Hutu and Tutsi) generals. This was initially celebrated on the streets of Bujumbura but it did not last longer than one day. The coup plotters probably overestimated the support for the anti-Nkurunziza movement within the armed forces (particularly in battalions located outside the capital). In addition, there were indications that the coup attempt was probably infiltrated from the very start by leading army generals, most notably the army chief of staff, General Prime Niyongabo. Several coup plotters were arrested but others, including Niyombare, managed to escape, mostly to Rwanda. In December, Niyombare and other army deserters set up the *armed rebel movement* 'Forces Républicaines du Burundi' (FOREBU), which declared an armed struggle to topple the Nkurunziza government. The coup allowed Nkurunziza to identify his allies and his opponents. Independent media were closed down. Civil society leaders left the country or were arrested. Grenade attacks added to a general atmosphere of fear and insecurity. Many real and suspected opponents – accused of being 'putchistes' – were arrested, tortured and forcibly disappeared. On 11 September, army chief of staff Niyongabo was ambushed but narrowly escaped an assassination attempt.

In the run-up to the general elections, the *political opposition* failed to unite and to present a credible alternative to a continuation of CNDD-FDD rule. However, the leaders of two unrecognised wings of opposition parties – Agathon Rwasa, self-declared opposition leader and historical leader of the 'Forces Nationales de Libération' (FNL) and Charles Nditije of Burundi's former single party, 'Unité pour le Progrès National' – set up a coalition, *'Abigenga Mizero y'Abarundi'* (*Independents – Hope of Burundians*) and introduced joint lists of 'independent' candidates. Shortly before the elections, however, the coalition asked its supporters to boycott them. Dissidents within the dominant party openly distanced themselves from the increasingly more militarist Nkurunziza regime and sought to join forces with the opposition, but too late to make a difference. In March, Hussein Radjabu, Nkurunziza's long-standing ally at the time of the CNDD-FDD rebellion, who had fallen out with the president and had been sentenced to a lengthy prison term in 2007, escaped from Mpimba central prison. He was the unofficial leader of the 'Union pour la Paix et la Démocratie' (UPD) and joined other opposition leaders in exile. Opposition politicians who remained in Burundi continued to be harassed, either through judicial proceedings or by the intimidation of their members. In January, Frédéric Bamvuginyumvira, vice president of the 'Front pour la Démocratie' (FRODEBU), was found guilty of corruption. In March, the wife of Agathon Rwasa narrowly escaped assassination when she was shot in a hairdressing salon in Bujumbura. In May, shortly after the failed coup, UPD chairperson Zed Feruzi was assassinated by unidentified gunmen in the capital city.

Because of the mounting tensions, repeated calls were made by the opposition, civil society and some international partners for the *general elections* to be delayed and for a genuine dialogue to take place to create acceptable conditions for elections. Legislative and communal elections were delayed by about one month and took place on 29 June. After a short delay, presidential elections were held on 21 July and Senate elections took place on 24 July. However, no progress was made in the dialogue between government and opposition. Most election observation missions suspended their operations prior to the elections. Several donors also withdrew their financial support for the elections. Two (out of five) members of the Electoral Commission fled to Rwanda. Although no major incidents were reported on election day, the legislative elections lacked credibility because of the context of instability and insecurity in which they were held. The CNDD-FDD won around 75% of the (valid) votes. The official results indicated that 13.8% of the (valid) votes had been cast for the 'Abigenga Mizero' coalition – to its own surprise and despite its boycott. After coopting additional women, Tutsi and Twa minority MPS to meet the constitutional quota requirement, 'Abigenga Mizero' thus took 30 seats (out of 121) in the *National Assembly*. The government hoped that the *ad hoc* coalition opposition might accept the result and take up its seats, thus showing the government's best intentions to have a multi-party parliament and a broad-based coalition government. This 'carrot' put the cohesion of 'Abigenga Mizero' under severe pressure. After some initial hesitation, and although many of his party members in rural areas had been harassed and intimidated since the 2010 elections, Rwasa accepted the offer and became vice president of the National Assembly. Coalition partner Nditije, however, instructed his elected candidates not to take up their seats, and most – but not all – of them obeyed. Nkurunziza obtained approximately 74% of the valid votes cast in the *presidential elections* and was sworn in for a third term in office, The ceremony took place under strict security, on 20 August, two weeks after his close aide, General *Adolphe Nshimirimana* had been ambushed and assassinated in Bujumbura and after the reprisal killing of former (Tutsi) chief of staff Jean Bikomagu and the attempted assassination of the internationally celebrated human rights activist Pierre-Claver Mbonimpa. In the new *CNDD-FDD dominated government*, five (out of 20) ministers belonged to Rwasa's FNL. The government's composition was fully in line with constitutional requirements in terms of gender, ethnic and political party representation. While real power rested with a group of generals loyal to Nkurunziza, the government included Minister of Public Security Alain Guillaume Bunyoni and Minister of Foreign Affairs Alain-Aimé Nyamitwe as its strongmen.

After the elections, the government did not show any intention to start a genuine dialogue with the opposition. Most opposition leaders – including many 'frondeurs' – went into exile, most of them to Rwanda or Belgium. In July, a new opposition coalition, the 'Conseil National pour le Respect de l'Accord d'Arusha et l'Etat de Droit' (*CNARED*), was established under the leadership of long-standing opposition leader Léonard Nyangoma. CNARED requested internationally mediated negotiations with the government on the release of political prisoners, the restoration of the independent media and the establishment of an interim government that should prepare new elections. Above all, CNARED insisted on the need to respect the Arusha Peace and Reconciliation Agreement of August 2000, which, together with additional peace agreements signed in 2003 and 2006, had allowed Burundi to enjoy a decade of peace after a decade of civil war. The government, however, refused to recognize CNARED, which it considered to be responsible for the coup d'etat and for terrorist attacks threatening the security of the state. CNARED at no point claimed responsibility for military operations against the government, although there were indications of some personal links between some of its members and newly established *armed rebel movements*. Apart from FOREBU, the armed movement 'Résistance pour un Etat de Droit' (*RED-TABARA*) declared an armed struggle to topple the Nkurunziza government. The security situation continued to deteriorate. On 11 December, an armed attack was staged against three military camps in and around Burumbura. This operation was largely unsuccessful but led to massive arrests in predominantly Tutsi-dominated neighbourhoods in the capital. Dozens of young men were reportedly tortured, executed or forcibly disappeared. Reports of mass graves remained unverified by an independent inquiry. More than at any time during the pre- and post-electoral crisis, warnings of a risk of genocide appeared in the international media and diplomatic circles. The government insisted that no international inquiry was needed and that the national law enforcement agencies, the judiciary and the *Truth and Reconciliation Commission* (TRC) were in charge of restoring law and order and of conducting inquiries into alleged human rights violations. In reality, because of the insecurity and the political crisis, the TRC, which had been established in 2014, was not able to conduct any inquiries or hearings into Burundi's legacy of past atrocities.

According to UNHCR figures, more than 200,000 Burundians had left the country by the end of December, most of them for neighbouring countries: Tanzania (120,000), Rwanda (70,000), the DRC (20,000) and Uganda (20,000), demonstrating but one aspect of the increasingly important regional and international dimensions of the Burundian political, security and humanitarian crisis.

Foreign Affairs

More than ever since the end of the peace process, Burundi was the subject of intense diplomatic activity at various levels. Many high-level delegations representing bilateral partners and intergovernmental institutions visited the country. After many years of active UN involvement with political developments in Burundi, the diplomatic lead was now taken by regional African bodies in trying to solve the crisis through dialogue.

First, the *EAC* took a leading role in trying to find a political solution. A first extraordinary summit on the situation in Burundi was held in Dar es Salaam on

13 May but was suspended after the military coup attempt in Bujumbura. The EAC logically condemned the coup, although, at the same time, EAC member states were strongly divided on the desirability of an additional term in office for Nkurunziza. Burundi's most important ally turned out to be *Tanzania*. After some initial hesitation and ambiguous statements, the Tanzanian government – which also facilitated Nkurunziza's return to Burundi after the coup – chose not to insist on a withdrawal of the candidature of the incumbent president. During a second extraordinary EAC summit on Burundi on 31 May, Tanzania insisted that the EAC should not openly call for Nkurunziza not to run. This was a major diplomatic victory for the Burundian government. Tanzania's position may well have been inspired by its tense relations with Rwanda and its ambition to maintain regional leadership at the EAC level. The Burundian crisis deepened the rift within the EAC. A third emergency summit on Burundi on 6 July confirmed the EAC's silence on the third term issue and appointed Uganda's President Museveni as facilitator on the Burundian crisis. After a short visit to Burundi on 14 July, Museveni failed to take any meaningful initiative until 28 December, when a Burundian dialogue meeting was held in Kampala (Uganda), at which the government, civil society and CNARED were present, but follow-up to the meeting remained very uncertain. Contrary to most other observer missions, who suspended their activities, the EAC did observe the legislative, local and presidential elections. Civil society organisations filed a case at the EAC Court of Justice challenging Nkurunziza's candidacy. The Court of Justice turned down the request for interim orders but did not deal with the merits of the case. As indicated above, within the EAC, diplomatic relations between Burundi and *Rwanda* importantly worsened towards the end of the year. The government openly accused Rwanda of supporting the armed opposition in an attempt to install a new government led by a Kagame appointee.

The *AU* repeatedly expressed concern at the crisis in Burundi, but AU opinions clearly differed on the type of involvement needed with the Burundian crisis. AU Commission chairperson Nkosazana Dlamini-Zuma visited in Burundi in March and spoke out clearly in favour of the need to respect the two-term limit laid down in the Arusha Agreement. Shortly after her mission, AU ambassador Boubacar Gaoussou Diarra was recalled to Addis Ababa (Ethiopia) for consultations and did not return to Bujumbura. After the Constitutional Court judgment, chairperson Zuma noted that all other interpretations of the Constitution differed from that made by the Court. The AU Peace and Security Council (AUPSC), however, urged all Burundians stakeholders to respect the Court's ruling. In June, the AUPSC decided to deploy human rights observers but no memorandum had been agreed upon to determine the mandate and the powers of those observers by year's end. Shortly after the 11 December events (see above), the AUPSC – at ambassadorial level – decided to authorise the deployment of an African Prevention and Protection Mission in Burundi (*MAPROBU*) for a period of six months with an initial strength of 5,000 military personnel and police. Burundi – not surprisingly – rejected the decision. Parliament held an extraordinary session, demonstrations were organised by CNDD-FDD, and the government informed the AU that it did not authorise the deployment of MAPROBU. As a result, the decision was referred to the AU Summit set for early 2016. If the Summit were to confirm the AUPSC decision, it would be an unprecedented step by the AU under its 'responsibility to protect' norm.

The *UN* political presence in Burundi (BNUB) was closed down and was replaced by the UN Electoral Observation Mission (MENUB), which started its activities in January, despite some delay following a disagreement with the government on the precise terms of the status-of-mission agreement. The government was absent at the official MENUB inauguration. On 13 March, a UNSC mission led by Angola, France and the USA visited Burundi. The mission strongly insisted on the need to respect the Constitution and the Arusha Agreement. In late April, in an effort to help defuse the situation, the UN Secretary-General dispatched his Special Envoy on the Great Lakes Region Said Djinnit to Bujumbura. Djinnit organised talks with political leaders, civil society representatives and religious leaders. In June, a number of political parties, disturbed by Djinnit's silence (perceived as tacit acceptance) on the third term issue, requested the UN Secretary-General to recall Djinnit. The government actively lobbied *Russia* and *China*, hoping to find allies against interference with what it considered to be strictly internal affairs. On 12 November, the UNSC adopted a resolution on Burundi, calling for a political solution to the crisis and expressing its full support for the mediation efforts led by President Museveni on behalf of the EAC. The absence of any explicit reference to possible sanctions was greeted as a diplomatic victory by the government.

In January, the *EU* signed an agreement with the government for € 8 m of support for the elections. On 28 May, the EU election observation mission suspended its activities, citing the many factors that made credible elections impossible. In September, the European Council adopted travel restrictions and an assets freeze in respect of four persons – three on the government side, one on the opposition side – whose activities "undermined democracy" or "obstructed efforts to achieve a political solution to the crisis". In October, in addition to individual sanctions, the EU also invited the Burundian government for consultations in accordance with the procedure provided for under Article 96 of the EU-ACP partnership agreement. The dialogue, whose objective was to encourage Burundi to take measures in the areas of democracy, human rights and the rule of law, took place in December in Brussels (Belgium), but did not yield any result. The EU was therefore preparing for a next step in the aid sanctions procedure. At the same time, the EU gave major importance to streamlining its approach with the AU.

In November, individual sanctions were also imposed against four individuals – two on the side of the government, including Minister of Public Security Bunyoni and two on the side of the opposition, including General Niyombare – by the *USA*, which, throughout the year, took the lead in the diplomatic campaign against Nkurunziza's third term. Also in November, in a remarkable video message,

US President Obama spoke directly to the Burundian people asking them to preserve peace in the country. Earlier in the year, at the height of the popular demonstrations, over 600 university students sought shelter and security beneath the wall of the US embassy in Bujumbura after the government closed down university campus, which it saw as too opposition-friendly. In October, Obama announced the suspension of Burundi as a beneficiary under AGOA.

Burundi remained actively involved in *peacekeeping* operations on the African continent. Despite the instability back home, the Burundian army continued to contribute some 5,400 troops to AMISOM (the AU Mission in Som alia) and some 1,100 troops and police officers to MINUSCA (the UN Mission in the CAR). In June, over 50 Burundian military were killed during an attack by al-Shabaab Islamists on an AMISOM base.

Socioeconomic Developments

Tax collection fell significantly. In October, Burundi's revenue authority, the 'Office Burundais des Recettes', reported that taxes collected so far were 17% below the 2014 figures. This was the inevitable consequence of the impact the political turmoil had on economic activity, in particular in the capital city: shops and markets closed down, several economic operators left the country, transport difficulties were caused by road blocks, etc. In the countryside, the informal economy was also strongly affected by movements of refugees and IDPs.

Agriculture continued to account for almost 40% of GDP, employing more than 80% of the population. In the first half of the year, commercial tea production benefited from investment and production rose by 8% compared with 2014. The coffee sector suffered from the crisis and from a fall in coffee prices (approximately 40% over 12 months). In addition, agriculture was also affected by some excessive rains, resulting in the destruction of crops and landslides. In November, Jean de Dieu Mutabazi, director general of the 'Autorité de Régulation de la Filière Café du Burundi' (ARFIC), announced a campaign to plant 4.5 m additional coffee plants. Mutabazi had been appointed in September, at the same time as the new head of the 'Office du Thé', Jacques Bigirimana. There was a general perception that both were being rewarded for their politically useful role as government-friendly opposition leaders.

Despite the adoption of a new *mining code* in 2014, the exploitation of industrial mines remained stalled. Local civil society groups feared that the new legislation adopted to implement the mining code was giving rise to an increased risk of corruption, despite Burundi's formal commitment, in February, to the Extractive Industries Transparency Initiative standard.

After several years of annual *GDP growth* of between 4% and 5%, it was estimated that the political turmoil would in a negative growth of over 7%. With a

GDP of $ 315 per capita, Burundi officially became the poorest country in the world, according to IMF figures.

In March, the IMF completed the sixth review of Burundi's *ECF* arrangement and concluded that the programme remained on track. Later in the year, the IMF announced that the seventh and eighth reviews were not possible and that the programme was now off track.

Burundi more or less consolidated its position on the World Bank's *Doing Business Index* (ranked 152th out of 189 countries, compared with 151st in 2014). Burundi's ranking fell slightly on most indicators, but improved on investors' access to electricity. On the Global Competitiveness Index of the World Economic Forum, Burundi was ranked 139th (out of 144 countries).

Consumer price inflation increased to 7% by the end of the year (compared with 4.4% in 2014). Inflation was particularly high in food prices. The *Burundian franc* officially remained relatively stable, but the gap between official and non-official exchange rates increased significantly, indicating a further depreciation of the franc.

The *2016 budget*, approved in parliament in late December, was based on an expected 44% drop in financial aid. In September, Belgium, Burundi's most important bilateral aid partner, announced a suspension and reorientation of all aid that was likely to support the government or its perceived domestic legitimacy. Other donors were expected to adopt similar positions if – as was expected – negotiations with the EU under the Article 96 sanctioning mechanism of the EU-ACP partnership agreement (see above) were unsuccessful. As a result, parliament adopted an austerity budget, which many observers nevertheless expected to be unrealistic. Expenditure was budgeted at $ 811 m, compared with $ 982 m in December 2014 (a decrease of 17.4%). The government announced a combination of external and domestic borrowing to cover the $ 82 m deficit.

Comoros

Rolf Hofmeier

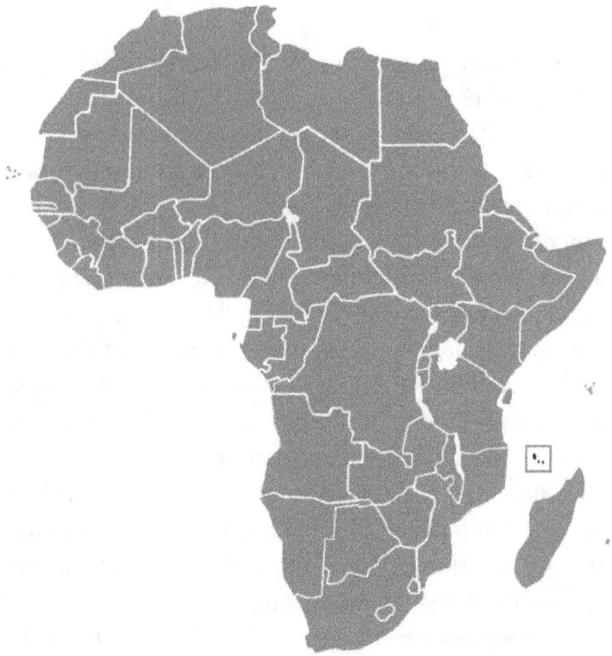

Somewhat delayed triple elections in early 2015 set the political scene for the ensuing year. Newly-forged political alliances were subsequently gearing up for the next presidential and gubernatorial elections in early 2016. President Dhoinine's ruling camp was mainly confronted by the renewed presidential ambitions of his predecessor and former mentor, Sambi, but the latter's constitutional eligibility as a candidate remained a strong bone of contention. Despite some signs of a possible re-emergence of the vicious political confrontations that had characterised the country during its often turbulent past, 2015 turned out to be another year of relatively calm political normalcy with no major upheavals. The long-standing frictions between the three 'autonomous' islands of the 'Union des Comores' and their political elites were still in evidence, but caused no tangible problems. The ambivalent relationship with France remained unchanged, given the enduring contentious Mayotte issue. Economically, it was another difficult year with slow growth, continuing power and water outages, accumulated salary arrears in the public sector and several strikes. The government's socioeconomic performance was considered rather unsatisfactory.

 | DOI 10.1163/9789004333239_032

Domestic Politics

Simultaneous *triple elections* for the National Assembly, three island councils and, as an innovation, 54 communal councils had originally been scheduled for November 2014, but had been postponed as a result of severe preparation problems, and were held on 25 January and 22 February. According to the Electoral Commission, 275,000 voters (fewer than in 2010) had been registered and a total of 805 candidates were allowed to stand (204 for the National Assembly, 353 for the island councils and the rest for the communal councils). Twenty-three political parties and a substantial number of independent candidates entered the fray for the first election round. The volatile *political scene* remained characterised by a plethora of small parties, practically all based on loyalty to particular individual leaders and not on articulated party programmes or specific ideologies. Only a few of the political parties were of significant importance at the national level, although they had varying degrees of support on particular islands. The atmosphere during the campaign period remained generally calm and devoid of significant irregularities. The same was true of the conduct of the elections, which were given a general sign of approval by several international observer groups.

The *first round of voting*, on 25 January, served to directly elect all island councillors and to reduce the number of candidates vying for the 24 directly-elected seats in the National Assembly. Only three candidates managed to obtain an absolute majority in their constituencies and thus to secure a mandate, while in all other constituencies the two frontrunners had to face each other in a *second round* on 22 February, when communal councillors were also elected. Only one woman was successful in becoming an MP. Voter turn-out was a record high at 71% in the first round and 73% in the second.

Altogether, six political parties, plus three independent candidates, won *seats* in the *National Assembly*. The 'Union pour le Développement des Comores' (UPDC) of President *Ikililou Dhoinine* took a narrow lead with eight MPs, closely followed by seven MPs from the 'Juwa' (Sun) party of former president *Ahmed Abdallah Sambi*. The 'Convention pour le Renouveau des Comores' (CRC) of another former president (and a leader of the 1999 putsch), *Azali Assoumani*, won two parliamentary seats, as did the 'Rassemblement Démocratique des Comores' (RDC) of Mouigni Baraka, the governor of the main island Ngazidja (Grande Comore). One seat each was won the 'Parti pour l'Entente des Comores' (PEC), closely associated with Sambi, and the 'Rassemblement pour un Développement Harmonisé et Integré' (RADHI), a splinter group of the CRC. In addition, the yet-to-be-installed new island councils were to nominate nine supplementary MPs (three from each island). Juwa was at pains to reject existing perceptions that it was a Shiite party, which were based on Sambi's past close links with Iran.

The relative strength of the parties varied considerably between the islands. The situation was most diverse on *Ngazidja*, whose 11 MPs were spread quite equally between all six parties, while Juwa had five out of nine MPs from *Anjouan*, Sambi's home island, and three out of four MPs from *Mohéli*, Dhoinine's home island, represented the UPDC. This pattern clearly reflected the continuing political rivalries and differing island identities in the archipelago. Similar rivalries for local power positions without discernible differences in political programmes also pertained in the island councils, where many independents served as councillors. In Moroni Mohamed Daoud (aka Kiki), whose UPDC-affiliated 'Orange' party had done very badly in the elections, was elected as mayor. During the second half of March *sharp tensions* arose in both the *island councils* of *Anjouan* and *Ngazidja* over the elections of the respective council presidents and the MPs in the National Assembly. The Ngazidja council was paralysed for over a week and a council president eventually elected with a Juwa-RDC alliance, while UPDC and its allies boycotted the session. In the Anjouan council all positions were taken by the Juwa majority, but a petition by the UPDC-allied opposition to the Constitutional Court temporarily invalidated the election of three Juwa-MPs.

In this confrontational climate, the *opening session* of the newly elected *National Assembly* on 3 April led to physical confrontations and the use of security personnel to remove opposition MPs. In the absence of Juwa and its allies, only the 16 remaining MPs elected Abdou Ousseni (UPDC), a former justice minister, as parliamentary president. Sambi denounced this as a "parliamentary putsch", but a few weeks later the alliance between Juwa and the RDC that had existed since the elections broke up, apparently under heavy pressure from the government on Governor Baraka. Four RDC MPs returned to parliament and moved over to the coalition around the UPDC, thus ensuring a solid majority.

On 29 April, President Dhoinine announced a small *government reshuffle* in the aftermath of the elections. All three vice presidents kept their portfolios. Of the seven ministers (of whom two were women) there were four new faces. The RADHI leader, Houmed Msaidié, was given the Interior Ministry. Vice President Fouad Mohadji, a Sambi supporter, remained responsible for health and social affairs, while Vice President Mohamed Ali Soilihi, the president's closest collaborator, kept the finance portfolio.

For the remainder of the year, all political discussions and the formation of personal and party alliances were already strongly focused on the *upcoming presidential and gubernatorial elections*, which were set in mid-August for 21 February and 10 April 2016. Dhoinine was constitutionally barred from seeking another term and the field for potential candidates appeared wide open. The constitutional principle of a *presidency rotating between the islands* had been adhered to for one full cycle, with consecutive presidents from Ngazidja, Anjouan and Mohéli; the next president was consequently expected to hail from Ngazidja. Former president *Sambi*, originating from Anjouan, nevertheless persisted in his ambition to become a presidential candidate and repeatedly demanded a public debate about amending the relevant Article 13 of the Constitution, calling for a referendum or a national convention of all political groups to undertake a general review of the achievements of 40 years of independence and of 15 years of the Fomboni Constitution. This idea was not rejected outright by the government, but was considered unfeasible before the coming election. Sambi and his followers argued strongly that the current constitutional principle ('tournante') perpetuated the precedence of separate island identities over a common national democratic consensus. Some political actors even advocated that, as a matter of principle, the next president should originate from Mayotte, the fourth Comorian island, but a fully-integrated French département since 2011 (see below), although this idea only gained partial support.

Concrete *preparations for the elections* got underway in September with a revision of the electoral register (300,000 voters were eventually registered) and the installation of island electoral commissions. It was envisaged that, for the first time, Comorians in the diaspora (up to 100,000 voters were estimated to be in France) would be able to vote, but this was still uncertain at year's end. Doubts were raised about the competency and financial resources of the National Electoral Commission to guarantee the competent conduct of the entire election process. Formal *candidacy declarations* (for the presidency and island governorships) had to be submitted by 21 December and the Constitutional Court almost immediately rejected three presidential candidates, including Sambi. Juwa criticised this decision as catastrophic for the unity of the country, but nevertheless accepted the ruling, which was not unexpected. The Constitutional Court validated record numbers of 15 gubernatorial candidates each for Anjouan and Ngazidja, and 11 for Mohéli, while 25 presidential candidates were listed to enter the primary contest on Ngazidja, which would select the three frontrunners who would battle it out nationally in the second round.

All major and some smaller political parties had *listed candidates*, but many were running as independents. Only one woman, residing in France, was campaigning as a diaspora candidate. With Sambi eliminated from the contest, he was now backing the PEC president Fahmi Said Ibrahim, his former foreign minister. Vice President Soilihi entered the fray as the candidate of the ruling UPDC and President Dhoinine. Other prominent candidates were former president Assoumani and Governor Baraka, plus a host of other seasoned politicians. On Ngazidja the gubernatorial competition was wide open, while on Anjouan Governor Anissi Chamdissine, who had formerly been a Juwa member, was seeking re-election for the UPDC. On Mohéli, the president's wife was vying for the governorship, while Governor Mohamed Ali Said was disqualified by the Constitutional Court from seeking re-election, having already served two terms. The main battle lines in the coming contests were to be between the ruling UPDC with around a dozen allied groups, the Juwa-PEC alliance (plus three smaller parties), and intermediate groups (such as the CRC and RDC), but this left room for many independents and shifting alliances at the local level.

In January, repeatedly postponed judicial proceedings finally took place in a special state security court in the case of a failed *coup attempt* in April 2013. Of the 15 suspects, two alleged leaders were given ten-year prison terms, while several others got between two- and six-year terms and some were released.

Foreign Affairs

The Comoros' long-standing conflict with *France* over the status of *Mayotte*, the archipelago's fourth island, continued to be a national focus, but without materially jeopardising the delicate relations with the former colonial power. January marked 20 years since the introduction of the infamous 'visa Balladur', which prevented Comorians from legally entering Mayotte and was regarded as having caused an estimated 20,000 deaths during perilous sea voyages on small boats. All Comorian governments had always insisted that Mayotte remained an integral part of the Comoros under international law. This was repeated, as usual, in the president'cs speech at the UN General Assembly in September, while he nevertheless stressed the existence of good relations between Comoros and France resulting from the country's traditional substantial dependence on France as a major economic partner and aid donor. On 1 August, the government withdrew its national team from the 9th Indian Ocean Island Games in the French overseas département of La Réunion in protest against the Mayotte team parading under a French flag during the opening ceremony, thereby contravening earlier practices. The government subsequently felt humiliated, however, when, in what it regarded as a political manoeuvre, the next Games in 2019 were awarded to Mauritius, although Comoros had long been earmarked.

The *AU*, as had been the case since the late 1990s, continued to be concerned about the maintenance of peace and political stability in Comoros. With regard to Sambi's insistent attempts to bring about amendments to the Constitution, AU spokespersons on several occasions stressed the importance of sticking to the current constitution and warned that Sambi's ambitions risked endangering the country's stability. On 30 November, former president Kikwete of Tanzania, acting as emissary of the AU, held talks with all political camps about the election and obtained Sambi's promise to accept the final verdict of the Constitutional Court about his candidacy.

Within the generally very limited scope available to it, the government continued to pursue an *open-door policy* and attempted to maintain equally cordial relations with Western powers (particularly France and the USA) and with China, Iran and many Arab countries in the expectation of attracting aid or commercial investments from these diverse sources, although not many investments had so far actually materialised. In early May, the newly appointed foreign minister stressed that priority was to be given to strengthening *cooperation within the region*. In February, Comoros hosted a ministerial council meeting of the East African Standby Force. A Comorian-Tanzanian Economic Forum took place in late April in the hope of attracting new investors from that quarter and of possibly diversifying from concentrating on seeking Arab investments, as hitherto. A military assistance agreement was signed with *China* in February, and China offered to further expand its bilateral assistance programmes (e.g. construction of a new port on Mohéli). Of significant importance was growing influence and assistance from *Saudi Arabia*, which provided substantial budgetary aid of € 40 m in the wake of Dhoinine's visit to Riyadh in early November. Simmering latent competition for influence between Saudi Arabia and Iran (in the latter case largely originating from Sambi's presidency and links) was suddenly terminated when Comoros joined the new Saudi-led international anti-terror alliance in mid-December and subsequently contemplated breaking off relations with Iran altogether. During the year, the president's most notable international activities were his participation in the AU, Arab League and China-Africa summits and in the UN General Assembly.

Socioeconomic Developments

The macroeconomic situation continued to be difficult, and it was another year that brought many hardships to most of the population. Faced by entrenched social resistance, the government was unable to implement essential structural reforms, which were seriously needed to improve economic efficiency, particularly in the public sector. Widespread social dissatisfaction resulted from what was widely perceived as poor government performance. The *GDP growth rate* was estimated at around only 1%, well below the population growth rate and a significant slowdown compared with 2013 (3.5%) and 2014 (2.0%). Average *inflation* for the year remained modest at around 2%. This was again largely due to the restraining effect of membership of the franc zone, whereby the franc comorien (FrC) remained pegged to the euro and supported by France (at FrC 492 : € 1). Substantial *remittances* from the large Comorian diaspora, which accounted for about a quarter of GDP, and inflows of aid revenue remained essential to counterbalance the traditional enormous *structural trade deficit*. The value of imported goods was about ten times higher than export income (practically all from cloves, vanilla and ylang-ylang). The import bill was mainly burdened by Comoros' heavy dependence on importing food staples and all of its energy requirements.

IMF missions in June and September assessed the Comoros' financial and economic performance, but no new credit arrangement or staff-monitored programme was concluded during the year; the last ECF had already expired in December 2013. The IMF viewed the immediate *outlook for the economy* as *difficult* and identified as key challenges the mobilisation of additional revenue and the containment of lower priority spending in order to close the considerable fiscal financing gap. The long existing crisis in the electricity sector and the slow implementation of the public investment programme were seen to have adversely affected economic activity and tax revenue. Unbudgeted increases in the wage bill and the exhaustion of deposits from the Economic Citizenship programme had limited the government's ability to finance itself domestically.

Public sector salary arrears, quite a common feature in the past, had again occurred since mid-2014 and eventually accumulated to four months' worth of outstanding payments. In view of the coming elections, the budget aid from Saudi Arabia (in November) was largely used to settle these arrears, but they were not entirely eliminated. The difficult situation also provoked a long teachers *strike* in March and April and a six-month strike (until the year's end) by medical staff at the main hospital. Continued *outages of electricity and water*, sometimes for several weeks, also made life precarious for most of the population and were a major cause of discontent with the government. This twice led to the organisation of public protests in the form of so-called *'ville morte'* (dead city) in Moroni by angry social groups.

Again, only very limited progress was made on a fundamental reform or privatisation of notoriously badly managed *parastatal companies*, particularly key public utilities (electricity, water and telecoms). This had long been demanded by the IMF and the World Bank, but in vain. Renewed efforts to improve the performance of *Ma-Mwe*, the deficient power and water company, were undertaken with external technical support and the installation of new generators, but the results remained inadequate. The long planned and very controversially discussed privatisation of *'Comores Télécom'* was finally abandoned by the government in the face of continued resistance from politicians and trade unions, who feared the inevitable loss of many jobs. Instead, a process was started in April to find an investor for a second mobile telecoms company with the intention of thus creating a competitive situation. Following a restricted tender process, a second telecoms licence was eventually awarded on 1 October to the Malagasy company *Telma*, owned by a French businessman, and finally concluded in mid-December upon payment of FrC 7 bn.

No tangible progress was made with regard to hopes for eventual success in *oil and gas* exploration in Comoros' extensive coastal waters. Expectations had recently risen following substantial hydrocarbon finds along the East African Coast, but the start of concrete exploration activities was slow to materialise. Following on from two exploration licences awarded in 2013, a third production-sharing contract was signed in November with the Texan company Rhino Resources.

Djibouti

Nicole Hirt

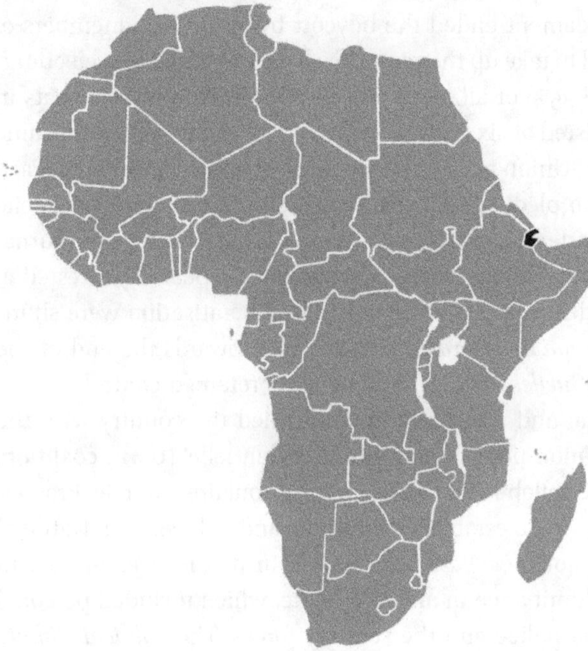

Early in the year, there was some hope for a process of cautious democratisation when the candidates of the opposition coalition ended their boycott and took their seats in parliament. However, harassment of the opposition continued and the situation deteriorated rapidly towards the end of the year, when President Ismaïl Omar Guelleh declared his candidacy for a fourth term in office. Violent clashes occurred on 21 December between security forces and members of the Yonis-Moussa clan who had gathered for a religious celebration, which resulted in more than 100 casualties. On the same day, police attacked the opposition coalition's leadership during a meeting and three politicians were seriously injured. Violent clashes continued between government forces and a militant wing of the 'Front pour la Restoration de l'Unité et de la Démocratie' (FRUD) in the Afar-inhabited north. China and Djibouti reached an agreement on the construction of a naval base, which further strengthened the country's position as a centre of international military facilities. Economic life was marked by substantial FDI and ambitious infrastructure projects, while endemic poverty and unemployment were not alleviated and standards of nutrition deteriorated due to worsening drought conditions.

 | DOI 10.1163/9789004333239_033

Domestic Politics

At the beginning of the year, there was some optimism that cautious democratic reforms might be introduced following the signature of a formal accord between the government and the 'Union pour le Salut National' (USN) opposition coalition at the end of 2014. This agreement ended the boycott by opposition members of parliament, who had refused to take up the seats they had won in the 2013 elections. The opposition had secured 35% of all votes, but were awarded only ten seats in the assembly. The USN consisted of six parties, including the 'Alliance Républicaine pour le Développement', the 'Union pour la Démocratie et la Justice' and the 'Parti National Démocratique', who pledged to strive for an end to the country's social misery and for a multi-party democracy. The coalition's spokesperson was journalist and political activist Daher Ahmed Farah, who had been repeatedly arrested in recent years. Hopes for modest reforms and gradual democratisation were short-lived, and the *political situation deteriorated substantially* towards the end of the year. *President Ismaïl Omar Guelleh* (widely dubbed IOG) retained control over all aspects of Djibouti's political and economic life and ruled the country with the support of the governing 'Union pour la Majorité Presidentielle' (UMP) coalition, which was dominated by Guelleh's 'Rassemblement Populaire pour le Progrès' (RPP). Guelleh's earlier promises to establish a reformed and independent National Election Commission were not met. Parliament's role in politics was limited in the face of the president's dominance in affairs of state, which included personal control over the military, the police and the security forces. The *political climate remained repressive* and opposition politicians and human rights activists were frequently harassed. *Press freedom* was also strictly limited; the government controlled the state-owned radio and television and the newspaper 'La Nation'. No independent media were allowed to work in the country, but the opposition Internet radio station 'La Voix de Djibouti' broadcast from France. Djibouti was ranked 170th out of 180 countries in Reporters Without Borders' 2015 press freedom report.

On 3 December, Guelleh announced in a speech broadcast by the state media that he would run for a *fourth presidential term* in the presidential elections scheduled for April 2016. This broke with his earlier assurances that he would not run for the presidency again. On 14 December, the opposition organised peaceful protests against Guelleh's candidacy, which was followed by the arrest of 50 opposition members in Djibouti Ville.

Harassment of the political opposition and human rights activists intensified towards the end of the year. In November, USN members were attacked with tear gas by security forces during an election rally, and six minors were arrested as they celebrated the Day of African Youth at the headquarters of a USN member party in Djibouti Ville. Violence culminated on 21 December, when security forces stormed a meeting of the USN party leadership and fired at the politicians with live ammunition, critically wounding three parliamentarians. Among the injured were USN leader Ahmed Yousouf and the party's secretary-general Abdourahman Mohamed

Guelleh. The third victim, the parliamentarian and secretary general of Djibouti's human rights league Said Hussein, managed to flee to Paris, where he gave an eyewitness account to 'Radio France Internationale'. He stated that the USN's meeting place was approached by heavily armed men, whose intention was "not to neutralize us but to kill us". He himself was shot in the throat and was brought to a French military hospital, from where he escaped to Ethiopia. According to Djibouti's public prosecutor, 17 people were arrested, including the secretary-general of the USN coalition.

Earlier on the same day, security forces had stormed a religious celebration of the *Yonis-Moussa clan* in Balbala, a suburb of Djibouti Ville. Members of the clan had gathered to honour the founder of their clan, when police fired into the crowd. The government announced that seven people had been killed and 23 injured, while the opposition and human rights organisations reported 25 dead and up to 100 persons wounded. USN representatives abroad stated that the assault had a political background because *Abdourahman Boreh*, an exiled businessman and arch rival of Guelleh, who acted as the USN's head of external relations, belonged to the Yonis-Moussa clan. On the other hand, Minister of Interior Hassan Omar Mohamed called the violence an "act intended to destabilize our nation" orchestrated by malicious individuals receiving instructions from abroad, most probably referring to Boreh. At the end of the month, human rights activist Omar Ali Ewado was arrested after publishing a list of the victims' names. On 31 December, Parliament approved a new *emergency law* that facilitated the extension of house arrest and the dissolution of 'radical groups'.

The *trial of Boreh* at the London Court of Arbitration, where Djibouti had brought a charge of corruption against him, continued and no verdict had been reached by year's end. In October, Guelleh declined to appear as the key witness, claiming that he had more pressing obligations at home.

During the spring, various *clashes between government troops and FRUD-Combattant*, the militant wing of the FRUD, occurred in the Obock region inhabited by the Afar minority. In April, Prime Minster Abdoulkader Mohammed Kamil tried without success to persuade Afar elders to stop supporting the militant movement. In June, the army shelled FRUD posts in the Mablas mountains and launched an unsuccessful attack against FRUD positions north-west of Tadjourah in an attempt to oust the group from an area around the Galafi border post between Djibouti and Ethiopia.

Foreign Affairs

Djibouti continued to maintain close relations with most neighbouring countries in the volatile Horn of Africa and focused on strengthening its strategic position in the wider regional and international context. The small country played an active role in supporting international anti-terrorism activities in the region. After the signing of the mediation agreement between Djibouti and *Eritrea* in 2010, no progress had been made towards a final demarcation of the contested border, and Qatari military observers continued to monitor it. The Eritrean government refused to hand over Djiboutian prisoners of war and Qatar, becoming increasingly frustrated with the stalled mediation process, considered handing the case over to the UN. Djibouti's government took a close interest in developments in *Somalia* and continued to support the AU peacekeeping mission, AMISOM. In January, a Djiboutian contingent of 960 troops that had been stationed at Beletweyne was replaced after three years of duty. Relations with the self-declared Republic of *Somaliland* also remained close. However, Djibouti temporarily closed its border with the territory in February, following threats by al-Shabaab to carry out acts of terror. In August, Somaliland's foreign bureau declared that Djibouti was about to open an *official diplomatic office*, following Ethiopia's and Turkey's example.

Djibouti and *Ethiopia* remained mutually interdependent and maintained close and cordial relations, including an *accelerating process of economic integration*. This was shown in the opening of the first section of the Chinese-constructed and financed new *Ethiopian Djiboutian Railway* in October, the signing of an agreement on a *fuel pipeline* from Djibouti port to Ethiopia's capital, Addis Ababa, in September and Ethiopian electric power support to Djibouti. In early February, the two countries held a high-level Joint Commission meeting, in which Djibouti's President Guelleh and Ethiopian Prime Minister Hailemariam Dessalegn underscored their willingness to enhance bilateral cooperation in the political, economic and social sectors. In mid-February, Hailemariam addressed Djibouti's National Assembly, promoting the idea of *increased political integration*. However, his speech fell short of indicating a clear picture of the desired form of political arrangement. The two leaders also remained united in their anti-Eritrea stance, and in a joint statement on 9 February they condemned the country for its "continuous destabilisation policy", demanding that the international community tighten sanctions.

Because of its important strategic location, Djibouti continued to host various *military bases* that served the purposes of surveilling international maritime routes, controlling piracy and fighting militant Islamist groups. The *USA* continued to station about 4,000 troops and civilian personnel at Camp Lemmonier, which also served as one of the world's largest *drone bases* for targeted assassination attacks on radical Islamists. US Secretary of State John Kerry paid a visit to Djibouti on 6 May and held talks with Guelleh, whom he thanked for his support in the evacuation of Yemeni-American families from conflict-stricken Yemen, praising him as a reliable ally in the region. However, the day after Kelly's visit Djibouti's government told the Americans that they had to evacuate a smaller *military base at Obock*, which hosted a minor contingent of US troops, because it was intended to host 10,000 Chinese troops in the near future. Throughout the year, *China* and Djibouti held negotiations related to the establishment of China's first military base on African soil, and Guelleh met his Chinese counterpart on the side-lines of the China-Africa

Cooperation summit in South Africa in early December. Djibouti's Foreign Minister Mahamoud Ali Youssouf announced during the same meeting that the two countries had come to an agreement and China would establish a military base near Obock with the purpose of fighting piracy and securing Chinese ships on their passage through the Bab al-Mandeb Strait. China reportedly agreed to pay an annual sum of $ 100 m per annum in rent compared with the $ 63 m paid by the USA. However, *Russian plans* to install naval facilities in the country seemed to have been postponed for the time being. *France* abandoned initial plans to cut the number of its troops stationed in Djibouti from 1,900 to 900 by 2017 following an intervention by French President François Hollande and concerns expressed by the Djiboutian government, and was now considering a troop reduction to 1,300 by 2018. With the small *Japanese military camp* and the presence of the EU's anti-piracy Operation Atalanta, Djibouti's territory was without doubt the most internationalised military zone in the world.

The international military presence in the country was often combined with aid programmes and private foreign investments, which constituted a stable influx of foreign currency. It seemed that strategic interests prevented the democratic nations with a military presence in Djibouti from expressing strong criticism of Guelleh's repeated *violations of human rights*. It was only after violence had culminated in the December shootings by police and security forces, that the USA urged Djibouti's government to immediately release the arrested opposition leaders, "respect its citizens' rights to freedom of expression and peaceful assembly and association, and exercise restraint", and encouraged both government and opposition parties to re-engage in political dialogue.

Djibouti's formerly close relations with the *United Arab Emirates* deteriorated sharply following Guelleh's cancellation of the port management contract with Dubai-based DP World, which was related to the personal conflict between Guelleh and former port manager Boreh, and in May the countries *severed diplomatic ties*. This led to a deterioration of relations with *Saudi Arabia*, which declared Djibouti's foreign minister persona non grata. Guelleh tried to mend these ties by loosening relations with *Iran*.

Socioeconomic Developments

The transformation of Djibouti into a modern city state and international service centre continued, as did *substantial inflows of FDI* for major infrastructural projects. This process was accelerated by the agreement with *China* about its future military base at Obock, since China was ready to engage massively in Djibouti's infrastructural development. In addition, *Ethiopia*'s continuing economic boom contributed to the acceleration of infrastructural development in Djibouti. In September, the two countries signed a $ 1.55 bn agreement for the construction of the *Horn of Africa*

Pipeline, designed to transport gasoline, diesel and jet fuel from Djibouti's port to central Ethiopia. China pledged finance for a *new railway from Djibouti to Addis Ababa* at a cost of $ 4 bn and engaged in the construction of the project via the China Railway Group and the China Civil Engineering Construction Corporation. It was intended to replace the partially defunct Ethio-Djibouti Railway, constructed by France in the late nineteenth century, by 2016. However, because of the deteriorating food situation in Ethiopia, the railway was partially put into service in October in order to deliver food aid to drought-affected areas. Ethiopia continued to deliver *electricity* to Djibouti, but progress was made with the government's ambitious plans to invest in *renewable energy* in order to become a self-sufficient energy producer. Djibouti's electricity costs were among the highest in the world. In July, Energy Minister Ali Mahmoud Yacoub signed a memorandum of understanding with Shanghai Electric for the construction of a 60 MW *wind farm* and, in October, solar developer Sky Power announced an agreement with Djibouti for the development of *solar projects* worth about $ 440 m, along with corporate social responsibility investments of $ 11 m towards education, training, research and development. The government also pursued its plans to develop the country's high *geothermal potential* with the help of $ 31 m secured from the World Bank, the AfDB and other multilateral lenders to facilitate exploratory drilling.

The strategic development outlook *'Djibouti Vision 2035'* was further pursued by the government, although it seemed that there was a stronger focus on infrastructure development than on poverty reduction. There was a *large discrepancy* between the flourishing investment economy, high currency influx through the international military bases and FDI and the prevailing high levels of poverty and unemployment and low levels of education among the general population.

Macroeconomic performance was satisfactory, with a progressively positive GDP growth rate of 6.5% and IMF estimates of an annual growth of 7% over the coming four years. Consumer price *inflation* remained low and stood at 2.6% at the end of the year. The *fiscal deficit* was projected to rise from 12.2% of GDP in 2014 to 16.5% in 2015 as a result of the government's high public investment spending. The deficit was financed by substantial FDI and by loans. *Foreign exchange reserves* increased further to $ 409 m in July. The Djibouti franc (Dfr) remained pegged to the US dollar at a rate of Dfr 177 : $ 1 under a currency board arrangement. The *structural trade deficit* persisted and the IMF estimated exports of goods and services to amount to $ 601 m compared with imports worth $ 1,318 m. The fiscal deficit on a commitment basis was estimated at 16.5% of GDP.

The government's efforts to mobilise revenues continued to be hampered by extensive tax exemptions for FDI projects. In June, the government organised a tax conference where it discussed a *comprehensive tax reform* with stakeholders, including the private sector and civil society. The IMF commended such a reform with the aim of achieving a transparent tax regime and reducing tax exemptions.

The general *business environment* remained heavily restricted, and Djibouti was ranked 171st (out of 189 listed countries) in the World Bank's 'Doing Business 2015' assessment. The World Bank supported several small programmes to improve the local private sector.

The *IMF* did not enter into a new ECF agreement with Djibouti and noted that the country's high external debt meant that the scope for additional borrowing was extremely limited. It recommended that the authorities strengthen public capacity to manage the ambitious investment programmes that were in place and urged the government to ensure the implementation of a sustainable fiscal and external debt path, including limitation of additional borrowing. It stated that Djibouti's poor were insufficiently protected and expressed concerns about the persistence of endemic poverty and unemployment. It recommended a focus on projects that would foster growth through job creation and poverty reduction, and investment in labour intensive sectors such as fishing and tourism.

42% of the population continued to be living in extreme *poverty*, and the *unemployment* rate was once more estimated at over 50%. The *food situation* had deteriorated rapidly during the past decade as a result of climate change and increased drought, which led to a loss of 70% of all cattle and increased the country's heavy dependence on food imports. 67,000 people were receiving food aid from WFP or were employed in food-for-work programmes. It was estimated that this number might double in the near future as a consequence of the even worse drought conditions that plagued the Horn region throughout the year. The *climate* conditions contributed to the increasing exodus from rural areas, with more than 85% of the country's population already living in the greater Djibouti Ville area. Rangeland conditions and water availability were specifically poor in the Obock and Ali Sabieh regions. FAO reports indicated that about 230,000 people were in need of *humanitarian assistance*, including more than half of the rural population, mainly small-scale farmers and herders in the north-west and south-east of the country. In addition, about 56,000 *refugees from Somalia and Yemen*, hosted in camps, were suffering from food insecurity. Djibouti's chronically deficient socioeconomic standard was reflected in its low 2015 *HDI* ranking (168th out of 188 countries).

The government's *dispute with DP World* remained unresolved. Guelleh had unilaterally revoked the 20-year management contract with the Dubai-based company for the Doraleh container terminal in 2014, claiming that DP World had received illegal favours from former port director Boreh, whom the government was suing for corruption at the London Court of Arbitration. Meanwhile, DP World continued its regular port management activities.

Eritrea

Nicole Hirt

Eritrea's autocratic political system and its command economy prevailed, and the mass youth exodus caused by the open-ended national service system continued unabatedly. The regime continued to host Ethiopian rebel groups on its soil, but in September the commander of the Tigray People's Democratic Movement, which had served as a security force for President Isaias defected to Ethiopia with hundreds of troops. The government introduced a new penal code, but the human rights situation remained alarming, as was confirmed by the UN Commission of Inquiry on Human Rights in Eritrea in its report published in the summer. Diaspora Eritreans were deeply divided between supporters and opponents of the homeland regime. Eritrea joined the Saudi-led anti-Houthi campaign in Yemen in the spring. The government lobbied European politicians concerned about the influx of Eritrean refugees to Europe, and the EU granted € 200 m in fresh development aid.

 | DOI 10.1163/9789004333239_034

Domestic Politics

Eritrea remained an autocracy under the firm control of President Isaias Afewerki. No progress was made on the drafting of a new constitution that he had announced in 2014. In March, *Yemane Gebremeskel* was appointed as *Minister of Information*, a post that had remained vacant for more than two years. He had served as head of the President's Office for more than two decades, and so his appointment could be seen as a demotion. There were rumours of the *'freezing' of Minister of Mines and Energy General Sebhat Ephrem*, appointed in 2014, with the implication that he did not exercise any actual power in his current position. His former post of minister of defence remained vacant. The cabinet met twice during the year, in April and November. Part of the discussion at the November meeting was around possible remedies for the expected poor harvest following inadequate rains.

In January, Brigadier General Gebrehiwet Zemichael passed away. He had been in charge of the militias, armed groups of elderly civilians who had to undergo military training and patrol their neighbourhoods. There was no news about his replacement or about possible changes in the leadership of the five military command zones. However, the chief of staff and unofficial head of the Ministry of Defence, *Major General Phillipos Weldeyohannes, retained his powerful position.*

In early September, Commander Molla Asghedom, the leader of the *Tigray People's Democratic Movement* (TPDM), locally known by its Tigrinya acronym 'Demhit', defected to Ethiopia with approximately 700 fighters. Eritrea had been hosting and training the anti-Ethiopian government rebel group for 13 years, with maintenance costs reportedly being covered by income from the Bisha gold mine. However, the TPDM had rarely carried out military operations against Ethiopian troops, but was rather engaged in supporting the Eritrean military security apparatus by rounding up Eritrean draft dodgers. Ethiopian media reported that Molla had cooperated with the Ethiopian security apparatus for more than a year, and that the TPDM had infiltrated all levels of the Eritrean military and government. The TPDM leader defected only three days after a *coalition of Ethiopian opposition groups*, named 'Ethiopian National Salvation', was formed in Asmara. The coalition consisted of TPDM, 'Arbegnoch Ginbot 7' and the little known Afar People's Liberation Movement and Amhara Democratic Force Movement. The prominent leader of Ginbot 7, Professor Berhanu Negga, a former leader of the Coalition for Unity and Democracy and winner of the mayoralty of Addis Ababa in Ethiopia's controversial 2005 elections, had been appointed leader of the coalition, obviously much to the dismay of Molla Asghedom. The defection was a blow to President Isaias, who had considered the TPDM leader as his personal confidant.

The *mass exodus of Eritrean youth* continued as in previous years. UNHCR Ethiopia expected an increase of registered Eritrean refugees from 106,670 in January to 131,660 in December; the equivalent numbers given by UNHCR Sudan were 117,320 and 125,530, respectively. This meant that close to 3,000 Eritreans fled their country every month, many of them unaccompanied minors. The *smuggling and trafficking of Eritreans* from Sudan to Libya and Egypt with the involvement of the Rashaida tribe and corrupt Eritrean and Sudanese officials remained an issue of concern, especially in eastern Sudan, where numerous Eritreans were abducted from refugee camps. The Sudanese authorities made some effort to curb the activities of people traffickers in the framework of the multilateral *Khartoum Process*, but the Eritrean government's response to the population outflow was ambivalent. On the one hand, government representatives, including presidential adviser Yemane Gebreab, downplayed the refugee movement and claimed that a high proportion of the refugees were Ethiopians masquerading as Eritreans. On the other, the Ministry of Foreign Affairs complained in a letter to the UNSC in July that organised people trafficking gangs were behind the Eritrean exodus in order "to prevent Eritrea and its people from defending their sovereignty by dispersing and debilitating their human resources".

The *human rights* situation remained abysmal and the population enjoyed no civil liberties. Eritrea continued to be ranked lowest in Reporters Without Borders' press freedom report and 23 *journalists remained behind bars* without due process, which made Eritrea the country with the third-largest number of jailed journalists behind China and Iran. The surviving members of the G15, a group of leading People's Front for Democracy and Justice (PFDJ) officials who had demanded reforms in 2001, remained behind bars without due process. *Violations of religious freedom* also continued: Pentecostal churches and Jehovah's Witnesses were banned and their members systematically persecuted, while state involvement in the religious affairs of the Orthodox Church and the Muslim community continued. On 21 December, the head of the Orthodox Church, Abune Dioskoros, died. He had been appointed in 2007, after government pressure led to the dismissal of his predecessor, Abune Antonios, who had remained under house arrest ever since. In June, the *Commission of Inquiry on Human Rights in Eritrea* (COIE), established by the UN Human Rights Council, issued a comprehensive report. The main findings were that systematic, widespread and gross human rights violations were being committed in Eritrea and that the main perpetrators could be identified as the Eritrean defence forces, the national security office, the police, the ruling PFDJ and the president himself. The COIE pointed out that there was no independent judiciary, prison conditions were extremely harsh and torture and mistreatment widespread. It also decried *open-ended national service* as a form of systematic forced labour and concluded that these violations, especially in relation to extrajudicial executions, torture and forced labour, might constitute crimes against humanity.

In January, the clandestine resistance movement 'Arbi Harnet' (Freedom Friday) reported that the authorities had retaliated against families of elderly citizens who had refused to join the neighbourhood militia by confiscating the family's food coupons. In March, the government started a programme of *house demolitions* in suburbs of Asmara as well as in Adi Qeyih (Southern Region). When secondary school students in Adi Qeyih protested against the arbitrary destruction of hundreds of homes, security forces killed at least two people and injured 13. Many of the affected houses had been financed by remittances from national service conscripts who had fled the country.

Eritrea's *judicial system* remained in a poor state and the formal court system continued to suffer from government interference. In May, new civil, penal, civil procedure and penal procedure codes were introduced to replace the transitional law codes inherited from Ethiopia. The *new laws* were supposed to incorporate sources of customary law, but it was unclear how far the new penal code would be implemented, since there was a severe shortage of qualified judicial personnel, and imprisonment for political reasons as well as arrests for alleged criminal offences regularly took place without any formal legal process. *Corruption* remained endemic, especially since many public sector employees were national service recruits whose wages did not cover their cost of living. High-ranking PFDJ cadres and military personnel were involved in *contraband trade and trafficking conscripts* over the borders. TI's Corruption Perception Index ranked Eritrea as highly corrupt (154th out of 167 countries).

The Eritrean diaspora was deeply split between government supporters and opponents. Pro- and anti-government *diaspora groups organised demonstrations* in Geneva (Switzerland) in June either to condemn or to praise the work of the COIE. Threats against COIE representatives by a group of regime supporters were taken so seriously that security forces were doubled for their protection. On the other hand, several thousand Eritreans who supported the political and/or civil society opposition organised a demonstration in Geneva on 26 June in support of the COIE's work and findings. In November, various opposition parties and civil society organisations participated in a workshop in Frankfurt (Germany) to exchange views.

Foreign Affairs

The *targeted sanctions* imposed on Eritrea by the UNSC in December 2009 (resolution 1907/2009) and in December 2011 (resolution 2023/2011) were not annulled, as the Eritrean government had repeatedly demanded. In a letter to the UNSC dated 22 September, the Somalia Eritrea Monitoring Group (SEMG) stated that it had found no evidence of Eritrean support for the Somali al-Shabaab *militias*. However, the government hosted, trained and supported militant Ethiopian opposition groups (TPDM and Ginbot 7) on its soil and had furthermore entered into a new strategic *military partnership with Saudi Arabia and the UAE*. Saudi Arabia and Eritrea had in fact come to an agreement on fighting terrorism, illegal trade and piracy in the Red Sea during a two-day visit by President Isaias to Riyadh in late April. The arrangement included the government's permission to grant the use of Eritrean land, airspace and territorial waters to the Arab anti-Houthi coalition in its military campaign in Yemen in exchange for monetary compensation and fuel deliveries. A few hundred Eritrean soldiers were also apparently embedded in a UAE contingent fighting the Houthis on Yemeni soil, which would constitute a *severe breach of the sanctions* regime. The SEMG also confirmed that the Eritrean government had failed to acknowledge that it held Djiboutian prisoners of war, and no progress was made in resolving Eritrea's conflict with *Djibouti*. President Isaias travelled to Riyadh again on 21 December and discussed means of coordinating the fight against terrorism with the Saudi Arabian king and his defence minister. The visit followed a one-day stopover by the emir of *Qatar*, Sheikh Tamim bin Hamad Al-Thani, in Asmara on 18 December, during which he promised increased investment in Eritrea. Qatar and Saudi Arabia had improved their mutual relations and were working on a joint strategy to counter the growing strength of Iranian proxy groups, including the Houthis in Yemen. Given that Eritrean–Qatari relations had deteriorated significantly after the retirement of the current emir's father and predecessor Sheikh Hamad bin Khalifa and that it was highly unusual for a Qatari head of state to visit Eritrea, it seemed that the Gulf states involved in the anti-Houthi campaign considered Eritrea as an important strategic ally. Eritrea's willingness to make a political shift from cooperating with Iran's pro-Houthi alliance could be seen as an attempt to overcome its international isolation and to secure fresh funds from the oil-rich Arab nations.

Ethiopia was worried about the Eritrean rapprochement with Saudi Arabia and other Gulf states. In December, Ethiopia's Prime Minister Hailemariam Dessalegn warned in an interview that Saudi Arabia and the UAE would have to bear the consequences of Ethiopia's response if their operations in and around Eritrea's port of Assab supported the "Eritrean regime's destabilisation agenda against Ethiopia".

The *stalemate between Eritrea and Ethiopia* continued, and no fresh initiatives were started to overcome the political standstill over their unresolved border issue. Ethiopia continued to reject the implementation of the 2002 Eritrea Ethiopia Boundary Commission's verdict and did not hand the territory surrounding the border town of Badme over to Eritrea, while Asmara instrumentalised the no-war-no-peace situation to justify the open-ended national service imposed on its population. On 21 March, social media reports indicated that the Sudanese 'Al Sahafa' newspaper had reported an *air attack* carried out by the Ethiopian air force on the Bisha mine in Eritrea, a joint-venture of the state-owned Eritrean Mining Company ENAMCO and the Canadian Nevsun Mining Corporation. Several Ethiopian radio stations confirmed the attack and the Ethiopian newspaper 'Awramba Times' quoted an unnamed high-ranking military officer who claimed that the Ethiopian air force had bombed targets inside Eritrea. One day later, Nevsun confirmed that "an act of vandalism" had occurred at the Bisha mine, but asserted that the impact had been minimal and no one had been hurt. Neither the Eritrean nor the Ethiopian government had anything to say about these events. One possible explanation for the incident was that it had been an act of sabotage, possibly from within the Eritrean military.

Eritrean–Sudanese relations remained close and Sudan's President Omar al-Bashir was probably acting as a broker in Eritrea's deal with Saudi Arabia and the UAE to join the anti-Houthi campaign. Isaias travelled to Khartoum for a working visit on 11–13 June and met with al-Bashir and Sudanese government officials to discuss economic cooperation and shared security issues. However, Isaias had failed to attend al-Bashir's swearing-in ceremony ten days earlier, in contrast to numerous African leaders, including Ethiopia's Prime Minister Hailemariam. Similarly, Isaias had avoided the third COMESA-EAC-SADC Tripartite Summit in Sharm al-Sheikh (Egypt) on 10 June, where al-Bashir, Hailemariam and Egypt's President Abdel Fattah el-Sisi had met for tripartite consultations concerning the Nile water conflict. Isaias had been invited to attend the meeting by Egypt's Foreign Minister Sameh Shoukry, who visited Eritrea on 7 May to discuss the Yemen crisis and Red Sea security. On 25–27 April, a *South Sudanese* delegation headed by the government's chief negotiator Nhial Deng Nhial visited Asmara and delivered a message from President Salva Kiir. Isaias warned his guests to be aware of the possible negative consequences of foreign intervention in the South Sudanese conflict, probably referring to Ethiopia's prominent role in the conflict mediation process. In the past, the South Sudanese government had accused Eritrea of supporting armed oppositions groups such as the South Sudan Democratic Movement led by late George Athor Deng.

There were no high-level meetings between Eritrean and Russian officials during the year and *no indications of Russian investment* in Eritrea's emerging mining industry, a prospect that had been presented by Russia's Foreign Minister Sergei Lavrov in 2014.

Israel continued to hold thousands of Eritrean refugees at the Holot facility under prison-like conditions and expelled Eritrean 'infiltrators' to the allegedly secure host countries Uganda and Rwanda. Israeli investigators found out that Eritreans arriving in Rwanda were trafficked to Uganda immediately after their arrival with the cooperation of Israeli authorities; most of them were living in precarious conditions in Kampala without secured refugee status.

The numbers of *Eritrean refugees* reaching *Europe* via the Mediterranean soared to more than 30,000 in 2014 and a similar number in 2015, with Sweden, Germany, Switzerland, the Netherlands and Norway receiving the highest number of asylum applications filed by Eritreans. As a consequence, several European leaders sought to improve relations with the regime in Asmara in order to curb the refugee influx. A number of *European delegations* travelled to Asmara to call for political reforms, respect for human rights and a reorganisation of the national service system, in exchange for financial support. An Italian delegation that included the Directors of International Cooperation and Migration Issues held talks with the Eritrean government on 24–26 March and received promises from presidential adviser Yemane Gebreab that Eritrea would be a democracy in three to five years' time. In May, a Norwegian secretary of state tried unsuccessfully to broker a deal with the Eritrean government to accept the repatriation of refugees from Norway. A precondition for such a deal would have been a guarantee that Eritrea respected the human rights of the returnees and granted international fact-finding missions access to the country. Germany's Minister for International Cooperation and Development Gerd Müller visited Asmara on 15 December and met Isaias to discuss human rights, the national service and the problem of the refugee exodus. Eritrean embassies, consulates and government middlemen in the diaspora faced no tangible restraints regarding the collection of the 2% *diaspora tax* levied by the regime on diaspora Eritreans' incomes, although these activities were restricted under the 2011 sanctions regime.

Relations between the *USA* and Eritrea remained poor and no ambassadors were exchanged. However, the American chief of mission in Asmara, Louis Mazel, tried to improve relations by publicly painting a positive picture of the situation in Eritrea. In December, he posted on his Facebook page an extremely optimistic report of his impressions during a government-guided visit to the Bisha mine, without reflecting critical reports by human rights organisations that had deplored the use of forced labour and poor working conditions for local labourers employed at the extraction site.

Socioeconomic Developments

The Eritrean economy remained firmly under the control of the ruling PFDJ and the high-ranking military, and private small business activities were strictly controlled. On 3 November, the Bank of Eritrea issued a decree (legal notice 124/2015) noting that a *currency reform* was underway and that all citizens had to exchange the nakfa (ERN) notes in their possession for new government-issued bank notes on a one-for-one basis. This process was to be conducted over a period of six weeks. Significantly, each individual was allowed to exchange only ERN 20,000 in cash, and any remaining amount in his or her possession had to be deposited in a national bank. Reasons given for this reform were that it would contain the black market and inflation and combat corruption and trade in contraband by controlling illicit business activities. During previous years, many PFDJ-loyal business people, military personnel and party cadres had amassed large sums of money in cash either through contraband trade, corruption and people smuggling or through black-market transactions. In addition, the vast majority of diaspora Eritreans, instead of using state-owned exchange bureaus, sent their private remittances through the Hawala system, which gave them a rate of between ERN 50 and ERN 58 to the dollar, while the official exchange rate had been fixed at ERN 15 : $ 1 for years. By obliging people to deposit sums exceeding ERN 20,000 in a bank account, the government forced its citizens either to reveal how much money they had and face possible punishment for being involved in illicit activities, or to forfeit the fortune they had amassed. During the exchange process, which lasted until the end of the year, many people who turned in their nakfa notes did not receive any new currency, especially in the rural areas, and were told to wait till later. In addition, a new rule was introduced that limited the amount that could be withdrawn from private bank accounts to ERN 5,000 per family per month, no matter what the size of the family.

Shortages of basic consumer goods and fuel continued, regular electricity blackouts even in the capital Asmara remained common, and no investments were made in urban infrastructure projects. It was expected that the *chronic food insecurity* prevailing in the country might increase dramatically due to failed rains related to the El Niño weather phenomenon. FAO reports indicated that Eritrean coastal areas received almost no rain, and that rainfall throughout the country was 30%–35% below average. As usual, the government did not publish any nutrition-related data and denied aid agencies access to its territory. President Isaias publicly denied the existence of any foot shortages in his New Year interview, rejecting UN food aid for the country's citizens. The Global Huger Index 2015 did not rank Eritrea due to a lack of data; it had consistently described the nutritional situation in the country as "extremely alarming" in recent years.

The *Warsay-Yikealo Development Campaign*, introduced in 2002 as a form of open-ended *national service* for all Eritreans of productive age, remained in place and no demobilisation took place. National service conscripts were employed in infrastructure projects run by PFDJ-owned construction companies, in military-run agricultural farms, and in the public administration. Presidential adviser Yemane Gebreab promised Western delegations that the latest round of recruits would be demobilised after serving 18 months (the original duration of the service), but state media did not publish this news inside the country.

The EU resumed *development aid*, which had been terminated in 2011 by request of the Eritrean government. The decision to resume support to the autocratic government had been controversial, and the decision was driven by the desire of many European countries to curb the influx of Eritrean refugees. The EU granted € 200 m in long-term support to promote poverty reduction and socio-economic development through the 11th EDF between 2016 and 2020. The money was intended to be channelled to the areas of energy and governance. Some of the reasons given for this decision were that a more efficient energy network would have a broad positive effect on social and economic development, and that the government should be enabled to improve its management of public finances.

As usual, statistical data were unreliable and erratic. According to UNICEF data, under-five mortality stood at a low of 50 out of 1,000 live births, but only one-third of all births were attended by skilled health personnel. Two-thirds of all children of primary school age were out of *school*, and only 22% attended secondary education. Surprisingly, the literacy rate for 15–24-year-olds was indicated as being 90%. *Inflation* was 11.6% (2014) and the economy grew by 2.1%, but *exports* depended almost exclusively on *copper* produced at the Bisha mine. The current account balance was estimated at –2.23% of GDP.

Ethiopia

Jon Abbink

The main political events of the year were the May national parliamentary elections and the massive Oromo revolt against the Addis Ababa Masterplan, which had aimed to incorporate Oromo farmlands. The elections were won, as expected, by the ruling EPRDF, with none of the 547 seats conceded to the opposition. It was a lacklustre and subdued event, with little international press coverage, and was regarded with deep scepticism and scorn by Ethiopian opposition parties, independent observers and most of the international community. The Oromo revolt led to major upheaval, with some 400 people killed and the government's land policy at risk.

Controversies over the closed political process, the impunity of the security forces, media repression, land issues and large-scale land investment schemes continued, turning violent in some places.

There were visits by some prominent world leaders and ministers, among them US President Barack Obama, who also attended a meeting at the AU headquarters in Addis Ababa.

 | DOI 10.1163/9789004333239_035

Ethiopia received tens of thousands of refugees from surrounding countries – Somalia, Eritrea and South Sudan (in the wake of the civil war there) – cared for mostly by UNHCR, and saw an almost equal number of out-migrants.

Relations with its neighbours, except Eritrea, were stable and rather cooperative, with a closer bond emerging with Djibouti. The Nile issue was unresolved, however, despite some signs of more cooperation between the Nile Basin countries.

In the economic domain, GDP growth and massive infrastructure growth proceeded, with the Gibe III hydro-power dam lake starting to fill up, amidst ongoing controversy over its negative effects on the environment and the livelihoods of downstream peoples. The second Growth and Transformation Plan (GTP) for 2015–20 was promulgated in September, but was not published, still being fine-tuned by policymakers. In effect, it meant continuity with GTP I, with no policy changes. Donor countries and the IMF and World Bank had no qualms about keeping donor funds flowing, despite serious repression of human rights, a restrictive private business environment, growing environmental problems and unsolved food security issues.

Domestic Affairs

Domestically, two events stood out: the May parliamentary elections and the Oromo farmers' revolt around Addis Ababa, resulting in death and destruction.

The *elections* for the Ethiopian House of People's Representatives took place on 24 May. They were preceded by a subdued and very lacklustre electoral campaign, in which the ruling Ethiopian Peoples' Revolutionary Democratic Front (EPRDF), in power since 1991, held all the trump cards. Many opposition party candidates were forbidden from running by the National Electoral Board. There were a few debates on national television, but campaigning by opposition groups was severely curtailed and hindered, notably outside the capital. Several opposition demonstrations were violently put down, as on 18 January in Addis Ababa, with dozens or people seriously injured. No foreign observers attended on election day, apart from an AU delegation, and a sense of competition was absent. Several prominent opposition leaders, including of the Unity for Democracy and Justice (UDJ) party, were jailed before the elections.

The elections themselves were well organised and largely peaceful, with voters having been urged if not compelled to vote by the authorities. Although a significant part of the population voted out of conviction, many others had no trust in the secrecy of the ballot and voted for the ruling party, unwilling to take a risk. Still, more than 500 members of the Ethiopian Federal Democratic Unity Forum or *Medreq* coalition were arrested at polling stations in Oromia region before and on election day, and 46 people were beaten and injured during the elections; six people sustained gunshot wounds and two were reported killed. The report by the

AU group praised the "peaceful and orderly" conduct of the elections but fell short of endorsing them as democratic or competitive.

The elections led to *a win of all the 547 seats for the EPRDF* and its various constituent (ethnic) parts, and they also took 100% of the seats in the 108-member *House of Federation* and the nine state regional assemblies. This result, declared on 22 June, was received with suspicion and scepticism across the board. Not all voters had voted for the ruling party, but the 'first-past-the-post' system meant that representation of opposition voices was impossible. Election Board officials and local authorities were anxious to prevent an opposition party win in their constituency and used all means to prevent it. The main opposition parties, the Medreq coalition (consisting of the Oromo Federalist Congress [OFC], Oromo National Congress, Arena-Tigray, the Ethiopian Social Democratic Party-Southern Ethiopia Unity Party, the All-Ethiopia Unity Party, and the Unity for Democracy and Justice [UDJ]), plus the independent 'Semayawi' (Blue) Party (mainly with a younger constituency), were disappointed if not appalled, although they had seen it coming. Neither of them secured a seat. The result had little credibility and effectively made the political process, let alone 'democracy', in Ethiopia irrelevant, with the ruling party positioning itself, in the words of opposition, for "continued eating" and "perpetual" power. The EPRDF showed no desire to engage in any national dialogue or debate about policy alternatives and the parliamentary sessions after May reflected this. A further post-election media crackdown also followed, with critical or independent journalists not tolerated and the Internet seriously censored. On global indexes, Ethiopia scored worst in Africa for Internet use and freedom.

Internationally, the response to the elections was muted. The US government and the EU showed no interest and issued cautious statements that they, respectively, "... remain committed to working with the Ethiopian Government" and "... look forward to continuing and deepening ... partnership".

Opposition politicians continued to be intimidated and targeted by the regime. Four opposition party members were reportedly killed in the post-election months. OFC leader Beqele Gerba, who was released in March after serving a four-year jail term, was arrested again on 25 December in connection with his alleged role in the Oromo protests against the land confiscation around Addis Ababa. Again, the charges had little evidence to stand on.

In the post-election consolidation of the regime, Prime Minister Hailemariam Dessalegn, seen as a transitional figure after the death of former prime minister Meles Zenawi in 2012, was able to consolidate his position and was re-elected as leader of the EPRDF and as prime minister. He went through a severe internal party grilling (performance evaluation session, or *gimgema*) on 11 May, but survived it. After an EPRDF congress in August, consolidating the policies followed thus far, a new cabinet was installed in October, with a reshuffle of some personnel and many new state ministers positions (bringing the total to about 80), with their own lavish budgets for new four-wheel drive cars and office furniture.

A major crisis was precipitated by *mass Oromo protests* in November–December against 'land development' and investments around the capital in connection with the Addis Ababa Master Plan, which envisaged steady expansion of the metropolis into surrounding areas inhabited mainly by Oromo farmers. (The master plan potentially encompassed an area at least ten times the current size of the capital.) In November, Oromo in and around the villages of Wolenkomi, Yubdo, Chanqa, Finch'a, Ginch'i, and some other places protested publicly against encroaching private investors who said they were acting under the Master Plan. Their slogans were: "Oromiya is not for sale", "Killing is not an answer to our grievances", and "We want genuine self-rule". With all land in Ethiopia being state-owned, the Addis Ababa Masterplan was legal, and failed only in its authoritarian implementation and by not providing compensation for farmers losing their land. Students at Addis Ababa, Haromaya and other universities staged protests in solidarity.

In the ensuing clashes, around *400 people were killed by the security forces*, including children and pregnant women, and in some confrontations several policemen also died. About 3,500 people were arrested. Journalists covering the protests, including Feqadu Mirkana of state-run Oromia Radio-TV, were also arrested. Among the foreign-owned farms that were attacked and burnt down was Solagrow, a Dutch farm that had fenced off 100 ha of communal grazing land from local people. The owner, operating under a government lease, lost a $ 300,000 investment. There was criticism within the EPRDF of its Oromo branch, the Oromo Peoples' Democratic Organisation, and some of its 'corrupt members', who were said to be responsible for the problems. The prime minister said on 20 December that the "recent question raised by the people of Oromia was a legitimate one", and that the Master Plan should have been drawn up "in consultation with the people of Oromia". But he added that "merciless legitimate action against any force bent on destabilizing the area" would be used. The Master Plan was suspended, but of consultations nothing was heard. The prime minister's statement that "the ruling party has never imposed a single developmental plan on the public without its will" was incorrect and accepted by few.

Press and media freedoms continued to suffer, with no real independent opinions allowed to flourish. Internet, telephone and e-mail traffic was seriously monitored with the help of sophisticated surveillance technology (e.g., with Chinese expertise and Germany's Trovicor data interception software) and a repressive police apparatus, leading to the arrest of more independent journalists and bloggers as well as periodic closures of social media sites. The state-run Ethio-Telecom Corporation was the only Internet provider that was allowed to operate. A widespread network of paid informants and an extensive phone tapping system restricted free speech, even in the private sphere and security forces generally acted with impunity.

Ethiopia was 4th on the global list of *'most censored' countries* drawn up by the Committee to Protect Journalists, with 17 journalists in jail, others forced into exile, and court cases ongoing against several bloggers. A prominent jailed journalist,

Temesgen Dessalegn, was denied medical treatment. Five of the 17 in prison were released before a visit by US President Barack Obama in July. Evidence of reporters' wrongdoing was very slim if not non-existent, and their convictions reflected government/party intolerance of any criticism.

Political freedoms further declined on all indexes, with the Freedom House Index again rating Ethiopia 'not free', with civil liberties and political rights a low 6 on a scale of 7.

In July, the *Federal High Court sentenced 18 Muslim activists* connected to the wave of Muslim public protests against "government interference in their internal affairs" in 2012–14. While these protests had been largely peaceful, the government saw elements of radicalisation and threats to public order and the delicate balance between faith communities. It had condemned the ideological and financial links of Muslim institutions such as the Awoliya Muslim College and some Muslim NGOs with foreign powers such as Saudi Arabia and Qatar. While the evidence against the Muslim leaders, detained since late 2012, was slight and circumstantial, they received jail sentences of five to 22 years for "terrorism and conspiracy to create an Islamic state".

In the domain of higher education, *academic freedom was restricted*, and university teachers and students walked a tightrope. The government continued to put party members in charge of university presidencies and suppressed critical public discourse, regularly accusing the university community of being 'pro-opposition'. Several academics critical of the government were denied tenure or contract renewal after retirement age. In March, philosophy professor Dagnachew Assefa was fired, apparently for criticism of the government. There was also strong pressure on students to join the EPRDF, with the prospect of securing a job. Curricula and research were increasingly monitored by the Ministry of Education, and freedom of assembly of staff and students was restricted.

The political situation in the rest of the country was marked by armed peace but also by several *low-key armed insurgencies*, with the *Ogaden problem* in the Somali Regional State continuing. While a part of the Ogaden National Liberation Front (ONLF) submitted and sought a compromise with the government after negotiations, another part continued its rebellion, but much weakened. The government played on clan-group differences in the Somali population (about 45% of the Somali Region's population belong to the Ogaden clan-family). On 26–29 May, armed clashes led to dozens of people being killed, with accusations of mass repression and rape of civilians, including, for example, in Shilaabo district, where government special forces, the 'Liyyu Police', were said to be involved. Its former commander Abdi Mohamed Omar (of the Reer Abdullah–Ogaden clan) continued as Somali Region president. The federal government was bent on keeping this region under complete control because of its proven large natural gas deposits and expected oil finds.

In the restive *Gambella region* in the West, insurgency by disgruntled and marginalised Anywa people (who had lost much of their land to government-supported investors and were threatened by the ongoing influx of Nuer people into their area) continued. Tensions between Nuer and Anywa remained at dangerous levels. The Majangir minority in Gambela also continued to suffer from government repression and land dispossession. In South Omo, a violent clash in May led to the security forces killing about 50 local people.

As well as the ONLF, there were smaller movements such as the Benishangul People's Liberation Movement, the Gambella People's Liberation Movement, the Oromo Liberation Front and the Sidama National Liberation Front. In October they concluded an alliance, the People's Alliance for Freedom and Democracy. In the north there was a movement allied to the Ginbot-7 party, with a base in Asmara (Eritrea). But none of these insurgency movements were regime-threatening.

Ethnic clashes occurred here and there in the country, revealing the unresolved problem of ethnic conflict management in the political system. On 12 December, a major confrontation between Oromo and Amhara in Ameya *woreda* (district) of Oromiya State erupted, with at least five people killed, ten houses burnt down, and many families dispossessed and fleeing. It was allegedly instigated by local (Oromo) government officials. Ongoing clashes also occurred between some ethnic groups in the south-west.

On 21 April, *public protests* erupted in Addis Ababa, following the circulation of a disturbing video recording of ISIS ('Islamic State') adherents decapitating what were probably Ethiopian Christian migrants in Libya. Demonstrators took to the streets and scuffles with the police followed, ending in a repression of the protest, with 48 people injured and hundreds arrested.

Overall, *religious relations* were accommodative, but tensions between Orthodox Christians, Pentecostal-Evangelical Christians and Muslims of various denominations remained present; strong rivalry continued under the surface and openly on Internet sites, with harsh polemical attacks. Several groups of ISIS sympathisers emerged and a number of them were arrested. On 11 December, a grenade exploded in the compound of the Anwar (Grand) Mosque in Addis Ababa, injuring 24 people. The attack was probably related to intra-Muslim rivalries.

Foreign Affairs

Ethiopia maintained good bilateral relations with Somaliland, the Somali Transitional Federal Government (TGF), which it supported militarily, Kenya, Djibouti and Sudan. It opened new talks with *Somaliland* on the future use of Berbera port. With *Kenya* there were some tensions over policy in southern Somalia.

Relations with *Eritrea* remained at a low ebb – in fact were absent – because of the continued stalemate on the border demarcation issue, now entering its 13th year. There were no new initiatives or pressure to resolve the matter, except that the Ethiopian prime minister said he would be prepared to meet and talk with the Eritrean president. The latter refused. The stream of Eritrean migrants/refugees into northern Ethiopia continued (although the majority exited via Sudan). Refugee camps were maintained in the Tigray region to accommodate them. In September, a remarkable episode unfolded when the core of the Tigray Peoples Democratic Movement (TPDM), a formerly anti-Ethiopian government group located in Eritrea under the protection of the Eritrean regime, defected to Ethiopia. Under its leader Captain Molla Asghedom, the force of about 700 men battled Eritrean border forces near Umm-Hajer and Seq al-Ketir, and entered Ethiopia via Sudan. The background to this event seems to have been the refusal of the TPDM to ally with the anti-EPRDF Ginbot-7 movement led by Berhanu Nega, which operated from Asmara, and wanted to unite all factions.

There were government negotiations with *Sudan* on finalising border corrections on the 725 km border between the two countries, including in the Al-Fashaga agricultural area east of Gedaref. Informal reports of Ethiopia giving land to Sudan led to these negotiations being contested.

Ethiopia remained the *key player in IGAD*. Ethiopia's representative Seyoum Mesfin (ambassador to China) was involved in IGAD-sponsored mediation talks between the combatants in South Sudan (SPLM and SPLM-In-Opposition) to reach a compromise, but these talks ended in failure early in the year.

The *Nile issue* stayed high on the agenda, with Ethiopia making conciliatory noises to Egypt but not changing its policy of unilateral hydro-thermal energy structure expansion via the Grand Renaissance Dam, about 45 km from the Sudanese border. The work on this project progressed, but slowly because of insecure funding (mainly domestic, as international partners had withdrawn). Egypt's concerns about the water level of the Nile were not alleviated, despite a rhetoric of cooperation and 'win-win'. On 23 March, the leaders of *Egypt, Ethiopia and Sudan signed a Declaration of Principles* in Khartoum (Sudan) on the regulation of Nile water use. It was a political deal, sidestepping the controversies ahead. Under the declaration, a technical committee was appointed by the three countries to oversee the dam's construction, but it would "... not be allowed to visit the dam or to witness the work on the site", thus precluding an evidence-based assessment of the dam's environmental impact.

With Addis Ababa as the *headquarters of the AU*, Ethiopia played a prominent role in Africa, but one growing problem, also voiced by some African diplomats, was the restrictive security regime around the AU, with the Ethiopians monitoring and screening visitors, suppressing free reporting and constraining media. This had a negative effect on the AU itself.

China, the EU and India remained major economic and trade partners of Ethiopia, providing most of the FDI, although the Chinese involvement was slowing down.

Ethiopia was visited by a number of *foreign dignitaries and delegations*. In January, Egypt's President Abdel-Fatah al-Sisi was in Addis Ababa to attend the AU summit opening session and consult with Ethiopian leaders (his visit being cut short by terrorist attacks in the Sinai by ISIS-affiliated groups). In the same month, Turkish leader Recep Tayyip Erdoğan paid an official visit, accompanied by ministers, bureaucrats and businesspeople. On 13–17 February, Seán Sherlock, the Irish minister of state for development, trade promotion and north-south co-operation, visited Ethiopia for talks on trade and investment opportunities, and Irina Bokova, head of UNESCO, visited on 23 March. She participated in the Women in Parliaments Global Forum Summit at the AU headquarters, and also met with Ethiopian Prime Minister Hailemariam and President Mulatu Demeqe. Also in March, Gil Haskel, head of Israel's Agency of International Cooperation MASHAV, came for a tour of agricultural projects, on which he was accompanied by Israel's ambassador in Ethiopia, Belaynesh Zevadia, and met with Ethiopia's Foreign Minister Tedros Adhanom.

On 16–17 April, Rwandan President Paul Kagame made a state visit, to discuss regional cooperation, trade and investment and "learning from both nations' experiences in peace and security", in which these two authoritarian governments did indeed have much in common. July saw a visit by two ministers of state from India.

A Japanese Development Ministry team including the permanent secretary of the Ministry of Industry and Trade (MIT) and the deputy permanent secretary of the Ministry of Finance visited Ethiopia from 28 September to 1 October to promote the *Kaizen* management system among government and companies. (The Kaizen system was included in the GTP II Plan.)

On 20–21 October, EU foreign affairs representative Federica Mogherini visited Addis Ababa for meetings with the AU (on the African Peace Facility, AMISOM and other security issues) and the Ethiopian government to discuss "economic growth, investments, climate change and migration issues". On 23 October, a Swiss delegation led by President Simonetta Sommaruga arrived to discuss the intensification of Swiss-Ethiopian bilateral relations. In December, French Minister of State for Foreign Trade Matthias Fekl visited the country for similar purposes, accompanied by a delegation representing some 40 French businesses.

October also saw a visit by fashion and entertainment world icon Victoria Beckham, active in philanthropic work, who visited youth groups and met with the Ethiopian minister of health. Another humanitarian visit was by Belgium's Queen Mathilde, honorary chair of UNICEF-Belgium, who was in Ethiopia on 9–12 November, visiting projects regarding the survival and wellbeing of children.

From the north-east African region, Addis Ababa was visited by politicians from *Somalia*, including on 9 March the new Somali TFG prime minister, Omar Abidrashid Ali Sharmarke, to discuss regional security and defence issues, and later in the year Abdikarim Guled, head of the Galmudug Interim Administration, and Puntland leader Abdiweli Mohamed Ali.

Prime Minister Hailemariam made a number of foreign visits. On 7 February, he was in Djibouti for talks with President Ismail Omar Guelleh, concluding cooperation agreements on economic integration, transport (new railroad links), power and energy, and foreign relations. On 8 June, he was present for the second day of the summit of G7 nations in Germany, and he visited Rwanda in August, following up on Kagame's visit to Addis Ababa in April. He went to China in September, for talks on economic cooperation and to attend the 70th anniversary of the end of WWII in Asia, and was in India on 26–29 October for the India-Africa Forum Summit. Finally, in December, Hailemariam attended the UN COP-21 Paris climate change summit.

A foreign policy highlight of the year was the visit on 27–28 July to Addis Ababa by *US President Barack Obama*, as part of a brief African tour. His planned visit was contested by a large part of the Ethiopian-American community, which in general remained very critical of the Addis Ababa regime. Obama was the first US president to visit the country. He met with Hailemariam and addressed the AU meeting at AU headquarters on 28 July on the subjects of economic opportunities in and for Africa and the need for the continent to have a democratic political future. In what was widely seen by opposition groups and analysts as a propaganda coup for the Ethiopian government, Obama gave a speech on Ethiopia in which he spoke of the "legitimately elected government" and referred in only subdued terms to the problematic human rights situation and political and media repression. He lauded the country's major role in battling *al-Shabaab* terror in the region.

Socioeconomic Developments

A *major drought* severely impacted food production and threw millions of people into dangerous, food-insecure conditions. According to UNICEF, toward the end of the year the total number of people affected was 10.2 m (of whom 5.7 m were children). Food, clean water, medical treatment, etc. had to be provided in aid. Cognisant of Ethiopia's problematic image as the perennial hunger country of Africa, the government was reluctant to publicise the situation, but again asked international donors for massive *food and humanitarian aid*, requesting $ 596 m in October. It said it had itself allocated $ 192 m to combat the crisis. In December, the government revised the amount needed to $ 1.4 bn, with a request that donors please pay.

The 'El Niño-effect' was blamed for the drought, but the crisis showed again that *agricultural production* and distribution were still not effective. The systemic lack of land property rights and the restriction of the small-holder sector did not stimulate local agrarian entrepreneurship and disadvantaged small farmers, and agro-pastoral production systems were similarly undermined. In addition, uncontrolled population growth played its part.

The various large-scale *land investment schemes* by both foreigners and local investors were not universally successful, and many collapsed for lack of preparation and failure to realise investment plans. Domestic agrarian investors tended to be urbanites who acquired land lease concessions for investment through agencies in the capital and engaged local former farmers and labourers for low wages, which only partly compensated them for the attendant loss of their land. The government became more cautious regarding allocation of land for investment and formulated somewhat stricter conditions for those leasing it.

An important development was the promulgation in September of the second phase of the *Growth and Transformation Plan* (GTP II). In this new five-year plan (2015–20), further GDP growth was foreseen, with expansion and commercialisation of agriculture, and infrastructural and hydro-energy construction, despite the criticism of social and ecological impacts by experts over recent years. More emphasis was also placed on industrial development and the interest of foreign parties in industrial investment steadily grew over the year. The GTP II also hinted at a renewed emphasis on manufacturing, with top party people and policy advisors aiming at a ten-year trajectory to make Ethiopia a major manufacturing hub with the sector as the main absorber of the approximately 2 m people entering the labour market every year. Major attractions for global investors were the very low wage costs and the availability of subsidised facilities in the first few years. Hindrances were the difficult and unpredictable regulatory environment and the government obsession with control. Industrial development was manifested in the planned construction of several new industrial parks in the cities of Hawassa (built by the Chinese and to be inaugurated in 2016), Dire Dawa, Kombolcha and Meqelle (in the north) and Adama (or Nazret). They would offer land at $ 1 per square metre a month to factories investing.

On 21 September, the Chinese–built Addis Ababa Light-Rail was opened in the capital, a two-line 34 km urban transport system, and one of the first in Africa, built with a Chinese loan of $ 475 m. Tickets were affordable at ETB (birr) 6 ($ 0.3) and state-subsidised.

The 1,870-MW *hydropower dam Gibe-III* reached completion and started producing electricity in October. Fears were expressed by various experts that it might suffer from silting up, as had happened with the Gilgel-Gibe I dam, and be vulnerable to periodic droughts. The reduction in the downstream flow of the Omo River had already affected various local peoples: the pastures and food retreat cultivation systems of the Bodi, Mursi, Kara, Nyangatom and Kwegu were impacted, with food insecurity and hunger as a result. The previously announced 'controlled flood release' did not occur, further undermining agriculture. Plans for building the *Gibe-IV* and *Gibe V* dams on the Omo, south of Gibe-III, were reconfirmed, again with a non-transparent bidding process and informal consent given by the government to the Italian construction company Salini to build the Gibe IV as well. Nothing was heard of environmental and social impact studies. Not all water management experts understood the logic of this dam, and local people were again shocked at these non-negotiated plans and the possibly devastating impact on their lands and livelihoods.

On 28–29 October, an 'Ethiopia Summit' was held at the Sheraton Hotel, Addis Ababa, organised by the UK's *Economist Intelligence Unit* and attended by government officials, global business executives and leading journalists, on the country's prospects for 'market potential', the telecoms sector, energy policy and manufacturing.

In March, Hailemariam announced *gas production and exports* from the Kalub and Hilala fields in the Ogaden Basin (estimated reserve: 4.7 trn cubic ft), scheduled to begin in 2017. The Chinese company GCL-Poly Petroleum Investments was the partner, and a $ 4 bn pipeline would be built to export the gas via to Djibouti.

In the south, relentless but risky *restructuring of the countryside* continued, including relocation and resettlement of local peoples, massive land clearance and the expansion of sugar plantations along the Omo River, run by MeTEC, the military-industrial complex of the EPRDF party, and the state-owned Ethiopian Sugar Corporation. It was a conflict-ridden process, strongly opposed by native populations in the area, who stood to lose everything in return for only marginal jobs for some of them – as guards, for example. Reports of abuse of local populations' rights in the Omo Valley induced the global retail company Hennes & Mauritz to state in January that it would stop using any cotton from this area, following a similar statement by the German company Tchibo a week earlier, and Turkish Ayka Investment was contemplating doing likewise.

Ethiopia's *economic growth*, as measured in GDP increment, continued; the IMF figure (not corrected for 2.7% population growth) was 8.7%, and GDP reached about $ 61.5 bn. The GDP per capita (current prices) was reported to be $ 597. Annual inflation was still high, at 10.4% (IMF figure). The World Bank (again) noted that the Ethiopian birr was overvalued.

Estimates of development were again variable and primarily measured quantitatively, based mostly on local data provided by the Central Statistical Authority and the IMF and World Bank figures. These showed that poverty, defined as $ 1.25 a day purchasing power, fell during the year by 2%–3%, and applied to 29.5% of the total population. Good qualitative measurements of poverty and well-being were, however, lacking or not considered, and some groups (the urban poor, pastoralists, some farming and occupational groups, and the unemployed) experienced a decline in food security, income and level of well-being.

External debt grew to about 23.4% of GDP, while the budget deficit (budget year ending 30 June) was limited to 2.8%, due to significant capital inflows (mostly donor money to the tune of $ 3.8 bn, of which about 10% was 'humanitarian aid') and an alleged 50% increase in FDI, which reached about $ 2.2 bn. Ethiopia retained one of the highest aid-per-capita ratios at $ 40.5. This was explained by its being seen as the most prominent country in Eastern Africa due to its relative stability and the size of its population, economy and army, and its role in African peacekeeping missions (including AMISOM, and in Darfur-Sudan). The government again effectively harvested the donor money, but this meant in effect that the country was as dependent as ever on external support, while at the same time its totalitarian state-developmental regime was further entrenched.

Remittances from Ethiopians overseas via the Commercial Bank of Ethiopia, the country's largest bank, reached a record estimated $ 3.7 bn, some 40% from the USA. This far surpassed export revenues, and was thus was the country's largest source of income. In addition, substantial unregistered sums also entered the country.

In January, it appeared that the World Bank, a major supporter of Ethiopia's authoritarian development trajectory, had ignored an internal report from its own Inspection Panel on the *abuse of World Bank funds* for Ethiopia's alleged forced relocations/evictions of local people. The report had said there was an 'operational link' between the World Bank-funded programme called 'Protection of Basic Services' and the controversial government 'villagisation' campaign, and noted that "failing to acknowledge this link and take action to protect affected communities constituted a violation of its own policies on project appraisal, risk assessment, financial analysis and protection of indigenous peoples". Similar criticism of the World Bank's involvement in other southern regions, jeopardising the rights of local people, were also heard – and ignored.

In general, the paradox of *GDP growth amidst conditions of serious agrarian under-production, food insecurity and outmigration* of unemployed and dispossessed people was again stark, showing the serious imbalances and inequalities in the national economy, which benefited some sections of the population and hurt others. Ethiopia ranked 173rd of 197 – countries on the HDI. The GINI-coefficient went from 30.1 to 33.3 (for what the incomplete statistical data are worth), indicating increased income inequality.

Ethiopia's *main exports* were gold (21% of total exports), coffee (19%) followed by flowers, live animals, oilseeds and khat. Export revenues totalled caround $ 2.9 bn.

On the *Index of Economic Freedom* (Heritage Foundation), Ethiopia's position was unchanged: 37th in Africa (and 148th in the world), meaning '*mostly unfree*'. Some progress was achieved in public finance management and trade freedom. On TI's Corruption Perception Index, it was 103rd of 168 countries, statistically a two place improvement, but not matched in the public's perception, especially regarding the elites / ruling party members, who had unfair privileges in access to credit, land lease contracts and jobs. A consistent though subdued stream of complaints about this was registered, and much everyday corruption and nepotism stayed out of the books.

Financial freedom was restricted by government efforts to keep a grip on the national economy. Negotiations on WTO membership were again stalled, with Ethiopia – taking a nationalist economic stance – not prepared to open up its financial and banking sector to international capital.

In September, the *IMF* concluded its 2015 *Article IV consultation*, which, while praising overall 'macroeconomic performance', resulted in warnings of too high inflation and high borrowing by public enterprises "with attendant risks of external debt distress". They also advised "decisive action to strengthen the business climate" and "enhance external competitiveness, less burdensome regulation, and easier private sector access to credit and foreign exchange". This was directed at the very dominant hold that the party-state retained over the national economy to the detriment of the private sector. Again, in good IMF fashion, nothing was said on the social and environmental aspects of the growth model, or about overall developmental equity or income distribution patterns.

On 13 August Ethiopia announced a climate resilience strategy plan for the agriculture, forestry, water, irrigation and energy sectors at a meeting with a delegation of the Global Green Growth Institute. It was said to be part of the government's vision to build a climate resilient green economy.

Ethiopia's *population* reached an estimated 92.3 m, continuing a major growth rate. Urbanisation accelerated.

Outmigration, aided by human traffickers, continued in the tens of thousands. UNHCR figures revealed that 82,268 Ethiopian migrants made the crossing to Yemen (70,845 of them young men), the highest number on record apart from in 2012. The numbers were surprising in view of the great domestic turmoil and insecurity in Yemen. Motives were repression, exclusion, poverty, lack of jobs and the indebtedness of farmers (who were unable to pay back obligatory loans for fertilizer, for example). Ports of embarkation were Obock and Bosaso. There was also legal outmigration of young Ethiopian females for domestic work in the Gulf States. In the context of migration, human trafficking remained a serious but under-documented problem.

Ethiopia itself also accommodated around 100,000 *new refugee arrivals* from neighbouring countries (mostly South Sudan), bringing the total number to 773, 759 (UNHCR figure), who were cared for with a UNHCR budget of $ 270 m.

Kenya

Gabrielle Lynch

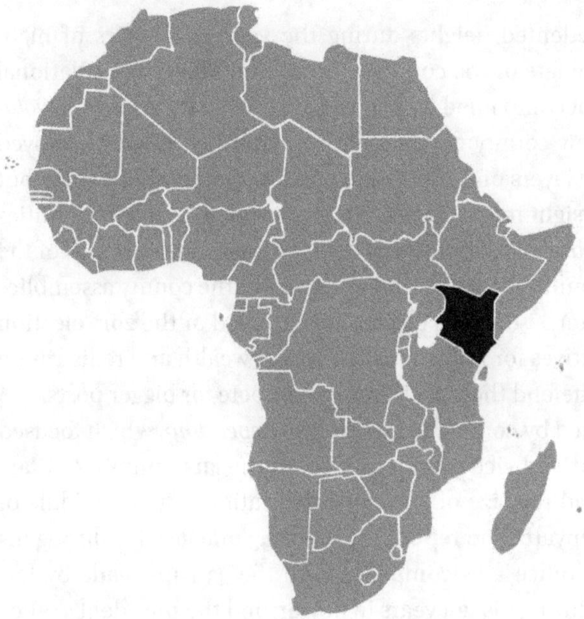

Dominant issues in 2015 were corruption, devolution and insecurity. Spiralling corruption was fuelled by the internal dynamics of the Jubilee Alliance government, and by the devolution of power to 47 new county governments – the latter providing new opportunities and incentives for graft. This crisis was a source of popular frustration and anger. It also further strained relations between the government and the political opposition, prominent civil society organisations and the media. These relations had already been severely tested by ongoing claims that the government was using the threat of insecurity and terrorism to delegitimise criticism, close the political space and undermine the gains of a reformist constitution – from the devolution of power and reform of the judiciary and police service to a new Bill of Rights. Certainly, a number of terrorist attacks were claimed by al-Shabaab, a radical Islamist group based in Somalia, although most now occurred in northern Kenya, rather than in Nairobi or at the Coast. However, while northern Kenya had long been regarded as politically and economically marginal, attempts to open up the northern corridor for the exploitation of new resources – together with incursions by al-Shabaab and the establishment of new county governments – ensured

 | DOI 10.1163/9789004333239_036

that insecurity in the region now had significant implications, not just for local residents, but for the country and the larger region.

Domestic Politics

Corruption reached unprecedented heights during the year, as a series of high-profile scandals – such as the fate of the country's Eurobond billions and National Youth Service funds – were accompanied by a localisation of graft through *devolution*. Regarding the latter, new county governments (established in 2013) enjoyed substantial budgets and new layers of fundraising, procurement and planning, but lacked institutionalised oversight mechanisms, which provided new opportunities for graft. At the same time, political aspirants became increasingly conscious of the resources and powers that county governors and members of the county assemblies enjoyed, which increased interest in these elected posts ahead of the 2017 election and provided perverse incentives for politicians to acquire wealth and redistribute patronage in their efforts to defend their positions or compete for bigger posts.

This crisis was accompanied by complaints of *excessive spending*, which focused on the office of the president and vice president, and on the large number of taxpayer-funded *foreign trips* and the size of travelling delegations. By the middle of the year, President Uhuru Kenyatta had reportedly made 43 official trips during his first two-and-a-half years in office – as compared with the 33 trips made by former president Mwai Kibaki during his ten years in power; and the president's office spent KES (shilling) 3.1 bn on travel and hospitality in 2014/15 – a 75% increase from 2013/14.

The apparent selfishness of the political elite fuelled popular frustration and anger, but also hopelessness and apathy, as many questioned what could be done to address these problems, given the failure of peaceful transfers of power in 2003 and 2013 and the inauguration of a new reformist constitution in 2010 to tackle them. At the same time, this context reinvigorated the *political opposition* as veteran opposition leader, Raila Odinga, and the Coalition for Reform and Democracy (CORD) adopted an *anti-graft platform*. However, this positioning was dismissed by Jubilee stalwarts, who questioned Odinga's own record as prime minister between 2008 and 2013; it was also undermined by the fact that corruption appeared to be as bad in CORD as in Jubilee-controlled county governments.

At the same time, Kenyatta publicly lambasted corrupt officials and politicians, and announced a series of *anti-corruption drives*. In his annual state of the nation address in March, the president recognised that "the time has come to send a strong signal to the country that [his] administration will accept nothing less than the highest standard of integrity from those that hold high office". More proactively, he directed officials adversely mentioned in an Ethics and Anti-Corruption Commission (EACC) report to step aside for 60 days to facilitate investigations. This action was initially welcomed, but investigations bore little fruit and most officials stepped back into their offices once the deadline had passed. Notable exceptions included Charity Ngilu, a veteran politician and cabinet secretary for land, who was still suspended from office by the year's end.

Anti-corruption efforts were undermined by problems within the *EACC*. In May, the president suspended the EACC's commissioners, including the chairman, Mumo Matemu, following allegations that the team had been bribed to stop a number of investigations. However, this left the EACC without commissioners until November, when a new team headed by Philip K.B. Kinisu, former head of a consultancy firm, was appointed by the president.

More fundamentally, anti-corruption efforts were limited by dynamics within the *Jubilee Alliance*. The main partners in this ruling coalition were Kenyatta's The National Alliance (TNA) and William Ruto's United Republican Party (UPR); and reports suggested that a desire to maintain this *winning coalition* into the 2017 election rendered it impolitic for Kenyatta to publicly admonish or punish those in the URP, which then emboldened those in TNA. This reality ensured that vulnerable officials were generally those who sat outside of either camp, including Ngilu, who had entered the Jubilee Alliance as head of the Narc-Kenya party. However, so public did the corruption crisis become that even Anne Waiguru – a close ally of Kenyatta and cabinet secretary for devolution and planning, who was named in the National Youth Service scandal – finally succumbed to pressure and resigned in November, citing poor health.

The need to maintain the ruling alliance not only undermined the government's efforts to tackle corruption, but also ensured that the *ICC*'s intervention remained a key political issue. The ICC had confirmed charges against Kenyatta, Ruto and two others in 2012; Kenyatta and Ruto were then elected president and deputy president, respectively, on an anti-ICC platform. However, in December 2014, charges against Kenyatta had been dropped, leaving only Ruto and a vernacular radio presenter, Joshua arap Sang, to face charges of crimes against humanity for their alleged involvement in the post-election violence of 2007/8. In turn, a number of URP leaders argued that the government had become less vocal in its criticism of the ICC following Kenyatta's reprieve, and was not doing enough to "save their son". In response, a number of TNA politicians reconfirmed their commitment to defeat the ICC. This included a public apology to Ruto and Sang by Gatundu South MP Moses Kuria, who claimed that he had been part of a team that had 'fixed' the duo by procuring false witnesses. Kuria later clarified that he did not know any ICC witnesses, but had coached five witnesses to give evidence before two national commissions of inquiry in 2008, whose findings and recommendations had then prompted and fed into the ICC investigations.

Allegations of ICC *witness intimidation* and *bribery* continued to dog Ruto, with attention focused on the suspicious death of Meshack Yebei, who was rumoured to be an ICC witness. Yebei had gone missing from his home in December 2014 and a badly mutilated body was found relatively nearby in January. However, DNA tests revealed the body to be that of another missing man, and it was not until March that Yebei's body was finally found around 600 km away. The ICC insisted that Yebei was not on their witness list, but a local human rights activist, Ken Wafula, argued that Yebei had been about to turn prosecution witness. Wafula's explanation was that Yebei had been involved in the intimidation and bribery of witnesses in Ruto's case, that he had subsequently fallen out with his former allies, and had then been killed by Ruto's henchmen. However, the story was further confused by counter-claims that Yebei was actually lined up to be a key witness for Ruto's defence. This case epitomised the rumours that surrounded the fate of ICC witnesses. The debate was extended by an ongoing legal battle between the ICC's Office of the Prosecution (OTP) and Ruto's defence team regarding the legality of using recorded statements made by witnesses but who had subsequently recanted their testimony.

In addition to politicking around the ICC's intervention, efforts to consolidate the Jubilee Alliance led Kenyatta and Ruto to form the new *Jubilee Alliance Party* (JAP). This initiative suffered problems from the start due to the unwillingness of many TNA and URP politicians to be drawn into a party over which they enjoyed little control. The JAP's first test occurred during a *by-election* in Kajiado in the southern Rift Valley. This seat had become free after the incumbent MP and retired army general, Joseph Nkaissery, was appointed cabinet secretary for interior and coordination of national government. Competition between the JAP and CORD in Kajiado was fuelled by the fact that, although Nkaissery had been elected on an Orange Democratic Movement (ODM) ticket, he had been appointed head of national security, while Ruto had expended significant energy trying to unite the Rift Valley vote. Ultimately, the ODM candidate, Memusi Kanchory, secured a narrow victory amidst claims of local resistance to Ruto's efforts to impose an unpopular JAP candidate.

Factions of the Jubilee Alliance also tried to extend their reach into other potential swing areas; most notably counties at the *Coast*. To this end, both Kenyatta and Ruto made a number of visits to the area when reports suggested that separate visits reflected efforts by TNA and URP adherents to build up parallel support bases, which provided further insights into uncertainties surrounding the JAP's future.

Spiralling corruption was also connected to ongoing *insecurity*, as corruption and mismanagement in the sugar industry, for example, together with high import tariffs and associated high prices, encouraged *smuggling* sugar from elsewhere in the world across the Somali border into Kenya – an illicit trade that al-Shabaab probably continued to benefit from, with overloaded trucks also allegedly carrying illegal weapons.

Al-Shabaab claimed a series of *terrorist attacks* in northern Kenya. Most notably: in April, armed gunmen killed 148 students at Moi University campus in Garissa; in July, 14 people were killed at a residential area next to a quarry in Mandera; and in November, 28 passengers on a bus from Nairobi to Mandera were shot. In each case, attacks targeted *non-Muslims* and those regarded as 'outsiders' or non-residents. For example, in the case of the November bus attack, non-Muslims were separated from a total of 60 passengers and then executed by the side of the road. These efforts to separate people faced resistance, however, and, in December, several Muslim passengers on a second bus that was attacked gave headscarves to their fellow passengers to help conceal their identity.

These attacks led to a significant loss of life and also sustained popular fears of further attacks, and fed into *criticism of the Jubilee Alliance government*. Many complained that the government was not doing enough to prevent attacks; that its response when they occurred was woefully inadequate; and that it did not do enough to honour or remember those killed. This debate reached a peak around the *Garissa attack* in April when – although there had been intelligence of a possible attack around the Easter holiday – it still took an elite response squad 11 hours to reach the campus, in part because a designated police helicopter was being used by a security officer's relatives, while the only *public memorial* held was organised by civil society activists rather than by the government.

Northern Kenya was also disproportionately affected by other forms of *insecurity*. In August, the UN announced that, in the first six months of the year, 310 people had been killed and over 215,000 had been displaced in the area as a result of inter-communal conflicts ranging from unresolved border disputes and cattle rustling to competition over land and water resources, and political contests – problems that continued into the second half of the year. However, while insecurity in the area had long been considered as of marginal political and economic importance, it now had significant ramifications for the country and region. This was due to the centrality of northern Kenya to economic plans, but also because devolution had increased the area's importance as a potential 'swing' district, while the powers invested in new county governments had increased political interest in these local-level seats. Finally, following Kenya's military invasion of Somalia in October 2011, al-Shabaab had responded with an escalation of attacks on Kenyan soil and had become increasingly adept at drawing upon the local frustrations of Kenya's historically marginalised *Muslim populations* in former Northern Eastern and Coast provinces, and in Nairobi. As a result, insecurity in northern Kenya was increasingly seen as having serious implications for national and regional security: both as a source of new recruits for al-Shabaab, and as a site of possible future terrorist attacks.

The government continued to face strained relations with *civil society organisations* and *media* outlets as a result of a widespread perception that it was using the threat of terrorism to close the political space, whilst simultaneously attempting to quell critical voices and encourage self-censorship in ways that would allow Kenya to retain its international image as a relatively free and open society. Principal targets included *NGOs* that called for the accountability of those involved in the post-election violence of 2007/8 and within the security sector. For example, in June, the government froze the bank accounts of Haki Africa and Muslims for Human Rights

(MUHURI) – two local human rights organisations that were helping to document abuses by the security services during counter-terrorism campaigns. However, the ban was later lifted after the High Court ruled that the organisations had no case to answer. Subsequently, the NGO Coordination Board announced it would deregister 957 NGOs if they failed to present full audited accounts within a fortnight. This included the Kenya Human Rights Commission, one of the country's most famous NGOs, which had long pushed for an end to impunity for a range of crimes including election-related violence, extra-judicial killings and torture, and grand corruption.

In contrast, disagreements between the government and commercial *media* outlets proved less visible as private threats to redirect government advertising and to use a 2013 Media Bill continued to encourage substantial *self-censorship* by individual journalists, editors and media houses. In April, the popular satirist, Gado, whose political cartoons had long appeared in the 'Daily Nation' (the country's leading national newspaper) was rumoured to have been sacked. However, Gado publicly countered these claims and insisted that he had taken a voluntary sabbatical.

The implementation of the *2010 Constitution* was another area of contention. In particular, opposition politicians and civil society activists argued that the government was trying to roll back certain reforms – in the *judiciary*, for example, by publicly attacking key figures and courts – and to undermine other reforms, such as in the security sector. The main focus for *security sector* reform was the public vetting of police officers by the National Police Service Commission. Hearings sought to increase public confidence in this critical institution and around 2,000 officers had been vetted by the end of the year. However, the process clearly failed to stir the same kind of excitement as the vetting of top judges in 2011, and made little difference to public confidence levels. In this context, *corruption within the police force* continued to be a source of widespread frustration. However, many Kenyans held much more ambivalent attitudes about *human rights abuses by police officers* despite a clear increase in the number of extra-judicial killings. Indeed, the latter appeared to be almost acceptable to many – the common idea being that youth killed in urban slums were actual or likely criminals, while residents of northern Kenya were similarly dehumanised as suspected terrorists.

The *Truth Justice and Reconciliation Commission* (TJRC) report, which had been pending before the National Assembly since July 2013, was not discussed. However, towards the end of the year, Hon. Abdullahi Dirie, MP for Wajir South, brought a *petition* before the National Assembly on behalf of the National Victims and Survivors Network. The petition requested that the National Assembly adopt the report and allocate "sufficient budget for the immediate and effective implementation of the recommendations contained in the report, in particular reparations of victims". Members pledged to prioritise debate of the report when the National Assembly reconvened in February 2016. At the same time, the government sought to draw attention away from the TJRC and demands for both punitive and *repara-*

tive justice for past wrongs, by prioritising the latter through the establishment of a National Reparations Fund.

In December, the Independent Electoral and Boundaries Commission (IEBC) announced that the country's next *general election* would be held in August 2017. However, even midway through the electoral cycle, the credibility of forthcoming polls remained a critical political issue, as opposition politicians and civil society activists insisted on the need for electoral reforms before they took place. These demands were reinforced by ongoing revelations regarding corruption in the Interim Independent Electoral Commission of Kenya (IIEC); the IIEC had been superseded by the IEBC, but the latter had retained many of the IIEC's structures and officials – including the chair, Ahmed Issack Hassan.

Foreign Affairs

Deputy President Ruto and radio presenter Sang continued to face charges at the *ICC* of crimes against humanity of murder, forcible transfer and persecution as an indirect co-perpetrator, and contributor to the commission, of crimes, respectively. These crimes had allegedly been committed by 'Kalenjin warriors' against government supporters in parts of the Rift Valley between December 2007 and February 2008 as part of a plan by ODM politicians to gain power and punish and drive out government supporters, who predominantly hailed from the Kikuyu and Kisii communities. The duo travelled regularly to and from The Hague to hear prosecution witnesses. Moreover, while the Kenyan government continued to insist that it was complying with the Court, it simultaneously sought to mobilise pan-African opposition to it, and to *counter-shame* the Court by depicting the OTP's charges as baseless and biased, and as detrimental to regional peace and development on the basis that the charges targeted democratically elected leaders of a regional powerhouse in an area wracked by terrorism.

The Kenyan government simultaneously sought to weaken the ICC's case against Ruto and Sang by lobbying through the *Assembly of State Parties* (ASP) for changes to the Court's rules and regulations (the ASP acts as the Court's oversight and legislative body and is comprised of state representatives that have ratified the Statue of Rome). This included Kenya's successful efforts to push the ASP to adopt a report reaffirming that recanted testimony could not be used, following an earlier decision by the ICC trial judges that permitted the OTP to use five recanted witness statements.

With Kenyatta freed of charges at the ICC, relations between the government and the country's main donors – the *USA* and *UK* – continued to thaw. In the run-up to the 2013 elections, the Jubilee Alliance had accused 'the West' of being behind Kenyatta and Ruto's troubles at the ICC, leading to increasingly strained relations. Two years later, the context had changed significantly, as was embodied by *President*

Barack Obama's first visit to Kenya in July, when several agreements were signed, including on the extension of visa validity for Kenyan visitors to the USA from one to five years. This shift was the result of shared interests: the UK and USA wanted to remain relevant in the country and region, while the government benefited from the aid given; and the UK and USA had an interest in helping Kenya to fight al-Shabaab as part of their global 'war on terror'.

For the UK, a desire to remain relevant was largely informed by historic links and substantial business interests, while, for the USA, it was also motivated by a felt need to sustain the country's position as the global powerhouse against a rising *China*. In this vein, Obama argued (in an interview for the BBC) that China had been "able to funnel an awful lot of money into Africa, basically in exchange for raw materials that are being extracted from Africa", and that "the United States has to have a presence [in the region] to promote the values that we care about".

For the UK, this shift in relations was also facilitated by a change of personnel. The *UK High Commissioner* Christian Turner had become a controversial figure during the 2013 election, when he had been accused of interfering in domestic politics. In December, Turner was replaced by Nic Hailey, who received a warm welcome and – more notably – quickly signed a much needed extension for the UK's military training facility in Laikipia.

Kenya's armed forces continued to be involved in neighbouring Somalia as part of the *AU Mission in Somalia* (AMISOM), which was primarily funded by the EU with additional support from the USA. However, little was known about *Kenya Defence Force* (KDF) operations, the number of al-Shabaab or civilian casualties, or the numbers of Kenyan soldiers who were killed or injured. In 2014, al-Shabaab had declared that their struggle had turned fully to Kenya in response to the country's invasion of Somalia and alleged 'atrocities' by KDF soldiers, and they continued to cite the ongoing invasion – together with "the suffering of Muslim communities in Kenya" – as the reason for their efforts to establish cells in, and to conduct attacks on Kenyan soil.

Beyond traditional donors, Kenya continued to reach out to neighbouring countries in the *EAC*, and to other potential diplomatic allies and trading partners. In the EAC, Kenya retained close relations with the so-called 'coalition of the willing' – namely President Museveni and the Ugandan government and President Kagame and the Rwandan government. In August, Kenya and *Uganda* signed a new *trade deal* that allowed Uganda to export sugar into Kenya, and Kenya to export beef into Uganda. In 2012, Kenya had blocked sugar imports from Uganda in violation of the EAC common market protocol, following allegations that Uganda was exporting cheap imported sugar into Kenya so as to undercut domestic producers. The two governments hailed the agreement as evidence of closer relations; however, CORD politicians argued that the deal would render Kenyan sugar unproductive and rallied farmers to reject it.

These wrangles over regional economic deals fed into the *presidential election campaigns* ahead of Uganda's general election in February 2016, when Odinga supported the failed efforts of opposition leaders, Kizza Besigye and Amama Mbabazi, to agree on a shared candidate through The Democratic Alliance (TDA). Ruto meanwhile joined Museveni on the campaign trail in eastern Uganda in an effort to mobilise his Kalenjin kinsmen from the local Sebei community to vote for the incumbent president. Kenyan politicians also got involved in elections in neighbouring *Tanzania* as Odinga came out to campaign for his long-term friend and successful 'Chama Cha Mapinduzi' candidate, John Magafuli.

East African partnerships also included plans for improved regional *infrastructure networks*, most notably, through a new *standard gauge railway* (SGR) from Mombasa in Kenya to Kampala in Uganda and Kigali in Rwanda; the Lamu Port Southern Sudan-Ethiopia Transport Corridor (LAPSSET), which included plans for a new road, railway and pipeline across three countries, and a port and oil refinery in Lamu; and a new *oil pipeline* from the Ugandan oil town of Hoima to the Kenyan oil town of Lokichar and Lamu port. However, while Kenya and Uganda renewed their commitment to their joint infrastructure projects – and work on the SGR continued at an impressive pace – Uganda went on to sign a separate agreement with Tanzania that paved the way for a possible pipeline from Hoima to Tanga in Tanzania. Given the size of Uganda's oil fields and the low price of oil, it was clear that Uganda would not need two pipelines, which raised questions regarding the future of a Hoima-Lokichar-Lamu line. Uganda's preference for the Tanzanian route seems to have been informed by rising insecurity in northern Kenya and the possibility that a pipeline could become a focus of terrorist activity.

Various state visits and international meetings helped raise Kenya's profile on the global stage. They included a high-profile visit by *Pope Francis* in July, while, in December, Kenya hosted the WTO's 10th Ministerial Conference. The latter led to the *'Nairobi package'*, which included a number of decisions that were hailed as benefiting relatively underdeveloped agricultural exporters such as Kenya. The government also had a visible presence at a number of large international conferences including the 3rd International Conference on Financing for Development in Addis Ababa (Ethiopia); the 2030 Agenda for Sustainable Development Goals conference in New York; and the UN Conference on Climate Change (COP 21) in Paris.

Socioeconomic Developments

At the beginning of the 2015/16 financial year, the government forecast an *economic growth* rate of between 6.5% and 7%. However, the Treasury later reduced this prediction to between 5.8% and 6%, citing the global economic crisis, the knock-on effect of travel warnings, adverse weather patterns, insecurity and population growth. However, while growth rates fell short of early optimistic predictions, most sectors continued to grow, with the World Bank estimating an overall growth rate of 5.4% by the year's end. This increase was associated with further expansion of the country's *middle class* and consumer culture. As a result, new franchises – for example, of coffee shops such as Java and Art Caffe, and of food outlets such as KFC – opened across the country, while Nairobi witnessed the reopening of Westgate mall after a terrorist attack in 2013, and the opening of Garden City Mall with over 50 retail outlets. More Kenyans also began to use *air travel*, which was facilitated by the extension of Jambojet's low cost domestic flight schedules, and by the opening of a new terminal at Jomo Kenyatta International Airport; this also prompted the entry of Fast Jet Kenya into the Kenyan market, with a licence to operate a number of domestic scheduled flights.

Adverse weather included the *El Niño* weather phenomenon, which peaked in the last three months of the year. Experts had suggested that Kenya might witness the strongest El Niño rains since 1950, following similar weather events in 1972–3, 1982–3, and most recently in 1997–8, when the excessive rains are estimated to have caused $ 1.2 bn-worth of damage to crops and infrastructure. In turn, Kenya's Meteorological Service warned that the rains might interfere with harvesting in the Rift Valley, especially in Trans Nzoia, Kenya's agricultural heartland. Fortunately, the El Niño rains were not as strong as had been feared, and the agricultural sector continued to grow during the year.

While the economy continued to diversify with the growth of the retail, service and IT industries, *public infrastructure* investment once again proved to be the strongest sector. This reflected the government's development plans, which continued to be articulated through *Vision 2030* – a plan that had been initiated under former president Kibaki and which included a series of ambitious and high-profile infrastructure projects, such as the SGR and LAPSSET. However, the future of the latter became increasingly uncertain. The initial plan was predicated on South Sudan's participation in the *oil pipeline* project, but the renewal of conflict in South Sudan, together with an agreement between Juba (South Sudan) and Khartoum (Sudan) on the use of the existing pipeline running from South to North Sudan, threw doubt on the willingness of foreign investors to finance a southern route. In addition, rumours circulated that South Sudan was considering the development of a new pipeline through Ethiopia and Djibouti rather than through Kenya. And furthermore, low oil prices, together with the possibility that Uganda might not contribute to a pipeline through Kenya, ensured that the original pipeline envisaged by LAPSSET appeared less feasible, while even the likelihood of a Kenyan pipeline from Lokichar to Lamu was brought into question. These regional developments also meant that even less ambitious plans were likely to be increasingly dependent on support from *China*, which was already involved in helping to build the Lamu port and the SGR.

Development projects came into direct tension with *conservation* efforts. The worst affected was *Nairobi National Park*, with agreements reached between various ministries and the Kenya Wildlife Service that allowed the SGR to cut deep into the Park, and for Nairobi's southern by-pass to hive off another area. Community groups and conservationists also raised questions regarding the construction of a new *coal-fired power station* in Lamu. Thus, while the government praised the economic benefits including new jobs, others raised concerns about the distribution of benefits and harms, and the environmental and human health costs.

Conservation and tourism were also troubled by high levels of *wildlife poaching*, with elephants, rhinos and lions as the main targets. Indeed, the exception to a story of steady growth across Kenya's economic sectors was the *tourism sector*, which continued to be affected by insecurity, and by the rise of alternative safari and beach destinations in East and Southern Africa. Media reports of terrorist attacks in 2014 in areas such as Lamu County – also home to Lamu Island, one of the country's most famous tourist havens – and the imposition, and then extension, of *travel warnings*, prompted a slump in the tourism industry. Moreover, while some countries – such as the USA – lifted their warnings, others – such as the UK – kept them in place. These warnings and more general security concerns continued to exert a heavy toll on the sector: for most foreign tourists the Kenyan Coast is a fairly homogenous entity, while al-Shabaab attacks constituted part of an accumulative process by which the coastal strip – and indeed Kenya – was painted as an uncertain and insecure place.

Despite significant economic growth across most sectors, Kenya's *budget deficit* increased, raising red flags as it came in the wake of the country's successful entry into the *Eurobond* market in 2014, through which the government had raised KES 250 bn. In a series of articles, the economist David Ndii argued that an 'elusive KES 140 bn' was not reflected in the government's bank deposits and that, given the government had sufficient funds for existing budget lines, the money must have been pocketed by politicians and officials through the inflation of various project expenditures. The second-largest *corruption scandal* of the year involved the *National Youth Service*, following reports of an estimated KES 791 mn lost in suspicious payments to private companies. In addition, in February, two directors of Smith and Ouzman, a small British printing company, were sentenced by a UK court for corruptly agreeing to make payments to officials employed at the IIEC as an inducement to favour Smith and Ouzman in relation to the award and payment of printing contracts. The case highlighted the international nature of much corruption, but also reminded Kenyans of the fact that IIEC officials under the leadership of the current IEBC chairman had allegedly received bribes, which renewed demands for the chairman and his team to be replaced.

Corruption even hit the country's *athletics* sector – usually a source of national pride and common identity – when the International Association of Athletics Federation suspended three Kenyan officials for their alleged involvement in the subversion of anti-doping controls. The *banking sector* was also not immune, with reports suggesting that the collapse of *Imperial Bank* was the result of massive fraud by staff. The Bank's collapse prompted the closure of branches countrywide and a freeze in all operations except the servicing of debts, while owners of over 50,000 deposit accounts waited for a decision by the Kenya Deposit Insurance Corporation to know how much of their money they would get back.

Many citizens also complained of high levels of *inequality* and a lack of jobs, and questioned the benefits brought by economic growth in and of itself. Citizens also suffered from relatively high *inflation* rates, ranging between 6% and 8%, largely due to high food prices and a weak currency. Such popular complaints were embodied in a five-week *teachers strike* over low pay and high costs of living. An industrial court ruled that teachers should receive a 50% pay increase, but the Kenyan government argued that they had insufficient funds to pay the teachers, who eventually went back to work after the Kenya National Union of Teachers gave the government and the Teachers' Service Commission more time to sign a collective bargaining agreement. The country also continued to feel the impact of having had one of the highest population growth rates in the world in the 1980s, which now fed through into a youth bulge and to further strains on land ownership in agricultural areas and large numbers of new entrants into the country's labour market.

Rwanda

Susan Thomson

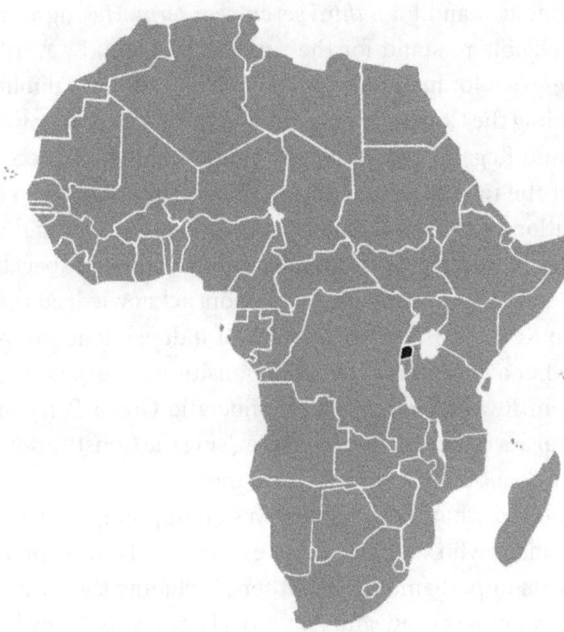

The ruling RPF continued to maintain strict controls on public life. The regime, led by President Kagame, faced little internal political opposition, and he commanded the loyalty of the bulk of the armed forces. Progress continued in the fields of public service delivery. The government oversaw orchestrated revisions to the 2003 Constitution to allow Kagame to stand for a third term in office. Foreign aid disbursements held steady in 2014–15, as donors continued to support the government's ambitious development agenda. Relations with donors remained tense, notably because they continued to chastise the government for its ongoing political repression, while also expressing disappointment at Kagame's decision to run for a third term. Bilateral relations with both Burundi and the DRC were strained. The economy remained resilient: despite an ambitious development programme, the effects of no new foreign aid combined with cheaper global energy costs and lower domestic public spending, economic growth remained a relatively healthy 6.5%.

 | DOI 10.1163/9789004333239_037

Domestic Politics

The ruling *Rwandan Patriotic Front* (RPF) continued to dominate all levels of socio-political life. For the first time in six years, President Paul Kagame did not reshuffle his cabinet. The government's energies were instead focused on revising the Constitution to allow for Kagame to stand for a *third seven-year term*. Having won in 2003 and 2010, he was not eligible to stand for the presidency again. By April, the pro-regime media and several senior members of the cabinet had made public statements in support of amending the Constitution to allow a third term, citing the RPF's majority in parliament and Kagame's track record in maintaining high economic growth since the end of the 1994 genocide. Rwanda's foreign donors spoke against amending the Constitution to allow for a third presidential term, citing the government's poor record on key human rights issues, including freedom of speech and assembly, and political openness and competition. Donors acknowledged the lack of an obvious successor to Kagame as well as the lack of independent governance institutions able to weather a potentially fractious transition in 2017. Of the six political parties operating in Rwanda, only one (Democratic Green Party of Rwanda, DGPR) was willing to raise a critical voice against revising the Constitution. The others operated as part of a coalition of parties loyal to the RPF.

In July, parliamentarians received what they claimed was an unprompted petition from more than 3.7 m Rwandans who supported the revision. Of the five opposition parties, only two held seats in parliament. The others, including the DGPR, had no elected representatives. Members of Rwanda's political opposition in exile, notably those from the *Rwandan National Congress* (RNC) and the *FDU-Inkingi*, both called on Rwanda's donors and internal political opposition to stop what they considered to be RPF manoeuvring to allow the ruling party to hold on to the presidency indefinitely.

In October, the RPF-dominated parliament endorsed *Article 172*. This ruling meant that Kagame was exempt from the constitutional limit of two presidential terms. Article 172 was revised to acknowledge Kagame's popularity as president (he had won previous elections with some 90% of the popular vote). It was a move regime allies praised and critics pilloried as the revision meant that only Kagame could stand for more than a third term of seven years and it also allowed him to compete for an additional two five-year terms. In a nod to the concerns of foreign aid donors, the amendment was put to a referendum in December. Ninety-eight per cent of eligible voters voted to lift term limits. The *EU Representative for Foreign Affairs* stated in early December that the fact that the constitutional amendments applied to only one person weakened Rwanda's transition to democracy. Such criticism fell on deaf ears as the vote paved the way for Kagame to hold the presidency until 2034. In his New Year's Eve state of the union address, Kagame confirmed that he "… humbly accepts the will of the Rwandan people" and would run for the presidency again.

Several recently retired or former *army officers remained in prison* charged with inciting violence or insulting the president. The trial of three senior officers – retired Brigadier General Frank Rusagara, Colonel Tom Byabagamba and demobilised Sergeant Francois Kabayiza – resumed at the military high court in December, following numerous procedural adjournments during the year. They were charged with "inciting insurrection and public disorder" as well as "tarnishing Rwanda's reputation". Human Rights Watch believed the latter accusation to be related to alleged contact with opposition groups in exile, mostly likely the *RNC*, founded in 2009 by former senior founding members of the RPF, most of whom had since fallen out with Kagame and the RPF. Ironically, international and regional political analysts believed the RNC posed no serious political or military threat, noting that the party had been unable to raise significant financial or moral support from Rwandans living in the diaspora, thus limiting its influence abroad and at home. Both Kabayiza and Rusagara had been forcibly retired in 2013 as part of a broader government effort to remove soldiers who had fallen out with the regime and to eliminate dissent in the ranks.

These *military shake-ups* sustained a broader mood of *domestic disillusionment* with the RPF. Members of the RPF's core constituency – urban, educated and English-speaking Tutsi – felt that Kagame had lost his vision for ethnic unity and economic prosperity for all Rwandans. There was in addition an on-going government tendency to scapegoat the political opposition and unfairly target regime critics through disappearance, and an increasing tolerance of nepotism and bribery among members of the ruling clique. In December, TI acknowledged this trend in its 2015 *Corruption Perceptions Index*, noting that Rwandans regularly paid bribes for basic services. At the same time, it declared Rwanda the least corrupt country in East Africa, and 44th best performer out of the 168 countries surveyed worldwide.

International and domestic human rights organisations regularly accused the RPF government of *harassment and intimidation of political opponents and journalists*. The RPF continued to acknowledge its control of the political sphere, citing state security, national ethnic unity and economic growth as priorities over political freedoms. Opposition parties remained constrained in their activities. Victoire Ingabire, president of the FDU-Inkingi party, remained in prison for the second year of an eight-year sentence for endangering state security and promoting ethnic divisionism. In June, Ingabire launched an appeal before the African Court on Human and Peoples' Rights, a regional human rights body operating under the aegis of the AU. Rwanda signed the Charter of the court in 2013, and the Ingabire case marked its first appearance before the regional body. The case was pending at the end of the year.

The *media* remained tightly controlled, and thus dominated by pro-government views. Tight restrictions on independent journalism, first introduced in 2009, remained in place. At the same time, several private radio stations were able to engage in frank political discussion provided the Ministry of Youth and Information and Communications Technology awarded the necessary approvals in advance, and an RPF representative was invited to join the discussion. *Self-censorship* continued, with many journalists unable or unwilling to engage in reporting on politically sensitive issues. In June 2015, Reporters Without Borders reported that Rwanda ranked 161st out of 180 countries in its Press Freedom Index, a one-place improvement over its 2014 ranking of 160th. In May, the Rwanda Utilities Regulatory Authority (RURA) banned the Kinyarwanda-language service of the British Broadcasting Corporation (BBC). This came on the heels of the October 2014 suspension of the BBC's service in Rwanda, following the release of the controversial documentary 'Rwanda: The Untold Story', which covered the role of the RPF in the 1994 genocide, and the revenge killings its soldiers had perpetrated before, during and after the genocide.

The media self-regulatory body, the Rwanda Media Commission (RMC), objected to the banning of the BBC, and its president, *Fred Muvunyi*, challenged the RURA for suspending the BBC service without consulting the RMC. Muvunyi then became the target of a systematic smear campaign on social media, when journalists close to the government argued against the need for the RMC. It had been created in September 2013 in response to international criticism of the lack of press freedoms in Rwanda, with a limited mandate to issue press accreditations and regulate media content on the basis of a code of professional ethics. In May, Muvunyi resigned his position as the head of the RMC, claiming government interference in his work. In his resignation, Muvunyi cited the BBC ban and the difficulties the RMC had in publishing a report on the state of the media in Rwanda. International consultants had drafted the report following the suspension of the BBC service in 2014, with funding from UNDP. The government blocked publication of the final report, leading to Muvunyi's flight into exile in late May.

Civil society remained cowed as state intimidation, harassment and infiltration continued unabated. The sole independent *human rights* group, the 'Ligue Rwandaise pour la Promotion et la Défense des Droits de l'Homme' (LIPRODHOR), had taken legal action against the government in 2014 in protest at a takeover of its leadership by members of the ruling RPF. In March, the appeal of the ousted LIPRODHOR leaders failed, as the Supreme Court ruled their case unconstitutional on procedural grounds. Another active independent human rights organisation, the Human Rights League in the Great Lakes Region (LDGL) experienced leadership setbacks and internal wrangling, leading to the cessation of its work in November. The closure of LDGL offices followed the questioning of its executive secretary, Epimack Kwokwo, and other newly elected members of the management team by immigration officials and police in October. The questioning concerned administrative and organisational matters, leading some of LDGL's leadership to fear for their safety. In 2014, two low-ranking policemen accused of the 2013 murder of TI Rwanda staff member Gustave Makonene had pleaded guilty to his murder. They were each sentenced to 20 years' imprisonment in January.

In November, Rwanda presented its human rights report to the *UN Universal Periodic Review* (UPR) mechanism. In an unusual turn for a government historically allergic to criticism, it addressed some of the concerns of Maina Kiai, the UN Special Rapporteur on the rights of freedom of peaceful assembly and association, in its UPR submission, receiving praise from the UN in December for implementing 63 of 67 recommendations made to Rwanda during its 2011 submission to the UPR. The most notable achievement was Rwanda' accession to the Optional Protocol to the *UN Convention against Torture* in June.

In December, the *International Criminal Tribunal for Rwanda* (ICTR) closed its doors. The final judgement was announced in December in the case of Pauline Nyiramasuhuko, the former minister of family and women's development. She was the first woman to be convicted of genocide by an international court. With the closure of the ICTR, the Rwandan government stepped up its efforts to call foreign courts to hold Rwandan genocide suspects accountable for their crimes. Domestic courts in several foreign countries tried Rwandans for genocide crimes under the principle of *universal jurisdiction*, and further cases were pending. In January, a Norwegian appeal court upheld the conviction of Sadi Bugingo, who had been sentenced to 21 years' imprisonment in 2013 for his complicity in the 1994 genocide. In 2014, the ICTR had transferred the case of Wenceslas Munyeshyaka, a priest accused of genocide and crimes, to France, where he had fled into exile in 1996, but in October, *France* dismissed the case for lack of evidence, once again straining relations between Paris and Kigali. In December, a *German* court handed down a life sentence without parole to Onesphore Rwabukombe for his role in ordering the killing of Tutsi during the 1994 genocide. With the closure of the ICTR, the *UN mechanism for international criminal tribunals* ramped up its efforts to track and arrest Rwandans living abroad who were accused of genocide and crimes against humanity.

In June, Emmanuel Karenzi Karake, head of Rwanda's intelligence services, was arrested on a European arrest warrant issued by a Spanish judge. In 2008, a Spanish court had indicted some 40 senior members of the RPF for war crimes and violations of international law dating back as far as 1990. The RPF protested against Karake's arrest, saying it was a violation of national sovereignty. The case was dropped in October, when a Spanish court stayed the case against Karake and others in the original indictment because of changes in Spain's universal jurisdiction laws. Kigali received news of Karake's release as an expression of vindication of its role in stopping the genocide.

Rwandan courts continued to try individuals alleged to have threatened state security or made ethnic divisionist or genocide denial claims in public. The most prominent case was against internationally acclaimed singer Kizito Mihigo, journalist Cassien Ntamuhanga, and co-defendants Agnès Niyibizi and Jean-Paul Dukuzumuremyi. They were charged with offences against the state and complicity in terrorist acts for allegedly collaborating with members of Rwanda's external political opposition. During sentencing in February, Mihigo received ten years, Ntamuhangu 25 years and Dukuzumuremyi 30 years for their respective crimes against state security. Niyibizi was acquitted.

Foreign Affairs

Rwanda's foreign affairs were dominated by its presumed military presence in *Burundi*. Rwanda also maintained its military involvement in the *eastern DRC*. While Rwanda had had tense relations with the DRC since the end of the 1994 genocide, it had maintained cordial diplomatic ties with Burundi. This changed in April, when Burundi experienced an outbreak of political violence, resulting in the arrival of 25,000 refugees in southern Rwanda. The violence occurred following a failed coup attempt by factions of the Burundian army after an announcement by Burundi's President Pierre Nkurunziza that he would stand for a third term. In May, Kagame condemned Nkurunziza's heavy-handed response to opposition protests. By June, some 70,000 Burundians had sought refuge in Rwanda, fuelling social and ethnic tensions in host communities. In October, Burundian officials close to Nkurunziza accused Rwanda of training rebels who were aiming to overthrow his government, and of harbouring General Godefroid Niyombare, who had led an attempted coup in Burundi in May. Also in October, Burundi's presidential spokesperson Willy Nyamitwe and Burundian Foreign Minister Alain Aimé Nyamitwe repeatedly suggested that Rwanda was acting as a rear base for Niyombare and other coup plotters, as well as providing training, arms and recruits for a possible new rebellion in Burundi. Rwanda denied all allegations. The implications of political instability in Burundi were felt across the region. The *AU*, the regional body responsible for brokering peace in Burundi, proposed a *Protection and Prevention Mission* in December, but the proposal fell on deaf ears as the Nkurunziza government rejected it as meddling in domestic affairs. A similar affirmation of the need to respect Burundian sovereignty was made by Kagame in August, when asked by Western diplomats if his government was meddling in Burundian politics. In July, the *UNSC* called on all sides in the Burundian conflict to recommit to internationally brokered peace talks. Regional leaders, including Kagame, scoffed at the idea, highlighting the political realities of regional peacekeeping in Africa's Great Lakes.

In February, the *Congolese army* (FARDC) announced its intention to launch a military campaign against the *Forces Démocratiques pour la Libération du Rwanda* (FDLR), a Hutu-dominated rebel group whose leaders had participated in the 1994 genocide. Although its stated mission was to use military pressure to force an 'inter-Rwandan dialogue', its actual mission seemed to be to destabilise Rwanda's security. International and regional analysts agreed that the FDLR, an underfunded force of approximately 1,500–2,000 rebels, was too weak to challenge Rwanda's internal security. In January, the *UN Stabilization Mission in the DRC* (MONUSCO) had issued an ultimatum to FDLR's leadership to disarm voluntarily. Rwanda had long pushed for Congo to take military action against the FDLR, citing internal security concerns. Didier Etumba, FARDC's chief of staff, announced that the operation was unilateral, with UN forces providing logistical and other non-combat support. By the end of February, Western diplomats, led by the USA and the EU, were quick to complain, as the head of the operation, General Bruno Mandevu, was red-listed in the UN's internal vetting system for UN-FARDC collaboration. Mandevu had a record of alleged human rights abuses, which raised concerns about the nature of the mission to disarm FDLR rebels. Later in February, Congolese President Joseph Kabila affirmed his country's commitment to conducting unilateral operations against the FDLR. Kabila accused MONUSCO officials of meddling in Congolese affairs and of violating the country's sovereignty. In September, the defence ministers of the DRC and Rwanda, Aimé Ngoy Mukena and James Kabarebe, met in Kigali for talks centred on the threat posed to both countries by the FDLR and the repatriation to the DRC of former combatants of the now defunct *M23 militia*, which had received financial, military and moral support from the Rwandan government. The talks ended with no specific deals in place.

In October, Maman Sambo Sidikou of Niger succeeded Martin Kobler as the head of MONUSCO. Sidikou continued his predecessor's policy of cautious scepticism of the FDLR's stated intention to disarm, a position welcomed by Rwanda's long-term strategy of refusing to enter into peace talks with the rebel group. Rwanda sought the full demobilisation of the FDLR.

Diplomatic relations with *Tanzania* improved. In late 2013, the then Tanzanian president, Jakaya Kikwete, had called for Rwanda to sit down for peace talks with the FDLR. Affronted by the suggestion, Rwanda had moved to diplomatically isolate Tanzania for its 'meddling' in national security issues dear to Kigali. In April, presidents Kagame and Kikwete met in Nairobi (Kenya) to discuss both the political violence in Burundi and regional economic integration through the *EAC*, of which Kikwete had become the chairman in February. Kikwete's pet projects included a railway linking Kigali to Tanzania's seaport in Dar es Salaam and a regional railroad had been a priority of Kagame's since 1994, as landlocked Rwanda experienced high tariffs and delays in importing commodities by road. The two men agreed during their April meeting to focus on issues of mutual economic benefit, rather than tackling sensitive topics such as the demobilisation of the FDLR.

Diplomatic relations with *South Africa* resumed. In 2014, both countries had recalled their ambassadors in a spat concerning the murder trial of Rwandan dissident Patrick Karegeya, and the subsequent attempt on the life of Faustin Nyamwasa Kayumba. In May 2014, South Africa had expelled three Rwandan diplomats for alleged ties to the second attempted murder of Nyamwasa in Johannesburg. South Africa and Rwanda maintained a reduced diplomatic presence in Kigali and Pretoria (South Africa), respectively, with only ambassadors in place without consular staff.

Rwanda and South Africa were the main contributors to *peacekeeping operations in South Sudan*, and South Africa maintained a key peacekeeping presence in the DRC.

Relations with many of Rwanda's *bi- and multilateral aid donors* – including the USA, the UK and the EU – remained stable in 2015, despite some terse statements from the EU and the US about Kagame's bid to stand for a third term in office. *Aid flows* accounted for some 40% of Rwanda's overall budget. The threat of foreign aid reductions also ushered in a change in the way foreign relations were managed, with donors providing payments to specific projects rather than general budget support. The resumption of reduced and conditional aid flows in 2014 had signalled an international community that no longer engaged Kigali on its own terms but rather through conditionalities. This trend continued in May, as the *US Subcommittee on Africa* held a special session to discuss American relations with Rwanda. The hearings did not result in the USA reducing its foreign or military aid to the country. In January, *Belgium* postponed the disbursement of € 40 m in aid, citing Rwanda's failure to meet certain governance indicators. In December, the *EU* condemned the RPF government for its willingness to amend the Constitution but did not link its criticism to suspension or postponement of the € 460 m it had committed in 2014 to support the security sector, health and agriculture up to 2020. In January, Christine Lagarde, managing director of the IMF, visited Rwanda to assure the government of the IMF's continued support for its economic policy.

The government also continued to consolidate its diplomatic and economic relations with *China*. In May, it welcomed the opening of a Chinese clothing factory, whose construction fulfilled the Chinese ambassador's 2014 promise to invest in Rwanda. Relations with *France* warmed: in April, the French government declassified key documents about its role in failing to stop the 1994 genocide. Kigali welcomed the move, while noting that France had played an indirect role in the loss of Tutsi lives in 1994. Kagame spoke to French media in February, saying that he considered France to be an important ally in Rwanda's post-genocide reconstruction.

Socioeconomic Developments

The government continued its efforts to showcase its *social reconciliation and economic development policies* to international audiences following the domestic events and international activities related to the commemoration of the 20th anniversary of the 1994 genocide. Throughout the year, the government highlighted its ambitious development plans, including improved institutional governance and technocratic competence, a zero-tolerance policy on corruption, and continued economic growth. The government intensified its public commitment to private-sector growth and infrastructure development, despite the continued threat of shortfalls in donor revenue. The *Second Economic Development and Poverty Reduction Strategy* (EDPRS 2) remained the core of the government's economic policy.

The EDPRS is the development framework through which the government is funding its ambitious *Vision 2020* policy, which aims to develop Rwanda into a knowledge-based middle-income country by 2020. In February, the *World Bank* cautioned Rwanda on its development plans, highlighting the need to moderate expectations and goals, given shortfalls in domestic revenue and lower than expected aid flows. In March, the government announced a series of efforts to improve the business environment and encourage private-sector development. The statement was seen as a reaction to the EDPRS 2 requirement that the government shift responsibility for economic growth and development to the private sector. The government had been involved in all areas of the economy since the 1994 genocide, and it met the suggestion with considerable concern. In a press conference in March, Minister of Finance and Economic Planning Claver Gatete reminded World Bank officials of Rwanda's technically competent public service and low levels of institutional corruption. In May, the government announced its intention to attract $ 1.2 bn in *FDI* through tax breaks and other incentives. World Bank officials received the news with scepticism as Rwanda had averaged FDI flows of approximately $ 350 m per annum since 2010.

Also in May, the IMF completed its third review of Rwanda's economic performance under the *Policy Support Initiative* and gave a satisfactory rating. The IMF's report noted that Rwanda's economic growth was uneven, notably in revenue generation. The *2015/16 budget*, released in May, contained a number of innovations to improve *Rwanda's tax base*. These included increased fuel levies to fund road maintenance, and import levies. Other efforts to modernise the financial sector included a new initial public offering (IPO) of the RPF-owned investment company Crystal Telecom, which raised $ 40 m in June, and marked an important test for the government. The IPO highlighted the challenge of promoting private-sector solutions for a public-sector development agenda, as the government would need to step back at some point if it was to attract private investors.

The primary challenge for the government to maintain robust economic growth remained *infrastructure deficiencies*. In October, Tanzania announced it had begun construction of a new port in Bagamoyo, 75 km north of the capital Dar es Salaam. This news followed the April announcement that the Tanzanian government would begin work on the rail link between Dar es Salaam and Rwanda and Burundi. In May, Kagame commissioned a *28-MW hydropower plant* known as Nyabarongo II in efforts to improve Rwanda's electricity supply. Power shortages were a drag on economic growth throughout the year, and the government was keen to support its fledging industrial sector with a ready supply of electricity. In September, the RURA sharply *increased electricity and water prices* for households and small businesses by 35% and 19%, respectively. Industrial consumers were not affected. The government promised to use the revenue gained through the price rises to invest in grid upgrades and new water infrastructure.

In September, the World Bank's *Doing Business Index* reported that Rwanda had fallen seven points from its 2014 position to 62nd out of 189 countries. The Rwandan Development Board incorrectly reported Rwanda's ranking as 46th out of 189 countries. In October, the government released its household poverty survey, showing that *poverty* had declined from a national headcount of 45% in 2011 to 39% in 2014. Critics of the government accused it of manipulating the poverty data by using a different methodology to measure household poverty from that used for the 2011 data set. In August, UNDP released an assessment of country progress towards the *MDGs*. Rwanda was one of a handful of low-income countries that met its goals with respect to gender equality in primary and secondary education, primary school enrolment rates, reductions in HIV/AIDS and malaria prevalence, maternal mortality, and climatic shocks, and improving access to the financial sector for low-income earners. In July, the World Bank reported that Rwanda's *GDP per capita* had risen to $ 718, up from 2014 but still short of the government's 2020 target of $ 1,000 per person per annum.

Throughout the year, the government continued the implementation of the third phase of its *National Land Use and Development Master Plan*, first introduced in January 2010. The plan had three phases: first, the merger of the local land usage policies devised in 1998 with the Master Plan; second, the creation of an urban development plan; and third, the implementation of the Master plan, once the peasantry had been taught how to use their land efficiently. In the second phase, representatives of the Rwanda National Resources Authority joined the small (less than 0.5 ha) plots of rural peasants into larger, more economically viable plots that could then be used for cash crops. As in 2014, the government had *stripped the titles of countless subsistence farmers*, entrusting control of land use to local government officials and effectively leaving subsistence farmers landless. The government also released a new website called the National Land Use Planning Portal in March, which provided online access to land-use plans and other spatial data. Critics of the website noted that many rural Rwandans, who made up 85% of the population, did not have access to the Internet.

Finance Minister Claver Gatete presented a *reduced budget* in May. Foreign aid cuts prompted the government to reduce both capital expenditure and government spending by 4%. The *GDP growth rate* remained robust at 7.6% (compared with 6.5% in 2014), despite the threat of a reduction in foreign aid, while average *inflation* rose to 2.1% (compared with 1.8% in 2014).

Seychelles

Rolf Hofmeier

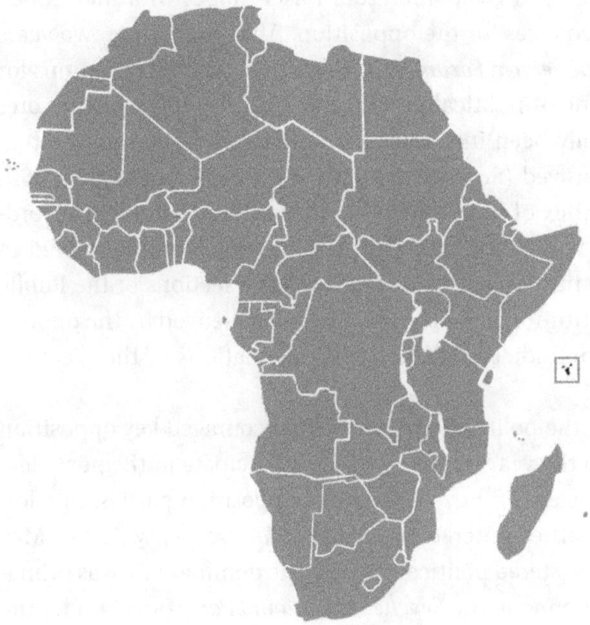

Following three unusually quiet years politically, 2015 saw a sudden flurry of renewed political activity. With the creation of several new political parties, President Michel and his long-ruling Parti Lepep were now confronted with a total of seven officially registered opposition parties. In presidential elections in December, Michel was forced into a second-round run-off against his main challenger, Ramkalawan, and only succeeded in winning another term by a few votes. On the international stage, the government continued its efforts to enhance the recognition of this tiny island nation and specifically to have it seen as a champion of the interests of small island developing states. Economic performance was again quite satisfactory, with somewhat higher growth, new record figures for the vital tourism industry, and further reforms to liberalise the economy and encourage small and medium-sized local enterprises, while also maintaining the population's remarkable level of social well-being. Seven years after the initiation of drastic economic reform measures, Seychelles continued to be praised by international organisations as a role model for successful reform-oriented policies.

 | DOI 10.1163/9789004333239_038

Domestic Politics

After years of animosity and distrust between the political opposition and *President James Michel* and his long-ruling *Parti Lepep* (PL, People's Party), amendments to the electoral legislation passed in December 2014 raised hopes of a more open political climate and fairer chances for the opposition. After more than two years of discussions in the *Electoral Reform Forum*, new more transparent regulations for the functioning and financing of political parties and for a new permanent voter registration system had finally been introduced. The long-criticised media situation had also markedly improved (Seychelles climbed seven places to rank 96th in the 2014 press freedom index of Reporters without Borders), although, according to the chairman of the national Media Commission, much still remained to be done. On 7 July, the Constitutional Court declared some sections of the Public Order Act 2013 to be unconstitutional; this Act had been challenged by the opposition, who claimed that it contradicted all the recommendations of the Electoral Reform Forum.

These notable changes in the political environment encouraged key opposition leaders to announce early in the year that they would participate in the next elections, in contrast to the 2011 election boycott by most opposition parties. In addition, several new political parties entered the *political landscape*, which in May consisted of eight officially registered political parties. The dominant PL was primarily faced by its traditional opponent, the *Seychelles National Party* (SNP) under the leadership of Wavel Ramkalawan. The Popular Democratic Movement (PDM) held a single opposition seat in the National Assembly; its chairman David Pierre was recognised to be the official leader of the parliamentary opposition. In May, a breakaway faction of the PL registered the new *'Lalyans Seselwa'* (Seychellois Alliance), led by Patrick Pillay, who had long been a high-ranking PL member (*inter alia* foreign minister 2005–2010). The new party was also supported by other former PL dignitaries and had as its treasurer V. Ramadoss, a wealthy Seychellois-Indian businessman, who had been PL treasurer and chairman of the Chamber of Commerce, but had clashed with Michel in 2012. Pillay emphasised that the PL under Michel had strayed too far from its former welfare-oriented course and had encouraged widening social division. The Seychelles Party for Social Justice and Democracy was registered in May and put up lawyer Alexia Amesbury as the country's first female presidential candidate.

As early as February, 71-year-old President Michel announced that he would seek another (third) term at the next elections, due in April 2016 at the latest. Subsequent speculation about a possible earlier election date was confirmed on 1 October, when Michel called for *presidential elections*, initially set for late November. After protests from opposition parties that this left insufficient time for preparation, the date was then moved to *3–5 December*. The PL was confident of winning once again and wanted to benefit from its dominance before

Pillay's dissident splinter group gained more ground. During its 29th congress on 5 June, the PL had already nominated Michel and Vice President Danny Faure as its official candidates. Simultaneously, 25 candidates (including 14 new ones) were selected for constituency seats in the next parliamentary election, due at the latest in September 2016. The SNP held its 22nd congress on 2 August, but left formal nominations deliberately open until the election date was officially set. Out of a total population of 93,000, 70,943 were registered to vote.

A total of *six candidates*, the highest number ever, entered the *presidential election contest*. Michel's opponents were Ramkalawan (making his fifth attempt at the presidency), Pillay, Pierre and Amesbury as party candidates and Philippe Boullé, running for the fourth time as an independent. The campaign atmosphere was quite animated, in sharp contrast to the previous elections in 2011, which had been overshadowed by the SNP boycott. There were some opposition complaints of intimidation of their candidates and of unequal coverage by the Seychelles Broadcasting Corporation, but by and large the election was conducted correctly, as reported by several external observer groups (AU, SADC, IOC, Commonwealth). The main tension centred on the question of whether Michel would win an absolute majority or be forced into a run-off. High voter turnout of 87.4% was testament to the wide interest.

The *official results* showed that the incumbent president had failed to obtain an absolute majority, but was a clear leader with 47.8% of the votes, while the 54-year-old Anglican priest Ramkalawan was in second place with a respectable 35.3% share of the votes. Pillay, the candidate of the PL dissidents, did rather well with 14.2% of the votes, while the scores of the other three candidates remained negligible. Pierre came last (with less than 1%), despite being the only current opposition MP.

A *second-round run-off* between Michel and Ramkalawan on *16–18 December* thus became necessary. All the eliminated candidates (except Pierre) and their parties rallied behind Ramkalawan and forged a joint grouping 'Linyon Sanzman' (Union for Change), which was also intended to serve as an umbrella organisation for the parliamentary elections in 2016. Michel was declared the narrow winner with 50.15% of the votes cast, having received only 193 more votes than his opponent, and was immediately sworn in for a new term on 20 December. Ramkalawan and the SNP quickly petitioned the Constitutional Court both for a recount and for an annulment due to alleged irregularities, but the petition cases were not to be heard before February 2016. The external election observers strongly recommended a change of the Constitution to the effect that the swearing-in ceremony would no longer be possible before the clarification of pending petition cases.

On 22 December, Michel held a first *cabinet meeting* with his unchanged government team of twelve ministers, which had been unanimously approved by the National Assembly. The cabinet had already been reshuffled on 26 January with a slight restructuring of some portfolios, the exit of two ministers and the appointment of four new ministers. Interior Minister Joel Morgan was moved to the Foreign Ministry, while former foreign minister Jean-Paul Adam was given responsibility for the Ministry of Finance and Trade.

Foreign Affairs

Within the limitations of its given narrow capacity, the government continued to pursue active public diplomacy to raise the visibility of its mini-state on the international stage. Seychelles specifically portrayed itself as a champion and natural leader of the group of Small Island Developing States (*SIDS*) at the global level, particularly raising concern about the inherent dangers of climate change for these countries. In support of the SIDS agenda, Seychelles continued to play an active part in attempts to strengthen the 39-member Alliance of Small Island States (*AOSIS*), whose presidency it was expected to assume in 2017. With respect to its geographical neighbourhood, the government remained an interested member of two relevant regional organisations, the *IOC* and *IORA*. On 26 April, Seychelles formally acceded to the *WTO* as its 161st member, thus bringing two decades of strenuous negotiations to an end. The government also continued to campaign internationally for Seychelles to be a candidate for a non-permanent African seat on the *UNSC* in 2017/18, despite its extremely limited diplomatic network.

India's Prime Minister Narendra Modi visited Seychelles in March at the beginning of a wider Indian Ocean tour, while Michel was in India in late August for an official state visit. On both occasions, several cooperation agreements, including defence and maritime security matters, were signed. Not to be outdone by India, *China* also continued to maintain cordial relations and to seek to exert some influence on Seychelles with its important geo-strategic position in the midst of the Indian Ocean. Vice President Faure visited China in April and discussed *inter alia* direct air links and linking Seychelles with the Chinese concept of a maritime silk road. The president of the tiny Pacific Ocean state of *Palau*, Tommy Remengesau, was guest of honour during the National Day celebrations on 29 June; he had been invited in order to underline the cooperation between AOSIS member states. President Michel met Pope Francis during an official visit to the Vatican on 30 April and attended the AU summits and the UN General Assembly, but otherwise refrained from international appearances.

The threat from *Somali pirate activities* in the Indian Ocean in recent years had practically come to an end in 2014 and no longer posed a problem. Nevertheless, the Seychellois judicial system was still forced to deal with the fall-out from earlier acts of piracy. In March, nine Somali pirates were sentenced by the Supreme Court to 14 years in prison for acts of piracy committed in November 2013, bringing the number of Somali pirates still held in Seychellois prisons to 33, while 225 more had already been repatriated to Somalia, Puntland and Somaliland. Despite the decline in piracy, *maritime security* remained an issue of concern, with most attention shifting to the fight against *drug trafficking*, which was clearly on the increase. The UN Office on Drugs and Crimes sought support from Seychelles to combat drug trafficking from Asia on the high seas.

Socioeconomic Developments

The Seychellois economy again demonstrated remarkable resilience in the face of prolonged global uncertainties. The general *macroeconomic performance* continued to be quite satisfactory, with a slight acceleration of the growth rate, only moderate inflation and another fiscal surplus. The government proudly praised its consistent pursuance of reform-oriented programmes, which had been introduced in late 2008 as a kind of shock treatment to ward off the near-collapse of the then unsustainably indebted and welfare-oriented economy. The significant change of policy orientation towards a liberal market outlook and an investor-friendly climate had very effectively stabilised the situation and encouraged a new dynamism. The official unemployment rate was given at a low 4.2%. In the 2015 *HDI*, Seychelles was ranked 64th in the 'high' human development category, ranking highest in Africa (equal with Mauritius). The World Bank moved Seychelles into the category of high-income countries. In the World Economic Forum's Global Competitiveness Index 2015/16, Seychelles was ranked 97th (out of 140) and seventh in SSA. The World Bank's Doing Business Report 2016 showed the country in 95th position (out of 189) and 5th in SSA. *Corruption* was considered to be a lesser problem, as shown by Seychelles' slightly improved rank at 40th (out of 167) in TI's Corruption Perception Index (second in SSA, only behind Botswana). With an annual *per capita income* of about $ 25,000 (PPP), Seychelles was clearly in a different league from most of the rest of Africa. All MDGs were largely achieved; health and education services were of excellent quality. The high average income was, however, quite unevenly distributed as evidenced by a relatively high *Gini Index* of 45.6 (calculated by the Statistical Bureau on the basis of a 2013 Household Budget Survey); 39% of the population were estimated to be living below the national poverty line, calculated at $ 15.2 per adult equivalent per day (PPP) and 24% were estimated to be living on less than a lower food-poverty line.

Largely as a result of a strong recovery in the tourism sector, the projected *GDP growth rate* for 2015 was revised upwards to 4.3% (by the IMF), compared with 2.8% in 2014 and 6.6% in 2013. After a spike in *inflation* to 5.8% in March (from a 2014 average of 1.4%), consumer price inflation was brought down to 3.2% by the year's end (thus achieving an annual average of 4.3% for 2015). The *exchange rate* saw the partial reversal of the depreciation experienced in 2014 and appreciated by 6.7% against the dollar in the first three quarters of the year, with the annual average estimated to be Seychelles rupees 13.3 to the dollar. The Central Bank consistently maintained its policy of accumulating *foreign exchange reserves* to improve the country's external position; by the year's end reserves had grown to $ 536 m, equivalent to a comfortable 4.7 months' import coverage (compared with just a perilous two weeks' at the height of the 2008 crisis). The structural deficit of the tiny import-dependent island's *balance of trade* remained principally unchanged, with imports accounting to about double the value of exports (consisting mainly of tuna fish and re-exports of oil products). Falling prices of imported commodities (particularly oil) led to a reduction in the *current-account deficit* from 22% of GDP in 2014 to about 18%. The impressive level of *FDI*, considering the size of the country, was forecast to have declined to $ 184 m (from $ 227 m in 2014), in line with the government's strategy of improving local investment and creating opportunities for Seychellois businesses.

The key *tourism sector* had an exceptionally good year with a 19% increase in arrivals (17% increase in revenue) and a new record of 276,500 visitors. This was helped by the opening of new flight connections, specifically by direct flights from Paris, operated by Air Seychelles from July onwards. Traditional European markets (France, Germany, Italy) and Arab Gulf countries were primarily responsible for the increase, while recently growing new markets (Russia, China) declined or stagnated. On National Day, President Michel declared a moratorium on the construction of large luxury hotels by international investors, giving in to recurring public protests against such ventures. The tourism policy was oriented towards supporting the growth of small local hotels and safeguarding environmental concerns.

The government consistently maintained a policy of *strict fiscal discipline* in pursuit of its goal to gradually redress the huge public debt that had been accumulated during the earlier welfare-oriented socialist era. It remained well on track to achieve the set target of bringing *public debt* down to below 50% of GDP by 2018. By the year's end, aggregate public debt had been reduced to 62% of GDP. In February, a landmark discounted debt buy-back with eight major creditors had been arranged under the Paris Club; the released funds were used to establish a $ 30 m trust for ocean conservation. For the eighth consecutive year, an overall *budget surplus* was achieved. On the back of an impressive government revenue equivalent to 32% of GDP (with VAT as main source of income), the fiscal year 2015 was expected to end with a primary surplus of 3.8% of GDP. The 2016 budget, introduced in parliament on 23 December, remained consistent with this tight fiscal and monetary approach.

IMF missions in March and October conducted routine reviews of the SDR 11.445 m Extended Fund Facility (EFF) that had been approved in June 2014; by December this enabled disbursements of about $ 9.1 m. In the IMF's assessment, implementation of the EFF-supported programme had been strong, all quantitative performance criteria had been exceeded by comfortable margins and the structural reform agenda was proceeding well. The 2015 macroeconomic outcome was generally viewed as positive, including commendable progress in building external buffers for this formerly highly vulnerable economy. Both the AfDB and the World

Bank approved loans for Seychelles to support on-going reforms to boost shared prosperity by improving the business climate, particularly with regard to small and medium-sized enterprises.

The *offshore financial sector*, the country's third economic pillar after tourism and the *tuna fishing industry* (contributing about 10% to the economy), was faced by new problems arising in the context of a global trend of de-risking and of enhanced initiatives on financial integrity and tax transparency. In February, Seychelles became the 85th signatory of the OECD convention on mutual assistance on tax matters. This undermined the continuance of former well-established practices, although the government had already in the past rejected accusations that it tacitly facilitated money-laundering scams.

Again, no tangible progress was made with regard to the possibility of *oil* or *gas* finds in the Seychelles' extensive maritime zone. Some international companies had shown interest in the past and gathered seismic data, but with the prevailing global climate in the oil industry no prospects for starting exploratory drilling were in sight. The government continued to actively promote its concept of the specific values of a *'blue economy'*, centred on the abundant maritime resources of the country's large exclusive economic zone.

Somalia

Jon Abbink

Somalia remained a divided country on 'life support' from the international donor community in the political, financial and military domains. The Somali Federal Government (SFG) maintained itself in power and steadily but very slowly expanded its reach and influence in south central Somalia, supported by high inflows of donor funds. Somaliland remained an autonomous region, consistently refusing to consider merging politically with the rest of the country. Puntland, nominally under the Transitional Federal Government, remained an autonomous territory. Elections for the SFG presidency previously announced for 2015 were delayed by President Hassan Sheikh Mohamoud.

The SFG's building of nation-wide institutions was slow and marred by clan-divisions and corruption. Local regional states re-asserted their autonomy. Somaliland remained absorbed in internal political problems, including controversy over delayed elections.

The country's security problem – terror by the radical-jihadist movement al-Shabaab and the resulting instability – was not solved, and disruptive attacks remained a challenge to the normalisation and build-up of a cohesive nation and of governmental institutions. Terrorist action in the cities by these Islamists seemed to increase as their territorial control base was shrinking, and attacks were extended

 | DOI 10.1163/9789004333239_039

beyond the borders of Somalia, with Kenya being the main target. Many hundreds of people were killed in various attacks – non-combatant civilians, AMISOM soldiers and government personnel. No attacks took place in Ethiopia, prevented by heavy security surveillance there. In non-al-Shabaab areas, security improved.

The border conflict in the Sanaag, Sool and Ayn (Cayn) areas, between Somaliland and Puntland, was not solved, with Somaliland maintaining a troop presence in the disputed region.

There was economic growth, carried mainly by the private sector, but investments by 'diaspora' Somalis receded somewhat due to continued insecurity and the unpredictable business environment, and hindered by lack of infrastructure and corruption. The country's largest source of income was remittances from overseas Somalis.

Somalia suffered from severe humanitarian problems, including a high number of IDPs, drought and food insecurity, and millions of dollars in international food and medical aid poured into the country.

Domestic Politics

Somalia, divided in three autonomous political units – Somalia, Somaliland and Puntland – continued to grapple with the challenges of security, political institution-building and economic recovery. The state remained largely dysfunctional and precarious, propped up by donor funds and military assistance by the 22,000 strong African Union Mission in Somalia (AMISOM) force. The political elite in Mogadishu remained (too much) dominated by clan-based politics and cronyism and appeared not to take the building of the country seriously. Politics remained rooted in the cleavages of centrifugal Somali political culture.

Although presidential *elections*, with a direct popular vote, were scheduled for 2015, President Hassan Sheikh Mohamoud, leader of the Somali Federal Government (SFG) in Mogadishu, had them *delayed*, citing the lack of security and infrastructure. The SFG mandate was due to end in August 2016. In the background were unresolved issues over electoral procedure (the president said that a 'one man, one vote' system would not be possible), constitutional problems, and disputes between factions in the 275-member parliament. A growing number of MPs was uncomfortable over Mohamoud's rapprochement with the Islamist 'Damul Jadiid' (New Blood) group, a Somali off-shoot of the Muslim Brotherhood. This fuelled tensions between the parliament and the president during the year, and delayed progress towards national unity and institution-building. It thus appeared that the political process, notably in southern Somalia, remained unduly influenced by clan-based politics and political Islam, although neither ever brought anything good to the country. On 17 December, the leaders of the SFG, Puntland, South West State, Jubaland, Galmuduug and other regions finally decided on a mixed voting system for the 2016 elections, with the formation of upper and lower houses whose structure and size would be determined on the basis of clan representation and region. But details would be worked out at another meeting to be held in Kismayo in January 2016.

The year was marked by further appalling *violence* perpetrated by the *al-Shabaab* militant jihadist movement, which continued its killing spree despite the loss of more of its territory. It was difficult to see this movement's political agenda. They resorted to destruction and terror for its own sake, killing civilians, SFG officials and AMISOM personnel. In Mogadishu, they regularly used suicide bombers and car bombs to attack government facilities, military checkpoints and hotels. On 20 January, al-Shabaab killed Ali Jalil, the new mayor of Afghoye town, near Mogadishu. On 20 February, a car packed with explosives crashed into the security gate at the Central Hotel in the capital and exploded, killing several people. It was immediately followed by a female suicide bomber (an employee at the hotel reception) detonating an explosives belt, killing more than 40 people, including her colleagues, visiting ministers and other guests, notably in the hotel's mosque. Remarkably, this suicide bomber had grown up in the Netherlands and had returned to Somalia a year before. In May, al-Shabaab carried out a terror raid on the government quarter of Mogadishu, killing 17 people. On 26 July, al-Shabaab terrorists stormed the Jazeera Hotel, killing ten people and injuring dozens. On 21 September, al-Shabaab detonated a car bomb near the SFG presidential palace, killing 11 people, among them two Polish members of a UN group, and injuring over 20. Another hotel (the Sahafi), used by many Somali MPs, was attacked with a car bomb on 25 October and armed militants entered and killed 15 people.

In June, al-Shabaab militants overran an AMISOM base in Lego, killing some 50 Burundian troops and capturing military equipment. Another massive attack occurred in early September at the AMISOM base in Janale, 90 km south-east of Mogadishu, allegedly killing 70 AMISOM soldiers. On 11 June, an al-Shabaab unit ambushed an Ethiopian army convoy near the city of Baidoa, allegedly killing dozens and destroying 13 vehicles. Al-Shabaab also repeatedly took over various towns in the countryside – albeit temporarily. For instance, on 1 September they occupied Yaaqbariweyne and Muuro Gaabay, on 6 September Buqda, and on 7 September Kurtunwarey – to show their presence and deflect offensives by AMISOM and Somali government forces. These coordinated hit-and-run attacks and the occupation and even recapture of a number of small towns showed that the movement was far from defeated.

Kenyan security forces also prevented several planned al-Shabaab terror attacks within Kenya, including in Mombasa in early January.

In the areas under its control, al-Shabaab exercised repressive violence against civilians; for example, on 23 April they executed a man for "insulting the Prophet Muhammad", and on 6 September they beheaded a man in Qahira village (Bay region), for "spying for Ethiopia". Public killings and punishments such as stoning to death, amputation and floggings also continued on a regular basis.

The USA and several allies kept up the *pressure on al-Shabaab* by various operations (mostly covert) and drone attacks. On 3 February, Yusuf Dheeq, the leader of the Amniyat, al-Shabaab's internal security unit, was killed. On 8 March, there followed the elimination, in a drone strike near Bardheere, of Adan Garar, a senior member of al-Shabaab who had allegedly helped plan the 2013 West Gate shopping mall massacre in Nairobi (Kenya), although this action was not confirmed by the USA or Kenya. In November, al-Shabaab operative Abdirahman Sandhere 'Ukash' was killed in an air strike. The Somali army also arrested a significant number of al-Shabaab commanders during the year.

Overall, *more al-Shabaab-held territory was recaptured.* On 22 July, AMISOM and Somali troops drove them out of Bardere (Gedo region). Two days later, the town of Dinsoor (Bay region) was retaken from them in a new offensive called Operation Jubba Corridor. AMISOM forces recaptured the town of Wabho (central Somalia) on 21 October and, on 13 December, pro-SFG forces captured Barwaqo, near the Kenyan border. At the end of the year, al-Shabaab was still estimated to hold some 25% of southern Somalia.

Faced with territorial losses, al-Shabaab continued *recruiting* among young (mostly Somali) *Muslims in Kenya* and also made attempts in other countries (such as Tanzania). New recruits in Kenya were often ordered to attack Kenyan targets. A most appalling massacre occurred on 2 April at Garissa University College in north Kenya, where 148 people died. Christian students were especially targeted, being separated from the others and executed. In retaliation, Kenya later carried out several air raids on al-Shabaab bases in Somalia.

Several *abuses by SFG troops* and allied militia were also recorded, including extrajudicial killings, arbitrary arrests and cases of gender-based violence, including rape. This was usually ascribed to poor discipline and weak command control. Unresolved land occupation issues in the southern region (dating from the 1990s when many Hawiye clan-family people had taken land from other clan-groups) were not resolved and continued to foment tensions.

Somalia had some of the most intrepid reporters, but it remained a *difficult environment for journalists and the media,* not only because of insecurity but also as a result of government intimidation and interference. Radio and social media were important, television and Internet services less so, because of poor infrastructure. The media landscape was also fragmented. On the other hand, foreign-based Somali websites were numerous, providing the latest news and comments, but civil rights and freedom of expression were generally under pressure in Somalia, with frequent arrests of journalists and broadcasters, including in government-held areas. In al-Shabaab-held areas, there was no media freedom at all and Internet use continued to be suppressed.

The *death penalty* was maintained and was carried out (by firing squad) in a number of cases, in both Somalia and Somaliland.

Effective government action against the rule of terror by al-Shabaab was hampered by *continued political infighting* in the SFG and in the Somali national army (only some 18,000 strong), which had no unified command structure, and often defaulted on paying soldiers' salaries – one of its most invidious failures. Also, discord between the various constituent units of federal southern Somalia played a role. In November, armed forces of the two regions of Puntland and Galmuduug (although the federal constitution forbids such armies and militias) clashed in Galkayo in a territorial dispute, leaving more than 40 people killed, hundreds injured and thousands displaced. On 2 December (and again on 5 December), Puntland leader Abdiweli Mohamed Ali Gaas and then Galmuduug leader Abdikarim Hussein Guled signed a cease-fire agreement in Galkayo in the presence of SFG Prime Minister Omar Abdirashid Sharmarke, but no final deal was reached.

The ISIS ('Islamic State') terror movement attracted some following among al-Shabaab members, but the latter's leadership (seeing itself as an al-Qaida branch) did not pay allegiance to ISIS, despite some factions arguing for joining. In the Puntland Galgala (Golis) mountain area, the army clashed with al-Shabaab loyalists on 4–5 January, killing 20 militants, and again in November, in Diine-Digle village, with a further seven killed. Puntland forces lost seven dead. But the militants were not decisively uprooted from this inaccessible area. In October, a certain Sheikh Abdulqadir Mumi, an Islamist propagandist and former recruiter for al-Shabaab based in the Galgala Mountains, declared his allegiance to ISIS. It was not clear whether all of his 300 followers agreed, but by this ISIS established a presence in Somalia.

Tensions between the various *regional states* claiming status within the emerging Somali federation continued to subvert a common agenda. Among these were the Jubba State, Central State, Galmuduug (formed in 2015), the 'South West State' (centred in Merka), all 'interim', but claiming autonomy. Boundary issues and clan-group rivalries often prevented efficient administration and security policy. In South West State, for instance, the competition between the Habr Gedir-Hawiye and Bimal-Dir clan groups was not resolved.

Somaliland, a relatively effective independent polity with one-third of the total Somali population, dominated by the Isaaq clan family, fared better, but was mired in political problems by the (delayed) elections, party relations and institutional reforms. There was also renewed fighting in its eastern border region in the self-proclaimed but internally divided 'Khatumo state' (Dhulbahante clan area). Political unrest due to internal divisions within the ruling Kulmiye party preceded the choice of a new leader in November. In October. Party president, Ahmed Mohamed Mohamoud Silanyo, had chosen Muse Bihi Abdi, the party's chairman, as his successor, but this bypassed the party's electoral procedure and led to 12 senior government officials (including seven ministers) resigning. There was also struggle over *reform of the political system*: governance based on consensus (i.e., deal-making) politics and clan-based negotiations was to evolve into formal party-based and state-like structures, but clan-based affiliations inevitably remained strong and in tension with a representative party-based democratic model, which was pushed by donors.

Also in Somaliland, there was wrangling over the date of the June 2016 presidential and parliamentary elections, with the president proposing a delay, citing incomplete voter-registration, outstanding legislation and ongoing unrest in the eastern Sool-Sanaag regions, but it probably had more to do with strengthening the position of the ruling Kulmiye party over the two other political parties. Finally, the Constitutional Court decided on 26 August to set the election date for 27 March 2017, following an earlier decision of the Somaliland upper chamber, the 'Guurti' (House of Elders).

Foreign Affairs

Somalia's constituent parts maintained relatively separate foreign relations, with the SFG focusing on the international donor community, Ethiopia and Djibouti. Relations with *Kenya* were tense. Remarkably, on 22 November Somalia's federal parliament *voted to expel Kenya's 3,660 AMISOM troops* from Somalia following accusations by a Kenya-based human rights organisation that Kenyan Defence Force officials were illegally involved in Somalia's sugar and charcoal trade. Kenya denied the allegations. Somali MPs also protested against the building of a defensive wall on the Kenya–Somali border, meant to keep out al-Shabaab militants. Another dispute with Kenya continued over the *delimitation of territorial waters*, against a background of competing claims for oil exploration blocks. The SFG pushed ahead with its lawsuit at the International Court of Justice.

Relations with *Ethiopia* were close, notably in the political and security spheres, with both the SFG and Somaliland authorities developing more cooperation and economic bonds. Various Somali leaders paid visits to Addis Ababa, including on 9 March SFG Prime Minister Omar Abdirashid Ali Sharmarke and later in the year Abdikarim Guled, head of the Galmuduug Interim Administration, and Puntland leader Abdiweli Mohamed Ali. Somaliland renewed discussions with Ethiopia on expanding Berbera port for use by Ethiopian businesses. The SFG and Somaliland also extended cooperation and trade with *Djibouti*.

Relations between Somalia's federal government and *Turkey* continued to expand. In January, a military cooperation agreement between the two countries was signed, of which one element was a plan to establish a training base for the Somali National Army, seen as suffering from internal division and lack of professionalism. Turkey's President Recep Tayyip Erdoğan visited Mogadishu on 23–26 January to discuss economic relations and the opening of a new Turkish-funded hospital named after him. He saw Somalia as a future geo-strategic asset for Turkey's new expansionist foreign policy, as "… a sister nation at the heart of the Indian Ocean" and as a potential emerging market. Turkey remained one of the most important investors in Somalia.

Several *Gulf States*, including Qatar and the UAE, remained important players in Somali politics, each choosing their own clients, but with unclear results.

In May, the *USA*'s Secretary of State John Kerry paid a brief visit to Mogadishu, the first US officeholder to do so. Other visitors included Djibouti's President Guelleh on 21–22 February, UN High Commissioner for Refugees António Guterres on 8–9 May, and Qatar's Foreign Minister Khali bin Mohammed on 22 May.

International donors continued to provide massive funding to the SFG and AMISOM. The problem was that donor insistence on a Somali political model continued to prevent local-level clan-group deals and agreements from below – a process that would need time.

Somaliland continued its drive for *international recognition*, but its political problems and the stalling of institutional reforms and elections made its case more difficult. Only Ethiopia recognised Somaliland but the country had diplomatic missions of Kenya, South Africa and South Sudan. Djibouti and Turkey opened consulates in Hargeisa. In April, an Egyptian delegation led by the vice minister for Africa visited Hargeisa. Donor support – or interference – remained strong, despite lack of political recognition, and funded some 20% of the Somaliland budget.

Sea piracy continued to decline as a result of successful international naval operations and there were no attempted attacks on vessels passing Somali coasts during the year. The efforts of the international naval anti-piracy force and maritime and political bodies thus paid off, assisted by action from, notably, the Puntland government patrolling the coast with its navy, taking pirate land bases and getting former pirates engaged in alternative activities. Several court cases against suspected pirates were still ongoing, however, and there was no illusion that the danger of Somali piracy was gone forever; the social and economic development situation was not adequate to prevent it. In addition, some 46 crew members from previously captured vessels were still being held somewhere in Somalia.

Illegal fishing by foreign trawlers along the coasts also remained a problem. Some illegal vessels, including the Iranian fishing boat Siraj, were attacked in March by what appeared to be pirates. One armed clash between pirates and Puntland security forces at Harardheere (Muduug region) was reported in November. In the same month, the UNSC re-authorised an extension of the *EU Naval Force Somalia*.

Socioeconomic Developments

Lack of statistics meant that assessments of the Somali economy were based on estimates. The World Bank and IMF put the country's *GDP* at some $ 6 bn, an estimated 2.7% increase, showing a further recovery. Gross fixed capital formation accounted for only 8% of GDP; the rest was consumption expenditure. Imports dominated the economy, accounting for more than two-thirds of GDP, with exports contributing only 14%. The large trade deficit was financed by remittances and international aid. Annual income per capita was estimated at $ 435 (with Somalia ranked the fifth-poorest country in the world). The private sector was the mainstay of the economy.

The SFG's *budget* was around $ 251 m, mostly spent on the fledging government institutions and the army. The IMF made the first survey of Somalia's economy in 25 years in an initial Article IV consultation, and noted that figures showed a *current account deficit* of $ 644 m (11% of GDP), with FDI at $ 434 m, seen as lower than in 2014. FDI was mainly in electricity, telecommunications and hotels. *Inflation* was very low at 1.3%. The economy was largely US dollar-based, partly because of the problem caused by the fact that an estimated 90% of Somali shilling notes were forged. The IMF also estimated external debt at $ 5.3 bn (93% of GDP). *Corruption* was engrained, with Somalia ranked 167th, taking last place in the TI Corruption Perception Index.

The resilience and growth of the Somali economy was due to the versatility and inventiveness of the Somali private sector. Further growth was hampered by security problems and the weak political institutions and legal-regulatory environment.

Exports were limited and had a narrow base: livestock, hides, incense and myrrh, charcoal, bananas and wildlife products – a significant part of which was contraband. The country exported over 5 m sheep and goats (one of the highest figures in the world) to Saudi Arabia and the Gulf States. Total exports fell slightly to $ 533 m and total imports stood at $ 2.6 bn. Investment in production sectors and diversification of the economy was extremely limited, restricting the expansion of the economy in the longer term. Other general economic problems – unemployment at more than 50%, low levels of education and training, low tax revenues, and overconsumption of the mild narcotic khat – were not tackled.

Somaliland's economic data were to be distinguished from those of the rest of the country. Its *budget* amounted to a modest $ 251 m, although this was a rise of 30% compared with 2014. The central government would receive 72% of this sum. The main source of revenue (some 85%) was customs duties, mostly from Berbera port. Being still internationally unrecognised, Somaliland had no access to bilateral aid funds, but its economy showed increased diversification and investment.

Somaliland's GDP was estimated at around $ 1.5 bn. Its main export, as for the rest of Somalia, was livestock, destined for Middle Eastern countries (some 60% of GDP). Somaliland also suffered from the wider regional drought, with 240,000 people affected and some 35% of livestock being lost, throwing many families into poverty.

No official figures for *remittances from Somalis abroad* were available, they were the mainstay of the economy, and were largely handled by the Dahabshiil company, active in 155 countries. They were estimated to amount to between $ 1.5 bn and $ 1.8 bn., mostly transferred via an efficient, trust-based international system, and represented the largest source of income and half of Somalia's GDP.

In the country as a whole, *drought* and its disruption to production led to the continuation of *massive food insecurity*. By October, over 3.2 m people (one-third of the population) were in need of assistance, with over 855,000 food insecure. Surveys conducted late in the year by FAO indicated that over 300,000 children under the age of five were acutely malnourished. More than 1.3 m Somalis remained internally displaced.

There was a close link between insecurity and economic development. After the Garissa terror attack by al-Shabaab in April, for example, the Kenyan government announced a *remittances ban*: 13 Somali-owned money transfer agencies in Kenya were closed, and Somalis in Kenya could no longer send money to relatives in Somalia. SFG President Mohamoud lodged a protest against the closing of this "lifeline for millions of Somalis" and said the measure was counter-productive.

With new tools and the sophisticated cashless mobile phone banking system, the Somali business class and telecoms companies tried to circumvent the remittances ban. One method was a new handheld device called 'Camelcash', with a fingerprint scanner, Wi-Fi, a card reader and printer. Private *mobile financial services* were thus very popular: about 26% of the population reported using mobiles to pay bills – the highest rate in the world – and 32% used them to send or receive money.

In anticipation of future oil finds and the upgrading of the country's energy infrastructure, a privately funded $ 2 m petroleum storage facility was opened in December in Mogadishu, under the auspices of the Somali Fuel Company. It had seven tanks capable of storing 40 m litres of fuel each.

The general state of *education* was poor, with only four out of ten children in school – one of the worst enrolment rates in the world. However, efforts were launched to expand and improve primary school coverage. Higher education expanded but was largely in private hands. Al-Shabaab regularly attacked schools and also targeted children for recruitment to the militia and into forced marriages.

In the *health sector*, the federal government also underperformed but together with international organisations expanded its campaign to eradicate some public health risks, such as polio, with immunisation campaigns. Across the country, and among both IDPs and the rest of the population, *gender-based violence*, overwhelmingly towards women, remained a huge problem.

Several reports by local NGOs and UN branches offered information on the country's alarming *environmental problems*, which were not addressed in any national policy plan.

The *population* stood at some 10.9 m with a growth rate estimated at 2.4%. The number of Somalis migrating to neighbouring countries fell significantly compared with previous years. For example, the number of Somali arrivals in Yemen, their first port of call, was 10,162 for the entire year, the lowest figure in a decade (and a drop from 19,640 in 2014, according to UNHCR). By August, over 28,000 Somalis had reportedly returned to Somalia from war-torn Yemen and, in a remarkable reverse movement, several hundred Yemenis arrived in Somaliland (and Djibouti) as refugees from the war in their own country.

South Sudan

Daniel Large

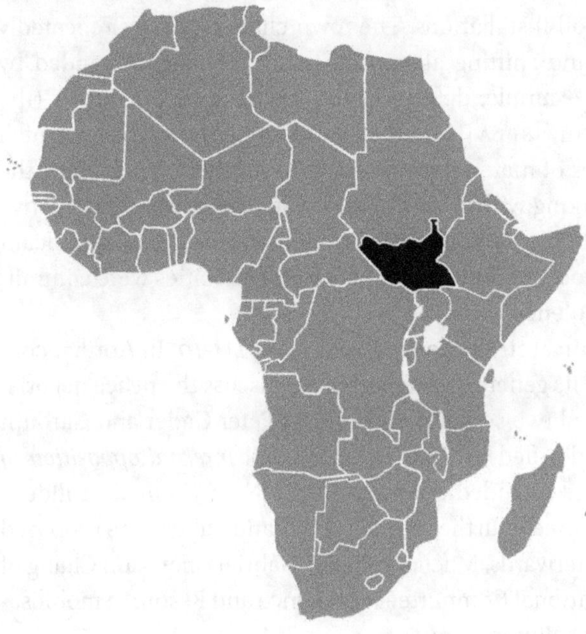

The year started with an escalation in South Sudan's civil war and, despite an agreement signed in August to stop the fighting, ended with formal peace but ongoing conflict. The August agreement officially created peace between the two main warring parties, but fighting and political struggle continued amidst a deteriorating humanitarian situation, a crisis in food production and the widening of low-level inter-communal conflict. Already hit by conflict, the oil industry further suffered from low international prices amidst severe economic crisis.

Domestic Politics

Much attention went into *peace negotiation efforts* in Addis Ababa (Ethiopia). Numerous deadlines in the negotiations, mediated by IGAD, came and went. President Salva Kiir Mayardit, for the Government of South Sudan, and Riek Machar Teny Dhurgon, for the Sudan People's Liberation Movement-In Opposition (SPLM-IO), signed another ceasefire agreement in February. It did not work. Nor did further face-to-face talks between the two leaders. While diplomacy continued in Addis Ababa, fighting continued in South Sudan and often the two were

 | DOI 10.1163/9789004333239_040

connected. The two parties again failed to come to an agreement by an IGAD deadline of 5 March, leading to a new *'IGAD-Plus' initiative*.

After the political process collapsed, government and allied forces mounted an offensive from April against the SPLM-IO in Jonglei, Unity and Upper Nile. The *surge in fighting* in Upper Nile saw heavy clashes around Malakal, its capital and gateway to the state's main oil installations. The town changed hands repeatedly and there were defections and shifting alliances. Shilluk forces commanded by General Johnson Olony, for example, defected from the government forces (the Sudan People's Liberation Army [SPLA]) and then fought with the SPLM-IO, which brought significant quantities of materiel to IO forces. In southern Unity state, the SPLA – and those forces working with it – engaged in the worst, most destructive campaign of the civil war to date, enabling the government to recapture a significant amount of territory. In the process, some of the war's worst atrocities were committed, including gross sexual violence.

Internal divisions and political strife characterised the *SPLM-IO*. In April, it convened a conference in Pagak, its general headquarters, to discuss the peace negotiations. In July, Machar removed two senior commanders, Peter Gadet and Garouth Gatkouth; fearing arrest, Gadet fled to Khartoum (Sudan). *Internal opposition to Machar's leadership* grew, and included a section of the Nuer Council of Elders. On 2 August, the SPLM-IO started a further Pagak consultation about the proposed IGAD agreement. Not long afterwards, Machar relieved Gabriel Changson Chang of his position as chair of the National Committee for Finance and Resource mobilisation; he later formed his own splinter group.

Throughout the year, there were *efforts to reunify the Sudan People's Liberation Movement* (*SPLM*) following the events of December 2013. These were led by Tanzania's ruling party, the 'Chama Cha Mapinduzi' (CCM) and South Africa's ruling African National Congress, who facilitated dialogue. Kiir, Machar and Deng Alor Kuol, the former cabinet affairs minister representing former detainees, signed a *Reunification Agreement* on 21 January in Arusha (Tanzania). On 1 June, five former detainees, including Kuol and former justice minister John Luk Jok, returned to Juba to meet Kiir. This advance guard was accompanied by South Africa's Deputy President Cyril Ramaphosa, the CCM secretary general, and the foreign ministers of Ethiopia and Kenya. On 3 June, Kiir revoked his previous orders and reinstated Kuol and Jok in the SPLM. In November, other members of the group, including Rebecca Nyandeng de Mabior, widow of the late SPLM leader John Garang de Mabior, Majak Agot, former deputy defence minister, and Oyah Deng Ajak, former minister of national security, returned to Juba.

Despite efforts to mend the SPLM, Kiir consolidated his position in the party. In January, the government announced that it would postpone elections, which had been scheduled for 30 June. In March, Parliament agreed an *extension of tenure* for the president, the National Legislature and the State Legislative Assemblies by three years, until 9 July 2018. The SPLM-IO and former detainees rejected these extensions as unconstitutional. In October, the SPLM was reformed following an extraordinary meeting of its National Liberation Council. The party dissolved its leadership structure and removed SPLM officials from their positions, with the exception of Kiir, who remained as chairman.

Beyond such elite politics, the *political climate deteriorated.* In March, a controversial new *National Security Service Bill* became law, despite lacking the president's signature. The authorities systematically sought to co-opt, capture or coerce civil society organisations and to enshrine control in legislation. In May, the National Legislative Assembly passed the *Non-Governmental Organisations Bill,* creating a regulatory framework for NGOs, but Kiir returned the bill for parliamentary scrutiny following concerns raised by civil society and members of the diplomatic community.

The *human rights* situation reached new lows. Aside from the fighting, National Security and SPLA Military Intelligence forces made arbitrary arrests and detained many suspected of supporting the opposition. A climate of fear, intimidation and violence greatly restricted the scope of independent media and civil society. *Journalists* were arrested and detained. At least six were killed, including a reporter, Peter Julius Moi, shot in August not long after Kiir threatened to kill journalists "working against South Sudan". There was a sharp deterioration in the state of *freedom of the press and association.* National Security shut down a number of media outlets, including the print edition of the 'Nation Mirror', 'The Citizen' and 'Al Rai'.

Relations between the government, armed opposition and the international presence deteriorated. Criticism of the belligerents from outside South Sudan was matched by criticism of the international community from within the country. The tone was set in January, when UN Secretary-General Ban Ki-moon criticised Kiir and Machar for putting their own interests first and failing to agree a power-sharing accord. In June, the head of the UN's Department of Peacekeeping Operations accused the Kiir government of refusing to cooperate with the UN and harassing its personnel; the UN resident humanitarian coordinator, Toby Lanzer, was declared persona non grata and branded an 'enemy' of South Sudan. After March, the *obstruction of humanitarian assistance and peacekeeping operations* escalated. By December, at least 43 humanitarian workers had been killed since mid-December 2013.

International pressure on the warring parties to stop fighting continued. In March, UNSC resolution 2206 created a system to impose *sanctions* against those contributing to the conflict. The sanctions committee created by the resolution designated six individuals for targeted sanctions. In June, the AU appointed former the Malian president, Alpha Oumar Konare, as AU High Representative for South Sudan, and the *AU Peace and Security Council* (AUPSC) called for "urgent steps" by the UN sanctions committee to take measures against warring parties in South Sudan who continued to defy efforts to end the conflict. On 24 July, *IGAD-Plus* proposed a new draft compromise agreement peace agreement and gave the two South

Sudanese parties until 17 August to sign a final deal. There was further *American pressure* to get a deal signed. In early August, US President Barack Obama warned Kiir and Machar that, if they failed to meet the 17 August deadline to sign the proposed compromise agreement, it would be necessary "to move forward with a different plan, and recognise that those leaders are incapable of creating the peace that is required". The USA submitted a draft resolution to the UNSC, calling for an arms embargo and further sanctions if peace was not agreed by 1 September.

This contributed to the headline event of the year, the so-called 'August peace agreement'. Machar signed this IGAD-mediated *Agreement on the Resolution of the Conflict in the Republic of South Sudan* on 17 August on behalf of the SPLM-IO, together with Pagan Amum Okiech on behalf of the 'former detainees'. This followed an IGAD Heads of State summit featuring a meeting between Kiir and Machar. Bending under heavy international pressure, Kiir eventually signed on 26 August. The agreement committed both parties to a permanent ceasefire, a power sharing Transitional Government of National Unity, and other provisions, such as the creation of a Commission for Truth, Reconciliation and Healing, a Compensation and Reparations Authority, and a Hybrid Court. Even as Kiir signed, however, the government circulated a document outlining detailed objections. These included opposition to central provisions of the agreement, such as the demilitarisation of Juba and the power-sharing structure of the executive.

Opposition to the agreement continued and deepened after its official signing. Divisions amongst South Sudan's political and military elite extended well beyond those formally negotiating on behalf of the government and the SPLM-IO, and arose in local settings in many parts of the country. Within government ranks, Chief of General Staff Lieutenant General Paul Malong Awan was vehemently critical and many also opposed the agreement within the SPLM-IO. One of the fiercest critics was the president himself. On 15 September, he said the agreement "attacked seriously the sovereignty of our country". Ominously echoing Sudan's former president Jaafar Nimeiri's critique of the 1972 Addis Ababa peace agreement when he was reneging on its terms, Kiir said that: "The IGAD proposed Compromise Peace Agreement is neither a Holy Bible nor Quran."

Despite generating hope in some quarters, in practice the agreement only created a formal framework for peace. The day after Machar signed, forces loyal to the SPLM-IO attacked a government garrison in Pageri, Eastern Equatoria, and, despite the formal ceasefire and ratification of the agreement by South Sudan's parliament on 10 September, SPLA conduct did not change in southern Unity, where government forces continued to attack SPLM-IO units. Nonetheless, *implementation of the peace deal* became a priority. The international community mobilised to support it, with reluctant, stop-start moves by the two parties to begin to implement selected aspects. In October, IGAD appointed the former president of Botswana, Festus Gontebanye Mogae, to lead the body created to oversee implementation of the agreement, the Joint Monitoring and Evaluation Commission (JMEC).

The government and the SPLM-IO signed a *permanent ceasefire* and transitional security arrangements, committing both to demilitarising Juba and other towns. In late November, the SPLA started to withdraw troops from Juba. Not long afterwards, the first meeting of the JMEC convened in Juba, but without SPLM-IO representation.

A political earthquake occurred on 2 October, when Kiir issued a decree announcing the *division of South Sudan*'s ten states into 28 new states. Modifying a proposal initially made by an influential group of Dinka leaders, the Jieng Council of Elders, this massively controversial redrawn political map was seen to create a form of *ethnic partition*, isolating Nuer communities in their own states and leaving Dinka in control of much of South Sudan. Unity and Upper Nile were each divided into three separate states, with the oil fields in Upper Nile coming, in effect, under Dinka control. The SPLM-IO and many other political parties condemned the announcement. In October, a new, predominantly Shilluk, group based in Wedokona, Upper Nile, formed to fight the 'unconstitutional' decree. IGAD also declared it to be against the spirit and letter of the peace agreement. Despite widespread opposition, Kiir continued with his plan.

The geography of *conflict expanded* as the year progressed, partly driven by the redrawn political map and other, inter-communal tensions. Fighting resumed in central and southern Unity in October, but low-level conflict was also spreading in other regions. *New rebel groups* appeared in Western Equatoria. The Arrow Boys mobilised amidst increased clashes between the SPLA and armed youths. Eastern Equatoria saw tensions. The situation in Northern Bahr el-Ghazal and Western Bahr el-Ghazal deteriorated, with government air strikes on 6 December and insecurity around Wau. Conflict also worsened in Jonglei in late December, especially in Pibor, after the appointment of a former deputy governor of Jonglei as governor of the proposed new Boma state.

The long delayed report of the *AU Commission of Inquiry on South Sudan*, created by the AUPSC in 2014, was finally released on 27 October (with a Separate Opinion by one member). A January meeting of the AUPSC had deferred consideration of the report. Finding *no evidence of the alleged coup* attempt against Kiir in December 2013, it concluded that "widespread and systematic" killings had occurred in Juba in December 2013, later spreading to other parts of South Sudan, and that these were coordinated and "could have been planned". South Sudan's Foreign Minister Barnaba Marial Benjamin rejected its findings, insisting that the conflict had been started by a coup attempt.

The August agreement failed to produce a meaningful reduction of violence. The year ended with continuing efforts to implement the agreement, ongoing low-level conflict and a worsening humanitarian situation. An SPLM-IO advance team entered Juba on 21 December led by Taban Deng Gai, its chief negotiator. Machar was supposed to return but did not. On Christmas Eve, new governors for the 28 states were appointed, and sworn in on 29 December. A *lack of political will* meant there had been minimal progress towards establishing the Transitional Government of National Unity.

Foreign Affairs

Much of South Sudan's foreign relations revolved around and concerned the conflict and the politics of fighting or negotiating peace. *International conflict mediation* backed by strong regional input evolved over the year. Early in the year, and in what it styled as supporting IGAD, *China* convened a consultative meeting of the two parties in Khartoum. The revised, expanded *IGAD-Plus* process, announced in March after 15 months of unsuccessful mediation, included the *UN*, the *EU*, the *Troika* (USA, UK and Norway), *China* and an *IGAD Partners Forum* (comprised of donor partners, with ministerial, ambassadorial and technical membership). The guiding approach appeared to be recognition that, without pressure, South Sudan's main warring parties would be unwilling to agree a peace deal and, in order to exert the necessary and coordinated pressure to push a deal through, IGAD needed wider international support. In June, IGAD-Plus was formally launched and supplied a 'synopsis' document to the parties setting out 'key provisions' of an agreement: *power-sharing, transitional governance and security arrangements.*

The *SPLM-IO* sought to secure regional and international support for its cause via diplomacy of its own. Machar was active in travelling to seek support. In mid-September, President Yoweri Museveni of Uganda visited Khartoum for talks about South Sudan's peace agreement but, shortly before he arrived, Machar was transported to Khartoum from Gambela, in western Ethiopia, by a Sudanese government plane. He then went to New York to participate in a UN high-level meeting on South Sudan. In October, he visited Washington, where US National Security Advisor Susan Rice cancelled a White House meeting citing the lack of commitment to implementing the peace process.

If much international engagement with the government of South Sudan concerned the quest for peace, much of Juba's foreign relations was aimed at addressing and circumventing international pressure, including over the issue of an arms embargo. On 10 September, for example, in an effort to secure *Russian support* at the UNSC, South Sudan's foreign minister and his Sudanese counterpart held talks with Russia's Foreign Minister Sergei Lavrov in Moscow. South Sudan wanted help in preventing the imposition of an arms embargo and widening sanctions. On 16 September, Russia and two non-permanent members of the UNSC blocked US moves to widen UN sanctions.

Kiir attended the AU Summit in South Africa in June. Vice-President James Wani Igga was sent to participate at the UN General Assembly in September. In early October, amidst ongoing friction, the White House cancelled a meeting with him and Pagan Amum. In late October, Kiir visited South Africa to brief President

Jacob Zuma on the peace deal, amidst stories that he was seeking medical treatment. Shortly afterwards, Kiir flew to *India* with a large delegation to participate in the India-Africa Forum Summit hosted by India's Prime Minister Narendra Modi in New Delhi. In November, Kiir, a Catholic, met *Pope Francis* in a private meeting in Kampala (Uganda). In early December, he went to Johannesburg (South Africa) to participate in the *6th Forum on China-Africa Cooperation*.

Juba's public diplomacy also sought to help address the domestic economic crisis. This included efforts to secure loans and renewed efforts to join the *EAC*. In March, *Sudan* and South Sudan's Joint Border Commission agreed to establish an escrow account to pay for border demarcation. As a measure of its economic stress, and with its payments to Khartoum falling behind, South Sudan tried to persuade Sudan to reduce the fees paid as part of its oil agreement. It signed an agreement to supply Sudan's Kosti power station with crude oil in return for electricity imports.

A further aspect of Juba's foreign relations was more difficult to pursue since it concerned military cooperation. Following the cooperation agreement with *Egypt* in March 2014, Juba continued military links with Cairo. In April, Chief of Staff Paul Malong Awan went to Cairo and met the Egyptian Defence Minister and Commander in Chief of Armed Forces General Sedki Sobhi. South Sudan's Minister of Defence Kuol Manyang Juuk followed up with a visit to Cairo in September.

In a year of further revelations and concern about the use of child soldiers in the conflict, South Sudan ratified the *Convention on the Rights of the Child*. It also became a party to the UN Convention against Torture and its Optional Protocol, and the Convention for the Elimination of Discrimination against Women and its Optional Protocol. In April, a hardly surprising announcement by South Sudan's justice minister stated that South Sudan would not sign the *Statute of Rome* and become a member of the ICC.

There was agreement to continue a cross-border humanitarian aid corridor, amid renewed accusations by South Sudan and Sudan about *cross-border intervention* and support for rebels in each other's territory. In October, after a meeting of their Joint Political and Security Mechanism, South Sudan and Sudan agreed to accept a proposal from the AU High-Level Implementation Panel for a safe militarised border zone along the South Sudan-Sudan border. South Sudan's military alliance with *Uganda* was renewed yet again in February. In October, however, Uganda announced that it would remove its forces and the withdrawal was finally completed in November. Apart from clandestine aid from Khartoum, regional support for Machar dwindled.

It was an acutely challenging year for *UN peacekeeping*. In May, the mandate of the UN Mission in South Sudan (*UNMISS*) was renewed to November, providing for a military component of up to 12,500 troops of all ranks and a police component of up to 1,323 personnel. In mid-December, the UNSC extended its mandate further to July 2016. It also extended the mandate of the *UN Interim Security Force for Abyei* until May 2016. UNMISS was challenged to implement its Chapter VII mandate to protect civilians. This included – but was by no means confined to – UMISS protection of six civilian sites housing more than 185,000 *IDPs*. UNMISS faced increasing requests for armed escorts for humanitarian convoys, a barometer of the levels of insecurity and danger facing international aid.

The dominant international response in South Sudan remained focused on a *humanitarian emergency*. There was some concern that 'development' in states not directly affected by conflict was being neglected, but the South Sudan Humanitarian Response Plan for 2015 focused almost entirely on humanitarian concerns. Efforts were made to scale up engagement to support the August peace agreement, and the UNMISS mandate was adjusted to support its implementation. The reality of conflict and a humanitarian emergency remained, however, rendering any serious peace-building effort hostage to the fate of the agreement.

Socioeconomic Developments

The human consequences of the war were severe. Beyond direct casualties (there being no proper record of fatalities), the total numbers of those experiencing *food insecurity and malnutrition* increased, with over 3.9 m facing severe food insecurity across South Sudan. As well as increasing, this spread to include areas previously considered relatively food secure, such as greater Equatoria region, Lakes, Northern Bahr el-Ghazal and Warrap. The conflict also had a massive impact on education and healthcare, with a significant contraction of what government role in these areas there had been in a country familiar with outsourcing such services to international agencies. In September, it was estimated that at least 55% of health facilities in Unity, Upper Nile and Jonglei were not functioning.

Government finances were badly affected by reduced *oil production* and exports. Oil production was lower than the approximate average for 2014 (around 165,000 b/d). Lower production resulted from the continuing complete shutdown of oil blocks in Unity and also from the further interruption of producing blocks in Upper Nile because of fighting. In May, for example, *China* evacuated some 400 workers from Paloch, Upper Nile, because of fighting; production later resumed when the SPLA regained control. South Sudan's income from oil was reduced not only by lower production but also by lower international oil prices and its fixed oil transit fee agreement with Sudan.

Spending pressures on the government grew. President Kiir replaced Finance Minister Aggrey Tisa Sabuni with David Deng Athorbei at the start of the year. In September, a *budget for the 2015/16 fiscal year* was finally passed and set total expenditure at SSP (pound) 10.3 bn ($ 3.55 bn at the then official exchange rate), a reduction of some 6% from the 2014/15 budget figure of SSP 11 bn. *Expenditure* continued to be dominated by security (SSP 4 bn of total expenditure), budgeted at substantially higher than education (SSP 800 m) and health (SSP 300 m). The *deficit* remained, being put at around SSP 3 bn.

The government faced fundamental economic problems. In May, Vice-President James Wani Igga implored regional leaders to save South Sudan from economic collapse. The government ran a monthly shortfall of at least $ 220 m, and borrowed to pay the public sector wage bill and other budget commitments, especially the priority defence and security sectors, and connected tribal patronage networks. *Public debt* rose significantly. The Ministry of Finance and Economic Planning admitted in June that debt was running at $ 4.2 bn, an increase of $ 700 m from January.

Inflation, foreign exchange and the exchange rate continued to be serious problems. The National Bureau of Statistics reported that the annual consumer price *inflation* rate increased by 109.9% between December 2014 and December 2015 (based on data from Juba and Wau). The price of staple foods – sorghum, beans, maize – reached record highs. The shortage of foreign exchange had a wide impact and hit business. In October, SABMiller, operating a factory on the outskirts of Juba producing a popular White Bull beer, cut production and laid off workers. A major problem it faced – as in South Sudan more generally – was the difference between the Bank of South Sudan's official *exchange rate* and the black market rate. While contributing to a major corruption scandal, the foreign exchange crisis finally led to the devaluation of the South Sudan pound on 15 December, and a floating rate was introduced. The official rate of SSP 2.96 : $ 1 moved to SSP 18.50.

In December, according to the UN Office for the Coordination of Humanitarian Affairs, there were about 1.66 m *IDPs* and 3.9 m people classified as 'severely food insecure' in South Sudan, as well as 645,992 *South Sudanese refugees* in neighbouring countries. Despite such large numbers of South Sudanese IDPs, the country also saw an increase in incoming refugees caused by fighting and instability in neighbouring countries. South Sudan was hosting some 265,700 refugees from the DRC, Ethiopia and the CAR, and importantly, Sudan. Forced out by fighting in South Kordofan and Blue Nile, *Sudanese refugees* continued arrive in Pariang, Unity State, and Maban, Upper Nile, so that the vast majority were encamped in parts of South Sudan where the conflict had been most intense.

Sudan

Laura James

The main domestic political preoccupation centred around attempts to hold a National Dialogue – seen as a means of dealing with the political crisis since the secession of South Sudan in 2011, which was expressed through civil war on the peripheries and anti-government demonstrations at the centre. The aim was to bring together the government, under the ruling National Congress Party (NCP), and both violent and non-violent opposition groups, in an inclusive process to discuss a common way forward. However, as the NCP regime, backed by the army and security services, reaffirmed its dominance in the country, inclusivity was progressively eroded. The opposition remained divided, marginalised and largely externalised, with key leaders exiled and meetings taking place abroad. The Sudanese government insisted that the long-planned National Dialogue should take place inside the country, with no external involvement, but failed to provide an enabling environment that would allow opposition and rebel groups to engage. The government was strengthened by rapprochement with the Gulf Arab states and their allies, in particular Saudi Arabia. Sudan was also part of the 'Muslim Alliance' against terrorism announced by Saudi Arabia in December. The *quid pro quo* for Sudan was both diplomatic and economic, with promises of agricultural investment. Sudan's more

 | DOI 10.1163/9789004333239_041

comfortable position in the Middle East region was complemented by relatively good relations with its immediate neighbours in Africa – most importantly, South Sudan, despite ongoing sources of tension. With regional linkages secured, Sudan was in a better position to manage relationships with global powers, although ties with the USA remained fraught. Sudan's economy continued to recover from the shock of South Sudanese secession. Monetary policy remained tight, but there were signs that fiscal discipline was slipping, and efforts at economic diversification and private sector development continued to flounder. The balance of payments also deteriorated sharply, causing further currency depreciation. Growth continued to be constrained by massive debt arrears, which limited options for new borrowing, and by US sanctions. Many of Sudan's peripheries continued to suffer from conflict and instability, with negative implications for overall livelihoods.

Domestic Politics

Political freedoms continued to be eroded. At the beginning of January, against opposition protest, the Constitution was amended to strengthen the National Intelligence and Security Services (NISS), legalising its recruitment of militia fighters, known as the Rapid Support Forces (RSF). Subsequently, the NISS sought to have one of the major historical opposition parties, the National Umma Party (NUP), dissolved. The power of President Omar al-Bashir was also boosted by the constitutional amendments, with provisions to allow him to appoint (formerly elected) state governors. The crackdown was particularly marked in the run-up to elections in April. Opposition figures were imprisoned or threatened, with the elderly chairman of the National Consensus Forces (NCF), Farouq Abu Issa, jailed for four months from December 2014 after signing up to the 'Sudan Call' for democratic transformation in the country, together with leaders of the NUP and the rebel Sudanese Revolutionary Front (SRF) and civil society leaders. The frequency of arrests and interrogations of journalists was also stepped up and, for the first time, many newspaper issues were seized in order to suppress articles on social as well as political issues. Pro-opposition civil society groups, such as the Sudanese Writers' Union, also had their licences revoked. Although the government formally agreed in September to end political detentions and censorship, and to ensure opposition freedoms, this undertaking was immediately broken, with further newspaper issues seized and activists arrested or prevented from travelling abroad. Two South Sudanese pastors were held for three months without trial on charges of espionage and sedition and, when they were eventually acquitted in August, they were prevented from leaving the country.

The government went ahead with *presidential and parliamentary elections* on 13–15 April, despite opposition and rebel demands that they should be postponed until after the completion of the National Dialogue. The polls were boycotted by most anti-government groupings, such as the NCF (including the NUP under Sadiq al-Mahdi) and the Reform Now Movement, established by Ghazi Salahedeen al-Atabani, an NCP defector. Many external bodies, including the EU, also refused to monitor the elections. An *AU* investigation team recommended that the AU should not send a monitoring mission, saying that the restrictive environment would make it impossible to hold credible elections, and advocated a delay to the polls; however, the AU overruled this advice and sent monitors. Al-Bashir won a new five-year term, with 94% of the vote, against a field of unknowns. The official turnout figure was 46%, but unofficial estimates were significantly lower, even though voting was extended by an additional day. The NCP also had a landslide victory in the National Assembly, winning 323 seats out of 426; the only significant opposition party to engage, the Democratic Unionist Party (DUP) under Mohammed Osman al-Mirghani, won just 25 seats. The DUP, which was a partner in the outgoing government, had already endorsed al-Bashir's bid for a new term, although at the cost of significant internal divisions and controversial expulsions.

The election victory further strengthened al-Bashir's position, although the fact that it took almost two months to negotiate the formation of a new government demonstrated that he still had to reckon with opposing regime views from both the highly influential military/security apparatus and the NCP party cadres. The *new cabinet*, named on 7 June after repeated failures to reach a consensus, also included 30% representation from opposition groupings that had participated in the polls, including the DUP. The overall line-up reinforced the impression of a *consolidation of presidential power*, including the appointment of a key loyalist and former presidential assistant, Ibrahim Ghandour, as foreign minister. The one exception was the loss of the president's close ally and defence minister, Abdelrahim Mohammed Hussein, who was not replaced until August (suggesting further hard bargaining). Hussein, who, like the president, had been indicted for war crimes in Darfur by the ICC, became governor of Khartoum – still a highly significant role. The week before the new government was announced, the chief of staff and other key military officers were also reshuffled, reflecting a broader realignment of power. Islamists and party cadres were further side-lined, with military-linked pragmatists, such as First Vice President Bakri Hassan Saleh, forming the backbone of the regime.

It was only after the new government had been announced that attention returned to the much-delayed *National Dialogue*, which was launched at a General Assembly dominated by government and allied nominees on 20 August. There had been ongoing efforts to start the process with a preparatory meeting in Addis Ababa (Ethiopia), under the aegis of the AU High-Level Implementation Panel for Sudan (AUHIP), headed by former South African president Thabo Mbeki. The purpose of this meeting would have been to agree rules of procedure, including safeguards for rebel and opposition groups. However, the government had in March at the last minute refused to attend, citing the nearness of elections and complaining of the selection of invitees from among the National Dialogue coordination body, known as the 7+7, with seven representatives from pro-government parties and seven from opposition groups – although the latter excluded the most important anti-government forces.

On 25 August, there was a renewed call by the AU Peace and Security Council (AUPSC), following its meeting with the 'Sudan Call' opposition holdouts, for an external *preparatory meeting*. However, the government vehemently rejected this and announced that it would proceed on its own, declaring that the enabling environment was already in place. Rebel forces were invited to participate and were offered a two-month ceasefire, but this was not taken seriously, and the president declared that the dialogue would go forward with whoever chose to attend. Of the main opposition forces, only the DUP and two Islamist groupings with strong historic linkages to the NCP – Hassan al-Turabi's Popular Congress Party and Al-Tayeb Mustafa's Just Peace Forum – decided to take part. A government-dominated National Dialogue therefore began on 10 October, and committee work proceeded through the end of the year. Meanwhile, the 'Sudan Call' opposition forces announced in November that they would "liquidate" the current regime and establish a transitional government, through a popular uprising if not through dialogue. This changed nothing on the ground.

Although the National Dialogue had originally been advocated as a comprehensive solution to Sudan's conflicts, in tandem with AUHIP-mediated peace talks, the failure to achieve a ceasefire or bring in the rebel groups through a preparatory meeting meant that the *fighting in Sudan's peripheries* rumbled on through the year. The rebels accused the government of offering empty guarantees; the government blamed the rebels for setting preconditions. Several rounds of *attempted peace talks* throughout the year, focused on achieving at least a cessation of hostilities and arrangements for humanitarian access, made no progress. One core tension was between the government's insistence on separating the questions of Darfur and the 'Two Areas' of South Kordofan and Blue Nile, while the rebel groups sought to present a united front and cooperate with the non-violent opposition in demanding a comprehensive approach. This was somewhat undermined in October, however, when an argument broke out within the SRF rebel alliance over whether the chairmanship should pass on from Malik Agar, leader of the Sudan People's Liberation Movement-North (SPLM-N), centred in the Two Areas, to Gibril Ibrahim, head of the main faction of the Justice and Equality Movement (JEM) – a more Islamist-leaning rebel group of Darfuri origins. The issue was still being contested at the end of the year. In November, the AUHIP hosted further talks between the government and the SRF, but the former insisted on separating the negotiating tracks for the Two Areas and Darfur, refusing to attend the joint opening session. Both tracks were soon suspended, with a failure to agree any common ground. A last-ditch attempt to hold a belated National Dialogue preparatory meeting in Addis Ababa, just to bring the SRF into the process, also floundered.

The confrontation between the Sudan Armed Forces (SAF) and the SPLM-N continued in the *Two Areas*, with the SPLM-N retaining territory in the Nuba Mountains and south of the Blue Nile capital, Damazin, near the South Sudan border. Fighting peaked in January, and again in August. The rebels also shelled the South Kordofan capital, Kadugli, during the elections in April. The result was an ongoing humanitarian crisis, but no real change in the balance of power between the two sides. In *Abyei*, another small border area disputed between Sudan and South Sudan, the presence of the United Nations Interim Security Force for Abyei (UNISFA), made up of Ethiopian troops, inhibited large-scale violence. Nevertheless, there were smaller attacks, after one of which, in May, UNISFA forces apprehended an individual claiming to be a Sudanese intelligence officer. In November, there was also an attack on the residence of the Ngok Dinka paramount chief, which was strongly condemned by the UNSC.

The conflict in *Darfur* proved even more intractable, in part because of the fragmentation of the violence. In January, the Doha Document for Peace in Darfur (DDPD), which had been rejected by all of the major rebel groups, was incorporated into the Sudanese Constitution. This was at a time when fighting had intensified further, with 100,000 new displacements in January alone (adding to the 2 m long-term internally displaced persons), as the SAF and government-allied militias, including the RSF, launched a renewed assault on the positions of several factions of the rebel Sudan Liberation Movement (SLM) in Eastern Jebel Marra, including the principal groupings led by Minni Minnawi and Abdelwahed al-Nur. There was another peak in displacements in South Darfur in November.

In addition to the direct conflict between government and rebels, there was also a growth in *localised violence* and lawlessness (including attacks on civilians and kidnappings for ransom), as well as inter-tribal fighting. The most significant outbreaks were between the Rizeigat and the Ma'alia tribes, in East Darfur, which rumbled on throughout the year, despite attempted reconciliation conferences, with the Ma'alia blaming the government for the conflict. However, significant clashes and casualties were also reported across the Darfur region between the Falata and Masalit, Berti and Zayadia, Birgat and Khazam, Falata and Salamat, and Rizeigat and Misseriya. The violence reflected the influx of weapons into the region in recent years, as well as, in many cases, competition over the lands of farming communities displaced as long ago as 2003. Despite all this, al-Bashir continued to call for the UN-AU Mission in Darfur (UNAMID) to leave Darfur, arguing that the only remaining conflicts were local and amenable to traditional resolution.

On the political side, the Liberation and Justice Movement (LJM), under Tijani al-Sissi, the traditional leader of the Fur people, continued to work with the NCP regime and to control the *Darfur Regional Authority*. The LJM, made up of small breakaway factions from the SLM and JEM, had been formed specifically to sign the DDPD in 2011. By early 2015, however, it was under intense internal pressure, with al-Sissi coming in for strong criticism from Secretary-General Bahar Idriss Abu Garda, and others, including with accusations of corruption. The LJM nevertheless continued cooperation with the NCP through elections, with only a brief suspension in June as part of the negotiations for ministerial portfolios in the new government. This pressure, however, was much less effective than that exerted on the government by a far more dangerous ally, Musa Hilal, the chief of the Mahameed tribe and leader of the *Sudanese Revolutionary Awakening Council*, a key figure in the former 'Janjaweed' militias. Hilal threatened an election boycott, demanded to be allowed to form his own political party, and demonstrated his influence even in Khartoum when he arrived to a vociferous reception from his supporters at the end of May, to attend al-Bashir's inauguration. These tactics clearly paid off; shortly after Hilal met with the head of the NISS in June, his arch-enemy, Osman Kibir, the longstanding governor of North Darfur, was removed in the reshuffle. It was also confirmed that in April 2016 the promised *referendum* would take place on whether Darfur should be one region (as desired by al-Sissi and the rebels) or five states (as preferred by Hilal and most Arab tribes) – with the latter seeming to be in a much stronger position.

Foreign Affairs

In March, al-Bashir visited *Saudi Arabia* for talks with King Salman, and shortly afterwards the SAF announced that ground troops were on the way to take part in the Saudi-led 'Operation Decisive Storm' against the Iran-backed Houthi rebels in *Yemen*. At the beginning of April, it was stated that the Sudanese air force was also participating. President Hadi of Yemen visited Khartoum in August, and soon afterwards the government confirmed that it was preparing to send additional forces to support the operation – a promise repeated by the defence minister in December. Up to 10,000 men were reportedly promised, though actual deployment was probably much lower. Al-Bashir, who had previously been cold-shouldered on trips to Riyadh, visited the king again in May, July and November, with high-level economic delegations. Sudan's 'Arab Food Security Initiative' to encourage *Gulf agricultural investment* took on a new lease of life. This new departure was further enabled by the rapprochement between Saudi Arabia and *Qatar*, which remained an important Sudanese ally. It did, however, necessitate a firmer cutting of ties with Saudi Arabia's current arch-enemy, *Iran*, a long-term military supplier for Khartoum. In March, Foreign Minister Ali Karti denied that the two countries had ever been allied.

In February, al-Bashir also paid an official visit to the *UAE* – where bilateral relations had previously deteriorated owing to the two countries' support for rival governments in Libya. He took a large delegation, including economic-sector ministers as well as those relevant to his stated purpose of discussing cooperation against *ISIS*, including in Libya. A rash of high-profile flights to join ISIS by Sudanese medical students in the middle of the year had boosted the government's activism in that area. A follow-up visit in November covered similar issues, and went well enough for al-Bashir to stay on for a week's holiday. By that time, Sudan's stance on *Libya* had also changed significantly. In January, the internationally recognised government in Benghazi was banning the entry of Sudanese citizens and threatening to shoot down aircraft, and as late as April detained the Sudanese consul. At the end of May, however, correspondence resumed between the Libyan prime minister and al-Bashir, and in October the Foreign Ministry expressed support for a UN-brokered deal proposing a national unity government for Libya.

Closer to home, there continued to be major sources of tension with *South Sudan*: each government periodically accused the other of support for its respective rebel groups – with some justification, as historic linkages between al-Bashir's regime and the Southern Sudanese rebel leader Riek Machar certainly remained in play, while the SRF was reliably reported to be assisting the South Sudanese army against Machar. Each country hosted large numbers of refugees from the other: over 180,000 Southerners were estimated to be in Sudan, while about 260,000 Sudanese had fled in the opposite direction. In April, the government of South Sudan complained that the SAF was also engaging in cross-border bombing raids, and in May its security forces detained a Sudanese embassy employee, accusing him of espionage. However, these hostile moves were interspersed with much more positive rhetoric, and in April the South Sudan's President Salva Kiir described the two countries' differences as 'trivial'.

Both governments repeatedly expressed their intention of implementing the *cooperation agreements* they had signed in 2012. In March, they held technical discussions on border demarcation, and in October agreed to activate a buffer zone and deploy joint monitoring units – although, given the ongoing fighting and tensions in the border areas, little actually changed on the ground. Their common interest in keeping the oil from South Sudan flowing through Sudan, which earned the latter significant fees, kept the overall relationship from deteriorating beyond a certain point. In March, South Sudan sought to renegotiate these fixed payments, which were poorly suited to an era of lower international oil prices, but with little success. In August, Juba launched a new diplomatic push to improve bilateral relations.

Better relations with the South Sudanese government in Juba were closely linked to a cautious rapprochement with its closest ally, *Uganda*. In February, Uganda's President Museveni announced that he had expelled Sudanese rebel leaders; and in August al-Bashir called on Museveni to use his influence to persuade the rebels to take part in the National Dialogue. This process culminated in September with an unprecedented visit to Khartoum by Museveni, after which the two presidents declared their joint support for peace and stability in South Sudan. In December, Sudan's vice president paid a return visit to discuss outstanding security issues.

Sudan also managed to maintain a precarious balance in terms of its relationships with *Egypt and Ethiopia*, as the three countries sought, sometimes acrimoniously, to negotiate the mechanism for operating the new *Grand Ethiopian Renaissance Dam*. Khartoum largely played the role of mediator between the two opposing interests, hosting the signing of an initial cooperation deal in March, and a more significant

agreement in December. Bilateral relations with *Egypt* were generally cordial, as the Sudanese government supported Cairo in its crackdown on Islamist militants, despite protests from its own Islamist movement. There were periodic tensions over Egyptian fishermen or Sudanese miners who were arrested on the wrong side of the border, as well as over the long-disputed territory of the Halayeb triangle, and in November complaints surfaced about the mistreatment of Sudanese nationals in Cairo by the Egyptian security services. However, these were resolved by determined high-level cordiality. In July, Egypt's President al-Sisi offered cooperation in implementing al-Bashir's Arab Food Security Initiative, while in August al-Bashir himself attended the opening ceremony for the New Suez Canal, al-Sisi's pet project.

At the same time, Sudan also sought to retain recently established positive relations with *Ethiopia*, strengthening both political and economic ties. In February, al-Bashir paid a formal visit, and a dissident Ethiopian general who fled to Khartoum with his Eritrean forces in September was politely returned to the Ethiopian government. The two countries cooperated to address the problem of Sudanese and Ethiopian bandits ('shifta') operating in remote border areas, and in November announced plans to redraw the border itself, as well as establishing a free-trade zone. Moreover, a third country was held in balance with this relationship, as Sudan also managed to remain on terms with Ethiopia's enemy *Eritrea*, even after the September repatriation. Eritrea's President Afewerki paid an official visit in June, and al-Bashir met the Ethiopian finance minister at the beginning of October, seeking to smooth things over, a reasonable degree of amity with Eritrea being important for maintaining peace in eastern Sudan. Similarly, President Idriss Deby of *Chad* remained on-side with respect to the management of rebels, handing several Darfuri insurgents over to the Sudanese police in May, and bringing three SLM splinter groups with him to Khartoum to join the National Dialogue in October.

A complex diplomatic dance continued with the *USA*, alternating suspicion and détente. There were repeated visits to discuss 'normalisation' of bilateral ties, and, following a trip to Washington by the Sudanese foreign minister in February, the USA amended its Sudan sanctions regime to allow exports of personal communications equipment and software. However, the sanctions themselves were renewed in November, and US officials repeatedly criticised the country's human rights record and failure to reach agreement with rebels – while Sudanese officials continued to regard the USA with suspicion. Relations with European countries such as the UK, France and Germany, followed a broadly similar, but less high-profile, pattern. All three continued to provide facilities to Sudanese opposition groups.

An additional cause of tension with Western countries was the debate over an 'exit strategy' for *UNAMID*, which Sudan argued was no longer necessary. Relations with the UN were very bad at the beginning of the year, in the wake of the expulsions of two senior UN officials, and reached another low point in April after an attack on Nigerian peacekeepers, whom the government blamed for killing civilians in response. In October, a dispute over delays to shipping containers destined for the mission caused a further diplomatic fracas. Discussions of how UNAMID might withdraw from stable parts of Darfur began in February and continued throughout the year. However, in June the UNSC unanimously renewed the UNAMID mandate, tying the exit strategy to progress in the security and humanitarian situation.

This renewal was particularly disappointing for Sudan as it highlighted the limits of its support from UNSC permanent members Russia and China. Al-Bashir visited *China* in August, and military cooperation between the two countries continued, as did oil sector investment. *Russia* also sought to boost relations, promising military aid and inviting ministerial visits. Russian companies agreed to invest in natural gas, gold and uranium mining in Sudan, while in September Russia made an unsuccessful bid to become the new host of the bilateral Sudan-South Sudan dialogue. However, Russian opposition to the Saudi position in the Middle East set some limits on the possible partnership with Sudan.

Russia and China continued to prevent the UNSC from following up on the referral of al-Bashir and other Sudanese officials to the *ICC*, which was seen as increasingly illegitimate among non-Western governments. In January, the AU Executive Council drafted a resolution demanding that the UNSC should cancel the referral outright, and in October India was added to the list of countries allowing al-Bashir to visit. The most significant instance was al-Bashir's visit to South Africa, an ICC signatory, in June, when the government failed to arrest him and allowed him to leave the country, despite a local court ruling. This followed a visit to Khartoum by South Africa's President Zuma in January, and was succeeded by a meeting between the two leaders in Beijing (China) in September, which reportedly focused on ways to confront the ICC. Nevertheless, the South African government apparently asked whether someone other than al-Bashir could attend when it hosted the Forum of China-Africa Cooperation in December.

Socioeconomic Developments

The IMF estimated that Sudan's real *GDP growth* was around 3.5%, down slightly from 3.6% in 2014 – disappointing for a developing country, especially given that population growth was estimated at 3.1%. On balance, the drop in international oil prices benefitted Sudan, as it had been a net oil importer since the South Sudanese secession, and the substantial payments for use of the pipeline and export facilities that it received from South Sudan were not tied to price, being set at $ 24.10/ barrel – although, as Juba struggled financially, there is evidence that some oil was provided as payment in kind to Sudan's refinery and electricity plants, while part of the payment also went into arrears.

Sudan made ongoing efforts to boost its own modest *oil production* from 120,000 b/d to 150,000 b/d, signing a new agreement with the Chinese National Petroleum Company in January and commencing drilling in the new Al-Rawat oilfield, in White Nile state, in October. However, there was little progress. In a statement in September, the oil minister blamed the reluctance of the oil companies to engage in repair work, given the low oil prices. Sudan also sought to increase *gold mining*, most of which was done by small-scale traditional miners – who seemed to have been smuggling some of their output rather than following the legal requirement of selling it to the Central Bank. The government tried to encourage more large-scale foreign investment in the sector, granting gold exploration concessions to a Russian firm in July (to some controversy, given the inflated reserve figures that were cited, as well as the relatively low profile of the company in question), and to three other companies, including an Italian firm, in November. In March, a US NGO, Enough, demanded that the US government impose specific sanctions on Sudan's gold output, some of which had been linked to intensified local conflicts in Darfur.

An extremely good harvest in 2014/15 supported *agricultural output*, although poor mid-year rains, both in Sudan itself and in neighbouring Ethiopia, the source of most of the Nile water, led to predictions of famine in 2016. In September, FAO appealed to donors to contribute to help small farmers and pastoralists in Darfur and Kordofan. The government itself remained more focused on its efforts to encourage large-scale agricultural investment for export, hosting discussions in April with Egypt and Saudi Arabia on the president's 'Arab Food Security' proposal. A new draft agricultural law caused controversy in June, as discontented MPs from the Gezira farming area demanded that it should be returned to parliament after the president refused to sign it. At mid-year, the IMF warned that expansionary fiscal policies to support agriculture had "injected considerable liquidity in the economy", but these must have been reined in, since, over the full year, money supply remained well under control.

The 2015 *budget*, as expected in an election year, did not introduce new taxes and kept in place existing subsidies on wheat and petrol. The finance minister forecast revenues of SDG (pound) 61.4 bn, up 33% from 2014, and expenditure of SDG 59.8 bn, up 30% – both relatively conservative increases in real terms, given the level of inflation. The latest IMF data estimated that the government in fact received significantly lower than planned revenue of SDG 50.8 bn, despite increases in taxes on tobacco in May, and spent slightly more than intended, at SDG 60.3 bn, despite lower-than-expected outlay on subsidies as a result of falling commodity prices. This boosted the fiscal deficit to an estimated 1.8% of GDP (the government claimed 1.2%), up from 1.1% in 2014, in what had been a steadily narrowing trend since secession. In a possible attempt to make up for this loss of fiscal discipline, the Finance Ministry in December mooted a *subsidy* reduction in the 2016 budget, but after strong negative public reaction and presidential intervention, conceded that this would not be done until there was a further shift in global oil prices. At the same time, the president responded to criticism of the high share of the budget allocated to the army and security services, saying that even more was needed. A draft *anti-corruption* law was approved by the cabinet in August, and sent on to parliament. However, there was no high-profile action against officials accused of corruption, with the president refusing to accept the resignation of one minister facing allegations in December.

The *trade deficit* widened sharply to $ 6.3 bn (from $ 4.9 bn in 2014). Imports rose slightly as a result of more spending on manufactured goods and machinery, despite cheaper fuel and wheat import bills. The value of oil exports halved, while non-oil exports also fell by 18%, including a 26% drop in earnings from gold. As a result, the *current account deficit* expanded sharply to $ 6 bn, compared with $ 3.5 bn in 2014. *FDI* continued to rise, but slowly, totalling just $ 1.7 bn. Large-scale government efforts to encourage agricultural investment by Arab Gulf allies – for instance, with the announcement of six free trade zones in February – had little concrete impact so far, despite the signing of a number of new agreements, including for dam construction. There were reports of some significant deposits into the Central Bank of Sudan in return for assistance in Yemen – with allegations in April of a $ 4 bn transfer from Saudi Arabia, although this was denied by Saudi officials. Whatever was provided was certainly not enough to balance the current account deficit, as foreign reserves declined by $ 38 m, while the Sudanese currency came under renewed pressure.

Despite all of the overblown reports of Gulf deposits, foreign currency remained in short supply, and there was also a steady *depreciation* of the Sudanese pound on the parallel market to SDG 11.6 : $ 1 by the end of December, from about SDG 8.8 : $ 1 in 2014. This compared with an official rate of SDG 6.1 : $ 1, and a rate of SDG 3.4 : $ 1 at the time of South Sudanese secession in July 2011. In October, when the SDG 10 : $ 1 barrier was breached, the police cracked down on currency traders, arresting several, which did nothing to reverse the trend.

Despite the combination of fiscal and currency pressures, however, the authorities did manage the money supply so as to bring *inflation* under control. By the end of the year, it stood at 12.6% – half the level seen in January. Average annual inflation was just under 18%, below target and significantly less than the 34% recorded in 2014 (when it was boosted by the late 2013 fuel subsidy cuts). The improvement was driven by a slower rise in food prices. Nevertheless, yet another year of double-digit inflation, at a time when wages and the broader economy were largely stagnant, was still extremely difficult for most households. They also suffered from shortages of subsidised flour in April, a rise in mobile telephone charges in May, and a lack of petrol in some states in June. In July, the governorate of Khartoum expressed its intention of increasing water and electricity tariffs to cover costs, while women took to the streets to protest about water shortages.

Many of Sudan's peripheries continued to suffer from conflict and instability, threatening both lives and livelihoods. In May, the UN and the Sudanese government launched a joint appeal asking donors to provide $ 1 bn to meet *humanitarian needs* for 5.4 m people across the country. Conflicts resulted in new displacements, especially in Darfur, where a number of IDP camps faced water shortages. They also disrupted the local economy: in September, the governor of South Kordofan threatened the death penalty for those trading with rebel areas. Conflict was also bound up with ongoing environmental degradation, linked to maladaptive livelihood strategies such as unsustainable grazing and deforestation, as well as to the impacts of climate change. Overall, the Sudanese population, which topped 38 m, saw only a slow improvement in key *development indicators*. The under-five mortality rate declined slightly, to 70.1 per 1000. The fall was part of an ongoing trend, but the rate remained well above the global average of 42.5 – and closer to the 83.2 seen in SSA than the 23.3 recorded in the MENA region. UNDP's 2015 Human Development Report put multidimensional poverty in Sudan at 53%, with 19.8% of the population living on less than $ 1.25 a day.

Tanzania

Kurt Hirschler and Rolf Hofmeier

The political scene was entirely focused on presidential and parliamentary elections in October. In a tight electoral contest with a strengthened opposition coalition, the long-ruling CCM party was able to defend a more than two-thirds majority in parliament and to see John Pombe Magufuli elected as the new president upon the expiry of President Kikwete's two-term mandate. The opposition proved unable to unseat the deeply-entrenched CCM system. Separate elections in semi-autonomous Zanzibar were declared void in dubious circumstances, with no crisis solution in sight before the year's end. A promised referendum on a new constitution was not held. Magufuli introduced an unforeseen new leadership style, stressing discipline, rigorous cost-saving measures and serious ant-corruption efforts in state institutions. This earned him popularity among the general public, but also raised questions about an emerging authoritarian streak. Relations with Western aid donors were slightly strained over dissatisfaction with a lack of reform measures and the Zanzibar election issue. Macroeconomic performance and growth continued to be strong, but managing the budget proved to be difficult.

 | DOI 10.1163/9789004333239_042

Domestic Politics

The *October elections* were the first in Tanzanian history that seemed to offer the faint possibility of an opposition victory. Numerous scandals had tarnished the image of the long-ruling CCM ('Chama cha Mapinduzi'/Party of the Revolution). In a reaction to the escrow account scandal in late 2014, President Jakaya Kikwete was forced to execute another *cabinet reshuffle* less than a year before the end of his final term. With the resignation of Energy Minister Sospeter Muhongo on 24 January, all senior officials who were implicated in the scandal had resigned or were dismissed, including two ministers, the attorney-general and some influential MPs and party cadres. This was Kikwete's seventh reshuffle in his ten-year tenure, all caused by alleged gross misbehaviour or underperformance of his ministers.

After an inclusive consultation process, the *Constitutional Review Commission* (CRC) had in 2013 compiled a draft for a new constitution, which had been intended to be discussed and finally adopted by a Constituent Assembly (CA) in October 2014. The CRC's draft had been supported by opposition parties; however, using its majority in the CA, CCM had changed the CRC's draft in some fundamental aspects. This draft was then to be submitted to a *referendum*, scheduled for 20 April. Doubts arose as to whether the referendum date could be met, given the slow pace of the biometric voter registration process, initially planned to start in November 2014, but delayed until February by the government's failure to provide the necessary funds. The National Electoral Commission (NEC) had initially planned to acquire 15,000 registration kits but this was reduced to just 8,000 by financial constraints. However, when registration started on 24 February, the NEC had received only 250 registration kits and it was not until mid-April that 3,000 more kits arrived. Consequently, on 2 April, NEC chairman Damian Lubuva announced that the referendum had to be postponed indefinitely. The voter registration process then continued until early August. The *postponement of the referendum* on the draft of a new constitution was received with satisfaction by opposition parties, the media and civil society organisations; for months they had called for a postponement and had demanded that the issue of the constitution needed to be addressed with consensus and should not be entangled with the election campaigning of competing political parties.

Unlike in many other African countries, there was no attempt to extend Kikwete's two constitutional terms, which were to end with general elections on 25 October. Therefore, CCM's internal selection process for a *presidential candidate* was crucial and turned out to be much more contentious than on any previous occasion. By 3 June, 42 CCM members, the highest-ever number of contestants, had picked up application forms. The unprecedented number of contestants was an indication of the *unpredictability of the selection process*. During recent years, no senior politician had been able to commend her- or himself as an obvious potential successor to Kikwete. Only the former prime minister, *Edward Lowassa*, was regarded by many as a 'natural' candidate. In 2008, he had had to resign following corruption allegations, which he had always denied. He had become the most controversial figure in CCM and among the population – condemned by many as the prototype of a corrupt politician, but celebrated by others as an innocent victim of intrigues and a gifted leader. In the run-up to the elections, the party was clearly split into a Lowassa-camp and an anti-Lowassa-camp. Although he never publicly indicated support for any of the contestants, Kikwete was assumed to favour Foreign Minister Bernard Membe, who came to be regarded as Lowassa's strongest opponent and the favourite of the anti-Lowassa-camp.

The *selection process* followed a well-established procedure. The nine-member party secretariat had to vet all applications using 13 criteria. On 10 July, the CCM National Security and Ethics Committee, led by party chairman Kikwete, scrutinised the applications and gave its recommendations to the 32-member Central Committee, which had to select five candidates from the original 38. The five were: Membe, Minister of Justice and former UN Deputy Secretary-General Asha-Rose Migiro, Minister of Works John Pombe Magufuli, AU Ambassador to the USA Amina Salum Ali and January Makamba, a young, albeit very influential politician, who had served as Kikwete's speech-writer and was the current deputy minster for communication. The *surprise omission of Lowassa* from this shortlist provoked massive protest from his many supporters and accusations of foul play by Kikwete. Despite an apparent split in the party, the large 378-member National Executive Committee continued according to procedures and approved three names to be forwarded to the highest party organ: Magufuli, Amina and Migiro. Although the selection depended mainly on political considerations, it was nevertheless surprising that two of the three recommended candidates were women. The CCM National Congress, consisting of about 2,100 members, met on 11–12 July and approved *Magufuli* as the party's *presidential candidate* with an overwhelming majority of 87% of the votes.

The 55-year old *Magufuli*, who had a PhD in chemistry, had been an MP since 1995 and had held several ministerial portfolios. He had earned public approval as minister of works, when he was seen responsible for successful road construction efforts over the past five years. Nicknamed 'bulldozer' for his record as public works minister, but also for his authoritarian leadership style, he had a reputation for being a hard worker who had never been involved in any scandals and was not well-connected in the innermost party circles. Magufuli named Minister of State for Union Affairs Samia Suluhu Hassan, from Zanzibar, as his running mate. Although the choice of a female candidate was widely welcomed, Hassan was also regarded critically for her hard-line stance as the CA's vice-chairperson. Zanzibar's current president, *Ali Mohamed Shein*, having served only one term, was nominated unopposed as *CCM's presidential candidate for Zanzibar*.

The *opposition alliance*, Coalition of the People's Constitution, (known by its Swahili acronym *UKAWA*), created in the CA context and consisting of CHADEMA ('Chama Cha Demokrasia na Maendeleo'; Party for Democracy and Progress), the CUF (Civic United Front), NCCR-Mageuzi (National Convention for Construction and Reform-Change) and the small NLD (National League for Democracy), had in October 2014 agreed to present a united front in the 2015 elections. Consensual agreement on the nomination of a joint presidential candidate nevertheless proved difficult and no choice had been made by mid-July. The political landscape then changed dramatically, when *Lowassa defected to CHADEMA* on 27 July. UKAWA had agreed to challenge CCM with joint candidates on presidential, parliamentary and council levels. On 4 August, Lowassa was nominated as *CHADEMA* and *UKAWA presidential candidate*. As expected, UKAWA nominated CUF's Seif Sharif Hamad as joint presidential candidate for Zanzibar. Lowassa's nomination posed several challenges for CHADEMA and UKAWA. The latter was only a somewhat loose coalition of parties with differing political agendas, mainly held together by their common support for the CRC's draft constitution and their criticism of CCM. CHADEMA in particular had over the years gained much of its support for its stance against the 'corrupt system' of the CCM government and had repeatedly named Lowassa as a key player. Before his defection, the new UKAWA presidential candidate had been a prominent figure in the rejection of the CRC draft and an uncompromising supporter of CCM's hard-line stance in the CA, the very factors that had initially led to the formation of UKAWA. No clear public explanation of UKAWA'S/Lowassa's position on the crucial constitution issue was given, and it remained unclear how the electorate would respond to the decision to embrace the former foe. The move was also controversial within CHADEMA's leadership, but awareness that Lowassa's unbroken popularity would bring them a strong push in the elections finally convinced party leaders. Nevertheless, a number of opposition politicians expressed their dissatisfaction with the decision and two of the most prominent stepped down in protest against the deal with Lowassa: CHADEMA's secretary-general, Wilbroad Slaa, who had been CHADEMA's relatively successful presidential candidate in 2010 and had been expected to become UKAWA's candidate in 2015, announced his resignation from CHADEMA and from active politics, and the CUF's long-standing chairman, Ibrahim Lipumba, resigned from his leadership post.

Several CCM members also defected from the ruling party and joined the Lowassa camp, among them the former prime minister Frederick Sumaye. Former EAC secretary-general Juma Mwapachu also returned his CCM membership card, but without joining CHADEMA. But what drew most attention was the crossing-over of one of CCM's founders and its former chief ideologist, 85-year old Kingunge Ngombale-Mwiru, to CHADEMA; where he actively supported Lowassa's rallies. Even so, despite several *prominent defections*, CCM managed to retain its unity and to actively rally behind Magufuli.

Of the 22 registered parties, only CCM, CHADEMA and six others nominated presidential candidates. With the exception of *ACT-Wazalendo* (Alliance for Change and Transparency-Patriots), none of the smaller parties was expected to gain any significant support. ACT-Wazalendo, only founded in 2014, was mainly associated with its charismatic leader Zitto Kabwe, a former leading member of CHADEMA and respected chairman of the National Assembly's Public Accounts Committee, who was forced out of CHADEMA in March, after a long leadership wrangle.

The *electoral campaign* started officially on 22 August for the Union and on 7 September for Zanzibar. Apart from some minor incidents, campaign rallies were peaceful, but sporadic clashes between supporters of the two main camps left at least one person dead and several injured. Security forces reportedly used tear gas to disperse CHADEMA members on some occasions, and opposition parties complained about arrests of their candidates in some areas. Both major camps went along with the widely expressed popular *demand for change*. Magufuli centred his campaign around his image as a results-oriented hard worker who would deliver and who had never been involved in any of the many CCM scandals – with the slogan 'Hapa kazi tu' (Here is only work); he deliberately kept a certain distance from the party. In an ironic twist, Magufuli was advocating stricter anti-corruption measures, while Lowassa was at pains to shed his image as a major corruption culprit. Both sides invested *enormous amounts of money* in their campaigns. CCM took full advantage of its incumbency, access to state resources and decade-long control of administrative structures. The state-owned *media* clearly favoured CCM, whereas private media reported in a more balanced way. Election reporting focussed mainly on the two main blocks and hardly covered the smaller parties and their candidates.

The elections were supervised by *two distinct electoral commissions*. The NEC was responsible for the election organisation on the Union level (presidency and parliament) both on the mainland and in Zanzibar and for the local council elections on the mainland. The Zanzibar Electoral Commission (ZEC) organised the elections of the Zanzibar president, the Zanzibar parliament (House of Representatives) and the Zanzibari local councils. The opposition's massive *distrust* of the electoral commissions culminated in its call upon voters to remain close to the polling stations on polling day in order to 'protect their votes' against alleged attempts by the commissions to rig the process.

By and large, *polling day* itself was peaceful, despite some minor incidents of disorder, missing materials and delayed opening of polling stations, but *tensions* increased soon after the polling stations closed. After first results from various polling stations had been released, police entered the CHADEMA tallying centre in Dar es Salaam and arrested more than 150 people for unlawfully posting results in social media. On 29 October, the data centre of the Legal and Human Rights Centre, which hosted the Tanzanian Civil Society Consortium on Election Observation (TACCEO) was raided by police, who temporarily arrested 36 data clerks and confiscated computers and mobile phones under Section 16 of the new Cybercrimes Act. These activities and a generally non-transparent handling of the tallying and tabulation of the results fuelled *allegations of vote rigging*.

In *Zanzibar*, things were even more dramatic. During the on-going counting process, ZEC chairman Jecha Salim Jecha *declared the election void* on 28 October, citing irregularities in Pemba, the CUF's stronghold, and announced that the exercise would have to be repeated. Two days before, CUF's Seif Hamad had publicly declared himself the winner, referring to accumulated results his party had received from all polling stations. Jecha's unilateral decision was challenged by some other ZEC members, who had not been consulted. It was also doubtful whether the ZEC had the formal competence to void the polls. Despite this dramatic turn, the situation remained calm. *International observer groups* from the EU, the AU, SADC and the Commonwealth and national observer groups protested against the ZEC chairman's decision. The CUF rejected a re-run and urged the ZEC to continue announcing the results. After an initial meeting between Kikwete and Hamad on 7 November, Hamad, Kikwete, Zanzibar's President Shein, former presidents Mwinyi and Mkapa and other high-ranking CCM-politicians were involved in several *closed-door meetings* aimed at overcoming the political impasse. Magufuli, however, remained conspicuously aloof, claiming to have no authority over Zanzibar's internal affairs. Although no solution was in sight by the end of the year, the population remained calm, although affected by drastically rising food prices caused by the prevailing uncertainty.

On 29 October, the NEC declared *Magufuli the winner* with 58.5% of the votes against 40% for Lowassa. It was the worst result for a CCM presidential candidate since the re-introduction of the multi-party system in 1992, and by far the best for an opposition candidate. The opposition was also comparably successful in the *parliamentary elections*. CHADEMA's overall percentage of parliamentary votes increased from 24% in 2010 to 32%, while CCM's fell from 60% to 55%. However, in the winner-takes-all electoral system, this increase in votes did not fully translate into a corresponding increase in seats. CHADEMA managed to win 34 constituencies, compared with 23 in 2010 and the CUF also increased its directly-elected MPS (mostly in Zanzibar) from 24 to 32. ACT-Wazalendo performed badly, winning only Kabwe's constituency, Kigoma-Urban. CCM scooped 196 seats (74% of the constituencies). Despite a united opposition and a widely perceived mood for change, CCM thus retained its *overwhelming two-thirds majority* in the National Assembly. The distribution of special seats for women (of which CCM got 66, CHADEMA 37 and CUF 10) was made proportionally to the number of constituencies won. Of the 264 directly-elected MPS, only 25 were women (CCM: 18, CHADEMA: 6, CUF: 1). Voter turnout was about 67%, a significant increase from 43% in 2010. The opposition generally performed well in most urban constituencies, while CCM retained its overwhelming support in rural areas. CCM proved more popular among women and older citizens, whereas UKAWA had most followers among young males and better-educated voters.

The results of the *town and district council elections* presented a similar picture. CCM was able to maintain its control over the vast majority of the councils, winning over 70% of all council seats. However, the opposition managed to win the majority of seats in important town and city councils (such as Dar es Salaam, Arusha, Mbeya and Moshi), while CCM was ahead in Dodoma and Mwanza. UKAWA refused to recognise the official results, claiming that the NEC had manipulated the count in favour of CCM, and boycotted Magufuli's inauguration as Tanzania's fifth president on 5 November. Samia Suluhu Hassan was sworn in as Tanzania's *first female vice-president*.

By several symbolic actions, Magufuli immediately indicated his determination to start a *new era* by implementing his 'Here is only work' slogan and no longer tolerating any 'business as usual' attitudes. A day after his inauguration, he unexpectedly visited the Finance Ministry and demanded information about absent officials. The following Monday, he fired the head of the National Hospital during another surprise visit, after he found patients sleeping on the floor and diagnostic machines out of order. In his crusade against civil servants' idleness, he continued *sacking dozens of officials*, both middle- and high-ranking; others were fired on allegations of corruption and misuse or theft of public property. On 16 December, Magufuli fired the long-serving director of the Prevention and Combating of Corruption Bureau, Edward Hoseah, for ineffectiveness.

A second major theme during his first weeks in office was to the *reduction of unnecessary public expenditure*. Magufuli ordered the suspension of all but essential foreign travel for government officials, and workshops for public servants in expensive hotels with generous allowances were banned. He cancelled the traditionally self-congratulatory Independence Day celebrations on 9 December: Tanzanians should not celebrate Independence, while the country suffered from cholera outbreaks. His call to use the holiday to clean-up the country was widely taken up and he participated personally by cleaning the fish-market area close to State House. In another symbolic move, he ordered a reduction in the cost of the parliament's inauguration party from $ 100,000 to $ 7,000, directing the rest of the money to buy hospital beds.

These measures brought the 'new broom' the expected public support. Magufuli's activities were also followed internationally with great attention, as he seemed to be setting new standards for cleaning-up a notoriously negligent and corrupt system, and was soon seen as a possible *role model for other African leaders*. Critics, however, doubted whether these popular and populist actions would be followed by more systematic approaches and structural reforms. In several cases, the desire of lower-level officials to show commitment to the Magufuli style led to dubious actions against subordinates, who were sanctioned for minor incidents. This new leadership style of directives and short-notice ultimatums given by Magufuli and subsequently by his ministers and other officials, as well as threats to dismiss and even jail subordinates if they failed to meet demands, also raised concerns about an *emerging authoritarian streak*.

On 19 November, Magufuli appointed the virtually unknown *Kassim Majaliwa* as his new *prime minister*. Majaliwa, a teacher by profession, had served in several government positions and been responsible for education as a deputy minister in the prime minister's office. His appointment was seen as an indication that improvements in the dilapidated education sector could become a top priority in Magufuli's first term. The composition of the new cabinet was eagerly awaited for weeks. Magufuli waited until 9 December to announce the names and portfolios of his ministers. In accordance with his cost-cutting policy, he presented a *drastically reduced cabinet* of only 18 ministries, with 34 ministers and deputies (compared with 60 under Kikwete). Initially, the key ministries of finance, education, tourism and public works remained vacant and were only filled on 23 December, since Magufuli took his time to find qualified individuals. Most of the ministers had already served in Kikwete's last cabinet, either as full ministers or as deputies.

Two controversial laws, the Cybercrimes Act and the Statistics Act, provoked national and international protests from opposition parties, civil society groups and academicians, as well as from the EU Delegation and the Development Partners Group. Experts were concerned that some provisions of the *Cybercrimes Act* could be used to restrict freedom of expression by criminalising the dissemination of false, deceptive, misleading or inaccurate information. The *Statistics Act* was criticised because it made it illegal to publish statistics unauthorised by the National Bureau of Statistics. Soon after the Cybercrime Act came into force in September, a student and a businessman were charged in separate cases for disseminating false information through social media networks. The Act was also cited by police to justify the arrest of TACCEO personnel during election observation on 29 October. After meetings with media and civil society stakeholders in June, the government withdrew two other controversial – but long-awaited – media bills, the Media Service Bill and the Right to Information Bill. Fears of a clampdown on *media* arose when the government banned a weekly newspaper, 'The East African', on 21 January for lacking proper registration, although it had been in the market for 20 years.

Foreign Affairs

On 20 February, Kikwete took over the rotating *EAC chairmanship* from Kenya. Since 2013, Tanzania had found itself somewhat isolated in the EAC due to its reluctance to follow Kenya's, Uganda's and Rwanda's fast pace in implementing joint projects, and to strained relations between Kikwete and Rwanda's President Kagame. During the year, relations with EAC partners improved considerably, without Tanzania giving up its somewhat hesitant stance towards an accelerated integration. The change from Kikwete to Magufuli raised hopes that Tanzania could become more active in the block.

Kenya's decision to ban Tanzanian tourist vehicles from accessing Nairobi Airport led to bilateral misgivings early in the year. The *tourism row* was then intensified by Tanzania's Civil Aviation Authority's decision to reduce the frequency of Kenya Airways flights to Tanzania by 67%. During a meeting in Windhoek (Namibia) on 21 March, Kikwete and Kenya's President Kenyatta agreed to lift the ban on

Tanzanian vehicles and to allow Kenya's airline to resume its normal flight schedule. Relations between the two countries remained cordial, with Kikwete being only the second foreign leader to address both houses of Kenya's parliament during his farewell state visit in early October. The two presidents agreed to scale up cooperation in the battles against terrorism, drug trafficking and poaching and signed several agreements, including to strengthen *co-operation in defence and security* by combating violent extremism, cross-border crime and human trafficking.

Relations with *Rwanda* improved significantly. In January, a UN report indicated that leaders of the Democratic Forces for the Liberation of Rwanda (FDLR) opposition militia had held several meetings in Tanzania since 2013 and that the Tanzanian government authorities were not investigating activities by and support for FDLR in Tanzania. Kikwete, however, declared his willingness to support a UN military offensive against the rebels. Kikwete and Rwanda's President Kagame met for the first time in two years during the February EAC summit; in March Kikwete attended a Northern Corridor project meeting in Kigali (Rwanda) at Kagame's invitation. Tanzania was not a member of the infrastructure project group, dubbed in 2013 the 'Coalition of the Willing' (Kenya, Uganda and Rwanda), which had explicitly excluded Tanzania and Burundi. On 26 March, Kagame launched the idea of a freight train route linking Dar es Salaam with the border town Rusumo and attended the Central Corridor High-Level Industry and Investor Forum in Dar es Salaam. The leadership change from Kikwete to Magufuli further eased the relationship. In December, Kagame congratulated Magufuli on his crackdown on tax evasion and inefficiency at Dar es Salaam port, which handled over 70% of Rwanda's deep-sea cargo.

Tanzania was regarded as an influential player in the *Burundi crisis*, owing to its good relations and protective role towards that country and its government, although its influence remained limited. During a visit to Bujumbura in March, Kikwete appealed to President Nkurunziza not to seek a third term and to respect the Arusha peace accord, which limited the presidential tenure to two terms. Responding to the escalation of violence that followed Nkurunziza's announcement that he would stand for a third term, Kikwete as EAC chairman sent a team of foreign ministers from Kenya, Uganda, Rwanda and Tanzania on a fact-finding mission to Burundi. The team was to prepare a report for an extraordinary EAC summit on 13 May in Dar es Salaam. At the summit, the presidents condemned the attempted military putsch on the same day in Bujumbura and called upon the authorities to postpone the elections. However, they remained silent on Nkurunziza's third-term ambitions. Tanzania initially opposed the decision of the AU Peace and Security Council to send a peace-keeping force to Burundi, and instead embarked on diplomatic efforts, with Kikwete, and later Magufuli and new Foreign Minister Augustine Mahiga, holding several meetings with Burundian officials. By the year's end, almost 120,000 *Burundian refugees* and more than 64,000 refugees from the DRC were living in overcrowded camps in western Tanzania.

Efforts to mediate in the *conflict in South Sudan* between the warring factions of the Sudan People's Liberation Movement (SPLM) had started in 2014 in Arusha with reconciliation talks between the main SPLM groupings. The talks, hosted by Kikwete and CCM, were concluded with the signing of a unification agreement on 21 January. CCM continued to facilitate the reconciliation process. On 30 November, Kikwete visited the *Comoros* as a special AU envoy in an effort to support the Comorian stabilisation process. He urged all stakeholders to work towards holding free, fair and transparent elections. On 5 May, two Tanzanian peacekeepers with the special *UN Force Intervention Brigade in the DRC* were killed and at least 13 others injured in an ambush, supposedly carried out by the Ugandan rebel group Allied Democratic Forces.

Relations with the *donor community* were ambivalent. The steps taken by the government in reaction to the escrow account scandal were welcomed by the *budget support group*, which in March started to release parts of the pledged general budget support that had been suspended in October 2014 in response to the scandal. Magufuli's determined actions against corruption, fraud and squandering of public resources were also well received by donors. However, concerns were raised about some other significant political developments, especially the nullifying of the elections in Zanzibar and the enforcement of the Cybercrimes Law and the Statistics Act. In a joint statement on 29 October, the election observer groups from the EU, the AU, SADC and the Commonwealth reacted with dismay to the voiding of the Zanzibari elections. On 9 November, the mission heads of 13 European states, the USA, Canada and the EU expressed their concern about arrests under the much-criticised Cybercrimes Act and called upon the government not to infringe fundamental human rights. The US *Millennium Challenge Corporation* (MCC) postponed the approval of Tanzania for a second envisaged compact because of the escrow account scandal. Unlike the budget support group, the MCC was not satisfied by the government's actions and on 17 September expressed continued concern about corruption. In December, the release of the envisaged $ 472 m for electricity projects was again postponed. Although no reasons were officially given, it was assumed that the nullification of the elections in Zanzibar and arrests under the Cybercrimes Law had influenced the decision.

Socioeconomic Developments

The overall *macroeconomic performance* was again quite satisfactory and in line with the strong continuous growth trend that had persisted since the early 2000s. Tanzania remained in the group of the fastest-growing and most consistently performing economies in Africa, although it was still characterised by a very low level of material wealth for the vast majority of the population. In the 2015 *HDI* (data for 2014), Tanzania was ranked 151st (out of 188 countries), in the 'low human development' category, whereas a year earlier it had been ranked 159th. On the basis of new national accounts data (revised in 2014), average *per capita income* (in nominal terms) was now estimated to have just passed the threshold of $ 1,000 per year – thus practically attaining the government's declared goal of reaching the status of a 'middle-income country' (defined by the threshold of a $ 1,045 per capita income). According to the 2015 HDI, the per capita income (in PPP terms) had been $ 2,411 in 2014 and a *Gini coefficient* of 38 showed a relatively modest level of unevenness of income distribution.

In the face of persistent global economic and financial uncertainties, Tanzania's economy continued to remain remarkably resilient. This was also partly due to the fact that the level of monetisation of the economy and the degree of trade openness with the rest of the world were still considerably lower than the average for SSA, thus shielding the country from negative repercussions. The *GDP growth rate* for 2015 was estimated at 7.1%, very similar to 2013 and 2014 (7.0%) and consistent with the growth trend of the last decade. Climatically, it was a difficult, but not disastrous year, with unfavourable weather conditions. The agricultural sector thus only expanded by 2.6% and the food stock of the National Food Reserve had to be run down to 180,000 tonnes by the year's end, compared with 460,000 tonnes in January. The main drivers of growth were the communications, mining and financial services sectors. Expectations of a faster and more fundamental transformation of the economy were increasingly linked with prospects for significant natural gas production, but with the depressed global oil markets it remained uncertain when the start of full commercial exploitation would finally get underway. Tanzania's ranking was practically unchanged at 120th (out of 140 countries) in the World Economic Forum's Global Competitiveness Index 2014–16, and at 139th (out of 189 countries) in the World Bank's Doing Business 2016 report.

Inflation had been successfully contained in 2014, thus opening the year with a 4.0% rate in January. Consumer price inflation then gradually rose to a high of 6.8% in December (average for 2015: 5.6%), largely driven by higher food prices resulting from poor weather conditions and by the effects of the *exchange rate depreciation*, which raised the domestic cost of imported goods. The shilling depreciated continuously throughout the year by about 24% against the dollar, attaining a rate of TSh 2,149 : $ 1 by the end of December. This was the combined effect of the global strength of the dollar, high liquidity in the domestic banking system, seasonally low export earnings, high repatriation of corporate dividends and delays in the mobilisation of expected external programme financing. The *structural trade deficit* was remarkably brought down by almost 30% from $ 5.6 bn (2014) to $ 4 bn, principally as a result of a significantly reduced (by 10.8%) import bill of $ 9,743 m, largely due to lower oil prices. Export earnings grew strongly by 7.6% to $ 5,725 m, mainly on account of manufactured goods, while traditional agricultural exports declined in value. On balance, and for the first time, almost 60% of Tanzania's import needs were covered by its own export earnings. The (preliminary) *current-account deficit* was thus estimated to have been considerably reduced from about $ 5 bn in 2014 to $ 3.1 bn, equivalent to an exceptionally low 7% of GDP. Gross *foreign reserves* remained more or less unchanged; at the end of June they amounted to $ 4.3 bn, sufficient to cover four months of imports of goods and services. While the *external debt* had previously been substantially reduced to a low of $ 4.2 bn in 2006 as a result of concerted debt cancellations under the HIPC initiative, it had in recent years been increasing again rather fast. The external debt stock reached a new high of $ 15.4 bn at year's end (compared with $ 14.2 bn at the end of 2014). The central government was accountable for around 80% of this debt. Almost half of the debt was owed to multilateral agencies and about 10% to bilateral donors, with the remainder composed of commercial debts and export credits. *FDI* inflows remained quite substantial, while *foreign exchange earnings* increased by 10.3% to $ 3.7 bn, mainly from travel and transportation services. *Tourism* earnings alone ($ 2.2 bn) from over 1.2 m visitors remained Tanzania's most important foreign exchange earner, even topping gold. The idea of raising funds with a Eurobond issue had been under discussion for years, but was again postponed because of unfavourable conditions on the international financial markets.

IMF missions visited Tanzania in March and September to conduct the second and third reviews of the country's performance under the current three-year *Policy Support Instrument* (*PSI*). Macroeconomic performance was judged to have remained strong and medium-term prospects were seen as favourable. Most assessment criteria under the PSI for June were met, but implementation was seen as having slowed ahead of the elections. Revenue and financing shortfalls, together with weak commitment controls, were identified to have led to the accumulation of further domestic arrears in the financial year 2014/15. While some progress on the achievement of structural reforms was noted, a number of benchmarks were detected as having been missed. Tanzania was seen as having a low risk of debt distress and to be eligible for more flexible debt conditionality. Tanzania's total national debt (external and domestic) of $ 19.4 bn by year's end was estimated to grow to around 43% of GDP in 2015–16.

On 11 June, Finance Minister Saada Mkuya submitted her *2015/16 budget* to parliament. Total expenditure was optimistically budgeted at TSh 22,495 bn (about $ 10 bn), a remarkable increase of 13% over the 2014/15 budget figures in view of clearly existing public finance problems. A high 74% share was foreseen for recurrent expenditure and only 26% for development programmes. The revenue forecast was composed of domestic tax and non-tax revenue (55% and 7%, respectively), domestic borrowing (27%) and external general budget support (GBS) and loans (10%). The GBS assumptions were drastically reduced compared with 2014/15 (24%) in reaction to the 2014 experience, when the group of development partners had withheld most of the budgeted GBS support as sign of disapproval over the lack of government action about a major corruption scandal. With increased efforts on domestic revenue generation, the tax share of GDP was expected to rise to 13%, still low by comparable SSA standards, and a target budget deficit of 4.2% of GDP was set. Budget priorities were given as financing the elections, completion of ongoing capital projects and special emphasis on rural electrification, water supply and human capital development. Towards the year's end, the new Maguful i government adopted a revised budget framework with a focus on curtailing non-priority current expenditures and postponing a number of not yet started investment projects, with the adjustments amounting to about 1% of GDP and aiming to maintain the deficit target.

The *2014/15 budget* had ended with an overall deficit that exceeded the target (3.8% of GDP) once the significant accumulation of expenditure arrears that had been building up in 2014 was taken into account. It also reflected shortfalls in revenue generation and financing, combined with weak expenditure controls. Even with the relaxation of the 2014 GBS freeze and the disbursement of delayed GBS funds in March, overall donor support fell somewhat short of expectations. The main shortfall, however, was due to $ 300 m less than planned external non-concessional borrowing, reflecting unfavourable conditions on international financial markets. The overall fiscal deficit was thus estimated to have attained around 4.5%, while the accumulated payment arrears had risen to about 1.1% of GDP. The new incoming government was tasked with settlement of existing verified arrears, mostly to suppliers and pension funds.

Optimistic expectations of a quick economic upturn in the near future, centred on the exploitation of Tanzania's substantial *natural gas resources*, were somewhat dampened with the realisation that a much longer time horizon was likely before full commercial benefits could be expected. This was due to the significant drop in global oil prices and the reluctance of international oil companies to commit substantial new investments. More exploration activities nevertheless continued and the volume of proven gas reserves was updated to 57 trn ft² (82% of which offshore), with more strikes being very probable. In August, the first gas from Mnazi Bay (near Mtwara) was transported to Dar es Salaam through the new Chinese-financed-and-built pipeline; this was a major step towards easing the long-endured problems of insufficient electricity generation and recurring *power failures*. After long delays, a new *Petroleum Act* guiding legislation on all aspects of the oil and gas industry was finally discussed in parliament and passed in July. The parastatal Tanzania Petroleum Development Company was to lose all regulatory functions and to become a commercial company, while separate state agencies were to regulate all upstream and downstream activities in the industry. The legislation built on experiences from Algeria and Norway, provided more transparency than hitherto and had no nationalistic bias (as had been feared by some observers). TANESCO, the heavily loss-making parastatal *power utility* continued to be a major financial burden on the government: by mid-year, TANESCO had accumulated arrears to its suppliers (mostly private energy producers) of TSh 700 bn, while the government had in turn run up substantial arrears to TANESCO. The IMF viewed a solution to TANESCO's financial misery as an upmost priority for the incoming government.

The improvement of the country's physical *infrastructure* continued to be a major focus of the government's development strategy, although the implementation of announced projects often remained rather uncertain. In October, preliminary works began for the construction of a large entirely new port near Bagamoyo, to be financed and constructed by China. New *mining* ventures were about to start production of nickel and uranium and were faced with protests from environmentalists. Gold production continued to contribute significantly to overall growth and exports, although declining in importance.

Uganda

Volker Weyel

The political temperature rose in anticipation of the presidential and parliamentary elections scheduled for early 2016. Opposition parties failed to unite, while the incumbent head of state enjoyed the unmistakable support of all the security forces and his party. Intimidation and chicanery were familiar ploys used by the state apparatus against critics. On this foundation, stability prevailed. Unstable conditions in the region affected Uganda, however, notably the situation in South Sudan. Events in Burundi generated a new influx of refugees, with others still arriving from South Sudan and the DRC. Uganda's international reputation corresponded to its role as an effective regional power and Pope Francis' visit brought the country into the international limelight. The economy slowed down, but still rested on relatively firm ground. Oil production had not yet started, and expectations were somewhat lowered in view of the worldwide slump in crude oil prices.

Domestic Politics

After a seemingly serious potential challenge to the nomination of President Yoweri Kaguta Museveni for another five-year term by the ruling *National Resistance Movement* (NRM) had been thwarted in 2014 by the ousting of Amama Mbabazi

 | DOI 10.1163/9789004333239_043

both as prime minister and as NRM secretary-general, in January Mbabazi also failed to be elected to the Central Executive Committee of the party by its National Executive Council. Nevertheless, he remained an NRM member, still bent on striving for selection as the party's national 'flag bearer', i.e. candidate for the presidency, announcing this in a YouTube video circulated on 15 June via social media. Six weeks later, he gave up on the NRM, but not on his candidacy. His long experience as a strategically placed insider in the NRM and government, including the intelligence services, as well as his networking capabilities, gave some credibility to his ambitions. Mbabazi was assisted by a group named the 'Go Forward' team.

The NRM held its party primaries to choose candidates for parliamentary seats and other elective offices at the end of October. They were marred not only by conspicuous irregularities and organisational flaws, but also by a number of violent incidents. Political convictions hardly played a role, the candidates being inspired by the prospect of access to power and sources of patronage. Given the dominance of the NRM, the party primaries in many constituencies predetermined the winners of the race for seats. A number of prominent incumbents failed in their bids for nomination. The losers' list included a well-known bush war 'historical', Minister for Constitutional Affairs Kahinda Otafiire, and Syda Bbumba, a former finance minister. Many of the losers decided to contest the parliamentary elections as independents. Though NRM rules called for the expulsion of members standing as independents against the party candidate, Museveni's attitude was less rigid; he was aware of the deficiencies of the primaries and knew that in the past the bulk of independent MPs had supported the government. About 15,000 delegates met for the National Conference from 30 October to 2 November in Kampala to elect party officials and to endorse Museveni as flag bearer.

Preparing for the 2016 contest, the Forum for Democratic Change (FDC), the major force among the *opposition parties*, decided to nominate again Dr Kizza Besigye, who had lost to Museveni in the 2001, 2006 and 2011 elections. He had hesitated to take part in an exercise which he deemed flawed. The two old parties, the Democratic Party (DP) and the Uganda People's Congress (UPC), did not field their own candidates and were in a dismal state. DP party president Norbert Mao, re-elected at a delegates' conference on 24 July in Entebbe, faced the resentment of a group centred around the ousted lord mayor of Kampala, Erias Lukwago. UPC internal wrangles even occupied the courts. Olara Otunnu, a former UN under-secretary-general, did not seek another term as UPC party leader. Among the candidates for succession was Jimmy Akena, a son of former president Milton Obote. The processing of the results from party district conferences held on 30 May was cut short when Akena's supporters, unimpeded by the police, occupied the party offices situated in Uganda House, a huge building owned by the Milton Obote Foundation, in the centre of Kampala. In a controversial development, Akena was later declared party president. This led Otunnu and his faction to seek a court ruling that Akena had been fraudulently elected. The struggle also had its pecuniary side since the UPC-linked Milton Obote Foundation, which deemed Akena to be a trespasser, held sway over finances. The political cleavage within the UPC was clear in Otunnu's stern opposition to Museveni while Akena entered an informal coalition with the president.

Intense endeavours to unite opposition groupings led to the creation of *The Democratic Alliance* (TDA) in June and to talks about the presentation of a single presidential candidate, which meant choosing either Besigye or Mbabazi. Neither of them was willing to cede his position, so eventually both were to enter the race. This was even seen as an advantage by some strategists, who calculated that in this way the full potential of both candidates could be exploited and thus the incumbent might attract less than 50% of the vote, forcing him into a run-off ballot (though neither of the two opposition candidates indicated a willingness to defer to whichever of them was in the lead). Besigye eventually stood as the FCD's flag bearer and Mbabazi as an independent supported by the TDA, which ultimately, however, consisted mainly of his Go Forward group and the DP plus Otunnu's UPC faction. Mbabazi and Besigye hardly had an opportunity to consult with voters since meetings and rallies were generally obstructed by the police, who occasionally used excessive force; Besigye and others were repeatedly put under preventive arrest.

Opposition and civil society groups had long debated whether to take part in the election as long as the *Electoral Commission* (EC), which was considered partisan, remained unchanged. Proposals forwarded through the Inter Party Organisation for Dialogue, a neutral platform, were ignored. Nevertheless, there were some changes in election procedures. In view of the fact that 48 persons picked up nomination forms to stand for the office of president, the nomination fee was raised from UGX (shilling) 8°m to UGX 20°m and the provision to fund candidates' campaigns was scrapped. On the other hand, the requirement for a candidate "to campaign in every district of Uganda" (the country comprising 112) for "at least one day in each" was removed.

For *nomination* at the EC on 3–4 November, one aspirant failed to satisfy the formal requirements and another, former Kampala mayor Nasser Ntege Sebagala, did not turn up as expected. Eight candidates were successfully nominated: Yoweri Kaguta Museveni, president since 1986 (NRM); Amama Mbabazi (Independent); Professor Venansius Baryamureeba, a former vice-chancellor of Makerere University (Independent); Dr Kizza Besigye Kifefe (FDC); Dr Abed Bwanika, a contestant in the 2006 and 2011 elections (People's Development Party); Joseph Mabirizi, a gospel evangelist (Independent); Maureen Faith Kyalya Waluube (Independent) and Major-General (rtd) Benon Buta Biraaro (Farmers Party of Uganda). Kyalya, a former presidential aide trying to capitalise on the perceived neglect of Busoga, made this the third contest with a female candidate. In 2006, Miria Kalule Obote, the widow of former president Obote, had stood for the UPC and in 2011 Beti Kamya had stood for the Uganda Federal Alliance.

The campaign for the presidential election officially started on 9 November (and for the parliamentary elections on 7 December), allowing for electioneering only from that date onwards. Museveni, however, had no inhibitions, justifying his travel and gatherings across the country as being in line with his official duties. Opposition candidates faced hidebound application of the rules, enforced by the police, and widespread chicanery. Early in the year, Inspector-General of the *Uganda Police Force* General Kale Kayihura had announced the use of more robust methods in public order management. Campaign activities were largely conducted peacefully, though there was a violent confrontation between Museveni supporters and Mbabazi supporters in Ntungamo in mid-December. There was a generally blatant massive police presence, and the existence of an auxiliary force called 'crime preventers' gave rise to controversy. At least 1.5 m people throughout the country were said to have been recruited as local intelligence gatherers and given basic training "to support the police". Though they were responsible for "community policing" in connection with terrorism, "child sacrifices, aggravated burglaries, assassinations, illicit drugs trade, rapes etc.", they were seen by many as a militia in the service of the ruling party, which made for an environment fraught with intimidation.

Parliamentary Speaker Rebecca Kadaga was relieved of responsibility in the '*rebel MPs*' issue. The Supreme Court ruled on 30 October that they were allowed to keep their seats, since after being expelled from the NRM they continued to be "members directly elected to represent their constituencies". Earlier, a constitutional amendment passed on 11 August and assented to by Museveni on 19 August permitted floor crossing by MPs within the last 12 months of the parliamentary term.

In August, Parliament sanctioned the formation of 43 *new counties*, effective retroactively from 1 July, pushing the number up to 249. Twelve towns became *municipalities* retrospectively on the same date (with seven more to attain that status on 1 July 2016). These measures boosted the number of legislators in the next parliament to well over 400. On 3 September, Parliament approved the creation of 23 *new districts*, bringing the total from 112 (including Kampala which has special status) to 135. This was to be implemented in stages, starting with four new districts on 1 July 2016, with the last seven scheduled for 1 July 2019.

The Public Finance Management Bill of 2014, which reformed the fiscal policy framework and established the Petroleum Fund, was signed into law on 23 February. Its new rule against supplementary budgets, however, was rescinded by a 12 November amendment, ratified two days later by the president. The Public Private Partnership Bill, which had been sent back to Parliament by Museveni in 2014, re-emerged. MPs eventually accepted that the executive would be in charge of all pertinent agreements whilst pointing out that they would continue to decide on the financing of projects. The bill was passed on 1 July and ratified by Museveni on 5 August.

Other major legislation included the Tobacco Control Act, aimed "to promote the health of persons and reduce tobacco related illnesses and deaths"; the bill was passed on 28 July and assented to by the president on 19 September.

The Anti-Corruption (Amendment) Act, passed on 7 July and approved by the president on 15 October, provided for mandatory confiscation of property of persons convicted of a corruption offence.

Among the bills passed by the 9th Parliament but not yet signed into law was the Non-Governmental Organisations Bill, approved on 26 November; "special obligations" imposed on NGOs included to "not engage in any act, which is prejudicial to the interests of Uganda and the dignity of the people of Uganda".

On 1 March, the president announced a *cabinet reshuffle*. Most office holders were reappointed but there were some notable newcomers, the 2016 elections casting their shadow ahead. With the newly appointed Minister of State for Youth and Children Affairs Evelyn Anite (born in 1984), and Minister of State for Planning David Bahati (born in 1973), the 'old man with the hat' was now reaching out to younger people. At the same time, he rewarded Anite for her being instrumental as NRM caucus spokesperson in 2014 in calling on Museveni "to offer himself" as the presidential candidate. In addition, the appointment of Bahati placated sympathisers with his homophobic initiatives but also required Bahati to obey cabinet discipline. Other important posts that were filled were those of minister of finance, with the independent-minded Maria Kiwanuka leaving and being followed by her state minister Matia Kasaija, a 'historical' and former deputy director in the 'movement' secretariat, and of attorney-general, with Peter Nyombi being replaced by his deputy Fredrick Ruhindi. The controversial Jim Muhwezi, who as health minister had been implicated in the Global Fund money scandal, fittingly now headed the Ministry of Information and National Guidance. Minister of Gender, Labour and Social Affairs Mary Karooro Okurut moved to the Ministry of Security, her replacement being Muruli Mukasa, a former minister of security. The education ministry was restructured as the Ministry of Education, Science, Technology and Sports and headed by 1974-born Jessica Rose Epel Alupo, formerly minister of state for youth and children's affairs. Dr Elioda Tumwesigye was appointed minister of health in place of Dr Ruhakana Rugunda, who had become prime minister in 2014, while Ronald Kibuule became minister of state for water, following Betty Bigombe who had returned to the World Bank in 2014. Abraham Byandala was demoted from minister of works, his part in the corruption case of the Mukono-Katosi road project having become suspicious, to minister without portfolio. Two-thirds of the senior ministers came from the Western Region, illustrating the president's way of making ministerial appointments a sort of reward for areas that voted for him; moreover, a strong emphasis on Kigezi was to counter the influence of Mbabazi, who hailed from that south-western sub-region.

Later in the year, the internal affairs portfolio fell vacant after the sudden death of Aronda Nyakairima. On 30 November, the president swore in Bukedea District Woman MP Rose Akol Okullo as his successor, advising her "to fight rampant corruption especially in the Department of Immigration and the Police". Concurrently,

NRM old hand Ali Kirunda Kivejinja, an octogenarian, was sworn in as third deputy prime minister and minister of East African affairs (a post that had been vacant since the demise of Eriya Kategaya on 2 March 2013) and Michael Werikhe, MP for a constituency in Mbale district, as minister of state for industry. All three appointees came from the Eastern Region, another NRM support base.

Following the 2014 Constitutional Court ruling that Museveni's re-appointment of *Chief Justice* Benjamin Odoki (who had reached the mandatory retirement age) was unconstitutional, the post was filled on 5 March by Supreme Court Judge Bart Magunda Katureebe, who was widely respected in the legal profession.

On 4 December, the Koogere oral tradition of the Basongora, Banyabindi and Batooro peoples in Western Uganda was inscribed by UNESCO on its List of Intangible *Cultural Heritage* in Need of Urgent Safeguarding. Named after Koogere, a female chief of Busongora about 1,500 years ago, it "conveys value, belief systems and collective memory". It was the fifth Ugandan element on this list, having started with the inscription in 2008 of barkcloth making, an ancient craft of the Baganda people, on the then Representative List of the Intangible Cultural Heritage of Humanity.

Former president Obote's foreign affairs minister Samuel Ngude *Odaka*, born in 1929 and hailing from Busia, died on 4 August. Minister of the Interior (appointed in 2013) and General Aronda *Nyakairima*, a former chief of defence forces, born in 1959 in Rukungiri district, died of acute heart failure aboard a plane returning from a visit to South Korea on 12 September. Major-General Ali *Bamuze*, former commander of the Uganda National Rescue Front II rebel group in West Nile, died on 4 October, aged 69.

Foreign Affairs

One of the most appalling events in modern history was recalled by Sam Kutesa, Ugandan president of the 69th session (2014/15) of the *UN General Assembly*, when he, together with UN Secretary-General Ban Ki-moon, unveiled the Ark of Return, the permanent memorial to honour victims of slavery and the transatlantic slave trade, at the UN headquarters in New York on 25 March. Beyond this symbolic duty, he chaired the General Assembly meeting on 27 July, which endorsed the Addis Ababa Action Agenda of the Third International Conference on Financing for Development held from 13–16 July in the Ethiopian capital. This was part of Kutesa's contribution towards reaching the global consensus on the landmark 2030 Agenda for Sustainable Development, declared by the Summit on Sustainable Development, a high-level plenary meeting of the 70th session of the General Assembly. The adoption ceremony on 25 September was presided over by Danish Prime Minister Lars Løkke Rasmussen and Uganda's President Museveni, whose countrymen held the presidency of the 70th and 69th General Assembly sessions, respectively. Kutesa had finished his term as president on 14 September and resumed his responsibilities as foreign minister, starting with a two-day visit to Washington.

Museveni's foreign travels included visits to Khartoum on 15–16 September in an attempt to mend fences with Sudan's President Omar al-Bashir, an ICC indictee, and to the third India-Africa Forum Summit on 26–29 October in New Delhi.

At home, the international highlight of the year was the brief *visit of Pope Francis* on 27–29 November, the pontiff arriving from Kenya and continuing to the CAR. He honoured the Christian martyrs killed, mostly in 1886, on the orders of Buganda's Kabaka Mwanga (and also met Mwanga's great-grandson Kabaka Mutebi). It was the third visit of a head of the Catholic Church, after Paul VI in 1969 and John Paul II in 1993.

The tenth in the series of *Northern Corridor Integration Projects Summits*, aimed at fast-tracking integration and facilitating the global competitiveness of the region, took place in Kampala on 6 June, members at that time being Kenya, Rwanda, South Sudan and Uganda. Burundi and Tanzania were observers. The three other summit meetings during the year were held in Kigali (Rwanda) and Nairobi (Kenya).

The heads of *intelligence and security services* of IGAD and EAC member states, having met first from 28 February to 1 March in Djibouti, held their second meeting on 14–15 July in Kampala. During the third meeting from 7–8 December at AU headquarters in Addis Ababa, an agreement was signed to establish the Eastern Africa Fusion and Liaison Unit (EA-FLU) in Uganda, and Uganda also became the first country to hold the EA-FLU chair, for a one-year term.

Affirming its entrenched role as regional power, Uganda took a stand in two crises besetting the neighbourhood. Ugandan troops in *South Sudan*, claiming to have helped avert genocide, effectively buttressed President Salva Kiir's government. The Uganda Peoples' Defence Forces (UPDF) were withdrawn after the 17 August peace deal between the warring parties and in line with UNSC resolution 2241 of 9 October. The last Ugandan soldiers left at the end of October. The situation in the country remained fragile, however. Meanwhile, Museveni's mediation in *Burundi*, with which an EAC emergency summit held on 6 July in Dar es Salaam had entrusted him, was hardly impressive. Oppositionists in the Burundian capital, Bujumbura, where the crisis had unfolded as a result of President Nkurunziza's disregard of term limits, denounced Museveni's own record over this issue. He delegated his task to Defence Minister Crispus Kiyonga, but the crisis gained even more momentum. On 28 December, Museveni presided over the relaunch of the intra-Burundian dialogue in Entebbe.

The still brittle situation in South Sudan and Burundi caused an influx of more *refugees*. During the year, 46,750 people arrived from South Sudan and 19,110 fled the turmoil in Burundi, while 33,607 were driven by the DRC's 'silent emergency'. This brought the total of registered refugees and asylum seekers, hosted with the assistance of UNHCR, to 512,966, making Uganda the country with the third-highest refugee population in Africa (after Ethiopia and Kenya).

The total number of repatriations to the *DRC* of ex-M-23 fighters cantoned in Bihanga camp in Kamwenge district reached only 195 by years' end, with about 1,000 showing no inclination to return.

Brigadier Muhoozi Kainerugaba, head of the UPDF's Special Forces Command (SFC) and son of President Museveni, called for the fostering of US-Ugandan ties in order to foil regional threats and international terrorism in a keynote speech at a training centre on asymmetric warfare in Mississippi in March. Also in March, Uganda was host to the two-week multinational command post exercise Eastern Accord of the US Africa Command (*AFRICOM*), which also involved soldiers from neighbouring countries. A one-year counter-terrorism training programme for an SFC elite unit conducted by the US Navy Seals concluded in August at Sera Kasenyi SFC Training School near Entebbe. A medical readiness training exercise involving US and Ugandan military personnel took place on 14–25 September in Jinja. Various trainings carried out by US marines, among others, aimed to augment UPDF capabilities in information operations, engineering and logistics, combat medicine and basic demolition. AFRICOM commander General David Rodriguez, visiting Kampala on 30 September, awarded the Legion of Merit to Chief of Defence Forces General Katumba Wamala and five other senior UPDF officers for their leadership in the AU Mission in Somalia (AMISOM); since 1942, the order had been awarded to fewer than 200 non-US military personnel.

In *Somalia*, AMISOM made more substantial gains against al-Shabaab but its mandate nevertheless had to be extended. On 28 July, the UNSC authorised the AU by its resolution 2232 to maintain the deployment until 30 May 2016. AMISOM, which was substantially funded by the EU, continued to rely on Uganda as the leading troop contributor with more than 6,000 of over 21,000 uniformed personnel. Its troops were deployed in the regions of Banadir and Lower Shabelle. On 1 September, the anniversary of the death of al-Shabaab leader Ahmed Abdi Godane, al-Shabaab attacked the AMISOM base in Janaale (Lower Shabelle), killing at least 19 Ugandan soldiers.

UPDF soldiers, forming the bulk of the AU Regional Task Force (AU-RTF), which was supported by US Special Forces of 'Operation Observant Compass', continued their operations in the CAR against the remnants of the *Lord's Resistance Army* (LRA), although it was through local Séléka militia that US forces were able to take senior LRA commander Dominic Ongwen into custody on 6 January. He was transferred to the ICC detention centre in The Hague on 21 January, facing seven counts of crimes against humanity and war crimes. Almost ten years after the issuing of arrest warrants by the ICC, he was the first of the five indicted LRA leaders to be brought before the Court. Ongwen had been abducted as a child and forced to join the LRA. The remnants of another ICC indictee, Okot Odhiambo, assumed to have been killed by UPDF soldiers in the CAR in late 2013, were exhumed on 20 March and brought to Uganda, where his identity was confirmed. The AU renewed the mandate of the Regional Cooperation Initiative for the Elimination of the LRA on 18 May for a further year. The UNSC in its comprehensive Presidential Statement 2015/12 of

11 June commended "the significant progress made by the AU-RTF" and paid tribute "to the important role" of the UPDF. It also welcomed "the continued advisory and logistical support provided by the United States as well as funding provided by the European Union". On 23 October, US President Barack Obama authorised the extension of Operation Observant Compass for a further year. Nevertheless, the LRA, estimated to have 230 armed fighters at most, proved surprisingly resilient to pressure. The amnesty clause of the Ugandan Amnesty Act, reinstated in May 2013 for two years, was extended for two more years. Its purpose was to induce mainly LRA fighters to surrender, but it did not apply to top leaders.

The Islamist *Allied Democratic Forces* (ADF) continued to make their presence felt in the east of the DRC. Long-time ADF leader Jamil Mukulu was arrested on Tanzanian soil in April and extradited to Uganda in July.

While the debate on *homosexuality* was not a major issue within the country, the lobby abroad continued unabated. Funding from outside sources had allowed for publication of the glossy magazine 'Bombastic' at the end of 2104, and about 15,000 copies were distributed free of charge. Randy Berry, appointed in February as the first Special Envoy of the US State Department for the Human Rights of LGBTI Persons, visited Uganda on 13–15 July to meet government and civil society representatives. Lesbian activist Kasha Jacqueline Nabagesera, initiator of 'Bombastic', made it to the cover of 'Time' magazine's Europe edition in June. On 30 November in Stockholm, she was able to add the 'Right Livelihood Award' aka 'Alternative Nobel Price' to her list of honours. The award carried a prize of SEK 1 m ($ 114,580) plus travel facilitation to enable her to propagate her views in various countries. Western involvements included a regional project aimed at promoting social tolerance and the rights of LGBTI people and other disadvantaged groups, for which the German government had pledged € 5.6 m for 2010–16.

Socioeconomic Developments

In a difficult global and regional environment, the *economy* fared well, though the shilling depreciated by 17.5% against the dollar over the calendar year (partly due to the strengthening of the US dollar). From July 2014 to June 2015, i.e. in financial year 2014/15, real *GDP* grew by 5%, failing to reach the anticipated 6.1%. GDP growth of 5.8% was predicted for 2015/16, with a return to 6%-6.5% anticipated in the medium term. The average annual *inflation* rate for the calendar year was 5.2%, rising from 4.3% in 2014. The stock of *foreign currency reserves* was adequate, corresponding to four months of imports. In a letter of intent to the IMF dated 12 June, new Finance Minister Kasaija described the reduction of "the infrastructure gap" as crucial to "our growth and development strategy". The upgrading of the transportation network and power generation were seen as major tasks ahead, with the infrastructure overhaul expected to take a decade at a cost of $ 11 bn, to be financed through public investment and public-private-partnership arrangements, according to the IMF.

The *IMF Executive Board*, which completed its fourth and fifth *reviews* under the advisory Policy Support Instrument (PSI) running since 2013, stated on 18 November that the performance under the PSI was 'positive'. Its team noted an unprecedented upsurge of 1.25 percentage points of GDP in *tax collection* during 2014/15, higher than the projected 0.5, but the domestic revenue to GDP ratio of about 13% was still low by international standards. In the IMF's opinion, it should be enhanced, together with "diversifying exports", "improving governance" and "strengthening social protection" in order to achieve "inclusive growth". As a tool to widen the tax base, in view of the informal sector accounting for almost half of economic output, the government decided that trading licences were to be given only to businesses with a Tax Identification Number.

On 3 March, the government submitted a *supplementary budget* for 2014/15 of UGX 847 bn (then $ 292 m), a large part of it having already been spent, including on campaign sweeteners such as bolstering civil service pensions. On 18 June, a second supplementary schedule was laid on parliament's table, followed by a third on 14 July, amounting to UGX 147 bn and UGX 128 bn, respectively.

According to the new Public Finance Management Act, the budget for the new financial year, commencing on 1 July, was approved at the end of May and Finance Minister Kasaija read his first budget on 11 June under the theme 'Maintaining Infrastructure Investment and Promoting Excellence in Public Service Delivery'. His presentation was preceded by Museveni's launch of the *Second National Development Plan* (2015/16–2019/20), "designed to propel Uganda towards middle income status by 2020", and by the *UN Development Assistance Framework 2015–2020*.

The *2015/16 budget* foresaw a total expenditure of UGX 23,972 bn (then roughly $ 7.6 bn), with 76.4% to be financed from domestic resources. The 23.6% external financing was expected to consist of UGX 5,649 bn in grants and loans; of which only UGX 1,095 bn (19.4%) would be grants, UGX 1,326 bn (23.5%) concessional and UGX 3,228 bn (57.1%) non-concessional loans. The steep increase in the budget total from UGX 15 trn (originally appropriated for 2014/15) to almost UGX 24 trn led to confusion even among experts and was explained with the new requirement to include in the books old roll-over bonds of around UGX 6 trn. The three sectors with the highest allocations were infrastructure (works and transport), education and security. Consumers were alerted to "modest adjustments" in excise duties, classically on items such as fuel, beer and cigarettes; motor vehicle lubricants were tagged with 5% excise.

Reflecting the global slump in crude *oil* prices, activities in the sector decelerated but did not stop. VAT exemption for oil production, lobbied for by the investors holding exploration rights (French Total, British-Irish Tullow and Chinese CNOOC), was granted. In June, Uganda and Tullow settled their capital gains tax dispute, the oil company agreeing to pay $ 250 m (of which $ 142 m had already been paid) instead of the $ 407 m that had been demanded. A subsidiary of the Russian state-owned conglomerate Rostec (which also produces military hardware) won the contract to build an oil refinery, not expected to become operational before 2020, a $ 4 bn venture.

A new managing director, Major-General James Mugira, was appointed to the commercial arm of the UPDF, the National Enterprise Corporation (*NEC*), in April. Since the end of 2011, he had been manager of the NEC subsidiary Luwero Industries, which manufactures mainly ammunition and spare parts. On 14 November, the groundbreaking ceremony, when the soil was first turned for the start of construction of the 'Kyoga Dynamics' factory for commercial emulsion explosives, set up with Chinese assistance, took place in Nakasongola.

Allen Kagina, commissioner general of the Uganda Revenue Authority from 2004 to 2014, and credited with having transformed a corrupt body into a reputable tax collector, was appointed executive director of the Uganda National Roads Authority (*UNRA*) with effect from 1 May. The UNRA was seen to be in need of her energetic approach to reform.

Emmanuel Tumusiime-Mutebile, governor of the *Bank of Uganda* since January 2001, was re-appointed in December for a further five-year term. He was widely perceived as standing for a prudent fiscal and economic policy.

TI's 2015 *Corruption Perceptions Index* put Uganda at 139th of 168 countries (compared with 142nd of 175 in 2014), equal with Kenya, and again scoring worse than Rwanda and Tanzania, but better than Burundi and South Sudan. Corruption, as noted by the IMF, continued "to affect the business climate".

PART 6

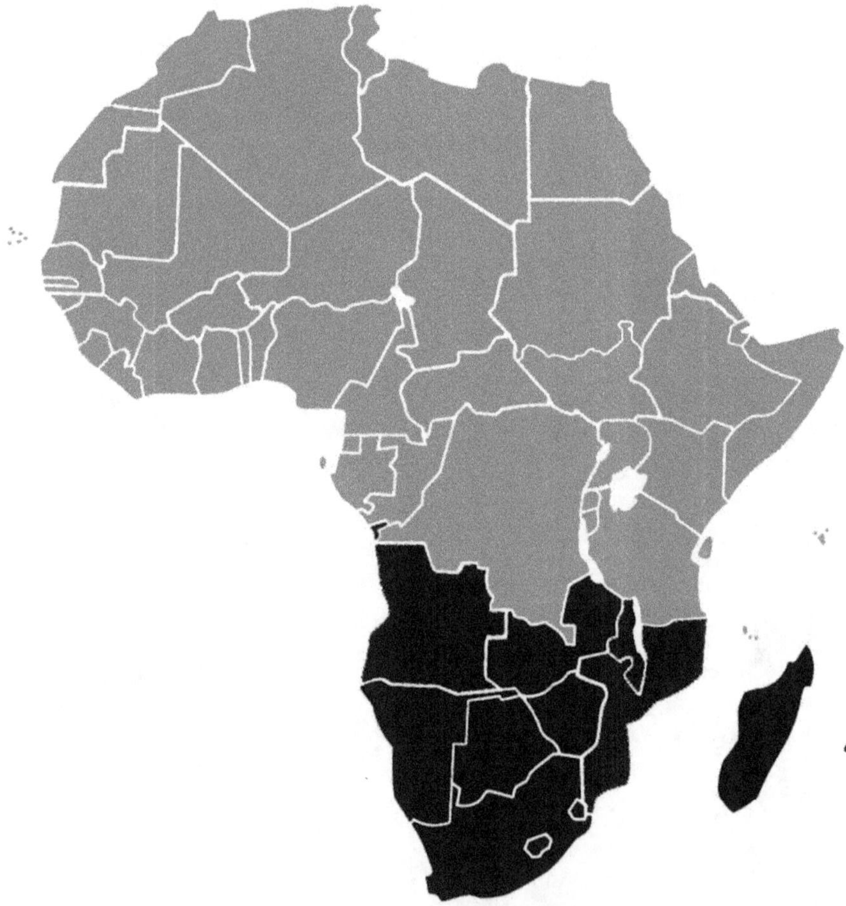

Southern Africa

Henning Melber

After several elections in 2014, the sub-region was politically less absorbed in domestic policy campaigns that would change governments or governance. But the relative absence of political contestation on the domestic front did not prevent a degree of policy turmoil in some countries. Scandals under the Zuma administration continued to make headlines in South Africa and that country experienced more economic decline than any other in the region. The Angolan economy was also hard hit as a result of the drastic slump in oil prices, and human rights there also deteriorated further. These two economic powerhouses in the sub-region thereby affected the overall economic performance of neighbouring countries, as did the general decline of commodity prices on the world market, which had a negative effect on the resource-based economies. In addition, floods and drought hit many rural communities in most countries and water shortages seriously impacted on the living conditions in urban areas too. The ecological vulnerability of the sub-region to the effects of climate change became ever more visible and indicated serious challenges for the future, while concerted sub-regional efforts continued to lack the necessary political will to meet the challenges. After several years of high economic growth, meagre times seemed to be arriving with few precautionary measures in place.

Elections, Democracy and Human Rights

In *Zambia presidential by-elections* on 20 January were triggered by the death in office of President Sata in October 2014. Eleven candidates competed to take over for the remainder of the presidential term, due to end in 2016. After a campaign period that saw only a few noteworthy violent incidents, the ruling Patriotic Front's Edgar Lungu won by a narrow margin of less than 28,000 votes ahead of Hakainde Hichilema of the opposition United Party for National Development. Despite the tight result, the election was recognised as credible with only minor infringements recorded, though in the end Hichilema refused to accept defeat. Despite being only a temporary caretaker, the newly elected president used his authority to carry out major cabinet re-shuffles.

In *Lesotho general elections* were held on 28 February in the midst of continued security concerns, which necessitated SADC involvement in the electoral process, with police forces from five member states deployed to the country to reduce risks. The results were unable to overcome the deep political divide. A new majority replaced the previous beleaguered government but was just too small to exercise

 | DOI 10.1163/9789004333239_044

sufficient authority. Phakalita Mosisili of the Democratic Congress, who managed as the new prime minister to lead a seven-party alliance, was not able to gain a decisive upper hand over Tom Thabane's defeated All Basotho Congress, which had only one parliamentary seat fewer than Mosilisi's party. The volatile political situation remained violent, culminating on 25 June in the assassination of the army's controversial commander Brigadier Mahoa, one of the key figures in the power struggle by members of the defence force, who were arrested and faced trial for high treason. Opposition politicians again fled to South Africa and boycotted parliament, which paralysed politics in a fragile security situation.

In *Madagascar*, the government lacked the political stability that was needed and hoped for after years of struggle over a negotiated return to constitutionally elected political leadership. Prime Minister Roger Kolo's government resigned on 13 January as a result of strained relations with President Hery Martial Rajaonarimampianina, who appointed General Jean Ravelonarivo to succeed Kolo in an effort to further integrate and co-opt the military into civilian political structures. The president survived an impeachment vote by a ruling of the High Constitutional Court, but the year ended with growing concerns that the desired reconciliation and consolidation of democratic rule were far from being a foregone conclusion.

Following the unexpected results of a snap-election at the end of 2014 in *Mauritius*, the new government saw the return of the long-serving elder statesman, Prime Minister Sir Anerood Jugnauth, to political power as head of the 'Alliance Lepep'. The year also witnessed the political demise of the former prime minister, Navin Ramgoolan, who not only failed to be re-elected but also faced criminal prosecution for his suspected involvement in money laundering and other dubious financial transactions. A similar fate awaited Prime Minister Jugnauth's son, the cabinet minister Pravind Jugnauth, who was convicted for a 'conflict of interest' during his time as finance minister. The image of the island state in the Indian Ocean, considered a role model for democracy and good governance, seemed to be less pristine than many thought, despite continuing to be ranked top in all Africa surveys. At least, with Ameenah Gurib-Fakim, another woman joined the ranks of African presidents, though the post was largely ceremonial.

In *Mozambique*, President Filipe Nyusi stood the test of his first year in office after being sworn in on 15 January. He was initially confronted with the obstructive influence of the old guard allied to former president Armando Guebuza, who only reluctantly vacated the party presidency in favour of Nyusi on 29 March. But the main political challenges were caused by Renamo and its leader Afonso Dhlakama, who decided to return to the bush and instigate new acts of aggression, which in turn provoked a response by the army, leading to armed skirmishes erupting again between Renamo guerrillas and government soldiers. Talks between the parties were abandoned and dialogue was again assigned to the distant future.

In *Namibia*, newly elected President Hage Geingob resumed office on Independence Day (21 March) and faced a much easier task. Not only had the South

West African People's Organisation (SWAPO of Namibia) consolidated its political hegemony even further with 80% of the votes in the parliamentary elections at the end of November 2014, but Geingob also gained further recognition in the parallel presidential elections, when he took 86% of the votes. In the absence of any meaningful opposition, SWAPO politics faced no serious challenges from outside the party. In a surprise move, when former president Hifikepunye Pohamba left office he also gave up the party presidency in favour of his successor. In the absence of any party rules for such a scenario, Geingob, who was the party's deputy president also became party president and continued to hold both positions. Not everyone in the party seemed satisfied with such a monopoly of political power, and policy differences also led to the suspension of a group of activists from the party's Youth League and created divisions in public opinion.

Politics in *Botswana* were rather unspectacular and it was a case of 'business as usual', while parties in *Malawi* continued to be much occupied with internal conflicts and power struggles. Both countries experienced major corruption scandals, however, which had political implications. In *Swaziland*, where self-enrichment continued to remain a royal privilege, King Mswati continued to show little to no willingness to enter into serious dialogue with the political opposition but rather continued to rule by state terror. Prohibition of meaningful political activity was justified on the basis of a terrorism act, which was used as instrument to prosecute those trying to mobilise against the undemocratic rule of the royal family. Two local trade unionists who had been in prison for 14 months were finally released on bail in July, not least as a result of international protest, while the country's overall human rights record remained appalling.

South Africa was kept abuzz with new scandals under the Zuma administration. President Jacob Zuma's State of the Nation Address on 12 February ended in chaos and physical violence when opposition MPs interrupted his speech and urged him to respond to the demand that he pay for considerable additions to his private retirement village, which had been financed under false premises by state funds. For the first time, a motion of no confidence in a president was tabled on 17 March. Various activities and organisations of the country's highly active and politicised civil society culminated in the emergence of a militant countrywide student protest movement that soon addressed issues beyond student politics. It began with mobilisation against a statue of Cecil Rhodes at the University of Cape Town but escalated into a campaign against the planned increase in tuition fees. The massive resistance forced the government to withdraw its plans towards end of the year, but campus life did not return to normal and much damage was done to the infrastructure of some universities. More harm was caused by the increased 'state capture' under the Zuma administration, when dubious transactions and even the shuffling of cabinet posts and other important offices in politics and the economy were revealed to have been decided under the influence of an Indian family operating locally. The revelations also impacted negatively on the economy (see more below).

This 'Zumatocracy' increased internal party frictions and raised the question of the presidential succession and Zuma's role after retirement.

In *Angola*, speculation continued over who would succeed President José Eduardo dos Santos, who had been head of state since 1979 – a year longer than even his counterpart in neighbouring Zimbabwe. Evidence seemed to grow that he and the family clan in charge of the country's economy were starting to prepare for a possible hand-over to one of his direct descendants, one candidate being his daughter Isabel dos Santos, who had emerged as the continent's richest woman, largely as a beneficiary of the 'oiligarchy'. The human rights situation deteriorated further and reached an all-time low since the end of the internal military conflict some 15 years before. Several prominent activists were arrested, prosecuted and sentenced, most notably the investigative journalist, activist and regime critic Rafael Marques de Morais, who faced 24 criminal defamation charges for allegations he had made in a book that leading military generals were involved in illicit diamond trading and extra-judicial killings. Threatened with long-term imprisonment, he was forced to retract some of the views he had expressed earlier, while an international solidarity campaigned mobilised for his release. Morais was sentenced at the end of May to six months in prison, suspended for two years. The police and military forces used ruthless violence to suppress political dissent, culminating in the killing of some demonstrators and the arrest and trial of many more. On 20 June, 17 members of a Luanda book club were jailed for reading the 'wrong' book. They were accused of conspiracy and high treason for plotting a coup and planning the assassination of the president and others, and faced long prison sentences. The atmosphere of growing repression continued to affect any civil rights movement as the Angolan regime became increasingly totalitarian and left no doubt as to the monopoly of power held by the MPLA and the dos Santos family in both politics and the economy.

In *Zimbabwe*, the governing ZANU-PF further consolidated the political hegemony it had regained under the gerontocratic rule of Robert Mugabe by winning a number of by-elections during the year, while the opposition MDC parties continued to decline as a result of factionalism, in-fighting and party splits. ZANU-PF was more occupied with the internal wrangles over the succession to President Mugabe than with fighting any political opposition outside the party. Several competitors kept party and public speculation busy with factional mobilisation. The rivalries escalated and culminated towards the end of the year, when the party's 15th annual National People's Conference became the forum for bitter fighting and did not announce any final resolutions. Ironically, absorption in continued internal fighting had a positive side effect in that it sapped the energy to do much further harm by the repression of opposition forces, so the human rights situation did not deteriorate any further, though human rights activists remained at risk being harassed by the police, and civil rights such as freedom of expression and assembly, as well as press freedom, remained under siege.

Several other countries between A (Angola) and Z (Zimbabwe) in the sub-region made little to no progress in terms of the protection and promotion of fundamental freedoms and civil and political rights. Xenophobia and the rights of indigenous minorities, as well as gender-based violence and gay and lesbian rights remained unresolved issues in most countries of the sub-region. *South Africa* was criticised for its voting behaviour on human rights related issues in the UN: it voted in the General Assembly against mandating the UN to deal with issues surrounding privacy and the surveillance of citizens. It abstained from votes related to human rights violations perpetrated in Iran and North Korea and voted to prevent condemnation of human rights abuses in Burma and Zimbabwe. The *ICC* remained another contentious issue. Following the AU's critical views on the role of the Court, South Africa ignored the indictment of Sudan's President al-Bashir when he attended the AU summit in Johannesburg in mid-June. The government argued that as a head of state participating in the summit, al-Bashir was covered by diplomatic immunity. While a South African high court was in session over an urgent appeal by a human rights organisation to extradite the Sudanese president, he was allowed hastily to leave the country from a military airport, pre-empting the ruling of the court that South Africa was obliged as a signatory to the Rome Statutes to comply with the ICC arrest warrant. The North Gauteng High Court refused the government leave of appeal on 16 September. In October, news was leaked that the ANC planned to leave the ICC. In a similar vein, *Namibia* massively criticised the ICC from mid-year, when President Geingob in his speech at the AU summit called the ICC an "abomination". Namibia's cabinet declared in November that it supported an initiative to terminate the country's membership in the ICC, though no concrete steps followed immediately. Notably, *Botswana* was the only country in the sub-region to articulate a dissenting view and welcomed the ruling on al-Bashir.

Almost ironically, all three countries received almost equal positive acknowledgment of their performance in terms of good governance, while the aggregated results of the sub-region once again scored best in the annual *Mo Ibrahim Index* for overall governance. Mauritius (rank 1/score 79.9) remained the top ranked of all 54 countries and Mauritius, Botswana (3/74.2), South Africa (4/73.0) and Namibia (5/70.4) were four of the five top scorers from the SADC region, followed by Lesotho (10/61.1), Zambia (12/59.5), Malawi (17/56.7), Mozambique (21/52.3), Swaziland (28/49.6), Madagascar (29/49.1), Angola (43/40.8) and Zimbabwe (44/40.4). Compared with the 2011 data, the biggest improvements were recorded for Zimbabwe (+4.6) and the biggest deterioration for Mozambique (−2.2). As usual, the scores given for the four components that contributed to the overall score (safety and rule of law, participation and human rights, sustainable economic opportunity and human development) occasionally left one wondering where the reality check of such surveys might be and what their value is. But what can be deduced is that the sub-region again compared favourably with the other parts of the continent, with eight of its 12 countries attaining above the average score of 50.1.

The *Fragile States Index* for 2015 also ranked most countries of the sub-region high among African states, with Mauritius (ranked 145th out of 178) topping the continental chart in the category 'stable', followed by Botswana and South Africa (122nd and 113th) in the 'low warning' category, Namibia and Lesotho (106th and 66th) in the 'warning' category, Madagascar (56th), Zambia (53rd), Swaziland (48th), Malawi (45th), Mozambique (45th) and Angola (41st) classified as 'high warning' and Zimbabwe (16th) as 'alert'. As always, the relevance and reliability of such rankings and the criteria applied remained the subject of controversy, but they often add to and shape perceptions, mainly by outside observers, and so should not be dismissed lightly.

Socioeconomic Developments

Apart from Swaziland, all countries in the sub-region were ranked on the list of 168 countries published in TI's *Corruption Perceptions Index* issued for 2015, with Botswana again being the top scorer (ranked 28th/score 63), followed by Mauritius and Namibia (equal 45th/53), Lesotho and South Africa (equal 61st/44), Zambia (76th/38), Malawi and Mozambique (equal 112th/31), Zimbabwe (150th/21) and Angola (163rd/15).

Party policies in *South Africa* guided by the purely personal motivations of President Jacob Zuma caused considerable economic damage. His replacement of a trusted finance minister with a hardly competent Zuma loyalist in early December caused a massive crisis and the exchange value of the rand plummeted to an all-time low. The domestic and international turmoil this created – in combination with internal party pressure – forced Zuma to revoke his decision within less than two days and to reinstate the former finance minister Pravin Gordhan in an effort to limit the damage. Speculation continued, however, as to the motives for such an ill-conceived political manoeuvre, which did a lot of harm and fuelled suspicions of attempts to cover up investigations into financial irregularities on a grand scale perpetrated by state officials. The role of the Indian Gupta family, allied to the Zuma family in activities labelled 'state capture', also became a topic of growing interest and concern that spilled over into 2016 and damaged government policy and had a negative impact on the economy, which was heading for a recession.

The dramatic drop in world oil prices had devastating consequences for the economy of *Angola*. Revenue from oil production, which had amounted to more than two-thirds of government's annual budget, was reduced to slightly more than one-third. However, the crisis did not affect the self-serving mentality of the dos Santos clan and those benefitting from their closeness to the political inner circle, but did have major implications for the country's purchasing power and hence also for neighbouring economies, particularly *Namibia*, whose exports to Angola (previously its fifth most important market) decreased from N$ 4.7 bn in 2014 to N$ 2.6 bn.

Angolan visitors and businesses in Namibia also declined markedly, which affected the Namibian retail and services sectors. The fall in demand in Angola also impacted negatively on Namibia's harbour facilities at Walvis Bay, which operated well below its capacity as fewer imports were routed to Angola.

Despite regaining some sort of relative political stability under ZANU-PF, *Zimbabwe*'s economic performance remained lacklustre. While restrictions that had been placed on foreign companies to enforce indigenisation were partly revoked in an effort to regain foreign investor confidence, towards the end of the year new plans for indigenisation again discouraged potential investment from abroad with the announcement of additional tax burdens. Internal party rivalries and competition for the succession to Mugabe also seemed to affect the coherence, or rather lack of coherence, of the country's economic policy.

With the biggest economies in the sub-region ailing, other SADC members received few benefits from interaction. *Climate related factors* added to the constraints. Parts of the sub-region suffered from the effects of floods early in the year (particularly Malawi and parts of Zimbabwe, but also Madagascar in the aftermath of cyclone Chedza). The effects of the worst El Niño ever recorded manifested later in lack of rainfall, which resulted in droughts mainly affecting south-eastern Angola, southern Botswana, Lesotho, southern Malawi, central and southern Mozambique, large parts of Namibia and South Africa, Swaziland, eastern Zambia, and north-eastern Zimbabwe.

As a result, harvests in all countries were severely affected and *food insecurity* reached considerable proportions, as reported in FAO's Global Information and Warning System. In Angola, an estimated 460,000 people were affected by crop losses and livestock death. Botswana's aggregate cereal crop stood at some 9,000 tonnes, a fall from the already reduced output in 2014, and livestock farmers faced massive shortages of water and grazing. In Lesotho, the estimated number of persons requiring food assistance doubled to some 450,000. In Madagascar, floods at the beginning of the year affected more than half a million people, of whom FAO assessed some 170,000 to be severely food insecure. Crop damage resulted in lower rice production. In Malawi, about 2.8 m people (up from 640,000 in 2014) were dependent upon food assistance as a combined result of the floods early in the year and the subsequent drought. In Mozambique, erratic rainfall was followed at year's end by heavy downpours causing floods in central parts of the country with crop losses and damage to infrastructure, mainly in the Zambezia and Manica provinces. Namibia experienced a combination of above-average temperatures and lack of rain, which affected mainly rain-fed crops in the communal sector (with a 73% fall in production) but also commercial maize production under irrigation (with 46% drop) and half of dry land commercial farmers, who saw total crop failure. Total cereal output fell by over 40%, while livestock conditions deteriorated. The number of food insecure people tripled to almost 400,000. Five provinces in South Africa (North West, KwaZulu-Natal, Mpumalanga, Limpopo and the Free State) were declared drought disaster areas. Maize production fell by 30% to an estimated 10.5 m tonnes. This resulted in a sharp decline in maize exports from 1.7 m tonnes in 2014 to 450,000 tonnes. Poor rainfall in Swaziland, mainly in the southern and eastern regions, contributed to a drop of more than 30% in the maize harvest and an increase in food insecurity from 3% to 5.5% of the population. The maize harvest in Zambia fell by one-fifth to 2.7 m tonnes as a result of severe dry spells and the number of people requiring food assistance more than doubled to 800,000, mainly in the Western and Eastern provinces. Zimbabwe's cereal production fell by 50% to 870,000 tonnes, with the southern and western provinces of Midlands, Masvingo, and Matabeleland the worst hit by crop losses, experiencing harvests down by between 66% and 84%. An estimated 1.5 m people were considered food insecure, three times more than in 2014. Given the general weather conditions, by year's end, forecasts for future maize harvests were bleak and the sub-region's agricultural production would not be enough to feed the people. SADC white maize import requirements faced a supply impasse. An additional problem was the incompatibility of US and South African genetically modified (GM) maize varieties, which were asynchronous, and this impacted negatively on the supply from US imports.

A SADC Extraordinary Summit of Heads of State and Government took place on 29 April in Harare (Zimbabwe) to adopt a revised *Regional Indicative Strategy Development Plan* (RISDP) for 2015–20. It coincided with the adoption of a *SADC industrial development strategy* for 2015–63 as the main focus at the same summit, aligned to the continental vision Agenda 2063. This was declared a transformational programme based on the pillars industrialisation, competitiveness and regional integration and was considered a top priority in the implementation of the revised RISDP. It included the following quantitative goals: to increase the regional growth rate of real GDP from 4% to a minimum of 7% annually; to double the share of manufacturing value added (MVA) in GDP to 30% by 2030 and 40% by 2050; to increase the share of medium-and-high technology production in MVA from less than 15% to 30% by 2030 and 50% by 2050; to increase manufactured exports from less than 20% to at least 50% by 2030; and to increase industrial employment to 40% of total employment by 2030. However, given the constraints in terms of infrastructure, including transport routes, communications, and even more the insecure water and energy supply, the catalogue adopted sounded once again more like wishful thinking than a realistic strategy. Similarly, the Tripartite Free Trade Agreement signed between COMESA, EAC and SADC member states in early June had so far achieved little beyond the rhetoric level of declaration. Given the dramatic drop in commodity prices since 2014 and the slow down of economic growth in most countries, not least in South Africa, the regional engine of economic development and growth, the implementation of the new programmatic strategies would face a tough uphill battle. Some rather drastic falls in currency exchange rates contributed further to the challenges: while this allowed commodity-exporting countries to manage declining terms-of-trade shocks to a large extent, it added pressure on imports and negatively affected local consumption. Global external shocks remained a risk variable directly impacting sub-regional and national level economies.

Sub-regional Organisations

All 12 countries in the sub-region were members of SADC (whose 15 member states also include the DRC, Seychelles and Tanzania). The 35th *annual SADC Summit* of Heads of State and Government was held on 17–18 August in Gaborone (Botswana), where President Ian Khama of Botswana became the elected chairperson with King Mswati III of Swaziland as deputy chairperson and designated successor for the following year. Mozambique's President Filipe Jacinto Nyusi and Tanzania's President Jakaya Mrisho Kikwete were elected as chairperson and deputy chairperson, respectively, of the SADC Organ on Politics, Defence and Security Cooperation. The Summit approved the SADC Regional Counter Terrorism Strategy and the resolution on the establishment of the Southern African Development Community Administrative Tribunal and adopted the Declaration on Youth Development and Empowerment.

Ahead of the 35th ordinary SADC annual summit, 19 partners from the NGO sector united in the Coalition for an Effective SADC Tribunal issued a statement on 14 August in which they bemoaned the disbanding of the old *SADC Tribunal* and the adoption of a new Protocol by the heads of state without consultation. The new Protocol shifted the focus of the Tribunal exclusively to the level of governments and removed access by individuals and legal representatives, thus aborting its human rights mandate. The coalition urged reconsideration of the decision, which it criticised for its disregard of judicial independence and separation of powers and its lack of respect for the rule of law.

SACU, the oldest customs union, now in existence for more than a century, which included South Africa and the so-called BLNS states, Botswana, Lesotho, Namibia and Swaziland, remained ailing. The Council of Ministers, intended to be its supreme decision-making authority and tasked to meet at least once in each quarter of the financial year, remained dormant. As a working paper of the South African Trade Law Centre (tralac) by Gerhard Erasmus diagnosed: "SACU is in an impasse about its impasse." The SACU Tariff Board had never become operational, nor had an agreement been reached on joint institutions or the adoption of a common policy. Despite a formula adopted in an agreement in 2002, nothing had happened since then, which was for Erasmus "the main reason why the Organization is in limbo". The consequence was the emergence of substitute structures and procedures for SACU operations. While SACU tariff policy was intended to be a collective affair, with a supra-national institution determining the common external tariff, the South African International Trade Administration Commission (ITAC) emerged as a kind of handling agent, despite its being a national state organ. Although SACU headquarters were located in Windhoek (South Africa), decisions were taken elsewhere on the basis of a revenue sharing arrangement, which South Africa had long considered was to its disadvantage. With the economic decline, the regional hegemon was less inclined to behave generously, while the other SACU states remained suspicious of the South African hegemonic role. The lack of autonomy over tariff policy, and the absence of a SACU tribunal as a body to decide on differences over the application or interpretation of the SACU agreement had created an atmosphere of suspicion and mistrust. Having no dispute settlement mechanism, SACU members were mainly concerned to maintain revenue based on the established revenue sharing formula, which was increasingly questioned by South Africa. At the same time, South African economic policy decisions remained a unilateral matter, despite its effects on SACU member states through the impact other agreements had on them.

A case in point had been South Africa's negotiations with the USA over *AGOA*, as summarised in another tralac paper by Erasmus, in which he recapitulated the negotiations during the year and their implications for the other SACU partners. The US Senate decided in March to include South Africa in the re-authorised AGOA over the coming ten years under "strict terms". This included, among other things, a demand for the removal of trade barriers on US exports, particularly chicken. In November, US President Barack Obama issued an ultimatum to South Africa to remove trade barriers on US chicken, beef and pork, to make American poultry and other products available on store shelves. The South African institution to respond was ITAC, the same that was in charge over SACU matters. But AGOA negotiations were run unilaterally, despite their effects on SACU states. Free US exports to South Africa directly affected the economies of the BLNS countries as fellow SACU member states. Namibian chicken producers followed the negotiations with concern and started to take matters to court. After all, article 31 of the SACU Agreement stated clearly, "No Member State shall negotiate and enter into new preferential trade agreements with third parties or amend existing agreements without the consent of other Member States." The ongoing AGOA negotiations, which had not been concluded by the end of the year, were just another indication how little a sub-regional common understanding and policy had developed. This bias in interests was visible not only in trade, but also more generally in politics. Despite being originally regarded with much hope and expectation, SADC and related sub-regional networks had not yet made much progress towards prioritising collective interests over national ones.

Angola

Jon Schubert

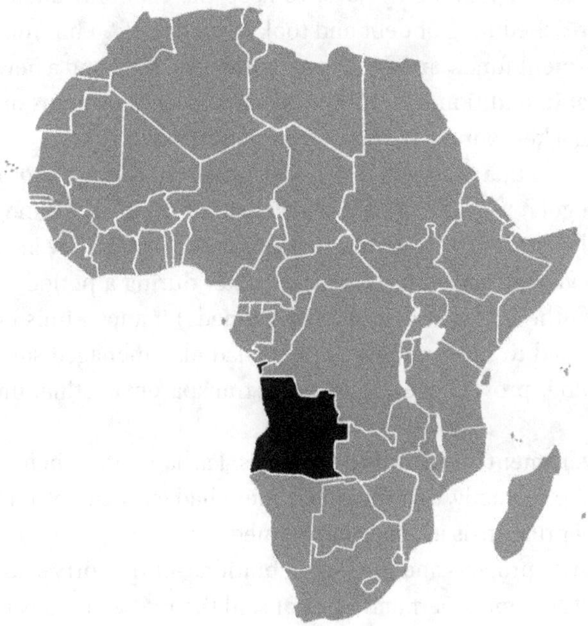

This was a year of crisis, with falling oil prices causing a rapid deterioration in the economy. Domestic politics were shaped by the impact of the economic downturn, but rather than tackling the crisis head-on, the authorities unleashed the most violent persecution of suspected 'internal enemies' since the end of the war. Internationally, Angola multiplied its overtures to new and old creditors but all socioeconomic areas saw significant decline, with negative consequences for large parts of the population, including a hitherto relatively well-off, nascent urban middle class.

Domestic Politics

In January, the government announced revisions to the state budget (Orçamento Geral do Estado, OGE), which had been approved only weeks before the beginning of the year. The budget had been based on an oil price of $ 81 per barrel, but with oil prices plummeting, cuts were necessary. On 9 February, Finance Minister Armando Manuel presented a *revised budget* with a benchmark price of $ 40 per barrel, which would necessitate cutting public expenditure by one-third. Although

 | DOI 10.1163/9789004333239_045

Manuel guaranteed that health and education, as well as the salaries of public service workers would not be affected, the government soon afterwards announced a public sector hiring freeze; state-owned companies were told to cut running costs by 30% and investments by half, while government departments were also instructed to immediately reduce spending by 50%. To keep the economy afloat, the government asked for a rescheduling of debt and took out *loans* of $ 1 bn from commercial banks and investment funds, another $ 500 m from the IMF, and a new $ 2 bn credit line from China. In addition, the authorities imposed restrictions on currency exchange, including a 'temporary' currency transaction tax.

At the end of January, José de Lima Massano resigned as governor of the *Central Bank* ('Banco Nacional de Angola', BNA), to pre-empt criticism of the Bank's handling of the crisis; in his stead, José Pedro de Morais was appointed as the new BNA governor. De Morais had previously served as finance minister during a period of booming oil prices. Although the fact that he had been named 'Finance Minister of the Year' (2008) was intended to reassure investors, he had also managed substantial Chinese loans of dubious provenance and even less transparent destination during that time.

UNITA lambasted the government's reaction to the crisis. Parliamentary bench leader Raúl Danda stated, quite correctly, that the government had learned nothing from the previous, shorter, oil price crisis in 2009, and blamed *corruption and profligate spending* on useless prestige projects and public celebrations for the sorry state of the national economy. UNITA deputy Fernando Heitor said the revised OGE was a document "without financial sanity or economic rationality", while the second-largest opposition party, 'Convergência Ampla de Salvação de Angola – Coligação Eleitoral', also said the government had "lost its way" frantically trying to cover up the holes in the budget created by its "wasteful spending".

In fact, *spending priorities* in the revised budget included the building of a memorial to the battle of Cuito Cuanavale, at an estimated cost of $ 7.5 m, $ 73 m for 'Non-Specified Recreation, Culture, and Religious Matters' at the president's 'Office for Special Works', a $ 62.5 m private jet, and $ 13.6 m for the acquisition of new furniture and equipment for the presidential palace – the last budget item being five times more than the budget for the construction of 24,000 social housing units and infrastructure for a further 30,000 houses in Luanda's peripheral Zango and Sapú districts. *Military spending* also remained the highest in Africa.

On 2 July, opening the meeting of the Central Committee of the ruling 'Movimento Popular de Libertação de Angola' (*MPLA*), President José Eduardo dos Santos, now in his 36th year in power, said the selection of *candidates for the 2017 elections* would require profound reflection: "In certain restricted circles it was almost a given that the President of the Republic would not see his current mandate through till the end, but it is evident that it is not sensible to envisage this option under the current circumstances." In conjunction with the waning popularity of Vice President Manuel Vicente, who was also blamed for mismanagement in his previous function as CEO of state oil company Sonangol (see below), this statement by the President was taken as an indicator of his intention to cling on to power beyond his current mandate, with a view to building up one of his children as potential successor in 2022.

Isaías Samakuva, president of the major opposition party 'União Nacional pela Independência Total de Angola' (*UNITA*) announced in June that he was not seeking re-election as party leader. At the party congress on 5 December, however, he was re-elected for a third term with 82.8% of the votes. Commentators remarked that this failure to renew the party leadership was probably the best gift UNITA could have given President dos Santos for the 2017 elections. The historic but now marginalised 'Frente Nacional de Libertação de Angola' (*FNLA*) continued to be beset by internal wrangling; at the party congress in February, confrontations between its two 'wings', led by Ngola Kabangu and Lucas Ngonda, led to the death of one party member.

In this atmosphere of crisis, the government cracked down on any perceived challenge to the regime. One of the measures taken was the signing into law in March of a presidential decree on the *regulation of NGOs*, which effectively restricted their financial and operational autonomy. In February, following the arrest of a local activist of the Lunda provinces autonomy movement, police attacked demonstrators calling for the activist's release in the town of Cafunfo, injuring several and detaining 20. Another Lunda activist, Rafael Muambumba, was released in June after a month in prison for "possession of seditious materials"; Muambumba claimed that he was regularly tortured during his imprisonment. *Forced demolitions* of informal houses and the eviction of residents continued in Luanda's Bairro Operário and Chicala neighbourhoods, as well as in Benguela and Lubango.

In April, police descended upon *Cabinda city* to prevent a demonstration against the detention of two local activists the month before; in March, José Marcos Mavungo and his lawyer Arão Bula Tempo had been arrested on allegations of "crimes against state security" but were still awaiting formal charges. Tempo was eventually "conditionally" released in May; Mavungo finally went on trial in late August, with the public prosecutor asking for 12 years' imprisonment for "inciting rebellion". His 'crime' was having called for a demonstration in Cabinda, though he was arrested on the eve of the protest. After a trial lasting a month, and despite the prosecution's failure to produce any evidence against him, Mavungo was sentenced to six years in prison.

In March, a trial opened in Luanda against human rights activist and investigative journalist *Rafael Marques*. In 2010, Marques had published a book in Portugal documenting the widespread and systematic abuse of the human rights of the local population and artisanal miners at the hands of private and public security forces in the diamond-producing Lunda provinces. When an earlier libel suit brought by the Angolan generals who owned the private security outfits was dismissed in Portugal, the plaintiffs launched a civil lawsuit against Marques in Luanda for "criminal defamation". After postponement and a month of hearings, Marques announced on 21 May that an agreement had been reached under which he would not retract his statements but would admit that he had never contacted the generals directly but had only communicated with their companies. In addition, Marques voluntarily agreed not to republish the book (his editor in Portugal had already made the e-book available free of charge in support of the author). In return, the generals dropped the suit as this face-saving deal spared them from having to testify in court and the public exposure of further evidence of the human rights abuses. Four days later, however, the Public Ministry (Attorney General) declared that Marques's statement amounted to a 'confession' and pressed charges in a criminal lawsuit; on 28 May, the activist was given a six-month suspended jail sentence.

In mid-April, news also emerged of a *massacre at Mt Sumi*, in Huambo province. José Julino Kalupeteca, the leader of the sect 'A Luz do Mundo' (The Light of the World), a millennial offshoot of the Adventist Church, had been camping on the mountain with about 4,000 followers, praying, singing, and awaiting the end of the world. When Kalupeteca's followers peacefully turned away census agents, the police returned a week later to arrest the group's leader, and a violent confrontation ensued between security forces and Kalupeteca's 'guard', in which, officially, between four and nine policemen and 13 members of the sect were killed; Kalupeteca himself was severely beaten and arrested, and was still awaiting trial at year's end. However, police rapid response units and army troops then moved in on the camp with assault weapons and set the huts on fire, allegedly killing a large number of pilgrims indiscriminately, including women and children. While President dos Santos stated that Kalupeteca and his followers presented a threat to peace and national unity, the opposition party UNITA claimed that at least 1,080 people had been killed and buried in mass graves; Rafael Marques also reported having heard of mass killings from army officers involved in the raid, and that followers who escaped the massacre were being hunted down across the country. However, the army sealed off the hill declaring it a military restricted area, only admitting a handful of parliamentarians two weeks later. The authorities rejected calls from both inside and outside Angola for an independent investigation – including statements by AI and UNHCR – with the government demanding an apology from the UN for violating the sovereignty of its legal institutions.

On 20 June, police in Luanda arrested 13 activists who had been "caught in the act" of reading books about peaceful political action. Two more were arrested on 22 June. The authorities then searched their homes and seized their personal computers and phones, and declared that the detainees had been "preparing acts aimed at disrupting public order and security in the country". 'Evidence' produced over the following months included the fact that one of the detainees was an army captain who had previously studied with one of the activists – 'proof' of the subversion of parts of the state security forces – as well as a public discussion on Facebook in which lawyer Albano Pedro, an individual completely unrelated to the detainees, asked people to speculate on the composition of an ideal '*Government of National Salvation*' to lead the country. There were suggestions that it should include some of these 'revús' (young 'revolutionary' activists), and also that the above-mentioned Kalupeteca might become president of the Republic, Rafael Marques minister of justice, and rapper MCK minister of culture. Attorney General João Maria de Sousa also claimed that the activists were manipulated by foreign embassies in Luanda and had been promised $ 100 m to overthrow President dos Santos.

The 15 detainees awaited trial for months, many in solitary confinement and without being allowed visits from family members or their lawyers; two women activists were also indicted as co-conspirators but were awaiting trial without detention. First the families of the accused, then a larger part of Luandan society, started calling for the release of the '*15+2 activists*'. A protest march by the mothers and wives of the detainees in August was violently put down by police using batons and dogs; further protests were declared 'unconstitutional' by Luanda governor Graciano Domingos. After the 90-day maximum period of 'preventive detention' had passed without any hearing, several detainees started a *hunger strike*. One of the prisoners, the well-known rapper and activist Luaty Beirão, persisted the longest. After 20 days, his condition deteriorated critically, prompting widespread domestic and international appeals for his release. A peaceful vigil in front of the Sagrada Família Church in central Luanda attracted an impressive number of people, including many of the middle class traditionally affiliated with the MPLA, who had hitherto preferred to stay out of politics. The vigil dispersed voluntarily after the police entered the square with dogs and water cannon; the next week, however, a follow-up vigil at the São Domingos Church was violently dispersed by the police, who entered the church during the service to arrest demonstrators. The Angolan bishops sent a note to the Holy See reporting this violation of church rights, but the government found more compliant priests who publicly affirmed that there had been no police intrusion. During the hunger strike, it was also revealed that the prosecution had falsified Beirão's declarations so that in case of his death, 'proof' of his intentions to overthrow the government could have been produced. When the authorities finally announced a date for the beginning of the trial, Beirão gave up his hunger strike after a symbolic 36 days, one day for every year President dos Santos had been in power, much to the relief of his family and friends, as well as many in the regime who feared nothing more having than the death of a martyr on their hands.

The *trial of the activists* started on 16 November. The MPLA's Political Bureau formally condemned any attempts by "certain national and international circles to put pressure on the Angolan authorities" to demand the release of "citizens formally accused of preparatory acts of rebellion with the intent to overthrow, in an unconstitutional way, the legitimately constituted government of Angola". A 'spontaneously formed' civil society movement, the '*Group Justice Without Pressure*' demonstrated in front of the tribunal, intimidating and physically assaulting independent journalists trying to cover the trial. Failing to produce any evidence of an actual criminal act, the prosecution leaked to the press videos of the accused that were doctored to show 'evidence' of their intent to violently overthrow the government. From the beginning, access to the courtroom was limited, as military intelligence agents filled over half of the available seats. AI condemned the exclusion of relatives and independent reporters from the proceedings, only to be attacked by Angola's newly nominated 'roving ambassador for the promotion of the government's image', Luvualu de Carvalho, who stated that the courtroom was "not a football stadium" and that, although seats were limited, access was guaranteed to the lawyers and family members of the accused. This was the same ambassador who in November claimed that the activists had planned to rally children at demonstrations, provoking security forces into killing them, which in turn would mobilise "Western powers, preferably NATO" to bomb Angola. This was denied by NATO headquarters the following day, in a statement that NATO had no intention of intervening in Angola and had, in fact, no interest in events in the country. To ease international and domestic pressure, on 15 December the Constitutional Court approved the transfer of the prisoners to *house arrest*, where they were still awaiting the continuation of this sham trial at the end of the year.

Restrictions on the reporting of these trials and the events at Mt Sumi were accompanied by concerted propaganda in the state-controlled media, as well as the routine, systematic harassment of independent journalists. Several issues of independent weeklies deemed too critical of the government were simply not printed because of alleged technical problems at the press. Overall, *press freedom* was thus still under threat. Furthermore, in his end-of-year speech, dos Santos reiterated his intention to pass a bill on information and communication technologies that would criminalise most forms of critical expression on social networks in Angola.

Foreign Affairs

Angola's actions on the international scene were chiefly determined by economic concerns and the need to find additional sources of loans. *China*'s importance grew further. After dos Santos negotiated a new $ 2 bn loan early in the year, a state visit to China in June further strengthened bilateral ties. One of the eight treaties signed was a financial assistance agreement, allegedly for $ 25 bn, but the modalities of the deal were not disclosed, which was criticised by the opposition. Thus, China was poised to overtake Portugal as Angola's main source of imports by the end of the year. The only cloud on the horizon was the arrest in October of Chinese-Angolan businessman Sam Pa in Beijing. Sam Pa was a key figure in the business ventures of the obscure 'Queensway Group', involving high-level Angolan politicians and Chinese generals.

Angola's imports from *Portugal* fell by about a third. More importantly, the many Portuguese companies operating in Angola faced payment arrears from the Angolan government, and had to let go most of their expatriate (Portuguese) staff. The 'new returnees', the about 200,000 Portuguese economic migrants who had been flocking to Angola in recent years in search of economic opportunities, now returned to Portugal in droves – about 500 per month in the construction sector alone – thereby reversing net migration flows. The situation was so bad that in March the Portuguese government extended a € 500 m credit line to Portuguese small and medium enterprises operating in, or exporting to, Angola to stave off bankruptcy. While the high-level investment of Angolan individuals in key assets of the Portuguese banking and media sectors continued, this reversal of fortunes also cooled the hitherto rather subservient enthusiasm of the Portuguese authorities to defend Angola's reputation at all costs. Thus, when AI Portugal condemned human rights violations in Angola, and Portuguese newspaper 'Público' called the Angolan government 'fascist', comparing its methods to the Salazar dictatorship, there was, unlike in previous years, no outcry from the Portuguese authorities.

Relations with *Brazil*, Angola's second Lusophone partner, were also affected by the crisis when Angola had to cancel its order for seven gunships for its navy because of its inability to pay. Moreover, investigations in Brazil into bribery and influence peddling by former president Luís Inácio 'Lula' da Silva and President Dilma Rousseff involving the major companies Petrobras and Odebrecht caused suspicion that Lula had lobbied on behalf of Brazilian companies during previous state visits to Angola. Most Brazilian credit lines to Angola since 2007 had been executed by Odebrecht and had benefited from very low interest rates. In addition, a Brazilian tribunal condemned Odebrecht for 'slavery-like' working conditions in its Angolan biofuels venture Biocom, in Malange. The judge found that Odebrecht had violated the most basic standards of safety and hygiene, respect and food, and that the contracting of Brazilian workers on 'ordinary' (i.e. visitor) visas constituted the crime of soliciting and trafficking. However, as the inquiry was opened by the Brazilian Public Ministry, the sentence only related to the treatment of its Brazilian workers and not to the majority of its Angolan staff.

In July, President François Hollande of *France* visited Luanda with a retinue of 50 high-level representatives of major French companies and returned with contracts worth over € 1 bn; no mention was made, however, of the disastrous human rights situation in Angola. In September, dos Santos also visited *Russia* with a view to negotiating a new loan agreement.

In February, a military mission of the German navy visited Luanda to carry out a joint naval exercise and reinforce naval cooperation with a view to combating piracy in the Gulf of Guinea. This strengthening of bilateral ties on the back of the sale of naval patrol boats by *Germany* to Angola was criticised in both countries; both the timing of the acquisitions in a year of budget cuts and food insecurity, and the sale of offensive military equipment to a country with a poor human rights record were questioned.

It was revealed in July that Angola had not paid any salaries to the Cuban state company Antex for the past three years. Under bilateral agreements, *Cuba* had been sending to Angola medical doctors and health professionals, who made up 42% and 70% of the healthcare workforce, respectively, as well as university professors, to make up for the Angolan skills shortage. Antex had recruited and employed these professionals, but then had to pay for their salaries out of its own funds. Faced with mounting arrears in payments from the Angolan side, Antex decided to withdraw its personnel from Angola.

Slightly closer to home, *Equatorial Guinea* hosted the African Cup of Nations (football). When opposition members called for protests and a boycott of the tournament (and were immediately imprisoned for it), President dos Santos decided in January to help out a fellow dictator in need by sending Angolan police to help "maintain public order". Another friendly neighbouring autocrat, President Denis Sassou-Nguesso of the *Republic of Congo*, visited Luanda in March to reinforce "ties of friendship and cooperation" and assess cooperation potential in the areas of defence and security, transport, fishing, oil exploration, and geology and mines.

Finally, in what sounded by then like a running joke, Minister of Commerce Pacavira announced in March that Angola would join the *SADC* free trade zone "in 2017". Despite yearly statements of intent, Angola had repeatedly postponed its membership of the zone since the latter's creation in 2008. Overall, in parallel to its diminishing economic attractiveness, Angola's light on the international scene thus lost some of its sparkle, with fewer ambitious bilateral or multilateral diplomatic initiatives taken.

Socioeconomic Developments

Following the adjusted budget, a presidential decree imposed cuts of one-third to budget spending in March. With *oil revenues* officially falling from 70% to 36.5% of government revenues, economic growth would be slower, at 6.6% of GDP instead of the initially projected 9.7%, and inflation would be maintained at between 7% and 9%. This proved to be largely wishful thinking, as the disastrous effects of the oil price slump were felt across all sectors of the Angolan economy; a Ministry of Finance report in May revealed, for example, that the revenues for that month were 85% lower than in May 2014. As the government cut fuel subsidies, *fuel prices* at the pump rose on 1 January and 1 May, which in turn led to a rise in fuel theft and customers fleeing without paying. A further rise was announced on 31 December; this 'New Year's Eve present' was complemented by the announced electricity and water price hikes in Luanda and Benguela.

The ubiquitous 'candongueiro', *collective taxis*, upon which a majority of Luanda's population depended for their mobility, were initially barred by the government from raising their fares. In May, however, the Luandan Transporter's Association (ATL) reached an agreement with the local government allowing them to increase their prices by 50% to compensate for the higher fuel prices. This affected the poorest segment of the population, who spent a large part of their disposable income on transport, and led to widespread discontent among passengers. Despite higher fares, taxi drivers called for a *strike* in early October, to complain about the lack of stations and persistent harassment and bribe-taking by the traffic police. As striking drivers attacked strike-breakers, the police intervened and arrested 143 strikers. The ATL asked for 'clemency', claiming that persons unknown had incited the violence and acts of vandalism.

Although the Central Bank liberalised the acquisition of hard *currency* by commercial banks in February, the kwanza was subject to inflationary pressures: the exchange rate to the US dollar, contained at around 95:1 over previous years, rose over the year from 105 to 135 in commercial banks. However, as banks started limiting their sales of dollars to the general public, the black market in dollars boomed again, with street rates rising quickly from 150 to about 290 at year's end.

Dollar inflows were not only reduced because of lower oil earnings; in November the US Federal Reserve suspended the sale of US dollars to *Angolan banks* for the 'systematic violation' of regulatory practices and money laundering. Indeed, the oligopolistic structure of the banking sector did not bode well for the transparency of financial activities. The liberal attribution of credits to politically connected persons led to an "exponential increase" in bad loans, according to consulting firm KPMG. A report published in November alerted to the fact that of the global credit volume of € 20 bn given by Angolan banks, 60%–70% was held by the 20 largest creditors.

Despite this threat of a banking crisis, in November the government successfully launched its first, $ 1.5 bn *Eurobond*. This had been in the pipeline since 2011, but the issue received a lower, 'junk' bond rating from the leading ratings agencies because of the precarious state of the economy. Nonetheless, Finance Minister Manuel announced that demand for the bonds was five times higher than the amount available, though the success of the issue came too late in the year for potential positive effects to be felt.

As another consequence of the reduced dollar inflows, imports were slashed and *consumer prices* started to rise significantly from as early as January, with the 'cesta básica' (the reference food basket of nine basic items) priced at $ 50 as early as March. Food importers were sitting on stacks of kwanzas but with no or increasingly expensive access to dollars to pay for their shipments. Moreover, the government held on to rigid import quotas introduced in 2014 to encourage local production and import substitution, which drove prices up further. As the local supply of *agricultural products* and processed food was still far from sufficient to cover domestic demand beyond subsistence level, illegal food imports increased. Rather than turning a blind eye, the authorities cracked down on illegal imports: in August, for example, the governor of Lubango ordered the destruction of 11,000 'illegal' eggs. The authorities blamed both inflation and the hike in consumer prices on 'speculators' and false information, but repeatedly "affirming the inexistence of objective reasons" for "certain economic agents" to raise prices, as Minister of Commerce Rosa Pacavira did in January, did precious little to mitigate the effects of the crisis.

The *Sovereign Wealth Fund*, created in 2011 amidst great fanfare and soon handed over to the president's son, José Filomeno 'Zénú' dos Santos, also did little to buffer the Angolan economy against the downturn in oil prices. While Zénú announced "imminent" investments of $ 1.1 bn in energy, transport and other infrastructure, as well as $ 500 m in hotels and environmental projects, investigative reports uncovered that the fund had paid $ 100 m to Kijinga SA, a shell company that had no declared employees and was registered at the same address as Zénú's own investment bank. Even so, Zénú was presented to the public as the great "diversifier of the economy" to increase his eligibility as the president's eventual successor.

Despite the economic downturn, the *plundering of state assets* by the inner circle of the regime continued unhindered and reached new heights. In June, Vice President Manuel Vicente, together with his associates, generals 'Kopelipa' and 'Dino', sold some of the shares in oil exploration blocks held by their company, Nazaki, to Sonangol, thus selling their shares back to the company that – when Vicente was still CEO of Sonangol – had authorised Nazaki's acquisition of the shares in the first place. The sale price was not disclosed but was estimated at "several hundred million" US dollars, and the transaction was approved by President dos Santos. In the same vein, following a tender for new onshore oil exploration blocks in September, most of the concessions were awarded to hitherto largely unknown domestic enterprises, mostly owned by the president's closest entourage.

In June, the president's billionaire daughter, *Isabel dos Santos*, announced her acquisition of Portuguese engineering company Efacec; shortly after, it was revealed that Efacec would be the main supplier of equipment for three new electrical dams under construction in Angola. More importantly, in August President dos Santos authorised the Angolan public electricity distribution company ENDE to buy 40% of Winterfell for an undisclosed sum; when Winterfell then acquired 65% of Efacec in September for $ 200 m, state funds had effectively paid, as usual, for the private enrichment of the dos Santos family. Thus, in February, when *Swissleaks* revealed details on over 100,000 clients of the HSBC bank in Switzerland and the bank's complicity in tax evasion, Angolans were not overly surprised that the 31 account holders of Angolan nationality who held assets worth $ 36 m were all intimately linked to the commercial interests of the circles closest to the regime.

The *unabashed spending* of senior party and government figures continued despite the crisis. In June, a US entertainment channel ran a show called 'Say yes to the dress', showing the daughter of Minister of Territorial Administration Bornito de Sousa spending $ 200,000 on her wedding dress and the dresses for her bridesmaids. The reaction to the 'golden wedding dress affair' amongst Angolans on social media and internet forums was immediate and furious. Though de Sousa was an MPLA hardliner, he still enjoyed wide respect in urban society and had a reputation for probity, integrity and competence. His Facebook post in reaction to the reports betrayed an odd mixture of petulance, reality denial and sense of entitlement, which prompted many even of his erstwhile sympathisers to criticise him harshly, and quite openly in the comment thread. On 28 November, Portuguese media also reported that an Angolan entrepreneur, Pinto Paulino Manuel Conto, had spent € 200,000 on his daughter's 15th birthday celebrations in Loures, Portugal. Finally, at year's end, Isabel dos Santos's mobile operator Unitel invited the US American rapper Nicki Minaj to perform at its Christmas concert at a cost of $ 2 m. International human rights foundations publicly called on Minaj to cancel the concert but her performance went ahead unhindered, with the rapper dismissing her critics by posting photos of her and Isabel dos Santos on Instagram and gushing over dos Santos as a role model for "girl power" and business success.

In contrast to the country's leaders and their vehicles for private enrichment, productive sectors of the economy and the population at large suffered from the crisis. In the *construction* sector, Portuguese and Brazilian companies had to lay off expatriate personnel (see above), but the situation was equally dire for local staff. In July, for example, local and expat workers at Soares da Costa threatened to set trucks and housing containers on fire in protest because their salary payments were three months overdue.

The oil sector faced turbulences that went well beyond a simple drop in revenues. An internal report leaked in June revealed that the unsustainable business model of the state oil company *Sonangol*, hitherto always held up as a lone 'island of excellence' in Angola's skewed economic landscape, had led to its becoming "technically bankrupt". During the bonanza years, huge inflows of oil money were distributed through an ever-growing network of subcontractors. This outsourcing of basic and specialised services had provided ample opportunities for private gain, but the growing presence of 'phantom contracts' and in-house contracting proved to be wasteful and inefficient, and undermined Sonangol's core competences. In July, the company denied rumours of failure, claiming that the market signals from the first semester were "animating", and that its ambitious expansion plans for exploration in Brazil, Venezuela and Cuba would go ahead; it nevertheless announced cutbacks of $ 1 bn by the end of the year.

Similarly, Swiss-listed commodity giant Trafigura announced in December that it would have to write off losses of $ 244 m in its AEMR iron-mining venture in Cassinga because of low global commodity prices.

The underfunding of the *education system* was further accentuated by the budget cuts. Parents reported in February that the illegal trade in secondary school places had reached new heights, with administrators demanding up to $ 500 for a pupil's enrolment, despite the constitutional guarantee of free education. At the end of December, the teachers' union SINPROF said the state of the education system was "lamentable" and demanded that the government pay teachers their overdue salaries, which by year's end had reached close to $ 118 m.

The *health sector* was also suffering from budget cuts, though previous years had not seen significant improvements either. Angolan infant mortality was still the world's highest, with one in six children dying before the age of five, and above 30% of children showing physical signs of malnutrition such as reduced body height. In addition, Angolan sociologist Nelson Pestana stated that a UNICEF report on the wellbeing of children and women in Angola released in June, which already painted a rather grim picture, was, in fact, too optimistic as its statistics were based on official figures more concerned with painting a good picture of the government than with reflecting the realities. Malaria, tuberculosis and polio continued to take their toll on the population, and 14 cases of anthrax were recorded in Huíla province in June. Road traffic fatalities also remained amongst the world's highest, with 12 people killed on average per day on the streets of Luanda. The drought-stricken southern provinces faced severe *food shortages* and, as pleas to the government were of no avail, the Bishop of Namibe appealed in December to Caritas, the Catholic Church's humanitarian agency, for emergency relief.

Finally, in August, a new waste management model in Luanda transferred responsibility for rubbish removal from the provincial government to municipalities. However, as the total budget allocated amounted to one-third of the amount previously spent, Luanda faced a dramatic *rubbish crisis* from September onwards, with the city slowly being transformed into one huge open-air waste dump.

Botswana

David Sebudubudu and Keratilwe Bodilenyane

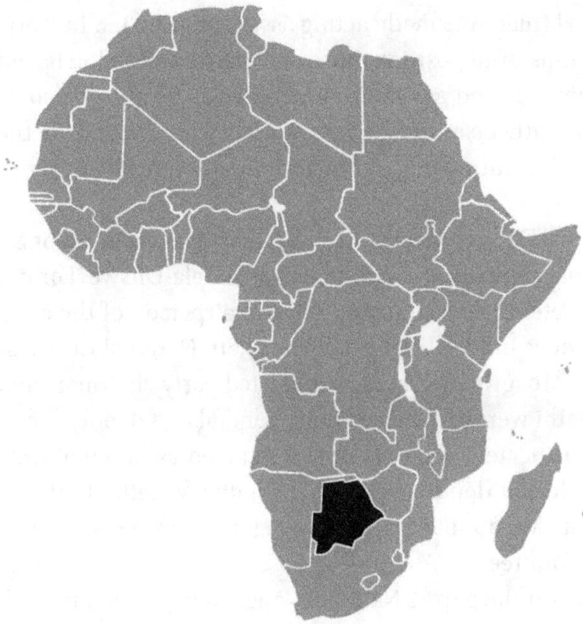

Compared with 2014, this was a quiet year on the domestic political scene. No major shift took place in the country's foreign policy, which continued to be underpinned by the values of good governance, democracy and respect for human rights. The economy experienced a slump in the demand for diamonds, and as a result barely grew. In response, the government announced an Economic Stimulus Programme (ESP), meant to boost economic growth, diversify the economy and generate employment. Longstanding socio-economic challenges continued to afflict the country's development prospects.

Domestic Politics

Forty-nine years into independence, the *Botswana Democratic Party* (BDP) continued to govern uninterrupted. Nothing dramatic happened politically following the closely contested general election of 2014. On 7 January, former vice president Mompati Merafhe passed away. On 1 March, President Ian Khama restructured the *cabinet*. Mokgweetsi Masisi who had become after the elections minister of education and skills development and vice president, was relieved of the

 | DOI 10.1163/9789004333239_046

ministerial portfolio to concentrate on the responsibilities of the vice presidency. Unity Dow was promoted from assistant minister to minister in the Ministry of Education and Skills Development and Kgotla Autlwetse was appointed assistant minister in the same ministry. Minister of Agriculture Christian Degraaf went on a two-month period of sick leave and his assistant, Patrick Ralotsia, was appointed acting minister, while Fedelis Molao was made acting assistant minister. In April, Degraaf was relieved of his ministerial position due to ill-health, and Ralotsia and Molao were confirmed as minister and assistant minister of agriculture, respectively. On 1 October, Kgotla Autlwetse and Fedelis Molao were moved to the Ministries of Agriculture, and Education and Skills Development, respectively, as assistant ministers.

The *BDP* held its 53rd National Council on 13–15 March, when it resolved, amongst other things, to review its primary election system, known as 'Bulela-Ditswe'. Former Member of Parliament (MP) Peter Siele was appointed as chairperson of the committee set to carry out the review. In July, the BDP held its 36th National Congress in Mmadinare. Vice President Mokgweetsi Masisi was elected party chairman, and Botsalo Ntuane and Shaw Kgathi were elected secretary general and deputy secretary general, respectively. As expected, Satar Dada was retained as national treasurer, and Jagdish Shah was elected deputy treasurer. Nonofho Molefhi, Botlogile Tshireletso, Unity Dow, Fidelis Molao and Daniel Kwelagobe became additional members of the executive committee.

The *Siele Report* was released at the party's National Congress in July. In line with some of the resolutions adopted at that time, the BDP in September mandated its Political Education and Election Committee to consider the prospects for political and electoral reforms. On 9–10 October, the party held a Special Congress in Gaborone, at which it considered the Siele Report. Following its consideration of the report, the party, amongst other things, reneged on a decision, taken at its 52nd National Council, not to welcome members who had resigned and stood as independent candidates ('Mekoko') in 2014. The party had experienced an unprecedented number of such cases owing in part to the challenges of its primary election system. Meanwhile, the BDP held its 15th National Women's Wing Congress in Lobatse on 10–12 April, at which it elected Minister of Health Dorcas Makgato as its chairperson. Makgato defeated Tshepo Wareus by 317 to 186 votes.

The *Botswana Congress Party* (BCP) held its 7th National Congress in Kanye on 18–20 July, when it elected its executive committee. Dumelang Saleshando was returned unopposed as party president. Kesitegile Gobotswang was elected deputy president, defeating Taolo Lucas by 467 votes to 442. Motsei Rapelana was elected party chairperson, and Kentse Rammidi and Tshegofatso Raditlhokwa were elected secretary general and deputy secretary general, respectively. Dennis Alexander was retained as treasurer whilst Dithapelo Keorapetse was elected publicity secretary. At this congress, the BCP decided to engage in cooperation talks with the *Umbrella for Democratic Change* (UDC). The BCP maintained its ties with the UK Labour Party and its members attended the party's annual conference in Manchester.

From 18 to 21 July, the *Botswana Movement for Democracy* (BMD) held its elective congress in Ghanzi, where it voted for its executive committee. Nehemiah Modubule was retained as party chairperson. Gilbert Mangole was elected secretary general and Tlamelo Botlhole deputy secretary general. Percy Bakwena was unchallenged as treasurer, with Keitumetse Sekhute as deputy treasurer. Tlamelo Mmatli was elected policy director. Meanwhile, Moeng Pheto, a former BDP MP, who resigned following his suspension, and stood as an independent parliamentary candidate in 2014, joined the BMD in March. Interestingly, in September Sydney Pilane, a founding member of the BMD who had left it in 2012, applied to rejoin the party, causing divisions within it. The *Botswana National Front* (BNF) held its conference in Goodhope on 18–21 July, when it discussed pertinent issues affecting the party.

A *by-election* was held in the Goodhope-Mabule constituency on 15 August, and was contested by three political parties, the BDP, BCP and UDC (the last of which is a coalition of three opposition parties, the BMD, BNF and Botswana People's Party). The by-election was caused by the resignation of UDC MP James Mathokgwane in May. On 24 July, Eric Molale resigned as minister of presidential affairs and public administration, and as a specially elected MP, in order to represent his party (BDP) in the by-election. Molale was re-appointed minister in the same ministry within a few hours of registering his name with the electoral authority. Consistent with its 2014 position, the Botswana Federation of Public Sector Unions (BOFEPUSU) supported the UDC candidate. Comfort Maruping was the BCP candidate. Kgosi Lotlamoreng II of the UDC won the election. In November, Molale was re-elected as a specially elected MP. Several council by-elections were also held and all were won by the opposition.

Meanwhile *corruption* continued to make headlines. In February, Parliament approved a motion, initiated by the MP for Goodhope, Mabule James Mathokgwane, to probe poor governance, including corruption and maladministration at Statistics Botswana through a parliamentary committee. In March, Parliament approved a motion to investigate claims of corruption and maladministration at the Botswana National Youth Centre. On 24 March, corruption charges levelled against Minister of Trade and Industry Vincent Seretse and Paul Paledi, a businessman and former BDP deputy treasurer, were withdrawn because two critical witnesses 'were not available'. In June, the accounts of a company owned by BDP MP Guma Moyo, and those of Minister of Youth, Sports and Culture Thapelo Olopeng, were frozen following a court decision. Guma and Olopeng were being investigated by the Directorate on Corruption and Economic Crime (DCEC) as they were "allegedly involved in bribery and corrupt dealings". By year's end, Olopeng, a close ally of President Khama, had not resigned from his ministerial position, and both Guma and Olopeng, who were business associates, had yet to be charged. In January, Minister of Finance and Development Planning Kenneth Matambo secured a high court order nullifying portions of a 2013 *parliamentary select committee report* that had investigated allegations of corruption and mismanagement at Fengyue Glass Manufacturing

(Botswana) Pty Ltd. The court found that the committee had violated the principles of natural justice in discharging its mandate. Meanwhile, Director General of Directorate of Intelligence and Security Services (DISS) Isaac Kgosi and his affairs continued to make newspaper headlines and to attract public interest, although no corruption charges were brought against him. Interestingly, media reports suggested that the DISS had threatened, intimidated and spied on officers of the DCEC who had investigated allegations of corruption against Kgosi. These reports were rebuffed by the DCEC director general. An Afro-Barometer Botswana Chapter survey released in March found that 81% of respondents considered government officials to be corrupt.

The *judiciary* became the subject of public attention. In August, Chief Justice Maruping Dibotelo reported four High Court judges, Oagile Dingake, Modiri Letsididi, Mercy Garekwe and Ranier Busang, to the police for drawing a housing allowance while residing in their official residences. In response, the four judges along with eight others, petitioned for Dibotelo's possible impeachment. Subsequently, President Khama suspended the four judges, and appointed a tribunal to investigate their possible removal, in line with Section 97(3) of the Constitution. The four judges challenged their suspension in court but without success. Consequently, in September there were calls in some quarters, for the chief justice to step down for causing 'loss of confidence' in the judiciary.

Relations between the government and BOFEPUSU continued to be frosty. In August, the High Court decided that it was unlawful for President Khama and the Directorate of Public Service Management to make declarations on the *public service* salary negotiations and other conditions of service outside the Public Service Bargaining Council (PSBC). The case was triggered by Khama's 2014 announcement of a 4% salary increment for civil servants whilst negotiations were yet to be concluded at the PSBC. Meanwhile, in April the government had awarded civil servants a salary increment of 6%. In December, BOFEPUSU affirmed its support for the UDC.

Minority rights continued to come to the fore. In February, the Botswana Network on Ethics Law and HIV/AIDS (BONELA) lauded the government's decision to extend its HIV/AIDS message to ostracised communities such as gays and sex workers. On 26 August, the Court of Appeal affirmed two High Court rulings that the government should provide foreign prison inmates with anti-retroviral therapy. Regarding the San/Basarwa, Survival International (SI) sustained its support for the plight of the Basarwa, and their campaign against Botswana's tourism sector, demanding the restoration of basic services within the Central Kalahari Game Reserve (CKGR), and that subsistence hunting within the Reserve be decriminalised. In February, SI lobbied British royals for support. Following SI's intensive campaign against Botswana's tourism, the government warmed up to the demands of residents of the CKGR. Subsequently, the First People of the Kalahari and its leaders gave SI a cold reception, despite having enjoyed SI support for years, in its campaign to resolve the plight of the residents of the CKGR.

Foreign Policy

Minister of Foreign Affairs and International Cooperation Pelonomi Venson-Moitoi led delegations to the 26th Ordinary Session of the Executive Council of the AU and the 24th Ordinary Session of the Assembly of Heads of State and Government of the AU on 30–31 January in Addis Ababa (Ethiopia), and to the High Level Segment of the 28th Regular Session of the UN Human Rights Council in Geneva on 2–6 March. She also attended the inauguration of Nigeria's President General Muhammadu Buhari on 29 May, and visited Qatar on 1–4 December.

Several official visits took place, affirming Botswana's friendly relations with other countries, including a visit on 9–11 March by President John Mahama of Ghana. *President Ian Khama* attended the inauguration of Namibia's President Hage Geingob on 21 March and a SADC Heads of State emergency meeting in Pretoria on 7 July to deliberate on political disorder in Lesotho. He visited France on 22–25 June and on 18 August assumed the position of chairperson of SADC at the organisation's 35th Ordinary Summit in Gaborone, a rotational position within the block. He visited Angola on 12–14 October and South Korea on 21–24 October, and attended the Commonwealth Heads of Government meeting in Malta on 27–29 November and the 21st Conference of the Parties (COP 21) to the UN Framework Convention on Climate Change in Paris from 30 November to 11 December. *Vice President Mokgweetsi Masisi* attended the 4th Tana High-Level Forum on Security in Africa on 18/19 April in Addis Ababa (Ethiopia), and the 70th session of the UN General Assembly from 25 September to 3 October in New York, and headed a delegation to the second summit of the Forum on China-Africa Cooperation in Johannesburg (South Africa) on 4–5 December.

Botswana continued to promote good governance, democracy and respect for human rights. On 30 April, Botswana denounced the Sudanese elections as not credible and, on 16 June, the government lauded a ruling of the South African North Gauteng High Court that Sudanese President *Omar al-Bashir* should be arrested when he attended the AU summit in that country on charges of crimes against humanity brought against him by the ICC. Al-Bashir evaded arrest. Botswana and South Africa are signatories to the ICC's Rome Statute.

Socioeconomic Developments

The country continued to show its susceptibility to global economic fluctuations, which resulted in a slump in the demand for diamonds. Botswana nevertheless stayed resolute in its commitment to *macro-economic stability*, and recorded positive ratings. In the 2015/2016 budget, revenue was set at P (pula) 55.38 bn against expenditure of P 54.15 bn, realising a surplus of P 1.23 bn. The main sources of revenue were minerals, customs and excise and non-minerals at 34.4%, 29.5% and 17.5%, respectively. This once again affirmed the importance of minerals to the Botswana economy. Foreign reserves grew by 7.3%, from P 79.1 bn in 2014 to P 84.9 bn by December. The yearly inflation rate was estimated at 3.1%, which is within the Bank of Botswana's medium-term range. GDP barely grew, standing at 1% instead of the projected 2.6%. Owing to a slump in economic activity, in October the government announced the ESP, which was geared towards enhancing economic growth, diversify the economy and generate employment.

The IMF Article IV Consultation, which took place from 7 to 12 December, noted that the country had experienced a slump in economic performance, and in response suggested reforms such as "prioritizing public investment in projects with a clear potential to enhance growth and human capital, while measures are being taken to improve execution capacity and efficiency". The IMF also reiterated that the tax base should be expanded. *International ratings* remained unspectacular. The World Economic Forum Global Competitiveness Report for 2015–2016 placed Botswana at 71st out of 140 countries. The Report identified "poor work ethic" as one of the major challenges that affected the business environment. Botswana was ranked 74th out of 189 countries in the 2015 World Bank Doing Business Report, while Moody's Investors Service maintained the country's credit rating at A2.

The government continued to make inexorable social challenges its key priority areas. It maintained its *social welfare programmes* targeted at vulnerable groups and reported that, as at June, it was supporting 32,860 destitute persons, 32,803 vulnerable children, 102,492 old age pensioners, 1,986 World War II veterans and 1,229 home-based patients. The 'Ipelegeng' Programme (short-term labour intensive works) targeted 64,191 recipients, monthly. The poverty rate remained at 20.7% and the national unemployment rate at 17.8%. Inequality also persisted. The country's Gini coefficient remained one of the highest in the world, estimated at 0.61.

The government continued its efforts to contain the *HIV/AIDS* menace. With a national prevalence rate of 18.5%, HIV/AIDS posed a threat to the country's development prospects. Mother to child transmission had fallen to less than 2% by March. As of April, the government reported that all pregnant women who were HIV positive were being provided with anti-retroviral treatment, irrespective of the level of their CD4. The government also stated that over 90% of HIV positive persons were receiving anti-retroviral treatment in November.

Lesotho

Roger Southall

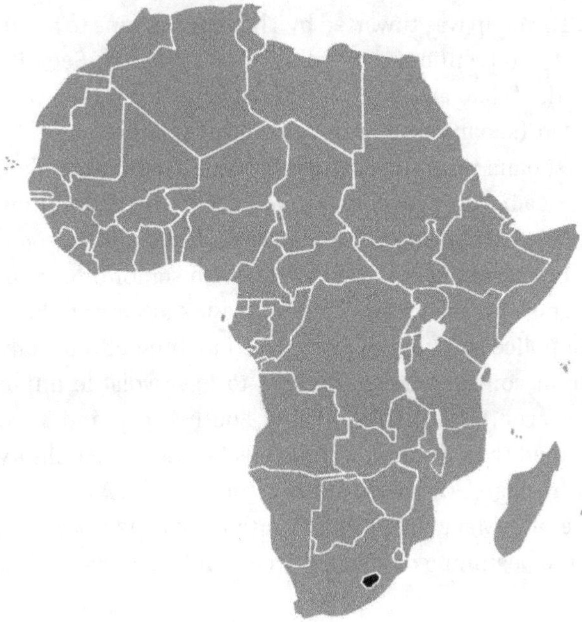

The political crisis that had gripped Lesotho following divisions within the coalition government led by Prime Minister Tom Thabane of the All Basotho Congress (ABC) had resulted in agreement, under pressure from SADC, that the country go to an early general election. This was held on 28 February, when a deeply divided country returned a deeply divided parliament. Although Thabane's ABC won only one less seat than the Democratic Congress (DC) of Phakalitha Mosisili, the latter was able to cobble together a coalition of seven political parties, which enabled him to form a government. However, any chance of a return to political stability was nullified by the reappointment on 21 May of Lieutenant-General Tlali Kamoli (allied to Mosisili) as commander of the Lesotho Defence Force (LDF), and the dismissal from the same post of Brigadier Maaparankoe Mahao (who had been appointed by Thabane). Opposition leaders fled to South Africa, Mahao was subsequently assassinated by members of the LDF, and opposition MPs boycotted Parliament. Intervention by the AU led to the appointment of a Commission of Inquiry into the new crisis under the auspices of SADC. As the country awaited its report, security remained fragile and the political arena continued in paralysis.

 | DOI 10.1163/9789004333239_047

Domestic Politics

The *election* was held against the background of a troubled security situation that had culminated in an apparent attempted coup by elements of the LDF, who in August 2014 had surrounded the official residence of Prime Minister Thabane after his dismissal of Kamoli. The coup was thwarted by Thabane's escape to South Africa and SADC's subsequent intervention. According to the Maseru Security Accord of 23 October 2014, both Mahao and Kamoli were to be exiled (along with Police Commissioner Khothatso Tsooana, who was aligned to Thabane) while the political crisis was resolved. Tsooana went to Algeria and Mahao to South Sudan, but Kamoli stayed in South Africa because no country could be found to host him. The ABC and the Basotho National Party (BNP), two parties in the Thabane coalition, alleged that from there he remained in close contact with senior officers of the LDF, who refused to recognise his dismissal. With Thabane's attempt to have Tsooana recalled to head the police rebuffed by SADC, the outcome of a bitterly contested, high stakes electoral contest was guaranteed to have volatile implications. For the moment, however, Deputy President of South Africa and SADC Facilitator Cyril Ramaphosa ruled that, because of tensions between the military and the police, SADC would be in charge of security during the election. As a result, 475 additional police from the DRC, Malawi, Namibia, South Africa and Swaziland were deployed in Lesotho at the beginning of election week, and were required to remain until 5 March.

As the *election results* were coming in, the ABC took an early lead in the lowlands and urban areas, with ABC candidates displacing Lesotho Congress for Democracy (LCD) candidates in constituencies previously held by that party. Indeed, only the LCD leader's constituency, and one other, remained in the party's hands. However, when the results from rural areas came in, the DC made up considerable lost ground. While the ABC won 40 (out of 80) constituency seats (contested under the British-style first-past-the-post system), the DC was a close runner-up with 37, with the remaining three seats being taken by the LCD (2) and the BNP (1). Crucially, however, the DC had won slightly more votes (218,573) than the ABC (215,022) out of the total of 563,972 cast, allowing it to get its nose ahead when it came to the calculation of the additional 40 seats for the 120 seat National Assembly, which were to be allocated under the Mixed Member Proportional Representation electoral system. This provided for compensatory seats to be allocated to political parties, taking into account those they had won in constituency contests, to provide for overall proportional representation. The eventual outcome saw the DC, with a total of 47 seats, just overhauling the ABC, with 46 seats, with the LCD winning a crucial 12 seats. Other seats fell to minor parties, namely the BNP (7), the Patriotic Front for Democracy (PFD) 2, and the Reformed Congress of Lesotho (RCL) 2, with the Basutoland Congress Party (BCP), Lesotho People's Congress (LPC), Marematlou Freedom Party (MFP) and the National Independent Party (NIP) winning one apiece.

Thabane's *three-party coalition* had been disrupted by his breach with Deputy Prime Minister Mothehjoa Metsing of the LCD over the latter's alleged receipt of bribes from a construction company. This, in effect, made the LCD available to the DC as a potential coalition partner. So it turned out, for when negotiations to form a winning coalition began, the LCD provided critical support to Mosisili. Because no party had won a majority, a coalition was inevitable. Given recent differences between the ABC and the LCD, the prospect of their coming together again was remote. Thus, although the DC had itself split from the LCD, this placed Mosisili at an advantage. When he proved able to attract the backing of the PFD, BCP, LPC, MFP and NIP alongside that of the LCD, he was able to announce the formation of a *seven-party coalition.* The new government was formally inaugurated on 17 March. Given that the previous coalition, composed of three parties, had collapsed in disarray, it seemed unlikely that this seven-party coalition would provide a recipe for stability. The immediate cost of it was revealed with the announcement of a new cabinet of fully 28 ministers (five more than in the previous parliament), along with seven deputy ministers. As leader of the largest party, Mosisili resumed his job as prime minister, with Mothetjoa Metsing reappearing in the deputy prime minister post he had occupied in the previous government. The coalition agreement provided *inter alia* for each party to be represented in the government according to their proportional strength. Furthermore, if a minister lost the confidence of his or her party, he or she would be dismissed, while if the prime minister lost confidence in a minister, he could only dismiss him or her after consultation with the leader of the party concerned. How this would work in the case of the dismissal of ministers belonging to parties with just one member was left hanging in the air.

With the new government installed, SADC withdrew from Lesotho – but was soon to be drawn back into the maelstrom of the country's turbulent politics. Kamoli returned to Lesotho on 29 March, clearly expecting to be reappointed to his post, while Mahao – albeit lacking the backing of most of the officer corps – formally remained *commander of the LDF* (their SADC enforced exile had led to the appointment of a temporary acting commander). Now, Mosisili acted to settle the matter. On 21 May, it was formally announced that Mahao's position as commander was terminated, with Kamoli re-appointed to take his place, his appointment being backdated to the date of his dismissal. In a related move, Tsooana was informed by the prime minister that his continuance as police commissioner was not in the national interest. Prior to this, *divisions within the army* had been publicly displayed when the wives of two soldiers who had been detained and tortured brought urgent applications to the High Court for them to be brought to court. The soldiers involved were part of a small group within the army who had been charged with intending to take part in a mutiny and conspiring to arrest or kill superior officers, with the intent, the charge sheet said, of installing Brigadier Mahao as commander of the LDF. The fact that Mahao was already legally commander of the LDF at the time of the alleged mutiny appeared immaterial. Further court cases saw other detainees, some of them senior officers, bringing further applications to the court in order to seek relief from torture. Despite the court ordering that those who had been subject to harsh treatment be granted medical treatment, the army claimed that, under military law, they were not eligible for bail.

It was after these various proceedings, on 25 June, that the *assassination of Brigadier Mahao* took place in broad daylight. He was ambushed by three vehicles, without registration numbers, 3 km from his farm, near Mokema village, while he was returning to his home in Maseru. Initially, Mahao was wounded in the arm, before being bundled into one of the vehicles and driven away, while two of his nephews who were with him were held at gunpoint by soldiers for 40 minutes. Mahao was subsequently killed, the LDF claiming that he had been resisting arrest. The injuries to the body released to the family included three wounds in addition to that on his arm. Mahao came from a highly placed family. At his funeral, his brother, Nqosa Mahao, who had recently become vice chancellor of the National University of Lesotho, appealed not only to King Letsie III, but also to President Zuma of South Africa, the AU, UN and other such bodies to press for a full investigation into the circumstances surrounding Mahao's death and linked it to the "wave of torture of scores of soldiers" being endured at the hands of "rogue elements" of the LDF. Already before, the leaders of the three *opposition parties* (Thabane of the ANC, Thesele 'Maseribane of the BNP, and Keketso Rantso of the RCL), had all fled to South Africa because of concerns for their security. There they met Cyril Ramaphosa on 6 June, and subsequently were joined by supporters for a demonstration on 14 June during the course of the AU Summit, coincidentally being held in Sandton. Their position, as expressed by Thabane, was that they could not return home without guarantees of safety from SADC. Opposition parties subsequently decided to boycott the proceedings of Parliament.

Mahao's assassination took place during the visit to Lesotho of a six-member SADC fact-finding mission. When it reported back, Cyril Ramaphosa was sent back to consult with Mosisili, who asked for SADC assistance in investigating Mahao's murder. However, SADC had pre-empted his request and had already decided there should be a *Commission of Inquiry*. When agreed, the terms of reference related principally to the alleged mutiny plot and alleged killings of supporters of the opposition; Mahao's death; the legality of his appointment as commander; and allegations that Kamoli's re-appointment had resulted in instability within the LDF and society more widely. The Commission, which was chaired by Mr Justice Mphaphi Pumaphi of the High Court of Botswana, was otherwise composed of legal, military and police figures from Botswana, Malawi, Namibia, South Africa and Zimbabwe. It began its hearings, which were followed avidly by the public, on 31 August, finally completing them on 23 October. Key figures – the prime minister, senior officers from the LDF, members of the opposition (including Thabane's son), journalists and representatives of civil society – were all subject to cross-examination, and unsurprisingly, gave highly conflicting evidence.

The *report of the Commission* was only presented to the Lesotho government in mid-January 2016. Prior to that, the government had sought to consolidate its power by replacing the principal secretaries of a wide array of departments with its own appointees. Meanwhile, the opposition continued to boycott Parliament, lawyers staged a two-day boycott of the courts to complain about intimidation by the LDF, and the army pressed ahead with its plans to prosecute some 24 soldiers for mutiny (which carries the death penalty). Another 20 soldiers, also wanted for detention by the LDF, had fled the country. By the end of the year, the security situation in Lesotho was as fragile as at any moment since the restoration of civilian rule in 1993, and peace was heavily dependent upon the future reactions of SADC.

Foreign Affairs

As ever, Lesotho's foreign affairs were largely determined by its relations with SADC, and South Africa in particular. Beyond the security situation, the principal issue concerned that of movement across the border with *South Africa*. Those who called for Lesotho to be incorporated into South Africa, remained a very small, if vocal minority. The concern of most was to be able to cross the border without undue delay and, for many Basotho, to be able to work in South Africa without hindrance. As the situation stood, border crossings – notably at Maseru Bridge, the country's main point of entry by road – could often take hours. Urgency was brought to the situation by a number of violent confrontations in April between taxi drivers from Lesotho and South Africa, which blocked Maseru Bridge. Hope for improvement was subsequently offered by South African Minister of Home Affairs Maulusi Gigaba announcing that his department would soon introduce a Lesotho Special Dispensation which, as well as regularising the position of undocumented Basotho in South Africa, would streamline border crossing requirements and procedures.

Warnings from beyond the region included that made by Ambassador, Matthew Harrington of the *USA*, who raised the prospect that unless human rights were observed and the security situation brought under control, the Millenium Challenge Corporation Board would need to reassess the eligibility of Lesotho for a second compact. Worth some $ 400 m, this was about a quarter of Lesotho's annual budget.

Socioeconomic Developments

The *budget*, largely inherited from the previous government, had estimated expenditure of M (maluti) 15.3 bn (the maluti is equivalent to the South African rand), and expected a fiscal deficit of 3.9% of GDP. Amidst the drama of the security situation, however, the country's desperate economic situation attracted little attention. Worse, when attention was paid to the economy, it was largely negative, focussing upon the high level of corruption and the poor investment climate: according to one report, Lesotho came last in ease of doing business among the five SACU countries, 13th out of the 15 SADC countries, and 128th out of 189 countries worldwide.

Madagascar

Richard R. Marcus

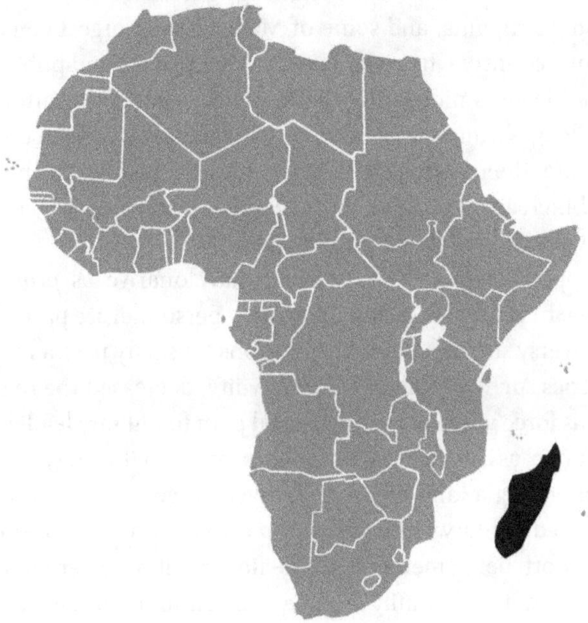

The government of Prime Minister Kolo resigned on 13 January at the end of a brief nine-month run marked by controversy. Kolo's relationship with President Rajaonarimampianina was strained and he was widely viewed as ineffectual in brokering the differences between the members of the highly factionalised government. General Jean Ravelonarivo was sworn in as prime minister three days later and the municipal elections of 31 July further strengthened the position of the president's New Forces for Madagascar (HVM) party. The economy of Madagascar continued to show sputtering growth amidst signs of new activity. The international community resumed support and lending continued to be robust. In a year of political fragility and modest economic growth, the state outperformed expectations and the government showed resilience and produced glimmers of hope for improved political and economic performance.

Domestic Politics

President Hery Martial Rajaonarimampianina began the year in a highly *precarious government situation*. The government of Prime Minister Roger Kolo was, from the

 | DOI 10.1163/9789004333239_048

outset, an unviable group appointed to appease political factions who found themselves on the losing side of the 2013 elections. Indeed, factionalism was the hallmark of the first legitimate government since the end of the 2009–13 political crisis. A medical doctor by training, Kolo was a technocrat with the support of critical business and civil society leaders. He was nonetheless a polarising figure, snubbed by the national business association, Fivmpama, and some of Madagascar's largest companies. This was significant in a country where the line between private and public sectors was often blurred and leaders moved fluidly between them. While intra-executive squabbles and challenges from would-be state leaders may have been the root of the government's failure, the growing challenges of rolling blackouts, chaotic traffic management and increasing protests in the capital, Antananarivo, and the largest port, Toamasina, were the visible cause of its undoing.

Rajaonarimampianina's appointment of General Jean Ravelonarivo as *prime minister* was clever and telling. In Madagascar, senior military personnel are part of the civil service. While controversy surrounds the implications for salary payments, this has, in contrast to countries such as Mali and Côte d'Ivoire, decreased the *role of the military* as an exogenous force while providing a legal path to military leadership in government. Ravelonarivo, as a leader in the public, private, civil society and military sectors, had been providing a kind of bridge between divergent interests and an uncomfortably disquieted military. His relationship with the president went back more than two decades, both being members of the Rotary Club – a veritable who's who of recent leaders – and having family members in common through the Arema party of former president Didier Ratsiraka and the current ruling party, 'Hery Vaovao ho an'i Madagasikara' (HVM). Ravelonarivo's appointment did not please everyone. He had distanced himself from politics during Marc Ravalomanana's presidency (2002–9), driving a wedge between himself and Ravalomanana's Tiako i Madagasikara (TIM) party. There was an active attempt by former presidents Andry Rajoelina and Zafy Albert to block him, and the influential former prime minister Camille Vital and some members of the military had expressed dismay at his promotion to general after years of working in the private sector. Far from being a compromise candidate, his appointment could never have been made a year earlier, but he nonetheless showed the strength to put together a cabinet largely comprised of well-respected technocrats.

A *lack of institutional consolidation* had long been the norm in Malagasy politics. What had not been the norm was that Rajaonarimampianina had come in as president without a personal political network on which he could rely. The Constitution ascribes an unusually large amount of power to the executive and Malagasy presidents have routinely exerted more power than the Constitution affords. The inability of the president to control the executive had led to inherent instability. Few analysts expected Rajaonarimampianina's presidency to survive the year and the critical story is how he succeeded. In 2013, presidential and parliamentary elections had been held concurrently and Andry Rajoelina's 'Miaraka Amin'i Prezida

Andry Rajoelina' (MAPAR) won an overwhelming parliamentary victory. President Rajaonarimampianina's HVM had not even been formed yet. Over the course of 2014 and 2015, individual leaders shifted their support from MAPAR and other parties to HVM, giving HVM parliamentary representation but not yet uncontested power. It is critical in Madagascar that the executive form a tight bond with private sector leaders, who play the role often played by civil society leaders in other countries, accompanied by a public relationship with the private, autonomous, but largely dominated press. Rajaonarimampianina was an accountant, not a captain of industry, but he had acquired positions on boards of directors in diverse industries, such as Blue Reef Investments, Fanampiana Ivoarana, Madagascar Investment Company, Madagascar Estates Development Partners, Winfair, Diamond Cement, National Tourism Development, Silhouette Cruises and Tropic-Group. More critically, he had won the support of influential people in the business community, including Alain Ramanantsoa and Tovo Ratovoarisoa, and he continued growing his own political network from existing confidants in Air Madagascar (where he had once served as chairman), the team he had worked with as minister of finance, the Rotary Club (where he had served in various capacities alongside Madagascar's private sector elite), and amongst fellow alumni of the 'Centre d'Études Diplomatiques et Stratégiques' in Paris.

Rajaonarimampianina's HVM faced new challenges. On 27 May, 121 of the 151 members of the parliament voted to impeach the president for what they saw as a violation of his responsibilities and failure to govern. Rajaonarimampianina immediately called the vote unconstitutional, citing the fact that only 80 legislators were present in session, a lack of due process and transparency, and an overstepping of legislative authority. Under the Constitution, a special High Court of Justice must hear calls for *impeachment*, but Rajaonarimampianina had failed to meet the 26 January deadline for establishing this Court. The impeachment thus went to the High Constitutional Court (HCC), presided over by the newly appointed constitutional scholar Jean-Eric Rakotoarisoa. On 12 June, the HCC ruled in favour of the president and overturned the impeachment vote.

With Rajaonarimampianina's position ratified, his HVM prevailed in the 31 July *municipal elections*, winning an overwhelming majority of the 1,600 contests, followed by Rajoelina's MAPAR, which gained victories in the important provincial cities of Toamasina, Mahajanga and Diego Suarez. However, the critical victory went to former president Marc Ravalomanana's TIM party in the capital, where his wife, Lalao Ravalomanana, won the mayor's office with 55.9% of the vote. The division between TIM in the capital, MAPAR in the provincial capitals, and HVM almost everywhere else set the stage for a potentially *volatile political future*, with the two preceding presidents poised to challenge each other and the sitting president. It became clear that the stability created by the new cabinet, the ratification of the president by the HCC, and the electoral victories in the municipalities were ephemeral. On 3 July Rajaonarimampianina was still able to say, "We are trying to strengthen this democracy through national reconciliation", but by year's end he had lost much of the good will he had built up and the message was lost. When the Malagasy Council for Reconciliation presented its draft to the president on 2 December, it had skirted the cabinet. The document reflected the influence of former heads of state, the Malagasy Council of Churches, and other civil society organisations but not that of the president or the prime minister. The inability of the prime minister to marshal competing forces inside and outside government began rumours that his days in the executive were numbered and his elite team would be disbanded.

Foreign Affairs

ODA rapidly increased. The EU as the largest donor announced on 23 November a € 518 m lending programme. The next-largest funder was the International Bank for Reconciliation and Development (World Bank), with loans of $ 95 m, followed by Japan, France and the USA. While former president Didier Ratsiraka (1975–93 and 1997–2002) had sought to maintain strong ties with France, the former colonial power, and former president Ravalomanana (2002–9) had sought to extend Anglophone relations, Rajaonarimampianina both further strengthened French ties and sought to diversify Madagascar's international positioning. *France's Ambassador* François Goldblatt was dismissed on 14 July. He was seen as a frank voice during a turbulent time. A 12 March tweet, in which he said, "Dismissal of the Director General of the Treasury: a very bad signal to donors for future directions of the executive", was seen as the final nail in his ambassadorial coffin. His approach was reflective of that of his predecessor, Jean-Christophe Belliard, Africa Director of Foreign Affairs for France, and considered one of the architects of President François Hollande's Africa policy. This was a sea change from the policies of former president Nicolas Sarkozy, and focused on more comprehensive approaches to the distribution of power and the empowerment of local leaders on the international stage both directly and through the AU.

The *USA* was quick to recognise the elections and Rajaonarimampianina's victory but slower than its counterparts in finding a path towards engagement. Its position was tenuous, given its close relationship to the ousted Ravalomanana, the stronger position it had taken against the transitional government, and its vocal questioning of Rajaonarimampianina during the electoral process. It was thus a landmark when US Ambassador Robert Yamate presented his credentials on 13 January as the first ambassador appointed by Washington to Madagascar since the recall of Ambassador Niels Marquardt on 7 June 2010. Yamate immediately made his presence felt, serving as as a go between for political adversaries during the trying political period of the May impeachment vote. On 15 September, a new American Cultural Center was opened, tasked to promote American values such as good governance, democracy, the rule of law, human rights, environmental protection and sustainable development, as well as the English language. Many hoped that the USA's increased engagement would lead to a renewal of inclusion under *AGOA*, which had been severed during the political crisis. This desire was realised and a new National AGOA Strategy was released on 9 April. The move was expected to create between $ 200 m and $ 300 m per year in export revenues and tens of thousands of jobs in Madagascar, particularly in the textiles sector. American businesses profited from the new US position even outside of AGOA, with new contracts awarded to MWH Global for infrastructure, water and energy projects and, on 24 July, a sizable contract to Symbion Power to build seven new power plants.

China continued to show interest but it remained predominantly confined to extractive resources – mining and timber – though with other small projects such as the opening of a hospital, donated by the Chinese government, on 25 June. Rajaonarimampianina inaugurated the building, in Anosiala Ambohidratrimo, a suburb of the capital. *Iran* and *Russia* also signalled increased interest. On 2 February, Hossein Amir-Abdollahian, Iran's deputy foreign minister for Arab and African affairs, and Rajaonarimampianina discussed prospects for a new Iranian ambassador and a desire to increase trade. On 8 April, Russian Foreign Minister Sergey Lavrov met with Foreign Minister Beatrice Atallah, producing a statement that the two countries had nearly identical views and pledging to work together on counter-terrorism efforts.

The *UN* had a substantial multi-agency presence, having played a significant role in coordination with *SADC* during the political crisis (2009–13) and having a transient SADC representative. SADC shifted its role from mediation to oversight. On 30 April, Madagascar submitted a progress update on the National Reconciliation Process to the SADC Summit, while formally thanking the organisation for its support in recent years. On 3 July, Rajaonarimampianina met with the AU and SADC chair, President Robert Mugabe of Zimbabwe, and both referred to Madagascar as a new but still fragile democracy. By year's end, SADC's largest efforts in Madagascar had shifted to El Niño induced food insecurity, which had gripped the region.

Socioeconomic Developments

Madagascar is one of the world's poorest countries and, after years of crisis, both the economy and the population remained highly *vulnerable to endogenous and exogenous shocks*. The country rose one place in the UNDP HDI rankings to 154th out of 186 countries, up from 153rd in 2014. Life expectancy rose from 64 to 65 years, but this masked a relatively high under-five mortality rate. With a steady Gross National Income of $ 1,328, Madagascar had one of the lowest fiscal yields in the world and the World Bank's World Data Indicator on poverty found that 87.7% of the population were living on $ 1.25 per day and 95% on under $ 2 per day. There was a marked slide during the political crisis of 2009–13, disproportionately impacting the majority rural population. Only 35% of the rural population had access to drinking water, compared with 78% of the urban population and only 14% of the total population had access to sanitation. While HIV/AIDS rates were low (0.4%), malaria rates continued to be high. During the political crisis, Madagascar had cut spending on social services by 23.5% to achieve economic stability. There was an increase in sectoral planning during the year and new policy process development around social services delivery.

Macroeconomic performance was mixed. GDP growth slowed slightly to 3.0%. Total investment as a percentage of GDP increased by 9.4%, while exports increased by 8.3%. At the same time, dependency on aid also increased. Capital expenditure was limited to 20% of total expenditure, of which 80% was donor financed. The budget deficit was allowed to slip slightly in an effort to confront public finance challenges. General government revenue increased by 5.4%, while total expenditure rose by 16.7%. This was largely made up for through borrowing, as evidenced by a 13.7% debt increase. Tax payments, both labour and commercial, remained steady while tax revenues increased by 19%, lagging behind the 21% post-conflict recovery expectation. In a "systematic country diagnostic" released on 25 August, the World Bank focused on the disconnect of the rural poor from the economy, low labour productivity, political instability, low investment and low inclusiveness as the country's greatest challenges, rotating these challenges around five priority themes: governance, public finance, private sector-led economy, poverty and environment, and human capital, all critical to Madagascar's development. Madagascar ranked 164th of 189 countries in the World Bank Ease of Doing Business rankings, with the greatest challenges being found in starting a business, protecting minority investors, paying taxes and construction permits. This reflected poorly on the expansion of private sector investment, particularly the diversification of foreign investment.

At the heart of economic development woes had been the on-going disjuncture between a highly entrepreneurial society with a strong low-level *private sector* and a narrow production sector with high foreign product dependency and an export sector confined to low-yield unprocessed goods. Tourism continued to stagnate, and the agricultural sector struggled in the face of shifting global market prices and natural disasters. By late August, there was significant locust infestation in the central highlands rice growing regions around Antirabe and Mandoto. *Food shortages* reached critical proportions. In a 3 November report, the UN found that nearly 1.9 m people in southern Madagascar did not have a secure food supply, with 450,000 facing severe shortages. Madagascar ended the year with a 7.4% *inflation* rate, but certain key goods, including the food staple, rice, continued to see marked increases in price. Thus, while aggregate inflation was in check, the average citizen felt the impact of increased food and transport costs.

Agriculture continued to be the largest sector, but *mining* continued to grow. Industrial mining was dominated by three large operators: QIT (majority owned by the UK-based Rio Tinto), Ambatovy (majority owned by the Canada-based Sherritt), and Kraoma. QIT had began production of its 70 m tonnes of ilmenite in 2009, with production covering about 2,000 ha in 2015. Sherritt continued to ramp up production towards its target of 60,000 tonnes of refined nickel and 5,600 tonnes of refined cobalt – a production level it expected to maintain for 30 years. A litany of new entrants successfully sought new mining exploration permits, including DNI Metals, Coal Mining Madagascar, and Energizer. Other large projects in development included those run by Toliara Sands, Mainland, Aziana and Holcim. Oil exploration remained active. Exxon withdrew from Madagascar in July but other companies increased exploration. including Madagascar Oil in April. The rise in industrial mining and oil was expected to significantly increase GDP and employment, but was already a nascent destabilising force, both politically and economically. In August, the government presented a new draft mining law. Controversy abounded as the new draft law increased royalties and mandated a 10% government stake that the World Bank said would decrease investment. Yet, with $ 230.1 bn worth of known resources in Madagascar, investors thus far appeared undeterred. The government struggled to govern a sector that offered apparent opportunities for extracting hard-to-trace funds. Madagascar had seen its suspension from the EITI lifted in June 2014. As a result, EITI published a Payment Reconciliation Report in January and a World Bank-sponsored 2015 Work Plan in April. These efforts were part of a larger struggle confronting Madagascar in the face of diminished governing capacity. Other sectors such as the illicit extraction of rosewood and, increasingly, the political economy of the beef industry presented similar challenges.

Malawi

George Dzimbiri and Lewis Dzimbiri

Heavy rainfalls caused floods in many southern parts of the country, killing 104 people and displacing thousands, and were followed by a hunger crisis. The withholding of aid by development and cooperating partners continued in response to massive looting of public funds in 2013. The government continued to adopt a zero-aid budget, which was largely to be financed by locally generated revenue. Lack of budgetary support crippled many operations in various sectors of government, particularly affecting hospitals and the judiciary. The Malawi kwacha fell drastically in value after it was floated on the market. Widespread public protests by civil society organisations and employees dominated social and economic media headlines as the local economy continued to sail through troubled waters.

Domestic Politics

Intra-and inter-party conflicts characterised the domestic scene. *Intra-party conflicts* were conspicuous in both the ruling Democratic People's Party (DPP) and opposition parties. In April, the battle for the leadership of the southern regional committee of the opposition Malawi Congress Party (MCP) refused

 | DOI 10.1163/9789004333239_049

to die down and took on a new twist after the Eston Kakhome camp obtained an injunction. The court order culminated into the closure of the MCP southern region headquarters in Blantyre, which became a no-go zone for the party's regional chairperson, Dennis Kathumba. In a related development, the opposition People's Party (PP) executive regional committee members and some members of parliament in the northern region removed former state president Joyce Banda from the party presidency in August and replaced her with former vice president Khumbo Kachale, citing lack of leadership. The initiative was taken amidst allegations that Banda had left for the USA after losing the May 2014 general elections and had not returned home. In May, the first vice president of the PP Sosten Gwengwe, left the party after losing the 2014 tripartite election, in which he stood as Banda's running mate. He announced that he was reviving his political career by joining the MCP. The trial of cashgate suspects was on-going and some were sentenced.

The ruling *DPP* was also beset by internal conflicts. In February, DPP youth cadets walked out of a meeting in Mzuzu convened by the minister of finance, economic planning and development and the deputy minister of defence, claiming that the two ministers were in no position to hear their problems. They were suspended from the party as a disciplinary measure for showing great disrespect to their elders. In June, President Peter Mutharika's advisor, Ben Phiri, threatened to resign for reasons unknown to the general public but State House quickly downplayed the emerging tensions. On 30 November, the DPP deputy director for women, Martha Chimpozo Kamanga, left the party to join the MCP, unusual in that defections were usually to ruling political parties. She claimed that the party was not progressive.

Inter-party conflicts emerged when, at the Blantyre Synod of the Church of Central Africa Presbyterian, serious allegations arose that the DPP and PP had sponsored candidates ahead of the Church's electoral General Assembly scheduled for August 24–27. It was alleged that the DPP had sponsored and manipulated the synod's general secretary while the PP had sided with his rival. The general secretary retained his seat amidst controversies over the irregular process. In June, chaos erupted in Parliament following rumours that the government had plotted to oust the speaker. This was quickly denied, though some felt that there was no smoke without fire. In a related development, former United Democratic Front (UDF) director of research Humphrey Mvula rejected an invitation by the Alliance for Democracy president Enock Chihana to join the party. The year also witnessed the formation of a *new party*. In July, former vice president Cassim Chilumpha formed the People's Assembly for Democracy and Development on a platform of devolution of power and creating a strong national economy.

The government was also in conflict with *civil society organisations* (CSOs) over various governance and economic management issues. On 25 November, media owners and managers in Malawi, through the Media Institute of Southern Africa

Malawi Chapter, petitioned President Mutharika on the delay in tabling the Access to Information Bill in the National Assembly. In the same month, over 16 key CSOs under the umbrella Civil and Political Space Platform advised Mutharika to watch his tongue and control his emotions when addressing issues raised by Malawians. They pointed out that the attitude he displayed on his return from the UN General Assembly had the potential to breed dictatorship in the country. Mutharika had held a press conference on 8 October, when he responded emotionally to growing criticisms of his allegedly over-sized delegation to the UN General Assembly at a time when the economy was crumbling. The Public Affairs Committee warned that the country risked a governance crisis and loss of popular trust because of the way the DPP administration had handled the sale of the Malawi Savings Bank in the face of public protest.

On 17 August, Mutharika announced a *cabinet reshuffle*, firing Minister of Health Paul Chibingu and Minister of Local Government Tarsizio Gowelo. They were replaced by Peter Kumpalume and Malison Ndau, respectively. In June, the government reshuffled principal secretaries: Chimwemwe Banda was moved from the Ministry of Information, Tourism and Culture to the Department of Disaster Management Affairs to replace Paul Chiunguzeni, who was moved to the Ministry of Defence, where he replaced Justin Saidi. The latter was moved to the Ministry of Information, Tourism and Culture.

Various *acts of legislation* kept Parliament busy. In May, The Reserve Bank of Malawi Amendment Bill was passed, which, among other things, reduced the limit of government borrowing from the Central Bank from the previous 20% to 10% of total borrowing. In a related development, Mutharika assented to the Marriage, Divorce and Family Relations Bill, bringing it into force in July. In June, the MCP and PP prevented the adoption of a government bill seeking authorisation to borrow about K (kwacha) 9.8 bn from the EIB to finance the upgrading of essential aviation safety and security equipment at Kamuzu and Chileka international airports. Minister of Finance Goodall Gondwe was forced to withdraw the bill temporarily so that it could be scrutinised by the Parliamentary Transport Committee. In addition, towards the end of June, the government rejected calls for a review of the proposed 10% tax on text messages and Internet services, arguing that the system was working perfectly without the tax in other countries. CSOs asked the government to review its decision on the basis that consumers were already paying heavily whenever they used communications services. In November, cabinet ministers unanimously rejected the draft Access to Information Bill that was intended to be tabled in parliament, claiming it was full of irregularities.

The Open Government Index released in March by the World Justice Project ranked Malawi 65th out of 102 countries. It was ranked 96th on the right to information, 89th on published laws and government data, 55th on complaints mechanisms and 26th on civic participation.

Foreign Affairs

Donors continued to withhold budgetary support following the cashgate scandal in 2013. This crippled many operations, particularly affecting government hospitals and the judiciary. On 11 September, donors announced that they would not support the seed component of the Farm Input Subsidy Program because of concerns about mismanagement of funds during the 2014 growing season. This meant that the Malawi government would have to raise about K 2.9 bn to fill the gap before the new growing season started at the onset of rains in November. However, *bi- and multi-lateral aid* continued to flow. On 4 June, the World Bank officially signed a financing agreement for $ 80 m (about K 36 bn) for emergency recovery projects after the floods that struck 15 of Malawi's 28 districts early in the year (see below). Finance Minister Gondwe said the project was important and timely as government would undertake some important recovery and rehabilitation work. On 15 May, the World Bank Group approved $ 80 m to help reconstruct critical public infrastructure, restore agricultural livelihoods and enhance food security following the floods. In a related development, on 9 June, the *AfDB* granted about K 13 bn ($ 29 m) as sector budget support for the protection of basic social services. The UN provided $ 9.2 m (about K 4.2 bn) for food, education and sanitation in Chikwawa, Nsanje and Phalombe, which had been hardest hit by the floods. On 15 June, the Global Fund endorsed a grant proposal for TB, HIV/AIDS and malaria campaigns running up to December 2017, despite concern over misuse of funds from previous budgets by the Ministry of Health and the National AIDS Commission.

On 15 May, the UK and Germany urged Malawi to burn the ivory that Mutharika was supposed to have burnt the previous month in order to send a signal to the rest of the world that Malawi was becoming an international leader in the protection of wildlife.

In April, 420 Malawians and nationals of Zimbabwe, Somalia, the DRC, Ethiopia and Zambia experienced xenophobic attacks in *South Africa*. The government hired over 20 coaches to bring home Malawians who were affected by the attacks.

Mutharika made several *foreign visits* during the year. In September, he went to the USA to attend a meeting of the UN General Assembly. He also attended the Commonwealth Heads of Government meeting in November in Malta. On 4 December, he went to South Africa to attend the Forum on China-Africa Cooperation after a successful visit to the UK.

On 8 June, the Chinese Beijing Xinwei Telecom Technologies Incorporated promised to revolutionise the telecommunication sector by investing up to K 87 bn ($ 200 m) to introduce comprehensive and cheap telephone, Internet and social media services in rural areas.

Socioeconomic Developments

The World Bank once again rated Malawi as the poorest country in the world with a gross national per capita income of $ 250. On 11 December, the Executive Board of the *IMF* concluded the 2015 Article IV consultation. The Board welcomed Malawi's commitment to the flexible exchange rate regime and the automatic fuel pricing mechanism, both of which had served Malawi well, and encouraged the authorities to implement structural reforms to remove supply bottlenecks, increase agricultural productivity and improve the business environment. They cautioned, however, that changes to the fuel import regime involving a greater role for the state-owned company should be transparent and include safeguards against the emergence of contingent liabilities for the budget. They also expressed concerns about the policy slippages that had prevented Malawi from achieving sustained growth and low inflation. They agreed that the outlook was subject to downside risks from continued weather-related supply shocks, the interruption of donor budget support, and weaker demand for Malawi's exports. Accordingly, they emphasised that restoration of macroeconomic stability was a critical priority. They also underlined the need for fiscal consolidation and tighter monetary policy, implementation of sound macroeconomic policies and structural reforms. They finally recommended broadening the tax base, strengthening tax compliance, and modernising tax administration and also stressed the need to accelerate public financial management reforms to restore trust and confidence in the budget process and foster donor re-engagement. The IMF warned Malawians to brace themselves for hard times in sourcing basic goods and services as a result of the government's failure to meet IMF targets. Their views came in light of the tough economic environment characterised by a skyrocketing inflation rate of 22.2% and high interest rates in commercial banks hovering between 32% and 37%, as well as a paltry GDP.

Price increases added to the cost of public utilities and services during the year. In September, water boards raised tariffs by 45% following government approval. Staple foods and other basic commodities were scarce. By March, maize was already in short supply in both government and private markets. The Agricultural Development and Marketing Corporation (ADMARC) started rationing maize to 20 kg per person instead of the normal 50 kg. Private traders took advantage of the looming hunger crisis to raise maize prices to K 160 per kg – 100% above ADMARC's selling price of K 80 per kg. Nevertheless, according to the basket of basic needs prepared by the Centre for Social Concern, the monthly cost of living in urban areas had fallen by 1.4% to K 118,663 in May from K 120,390 the month before. In May, maize prices went down by 11% and charcoal prices by 4%, but in September, ADMARC markets across the country were selling maize at K 110 per kg, representing a 37% increase. Thus, while the government was selling at K 5,500 per 50 kg bag of maize, the informal market was selling at K 8,000.

Electricity outages were a regular occurrence. The Electricity Supply Commission of Malawi (ESCOM) reduced power supply by 50%, leading to continued, longer and more intensive load shedding in most parts of the country. ESCOM announced in August that the generating of capacity at its Nkula and Tedzani Hydro-power stations had fallen by close to 50% as a result of low water levels in Lake Malawi. Water levels had become a catch-all for ESCOM. Both high and low levels of water in Lake Malawi and the Shire River were regular explanations for constant electricity blackouts.

The year saw the worst *floods* ever recorded in the country when between January and March many parts of southern Malawi (Chikwawa, Mulanje, Phalombe, Nsanje and Mwanza) were under water. Over 230,000 people were displaced and 104 were killed. This was a recipe for hunger. Malawi's post-disaster needs assessments report showed that the country required about K 215 bn ($ 494 m) for full recovery and reconstruction after the damage caused. The extensive damage to life and property prompted the president to declare a *State of Disaster*, appealing for local and international relief assistance. The flooded southern region experienced a cholera outbreak, with Nsanje, Phalombe and Chikwawa being hardest hit among the 15 flood districts. On the other hand, the local currency experienced a steep depreciation. In September, the exchange rate stood at K 615 to the dollar and by December, it was trading at K 670.

Tobacco earnings fell by $ 62 m following poor sales and reduced prices caused by the heavy rains and floods that hit most tobacco-producing districts. The Tobacco Association of Malawi lamented the low market prices for the leaf. There was also a battle among buyers, most of whom preferred contract tobacco and hence compromised prices for tobacco at auction: 85,277 kg of flue-cured tobacco was sold at auction, compared with 8.3 m kg traded on contract. The Tobacco Control Commission (TCC) reported earnings of $ 204.3 m compared with $ 183.4 m in 2014. As the tobacco market season opened in April at the Lilongwe auction floors, the TCC released minimum and maximum buying prices. The buying price of flue-cured tobacco, mostly reserved for large estates, ranged from $ 0.25 (K 129) to $ 4 (K 1,784) per kg compared with the 2014 minimum price of $ 2.65 (K 1,181). Dark-fired tobacco was sold at between $ 1 and $ 3.40 per kg compared with the 2014 price of $ 2.10. The buying price for barley, grown by the majority of Malawians, ranged from $ 0.85 (K 379) to $ 4.50 (K 2,700) per kg compared with the minimum in 2014 of $ 1.76 (K 784).

There was also a drop in the output of tea, soya and sugar. Economic commentators argued that the long-term impact of the underperformance of tea and sugar would be a decline in economic competitiveness and continued reliance on donor support. A Reserve Bank of Malawi report recorded a fall in *tea* revenue to $ 2.1 m from $ 4.4 m in 2014. Similarly a National Statistics Office monthly statistical bulletin indicated that, as of July, the total value of tea auctioned at Limbe amounted to

K 1.03 bn compared with K 1.2 bn in 2014. In addition, price fluctuations irked *soya bean* growers in their respective area markets. Farmers from Machinga, Mangochi and Mchinji accused the government of leaving them at the mercy of unscrupulous traders who were buying below the market price, at as low as K 130 per kg.

In May, Finance Minister Gondwe submitted the *national budget* for the 2015/16 financial year. He struggled to create a balanced budget because of the deficits caused by the absence of donors and the need for increased resources to buy food in the wake of the floods. Unlike in the past, the budget assumed no budget support. On 26 June, members of Parliament approved the K 930 bn budget, although opposition MPs cautioned the government against abuse and mismanagement of public resources. They also had reservations regarding the disposal of the wholly state-owned Malawi Savings Bank, claiming that this had been hurriedly undertaken without transparency in order to cushion political favourites who had obtained colossal loans from the bank that they were not able to repay.

Lack of funding and *shortages of medicines* affected health provision. The worst affected district hospitals were asking for medical supplies from rural health centres and clinics, while some health workers were raising questions about the capacity of the Central Medical Stores to ensuring the availability and regular supply of drugs. Painkillers, antibiotics, anti-malaria drugs and contraceptives were in desperately short supply. In July, the National Organisation of Nurses and Midwives (NONM) blamed the government for failing to address the crisis. The NONM said nurses were tired of witnessing preventable deaths in the country's public health institutions. Health service delivery in almost all the 28 districts in the country had slowed down following the government's decision to cut recurrent transaction allocations to districts health offices.

Labour disputes escalated as a result of disagreements between employers and employees in all sectors of the economy. Parliamentary secretarial staff disrupted business on 3 February, the second day of the mid-term budget review meeting, when they staged a strike after rejecting an 18% salary increase offered by the government. The staff resorted to industrial action after the Treasury failed to honour a Parliamentary Service Commission recommendation that salaries of National Assembly staff be raised by 24%. Also within the public service, judges and magistrates rejected a 22% pay rise in February. The development came barely a month after the end of a seven-week judiciary support staff strike that had paralysed the country's justice delivery systems between November and December 2014, but which had ended early January after the two parties agreed to resolve the matter. In a related development, the Civil Service Trade Union Mzuzu chapter protested over a salary raise on 11 February saying that the 45% salary increment awarded by government unfairly favoured employees in higher grades over lower level workers. On 6 March, employees of the Christian Health Association of Malawi (CHAM) started a strike that forced about half of the health facilities under the CHAM to discontinue their operations. The workers had given the government a seven-day ultimatum to address the disparities between their salary increments and those awarded to workers in government health facilities. They threatened to continue withholding their labour indefinitely if their grievances were not resolved quickly.

The year was also marked by a *series of fires* from July to November. Several markets, including Mzuzu, Salima, Lilongwe and Mchinji, which are major hubs for local and international traders, were completely destroyed. Merchants and the wider Malawi populace suspected politically motivated arson as the major explanation for the frequent market fires. The government promised an impartial investigation through the Ministry of Local Government.

Mauritius

Tor Sellström

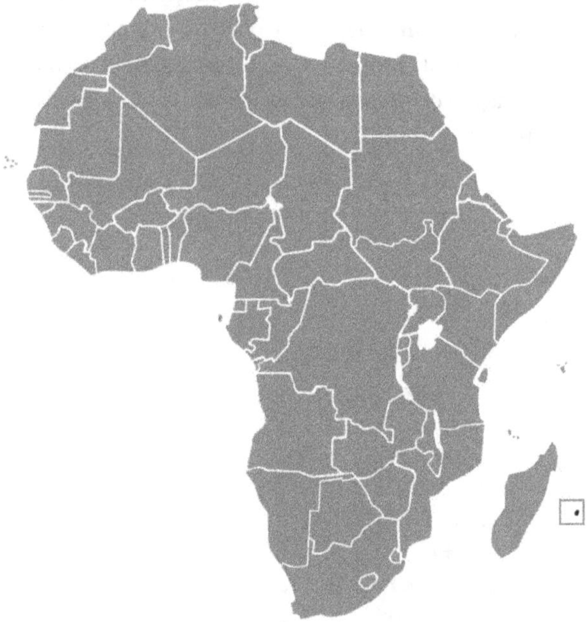

Domestically, the year was dominated by the electoral victories of the 'Alliance Lepep'; the arrest of ex-premier Ramgoolam; the crisis of the Labour and MMM parties; and the ramifications of several irregular financial schemes. In its foreign relations, Mauritius tried to balance the rising interests of India and China in the Indian Ocean and turn them to its advantage. The dispute with Britain over the Chagos archipelago also featured prominently. Despite a persistent economic slowdown, the financial services sector and tourism did well. As in 2014, the country ranked first in Africa with regard to governance and human development, although unemployment was relatively high and gender inequality deep-rooted.

Domestic Politics

As 2014 drew to a close, Prime Minister Navin Ramgoolam of the ruling Labour Party ('Parti Travailliste' – PTR) called for snap elections. Behind the initiative was a constitutional proposal, known as the Second Republic Project, drawn up with Paul Bérenger, the leader of the Mauritian Militant Movement ('Mouvement Militant Mauricien' – MMM). Largely seen as a scheme to advance the two leaders' personal

 | DOI 10.1163/9789004333239_050

interests, the result of the *parliamentary polls* on 10 December 2014 was, against expectations, a resounding rejection of the PTR-MMM alliance, which secured only 13 seats in the National Assembly (9 to the MMM and 4 to Labour) and the prime minister, son of the 'Father of the Nation', Sir Seewoosagur Ramgoolam, failed to retain the seat he had held for over two decades, while the opposition 'Alliance Lepep' (People's Alliance) won no fewer than 47 seats. The remaining two seats went to the local Organisation of the People of Rodrigues ('Organisation du Peuple de Rodrigues').

The 'Alliance Lepep' was headed by 84-year-old Sir *Anerood Jugnauth*, leader of the Militant Socialist Movement ('Mouvement Socialiste Militant' – MSM), a former prime minister (1982–95 and 2000–3) and president (2003–12), and widely credited for Mauritius' successful economic diversification. In addition to the MSM, the 'Alliance Lepep' was composed of Xavier-Luc Duval's Mauritian Social-Democratic Party ('Parti Mauricien Social Démocrate') and the newly formed Movement for Liberation ('Muvman Liberater'), a splinter from the MMM led by Ivan Collendavelloo. With Jugnauth as prime minister, the coalition government was sworn into office on 17 December 2014.

Shifting coalitions, party splits and re-alignments are common in Mauritius. Taking place within a restricted circle of dynastic families, electoral calculations and intrigues have over the years also become part of the domestic political landscape. Against this background, the outcome of the December 2014 elections was not exceptional. The immediate aftermath, however, certainly was. Launching what Prime Minister Jugnauth termed '*a clean-up campaign*', within weeks he either dismissed or demanded the resignation of some 20 senior state officials close to the Labour Party, including the governor of the central bank. In what critics saw as an aggressive score-settling course, many were replaced by members of the Jugnauth political clan and largely drawn from the Vaish caste of the Hindu community.

In February, these moves culminated with the arrest of former prime minister *Ramgoolam*, a turn of events that rocked the establishment and was to dominate the domestic political scene in 2015. No longer enjoying parliamentary immunity, Ramgoolam was taken into custody on 6 February after investigations into a 2011 burglary had led the police to the discovery of large amounts of cash at his Port Louis residence. Accused of 'conspiracy to do a wrongful act' and 'money laundering', he was released on bail the following day. The former premier denied any wrongdoing and declared that the money – which included new, consecutively numbered US dollar bills – represented campaign funds donated by Labour supporters. As he had stood down from the leadership of the Labour Party, the judicial case widened to include connections with a Ponzi scheme involving the British American Investment finance company. In mid-May, Ramgoolam was arrested again, and in October it was revealed that the British National Crime Agency had been asked to carry out further investigations into his alleged irregular activities.

At the same time, another high-profile affair caught up with the Jugnauth family. On 2 July, *Pravind Jugnauth*, the son of the prime minister, appointed in December 2014 as minister of technology, communication and innovation, was convicted on charges of 'conflict of interest' and given a 12-month suspended jail sentence. The charges dated back to his term as finance minister in 2009–11, when the government had purchased a private medical clinic (MedPoint) owned by Pravind's sister.

Against this backdrop, *municipal elections* were held on 14 June. The Labour Party argued that the polls would not be free and fair and boycotted the elections. This, in turn, led to an overwhelming victory for the ruling 'Alliance Lepep', which won all the 120 council seats. Although marred by low voter turnout (35.6%), the local elections confirmed Lepep's dominance and the crisis in the Labour and MMM parties, two major forces on the Mauritian post-independence political arena.

In late May, President Kailash Purryag, who in 2012 had been nominated by the former Ramgoolam administration, resigned from his mainly ceremonial post. In his place, the government proposed Ameenah Gurib-Fakim, a renowned bio-scientist and professor at the University of Mauritius. The nomination was approved by the National Assembly on 4 June with few dissenting voices and the following day Gurib-Fakim took office as the *first female president* of Mauritius and one of very few female heads of state in Africa.

Foreign Affairs

Mauritian foreign policy remained focused on Europe, India and China, as well as, increasingly, on Africa. As a member of both the Commonwealth and its French counterpart the OIF, it maintained close links with the two former colonial powers Britain and France. With influential national communities of Indian and Chinese descent and located in the middle of the Indian Ocean, it navigated the increasing regional rivalries between the two Asian giants, endeavouring to turn them to advantage. With regard to Africa, its membership of SADC, COMESA and other regional organisations offered opportunities. With the exception of the Chagos issue, Mauritius' foreign relations were by tradition primarily guided by *economic and financial considerations*. This was also the course followed by the new 'Alliance Lepep' government.

Mauritius maintained good relations with the United States, France and – despite the dispute over Chagos – the United Kingdom (UK). Approximately 50% of the country's exports went to the EU, with the *UK* and *France* as the principal destinations. France and the UK were also the leading tourism partners. More than a third of foreign visitors were French passport holders, including those from the French overseas department of Réunion, Mauritius' sister island in the Indian Ocean. Of international tourists, around 22% came from France, followed by those from the UK, representing 11%.

France's influence was only surpassed by that of *India*, particularly signified by Prime Minister Narendra Modi's visit on 11–13 March. During the visit, India – from where Mauritius sources almost a quarter of its imports – offered a concessional credit of $ 500 m and five bilateral agreements were signed, notably covering cooperation in the Indian Ocean and the construction of an airstrip and jetty facilities on the distant Agalega Islands, belonging to Mauritius, but located some 1,100 km to the north. Rumours about Indian interest in securing a naval base on Agalega had circulated for years, and many observers interpreted the agreement as part of an extended *security arrangement* between the two governments in Port Louis and New Delhi.

Throughout the year, Mauritius and India were negotiating a revision of their *Double Taxation Avoidance Agreement*, originally signed in 1983. A cornerstone in Mauritius' economic diversification and emergence as an international financial centre, the significance of the agreement was illustrated by the fact that Mauritius accounted for around 24% of FDI into India during the Indian fiscal year 2014/15, the biggest single FDI source and overtaking Singapore. Increasingly, however, the Indian authorities had expressed concern that the funds largely represented domestic capital routed through Mauritius to avoid Indian taxes, a malpractice known as 'round tripping'. Against this background, a revision of the agreement was raised by Modi during his visit in March, and in July it was initially reported that a consensus had been reached. By the end of the year, however, a revised text was still under discussion.

China viewed Mauritius as an important gateway to the African continent, with around 15% of Mauritius' imports sourced from China. In 2015 – a year in which China's presence in the Indian Ocean grew stronger, notably marked by the opening of a naval base in Djibouti in November – the already close links with the small island state developed further. In June, a bilateral civil aviation agreement made provision for as many as 28 return flights a week between the two countries, reflecting Mauritius' growing importance as a Chinese tourist destination. The total number of Chinese tourists was close to 90,000, representing 8% of international visitors and an increase of over 40% compared with 2014. In the process, China took fourth place among Mauritius' tourism partners, behind France/Réunion, the UK and South Africa. Chinese investments were also on the rise. In connection with the December FOCAC (Forum on China-Africa Cooperation) summit in Johannesburg, it was announced that the Jinfei Economic Trade and Cooperation Zone, north of Port Louis, would be re-designed and implemented. Modelled on China's coastal manufacturing regions, the ambitious industrial complex was originally launched in 2006, but had since fallen behind schedule.

With regard to Africa, the Jugnauth government pursued the 'Africa strategy' launched in 2012, focusing *inter alia* on regional integration, tax agreements and scholarships for African students. As part of the strategy, the Ramgoolam administration had in 2014 set up a *Mauritius-Africa Fund*, promoting Mauritian business ventures in the continent. By 2015, double taxation avoidance agreements had been concluded with 14 African nations. At the same time, 45 Mauritian companies had invested in 12 African countries, covering areas from agri-business and banking to communications and renewable energy. In his budget speech in March, Finance Minister Lutchmeenaraidoo announced that Madagascar, Ghana and Senegal intended to cooperate with Mauritius in developing Special Economic Zones in their countries.

Finally, the disputes with the UK over the forcibly exiled Chagossians and Mauritius' claim to sovereignty over the British-held *Chagos archipelago* featured prominently on the foreign policy agenda. Although significant progress was registered in both cases, neither of them was resolved. In 2014, a study commissioned by the UK had found that there were, in principle, no fundamental legal obstacles to a resettlement of the islanders. The Mauritius-based Chagos Refugees Group welcomed the finding, but noted that the right of return was conditional on a series of constitutional and other instruments, which had not been dealt with by year's end. Similarly, with regard to Mauritius' sovereignty claims, the Permanent Court of Arbitration in The Hague, Netherlands, ruled on 18 March that the establishment by the UK of a marine protected area around Chagos contravened its obligations under the UN Convention on the Law of the Sea. While the verdict was historic, the court did not pronounce on the cardinal issue of sovereignty. Meeting in Johannesburg in mid-June, the AU reiterated its position that the Chagos archipelago, including Diego Garcia, formed an integral part of Mauritius and, in his address to the UN General Assembly in early October, Prime Minister Jugnauth emphasised that it was high time the decolonisation of Africa was completed.

Socioeconomic Developments

A major factor behind the victory of the 'Alliance Lepep' in December 2014 was the *economic slowdown*, which had resulted in persistent unemployment and widening income disparities. For the period 2012–15, real GDP growth was around 3% per year. Although this compared favourably with most African countries, it revealed structural challenges in the transition towards an economy primarily driven by the tertiary sector. With prices down by almost 30%, *sugar production* contracted and, in general, faced an uncertain future as the EU sugar import quotas from the ACP states were set to be abolished in 2017.

Importantly, the *tertiary sector* continued to register above average growth, particularly with regard to financial and insurance activities, as well as information and communications technology (ICT). Mauritius maintained the objective of becoming a financial hub between Asia and Africa, and financial and insurance services registered a growth of 5.2%, contributing 10.3% to GDP. Tourism also continued to surge. With increasing numbers from China, the country welcomed 1.1 m visitors, an increase of 10% over 2014 and a record for the second consecutive year. In his budget speech in March, Finance Minister Lutchmeenaraidoo emphasised that Mauritius was at *a major crossroads*, noting that a GDP growth of 3% could not generate enough employment and improvement in living standards and that the creation of greater national wealth should also be concerned with better sharing. To achieve the objective of higher, inclusive growth, he outlined a policy that, in addition to the tertiary sector, would focus on the 'blue economy', prioritising opportunities for fishing and shipping, 13 so-called mega-projects across the country and small and medium enterprises. Among the mega-projects was the transformation of the Port Louis harbour into a major regional hub for transshipment, bunkering, petroleum storage etc.

In the third quarter, *unemployment* stood at 7.4%, about the same as in 2007, but almost double that of the early 1990s. Youth and women were particularly affected, largely due to a mismatch between education and the skills required in the changing labour market. *Income inequality* had increased between 2006 and 2012, with the Gini coefficient rising from 0.388 to 0.413, and preliminary estimates indicated a continuing trend over the period 2013–15. Affecting less than 1% of the population, extreme poverty as defined by the World Bank was, however, minimal. With regard to *human development*, the country remained within the UNDP 'high' category, marginally increasing its HDI score and ranking 63rd out of 188 countries – number 1 in Africa and well above the SSA average.

Mauritius' non-violent democratic traditions, strong public institutions and measures to protect against financial irregularities have meant that it has for many years been high on international indexes concerning *governance* and *transparency*, particularly when compared with continental Africa. Notwithstanding the 2014–15 political transition, as well as the Ramgoolam and Jugnauth cases and a number of other affairs, the Indian Ocean nation was again ranked number 1 out of 54 countries on the Ibrahim Index of African Governance (IIAG), a position it had retained every year since 2000. On TI's global Corruption Perception Index, it was placed 45th, up two places from 2014 and only surpassed in Africa by Botswana, Cabo Verde and Seychelles. At the same time, the World Bank ranked Mauritius 32nd in the world with regard to doing business, first in Africa and ahead of industrialised countries such as Italy and Japan. Although Ameenah Gurib-Fakim was appointed president in 2015, Mauritius continued to lag behind with regard to *gender equality*. Of 25 ministers in the 'Alliance Lepep' government, only three were women. In the African context, too, gender equality registered a decline. On the IIAG index for 2015, the sub-category 'gender' showed a drop of –7.9 points since 2011, making Mauritius 23rd of the 54 African countries, by far its lowest ranking in any sub-category.

Relative poverty notably affected the distant, semi-autonomous island of *Rodrigues*, Africa's easternmost inhabited land, located 600 km east of the main island and with a population of around 40,000. Based on small-scale fishing and subsistence farming, the economy of Rodrigues had been largely isolated from the country's post-independence boom and in 2015 the people of Rodrigues were earning 30%–50% less than the national average. To address the island's isolation and promote it as a tourism destination, the Jugnauth government announced *inter alia* the installation of a new submarine fibre optic cable linking Rodrigues to Mauritius and the rest of the world, the extension of the local airport and the acquisition of a new vessel for merchandise and passenger transport.

Mozambique

Joseph Hanlon

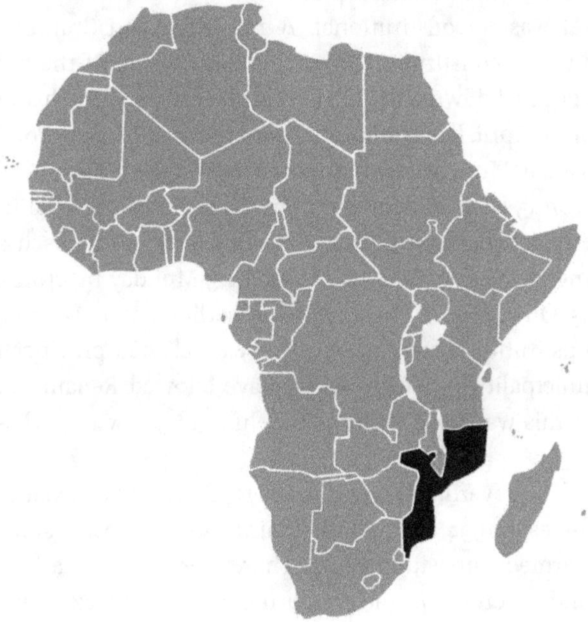

In his first year in office, President Filipe Nyusi faced a wide range of challenges. The armed opposition, Renamo, went back to war, while keeping its seats in parliament, and negotiations collapsed. Dramatically falling commodity prices raised questions about the use of the huge gas reserves; a dubious $ 850 m bond issue caused more headaches. The economy continued to grow, but poverty was not reduced, while Nyusi and the younger generation struggled to wrest power from the old guard.

Domestic Politics

Filipe Nyusi took office as *president* on 15 January but immediately faced a set of inherited problems, complicated by attempts by the old guard allied to former president Armando Guebuza to retain power. Still a member of the Frelimo party Political Commission, Guebuza was only pushed out as president of the party on 29 March and replaced by Nyusi. Economic issues dominated his first year, while opposition leader Afonso Dhlakama of Renamo was the main political issue. On 17 January, Dhlakama announced at a rally in Tete that he did not recognise the Nyusi government.

 | DOI 10.1163/9789004333239_051

Dhlakama demanded the right to name *governors* in the six provinces in which he claimed to have a majority, and in the longer term to move to elected governors, following the model of elected mayors and municipal assemblies at local level. Renamo tabled a bill in parliament and Dhlakama said in statements in February and March that he would govern by force in those provinces if parliament rejected it. Frelimo said the proposal was unconstitutional. A respected constitutional lawyer, Gilles Cistac, argued that a constitutionally acceptable version of the bill could be written, but he was gunned down and killed on the street on 3 March and Parliament rejected the bill on 30 April. Dhlakama and Nyusi met at a Maputo hotel on 7 and 9 February. The so-called 'Monday negotiations' between the government and Renamo continued, and on 15 June an agreement on the separation of political parties from the state was reached, but Renamo continued to refuse to discuss the demobilisation of its armed forces. On 23 August, after 113 Monday meetings, Dhlakama broke off the talks. On 31 July, at the end of the parliamentary session, Renamo had submitted a constitutional amendment to create elected provincial governments (similar to municipalities), which would have allowed Renamo to nominate five governors, but this was rejected by the Frelimo majority in parliament on 7 December.

With the tacit agreement of the government and the UN representative, Renamo had not demobilised all its forces in 1994 and had maintained military bases since then, thus always being an armed opposition party. There were confrontations between *Renamo guerrillas* and government soldiers during the year in Gaza, Tete, Sofala and Zambézia provinces. Fighting escalated in two areas, leading to schools closing and residents fleeing. Renamo announced it was opening a major new base in Raposo, Morrumbala district, Zambézia. Riot police set up a base nearby and there were regular confrontations. The other area of on-going conflict was in north-eastern Tete province, bordering Malawi, from where 3,000 refugees had fled to Malawi by the end of year. On 22 June, Dhlakama said he personally gave the order for a 14 June attack on government forces 3 km from the Renamo military base at Mucombedzi, Moatize district, Tete. On 12 and 25 September, Dhlakama's armed motorcade was ambushed in Manica and at least 23 people were killed. Dhlakama was unhurt, but retreated to his former bush headquarters near Mount Gorongosa in Sofala. Accompanied by mediators and journalists, he went from there to Beira on 8 October, but the next day the house was raided and his guards disarmed, so he returned to the bush. Interior Minister Jaime Monteiro announced that the raid marked the start of disarming Renamo.

Lourenço do Rosário, rector of the 'Universidade Politécnica' and one of the key mediators between Renamo and government, warned that, following the *collapse of the talks*, "there are people on both sides who think the best solution is military". In a speech on 2 October, he said that it was conflicts between the political and military within both Renamo and Frelimo that had killed the Monday talks and, in an interview with the weekly 'Savana' published on 2 October, he said that there were those on the government side who supported a "Savimbi solution" – killing Dhlakama and using military force to push Renamo generals to join the government army. In the same speech, do Rosário also blamed Armando Guebuza for following, after his 2009 re-election as president, "the one route that would aggravate the conflict" by saying, in effect, "dialogue is no longer important". Thus, "it was not by accident that the Renamo leader left Maputo for Nampula". The attacks on Dhlakama came when Nyusi tried to restart talks, and seemed intent on forcing Dhlakama into the bush and blocking dialogue. Some argued that Nyusi had lost control of the police and security services. Finally, he used the unusual platform of a 19 November graduation ceremony for prison guards to say: "I use this podium to instruct the pausing and reconsideration of compulsory disarmament." Thus he made clear that he was bypassing the security and police command to issue the order.

On 16 September, a Maputo court acquitted Carlos Nuno Castel-Branco, a prominent economist, and Fernando Mbanze, editor of the newsletter 'MediaFax', in a *libel case* concerning criticism of former president Armando Guebuza, libelling the president being a state security offence. 'MediaFax' had reprinted a Facebook post by Castel-Banco. The court analysed the post in detail but, although it was highly critical of Guebuza, could find nothing libellous in it.

From the middle of the year there was a spate of kidnappings and murders of people suffering from albinism arising out of a new belief that *body parts of albinos* had magic properties and could be used in ceremonies.

Mozambique was officially declared *free of land mines* at a ceremony in Maputo on 17 September.

Foreign Affairs

Xenophobic attacks in *South Africa* in April caused at least 2,000 Mozambicans to flee that country. South Africa's Kruger National Park reported in July that 80% of poachers arrested were Mozambican, and on 18 September former president Joaquim Chissano released statistics showing that over the past five-and-a-half years almost 500 Mozambicans had been intercepted while poaching in the park and shot dead by South African game rangers and security forces. There were still 32,000 Mozambicans working on South African mines, remitting $ 60 m annually to Mozambique. In 1970, there had been 113,000 Mozambicans working in South African mines, but by 2003 the number had fallen to 55,000, and was predicted to fall by 8% per year with South African restrictions on the number of foreign miners and the closure of some gold and platinum mines.

Mozambique continued to balance *British and Portuguese links.* Britain's minister for Africa visited Maputo in May and President Nyusi attended the Commonwealth summit on 29 November in Malta and stressed his commitment to the Commonwealth. But Nyusi also visited Portugal in July and went to the CPLP headquarters. He attended the AfDB's 50th annual meeting and backed the African Common Market.

In his first year as president, Nyusi made contact with most of the *neighbouring countries*. He made a state visit to South Africa in October and went to Zimbabwe in August and to Namibia for the investiture of President Hage Geingob on 21 March. Tanzanian President Jakaya Kikwete visited Maputo on 8 October and Nyusi attended the inauguration of his successor, John Pome Magufuli, in November. Nyusi and Kikwete called for the building of a second bridge over the Rovuma River, even though the first bridge, inaugurated in May 2010, was underused, partly because of the poor state of the access roads. Nyusi took over as chair of the SADC Organ on Politics, Defence and Security Cooperation on 18 August, which led him into attempts to find a solution to the Lesotho political crisis linked to the killing of Army Commander Maaparankoe Mahao in June. Lesotho's Prime Minister Pakalitha Mosisili came to Maputo to meet Nyusi on 6 October as part of this process.

SADC, COMESA and the EAC agreed to merge on 1 June at a meeting at Sharm El Sheikh (Egypt), but Mozambique did not sign up. Mozambique and Tanzania – both founder members of SADC – had never joined COMESA, although most SADC states were members of both. Mozambique said it would continue with negotiations and try to resolve its problems with COMESA, but would not join the merged body yet.

The Council of Governors of the Islamic Development Bank met in Maputo in June.

Socioeconomic Developments

The plummeting gas price delayed development of the huge gas fields on the coast of Cabo Delgado in the north, and combined with dramatically increased debt, devaluation, inflation, and a decline in aid to create an economic crisis and force Mozambique to take an IMF loan. GDP growth was expected to be down to 6.1% for the year. *Aid* continued to decline, in part because of donor anger over the Ematum bond issue (see below). President Nyusi himself noted that the fall in foreign aid had also led to reduced foreign reserves. Although, 14 donors, led by the World Bank, the EU, Britain and Sweden, continued to provide budget support and signed a new agreement on 21 September, five donors stopped budget support, largely in protest at the still unexplained Ematum bond. In August, the IMF predicted that foreign aid grants would be $ 824 m, but by December the estimate had been cut by 25% to $ 615 m. The government suspended negotiations on $ 2.2 bn in loans for infrastructure projects, the IMF revealed, and sent them back to ministries for reconsideration.

As part of his new government, Nyusi named Adriano Maleiane, a highly respected former governor of the Bank of Mozambique, as *finance minister*; he was chosen to try to clean up the mess left by former president Guebuza. On 20 November, Maleiane said that public foreign *debt* had grown dramatically between 2012 and 2014, from $ 4.8 bn to $ 7 bn. $ 1.5 bn of the new borrowing was made up of three loans. Two loans had been personally negotiated by Guebuza with China: $ 700 m for the Maputo-KaTembe bridge, which would be one of the largest suspension bridges in Africa (although engineers said a less dramatic bridge could have been built for half the price), and $ 300 m for the Maputo ring road. The third loan was the 2013 $ 850 m government guaranteed bond issue to buy tuna fishing boats at a cost of $ 230 m for a new tuna fishing company, Ematum, 33% owned by the state security services, 34% by the state, and 33% by the state fishing company Emopesca. Despite repeated demands, government had never explained what the remaining $ 620 m was for; some was said to be for coastal patrol boats and some for weapons, and it was widely believed some had gone to Guebuza's cronies. The outcry from donors and the IMF led the government to take onto its books $ 500 m of the debt. One of government's biggest domestic debts was made up of over $ 200 m in VAT rebates owed to companies. This issue had been dragging on for years, and Maleiane decided in July to pay the outstanding rebates with government bonds. Companies could hold the bonds and be paid over time, or sell the bonds to banks at a discount, typically of 10% to 20%. Not surprisingly, businesses were angry at being charged an extra penalty. Domestic public debt stood at $ 1 bn. Private foreign debt had remained almost constant over 2012–14, rising from $ 4.5 bn to $ 4.7 bn, but domestic private debt had risen to $ 4.4 bn.

This was also a period in which the US dollar was rising in value, so the metical (Mt) fell in value from Mt 36 : $ 1 in June to Mt 54 : $ 1 at the end of November. Most consumer goods in the capital Maputo were imported from South Africa, and the exchange rate fell from Mt 2.7 : ZAR (rand) 1 in June to Mt 3.8 : ZAR 1 in late November, although this had been reversed slightly by the end of the year. But this triggered *inflation*, which rose to 10.6% for the year. The standard lending facility rate (paid by commercial banks to borrow from the central bank) was raised from 7.5% in September to 9.75% in December.

All three *credit ratings* agencies downgraded Mozambique, largely due to the Ematum issue. Standard and Poor's downgraded Mozambique from B to B– in July, and in August Moody's downgraded Mozambique from B1 to B2 and changed the outlook to negative. On 31 October, Fitch revised the country's rating downwards from B+ to B because its fiscal profile had "deteriorated sharply over the past year, reflecting high budget deficits, a rapid rise in public debt, volatile government revenue and a widening wage bill". Moody's said the government had "run large fiscal deficits resulting from a high volume of government capital expenditures (16.5% of GDP in 2014), fast-growing current spending and decreasing grants from the international community". Ematum bond repayments started in 2015 at $ 200 m per year, doubling public debt service; Maliane announced on 18 June that he hoped to reschedule the repayments.

For the first time in a decade, Mozambique was forced to ask for a loan from the *IMF*. Several countries, including Mozambique, had stopped taking IMF loans a decade or more before because of the harshness of IMF conditions. Donors demanded that recipient countries should follow IMF programmes, so the IMF had created the Policy Support Instrument, which was to be negotiated with individual countries and had softer, unenforceable conditions. Going back to borrowing from the IMF meant that stricter conditions would be imposed. An IMF team visited Mozambique on 14–28 October and agreed a $ 286 m loan, which was approved by the Executive Board in December. The loan was needed to cover what the IMF called "short term challenges" to the economy (including falling exports due to falling commodity prices, while imports had "continued to grow at a fast pace of 17% year-on-year"), and excessively expansionary policies in the election year 2014, with electoral spending accounting for 0.9% of GDP, as well as Ematum. In a 4 December report, the IMF noted that "the pace of debt accumulation and the increase in public spending in recent years are not sustainable, also resulting from the poor quality of debt contracted and a lack of rigor in project selection criteria". As part of the new loan arrangement, the IMF imposed a stringent set of conditions, including "further fiscal adjustment, continued exchange rate flexibility, and tight liquidity management", as well as cutting spending, greater transparency in selecting public investment projects, and improved VAT management. The government had already promised more rigorous technical assessment of investment projects exceeding $ 50 m. One aspect of fiscal adjustment would be to cut tax exemptions for large corporations, especially VAT import exemptions, which were intended to attract investment. In a 3 December report, the IMF noted that, with the possible exception of Ematum, "there is no evidence of capital flight [because] domestic agents retained their savings in the country".

On 7 December, the Bank of Mozambique issued a new regulation that individuals would not be allowed to use credit cards for more than $ 13,000 in foreign expenditure per year. This was to apply to the total on all credit cards held by one individual. Uncontrolled credit and debit card *spending abroad* was one of the factors contributing to the recent sharp depreciation of the metical, and Bank of Mozambique Governor Ernesto Gove said on 30 November that this type of spending had risen dramatically. Bank cards had been used abroad to the tune of $ 300 m in 2012 but this had jumped to $ 800 m in 2014. The owner of one card (whom Gove did not name) had used it for $ 2 m in purchases abroad in a single year.

Mozambique has one of the largest natural *gas reserves* in Africa, but falling prices slowed decision-making and production was not expected to start until 2021 or 2022. More than $ 100 bn in investment would be required, mainly for the plants to produce liquefied natural gas (LNG). The gas field is split in two, with the half nearest the coast led by Anadarko of the USA and the half further offshore by ENI of Italy. After protracted negotiations and pressure from government, the two agreed on how to use the reserves that straddled their two exploitation zones, but after more than a year of discussions confusion remained over whether they would use a government-controlled logistics base in Pemba. In December, ENI submitted a proposal for its first liquification plant to be an offshore floating plant. Both ENI and Anadarko delayed final investment decisions (FID) because of falling LNG prices, large amounts of LNG coming on to the market, and drawn out negotiations with government; FIDs were not expected until 2016 or 2017. Anadako still had only partial agreements to sell its LNG and did not yet have binding contracts.

Eight of the 13 largest *investment projects* approved between 1990 and 2012 had not gone ahead, according to a study by the Instituto de Estudos Sociais e Económicos (IESE) released on 23 June, corresponding to 60% by value of projects approved. By number, only half of approved projects had gone ahead. Although the government's Investment Promotion Centre ('Centro de Promoção de Investimento') published reports of investments approved, it did not analyse what happened to them and the IESE study was the first to do this. The projects that had not proceeded, or which had already failed included biofuels, forestry and paper, coal, iron and steel, petrochemicals and a hydro-electric dam. Projects approved were valued at $ 35 bn, of which 37% was to be made up of foreign investment, 38% foreign bank loans, 19% domestic bank loans, and 6% domestic investment. The report argued that many projects were speculative, sometimes being given land much in excess of what they needed, and could not raise the necessary funding. Others were proposed by multinational companies simply to keep out competitors, and were never intended to be implemented.

Export data for 2014 was announced in mid-2015. Most of the $ 3.9 bn in exports came from mega-projects: aluminium ($ 1,052 m), coal ($ 491 m), electricity ($ 355 m), gas ($ 340 m) and heavy sands ($ 178 m). Traditional exports were led by tobacco ($ 250 m) followed by timber ($ 120 m), sugar ($ 81 m), cotton ($ 80 m), bananas ($ 49 m), prawns ($ 41 m) and cashew nuts ($ 17 m). A study by researchers at Eduardo Mondlane University concluded that, in the decade between 2003 and 2013, Mozambique had lost over $ 540 m in illegal exports of wood to China. Over 90% of timber exports went to China, most of them undeclared, according to deductions made by comparing official statistics from the two countries; China's imports were 5.7 times greater than the exports officially declared by the National Directorate of Land and Forests.

Montepuez was calculated to be the world's largest supplier of *rubies*, which are found in gravel in an ancient riverbed. The mine expects to process 10 m tonnes of rock per year, with an expected yield of between 1 gm and 35 gms of rubies per tonne. The huge Montepuez Ruby Mining mine – 400 km^2 (40,000 ha) – is 75% owned by the British company Gemfields and 25% by Mwiriti, which in turn is owned by Raimundo Pachinuapa.

The *Family Expenditure Survey* ('Inquérito ao Orçamento Familiar') released on 30 December by the National Statistics Institute ('Instituto Nacional de Estatística') revealed that *inequality* had doubled in just six years. The best-off 20% of Mozambicans spent 14 times as much as the poorest 20%, double the ratio of 7:1 just six years earlier. The survey showed that average per capita expenditure had risen by 40% in real terms in the past six years, but the big gainers were the better-off. In just six years, the top 20% of the population had seen their spending triple, rising from $ 1.93 per person per day to $ 5.88. By contrast, the poorest 20% had seen their spending rise from $ 0.29 per person per day to $ 0.43. If the population is divided into fifths by expenditure, their daily expenditure in dollars per person was $ 0.43, $ 0.75, $ 1.13, $ 1.80 and $ 5.88, suggesting that about half of Mozambicans were living on less than $ 1/day. The rural-urban gap had widened, with urban per capita spending increasing from 2.1 times to 2.5 times rural per capita spending. For rural people, this was not necessarily cash spending, as it included the market value of food they grew and ate and the value of self-built houses. The poorest provinces continued to be Zambézia, with average per capita expenditure of $ 0.82/day and Nampula with $ 0.88/day. "In Mozambique, income inequality has increased despite high rates of economic growth" and "few countries offer such a stark contrast as Mozambique," warned the IMF in a report dated 4 December. "Benefits of growth have not been broadly shared" and "geographical inequality (with much higher income levels in the southern provinces) could also become a source of political tension given that most of the natural resource wealth is located in the northern provinces." IMF resident representative Alex Segura-Ubiergo added that "high levels of inequality hamper government policies to reduce poverty [and] make it difficult to sustain growth" and "can lead to political instability". Mayke Huijbregts, UNICEF's child protection head for Mozambique, said in November that 43% of Mozambican children were suffering from chronic *malnutrition*, the same level as in 2008, and President Nyusi declared on 14 October that levels of poverty and malnutrition remained "unacceptably high".

The Family Expenditure Survey showed that 56% of families had mobile telephones while only 52% had a bed. The percentage of families with a bicycle had declined since 2009, from 38% to 33%, due to a move up to motorcycles (4% up to 8%) and cars (2% up to 4%). Also 10% of families had solar panels and 6% had computers. Illiteracy had fallen from 50% to 45%. But for the 15–19-year-old age group, it remained at 29% – surprising as the survey reported that only 13% said they had not been to school. Illiteracy rates for adults were 30% for men and 58% for women.

Panama disease, a devastating banana disease first identified in 2013 on the Matanuska plantation in Monapo, Nampula, was also identified in Chiure, Cabo Delgado and, on 12 October, the Ministry of Agriculture and Food Security banned all movement of banana saplings and cane from the two companies. The disease had not been successfully controlled and had the potential to wipe out all of

Mozambique's commercial banana production in the next decade. The disease was probably brought in with dirt on the boots or clothes of Matanuska workers from Asia. Matanuska is partly a Norwegian aid project, and the cost to Mozambique of Panama disease was likely to be far more than the value of Norfund investments in Mozambique.

Very heavy rains in Zambézia caused *floods* near Mocuba on 12 January that cut the main north-south road and washed away ten large metal pylons and 15 km of power line, cutting the only electricity line to the north and leaving Nampula, Niassa and Cabo Delgado provinces without electricity until 9 February. In contrast, as the El Niño weather pattern developed, there was *drought* in southern provinces, which threatened to destroy crops in Gaza and Inhambane. The Council of Ministers was told on 4 August that this meant that 138,000 people faced hunger. Rains should have started again in November, but the drought continued into a second rainy season. Southern Mozambique had unusually high temperatures and record highs were reached in South Africa.

Violence remained a common feature. Twenty kidnappings were reported, down from 30 the previous year. Journalist Paulo Machava, editor of the daily newsletter 'Diario de Noticias', was shot dead by unknown assailants on 28 August. Carlos Jeque, a lawyer and politician, was shot and injured on the Maputo ring road in Marracuene on 8 December. Toxic bacteria in beer killed 75 people in Chitima, Tete, on 9 January. They had been drinking a local beer, known as phombe, made from sorghum, maize bran and sugar. The dead included the woman who brewed the beer and all her family. The remains of the beer and the inputs were sent to a forensic lab in the USA, which discovered toxins from the bacterium Burkholderia Gladioli in the beer and the maize. The maize had been affected by flooding and had begun to rot, so could not be used as food, but it had been assumed that it could still be used for brewing. Of 256 people who drank the contaminated phombe, 232 fell ill and 75 died. Mozambique was one of the most dangerous countries in the world to be a pedestrian, according to WHO's 'Global Status Report on Road Safety 2013', published in March. It reported that Mozambique had a high road traffic death rate, with 56% of road deaths being pedestrians.

Namibia

Henning Melber

The year saw the ascendancy of the new Head of State Hage Geingob, perhaps the last member of the first generation of the former liberation movement SWAPO (South West Africa People's Organisation). He took over from Hifikepunye Pohamba, who was for his two terms in office awarded the Mo Ibrahim Prize for good governance. Geingob introduced several institutional innovations and expanded the senior level of the administration. This increased government expenditure and added to the growing fiscal stress. The economic fragility was also exacerbated by global economic volatility and other negative factors. Despite the limitations of the promised prosperity under Geingob, SWAPO further extended its political hegemony through regional and local elections in November. With hardly any opposition remaining in both national chambers and on regional and local authority levels, Namibian democracy de facto was dependent on one party. In terms of its foreign policy, Namibia clearly continued to turn more to the East and announced its planned withdrawal from the ICC.

 | DOI 10.1163/9789004333239_052

Domestic Politics

President-elect Hage Geingob had already taken several initiatives before his swearing in on 21 March. On 2 February, a *presidential council* was announced, composed of Geingob and his two predecessors, the previous prime ministers and their deputies. Nickey Iyambo was appointed as Namibia's first vice president. He had served in all cabinets over the previous 25 years and was the longest-serving minister of the first generation of post-Independence politicians. Among the eight additional MPs appointed with non-voting rights by the president were Pendukeni Iivula-Ithana and Jerry Ekandjo, the two internal party nominees for president who had lost to Geingob. He also resuscitated the fading political careers of Minister of Presidential Affairs Albert Kawana and Governor of the Hardap region Katrina Hanse-Himarwa as members of 'Team Hage'. The former deputy speaker and retired bishop Zephania Kameeta, also from the party's old guard, was brought back to take specific responsibility for the newly created portfolio of poverty eradication and social welfare. The *new cabinet* was announced on 19 March. Four new ministries were created and seven portfolios were renamed. The top-heavy executive structure seemed to represent an effort to reconcile internal party divisions and to secure loyalty. In particular, the expansion of the second-tier level of deputy ministers from 18 to 32 was most likely aimed at inclusivity. Added to the 28 cabinet members, this meant that almost 60% of all MPs were top government officials and led to an estimated 30% increase in the cost of government from N$ 50 m under the Pohamba administration to N$ 65 m. This generosity was widely considered a strategic investment in internal party stability to anchor Geingob's office as president in structures that create loyalty among the beneficiaries. Geingob also recruited several high-paid advisors to the Office of the President, whom he originally called the 'A-team', leaving the media and wider public wondering what role the ministers were supposed to play.

Amidst controversies as to the procedure and in a reportedly tense atmosphere, retired head of state Hifikepunye Pohamba in a surprise move handed over the *party presidency* to Geingob at a SWAPO central committee meeting on 18 April – well ahead of the scheduled elections at the next party congress in 2017. The politburo rejected Geingob's proposal that he be replaced as the party's vice president by a trusted office holder, and so he now held both party offices and the state presidency, which gave him a strong advantage over potential contenders for the next round of leadership contests in both the party and the state.

The president's first *State of the Nation Address*, given in parliament on 21 April showed a clear shift in language from the hitherto mainly party-dominated patriotic history, which had cultivated an exclusive narrative of SWAPO as the sole liberator. Geingob presented a more inclusive discourse. SWAPO was not mentioned once. Instead, the *Namibian house* was created as the new figurative core image and reference point and this metaphor continued to be a constant and integral feature of the president's public statements. However, while deliberately stressing the inclusivity of the nation-building project, Geingob promoted exclusionary tendencies by refusing to comment on gay rights. He also confirmed that those who had fought on the side of the South African army against SWAPO would not be eligible for war veteran status or for the pension awarded to those who had fought for SWAPO. Neither did the president show any inclination towards reconciliation with activists of the party's *Youth League*, four of whom (including the president) had been suspended the year before. They were finally expelled, reportedly at Geingob's instigation, at a meeting of the party's central committee, on 23 July. In August, they announced that they were starting legal proceedings against what they considered a violation of internal party disciplinary procedures.

Reconciliation did take place on other fronts, however. The former foreign minister, Hidipo Hamutenya, who had fallen out with the party leadership in 2004 in the battle for the country's presidency, had then established the Rally for Democracy and Progress (RDP) as an opposition party. After initial successes as the official opposition, it had faltered and become irrelevant. Hamutenya returned to SWAPO on 28 August and other previously higher-ranking SWAPO members who had joined him in the RDP followed his lead. At a SWAPO gathering on 21 November, Hamutenya urged the party to rally behind President Geingob. The collapse of the RDP was widely considered as another sign that the *SWAPO hegemony* was becoming further entrenched, with the cooptation of several leading opposition members.

In a surprise move, Geingob appointed Katuutire Kaura, the former president of the Democratic Turnhalle Alliance (DTA), on 25 September as advisor to the governor of the Kunene region – the only region in which SWAPO held no absolute majority until the forthcoming *regional council and local authority elections* on 27 November. The media expressed great concern that the opposition parties seemed weaker than ever and that election campaigns were largely absent. The only newsworthy items were internal SWAPO power struggles over the list of candidates: 26 of the 121 regional council constituencies and five of the 57 local authorities were left uncontested to SWAPO, which showed the organisational weakness of the opposition. Voter turnout for the 95 contested constituencies in the regional elections was 36.5%, an all-time low. SWAPO candidates took 112 elected regional council seats and won a clear majority in all 14 regions. All but two of the 42 members of the National Council were SWAPO representatives and SWAPO remained in firm control of 54 of the 57 local authorities. For many observers, this was a clear indication that there was not much democratic competition left in Namibia.

The *high treason trial* over the failed attempt at secession in the Eastern Caprivi region of 2 August 1999 finally ended with a verdict on 8 December. Of the originally more than 120 accused, around 30 were found guilty and received long jail sentences. More than 20 of those originally arrested had died in jail (bail was refused even for those suffering from serious medical conditions), while most others had had their charges dismissed during the course of the trial. Many of them had spent up to 16 years in prison. The judge harshly criticised the police for using torture to force those arrested to implicate others and to confess.

On 20 November, retired president Pohamba received the 2014 *Mo Ibrahim Prize* for African Leadership in Accra for his terms in office. The prize, given to heads of state in recognition of good governance, had not been awarded to anyone for several years. The media and the wider public applauded the recognition, despite having been rather critical of Pohamba in the past.

Foreign Affairs

Despite his appeal to cabinet members to limit their travel activities, President Geingob was absent from Namibia on a number of occasions during his first nine months in office. The *intensive presidential travel schedule* included visits to 19 cities in 14 countries. A working trip to Angola on 16 April was Geingob's first state visit. On 20 April, he attended the SADC Summit in Harare (Zimbabwe), followed by a working visit to South Africa where he met president Jacob Zuma on 6 May. On 29 May, he attended the inauguration of President Buhari in Nigeria and visited Mali, and on 10 June he was a co-signatory to the Sharm-el-Sheikh declaration launching the COMESA-EAC-SADC Tripartite Free Trade Agreement in Egypt. He made a state visit to Cuba on 14–16 September before visiting the USA to receive the African Political Leader Award on 18 September in Washington DC (jointly with the Gambian autocrat Jammeh) and an Honorary Doctorate at Fordham University in New York on 22 September, to deliver his maiden speech at the opening of the 70th UN General Assembly and to receive the Africa-America Institute Lifetime Achievements and Distinguished Alumnus Award, both on 29 September. He made an official state visit to Tanzania on 11–12 October, and attended the 3rd Africa-India Forum Summit in New Delhi at the end of October. On 27 November, Geingob left for a three-day general meeting of the Commonwealth Heads of State in Malta, followed by attendance at the COP 21 climate summit in Paris on 31 November and participation in a Global Africa Investment Summit in London on 1–2 December. The tour concluded with the China-Africa-Forum in Johannesburg (South Africa) on 4–5 December. The local newspaper 'The Namibian' reported on 18 December that, according to its own investigations, the president had earned an additional N$ 2.4 m in travel allowances during the year, and had flown more than 70,000 km at a minimum cost of N$ 3.5 m in airplane fuel.

For the *AU Summit* in Johannesburg on 14 June, Geingob had prepared a speech in which he praised Robert Mugabe as his role model and lashed out against the ICC as an abomination because of its undue interference in the internal affairs of sovereign states. During his state visit to Tanzania on 11–12 October, he lobbied for the withdrawal of Tanzania from the ICC. In line with recommendations already formulated earlier by the African National Congress in South Africa and SWAPO at home,

Minister of Information and government spokesman Tjekero Tweya announced at a press conference on 23 November that the government had decided to withdraw from the ICC as part of a reformulation of the country's foreign policy.

On 15 June, the foreign ministers of Namibia and *South Africa* signed an MoU concerning the allocation of a pledge made on the occasion of an earlier state visit by President Zuma in November 2013 for 100 m South African rand in drought relief, half to be spent on procurement of seeds and maize meal and half on drilling boreholes and related water projects. In a rare sign of international solidarity by members of the public, some 200 mainly younger people had demonstrated on 28 April against xenophobic attacks taking place in South Africa, and had marched on the South African High Commission in the Namibian capital, Windhoek, and handed over a petition, asserting that violence against any African was an attack on all Africans.

Friendly relations with *China*, officially termed an 'all-weather friendship', continued. On 30 March, a top-ranking Chinese military delegation led by State Councillor and Defence Minister Chang Wanquan met President Geingob in Windhoek, thereby reinforcing earlier rumours that the Chinese government intended to establish a naval base in Walvis Bay harbour. Questioned at a press conference the next day, Geingob mentioned that rumours might kill a country. Confronted with speculation during the BBC's 'Hard Talk' on 1 December, Geingob neither confirmed nor denied Chinese interest in the naval base. The US Embassy in Windhoek on 10 December categorically denied that the USA had approached the government with a view to obtaining a naval base in Walvis Bay, contrary to what Geingob had indicated during the 'Hard Talk' interview. Attending the China-Africa Forum Summit in Johannesburg on 4/5 December, Geingob met again with Chinese President Xi Jinping, whom he had already visited in 2014 when he had been prime minister. In his speech there, he emphasised that the partnership with China "is one built on long lasting and historic solidarity, as well as mutual respect. It is therefore offensive when we are lectured by certain nations and warned about the so-called Chinese colonization of Africa." He applauded a number of key Chinese investments in Namibia and praised as invaluable the two countries' deepening cooperation, especially with regard to infrastructure. Chinese companies had huge stakes in Namibian nuclear mining operations and were in control of large parts of the construction industry, dominating competition for public tenders in the sector such as for roads, railways, harbours, airports and office buildings.

Diplomatic relations with *Western countries* featured less prominently. French Minister for Ecology, Sustainable Development and Energy Ségolène Royal visited Namibia in early August and met with the president and her counterparts at the Ministry for Mines and Energy. The French mining giant Areva was among the major companies with operations in Namibia's uranium sector. Accusations of graft and a probe into dubious deals, which involved Geingob as a former Areva consultant, emerged in early December. Neither the company nor the president commented on their past relationship.

Relations with *Germany* were historically close but also precarious. During the year, both countries entered a new stage as the German government indicated that it was prepared to accept the term genocide as appropriate description of the atrocities committed against the anti-colonial resistance movement (1904–1907). At the end of the year, both countries appointed special representatives in order to seek a common ground with regard to dealing with their shared past. Meanwhile, representatives of German civil society and agencies of the descendants of the Namibian victim groups complained that they were not part of the negotiations.

Socioeconomic Developments

Overall, public concern over the government's economic policy and its expenditure rose considerably during the first months of the Geingob administration, and was also fuelled by the marked increase in the number of highly-paid senior officials and the expansion of the cabinet, alongside considerably increased benefits for political office bearers.

Average annual per capita income of $ 9,418 for the estimated population of 2.3 m put Namibia into the category of a higher middle-income country. According to the 2014 data presented in UNDP's Human Development Report (HDR) for 2015, it ranked along with Morocco as 126th out of 188 countries on the HDI index, with a value of 0.628, placing it in the *medium human development category*. But when the HDI is adjusted for inequality, it falls by 43.6% to 0.354, leading to a drop of 25 places (the second worst world-wide after Iran). On the basis of 2013 data, the HDR categorised 44.9% of the population as living in *multiple poverty* – 21.4% higher than the proportion of people living on a daily income of less than $ 1.25 and hence classified as 'extremely poor' on the basis of their monetary income. 'Multiple poverty', on the other hand, is a category that considers access to health and education facilities, sanitation, water and related services as factors contributing to destitution. A further 19.3% of the population were classified as close to multiple poverty. This means that almost two-thirds of the population were living in multiple poverty. Average life expectancy was 64.8 years (62 for men and 67.3 for women). This represented a gradual increase in life expectancy, returning to figures at Independence, and suggested that the worst effects of HIV/AIDS, with the accompanying decline of life expectancy, had been left behind.

New Minister of Finance Calle Schlettwein presented the annual *budgets* 2015/16 to 2017/18 on 31 March. Four key priorities were identified for guiding fiscal policy: inclusive growth, poverty reduction, wealth creation and service delivery, including accountability and value for money. For the year 2015/16, a revenue increase of 11.4% was forecaste (N$ 58.4 bn). Expenditure was expected to increase by 11.6% to

N$ 67.1 bn, of which 83.5% was allocated as an operational budget and 16.5% as a development budget for investment. Close to N$ 4 bn were earmarked as interest payments for debt servicing. Voting on expenditure again allocated the highest proportion to the two educational ministries, which received in total almost N$ 15 bn. The Ministry of Defence was, as in previous years, the second largest recipient of funds with N$ 7.2 bn, followed by the health ministry with N$ 6.5 bn and the police with N$ 4.7 bn. The policy of subsidies for state-owned enterprises continued unabated with transfers of approximately 14% of total spending, mainly to support operational activities. Investments from the development budget were mainly allocated to transport (N$ 2.8 bn), urban and rural development (N$ 1.3 bn) and agriculture, water and forestry (N$ 1.2 bn).

The ongoing *deficit* contributed to a further rise in the debt-to-GDP ratio, which was expected to double despite a major increase in GDP from the 2011 level of 16% to well above 30%. As observed in an analysis carried out by the local Institute for Public Policy Research (IPPR), "this trend is highly concerning and ultimately not sustainable". Total government guarantees were projected to increase to 11.3% of GDP by 2017/18, well beyond the original target of 10% maximum. As the IPPR commented, this highlighted the government's "continued utilization of all possible funding sources, to their maximum". Figures produced by the Bank of Namibia showed that at the end of November state *debt* had increased by 21% from N$ 32.2 bn in 2014 to N$ 39 bn, while foreign currency reserves were close to N$ 23.8 bn, compared with N$ 22.7 bn a year before. In October, the government raised a second Eurobond of US$ 750 m (equivalent to some N$ 10.4 bn at the exchange rate then), of which US$ 300 m would be used to support the foreign reserve position and US$ 450 m to finance development projects. By year's end, estimates suggested that, due to the additional borrowing, a lower than expected GDP growth and the unfavourable currency exchange rate (the N$ is pegged to the South African rand, which during the year depreciated by over 30%) debt had accumulated to account for over 35% of GDP, which government had originally declared the maximum ceiling for its fiscal policy. Financial observers expressed growing concern at the lack of fiscal prudence. In a press release on 24 September, the IMF summarised the Article IV Consultation and warned that, due to several factors, risks to a sound economy were increasing. Meanwhile, the trade deficit increased by over 100% in the third quarter of the year compared with 2014, and displayed vulnerability to external shocks.

On 3 November, Finance Minister Schlettwein presented a *mid-year budget review* to parliament and had bad news as regards the income from the SACU revenue fund, which had run an estimated deficit of N$ 7.6 bn in the 2014/15 financial year. This implied not only a downward adjustment of future SACU receipts (which account for a third of Namibia's total revenue), but also repayment of a N$ 3 bn share for the next financial year. He also announced a downward adjustment of 4.9% in revenue income to N$ 55.6 bn and necessary cost-saving measures to reduce expenditure, as well as re-allocation of funds between ministries to meet spending priorities.

Meanwhile, salary increases for civil servants were also announced to the tune of N$ 1 bn, while criticism of a highly-paid bloated public service (with some 100,000 employees) grew. The proposed introduction if a 'solidarity tax', originally applicable to monthly incomes over N$ 6,600 was heavily criticised by the public, who felt that first those better and best off should be taxed at a higher rate. Government then backtracked and announced that the idea would be thought through again – an indication that certain concerns were still under consideration by policy makers.

Soon after moving into office, president Geingob had announced an increase in the old-age pension for those over 60 years of age from N$ 600 to N$ 1,000 a month as a much welcome effort to reduce poverty. He also created a new ministry for poverty alleviation and declared the fight against poverty to be his government's top priority, but little was achieved during the year to ease the general misery, and *hunger* remained a daily experience for many ordinary Namibians. According to information presented at a Food and Nutrition Security strategic review workshop in early September, the UN State of Food Insecurity Report for 2015 showed that 42.3% of the population was undernourished in 2014, compared with 27.3% in 2002. These data contrasted with claims that poverty had been reduced by 11% during the previous decade. On 20 November, the local UNICEF representative announced that an estimated 270,000 children were living in poverty, with 140,000 of them in severe circumstances. A total of 880,000 Namibians (42%) were below the age of 18, while the same percentage of Namibians was classified by the FAO as malnourished.

The *school system* continued to perform dismally. After some positive trends in 2014, the end of year exams showed a decline in pass rates at senior school level. Grade 12 (school leaving) exams were passed by 6,056 students with results that allow access to university, i.e. about one- fifth fewer than in the previous year (7,536). Pass rates in the grade 10 exams required for access to senior school levels, were only obtained by some 20,000 out of 37,000 students (about 54%). Insufficiently trained and under-motivated teachers, lack of material infrastructure, and the unsupportive environment provided by the living conditions of many students were considered as contributing factors, as well as the inefficient spending of state funds.

Strong El Niño effects led to a massive *drought*. The municipality of Windhoek announced water restrictions in the capital towards the end of the year after several appeals to reduce household consumption showed little result. Water reserves fell dramatically and an emergency was looming. The situation in rural areas, which had suffered already from bad harvests in 2014, continued to deteriorate. An Agricultural Inputs and Household Food Security Situation report released in December by the National Early Warning and Food Information Unit warned that household *food security* had significantly weakened in the seven major northern communal crop-producing regions, as most households had exhausted their supplies from the poor harvest of the last season. Food insecurity was exacerbated by the fact that a large number of draught animals that were used to plough had died because of the drought. A hefty price increase for stable foods was predicted, which would further worsen the situation.

Natural resources were depleted not only with respect to extensive land use, underground minerals and fish along the coast, but also by *poaching*, which increased dramatically. By the end of the year a total of at least 80 rhinos had been killed illegally (mainly in the Etosha National Park), compared with the 25 registered in 2014, four in 2013 and two in 2012. A spectacular on-going court case implicated four Chinese citizens in smuggling rhino horns and other illegal hunting trophies and there were allegations that high-ranking officials were also involved in such organised crime. The Chinese-Namibian friendship seemed to be effective in multiple aspects, though growing sentiment among ordinary people seemed to suggest it was not welcomed by all.

South Africa

Sanusha Naidu

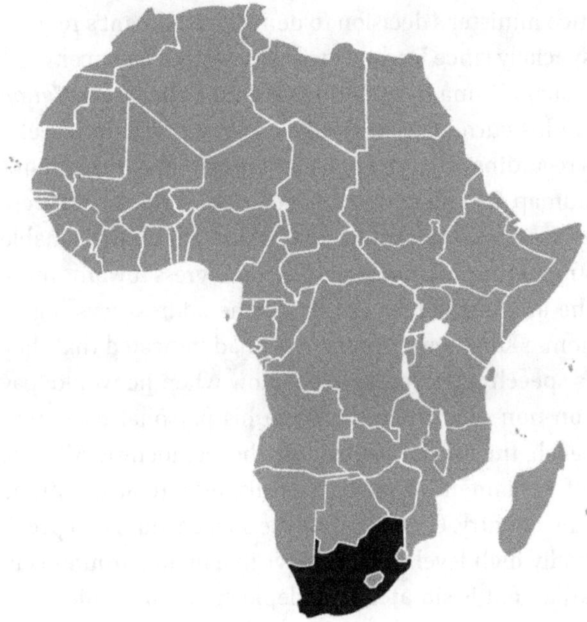

Following the 20th anniversary (in 2014) of its first democratic election, South Africa commemorated the 25th anniversary of Nelson Mandela's release from prison. Despite the symbolic significance of the occasion, harsh realities were a reminder of the limits to the transformation since then. As more scandals emerged in the public domain, the political, economic and social landscape underwent some sobering checks and balances that tested the vision of the Rainbow Nation.

Domestic Politics

The year started off with a critical test for the *Truth and Reconciliation Commission*. On 30 January, Eugene de Kock, the commander of the South African Police counterinsurgency unit under the apartheid government, commonly known as the Vlakplaas hit squad, which functioned as a paramilitary unit, was granted parole on medical grounds after being convicted and imprisoned for life. This brought mixed reactions, especially among the families of those who had been tortured and killed at the hands of Vlakplaas operatives, who protested against what they saw as a failure of justice. At the same time Justice Minister Tshililo Michael Masutha denied

 | DOI 10.1163/9789004333239_053

parole to Clive Derby-Lewis, who had been sentenced to life imprisonment for the assassination of Communist Party leader Chris Hani. Applying for medical parole on the grounds of lung cancer, Derby-Lewis filed an urgent application in May at the Pretoria High Court to have his case heard. The court ruled in his favour and ordered the Ministry of Correctional Service to release him on medical parole. The judge also found that the justice minister's decision to deny the applicant's request for a fifth time was flawed, especially since Derby-Lewis was in stage 4 cancer.

On 12 February, President Jacob Zuma delivered his eighth *State of the Nation Address* (SONA), the second in his current term in office. In the preceding weeks, there were high expectations regarding what the president might unveil as a political, economic and social roadmap for the country. Chief among the issues were calls for the creation of better economic conditions that would enable sustainable jobs, more government investment to stimulate growth, and progress towards more reliable energy access. But the atmosphere leading up to the address was highly politically charged. The Economic Freedom Fighters (EFF) had indicated that they would disrupt the president's speech with demands to know when he would 'pay back the money' expended on non-security upgrades to his personal residence, Nkandla. A day before the speech, the official opposition, the Democratic Alliance (DA), marched to the gates of Parliament to mark their displeasure at the Zuma government's governance of the country. On the day of the speech, unlike in previous years, there was an unusually high level of security visible in and around central Cape Town where the Parliament is situated. The deployment of public order police, riot squads, patrolling Nyalas (a locally manufactured 4×4 armoured personnel carrier), and the use of water canons in and around the vicinity of Parliament indicated a highly securitised environment. In addition, Parliament had ceded its authority to state intelligence services, which had taken control of the event and the entire accreditation process. One commentator observed that there was "a sense of unease", which added to "one's growing apprehension". Even before Zuma could deliver the speech, tensions were running high in the *National Assembly* because a jamming device had been installed to scramble all cellular networks and block communications. Opposition parties and the media protested against what they saw as a deliberate attempt to subvert the right to information, which they saw as an infringement of the Constitution. A chant of "Bring back the signal" lasted for about ten minutes before the mobile phone signal was restored. The rationale for blocking communications was bizarre: a comment in the 'Daily Maverick' said, "The misguided attempt to protect the president from embarrassment was in fact sabotage of his own speech, as anything he was announcing to the nation could not be transmitted through electronic communications." Speaker of the House Baleka Mbete promised to initiate an investigation into the communication fiasco, but the situation in the National Assembly spiraled out of control. A few minutes into the delivery of Zuma's speech, EFF MPs raised a point of order asking when he was going to pay back the money. This interruption led to protracted and heated debate as to whether SONA was the appropriate platform for raising such issues, which digressed into conflicting interpretations of the parliamentary rules handbook. The speaker issued warnings that disruptive MPs would be ejected from the house and eventually ruled Julius Malema, Floyd Shivambu and Mbuyiseni Ndlozi out of order and asked the sergeant at arms to remove them. The scenes that followed were surreal. *Scuffles* broke out between plain-clothes security personnel and EFF MPs and all of the EFF members were forcibly removed from the chamber, several being injured. There was also confusion as to whether the security forces that entered the house were actually parliamentary security personnel. The DA protested against the violent treatment of MPs and the presence of armed men, allegedly public order police, in the chamber, and staged a walkout. The MPs belonging to the United Democratic Movement, the Congress of the People and Agang also left. The speech continued, though overshadowed by the earlier chaos. Even though the president unveiled a nine-point development proposal as a roadmap for the country, the events of the evening led one journalist to write: "SONA 2015: The day our country broke".

Speaking outside the National Assembly, the leader of the EFF, Julius Malema, declared to the media that the EFF would continue to ask relevant questions, even if they were beaten up. He described the event as a sign of a police state, where in the absence of political answers the security apparatus intervened: "We've always said the ANC [African National Congress] has sent South Africa into a security state, so today it was confirmed." The SONA chaos also brought into focus the issue of *separation of powers* between the Executive and the Legislature.

On 17 March, the DA submitted a *motion of no confidence* in Zuma's leadership, which was debated in Parliament. An earlier action initiated by Agang SA had been withdrawn. Even though the motion was unsuccessful as the majority of ANC MPs voted against it, this was a significant step as it was the first time that a sitting president had faced such action.

Also in March, a group of students from the University of Cape Town (UCT) embarked on a campaign for the removal of a statue of Cecil John Rhodes. Calling themselves the 'Rhodes Must Fall' movement, the group declared that they would mobilise "for direct action against the reality of institutional racism" at UCT. The campaign soon morphed into a country-wide student protest across various universities targeting what was seen as a lack of racial transformation in the higher education sector. Several universities saw disruptions to their curriculum and the protests evolved into violent clashes that caused the destruction of university property.

April saw the resurgence of *xenophobic violence*. The attacks started in Durban and spread to Johannesburg. It was alleged that the situation was further aggravated by comments made by the Zulu King Goodwill Zwelithini. In a speech on 20 April, he demanded that foreigners "should go back to their countries". Local people looted foreign-owned shops, forcing many foreign nationals to relocate and seek protection in police stations. About 300 people were arrested for their involvement in the attacks. The unrest also saw the killing of Emmanuel Sithole, a Mozambican national, which caused a public outcry following the release of photographs of the assault in the 'Sunday Times'. Four suspects were arrested for the murder but it was not clear whether the attack was motivated by xenophobia or by some other kind of criminal intent. Some countries, including Malawi, initiated repatriation programmes, while others announced that they would evacuate their nationals from the country. Several thousand people took to the streets of Johannesburg to demonstrate against attacks on immigrants, but this had little effect. In October, there were sustained assaults on foreigners in Grahamstown and the Eastern Cape, which resulted in more than 500 people being displaced and more than 300 homes and shops looted. Reactions to the violence by government ministers did little to resolve the situation. Minister of Small Business Development Lindiwe Zulu responded to the violence with a comment that foreign business owners "cannot barricade themselves in and not share their practices with local business owners". The minister's comments drew strong widespread criticism. The government proposed a commission of inquiry into what had sparked the attacks and the alleged involvement of King Goodwill Zwelithini. In addition, it was felt by some that the economic competitiveness of foreigners was undermining the profit margins of local entrepreneurs and this perception was identified as one of the main causes for the violence.

On 9–10 May, the *DA national elective convention* took place in Port Elizabeth. In the months leading up to the congress, there were strong indications that Western Cape Premier Helen Zille was going to stand down as party leader and in April, she announced that she had decided not to stand for re-election. This sparked discussions around the need for the party to effectively address its internal struggle for racial transformation. The party's leader in Parliament, Mmusi Maimane, won a landslide victory to become the first ever elected black party leader. Being a pastor and running under a campaign slogan of 'Believe in tomorrow', Maimane's victory also coincided with the party's adoption of a new values charter

Towards the end of May, reports surfaced of allegations that South Africa had paid a $ 10 m bribe to win the bid to host the *2010 FIFA World Cup*. The allegations were made by one of FIFA's executives and former vice president Jack Warner, who was being investigated by the US authorities for bribery. Both the South African sports minister and the head of the bidding team, Danny Jordaan, rejected these claims as absurd, countering that it would not make sense to pay for votes four years after the bid was won, but the allegations continued to cast a shadow on the 2010 tournament. In the aftermath, Danny Jordaan, who was president of the South African Football Association, was appointed as mayor of the Nelson Mandela Municipality in *Port Elizabeth*, which the ANC had narrowly won in the 2011 local government elections, but which had been hamstrung by factional battles and was widely believed to be heading for an electoral defeat by the opposition DA in the

2016 local government elections. Jordaan's appointment was intended to resolve the political weakness of the ANC there and also to address financial issues with a view to restoring voter confidence.

On 28 May, National Police Minister Nkosinathi Nhleko released the findings of an investigation into the security upgrades of President Zuma's *Nkandla* residence. The minister had been tasked with determining whether the president was obliged to pay for some of the non-security upgrades, which included a swimming pool, a visitor centre, a cattle kraal and an amphitheatre. His report concluded that the president was not required to pay back any of the money, in direct contradiction to the public protector's report, which had found that Zuma had gained personally from the renovations and should therefore pay for some of the upgrades. Opposition parties denounced the findings of Nhleko's report as being biased, though domestic public opinion was divided.

On 25 June, Zuma released the keenly awaited report of the *Marikana Commission*, which had investigated the massacre at the Lonmin mine in 2012. It exonerated several political figures of being implicated, including Deputy President Cyril Ramaphosa, but it questioned the fitness of Police Commissioner Riah Phiyega to hold office. The Commission also found that those who had committed the killings, both police and strikers, as well as the failure of the mining company Lonmin to protect employees, should be investigated. Reactions to the Commission's findings were mixed. Opposition parties and civil society organisations pointed to inconsistencies in the Commission's report and some bias in favour of the mining company and political figures. The report was also criticised for failing to address the issue of compensation for the families of the victims and the widening gulf between mining companies and their workers.

The *court case against Julius Malema*, leader of the EFF, in which he was charged with fraud and corruption, was dismissed in August after the state prosecution team asked for another postponement of the case following several previous adjournments. The dismissal did not mean that the charges against Malema had been completely dropped and Malema noted that he would be prepared for them to be re-instated. At the same time, he and the EFF considered the charges represented a political witch-hunt against the party and its leader because they were challenging the Zuma government on its governance weaknesses.

Towards the end of August, eight former policemen who had been charged with the murder of a Mozambican national, Mido Macia, in February 2013, were found guilty and sentenced to 15 years each in prison. The case had caused domestic and international outrage and brought into focus the urgent need to address *police brutality*.

In September, the national police commissioner presented the annual *crime statistics* to Parliament. Overall, they showed a downward trend; there had been an increase in murder and aggravated robbery but a drop in the reporting of sexual offences. Think tanks were quick to point out that the drop in the reporting of sexual offences did not mean that fewer such acts were committed but was rather an indication that victims did not feel comfortable reporting such incidents and that there was a high level of distrust in the police. Discrepancies were also highlighted by organisations such as Africa Check, which challenged the validity of the statistics, noting that the figures were already six months old. This led to a call for crime statistics to be reported on a continuous basis.

Zuma announced a *cabinet reshuffle* on 22 September. With the death of Minister for Public Service and Administration Collins Chabane in March in a car accident, the post had to be filled. But the cabinet reshuffle also sparked various controversies regarding the timing of the shuffle and why certain portfolios were undergoing ministerial changes. Moving Minister of Mining Adv Ngoako Ramathlodi to fill Chabane's post, the president brought in a relatively unknown Free State MP, Mosebenzi Zwane, to take over the mining portfolio. The reshuffle caught industry actors and analysts off guard, leading to speculation that a faction known as the premier league in the ANC was seeking to extend its control of state resources.

On 14 October, Zuma announced the *suspension of Police Commissioner* Riah Phiyega, following the Marikana Commission's finding that she was unfit to hold the position. A commission of inquiry was set up to determine Phiyega's suitability to be police commissioner and allegations that she and others had misled the Marikana Commission regarding the events that had led to the killing of 34 miners in 2012. Phiyega described her suspension as malicious and vindictive and considered that the reasons for it ran deeper than the Marikana issue alone. It appeared that she had been trying to clean up the police ministry's awarding of tenders and contracts, which had apparently been granted without proper procedures. In an interview with the 'Sunday Times', Phiyega alleged that certain high-profile individuals were "hellbent" on undoing the tight financial controls in the South African Police Service for their own gain. It would seem that the relationship between Police Minister Nhleko and Phiyega was complex and it was further exacerbated when the police minister announced that Phiyega had been found guilty by a ministerial reference group of misconduct, perjury and fraud.

On 9–12 October, the ANC held its 4th *National General Council* (NGC) meeting at Gallagher Estate in Midrand. The meeting was convened to discuss the strategic, organisational and political issues facing the party. Primarily aimed at carrying out a mid-term review of resolutions agreed at the 53rd National Elective Conference in 2012, the NGC provided a platform to assess the direction of the party. Key issues were: 1) a drop in membership numbers and how to strengthen party support; 2) questions around Zuma serving a third term and his successor as the next ANC president; and 3) the impact of internal factionalism and divisions on ANC cohesion.

From mid October, university students embarked on a nation-wide protest against a proposed 10.5% increase in fees at the University of Witwatersrand (Wits). Hashtagged *#Feesmustfall*, the protests spread like wildfire across South

Africa's higher education sector and morphed into what some analysts and journalists saw as an unprecedented mass awakening of the country's youth in democratic South Africa. Sparked by the #Rhodesmustfall movement, which evolved into #Feesmustfall, the protests were about more than the inability to afford the costs of higher education. There was an outcry at the failure of the political system and the inability to lift the burden of being black and poor. Since most campuses were marred by violence and closed for several days into November, university authorities and government officials tried to find an amicable solution to the crisis, which brought the university calendar to a standstill and led to several universities postponing examinations. The situation reached a standoff on 21 October, when approximately 5,000 students marched to Parliament during the finance minister's medium term expenditure framework speech. They broke through barricades and occupied the parliamentary precinct area, demanding to be heard and asking for the higher education minister and the president to address them. The situation soon deteriorated into a standoff between police and student demonstrators, leading to violent altercations between students and police and security personnel, with the latter using stun and smoke grenades to disperse the students. Student leaders were arrested, among them the children of prominent anti-apartheid activists such as Frank Chikane. Some observers commented that the confrontation was reminiscent of the Soweto Uprising of 1976. The minister of higher education proposed a lower increase of 6%, but this did little to satisfy student demands. Eventually, the Department of Higher Education accepted that there would be no fee increase for 2016, but university authorities did not believe that this would solve the financial crisis, some indicating that repairing the damage done to university property would escalate costs.

In November, Parliament came to a standstill because of disruption caused by workers called on strike by the National Education Health and Allied Workers Union for better working conditions, delivery of performance bonuses and an end to outsourcing. Police used aggressive tactics to deal with protesting workers. Almost four weeks after workers went on strike and protracted negotiations with parliamentary management, a deal was negotiated and the strike ended.

On 9 December, afterwards labelled 9/12, Zuma announced the *removal of Finance Minister Nhlanhla Nene*, sending shockwaves through domestic and international markets. Nene's redeployment to the BRICS Bank was not seen as a legitimate reason to relieve the country's first black finance minister of his position. Nene was replaced by David van Rooyen, considered a relatively lightweight MP. With the economy already under strain and the currency weakening, the reaction from business, labour, former ANC stalwarts and ministers, and the general public led to a massive backlash condemning the decision. The domestic reaction and internal discussions in the ANC forced Zuma to replace van Rooyen with Pravin Gordhan, a previous finance minister considered as more market friendly. In the space of three days, South Africa had three different finance ministers. Speculation was rife that the abrupt removal of Nene had political causes. Nene was looking into wasteful spending in government departments and state-owned enterprises, as evidenced by his reluctance to fund the R (rand) 1 trn nuclear programme, his inquiry into the squandering of funds at the South African Broadcasting Corporation and his ruling against South African Airways in negotiations with Airbus. But there were also indications that the decision was affected by outside influence, namely that of the Indian Gupta family. EFF Deputy President Floyd Shivambu argued that the Guptas had established a solid network inside the ANC, with "disproportionate and decisive influence in what happens in the ruling party and the state". Zuma's decision to fire Nene led to country-wide demonstrations on 15 December under the slogan *#ZumamustFall*.

Foreign Affairs

Generally speaking, South Africa's international engagement continued with little change. In January, South Africa became *chair of the G77 and China* and coordinated the G77 and China positions in the negotiations for the 2030 Agenda for Sustainable Development, which was adopted at a UN Summit in September, and during the third International Conference on Financing for Development, which resulted in the Addis Ababa Action Agenda. During the same month, South Africa took part in the SADC election observer mission to Zambia.

During the 24th AU Summit in Addis Ababa (Ethiopia) in late January, South Africa was approached to host the 25th AU Assembly in July. Hosting the Assembly tested South Africa's obligations under international law. During the Summit, the NGO Southern African Litigation Centre (SALC) brought a court action with the aim of compelling the South African government to *arrest Sudanese President Omar al-Bashir* in an attempt to force South Africa to abide by its obligation as a signatory to the Rome Statute. The SALC legal team argued that South Africa had a constitutional duty to comply with international and domestic law and apply the arrest warrant issued by the ICC. The South African government's legal counsel argued that, under customary international law and treaty law, namely, the Host State Agreement under which the summit was held, al-Bashir had immunity. The court ruled in favour of SALC and ordered that the South African government had a duty to arrest al-Bashir. Meanwhile, as the case was being heard, al-Bashir had left the country. Responding to the court judgment, the government issued a press briefing in which Minister in the Presidency Jeff Radebe noted that detailed meetings had been held with the ICC regarding the al-Bashir issue. Radebe went on to say, "The ICC must have been aware that South Africa would, in the execution of the warrant, breach its existing treaty obligations with the AU. That must be the only plausible reason why the ICC had invited South Africa to consult with it. Having extended an invitation to South Africa to consult, the ICC had a duty to consult with good faith with South Africa and to assist it to comply with its obligations to the ICC and the AU." The al-Bashir issue led to calls at the ANC NGC conference to re-evaluate South Africa's membership of the ICC.

During the course of the year, Deputy President Cyril Ramaphosa continued to act as envoy on *mediation efforts in Lesotho* and South Sudan. His role as SADC facilitator on the unfolding political and security crisis in Lesotho resulted in elections being held in February. During the course of the year, Lesotho's political issues escalated with the apparent killing of an army general allegedly involved in a mutiny plot against the government of Prime Minister Mosilisi. A SADC Commission of Inquiry was set up to investigate the incident but it was experiencing serious setbacks by December due to the non-cooperation of some senior Lesotho officials. Ramaphosa had to calm tensions, which seemed to be delicately balanced by year's end. Some observers pointed to Ramaphosa's statesmanship and he was praised for his maturity in restoring some normalcy to Lesotho's political and security affairs through dialogue.

On 31 May, President Zuma made a working visit to Tanzania to participate in the EAC Heads of State Summit, where discussions revolved around the political and security situation in *Burundi*. Given the role that South Africa, and Zuma in particular, had played in negotiating the peace deal there in 2000 following the civil war, leaders of the EAC saw South Africa's role as pivotal in dealing with the current crisis. South Africa's position was informed by following a regional approach but the country's reticence regarding the situation sometimes raised questions over whether Pretoria was genuinely focused on resolving conflicts across the continent. This issue surfaced in December, when South Africa refused to be part of an AU-led 5,000-strong African Protection and Prevention Mission to Burundi (MAPROBU) to protect civilians and prevent the escalation of civil strife. Given that Zuma had been instrumental in proposing the African Capacity for Immediate Response to Crises (ACIRC), established by the AU in 2013 to enable volunteer states to respond quickly to such situations, sending troops under MAPROBU would appear to have been an ideal platform for Pretoria to demonstrate its commitment to ACIRC, but the Zuma government gave a weak response, citing lack of personnel. Some think-tanks saw this as a lost opportunity and were baffled since South Africa was also chair of the AU Peace and Security Commission. It also brought into question South Africa's credibility as a mediator.

In July, the Department of International Relations and Cooperation (DIRCO) launched *two foreign policy institutions*: the South African Association of Former Ambassadors, High Commissioners and Chief Representatives, and the South African Council on International Relations (SACOIR). The purpose of the former was to create a platform for former ambassadors, high commissioners and chief representatives to offer their extensive experience, expertise and institutional memory on international relations and diplomacy in the service of the execution of South Africa's foreign policy interests. The latter, SACOIR, was made up of members appointed from academia, business, civil society and labour, and was to serve as a consultative platform for South African think-tanks, academics and other relevant representatives of civil society to interact with DIRCO on the development and implementation of South Africa's foreign policy. SACOIR was also envisaged as helping to implement the recommendations of the National Development Plan on the country's foreign policy focus.

A *Foreign Service Bill* was tabled in Parliament on 4 November, having been approved by cabinet in August. The Bill provided for a single foreign service system and created an enabling legislative framework through which the foreign service would be managed and regulated by DIRCO. In addition the Bill, which was laid open for public comment, would enhance the efficiency, accountability and cost-effectiveness of capitalising on opportunities abroad to advance South Africa's foreign policy and developmental agenda. The Bill aimed to professionalise South Africa's diplomatic community.

South Africa attended the 3rd *India-Africa Forum Summit* hosted in New Delhi at the end of October. The Summit saw South Africa reaffirm relations with India under its new government. In early December, South Africa hosted the *Forum on China-Africa Cooperation* (FOCAC) in Johannesburg. Elevated to heads of state level, the Forum was preceded by a bilateral meeting between Beijing and Pretoria, which saw the signing of 26 investment and trade agreements worth about $ 6 bn. South Africa saw these agreements as important drivers for revitalising the domestic economy and stimulating growth for job creation. China pledged $ 60 bn in development finance and investments to Africa over a three-year period. South Africa saw the outcome of the FOCAC as part of its overall agenda in pushing for more cross-border investment aimed at regional integration.

On the trade front, *AGOA* threatened to derail relations between Pretoria and *Washington*. The tensions focused around the lack of openness of the South African economy to US imports, including the South African government's imposition of anti-dumping duties on chicken bone imports from the USA. In addition, South Africa wanted to protect the poultry industry against avian bird flu, which had been detected in the US sector. The South African poultry sector feared that local producers would not be able to compete with US imports and that the market would become flooded by US products. South Africa was given a deadline by which to adopt remedies to address the concerns raised by the US business sector and to remove barriers to chicken, beef and pork imports. There were also concerns that the proposed private security bill aimed at regulating the industry would prejudice US companies operating in the South African market, which created added fears that the US was trying through the trade facilitation processes under AGOA to interfere in domestic legislation. The tensions resulted in South Africa being cautioned that it could lose its trade preferences under AGOA. The USA gave South Africa a 31 December deadline to resolve the trade dispute.

Socioeconomic Developments

The South African economy had to navigate tricky terrain, which included falling commodity prices, rising unemployment, a weaker currency that had negative effects on the country's balance of payments, and the contagion effects from the drop in the Chinese economy. *Economic growth* was at 1.3%, down from 1.5% in 2014. GDP stood at almost R 4 trn. The two main factors that contributed to the contraction of the GDP output were the fall in agricultural production and the rise in the price of utilities (i.e. water, gas, and electricity). Agricultural production, particularly of field crops, was hampered by severe drought conditions and contracted by 8.4%, the largest decline since 1995.

Manufacturing also recorded a flat performance, with industry expanding marginally by 0.1%. *Mining*, however showed the highest level of growth with expansion of around 3%. The increase was mainly a result of increased platinum group metal (PGM) production. A low base had been created by the PGM miners' strike in 2014, but this led to a 46.2% rise in PGM production in 2015. Of the four major minerals (i.e. PGMs, iron ore, gold and coal), only PGMs recorded a production increase. Despite some modest growth, the sector also faced an uphill battle, with prices for key commodities down and production stymied by labour strikes and power shortages. In mid-December, one of the country's largest mining companies, Anglo American, announced plans to lay off more than 50% of its staff and sell off non-core assets in an effort to stem the double-digit decline in its share price.

By the end of the year, Stats SA had announced that South Africa had narrowly missed a recession. The South African Reserve Bank raised interest rates twice, lifting its benchmark rate by 25 basis points in both July and November in attempts to keep inflation below the 6% threshold and stimulate growth in the economy. The steady *depreciation of the currency* added a further burden. Following the Nene crisis in December, the South African rand fell to its lowest levels against the US dollar reaching almost R 18 : $ 1. The impact of Nene being recalled saw the rand lose almost 9% of its value against major currencies. Overall, the rand lost 30% of its value over the year. The move also impacted on the value of the Johannesburg Stock Exchange, which saw share prices fluctuate. Ratings agencies such as Standard and Poor's, Fitch and Moody's were all concerned about the lack of policy certainty having negative consequences for South Africa's economic outlook. In October, there were rumours that the country was facing a *credit downgrade*. In the first week of December, just before the finance minister was replaced, Fitch Ratings downgraded South Africa's credit rating to one level above junk status. The impact of Nene's removal from office caused more anxiety among international creditors, but the appointment of Pravin Gordhan seemed to relieve some of the nervousness.

Secure *energy supply* remained a challenge. In April, the energy minister announced 13 winning bids for the fourth round of the Renewable Energy

Independent Power Producer Procurement programme, established in 2011 to combat load shedding, diversify the energy mix, curb emissions and encourage greater private participation in the sector. In July, the Department of Energy had confirmed that it was ready to award a tender for the building of a nuclear power facility by the end of the year. The tender process was overshadowed, however, by comments made by former finance minister Nene in August, when he indicated that he would not sign off on the Zuma-led plan for a 9.6 GW nuclear power programme if it was unaffordable, and that he would not be swayed by political meddling, despite Zuma's assurance that the process would be a "fair, transparent, and competitive procurement process to select a strategic partner or partners to undertake the nuclear build programme". Cost estimates for a 9.6 GW nuclear programme ranged from $ 37 bn to $ 100 bn. By the end of the year, the tender for the nuclear facility had not been issued. Rumours were circulating that Russia's Rosatrom seemed to be the favoured bidder. The energy sector also saw strikes in the beginning of the year. Workers took industrial action at the Medupi Power Plant and Eskom contractors fired more than 1,000 workers for taking part in an illegal strike.

The *unemployment* rate increased to 26.4% in the first three months of the year from 24.3% in the previous quarter – the highest rate since 2005 – while employment grew at a slower 0.9%. In the three months to March, the number of unemployed went up by 626,000 to 5.535 m, from 4.909 m in the previous quarter. The expanded unemployment rate, including people who had stopped looking for work, increased by 1.5% to 36.1%, from 34.6% in Q4 2014. According to these figures, youth unemployment, at 63.1%, constituted a major crisis for the country. In the third quarter, 7,000 jobs were created in the formal sector according to Stats SA. Throughout the year, the country faced ongoing *service delivery protests*, mostly levelled at the inefficiency of local government bureaucracies. Inequality levels showed no improvement, according to TI's 2015 Corruption Perception Index report.

Swaziland

Marisha Ramdeen and Senzwesihle Ngubane

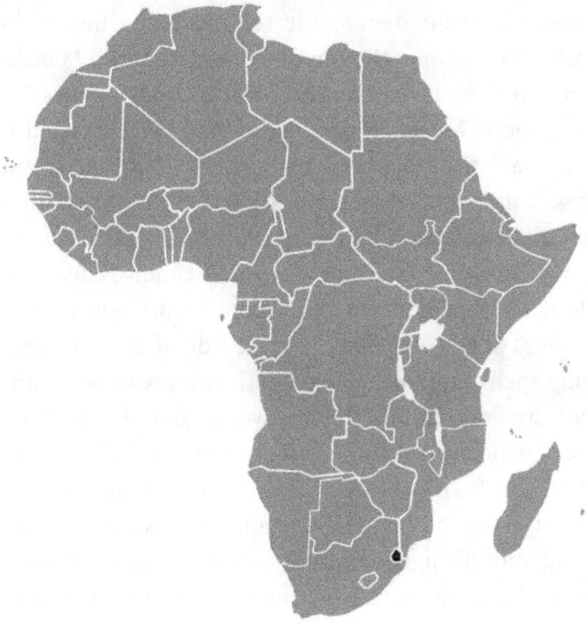

The royal family in the Kingdom of Swaziland remained bent on holding on to power and resisting any efforts towards social and political transformation, despite on-going calls for democratic reforms. The imprisonment of Mario Masuku and Maxwell Dlamini was widely criticised both locally and abroad, while the Suppression of Terrorism Act was challenged in court. The government's major infrastructural projects were disputed, and drought resulted in serious food insecurity. On the positive side, 2015 saw a decline in the HIV infection rate.

Domestic Politics

On the political front, the much anticipated dialogue between the government and some of the political formations inside Swaziland under the auspices of the Commonwealth did not produce the desired result. Under ceaseless pressure from the unions and opposition parties advocating *democratic reforms,* the Commonwealth positioned itself as an interlocutor for engagement between King Mswati, civil society organisations and opposition parties. A meeting expected to be held on 30 September did not take place. Senior Prince Masikela stated publicly

 | DOI 10.1163/9789004333239_054

"that chances of the political formations meeting the king were now slim following a report that they would be taking demands to his Majesty during the meeting". The prince further reiterated that no subject in Swaziland could take demands to the king and for this reason the meeting was cancelled.

The government's use of the *Suppression of Terrorism Act* of 2008 to deal with political opposition and those calling for democratic reforms came under the spotlight again. The act was used to continue the imprisonment of Mario Masuku and Maxwell Dlamini and remained a rallying call for local activists opposed to the Act, who demanded their release. Masuku and Dlamini had been arrested in May 2014 after attending a May Day rally. They were charged with subversion and terrorism, among other things, and accused of supporting the People's United Democratic Movement, which was banned under the Suppression of Terrorism Act. International pressure groups such as the International Trade Union Federation, British Trade Union Federation, and representatives from the Danish government and the African National Congress (ANC) weighed in on the side of the detainees, calling for their release. Having spent 14 months in jail and with pressure mounting on the government, they were granted bail by the Swaziland Supreme Court on 14 July. After their release, advocates took the opportunity to challenge the Suppression of Terrorism Act and the Subversive Activities Act of 1938 and the challenge began to be heard in court in September. Those against the two acts argued that they were unconstitutional and infringed the right to freedom of expression, since the definitions of 'terrorism' and 'sedition' were too vague and were applied even when people had legitimate rights to speak or act. In 2014, a *judicial crisis* had unfolded between Chief Justice Michael Ramodibedi and three high court judges who criticised some of his actions. He had issued warrants of arrest against them, which were ultimately not executed. On 17 June, the Chief Justice was finally fired for abuse of power by King Mswati.

The *Global Peace Index* ranked Swaziland 87th out of 162 countries. The Index measures three categories: the level of societal safety and security; the extent of domestic or international conflict; and the degree of militarisation. Out of a maximum of 5, Swaziland scored 3 for perceived criminality, 4 for murders, 4 for violent demonstrations, and 3.3 for political instability. In terms of governance related issues, Swaziland had very low ratings: on a scale of 1 to 10, it scored 1 for electoral processes, 2 for the functioning of government and 3 for political democracy.

The *human rights* record remained very poor. Basic individual freedoms continued to be affected by an alarmingly high rate of domestic abuse. The absence of an enabling legislation to protect and effectively prosecute sexual offences had crippled the ability of women to seek recourse in cases of such abuse. In 2009, Swaziland had passed the Sexual Offences and Domestic Violence Bill, but it had not yet become law. Child abuse was another main area of concern. Severe cases of corporal punishment were reported in the media. Although the Ministry of Education issued a directive to ban corporal punishment in schools, this was yet to be effectively implemented in most schools. Reports alleged that a 17-year-old pupil died and a 12-year-old suffered severe injuries after excessive beatings. There were also reports of child labour, which made headlines when the Department of Education issued a statement postponing the re-opening of schools in January indicating that the delay was due to ongoing national duties. This was an oblique reference to the annual weeding of the king's field, which was expected to be carried out by school-age children.

Foreign Affairs

The former president of Malawi, Bakili Muluzi, who had been appointed as the Special Commonwealth Envoy to Swaziland in 2014, engaged with the Swazi government to deal concretely with some of the issues relating to the conduct of democratic elections, as well as opening up space for dialogue between the government of King Mswati and those in the opposition.

Swaziland became one of only three countries in Africa to be deprived of receiving trade benefits under the *AGOA*. Among the reasons given were that Swaziland had not demonstrated progress on the protection of internationally recognised workers' rights, and had failed to make any meaningful progress on the protection of freedom of association and the rights to organise, as well as its excessive use of security forces and arbitrary arrests to stifle peaceful demonstrations. The impact of this decision was likely to be felt immediately on issues of socio-economic development. For instance, Tex Ray, a Taiwanese textile factory, closed down at the end of October as a result of the loss of AGOA, and labour unions anticipated the loss of 17,000 jobs.

Relations with the *EU* remained cordial, marked, for example, by a € 480 m grant allocated as development assistance. Despite such support, the EU also maintained pressure on the government with regard to human rights issues, as witnessed by the delegation of government ministers who were in Brussels on 21–25 September to respond to demands made by the European Parliament to improve the human and workers' rights situation in Swaziland.

King Mswati undertook two trips to Asia during the course of the year. He visited *Taiwan* on 15–20 May, where he met with dignitaries and presented a lecture at the Shih Chien University. Swaziland had enjoyed good relations with Taiwan for 45 years. During the visit, President Ma Ying-jeou met with King Mswati at a welcoming ceremony to discuss issues of mutual concern and to strengthen bilateral relations. The ceremony was also attended by senior Taiwanese government officials and foreign ambassadors to Taiwan. On 26–29 October, King Mswati attended the India-Africa Summit in New Delhi. He was one of ten African leaders at the Summit, which sought to initiate partnerships and deals worth $ 10.6 bn in loans and grants.

At the *SADC* summit in August, Swaziland was appointed to take the deputy chairmanship of the regional body, which automatically made Swaziland the incoming SADC chair for 2016. King Mswati had previously served as deputy chair of the SADC Organ on Politics, Defence and Security Cooperation in 2007 and as its chairman in 2008.

In *South Africa*, the National General Council of the governing ANC called, on the one hand, for a common programme among its political allies on Swaziland, while on the other recommending that the ANC engage all the political stakeholders to better understand the situation and to find out what future they envisaged for Swaziland. Such utterances should bode well for a region that had remained somewhat silent on the question of Swaziland with regard to providing a coherent and clear regional approach to taking better account of the current political situation. It was also hoped that these recommendations would cause the region and key countries such as South Africa to take note of initiatives such as that of the Commonwealth, so that the question of Swaziland might be decided within the region rather than elsewhere. Key too in this recommendation was a realisation of the need for those calling for reforms inside Swaziland to re-evaluate their options to date, consider issues that continued to divide them, and seek means to at least have a minimum agreed programme of action for change, in spite of existing political and leadership-related challenges.

Socioeconomic Developments

A majority of the estimated population of 1.268 m people continued to live below the *poverty* line, with an estimated 69% living on $ 1.25 or less a day. Life expectancy at birth was 48.7 years, in vast contrast to the global average of about 71 years. Drought and disease continued to be contributing factors to low life expectancy, the country having experienced severe *drought* in many areas during previous years, building up to a national emergency. The government was criticised for its slow action to avert this crisis by allocating only 3.5% of the budget rather than the 10% it had promised. As a result, households experienced loss of livestock and produce and this contributed to the poverty rate, as 84% of the country's poor were living in rural areas and surviving on subsistence agriculture. Consequently, the per capita rural income was about four times lower than in urban areas, and food consumption in the countryside was half that in the towns. About 66% of the population continued to be unable to meet basic food needs, with 43% living in chronic poverty. FAO and WFP carried out an assessment mission to determine the improvement of *maize production*. According to the report, Swaziland had experienced an extended dry period that had affected maize development, a situation compounded by the fact that manual labour and the shortage of farming equipment, such as tractors and other machinery contributed to insufficient levels of production. The report also indicated that an estimated 50,000 people were severely food insecure and in need of assistance while 18% were moderately food insecure.

Swaziland had the highest *HIV* prevalence rate in the world, at 27%, but, on a positive note, HIV infections were declining. The Swaziland HIV Estimates and Projections report indicated that the annual incidence rate among the 15–49-year-old age group was expected to drop from 2.9% in 2011 to 1.9% in 2015.

The sectors contributing most export revenue to the Swazi economy included agriculture, forestry, mining and manufacturing (textiles and refined sugar). According to the most recent economic outlook report by the AfDB, Swaziland's *GDP growth* had fallen from 3.0% in 2013 to 2.5% in 2014.

It was reported that approximately 700 jobs were lost when the mining company SG Iron at the *Ngwenya Iron Ore Mine* collapsed as a result of its $ 4 m debt. Reports also indicated that a loan of $ 10 m that had been taken out by King Mswati, which he had refused to pay back, had resulted in the liquidation. There was speculation that the money was spent on a plane, which was the subject of intense controversy. The plane was reportedly seized by the Canadian courts in January after a court application was brought by a Malaysian businessman who claimed that the king had failed to pay him a long-outstanding debt of $ 3.5 m for luxury upgrades to the plane. The Canadian court ruled that it would be returned if the government of Swaziland paid back the $ 3.5 m.

In areas of *infrastructural development*, the government had dedicated funds to projects but there were concerns regarding the financial returns from these projects. For instance, the *King Mswati International Airport*, built with an investment of $ 250 m and officially opened in October 2014, was not generating enough revenue. On average, only 194 passengers per day were recorded. At this rate, the airport was only receiving 23% of the 300,000 passengers per year that it needed to break even financially. Furthermore, it was reported that the Swazi government had backed a plan to build a *shipping port* at an estimated cost of $ 3 bn. The country has no coastline, but the plan was to build a 26 km canal from the Mozambican coast to Mlawula, where the port was to be constructed.

Zambia

Edalina Rodrigues Sanches

Edgar Lungu of the ruling Patriotic Front (PF) won the presidential by-elections by one of the narrowest margins ever against the runner-up, Hakainde Hichilema of the United Party for National Development (UPND). The elections were deemed free and fair, but levels of turnout reached a record low. Inonge Wina became the first female vice president and the PF was the major winner in the parliamentary by-elections. Parliament passed the Constitution of Zambia (Amendment) Bill, which changed the formula for winning presidential elections from a simple majority to 50% plus one. Eduard Lungu set himself an intensive travel programme to further and deepen bilateral relations with neighbouring countries in Southern Africa and with China. China remained a key investor, with important agreements reached in the technology, communications and transport sectors. Against falling copper prices, Zambia's currency continued to be devalued, the economy slowed down and unemployment increased in the mining sector. A new mining tax regime was approved. The electricity deficit rose dramatically, generating a severe power crisis, and electricity tariffs increased. The cost of living rose and only two out of the eight MDGs were attained.

 | DOI 10.1163/9789004333239_055

Domestic Politics

The *presidential by-election* followed the death of President Michael Sata on 28 October 2014. According to constitutional provisions, if the president's office becomes vacant by reason of his death, an election to the office of the president shall be held within 90 days from the date of the vacancy (Articles 38 and 34). Acting President Guy Scott announced 20 January as the date of the by-election. The winning candidate was to complete Sata's term until 2016. A total of *eleven candidates* successfully filed their nomination papers: Edgar Lungu (PF), Hakainde Hichilema (UPND), Edith Nawakwi (Forum for Democracy and Development; FDD), Nevers Mumba (Movement for Multi-Party Democracy; MMD), Tilyenji Kaunda (United National Independence Party), Eric Chanda (Fourth Revolution Party), Elias Chipimo Jr (National Restoration Party; NAREP), Godfrey Miyanda (Heritage Party), Daniel Pule (Christian Democratic Party), Ludwig Sondashi (Forum for Democratic Alternatives) and Peter Sinkamba (Green Party of Zambia).

The frontrunners were Lungu, who emerged from relative anonymity to be the PF presidential candidate at a highly divided and controversial General Conference, and Hichilema, the UPND founding leader and a contestant in all presidential elections since 2006. In terms of *campaign strategies*, Lungu heavily capitalised not only on former president Sata's popularity and charisma, but also on his reputation and achievements, especially in growing the economy. In fact, he frequently positioned himself as the guardian of the late president's legacy. According to Nicole Beardsworth, a South African political analyst, "The PF's campaign materials reflected this, giving Sata's face prominence and placing Edgar Lungu's smaller image below it in a symbolic sign of deference." Apart from pledges to continue with Sata's 'vision' and development programmes, Lungu promised to reduce fuel and staple food prices, to increase access to education, to expand social welfare cash transfer schemes to all rural districts, to ease land acquisitions by Zambians, to protect media freedom and to continue outlawing homosexuality (he had long been an opponent of gay rights). His campaign slogan, "Ifintu ni Lungu" ("Edgar Lungu is the real thing"), became popular among young people and went viral on social media. Meanwhile, Hichilema invited voters "to board Flight HH2015". He promised to enact a new constitution by 2016, to lower the cost of living by reducing the price of fuel, to create more jobs by changing the retirement age from 65 to 55 and to reduce the cost of fertiliser to allow farmers to increase their agricultural productivity, which in turn would reduce the cost of the staple foods. Hichilema also contested the way the government had been using the Public Order Act (POA) to limit political competition, arguing that it should be properly managed to allow people to express themselves. Moreover, he promised that the UPND would repeal the negative NGO Act, which had been criticised by national and international organisations for inhibiting NGOs' independence and freedom of action. In terms of *campaign resources*, Hichilema seemed able to access more resources than Lungu.

In particular, he used a helicopter to campaign in traditional PF strongholds, such as the provinces of Luapula, Muchinga and the Northern Province, which he had rarely visited in his previous presidential campaigns. Nevers Mumba of the MMD and Edith Nawakwi (FDD's president since 2005) also captured some media attention, being the first priest and the first woman, respectively, to run in presidential elections. Mumba promised that school education would be mandatory if he came to power and that he would also reintroduce agricultural subsidies, while Nawakwi's campaign focused on fighting corruption, which she promised to do by decentralising government.

The campaign period (19 November 2014 to 19 January) was considered relatively peaceful, apart from two incidents involving PF and UPND supporters. In Shiwa N'gandu, PF cadres tried to torch a helicopter carrying UPND leaders and the two parties clashed at the airport in Mongu, when the departure of Hichilema (UPND) coincided with the arrival of Interim President Scott (PF). The election was meant to take place on 20 January, but voting ultimately extended over four days and ended on 23 January because of the intensity of the rains. The Electoral Commission of Zambia (ECZ) announced the *final result* on 24 January, declaring Lungu the winner with 807,925 votes (48.3%) against Hichilema's 780,168 (46.7%), leaving a gap of 27,757 votes (1.6%). In terms of *electoral geography*, Lungu (PF) had the broadest geographical appeal, winning in six provinces and coming second in four. Hichilema (UPND) had the most dedicated voters, with Southern Province recording the highest voter turnout at 48.97%, followed by Northwestern Province with 38.2%, both UPND strongholds. Mumba came fourth nationwide and seventh in Eastern Province, the MMD's traditional stronghold. The picture was more complex in Central Province, and votes were also spread out more in urban areas and in the Lusaka and Copperbelt Provinces. *Turnout* declined to a historical low of 32.4% (down from 54% in 2011). Despite election day being declared a public holiday, only 1,671,662 out of the 5,166,084 eligible voters turned up at the polls.

Elections were declared *free and fair* by international observers hailing from the AU, SADC, COMESA and the Electoral Institute for Sustainable Democracy in Africa. Minor incidents were reported, including an attack on ECZ staff in Choma, but the election took place without any major clashes between parties. There were few reports of electoral malpractice, but the UPND complained that the Zambian Air Force had grounded its helicopters, which were meant to provide transport for its election observers. Hichilema eventually declared that the election had been 'stolen' and did not accept the results. In terms of *campaign finance*, the election cost an estimated K (kwacha) 344 m, with K 19 m coming from donor contributions from countries and institutions including Ireland, Japan, Sweden, UK, USA and the UNDP, and the rest being covered by the government.

Despite having little room for manoeuvre, since he inherited the MPs, ministers and PF officials chosen by Sata, Lungu stated that he would select his cabinet on the basis of merit. Changes in this matter were considerable throughout the year.

He originally appointed a cabinet of 21 ministries, retaining the defence portfolio himself. He removed five of the late President Sata's ministers (Guy Scott, Robert Sichinga, Mwansa Kapeya, Wylbur Simuusa and Emmanuel Chenda), who had not supported him during the power struggle in the PF. However, he kept nine ministers with their portfolios unchanged, notably Alexander Chikwanda (Finance), Joseph Kasonde (Health), Harry Kalaba (Foreign Affairs) and Jean Kapata (Tourism and Arts), and transferred several others to different portfolios, including Ngosa Simbyakula (Justice) Davies Mwila (Home Affairs) and Joseph Katema (Chief and Traditional Affairs). New entrants were Margaret Mwanakatwe (Commerce, Trade and Industry), Christabel Ngimbu (Lands, Natural Resources and Environment), Given Lubinda (Agriculture and Llivestock) and John Pahari (Local Government and Housing). Lungu then appointed over 30 deputy ministers (including five from the MMD), which was highly criticised by opposition parties who contested the duplication of several ministries.

Lungu's *second cabinet* included 25 ministries and was formed after Parliament approved the establishment of five new ministries on 1 October. He subsequently split five ministries into two, including Finance (Finance; Development Planning), Mines, Energy and Water Development (Energy and Water Development; Mines and Minerals Development), Agriculture and Livestock (Agriculture; Fisheries and Livestock), Transport, Works, Supply and Communication (Transport and Communication; Works and Supply) and Education, Science, Vocational Training and Early Education (General Education; Higher Education). In addition, Lungu moved child development to the Ministry of Youth, Sports and Child Development, and mother and child health to the Ministry of Health.

The upshot of the presidential by-election was also marked by action against members who had broken *party discipline*. In the MMD, at least 18 members were expelled for having supported either the PF or the UPND in the presidential by-election. The UPND expelled three MPs for backing the ruling PF party, while the ruling PF expelled members who had refused to campaign for Lungu. Parties also took a period to reorganise and to prepare themselves for the August 2016 general elections. The MMD held a policy conference aimed at renewing the party's policies in line with changing times to culminate in the 2016 MMD Manifesto, while the NAREP replaced its national secretary.

Several *parliamentary by-elections* were held: the first round in Chawama, Masaiti and Senga Hill (14 April), the second in Malambo, Petauke and Mulobezi (30 June), the third in Bangweulu (6 August) and finally the fourth in Lubansenshi and Solwezi West (4 September). The PF was the major winner, losing only in Solwezi West to the UPND.

The *Constitution of Zambia (Amendment) Bill 2015* was published in late July. It included 20 revisions, including a majoritarian system for the election of the president (50% plus one), the election of a vice president as the president's running mate, an increase in the number of MPs from 158 to 250 (156 elected and 94 chosen from party lists), the establishment of provincial assemblies, the establishment of two higher courts (appeal and constitutional), the introduction of dual citizenship, the establishment of a financing fund for political parties, the renaming of the police and the prisons service and the election of parliamentary secretaries, amongst other things. On 19 November, the bill was passed by Parliament after the second reading. In line with the Zambian law-making process, this phase involved a general debate, followed by a vote to channel the bill to the Committee on Legal Affairs, Governance, Human Rights and Gender to consider the text of the constitutional bills and to issue a report, generating a third reading before final approval by the president. In December, Parliament adopted the new Constitution with the amendments listed above except for Part 3, the bill of rights, which was to be adopted through a referendum in 2016.

Still related to electoral issues, six *new constituencies* were created in areas where the recent creation of new districts had resulted in constituencies spanning more than one district. The changes recommended by the ECZ implied the need to split the following constituencies: Siavonga (consisting of the old Siavonga and the new Chirundu Districts), Sinjembela (Shangombo and Sioma), Mansa Central (Mansa and Chembe), Kaoma Central (Kaoma and Nkeyema), Kapiri Mposhi (Kapiri Mposhi and Ngabwe) and Kapoche (Petauke and Sinda).

In terms of liberal and *civil rights*, the POA, which stipulates the parameters within which public meetings are held and thus parties' abilities to operate and to campaign in by-elections, remained contestable, as there were accusations of government misuse of the existing provisions. Despite the blocking of some critical websites, the Internet remained one of the freest spaces for journalists and bloggers to express criticism of the government, with freedom at a net rating of 40 (on a scale where 0 = most free to 100 = least free). Nevertheless, the media environment remained challenging (rated 'not free' according to Freedom House).

Foreign Policy

President Lungu had a busy travel schedule throughout the year. In his first 30 days in office, he travelled abroad four times (*Ethiopia, Zimbabwe, Angola* and *South Africa*). In contrast, the late President Sata did not leave Zambia in his first month in office, and former president Rupiah Banda (MMD) undertook one trip only. Visits were mainly aimed at strengthening cooperation with bordering countries and capturing investments for relevant sectors of the country's economy. In January, Lungu was in Addis Ababa (Ethiopia) to attend the 24th session of the AU Assembly. In February, he received President Jakaya Kikwete of Tanzania, the first visit by a foreign head of state during Lungu's presidency. The purpose of the two-day state visit was to discuss bilateral issues, including the restoration of the Tanzania-Zambia Railway Authority (TAZARA) and the

Tanzania-Zambia-Mafuta (TAZAMA) pipeline and the improvement of goods clearing at the Nakonde-Tunduma border. Lungu also travelled to Zimbabwe on 7 February to pay a traditional courtesy call on President Robert Mugabe, to Angola on 13 February to commission the renewed Benguela Railway, to address the Angolan National Assembly and to sign bilateral agreements on cross-border water and railway transport, and finally to South Africa on 25 February to meet President Jacob Zuma, to discuss bilateral, regional and international issues with a focus on the DRC, Madagascar and Lesotho.

In March, relevant travel included a trip to *Namibia* to attend the country's 25th Independence Day celebrations and the inauguration of President Hage Geingob, and a state visit to *China*. The visit to China received great media attention due to its outcomes: the main highlights were two bilateral agreements worth CNY (yuan) 400 m ($ 65 m) and an additional CNY 410 m under a framework for concessional loans and grants destined for the Zambia Information and Communication Technology Authority for the construction of communication towers in rural areas. Also, a range of investment agreements worth $ 800 m were established with mostly private sector companies in China, targeting projects including a new oil refinery, a cement plant and milling plants in all of Zambia's ten provinces. The Ministry of Foreign Affairs was set to open a consulate in Guangzhou in southern China, as most Zambians did business far from the embassy in Beijing. This was also the month in which Lungu ordered the Ministry of Foreign Affairs to waive visa fees for all Chinese tourists.

In April, Lungu visited Zimbabwe to attend the SADC Summit and officiate at the 56th Zimbabwe Trade Fair. In May, he was present at the *Extra-Ordinary Summit of Heads of State of the Great Lakes Region* held in Angola. In June, he attended the AU Summit in South Africa and Mozambique's 40th Independence Day celebrations. In July, he visited Malawi to attend its 51st Independence Day ceremonies and Uganda for a two-day state visit. Both President Museveni and Lungu manifested the will to strengthen and deepen cooperation between Uganda and Zambia. In August, Lungu participated in the SADC Heads of State and Government meeting during the official opening of the 35th Ordinary Summit in Gaborone (Botswana).

First Lady Esther Lungu was also quite active. In September, she participated in a series of meetings in Dallas (Texas) and New York. Among many other events, the George W. Bush Institute invited her to participate in high-profile engagements with other first ladies, focusing on women's empowerment, health, technology and other sectors. In New York, she attended a series of events including the Women and the New Sustainable Development Agenda (25 September). In October, she was in Saudi Arabia at the invitation of the Ministry of Health of the Kingdom of Saudi Arabia and Her Royal Highness Princess Latifa Bint Abulaziz Al Saud, the Saudi king's wife. She met the princess to discuss support for women's and children's programmes in Zambia. In December, she launched the Esther Lungu Foundation as a vehicle to carry out her humanitarian work.

Socioeconomic Developments

Zambia's *economic slow down* followed regional and global trends. According to World Bank estimates, SSA's GDP growth averaged 3.7%, down from 4.6% in 2014, while Zambia's GDP growth averaged 3.5%, down from 5.6%. After experiencing average growth rates of 8% between 2002 and 2010, the economy had steadily contracted ever since, being poorly diversified and heavily dependent on the performance of the mining sector. Copper contributed 9% to GDP and accounted for more than 70% of exports, with the economy being vulnerable to shifts in trading prices and demands at the global level because of its high dependence on this metal. Copper prices dropped to a six-year low and global demand for the metal (particularly from China, Zambia's main trading partner) declined. In the first half of the year, *copper export earnings* dropped to $ 2.6 bn, a fall of 29.9% compared with the same period in 2014. Annual *inflation* rose to 19.5% in November, up from 14.3% in October, driven by increases in prices for both food and non-food items. The *trade balance* posted a deficit of K 2.58 bn in October, from K 2.11 bn in September. In April, the cabinet approved the Income Tax (Amendment) Bill of 2015, seeking to implement changes to the mining tax regime and corporate income. *Mineral royalties* increased to 8% for underground mines and 20% for open cast mines. Corporate income tax for mining operations increased from zero to 30%.

Lack of rain and low water levels in all reservoirs (particularly in the Kariba dam on the border with Zimbabwe) triggered a severe power crisis, which affected both the general population and the mining sector. According to Minister of Mines, Energy and Water Development Christopher Yaluma, the electricity deficit rose from 560 MW in August to 985 MW in September. In response, the government decided to import electricity from a gas-fired generator based in Ressano Garcia in southern Mozambique. The Zambian government revealed that more than $ 40 m was spent on importing 148 MW of emergency power between September and December. In August, the cabinet approved an immediate increase in electricity tariffs for all categories of electricity users, excluding the 'life-line tariff' for residents using less than 500 kwh per month. It should be noted that Lungu had already in February approved an increase for all commercial consumers except for mines on condition that ZESCO, the state-owned power company, would freeze residential tariffs for two years. Nevertheless, in November, ZESCO proposed an increase in electricity tariffs of between 170% and 250%. ZESCO justified its new proposal by explaining that the new tariffs were intended to attract a portfolio of diversified generation projects and investors.

Power shortages, falling copper prices and changes in the tax regime made 2015 a particularly challenging year for the *mining sector*, affecting not only earnings but also the expansion of mining activities. Because of the need to restructure mining activities, thousands of workers lost their jobs: 1,675 from Konkola Copper Mines (Vedanta Resources Plc), over 3,000 from Mopani Copper Mines (Glencore Plc) and

1,640 from Luanshya Copper Mines (China Nonferrous Mining Corporation Ltd). With the 2016 general elections ahead, Lungu promised to create 10,000 jobs in the Copperbelt province by transforming Zambia into an agro-based economy involving ex-miners and supported by infrastructural development, namely construction of a new airport, roads and a water reticulation system.

The Jesuit Centre for Theological Reflection (JCTR) Basic Needs Basket revealed a general rise in the cost of living for most towns at the close of the year. Considering the two major cities, Lusaka and Kitwe, the JCTR registered the following increases: the Basic Needs Basket for Lusaka increased from K 3,715.47 in July to K 4,371.76 in December (17.6% increase), while the Kitwe Basic Needs Basket went up from K 2,768.69 in July to K 3,919.58 in December (41% increase). These rises resulted from price increases in food and non-food items, in particular the rise in the cost of maize meal, which increased from K 68.00 to over K 82.00 per 25-kg bag in some parts of the country, and the rise in energy costs. The government eventually stopped supplying millers with subsidised maize from the Food Reserve Agency, allegedly because millers had not reduced maize meal prices.

The *budget deficit* widened to K 20.5 bn (18.5% of GDP) in the first six months of the year, mainly due to expenditure on civil servants' salaries and infrastructure projects (the government had accumulated an overrun of K 1.9 bn on Link Zambia 8000). Despite its difficulties, Zambia hesitated to accept an *IMF* loan, with Finance Minister Alexander Chikwanda stating that "the IMF is not the best mechanism for helping countries which are down", and that "in some cases it even compounds" the difficulties. Still, two IMF teams visited the country in March and November. In a May Press release, the IMF encouraged the government to address infrastructure and electricity constraints, strengthen project selection and prioritise capital spending. It also called for sustained expenditure and revenue efforts, including efforts to contain the wage bill and target social spending. On the positive side, it commended the cabinet's decision to change the mining tax regime. Later, a press release issued in November stated that Zambia's authorities and the IMF staff would remain closely engaged in the period ahead and work on possible forms and timing of engagement.

The Zambian government still turned to the external market to seek out *multilateral assistance*. For instance, in May, Sweden announced it was unlocking $ 47.3 m in donor funds that it had frozen in 2010 after allegations of misappropriation. The move was seen as a clear victory for Lungu's anti-corruption platform. In December, the government approved a $ 275 m loan from the Industrial and Commercial Bank of China for the design and construction of 2,350 housing units for the security wings (police, prisons, immigration department and intelligence department).

2015 was also challenging in terms of *human development* achievements. Zambia only achieved two of the eight MDGs: MDG 2 (universal primary education) and part of MDG 6 (HIV/AIDS, malaria and other major diseases). It failed to achieve the targets set for MDG 1 (poverty and hunger), MDG 3 (gender equality), MDG 4 (child mortality), MDG 5 (maternal mortality), MDG 7 (environmental sustainability) and MDG 8 (global partnership for development). According to the 2015 *Social Progress Index* (an index that scores countries in terms of basic human needs, foundation of well-being and opportunity), Zambia ranked 105th out of 133 countries (with an index of 51.62), slightly better than its index of 50.48 in 2014. Zambia performed best on 'opportunity' (placed 80th) and worst on 'basic human needs' (placed 121st). According to WFP, Zambia had one of the highest rates of undernourished people in the world (48%). In absolute figures, the number of undernourished people had more than doubled in the last 20 years to 7.4 m people.

In a year with great economic and social challenges, there was some good news too. *Sugar production* reached a record high (424,024 tonnes), with Zambia Sugar recording the highest ever tonnage produced by a single sugar factory on the African continent in any given season. In April, the Supreme Court of Zambia upheld a 2011 High Court verdict that found Vedanta (Konkola Copper Mines) guilty of water pollution, which poisoned thousands of Chingola residents in 2006. This was seen as a landmark decision for the way mining pollution is regarded in Zambia.

Business with *China* continued to diversify. In January, a Chinese company that was exploring for diamonds in Mbala, Northern Province, reported that Zambia had "high grade diamonds in comparison to that of South African diamond mines". In April, China Jiangxi Corporation Zambia Ltd, responsible for expanding Lusaka's Kenneth Kaunda International Airport, announced that work would start in May. As in 2014, Zambia scored 38 in the Corruption Perceptions Index, even though its relative position improved from 85th out of 175 to 76th out of 168.

Zimbabwe

Amin Y. Kamete

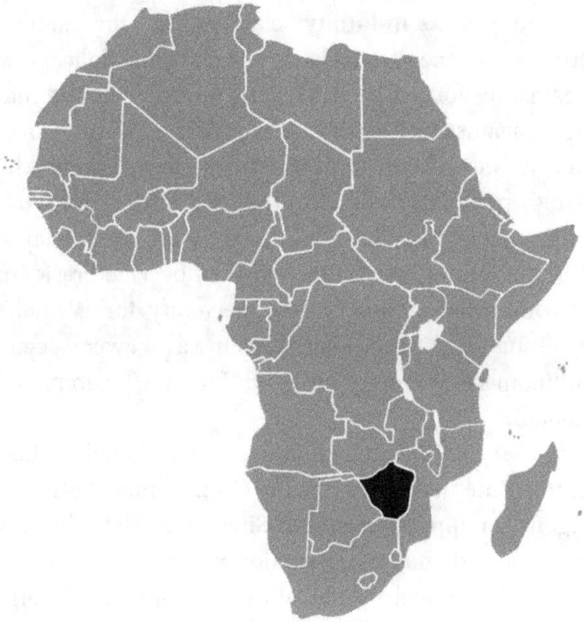

The year was dominated by factionalism in the Zimbabwe African National Union-Patriotic Front (ZANU-PF), with purges in the party becoming a regular occurrence. The intraparty fighting pitted the faction allegedly aligned with the president's wife against the camp loyal to one of the vice presidents. Relentless rumours about President Mugabe's health were a constant talking point throughout the year. As in previous years, much of Zimbabwe's foreign relations centred on controversies about 'illegal' western sanctions, an issue which again saw very little change in the positions of the key players. The economy showed signs of deterioration.

Domestic Politics

The year started with the fallout from the decimation of the *Mujuru faction.* Throughout the year, there were endless purges of perceived allies of ousted Vice President Joice Mujuru. On 14 January, the sacked political heavyweight, former ZANU-PF secretary for Administration and Presidential Affairs Minister *Didymus Mutasa,* issued a scathing press statement "on behalf of all the loyal members of ZANU-PF who are determined to restore the image of our party". The statement

 | DOI 10.1163/9789004333239_056

accused President Robert Mugabe and his wife of fanning hatred and division in the party. Mutasa described the congress that sacked him and other party members allegedly loyal to Mrs Mujuru as illegal, and the sackings as therefore null and void. He threatened legal action. Critics interpreted Mutasa's venomous statement as a case of sour grapes for his ouster. Quoting legal experts, state-controlled media ridiculed Mutasa's legal bid as "an exercise in futility", claiming that the planned application had no legal merit. In the face of attacks by his erstwhile colleagues, Mutasa continued his fight against his former party. On 30 January, he hinted that Mujuru would be filing a lawsuit against the president's wife, Grace Mugabe, over attacks that had led to the former's expulsion from the party. On 2 February, he said he would attend ZANU-PF's planned disciplinary hearing against him, out of his "enduring respect" for President Mugabe. The hearing had been delayed by Mrs Mugabe's absence. The disciplinary committee was led by Vice President Phelekezela Mphoko. Other committee members were secretary for Women's Affairs Grace Mugabe, ZANU-PF national commissar Saviour Kasukuwere, secretary for legal affairs Patrick Chinamasa, Secretary for Youth Pupurai Togarepi and politburo member Kembo Mohadi.

Unconfirmed reports of *Mugabe's poor health*, which were traditionally voiced at the beginning of the year, this time included his wife. On 22 January, Mugabe reported that she had undergone an appendectomy in Singapore. The following day, there were reports that Mugabe had undergone a major prostate cancer operation, also in Singapore, but this was denied by Mugabe's spokesperson, George Charamba, who said he had gone for "an annual review of his eyes". On his return, Mugabe did not mention his own operation, but disclosed that he and his family had undergone medical check-ups during their holiday. Rumours about Mrs Mugabe's health intensified with her continued absence from the country. On 9 February, the presidential spokesman denied reports that she was in a coma. In March, unconfirmed reports in the private media reported that she had received treatment for colon cancer. Amidst the reports and speculation about his wife, Mugabe's own health continued to be the subject of rumours, fuelled by his frequent trips to Singapore. After his return from annual leave in February, he had flown to the city-state three times by the end of April. Mrs Mugabe disappeared from public view and was not fulfilling her party obligations and other duties as head of the ZANU-PF Women's League, amid reports that she was ill. She was said to be seeking treatment abroad. On 3 June, she reappeared on the political scene and scoffed at reports of her poor health, insisting that she was as fit as a fiddle. *Mugabe's fall at the airport* escalated speculation on his health: on 4 February, on his arrival from Ethiopia, he missed a step and tumbled off the podium at Harare International Airport. The incident quickly became major news. According to reports, journalists at the scene were forced to delete pictures of the president lying on the ground. With videos of the fall going viral, the fallout from the incident lasted for some time, with government spin-doctors and detractors tussling over what actually happened. It was also reported that up to 27 members of the presidential security and advance team who stood by as Mugabe fell were suspended on 6 February. The opposition unsurprisingly capitalised on the event, using it as evidence to support their questioning Mugabe's fitness to rule.

Following the purging of Mujuru loyalists, *ZANU-PF factional fighting* took on a new dimension. By the second half of the year, it was being speculated that the alliance between Grace Mugabe and Vice President Emmerson Mnangagwa that had annihilated the Mujuru faction was unravelling. The increasingly influential Mrs Mugabe was said to be working with ZANU-PF's ambitious Young Turks, known as Generation 40 (G40). As in previous years, the factional wars were associated with ZANU-PF's fractious succession politics. There was speculation that rather than helping Mnangagwa become president, Mrs Mugabe was preparing herself for the position. Phelekezela Mphoko, the other vice president, was reported to be in the Grace Mugabe camp. On 8 August, President Mugabe denied for the first time speculation that he was lining up his wife to succeed him. The factional fighting pitted two formations against each other: the Mnangagwa-aligned 'Team Lacoste' and the Grace Mugabe-aligned G40. The most vocal members of the G40 formation were Higher Education Minister Jonathan Moyo; party national commissar, Saviour Kasukuwere; and Mugabe's nephew, Patrick Zhuwao. They were openly opposed to Mnangagwa, viewing him as unfit to run the party and country.

One of the high-profile public battles between the factions involved choosing a candidate for the *Harare East constituency*. The factions picked rival candidates and the case went all the way to the High Court. On 6 May, the court ruled that both candidates could contest the 10 June election. On 16 May, it was reported that the G40 faction had upstaged Mnangagwa's camp in the battle for the constituency. ZANU-PF officially chose G40's preferred candidate, Terence Mukupe, to represent the party over Mnangagwa loyalist Mavis Gumbo. Mnangagwa's woes were not helped by his political gaffes. In an interview with 'New Africa' magazine in September, he described the immensely popular late vice president Joshua Nkomo as a sell-out. This damaged Mnangagwa's image and presidential ambitions because it alienated Ndebele people both within and outside the ruling party. As the factional fighting intensified, the Mnangagwa camp reportedly tried to outflank the G40 when, on 12 November, it was reported that the *Masvingo provincial executive* was planning to be the first to endorse Mnangagwa as Mugabe's official number two ahead of the party's December conference. This was apparently in response to the G40's strategy to oust Mnangagwa. In October, the G40 were reported to be plotting to push for a constitutional amendment to re-introduce a clause that would compel ZANU-PF to have a woman in the party presidium. What fuelled speculation that this was targeted at Mnangagwa was the fact that Mphoko, the other vice president, appeared to be safe as his appointment was in accordance with the 1987 ZANU-ZAPU Unity Accord. The G40 appeared to have secured the support of two influential organs of the party: the Youth League and the Women's League, headed by Grace Mugabe.

The drama in the *factions of the* MDC (Movement for Democratic Change) spilled over into 2015. On 17 March, 17 opposition MPs and four senators were expelled from parliament by order of the Speaker of Parliament, Jacob Mudenda, after they broke away to form a new party. The 21 had been elected or nominated on MDC-T (Tsvangirai) tickets. They later split to form MDC Renewal, led by former finance minister Tendai Biti. As 14 of the MPs had been directly elected in the 2013 election, the expulsions triggered by-elections in their constituencies. The MDC-T would be able to appoint replacements for the other seven seats, which were allocated according to the proportion of votes cast in the 2013 election. Also on 17 March, Biti responded by vowing to challenge the expulsion in court, although his legal challenge would be unlikely to succeed. Biti also made allegations that MDC-T was working with ZANU-PF to destroy his MDC Renewal. This was hardly a believable allegation, given the tensions between MDC-T and ZANU-PF.

In a *series of by-elections* triggered by the expulsion of the MPs and senators, deaths of legislators, and the elevation of Mnangagwa to the vice presidency, ZANU-PF secured easy victories, beginning on 28 March, when it won Chirumhanzu-Zibangwe and Mount Darwin constituencies. On 10 June, ZANU-PF won all 16 contested seats in parliamentary by-elections and, on 20 December, won in Nkulumane, thereby improving its political presence in Bulawayo. The MDC-T boycotted all the by-elections, vowing not to take part in any future elections before the alignment of the Electoral Act with the new Constitution. The minor parties that contested the by-elections lost by huge margins.

Throughout the year, there was intense speculation about ousted Vice President *Joice Mujuru's political intentions.* Her allies, Rugare Gumbo and Didymus Mutasa, had indicated that she was going to form her own political party and in April Mutasa claimed that efforts were underway to form a party to be called Zimbabwe People First (ZPF), with Mujuru as its leader. Mutasa insisted the party would be the 'original' ZANU-PF. For some time, Mujuru maintained her silence and all political statements were made by Mutasa and Gumbo. Finally, in September, Mujuru came into the open about her future and gave the strongest indication that she would challenge President Mugabe. On 8 September, she unveiled her party manifesto, entitled *Blueprint to Unlock Investment and Leverage for Development* (BUILD). She claimed that BUILD reflected her party's 'proposal to translate our vision for a better Zimbabwe into reality'. In addition to economic issues, the manifesto contained other important provisions, including acknowledging dual citizenship and promoting and supporting press freedom. ZANU-PF loyalists ridiculed the manifesto, though it received favourable reviews from some commentators.

President Mugabe announced a *cabinet reshuffle* on 11 September, adding to the bloated cabinet. He appointed four new ministers and 10 deputies. Jonathan Moyo was moved to the Ministry of Higher and Tertiary Education from the Information,

Media and Broadcasting Services Ministry, where he was replaced by Christopher Mushowe. Saviour Kasukuwere was moved to the Ministry of Local Government Public Works and National Housing, being replaced at the Water and Climate Ministry by Oppah Muchinguri. Ignatius Chombo was moved from the Local Government Ministry and re-assigned to the Ministry of Home Affairs. Nyasha Chikwinya was appointed to take the lead at the Ministry of Women's Affairs. There had been speculation that Mugabe would bring his wife into the cabinet, to take over the Women's Affairs Ministry. Mugabe's nephew, Patrick Zhuwao was named minister of youth development, indigenisation and economic empowerment.

ZANU-PF's 15th Annual National People's Conference opened on 11 December in Victoria Falls. As expected, the party's factional in-fighting escalated, with accusations and counter-accusations of plots between the two camps. So vicious were the conflicts that Mugabe openly admitted that factionalists were "threatening to tear each other apart at this conference". There were reports that the G40 was trying to force Mnangagwa out of the race for the presidency by demoting him and replacing him in the presidium with Grace Mugabe. The influential Women's League had demanded in its resolutions to the conference that a woman be incorporated into the presidium by 2016. However, on 12 December, President Mugabe, in his closing speech, seemed to scuttle the plot by dismissing any plans of leadership change as 'dreams'. It is believed Mugabe saved Team Lacoste. In a departure from the norm, the conference ended on 12 December with no announcement of final resolutions. This was seen as an indication of the bruising factional in-fighting that had characterised ZANU-PF's succession politics throughout the year. Another significant development at the conference was the call by some delegates for a return to the Zimbabwe dollar.

Partly because of the factional conflicts in ZANU-PF, the *human rights situation* remained relatively stable during much of the year. However, there were reports that the government continued to violate human rights in defiance of protections enshrined in the new Constitution. According to HRW, the expected legislative framework and new or amended laws to improve human rights in line with the Constitution did not materialise. The organisation reported that police violated basic rights, such as freedom of expression and assembly, "using old laws that are inconsistent with the new constitution". Later in the year, there was some progress in the harmonisation of some pieces of legislation with the Constitution. According to the Zimbabwe Human Rights NGO Forum, by the end of the year the General Laws Amendment Bill of 2015 had addressed 125 Acts of Parliament and 51 Acts had been amended under the National Prosecuting Authority Act. An outstanding 116 Acts still required minor amendments, while 49 required substantial amendments.

Police harassment continued. Human rights activists faced severe restrictions on their work. Police frequently applied draconian laws such as the Public Order and Security Act and the Access to Information and Protection of Privacy Act to ban public meetings and gatherings. Journalists and opposition and other activists were prosecuted under these laws. Between October and December, the Zimbabwe Human Rights NGO Forum reported a cumulative total of 998 human rights violations. On 9 March, five armed men abducted 36-year-old journalist *Itai Dzamara*, a human rights activist, vocal Mugabe critic and leader of a protest group known as Occupy Africa Unity Square. At year's end, he had still not been found. The authorities consistently denied any government involvement. On 13 March, Dzamara's wife approached the High Court to compel the state to search for her husband. Judge David Mangota ordered the home affairs minister, the police commissioner-general and the director-general of the Central Intelligence Organization "to do all things necessary to determine Dzamara's whereabouts". The judge ordered the government to report to the court every two weeks on its progress with the case until Dzamara was found. They did not comply with the order.

There were violations of *freedoms of assembly and expression*. On 25 April, activists organised a car procession to raise awareness about Dzamara's disappearance. Police arrested 11 of the activists and detained them for six hours. They were released without charge. On 8 November, Highfield East MP Erick Murayi (MDC-T) and 16 others were arrested on charges of public violence and for holding a rally without police clearance. On the *press freedom* front, on 2 November police arrested three state media journalists who had published a report implicating senior police officers and Parks and Wildlife Authority rangers in the killing of elephants in Hwange National Park. On 12 November, the journalist Andrison Manyere was arrested in Harare for covering a demonstration by MDC-T activists against what they saw as reluctance by the Zimbabwe Electoral Commission to implement electoral reforms. He was later released without charge.

Foreign Affairs

With no major change in the country's domestic and foreign policy, there was little change in foreign relations. Relations with most African and Asian countries and organisations continued to be friendly. Relations with the OECD countries experienced some slight shifts. As had become the norm, ZANU-PF and the government blamed the country's deteriorating economic situation on 'illegal' western sanctions.

President Mugabe began the year as *Chairman of SADC*, a position he had assumed in August 2014. This role continued to be celebrated among his supporters and was used as an indication of his stature as a statesman. During his watch as SADC chairman, the *crisis in Lesotho* arose following the killing of the army commander in June. Mugabe expressed concern and worked to resolve the situation. His bid to diffuse the crisis included meetings with South Africa's Defence Minister Nosiviwe Mapisa-Nqakula, President Jacob Zuma's special envoy, in Harare on 30 June. As chairman of the bloc, Mugabe travelled extensively to countries in the region. This generated controversy with the opposition and critics complained about what they asserted was a waste of resources. In August, Mugabe handed over the SADC chairmanship to President Ian Khama of Botswana. While critics dismissed Mugabe's chairmanship as a non-event, his supporters defended his legacy at the helm of the organisation and the benefits to the country's international standing. Ironically, despite having its leader as chairman of SADC, Zimbabwe failed to pay its $ 2 m contribution for the year. Officials blamed the banking system, claiming that banks were "reluctant to conduct transactions from the country".

On 30 January, President Mugabe was appointed as the new *chairman of the AU*. While his supporters predictably celebrated, Mugabe's appointment drew criticism from Zimbabwean opposition parties and Mugabe critics. The MDC-T argued that he lacked "the political legitimacy to lead an Africa that should be looking to consolidate democracy and good governance", while the head of the ICG pointed out that the "elevation sends a negative signal of African solidarity with leaders who've misruled their countries". As was the case with his chairmanship of the SADC, Mugabe's tenure at the AU drew mixed review. His supporters hailed it as a success: the state-owned 'Sunday Mail' newspaper said that he had introduced processes and implemented plans that helped steer the AU into its current form. Critics, dismissed his tenure as a disaster, with 'The Zimbabwean' newspaper describing Mugabe as the AU's weakest leader in history. As head of the AU, Mugabe travelled extensively. During March, he made five trips to other African countries. Predictably, this brought criticism from people who saw it as a waste of money that the country could ill afford. Mugabe also faced harsh *criticism from abroad*. On 29 May, journalists confronted him during the inauguration of Nigerian President Muhammadu Buhari in Abuja and questioned him about his long stay in power. His supporters did not take kindly to this embarrassing encounter and the state media went into overdrive to denigrate the journalists.

While relations with most of Africa were good, the same could not be said of Zimbabwe's relations with *Botswana*. On 17 August, when Botswana's President Ian Khama took over as SADC chairman, he said he wanted the region "to be a beacon for democracy for Africa", and blasted "leaders who cling to power". Such were the relations between the two countries that observers interpreted the remarks as being directed at Zimbabwe. Relations with *South Africa* remained good. In April, President Mugabe paid his first state visit to South Africa since 1994 and the two countries strengthened bilateral relations with the signing of five agreements on 8 April. The agreements comprised the establishment of a binational commission to be led by the two heads of state; a memorandum of understanding on diplomatic consultations; a memorandum of understanding on trade cooperation; an agreement on mutual assistance between customs administrations; and an agreement on cooperation on water resources management.

On the international stage, Zimbabwe maintained good relations with *China.* On 1 December, China's President Xi Jinping arrived in Zimbabwe. He was easily the most prominent global leader to visit the country in many years. In an article in the state-controlled 'Herald' newspaper, Mr Xi said the two nations had a "deep and firm" friendship. On 22 December, Zimbabwe announced that the yuan would become the latest currency to be approved for public transactions in Zimbabwe. This was seen as part of the country's plans to increase trade with China. The decision was made following Beijing's confirmation that it would cancel $ 40 m of debts.

Zimbabwe strengthened relations with *Russia,* one of its traditional allies. On 4 January, state media reported that a high-powered Russian delegation would visit Zimbabwe that month to finalise some multi-million dollar projects aimed at improving water infrastructure in Harare and surrounding towns. They were aimed at dam construction, irrigation development and water management. In May, it was reported that Russian investors would be financing a $ 4 bn platinum mine in the Great Dyke. The investors said they would also carry out exploration for other minerals, which could add to their investment. This was in line with a 'roadmap' agreed in September 2014 during the visit of Russian Foreign Minister Sergei Lavrov.

Outside its circle of traditional allies and friends, Zimbabwe forged relations with *Belarus.* The two countries stepped up cooperation in sectors ranging from agriculture to mining. On 18 November, Mugabe approved a number of investment deals after his meeting with the visiting Viktor Sheiman, President Lukashenko's chief property manager. The deals covered agriculture, mining and agricultural equipment. Mugabe and Sheiman also discussed cooperation in electricity, road and bridge construction, housing and education.

There was no major shift in *relations with the EU.* The thaw continued, with the EU announcing a resumption of aid to Zimbabwe. On 16 February, the EU unveiled a $ 270 m aid package to support Zimbabwe's agriculture and health sectors. This marked the resumption of direct funding after more than ten years. However, the EU maintained its asset freeze and a travel ban on Mugabe and his wife, as well as an arms embargo. During the signing ceremony, EU Ambassador to Zimbabwe Philippe Van Damme cautioned that this move did not "mean that everything is suddenly sorted out and that we are entering a new honeymoon", pointing out that, although some obstacles had been cleared in the EU-Zimbabwe partnership, "new problems may emerge, old problems may reappear".

Zimbabwe's relations with the *UK* saw some activity. On 12 February, a UK private sector-led International Investor Delegation arrived in Zimbabwe to explore investment opportunities. The British Embassy claimed this signalled "the strengthening of business ties between the two countries". In March, DFID launched a programme to increase incomes and reduce poverty among smallholder farming households in chronically food and nutrition insecure districts and, on 7 September, approved new funding to support Zimbabwe's education sector. On 17 September, UK Foreign and Commonwealth Office Head of Central and Southern Africa Department Danae Dholakia, who was visiting Zimbabwe, met Minister of Water, Environment and Climate Oppah Muchinguri-Kashiri. According to the British Embassy in Harare, the two discussed, among other things, combating the illegal trade in wildlife; the UK's ongoing support to the water sector in Zimbabwe; and mitigating the impacts of global climate change on Zimbabwe in the context of the 21st Conference of Parties in Paris.

Relations with the US remained frosty. This became clear on 13 March, when two visiting US diplomats ruled out a change of policy with Zimbabwe. Speaking to reporters in Harare, Deputy Assistant Secretary of State for African Affairs Shannon Smith said the US would not relax travel bans and other sanctions against President Mugabe and his leadership during the year. However, on 3 July, speaking at the 239th US Independence Day anniversary in Harare, US Ambassador to Zimbabwe Bruce Wharton said his government was committed to the development of Zimbabwe and had embarked on various projects mutually beneficial to both countries. In a move that did not help bilateral relations, Mugabe was excluded from an AU meeting in July 2015 after he was snubbed by US President Barack Obama. Despite being the AU chairman, Mugabe was not among the leaders who met Obama at the AU headquarters in Addis Ababa (Ethiopia) on 28 July. Mugabe's spokesman said Mugabe was unmoved by Obama's visit to the AU and dismissed the event as like "a visit by any other visitor".

Relations with multilateral organisations were mixed. On 8 April, the management of the *IMF* completed the first review under the Staff-Monitored Program (SMP) with Zimbabwe. The IMF described the SMP as the "lynchpin of the authorities' roadmap for building a strong track record towards normalizing the relationship with Zimbabwe's creditors and mobilizing development partners' support". According to the IMF, the main objective of the programme was to strengthen Zimbabwe's external position as a prerequisite towards arrears clearance, normalisation of debt servicing, and restoring access to external financing. In September, the IMF indicated that, even if Zimbabwe undertook economic reforms, it would take at least three years before it could expect loans from international lenders. Zimbabwe stepped up its reengagement with creditors by, among other things, increasing payments to the *World Bank* and the *AfDB*. On 19 May, the World Bank urged Zimbabwe to urgently clear its arrears with the Bretton Woods Institutions and the AfDB in order to access the extra lines of credit necessary to fund the economy. The executive director of the World Bank's Africa Group, Louis Rene Peter Larose, pointed out that the resolution of Zimbabwe's debt overhang and the clearance of arrears needed "to be treated with the urgency it deserves".

Socioeconomic Developments

Zimbabwe faced some significant economic challenges during the year. *Economic indicators* reflected the challenges in the economy. Confirming signs of deflationary pressures, Reserve Bank of Zimbabwe figures showed that the December consumer price index was 98%. The year-on-year price increase was –2.4% compared with –0.2% in 2014. According to Economist Intelligence Unit (EIU) estimates, the real GDP growth was 0.2%, a sharp drop from 3.8% in 2014. The EIU put the nominal GDP at $ 13.9 bn, down from $ 14.2 bn. The current account balance was –$ 2.5 bn, up from –$ 1.0 bn, while total international reserves dropped to $ 297 m. In the budget statement, the finance minister estimated public and publicly guaranteed *debt burden* at $ 8.3 bn. The external debt consisted of debts of $ 1.4 bn. The arrears amounted to $ 5.4 bn, giving a total debt of $ 7.0 bn.

Zimbabwe performed poorly in a number of *world league tables*. In the World Bank's Doing Business 2016, the country was ranked 155th, down from 153rd in 2015 out of 189 economies. The World Economic Forum's Global Competitiveness Report 2014–15 ranked Zimbabwe 124th out of 144 countries. The Human Development Index for 2015 gave a figure of 0.509, which placed Zimbabwe 155th – an improvement from 156th in 2014.

On the humanitarian front, the country faced a number of challenges. In April, Masvingo Provincial Affairs Minister Shuvai Mahofa said the government would embark on the second relocation of nearly 3,000 Tokwe-Mukosi *flood victims* from the Nuanetsi Ranch to seven farms that had been identified for them in Mwenezi district. Each of the families would be allocated six hectares at the new plots. Another *cholera outbreak* hit the country. On 9 March, Health and Childcare Minister David Parirenyatwa announced that confirmed cholera cases had risen to 12, while three more suspected cases at Birchenough Bridge were still to be verified. By April, the situation appeared under control. Government and partners remained on alert following one new suspected cholera case in Manicaland Province and one suspected case in Mashonaland East Province.

Food security challenges resurfaced. According to the Vulnerability Assessment Committee (ZIMVAC) Report of 2015, maize production dropped by 49% from the average, with a likely cereal deficit of 650,000 tonnes. The crop production deficits were caused by poor rainfall distribution during the season. As a result 1.5 m people were at risk of food and livelihood insecurity. The ZIMVAC 2015 rural livelihoods assessment indicated that approximately 10% of the rural population were projected to be food-insecure for the period of October–December and that 16% of the rural population were projected to be food-insecure for the period of January–March 2016.

According to *demographic indicators* produced by the World Bank, the death rate for the period 2011–15 stood at ten deaths per 1,000 of population. Due to the worsening economic situation, there was an increasing flow of Zimbabweans into

South Africa and Botswana in search of better economic opportunities. UN estimates put the crude net migration rate at 4.35 migrants per 1,000 of population. Life expectancy for the total population was 51 years. The infant mortality rate was estimated at 47 deaths per 1000 live births (World Bank estimate). The literacy rate was a league-topping 91%, making Zimbabwe the leader in Africa.

According to the government, the *HIV/AIDS* epidemic remained "generalized, feminized and homogenous" and with continued declines in new infection rates, prevalence and AIDS-related mortality. UNAIDS figures showed that 1.6 m people were living with HIV. The prevalence rate among adults aged 15–49 was estimated at 16.7%. About 150,000 children aged 15 or under were living with HIV. Deaths due to AIDS were estimated at 39,000. There were 570,000 children aged 0–17 who had been orphaned by AIDS.

The *education and health* delivery systems continued to experience problems of staffing, equipment and funding. Health and education personnel remained a substantial part of the brain drain. Industrial action and threats of industrial action arising out of salary disputes were a constant feature throughout the year, further compromising these sectors. In September, teachers' unions threatened industrial action at the beginning of the third term. They wanted to force the government to address their concerns, which included working conditions and the withdrawal of salaries for more than 3,000 teachers found missing from their workstations during a human resources audit conducted by the Ministry of Primary and Secondary Education. On 27 December, government doctors gave their employer a five-day ultimatum to pay their December salaries and bonuses, threatening withdrawal of labour in the new year.

Job losses spiralled in the second half of the year as companies took advantage of a shock court ruling by the Supreme Court on 16 July that companies could lawfully terminate employees' contracts at any time without offering them packages, provided they had given them at least three months' notice. There was a flood of employment terminations as companies saw the termination of contracts on notice as a cost-effective way of firing workers without the need to give any explanation or conduct disciplinary hearings or take the costly retrenchment option. Figures for those who lost their jobs in July alone ranged from 20,000 to 25,000 in both private and state-run firms. Faced with the massive job losses, the government rushed to amend the labour laws. On 26 August, new labour regulations came into force that made it harder to retrench workers. Retrenchments could now only be allowed in specific circumstances, with a minimum retrenchment package of one month's pay for every two years of service. The regulations were backdated to July.

On 27 August, the 'Financial Gazette' reported that the government had abandoned its populist *indigenisation policy* "in a desperate attempt to lure offshore capital required to revive the country's disintegrating economy". The indigenisation law compelled foreign-owned companies to cede at least 51% of their shareholding in locally based companies to blacks or specific entities designated by government.

However, it appeared there was a reversal in the reversal. In October, the combative new indigenisation minister, Patrick Zhuwao, announced that Zimbabwe would be imposing an additional tax burden on foreign-owned companies. The proposed 10% empowerment levy to fund indigenisation and economic empowerment would be raised to 12.5% in 2017. The change in policy appeared to reflect the factional struggles within ZANU-PF. Zhuwao was a leading member of the G40 faction while Finance Minister Chinamasa was believed to be in the Mnangagwa camp.

On 26 November, Finance Minister Chinamasa presented the *2016 national budget* with the theme "Building a Conducive Environment that Attracts Foreign Direct Investment". Chinamasa proposed a $ 4 bn budget. At $ 3.7 bn, recurrent expenditure was 92.1% of the budget. Revenue was projected at $ 3.9 bn in 2016. The $ 150 m deficit (1.1% of GDP) was to be funded by local borrowing. Chinamasa projected a GDP growth rate at market prices of 2.7% for 2016. Although expenditure on wages was expected to fall to 80% of the total budget, it would still increase by 2.7% in 2016.

www.ingramcontent.com/pod-product-compliance
Lightning Source LLC
LaVergne TN
LVHW080115011026
849160LV00013B/1106